THE LEGAL PROFESSION AND
THE COMMON LAW

THE LEGAL PROFESSION AND THE COMMON LAW

HISTORICAL ESSAYS

J.H. BAKER

THE HAMBLEDON PRESS
LONDON   AND   RONCEVERTE

Published by The Hambledon Press, 1986

35 Gloucester Avenue, London NW1 7AX (U.K.)

309 Greenbrier Avenue, Ronceverte,
West Virginia 24970 (U.S.A.)

ISBN 0 907628 62 1

History Series 48

© John H. Baker 1986

British Library Cataloguing in Publication Data

Baker, J.H.
   The legal profession and the common law:
   historical essays. — (History series; 48)
   1. Law — England — History and critieism
   I. Title II. Series
   344.2'009   KD606

Library of Congress Cataloging-in-Publication Data

Baker, John Hamilton.
   The legal profession and the common law.

   Includes bibliographical references and index.
   1. Lawyers — Great Britain — History.
   2. Common law — Great Britain — History.
   I. Title
   KD460.B35   1986   349.41   85-30581
   ISBN 0 907628 62 1 (U.S.) 344.1

Printed and bound in Great Britain by
W.B.C., Bristol and Maesteg.

CONTENTS

List of Illustrations	vii
Acknowledgements	ix
Foreword	xi
Abbreviations	xiii
Table of Statutes	xvii
Table of Cases	xviii

I. THE LEGAL PROFESSION

1	The Inns of Court in 1388	3
2	Learning Exercises in the Medieval Inns of Court and Chancery	7
3	The Old Moot Book of Lincoln's Inn	25
4	Readings in Gray's Inn, their Decline and Disappearance	31
5	The Old Constitution of Gray's Inn	39
6	The Inns of Court and Chancery as Voluntary Associations	45
7	The English Legal Profession, 1450-1550	75
8	Counsellors and Barristers	99
9	Solicitors and the Law of Maintenance, 1590-1640	125

II. LEGAL INSTITUTIONS AND LITERATURE

10	The Changing Concept of a Court	153
11	The Pecunes	171
12	Coke's Notebooks and the Sources of his Reports	177
13	The Common Lawyers and the Chancery: 1616	205
14	The Newe Littleton	231
15	Sir Thomas Robinson, Chief Prothonotary of the Common Pleas	243

III. COMMON LAW AND PROCEDURE

16	Criminal Courts and Procedure at Common Law, 1550-1800	259
17	The Refinement of English Criminal Jurisprudence 1500-1848	303
18	Criminal Justice at Newgate, 1616-1627	325
19	The Law Merchant and the Common Law before 1700	341
20	Origins of the 'Doctrine' of Consideration, 1535-1585	369
21	New Light on Slade's Case	393

IV. THE TUDOR LEGAL TRANSFORMATION

| 22 | The Dark Age of English Legal History, 1500-1700 | 435 |
| 23 | English Law and the Renaissance | 461 |

| Index of Names | 477 |
| Index of Subjects | 487 |

LIST OF ILLUSTRATIONS

1	The Lincoln's Inn moot book		24
2	Legal London in about 1570		44
3	The Courts of King's Bench and Chancery, c. 1620		152
4	"Daungerous et absurd opinions affirme devant le roy"		170
5	Sir Edward Coke		176
6	Thomas Egerton, Lord Ellesmere	*facing*	210
7	Francis Bacon, Baron Verulam	*facing*	211
8	Edward Littleton, Baron Lyttelton of Munslow		230
9	Thomas Robinson's notebook		242
10	The Court of King's Bench, c. 1450-60		302
11	Sir Thomas Walmsley		392
12	Manuscript law reports	*facing*	454
13	Reporters in the Court of King's Bench, c. 1675	*facing*	455

ACKNOWLEDGEMENTS

The articles reprinted here appeared first in the following places and are reprinted by the kind permission of the original publishers.

1	*Law Quarterly Review*, 92 (1976), pp. 184-7.
2	This chapter appears here for the first time.
3	*Law Quarterly Review*, 95 (1979), pp. 507-12.
4	This chapter appears here for the first time.
5	*Graya*, 81 (1977), pp. 15-19.
6	*Quaderni Fiorentini per la storia del pensiero Giuridico Moderno*, 11/12 (1982-83) (Giuffrè, Milan), pp. 9-38.
7	*Lawyers in Early Modern Europe and America*, ed. Wilfred Prest (Croom Helm, London, 1981), pp. 16-41.
8	*Cambridge Law Journal*, 27 (1969), pp. 205-29.
9	*Cambridge Law Journal*, 32 (1973), pp. 56-80.
10	This chapter appears here for the first time, by permission of the Citadel Inn of Court.
11	*Law Quarterly Review*, 98 (1982), pp. 204-9.
12	*Cambridge Law Journal*, 30 (1972), pp. 59-86.
13	*The Irish Jurist*, 4 (1969), pp. 368-92.
14	*Cambridge Law Journal*, 33 (1974), pp. 145-55.
15	*Bodleian Library Record* (1978), pp. 27-40.
16	*Crime in England, 1550-1800*, ed. J.S. Cockburn (Methuen, London, 1977), pp. 15-49, 299-309.
17	*Crime and Criminal Justice in Europe and Canada*, ed. Louis A. Knafla (Waterloo, Ontario: Wilfred Laurier University Press, 1981 for the Calgary Institute for the Humanities), pp. 17-42.
18	*The Irish Jurist*, 8 (1973), pp. 307-22.
19	*Cambridge Law Journal*, 38 (1979), pp. 295-322.
20	*On the Laws and Customs of England: Essays in Honor of Samuel E. Thorne*, ed. M.S. Arnold, T.A. Green, S.A. Scully and S.D. White (University of North Carolina Press, Chapel Hill, 1981), pp. 336-58.

21 *Cambridge Law Journal*, 29 (1971), pt. 1, pp. 51-67; pt. 2, pp. 213-36.
22 *Legal History Studies*, ed. D. Jenkins (University of Wales Press, Cardiff, 1975), pp. 1-27.
23 *Cambridge Law Journal*, 44 (1985), pp. 46-61.

PERMISSIONS

The illustrations are reproduced by the kind permission of the following:

1 Cambridge University Library; 2 Guildhall Library, London; 3 Trustees of the British Museum; 4 Cambridge University Library; 5 The Rt Hon. the Earl of Leicester; 6 The Masters of the Bench of Lincoln's Inn; 7 National Portrait Gallery, London; 8 National Portrait Gallery, London; 9 Bodleian Library, Oxford; 10 The Masters of the Bench of the Inner Temple; 11 Dr J.H. Baker; 12 Cambridge University Library; 13 Bodleian Library, Oxford.

FOREWORD

This book contains some of the articles, notes and occasional lectures which I have written during the last sixteen years. The individual papers were written for a variety of purposes, and so there is not much uniformity or overall coherence in this collection; but I hope their reappearance in this form, with tables and indices, will render more accessible whatever is still of use.

If there is any recurring theme here, I suppose it is evidentiary, in that I have tried to demonstrate the range and value of manuscript sources in discovering what in 1972 still seemed to be a dark age of English legal history. Medievalists have, inevitably, always recognised the importance of records and manuscript literature. But the same has not been generally true of scholars writing on legal developments subsequent to the introduction of printing. It is not just that printing has a blinkering effect: there is the problem of volume, not to mention that of accessibility. After all, no one would question that Holdsworth had quite enough to keep him occupied without resorting to unprinted sources. Nevertheless, the printed law reports and reference books, singled out for publication by stationers serving the needs of practising lawyers, are by no means the best or the most revealing for historical purposes; and in any case, since practitioners until fairly recent times lived with manuscripts as much as with printed books, it seems reasonable to suppose that legal historians who emulate them will not only find new material but will also stumble upon questions which they had never thought to ask. Several of the papers printed here were indeed the result of chance discoveries — especially in the enormous surviving body of unpublished reports for the period 1550-1650. Although I have since wandered further into the earlier part of the "dark age", and spent more time with the plea rolls, the territory where my expedition began is still largely untrodden, and I hope others will explore it for themselves.

A secondary theme is the importance of the profession which made the law in the period before the Civil War, and of its unique legal university between London and Westminster. That area of study is opening more rapidly, and much has been revealed in the short time since my own earliest papers were written. Most of this recent work, however, has taken the form of social history. The rôle of the inns of court in creating, developing and hardening legal doctrine is touched on briefly in Part I, and in chapters 17 and 23, but requires further investigation.

If I were writing these pieces today, they would all be more or less different; but it is too late to rewrite them now, and I have contented myself with a few notes and comments to bring them up to date. Some misprints have been corrected, and cross-references to other articles included here have been amended as appropriate.

J.H. Baker

Cambridge,
December 1985

ABBREVIATIONS

Several different conventions are followed in the papers printed below. References composed of initial capitals are sometimes italicised and sometimes punctuated with stops, but in this table the initials alone are given. Law reports are cited in the usual manner: for guidance see the note on p. 259. Year books are cited by term, regnal year, folio and *placitum,* in that order.

AALH	Association of American Law Schools, *Select Essays in Anglo-American Legal History* (1907-09), three volumes.
AJLH	American Journal of Legal History.
Barnes, *Somerset*	T.G. Barnes, *Somerset 1625-1640* (1961).
Barrington, *Observations*	D. Barrington, *Observations on the more Ancient Statutes* (1775 ed.). [1st ed. 1766.]
BIHR	Bulletin of the Institute of Historical Research.
BL	British Library.
Black Books	Records of the Honorable Society of Lincoln's Inn: *The Black Books*, vols. I-IV (1897-1902).
Bl. Comm.	W. Blackstone, *Commentaries on the Laws of England* (several editions). [1st ed. 1765-69.]
BM	British Museum library, now called the British Library.
Bodl. Lib.	Bodleian Library, Oxford.
BR	Bancum Regis (King's Bench).
Br. Lib.	British Library.
Brit. Mus.	*see* BM.
Bro. Abr.; Brooke	R. Brooke, *La Graunde Abridgement* (1573). Entries are cited by title and case-number.
C1-3	Early Chancery Proceedings (PRO).
C33	Chancery Decree and Order Books (PRO).
C66	Patent Rolls (PRO).
C82	Chancery warrants (PRO).
C142	Inquisitions Post Mortem (PRO).
Camb. U.L.	Cambridge University Library.
CLJ	Cambridge Law Journal.
Cockburn, *Assizes*	J.S. Cockburn, *A History of English Assizes 1558-1714* (1972).
Co. Entr.	E. Coke, *A Booke of Entries* (1614).
Co. Inst.	E. Coke, *Institutes of the Laws of England* (1628-44), four parts.

Co. Litt.	E. Coke, *First Part of the Institutes* (1628), being a commentary on Littleton's *Tenures*.
Collectanea Juridica	F. Hargrave ed., *Collectanea Juridica* (1791-92), two volumes.
CP	*see also* Maitland, *CP*.
CP 40	Plea Rolls of the Court of Common Pleas (PRO).
CP 45	Remembrance Rolls of Prothonotaries of the Common Pleas (PRO).
Crompton, *Justice*	R. Crompton, *Loffice et auctoritie de Justices de Peace* (1617 ed.). [1st ed. 1584.]
Crown Circuit Companion	W. Stubbs and G. Talmash, *The Crown Circuit Companion* (6th ed., 1790). [1st ed. 1738.]
CRR	*Curia Regis Rolls* (HMSO).
CSPD	*Calendar of State Papers (Domestic Series)* (HMSO).
CUL	Cambridge University Library.
D	*Digest* of Justinian.
Dalton, *Countrey Justice*	M. Dalton, *The Countrey Justice* (several editions). [1st ed. 1618.]
E13	Plea Rolls of the Exchequer of Pleas (PRO).
E163	Exchequer Miscellanea (PRO).
Eden, *Principles*	[W. Eden], *Principles of Penal Law* (1771).
Fitz. Abr.; Fitzherbert	A. Fitzherbert, *La Graunde Abridgement* (1577 ed.). [1st ed. 1514-16.]
Fitz. N.B.	A. Fitzherbert, *La Nouvelle Natura Brevium* (1635 ed.). [1st ed. 1538.]
Foster, *Crown Law*	M. Foster, *Discourse upon .. the Crown Law* (1762).
GI	Gray's Inn.
Guide to Juries	Anon., *A Guide to Juries* (1703).
Hale, *Pleas* (HPC)	M. Hale, *A History of the Pleas of the Crown* (1736), two volumes. [Written *c.* 1670.]
Hawkins, *Pleas* (Pl. Cor.)	W. Hawkins, *Pleas of the Crown* (1771 ed.). [1st ed. 1716.]
HCJ	*Journals of the House of Commons.*
HEL	*see* Holdsworth, HEL.
HLJ	*Journals of the House of Lords.*
HLS	Harvard Law School.
HMC	Historical Manuscripts Commission.
Holdsworth, *History* (HEL)	W.S. Holdsworth, *History of English Law* (3rd ed., 1923-66), sixteen volumes.
ICLQ	International and Comparative Law Quarterly.
IND 1-	Common Pleas Docket Rolls (PRO).

Inner Temple Records	*A Calendar of the Inner Temple Records* (1896-1937), five volumes.
Inst.	*see* Co. Inst.
IT	Inner Temple.
ITR	*see Inner Temple Records*
JSPTL	Journal of the Society of Public Teachers of Law.
KB 27	Plea Rolls of the Court of King's Bench (PRO).
KB 30, 31	Records of the Court for Crown Cases Reserved (PRO).
KB 150	King's Bench Files of Warrants of Attorney (PRO).
Lambard, *Eirenarcha*	W. Lambard, *Eirenarcha: or of the Office of Justices of Peace* (1581).
LI	Lincoln's Inn.
LIBB	*see Black Books.*
LQR	Law Quarterly Review.
LRH	J.H. Baker ed., *Legal Records and the Historian* (1978).
Madan, *Thoughts*	M. Madan, *Thoughts on Executive Justice, with respect to our Criminal Laws* (2nd ed., 1785).
Maitland, *CP*	H.A.L. Fisher ed., *The Collected Papers of F.W. Maitland* (1911), three volumes.
Milsom, *Foundations*	S.F.C. Milsom, *Historical Foundations of the Common Law* (1969; 2nd ed., 1981).
MSR	W. Le Hardy ed., *Middlesex Sessions Records*, vols. III-IV (1937-41).
NYULR	New York University Law Review.
P & P	Past and Present.
PC2	Privy Council Registers (PRO).
PCC	Prerogative Court of Canterbury, registers of wills (PRO, formerly in Somerset House).
Pension Book	R.J. Fletcher ed., *The Pension Book of Gray's Inn* (1901-10), two volumes.
PM	F. Pollock and F.W. Maitland, *The History of English Law before the time of Edward I* (2nd ed., 1898), two volumes (reissued 1968).
PRO	Public Record Office, London.
PRO 30/23	Records of the Honourable Society of Serjeants' Inn, Chancery Lane (PRO).
Rastell, *Entrees*	W. Rastell, *A Collection of Entrees* (3rd ed., 1596). [1st ed. 1566.]
RHD	Revue Historique de Droit Français et Etranger.
Rolle Abr.	H. Rolle, *Un Abridgement des Plusiers Cases* (1668), two volumes.
Rot. Parl.	*Rotuli Parliamentorum* [1783], six volumes.

Rymer, *Foedera*	[T. Rymer], *Foedera* (G. Holmes and R. Sanderson ed., 1727-35), twenty volumes.
SC	Same case.
Seld. Soc.	Selden Society.
Sel. Ess. Anglo-Amer. Leg. Hist.	see AALH.
Shepp. Abr.	W. Sheppard, *A Grand Abridgement of the Law of England* (1675), four parts.
Simpson, *History of Contract*	A.W.B. Simpson, *A History of the Common Law of Contract: the rise of assumpsit* (1975).
Smith, *De Republica*	T. Smith, *De Republica Anglorum* (1583).
SP 1	State Papers of Henry VIII (PRO).
SP 14	State Papers of James I (PRO).
SP 16	State Papers of Charles I (PRO).
Spelman; *Spelman's Reports*	J.H. Baker ed., *The Reports of Sir John Spelman* (1977-78), Selden Soc. vols. 93-94.
SS	Selden Society.
SSSS	Selden Society, supplementary series.
Stat. Regn.	Statutes of the Realm.
State Trials	F. Hargrave and other ed., *State Trials*, vols. I-XXVII (1809-20).
STAC 2	Star Chamber Proceedings (PRO).
Staunford, *Plees*	W. Staunford (Staundeford), *Les Plees del Coron* (1574 ed.). [1st ed. 1557.]
STC	A.W. Pollard and G.R. Redgrave, *A Short-title Catalogue of Books ... 1475-1640* (1926). A new edition is in preparation.
Stephen, *History*	J.F. Stephen, *A History of the Criminal Law of England* (1883), three volumes.
Style Pr. Reg.	W. Style, *Regestum Practicale: or, the Practical Register* (1657; anr ed., 1694).
TRHS	Transactions of the Royal Historical Society.
UCL	University College London.
ULC	Cambridge University Library.
Vidian, *Entries*	A Vidian, *The Exact Pleader* (1684).
Vin. Abr.	C. Viner, *A General Abridgement of Law and Equity* (1741-53), twenty-three volumes.
Wallace, *Reporters*	J.W. Wallace, *The Reporters arranged and characterized* (4th ed., 1882).
YB	The year books. Most references are to the edition of 1679-80.

TABLE OF STATUTES

Magna Carta (1225)	158, 202, 261-2, 263, 268
52 Hen. III, Statute of Marlborough, c. 1	162
11 Edw. I, De mercatoribus	347
13 Edw. I, Statute of Westminster II, c. 24	402, 413, 423
13 Edw. I, Statute of Acton Burnel	347
28 Edw. I, Articuli super cartas, c. 11	106
1 Edw. III, stat. 2, c. 17	279
2 Edw. III (Northampton), c. 2	274
4 Edw. III, c. 2	274
27 Edw, III, stat. 1, c. 1	209, 215, 216
27 Edw. III, stat. 2 (Staple), c. 2	347
36 Edw. III, c. 15	282
12 Ric. II, c. 10	276
15 Ric. II, c. 2	270
17 Ric. II, c. 6	226
4 Hen. IV, c. 18	84
4 Hen. IV, c. 23	209, 215
7 Hen. IV, c. 14	101
13 Hen. IV, c. 7	270
2 Hen. V, c. 3	269
2 Hen. V, c. 4	276
3 Hen. VI, c. 4	101
15 Hen. VI, c. 4	226
1 Edw. IV, c. 2	279
8 Edw. IV, c. 2	101
17 Edw. IV, c. 2	353
1 Ric. III, c. 1	462
3 Hen. VII, c. 1	262
3 Hen. VII, c. 3	281
4 Hen. VII, c. 13	293
11 Hen. VII, c. 3	263
19 Hen. VII, c. 13	269
1 Hen. VIII, c. 6	263
14 & 15 Hen. VIII, c. 5	50
21 Hen. VIII, c. 11	262
22 Hen. VIII, c. 14	286
23 Hen. VIII, c. 10	55
23 Hen. VIII, c. 13	269
27 Hen. VIII, c. 10	462
27 Hen. VIII, c. 24	277
28 Hen. VIII, c. 15	267
31 Hen. VIII, c. 27	52
32 Hen. VIII, c. 3	286
32 Hen. VIII, c. 42	51
37 Hen. VIII, c. 8	309
1 Edw. VI, c. 12	293
5 & 6 Edw. VI, c. 11	289
1 & 2 Ph. & Mar., c. 10	286, 289
1 & 2 Ph. & Mar., c. 13	274, 281
2 & 3 Ph. & Mar., c. 10	274, 281
5 Eliz. I, c. 1	40, 128
13 Eliz. I, c. 1	202
13 Eliz. I, c. 29	48
18 Eliz. I, c. 12	166
27 Eliz. I, c. 8	418
31 Eliz. I, c. 1	418
39 Eliz. I, c. 4	297
3 Jac. I, c. 7	143-4, 147
21 Jac. I, c. 23	148
21 Jac. I, c. 23	112
16 Car. I, c. 10	267
22 & 23 Car. II, c. 25	271
29 Car. II, c. 9	279
4 & 5 Will. & Mar., c. 18	266
7 & 8 Will. & Mar., c. 3	268, 287, 288
1 Ann., stat. 2, c. 9	288
6 Ann., c. 9	293
4 Geo. I, c. 11	293
4 Geo. II, c. 26	282
4 Geo. II, c. 32	323
12 Geo. III, c. 20	284
19 Geo. III, c. 74	293, 298
21 Geo. III, c. 68	323
23 Geo. III, c. xxx	53
30 Geo. III, c. 48	294
59 Geo. III, c. 46	268
3 & 4 Will. IV, c. cx	53
6 & 7 Will. IV, c. 49	54
6 & 7 Will. IV, c. 114	287
11 & 12 Vict., c. 43	271
11 & 12 Vict., c. 78	327
36 & 37 Vict., c. 66 (Judicature Act 1873)	154, 229
38 & 39 Vict., c. 77 (Judicature Act 1875)	154
15 & 16 Geo. V, c. 49 (Judicature Act 1925)	229
London Government Act 1963 (c. 33)	61
Criminal Law Act 1967 (c. 33)	109
Courts Act 1971 (c. 23)	154, 273

TABLE OF CASES

(1) Year books and cases cited by year

Mich.	9 Hen. III, Fitz. Abr., *Ley* 78	401
	20 & 21 Edw. I (Rolls Ser.) 68	346
	21 & 22 Edw. I (Rolls Ser.) 74, 458	346, 347
	31 Edw. I, Fitz. Abr., *Voucher* 289	401
Hil.	4 Edw. II (26 Seld. Soc.) 127	346
Mich.	7 Edw. II (39 Seld. Soc.) 14	346, 347
Pas.	15 Edw. II, p. 464	106
	Anon. (1323)	347
Mich.	19 Edw. II, p. 626	347
Hil.	2 Edw. III, 5, pl. 4	174
	4 Edw. III, Lib. Ass., pl. 3	340
Trin.	10 Edw. III, 24, pl. 23	103
	12 Edw. III, Lib. Ass., pl. 5	272
	12 Edw. III, Lib. Ass., pl. 32	320
Trin.	12 Edw. III, Fitz. Abr., *Corone* 119	320
	13 Edw. III, Lib. Ass., pl. 6	335
	13 Edw. III, Fitz. Abr., *Prohibition* 11	211
	18 & 19 Edw. III (Rolls Ser.) 291	336
Mich.	20 Edw. III (Rolls Ser.), II, 555	167
Hil.	21 Edw. III, 7, pl. 20	102, 103, 104
Hil.	21 Edw. III, Fitz. Abr., *Barre* 271	279
	26 Edw. III, Lib. Ass., pl. 23	315
	26 Edw. III, Bro. Abr., *Corone* 217	336
	27 Edw. III, Lib. Ass., pl. 38	315
	27 Edw. III, Lib. Ass., pl. 39	331
Mich.	29 Edw. III, 47, pl. 13	3, 13
Mich.	30 Edw. III, 25	363
Trin.	32 Edw. III, Fitz. Abr., *Annuitie* 30	103, 104
Pas.	41 Edw. III, 10, pl. 5	398
Mich.	41 Edw. III, 19, pl. 3	103
Mich.	41 Edw. III, 31, pl. 36	167, 474
Pas.	42 Edw. III, 9, pl. 7	398
Hil.	48 Edw. III, 2, pl. 6	349
Hil.	48 Edw. III, 6, pl. 11	398
Hil.	49 Edw. III, 5, pl. 8	402, 407
Trin.	12 Ric. II (Ames) 7, pl. 5	398
Mich.	2 Hen. IV, 6, pl. 24	16
Pas.	2 Hen. IV, 18, pl. 6	363
Pas.	10 Hen. IV, Fitz. Abr., *Attaint* 60, 64	269
Mich.	11 Hen. IV, 13, pl. 30	331
Mich.	11 Hen. IV, 33, pl. 60	403
Hil.	11 Hen. IV, 47, pl. 21	386
Trin.	11 Hen. IV, 82, pl. 28	405
Hil.	13 Hen. IV, 17, pl. 12	119
	5 Hen. V, 4, pl. 10	351
Mich.	9 Hen. V, 14, pl. 23	384
Pas.	1 Hen. VI, 43, pl. 30	352
Mich.	2 Hen. VI, 5, pl. 3	106
Hil.	3 Hen. VI, 33, pl. 26	107, 123
Hil.	3 Hen. VI, 36, pl. 33	371, 403
Pas.	3 Hen. VI, 42, pl. 14	107
Trin.	3 Hen. VI, 53, pl. 24	113
Mich.	8 Hen. VI, 5, pl. 13	402
Hil.	8 Hen. VI, 19, pl. 6	166
Hil.	8 Hen. VI, 23, pl. 9	103, 104
Trin.	9 Hen. VI, 24, pl. 19	16
Mich.	9 Hen. VI, 37, pl. 12	172
Mich.	9 Hen. VI, 55, pl. 41	172
Mich.	11 Hen. VI, 10, pl. 24	113
Hil.	11 Hen. VI, 18, pl. 10	104
Pas.	11 Hen. VI, 43, pl. 30	384
Trin.	11 Hen. VI, 49, pl. 7	166
	14 Hen. VI, 18, pl. 58	104, 122
Mich.	19 Hen. VI, 30, pl. 56	113
Pas.	20 Hen. VI, 28, pl. 21	349
Trin.	20 Hen. VI, 34, pl. 4	104, 388
Trin.	20 Hen. VI, 37, pl. 6	84
Mich.	21 Hen. VI, 4, pl. 6	105, 107, 123
Mich.	21 Hen. VI, 15, pl. 30	113, 135
Hil.	21 Hen. VI, Fitz. Abr., *Corone* 455	335
Trin.	21 Hen. VI, 55, pl. 12	404
Trin.	28 Hen. VI, 12, pl. 28	113
Mich.	31 Hen. VI, 9, pl. 1	107
Hil.	32 Hen. VI, 33, pl. 28	172
Mich.	39 Hen. VI, 5, pl. 8	113
Mich.	39 Hen. VI, 21, pl. 31	103
Pas.	4 Edw. IV, 2, pl. 2	399
Pas.	4 Edw. IV, 11, pl. 18	283, 335

Table of Cases

xix

Long	5 Edw. IV, fo. 109ᵛ	159
Long	5 Edw. IV, fo. 320	172
Mich.	6 Edw. IV, 3, pl. 9	352
Trin.	7 Edw. IV, 10, pl. 1	171
Hil.	7 Edw. IV, 23, pl. 27	352
Pas.	8 Edw. IV, 5, pl. 17	279
Mich.	8 Edw. IV, 11, pl. 9	352
Pas.	9 Edw. IV, 5, pl. 20	83, 254
Trin.	9 Edw. IV, 27, pl. 40	286
Trin.	9 Edw. IV, 28, pl. 41	335
Hil.	9 Edw. IV, 48, pl. 3	103
Hil.	9 Edw. IV, 53, pl. 17	103
	49 Hen. VI, 14, pl. 9	320
Trin.	11 Edw. IV, 2-3, pl. 4	159, 400
Mich.	12 Edw. IV, 11, pl. 2	402
Mich.	13 Edw. IV, 4, pl. 9	402
Pas.	13 Edw. IV, 9, pl. 5	345, 347-8
Trin.	14 Edw. IV, 7, pl. 10	283, 335
Mich.	15 Edw. IV, 2, pl. 2	474
Mich.	15 Edw. IV, 14, pl. 18	349
Mich.	16 Edw. IV, 9, pl. 5	384
Trin.	17 Edw. IV, 4-5, pl. 4	384
Trin.	18 Edw. IV, 7, pl. 6	254
Trin.	18 Edw. IV, 10, pl. 29	5
Mich.	19 Edw. IV, 3, pl. 9	113, 135
Mich.	20 Edw. IV, 10, pl. 9	403
Mich.	21 Edw. IV, 28, pl. 2	351
Mich.	21 Edw. IV, 55, pl. 27	402
Mich.	21 Edw. IV, 65, pl. 42	31
Pas.	22 Edw. IV, 2, pl. 8	402
Pas.	22 Edw. IV, 7, pl. 20	402
Mich.	22 Edw. IV, 22, pl. 2	279
Mich.	22 Edw. IV, 37, pl. 6	208, 211
Mich.	1 Ric. III, 1, pl. 1	279
Mich.	2 Ric. III, 7, pl. 13	400
Mich.	2 Ric. III, 11, pl. 25	279
Mich.	2 Ric. III, 14, pl. 39	398
Mich.	2 Ric. III, 18, pl. 45	159
Mich.	2 Ric. III, 22, pl. 53	335
Hil.	1 Hen. VII, 10, pl. 10	463
Hil.	1 Hen. VII, 13, pl. 27	330
Pas.	4 Hen. VII, 7, pl. 4	109
Mich.	5 Hen. VII, 1, pl. 1	397
Pas.	5 Hen. VII, 20, pl. 1	113, 137
Pas.	6 Hen. VII, 1, pl. 1	166
Trin.	6 Hen. VII, 4, pl. 4	279
Mich.	6 Hen. VII, 7, pl. 14	398
	6 Hen. VII, Caryll Rep.	353
Mich.	10 Hen. VII, 8, pl. 15	166
Pas.	11 Hen. VII, 22, pl. 11	279
	14 Hen. VII, Fitz. N.B. 220	401
Trin.	15 Hen. VII, 11, pl. 21	32
Mich.	20 Hen. VII, 8, pl. 18	389, 399, 403, 413
Trin.	20 Hen. VII, Keil. 66	279
Hil.	21 Hen. VII, 12, pl. 13	398
Mich.	21 Hen. VII, 30, pl. 5	399
Mich.	21 Hen. VII, 40, pl. 62	113
Mich.	21 Hen. VII, 41, pl. 66	403, 468
Mich.	21 Hen. VII, Keil. 69, 77	385, 389
Mich.	7 Hen. VIII, Anon. (1515), Spelman Rep.	135
Pas.	7 & 8 Hen. VIII, Keil. 186	337
Mich.	12 Hen. VIII, 11, pl. 3	168, 428
Hil.	14 Hen. VIII, 16, pl. 3	281
Pas.	14 Hen. VIII, 31, pl. 8	399, 413
Pas.	22 Hen. VIII, Caryll jun. Rep.	166
Trin.	22 Hen. VIII, Yorke Rep.	376
	24 Hen. VIII, Pollard Rep.	376
Hil.	26 Hen. VIII, 9, pl. 1	166
Pas	27 Hen. VIII, 2, pl. 6	279
Trin.	27 Hen. VIII, 23, pl. 21	168, 429
Trin.	28 Hen. VIII, Dyer Rep.	376
Mich.	36 Hen. VIII, Gell MS.	88
	37 Hen. VIII, Bro. Abr., *Action sur le case*, pl. 4	429
	Anon. (1549)	135
	Anon. (1552)	281
	Anon. (1553)	276
	Anon. (1553)	413
	Anon. (1555)	274
	Anon. (1555)	296
	Anon. (1557)	415
	Anon. (1561)	293
	Anon. (1561)	336
	Anon. (1562)	312
	Anon. (1566)	442
	Anon. (1569)	402, 407
	Anon. (1571)	429
	Anon. (1572)	375
	Anon. (1572)	410, 422
	Anon. (1577)	370, 375
	Anon. (1578)	322
	Anon. (1579)	383
	Anon. (1580)	429
	Anon. (1581)	375
	Anon. (1582)	375
	Anon. (1582)	412
	Anon. (1584)	274
	Anon. (1584)	377
	Anon. (1584)	383 (two)
	Anon. (1587)	424, 426
	Anon. (1588)	322
	Anon. (1588)	370
	Anon. (1588)	426 (two)
	Anon. (1592)	419
	Anon. (1594)	415

xx   *The Legal Profession and the Common Law*

Anon. (1594)	426	Anon. (1646)	121
Anon. (1594)	429	Anon. (1646)	163
Anon. (1595)	424	Anon. (1647)	223
Anon. (1595)	428	Anon. (1648)	163
Anon. (1596)	416	Anon. (1650)	163-4
Anon. (1599)	415	Anon. (1661)	298
Anon. (1599)	418	Anon. (1663)	277
Anon. (1600)	142	Anon. (1666)	293
Anon. (1601)	142	Anon. (1668)	344, 360, 363, 364
Anon. (1603)	425		
Anon. (1616)	225	Anon. (1672)	439
Anon. (1617)	329	Anon. (1673)	432
Anon. (1620)	270	Anon. (1673)	442
Anon. (1627)	223	Anon. (1698)	300
Anon. (1629)	120	Anon. (1775)	290
Anon. (1631)	120		

(2) Cases cited by name

Aboas v. Raworth (c. 1666)	365	Bate v. Luce (n.d.)	365
Addis's case (1609)	211	Bawdes v. Amhurst (1715)	116
Albany's case (1585)	190	Baxter v. Read (1584)	389
Aldridge v. Woolridge (1597)	126	Baynard v. Maltby (1531)	351
Allen's case (1615)	213, 216-17	Beaulieu v. Finglam (1401)	363
		Becher v. Mountjoye (1573)	387
Allen v. Nash (1635)	452	Beckwith's case (1585)	194
Alston v. Pamphyn (1596)	418	Bedford v. Eyre (1559)	375
Alton Woods, Case of (1600)	190	Beecher v. Sturges (1596)	419
Annesley v. Kytley (1539)	372	see also Turgys	
Apsley's case (1615)	212-13	Belasyse v. Hester (1697)	364
Archer's case (1597)	190	Benet v. Kyng (1472)	87
Ashby v. White (1703)	457	Bestley v. Dixon (1610)	112
Ashford v. Thornton (1818)	268	Beswick v. Cunden (1596)	418
Ashhurst v. Thomas (c. 1628)	359, 365	Bigby v. Kennedy (1770)	262
Ashley's case (1611)	199	Bill v. Body (1560)	226
Astwick's case (1567)	211	Blanke v. Spinula (1520)	354, 400
Aswel v. Osborn (c. 1628)	359, 365	Blocke's case (1597)	426
Atkyns v. Longvile (1604)	203	Blofield v. Havers (1592)	202
Att.-Gen. v. B.B.C. (1980)	154	Blowlewell v. Turnwill (1637)	149
Att.-Gen. v. Glanvill (1616)	219	Bonham's case (1610)	184, 195
Att.-Gen. v. Hichecoke (1605)	142	Booreman v. Middle Temple (1641)	66, 67
Att.-Gen. v. Kinge (1596)	141	Bosyis v. Merewell (1292)	346
Att.-Gen. v. Parmeter (1607)	145	Boughton's case (n.d.)	111
Aubrey v. Flory (1321)	346, 347	Bracebridge's case (c. 1583)	389
		Bradford v. Woodhouse (1619)	113, 146
Babham v. Hampden (c. 1545)	108	Bredon's case (1597)	190
Baker (Sir John) his case (c. 1550)	187	Brickwood v. Fanshaw (1690)	121
Baker v. Bains (1826)	61	Broker's case (1490)	398
Bancroft's case (c. 1608)	184	Bromwich v. Lloyd (1698)	360, 365
Bandon's case (1313)	346	Brooke v. Harrald (1594)	137
Bankes v. Allen (1615)	112	Brooke v. Mountague (1605)	105, 122
Barkley v. Foster (1597)	417, 418	Broughton v. Prince (1589)	129, 131-4
Barnham v. Barrett (1602)	424-5	Brown v. Borlace (1697)	61
Bartlett v. Wright (1593)	475	Brown v. London (1669)	360
Barton v. Kyrkeby (1519)	68	Browne v. Cornely (1533)	372

Table of Cases

Brownlow v. Michel (1615)	207
Bryerley v. Staple Inn (1826)	61
Buckhurst (Lord) his case (1598)	190
Buckridge v. Shirley (1672)	439
Burgh v. Warnford (1553)	316
Burley v. Wisse (1601)	421
Burton (Andrew) his case (1637)	135
Burton v. Davy (1437)	352
Busshewell v. Rye (1546)	375
Butterye v. Goodman (1583)	382-3
Calmady's case (1574)	385
Calvin's case (1608)	183, 191, 194
Camond v. Jent (1596)	428
Cantok v. De Wyche (1294)	103
Cantrell v. Church (1601)	418
Capel's case (1592)	190
Carrier's case (1473)	345, 347-8
Carter v. Downich (1689)	362, 363, 364
Carye's case (1626)	111, 112, 133
Cawenfeld v. Elder (1546)	374
Chabnor v. Dyke (1589)	109
Chandler v. Meade (1705)	364
Chedington (Rector of) his case (1598)	190
Cholmeley v. Humble (1597)	190, 194
Churche v. Cantrell (1601)	428
Clapham's case (1627)	112
Clarke v. Martin (1702)	345
Clarke v. Robinson (c. 1662)	365
Claxton v. Swift (c. 1685)	365
Cleggatt v. Hammersly (1636)	133
Clement's Inn, Case of (1661)	67
Clement's Inn v. Ford (1632)	61
Clement's Inn v. Kellett (1678)	67
Cleymond v. Vincent (1520)	168, 428
Clifford v. Astrye (1642)	112
Clou v. Kellowe (1457)	60, 77
Cobat's case (1368)	264
Cobb v. Nore (1465)	185, 212
Collard v. Collard (1594)	203
College of Physicians v. Rose (1703)	117
Colson v. Cotton (1596)	417-8
Colt & Glover v. Coventry (Bishop) (1616)	207
Colvile v. Cutler (c. 1666)	365
Comberton's case (1313)	346
Commendams, Case of (1616)	207
Conservative Central Office v. Burrell (1982)	46
Constantine v. Barnes (1595)	136
Cook v. Pyne (n.d.)	384
Cooke's case (1581)	378
Copwode v. Staple Inn (c. 1527)	56
Corbet's case (1599)	190
Core v. May, executor of Woddye (1536-7)	351, 398, 399
Cory's case (n.d.)	112
Cottington v. Hulett (1588)	428
Cramlinton v. Evans (1689)	363
Crattendon's case (1599)	418
Crewe v. Curson (1582)	378
Crogate's case (1608)	184
Crouch v. Credit Foncier of England (1873)	344
Crowder v. Robinson (1577)	226
Cuppledike's case (1602)	190
Curle's case (n.d.)	184
Dacre (Lord), Re (1535)	167-8, 474
Darcy v. Allen, see Monopolies, Case of	
Daubeny v. Gore (1590)	182
Dean's case (1714)	122
Death v. Serwonters (1685)	365
Dederit v. Abbot of Ramsey (1315)	347
Derby (Earl of) his case (1598)	202
Devonshire (Earl of) his case (n.d.)	184
Digby v. Mountford (1575)	400
Digges' case (1600)	190
Doe d. Bennett v. Hale (1850)	116
Doige's case (1442)	104, 388, 389
Doket's case (1454)	135
Dolphyn v. Barne (1540)	354-5
Doughtey's case (1582)	202
Dowman's case (1583)	316
Dudley (Lord) v. Powles (1489)	397
Dunstable v. Le Bal (1278)	346
Duppa v. Jones (1602)	416, 427
Dynham v. Gylbert (1478)	77
Eaglechilde's case (1630)	360
Eason v. Newman (1596)	418, 420
Edgecomb v. Dee (1670)	432
Edie v. East India Co. (1760)	344
Edwards v. Burre (1573)	417, 422, 429
Egerton v. Margan (1610)	262
Elmer v. Thacker (1591)	182
Elyot v. Tofte (1513)	111
Englefield's case (1592)	202
Estrigge v. Owles (1588)	417
Eveleigh v. Parker (1640)	148
Evely v. Livermore (1646)	121

xxi

Ewers v. Benchkin (c. 1688)	366	Hadley v. Weymer (1500)	87
		Hagger's case (1598)	426
Finch v. Throgmorton (1591)	182	Halsequell v. Valance (1592)	135
Finch v. Throgmorton (1598)	208-9	Hare v. Browne (1586)	134
Fisher v. Sadler (1589)	138	Harford v. Gardiner (1588)	377
Five Knights' case (1627)	241	Harper v. Belfield (1594)	428
Flemish Merchants, Case of the (1313)	346	Hartilpoole v. Puttenham (1567)	107
		Harvy v. Stone (1539)	373, 376
Flower v. Flower (1597)	426	Harvye v. Facye (1596)	203
Fooly v. Preston (1586)	370	Hawley, Ex parte (n.d.)	112
Forster v. Alfray (1454)	60, 77	Heale v. Giddye (1591)	111-12, 134-5
Fortescue v. Coake (1616)	290		
Foster v. Scarlet (1587)	389	Heath v. Ridley (1614)	211, 215
Franklyn v. Boteler (1634)	112	Hele's case (1588)	216
Frisland's case (1596)	416	Hele, see also Heale	
Fulham v. Flemyng (1287)	347	Henstead's case (1594)	194
Fuller's case (1586)	370, 383	Herlakenden's case (1589)	182
Furnival's Inn v. Hardesty (1702)	64	Herne v. Roth (or Rolfe) (1634)	114, 141, 148-9
Furnival's Inn v. Leycrofte (c. 1487)	50, 65		
Furnival's Inn v. Pottyer (1499)	64	Hewton v. Forster (1536)	373
Fyneux v. Clyfford (1517)	379	Heydon's case (1584)	194
		Heydon v. Good (1600)	113, 141
Gage v. Johnson (1622)	113, 145	Hodge v. Vavisour (1612)	430
Gamford v. Nightingale (1605)	428	Hodges v. Steward (1695)	364
Gardiner v. Bellingham (1614)	410	Hogg v. Jackson (1601)	428-9
Gardner's case (1592)	271	Holcroft v. Beard (1600)	418
Gawod v. Bankes (1596)	428	Holiday v. Hicks (1600)	418
Gaywood v. Gent (1596)	428	Holmes v. Harryson (1549)	374
Gere v. Mone (1473)	87	Holt v. Oxenden (1542)	376
Germin v. Rolls (1596); see also Rolls	136, 138-40	Honesti v. Gerardin (1291)	346
		Horn's case (1456)	113, 135
Gerard (Lord) his case (1581)	384, 385	Howard v. Wood (1679)	431
Gibbon v. Budd (1863)	123	Howell v. Trevanion (1588)	370, 375, 387
Gibs v. Price (1650)	111, 112		
Giles v. Coulshill (1576)	89	Hudson's case (1558)	387
Gill v. Harewood (1587)	375	Huet v. Conquest (1616)	225
Glanvill v. Courtney (1616)	211-12, 215, 216-18	Hughes v. Robotham (1593)	410, 428
		Hull v. Daucomb (1425)	113
		Humfrey v. Humfrey (1577)	211
Goddard's case (1584)	186	Hunt v. Bate (1568)	378, 398
Godmanchester, Case of (1567)	165	Hunt v. Capell (1592)	190
Goodwin v. Gouldsmithe (1616)	217	Hunt v. Sone (1587)	415
Googe's case (1615)	214-15	Hurleston v. Lord Dacre (1568)	378
Gramson v. Bower (1584)	370, 378	Hyde v. Cormet (1594)	202
Graye (Lord) his case (1506)	399	Hyne v. Tanner (1597)	418
Gray's Inn v. Gargrave (1585)	64, 68, 69-70		
		Imber v. Wilking (1579)	193
Gren v. Berewyk (1311)	346	Inner Temple v. Ince (1677)	67
Grene v. Warde (n.d.)	352	Ireland v. Higgins (1589)	387
Gresham v. Tufold (1462)	63	Isack v. Barbour (1563)	370, 386
Grey (Lord) his case (1567)	372, 374, 377		
		Jordan's case (1535)	413
Grey v. Bolte (1544)	373	Jordan's case (1596)	429
Griggs v. Helhouse (1595)	429		

Kelloway v. Mere (1629)	114, 146	May v. Alvares (1595)	417
Kennedy v. Broun (1863)	123	May v. Cardwydin (1593)	419, 428
Kercher's case (1611)	430	Maydeford v. Love (1495)	87
Kinnersley v. Coper (c. 1589)	134	Maylard v. Kester (1599)	427
Knappe v. Comyn (1600)	356	Maynard v. Dyce (1542)	356, 357-8, 361, 362-3
Knappe v. Hedley (1600)	357, 358-9	Mayowe's case (1594)	190
Knight's case (1598)	194	Meane v. Peacher (1611)	430
Knight v. Rushworth (1596)	375	Messor v. Molyneux (1741)	123
Kyrryell v. Petillesdene (1446)	60	Michaell v. Dyas (1545)	352
		Michelbourne v. Burrell (1597)	415
Lane's case (1586)	159	Michell's case (1577)	211
Lane v. Cotton (1599)	133	Michell v. Cloutesham (1453)	60, 77
Lathebury v. Fitzherberd (1410)	124	Michell v. Dunsden (1595)	414
Lavandre v. Dele (1519)	354	Mildmay (Sir Anthony) his case (1614)	216
Leech v. Penton (1614)	113, 145, 147	Mildmay (Sir Walter) his case (1597)	202
Legate v. Pinchon (1611)	430	Mildmay v. Standish (1598)	190
Lethulier's case (1692)	364	Mildmay v. Standysh (1584)	376, 389
Levinz v. Randolph (1700)	64, 70	Milles v. Raynton (1600)	416, 428
Lewes v. Lany (1607)	119	Millington v. Burges (1587)	426
Lewes v. Style (1506)	138	Milton's case (1668)	360
Lilburne's case (1637)	267	Mingay v. Hammond (1618)	103
Lile v. Frencham (1587)	377, 383, 387	Monopolies, Case of (1602)	184, 192, 451, 455
Lincoln (Lord) his case (n.d.)	136		
Lincoln (Dean and Chapter) v. Barnard's Inn (1502)	56	Moor v. Row (c. 1630)	122
		Morgan v. Lloyd (1649)	281
Lincoln's Inn v. Bond (1770)	65	Moses v. Macferlan (1760)	432
Littleton's case (1602)	203	Mounsey v. Traves (c. 1621)	359, 365
Lloyd v. Gregory (n.d.)	188	Mounson (Lord) v. Bourne (1627)	159
Lloyd v. Loaring (1802)	65	Mounson v. Dawson (1630)	103
London (Chamberlain of) his case (1599)	194	Mounteagle (Lord) v. Worcester (1555)	399
London (City of) v. Goree (1676)	431	Mowenslowe v. Crowche (1531)	354
Lowys v. Lowys (1303)	347	Myddelton v. Foxley (1523)	352
Lucalli v. Foster (c. 1577)	356, 357	Myles v. Smythe (1595)	420
Lucy v. Walwyn (1561)	370, 379-81, 386		
		Nethersall's case (1596)	134
Lutwich v. Hussey (1583)	377, 416	Newcastle (Bailiffs of), Case of (1607)	166
Lyon's Inn v. Proctour (c. 1530)	65	Newman v. Gybbe (1549)	374
Magdalene College case (1615)	214	Norman v. Moore (1549)	374
Manser's case (1584)	186	Norman v. Sone (1594)	416
Manwood v. Worland (1557)	106, 111	Norwood v. Read (1558)	404, 428
Market Overt, Case of (1596)	194	Noys v. Downing (1663)	300
Markys v. Collys (1475)	88	Nurse v. Pounford (1631)	134
Marler v. Wilmer (1539)	372-3, 391		
Marsden v. Waithman (1826)	61	Oaste v. Taylor (1612)	359, 365, 366
Marsh v. Rainsford (1588)	120		
Martin v. Boure (1603)	356	Oklond v. Danvers (1311)	167
Martin v. Marshall (c. 1615)	159	Oliver v. Emsonne (1514)	103
Mason v. White (1699)	163	Omer's case (1608)	263
Mathews' case (1595)	429	Onely v. Kent (1577)	113, 138, 146
Matthews v. Hopkin (1665)	363		

Orwell v. Mortoft (1505)	385, 389, 399, 403, 413	Pynnok v. Clopton (1547)	374
		Pynnok v. Fyndern (1539)	372
		Pyrry v. Appowell (1545)	374
Osbourn v. Eden (1600)	113, 141		
Owtrede v. Whyte (1546)	374	Quasshe v. Skete (1538)	372
Oxford (Earl of) his case (1615)	208, 214-15	Quelch's case (c. 1610)	145
		Ramsey (Abbot of) v. Prior of Anglesey (1506)	398
Page's case (1585)	370		
Page's case (1591)	202	Rea (Lord) v. Ramsey (1631)	268
Paine v. Perramour (1596)	415	Read v. Rochforth (1556)	263
Palmer v. Boyer (1594)	112	Rege Inconsulto, Case of (1615)	207, 213
Palmer v. Randz (1599)	417	Rent v. Danyell (1549)	374, 376
Paramour v. Payne (1595); see also Paine	413, 420, 428	R. v. Abington (1586)	283, 288
		R. v. Abraham (1689)	273
Paston's case (1579)	401	R. v. Allen (1662)	299
Paston v. Genney (1471)	105, 400	R. v. Allyson (1679)	323
Payne v. Hyde (1596)	429	R. v. Alman (1765)	261
Peacham's case (1614)	207	R. v. Ames (1518)	305
Peare v. Jones (1634)	112	R. v. anon. (1539)	306
Pecke v. Redman (1555)	399-400	R. v. anon. (1553)	321
Peirson v. Ponuteis (1608)	360, 364	R. v. Ashfield (1623)	325
Pelham's case (1588)	190	R. v. Atwood (1617)	308, 326
Penrice v. Parker (1673)	121	R. v. Axtel (1660)	283, 288
Penros's case (1412)	119	R. v. Barbour (1490)	308
Perke v. Loveden (1601)	428, 429	R. v. Barnard's Inn (1836)	66
Phyllyp v. Heeth (1540)	373, 375	R. v. Bath (Mayor &c of) (1671)	101
Pickering, see Pykeryng		R. v. Berchet (1690)	266
Pigot's case (n.d.)	235	R. v. Blair (1689)	272
Pillesworth v. Feake (1602)	410, 427	R. v. Boothe (1602)	287
Pinchon's case (1611)	430	R. v. Bradshaw (1594)	201
Pinnel v. Cole (1602)	194	R. v. Bray (1627)	338
Pole's case (1425)	105, 107, 120	R. v. Bromwich (1666)	290
		R. v. Buckler (1551)	276
Pomeray v. Abbot of Buckfast (1442)	113, 135	R. v. Bull (1617)	335
		R. v. Bushell (1670)	270
Popham v. Prior of Breamore (1410)	405	R. v. Butterworth (1826)	61
		R. v. Carew (1660)	309
Pordage v. Cole (1669)	379	R. v. Carnabye (1641)	325
Porter's case (1592)	190	R. v. Cary (1597)	202
Postern's case (c. 1602)	142	R. v. Chandler (1702)	271
Powell's case (1618)	112	R. v. Charnock (1696)	283
Powell v. Preston (1601)	427	R. v. Chichester (1671)	270
Pratt v. Banks (1655)	149	R. v. Cobham (Lord) (1603)	201
Preston's case (1627)	134	R. v. Compton (1625)	296
Preston v. Tooley (1587)	370, 389	R. v. Cook (1774)	310
Primate v. Jackson (1664)	300	R. v. Cooke (1638)	325
Prince (Henry) his case (1606)	192	R. v. Cornwall (1591)	305
Prince's case (n.d.)	111	R. v. Cowley (1516)	337
Prince's case (n.d.)	235	R. v. Creyghton (1536)	306
Proclamations, Case of (1610)	199	R. v. Culliford (1704)	265
Prohibitions, Case of (1610)	199	R. v. Cusacke (1619)	362
Purslowe v. Tisdale (1600)	416	R. v. Dacre (1593)	201
Pykeryng v. Thurgoode (1532)	389, 413	R. v. Da Gama (1594)	201
Pylat v. FitzSibill (1308)	347	R. v. Davy (1536)	306

Table of Cases

R. v. Delarever (1536)	306, 308	R. v. Knightsbridge Crown Court (1981)	164
R. v. Delbridge (1618)	308, 326	R. v. Lambe (c. 1620)	307
R. v. Dennis (1557)	286	R. v. Langhorn (1679)	290
R. v. Devonshire (Duke of) (1687)	296	R. v. Latham (1673)	300
R. v. Devonshire (Earl of) (1596)	201	R. v. Leach (1664)	270
R. v. Deynes (1535)	307	R. v. Leighton (1708)	299
R. v. Doyle (1769)	294	R. v. Lenthal (1589)	306
R. v. Dunn (1765)	301	R. v. Lilburne (1653)	282
R. v. Dyer (1703)	271	R. v. Lincoln's Inn (1825)	66
R. v. Edgerley (1641)	273, 296	R. v. Lisle (1685)	294
R. v. Essex (Earl of) (1601)	201	R. v. Lomas (1694)	299
R. v. Fawkes (1605)	202	R. v. Long (1596)	298, 308, 326
R. v. Felton (1628)	294	R. v. Lopes (1594)	201
R. v. FitzHarris (1681)	252	R. v. Love (1651)	290
R. v. Foster (1616)	335	R. v. Mackalley (1611)	325
R. v. Foxby (1704)	298	R. v. Madan (1780)	297
R. v. Gardiner (1533)	306, 320-1	R. v. Mansell (1584)	270
R. v. Gardiner (1665)	300	R. v. Mapurley (1538)	306
R. v. Gargrave (1615)	299	R. v. Mason (1756)	287
R. v. Geary (1688)	292	R. v. Menville (1584)	201
R. v. Gibbons (1651)	272, 283	R. v. Moders (1663)	290
R. v. Godfrey (1616)	335	R. v. Moreley (1760)	271
R. v. Gore (1611)	317	R. v. Morley (Lord) (1666)	290
R. v. Gray's Inn (1780)	66	R. v. Moseley (1647)	288
R. v. Gwin (1672)	323	R. v. Norfolk (Duke of) (1571)	289
R. v. Hale (1741)	294	R. v. Nubolt (1511)	312
R. v. Halle (1536)	307	R. v. Oates (1688)	296
R. v. Hardy (1794)	288	R. v. Oneby (1727)	316
R. v. Harman (1619)	286, 289, 293	R. v. Page (1633)	261, 329
R. v. Harrison (1638)	295	R. v. Paine (1695)	290
R. v. Harrison (1660)	282, 283	R. v. Parker (1782)	323
R. v. Harvey (1660)	288	R. v. Peters (1660)	283
R. v. Harwood (1616)	334	R. v. Phorbes (1681)	299
R. v. Hatton (1354)	124	R. v. Plummer (1701)	317
R. v. Haydon (1618)	336	R. v. Porter (1703)	298
R. v. Hedges (1779)	323	R. v. Pursell (1590)	274
R. v. Hickman (1785)	323	R. v. Raleigh (1603)	288, 289, 290
R. v. Hodgson (c. 1700)	301	R. v. Ratcliffe (1746)	283
R. v. Holloway (1628)	325	R. v. Reason & Tranter (1722)	319
R. v. Holmes (1634)	325	R. v. Reynoldes (1618)	337
R. v. Hood (1666)	270	R. v. Rice (1616)	298
R. v. Huggins (1730)	317	R. v. Rogers (1532)	307
R. v. Humfrey (1607)	282	R. v. Rosewell (1684)	283, 288
R. v. Hunt (1627)	339-40	R. v. Roupell (1776)	279
R. v. Hurdman (1661)	288	R. v. Royley (1612)	319, 325
R. v. Isley (1785)	323	R. v. Rudd (1775)	291
R. v. James (1661)	283, 291	R. v. Russell (Lord) (1683)	290
R. v. Johnson (1686)	273	R. v. St Catharine's Hall (1791)	234
R. v. Jones (1665)	300	R. v. Salisbury (1554)	286
R. v. Joyner (1664)	316	R. v. Saunders & Archer (1574)	313, 335-6
R. v. Kareck (1616)	334	R. v. Saunders (1669)	299
R. v. Kinloch (1746)	300	R. v. Scott (1785)	293
R. v. Kirk (1699)	290		

R. v. Senior (1788)	73, 323
R. v. Shaftesbury (Earl of) (1681)	264, 282
R. v. Shaw (1785)	301
R. v. Sherleys (1557)	269
R. v. Shipley (1784)	311
R. v. Sidley (1663)	305
R. v. Smith (1681)	300
R. v. Standish (1670)	438
R. v. Stevens (1640)	308, 326
R. v. Strafford (1641)	239
R. v. Strickland (1617)	297
R. v. Sturgys (1539)	307
R. v. Taverner (1616)	273, 334
R. v. Templeman (1702)	284
R. v. Thatcher (1676)	290
R. v. Thomas (1554)	269, 289
R. v. Thomas (1613)	287, 293
R. v. Thorely (1672)	283
R. v. Throckmorton (1554)	288, 289
R. v. Tong (1662)	291
R. v. Tooke (1795)	289
R. v. Udall (1590)	288, 289
R. v. Vane (1661)	282, 286, 300
R. v. Waite (1743)	285
R. v. Wakeman (1679)	288
R. v. Walcot (1695)	295
R. v. Watlyngton (1499)	306
R. v. Weston (1536)	308
R. v. Wilkes (1770)	299
R. v. Windham (1667)	270
R. v. Wody (1470)	320
R. v. Wye (1595)	299
R. v. Wynne (1582)	321
R. v. Wynster (1605)	202
R. v. Wynyard (1539)	306
R. v. Yonge (1610)	322-3
Reynell's case (1617)	227
Reynold's case (1597)	134
Rich v. Holt (1609)	112
Rich v. Kneeland (1613)	363
Richards' case (1542)	363
Richards v. Bartlet (1584)	370
Right's case (1455)	405
Rioters' case (1681)	300
Rolls v. Germine (1596); see also Germyn	113
Rondel v. Worsley (1967)	122, 124
Rudder v. Price (1791)	415, 424
Rudston's case (1549)	109
Rudyard's case (1670)	168
Ruswell's case (1615)	212-13, 227
Rutton's case (1592)	426
Sackford v. Phillips (1594)	416
St Edmundsbury Diocesan Board v. Clark (1973)	155
St Mary Overy (Prior of) v. Culpeper (1523)	166
Sanderson v. Ekins (1588)	426
Sands v. Trevilian (1630)	114, 146
Sandys (Lady) her case (1640)	234
Sarsfield v. Witherley (1689)	363, 366
Scavage v. Tateham (1601)	281
Selden's case (1629)	241
Semayne's case (1604)	191
Serjeants' Inn v. Brown (1824)	61
Serle v. Rosse (1596)	429
Seymour v. Butterworth (1862)	60
Shackleton v. Grene (1596)	417
Sharington v. Strotton (1566)	376-7, 384
Sheffield v. Rise (1594)	410, 422
Shelley's case (1581)	183, 188, 189, 190, 194, 454, 455
Shepparde v. Becher (1600)	358, 359 363
Ship Money, Case of (1638)	241
Shipton v. Dogge, see Doige's case	
Shrewsbury (Earl of) his case (1610)	168
Shrewsbury (Earl of) v. Furnival's Inn (c. 1508)	56
Shuttleworth v. Bolton (n.d.)	455
Shuttleworth v. Garrett (1689)	431
Sidney Sussex College, Case of (1642)	234
Simcocke v. Payne (1601)	427, 428
Slade v. Morley (1602)	168, 188, 354, 357, 393-432, 438-9, 451, 454
Smeeton v. Collier (1847)	163
Smith's case (1600)	209
Smith v. Aiery (1705)	360
Smith v. Desmond (1965)	337
Smith v. Hitchcocke (1587)	375
Smith v. Kerr (1902)	57
Smith v. Smith (1584)	383
Smith v. Taylor (1771)	262
Smyth v. Bocher (1595)	410
Snagg v. Gray (1571)	111
Snigg v. Chambers (1647)	144
Snowe v. Jourdan (1572)	370, 387
Soly v. Perott (1547)	354
Somerset's case (1616)	207

Table of Cases

Spence v. Bryan (1468)	351
Spencer v. Hemmerde (1922)	430
Stanhope v. Blythe (1586)	111
Steadman v. Hockley (1846)	122
Stewart v. Hodges (1693)	360
Stone's case (1562)	330
Stone v. Mounford (1587)	134
Stone v. Withypoll (1588)	370, 377, 384
Stout v. Cowper (1699)	262
Strangborough v. Warner (1589)	383
Stratton v. Swanlond (1375)	398
Stubbings v. Rotheram (1595)	429
Stupholm v. Hart (1680)	122
Sturges, see Turgys	
Sturlyn v. Albany (1587)	377
Sukley v. Wyte (1543)	388
Sutton's Hospital, Case of (1612)	193
Sydenham v. Worlington (1585)	385, 389
Syms v. Newbury (1629)	122
Tailboys v. Sherman (1443)	404
Tailor v. Jeretrude (1452)	107
Tailour's case (1450)	113
Tanfield's case (n.d.)	415
Tayllor v. Kyme (1533)	372
Taylor v. Foster (1601)	415
Taylor v. Lodington (1593)	414
Teheran-Europe Co v. S.T. Belton Ltd (1968)	344
Thetford's case (c. 1589)	182
Thorneton v. Kempe (1596)	428
Thornhill v. Evans (1742)	122
Thorp v. Evans (1742)	122
Thorp v. Makerel (1318)	163
Thoroughgood's case (1584)	186, 194
Throckmorton v. Finch (1598); see also Finch	202
Thumansen v. Van Prussen (1600)	356, 357
Thursby v. Warren (1629)	114, 146, 147
Tito v. Waddell (1975)	155
Tisdall v. Bevington (n.d.)	127
Tompson v. Hollingsworth (1641)	223
Tooley v. Windham (1590)	377
Towll v. Hawkyns (1549)	355
Townsend v. Mayor of Oxford (1663)	66
Trobervil v. Brent (1611)	215
Trussell v. Mounslowe (c. 1596)	140
Turfote v. Pytcher (1543)	374
Turgys (or Sturges) v. Becher (1596); see also Beecher	414, 415, 419-20, 428
Turnaunt v. Bastard (1467)	56
Turnaunt v. Clerk (1467)	56
Turner v. Philipps (1791)	120
Turnor v. Nelethropp (1531)	400
Tusten v. Clotworthy (1600)	356
Tyll v. Brockhouse (1548)	375
Utber v. Couper (1654)	149
Vandeput v. Messam (n.d.)	366
Vanheath v. Turner (1621)	360, 363
Vaughan's case (1596)	194
Vaus v. Serle (1589)	134
Vavasour v. Puttenham (c. 1558)	106, 108
Veitch v. Russell (1842)	123
Vernon's case (1572)	177
Vynter's case (1465)	83, 254
Wade v. Braunch (1596)	413
Wakelin v. Coles (1739)	61
Walker v. Myddylton (1542)	351
Walkyn v. Butts (1683)	365
Walton's case (1567)	377
Warren v. Smith (1615)	214
Watkins' case (1425)	403
Webb's case (1577)	370, 389
West v. Stowell (1577)	382, 384
Whitehed v. Elderton (1530)	400, 410
Whorwood v. Gybbons (1587)	375, 415
Wild's case (1599)	194
Williams v. Williams (1596)	414, 415
Williams v. Williams (1693)	363
Wilson v. Pecke (1629)	141, 146-8
Winchcomb v. Goddard (1601)	298
Wiseman's case (1584)	186
Wiseman (Jane) her case (1598)	334
Wiseman v. Barnard (1585)	389
Woodford v. Deacon (1608)	410
Woodward v. Rowe (1666)	363
Worthington v. Garstone (1580)	113, 138
Wortley v. Savill (1600)	113, 141
Wraynham's case (1618)	211
Wright's case (1614)	211
Wright v. Fowler (1614)	215
Wright v. Green (1602)	429
Wyvell v. Frenche (1534)	372
Zangis v. Whiskeard (n.d.)	455
Zouch (Lord) his case (1603-4)	202, 454-5

I

THE LEGAL PROFESSION

1

THE INNS OF COURT IN 1388

Professor Simpson's discovery of a note concerning the 1425 call of serjeants [1] has, besides raising a puzzling question about the Outer Temple, shown that the four Inns of Court had already attained their superiority over the lesser inns which Fortescue collectively described as Inns of Chancery. But how new was that superior status in 1425? Had there been a time when Fortescue's distinction between greater and lesser inns could not have been made? Modern writers agree that the origins of the various inns lie somewhere in the fourteenth century, but the reluctance of any new evidence to present itself has kept the details of the story surprisingly obscure. The most we can say with confidence is that the town-houses where the apprentices of the Bench lived in term-time had acquired by the 1350s educational as well as purely residential functions,[2] and the inns had thereby become societies.

A happy discovery in the Bodleian Library enables a little of the story between the 1350s and 1425 to be revealed. A call of serjeants took place on or soon after 20 October 1388, no doubt occasioned by the upheavals which occurred in the judicial system earlier in the year. The event is mentioned in two manuscript Year Books, though the note was unfortunately omitted from the Ames Foundation edition of 12 Richard II.[3] In the Bodleian version the new serjeants' former Inns are stated:

"Nota quod a die sancti Michelis in Tres Septimanas termino supradicto Hugo Huls et Johannes Woderove de Greysynne Willelmus Crosby Willelmus Gascoyne Johannes Cassy Willelmus Bryncheley et Robertus Hyll interioris Templi et Willelmus Hankeforde medii templi dederunt aurum etc."

The note is of value for a number of reasons.

First, it establishes the details of the second recorded call of

---

[1] Brit.Lib., MS. Harley 5159, f. 35v; 89 L.Q.R. 32. The call took place on or soon after 17 June 1425 (not 1426).

[2] See M.29 Edw. 3, 47, pl. [13] ("ceo ne fuit unques excepcion in cest place, mes nous lavomus oy sovent enter les apprentices in hostelles"); Rot.Claus. 37 Edw. 3 [C54/201], m.20 ("Quia Ricardus de Norwico . . . apprentista de communi Banco nostro super erudicione sua inter alios apprentistas de eodem Banco apud London pro maiori parte anni personaliter moratur"). For learning exercises possibly conducted in these nascent societies, see the "Quaestiones compilatae de statutis" in Camb.Univ.Lib., MSS. Hh.2.8, ff. 115–123v; Ll.4.17, ff. 219–222v.

[3] Bodl.Lib., MS. Bodley 189, f. 32v; Lincoln's Inn, MS. Hale 77, f. 247v. These were MSS. *G* and *A* respectively in G. F. Deiser (ed.), *Year Books 12 Richard II* (1914).

serjeants, a call not mentioned in the reference books. And in so doing it confirms the paramount importance which then attached to the custom of distributing gold: the reporter (like his fifteenth-century successors) did not use the word "serjeant" at all, but merely noted the giving of gold. In this respect all the Year Book reporters followed the precedent set by him who reported the first recorded call on 26 January 1383:

> "Nota quod isto termino Hillarii Cherletoun Thirnyng Marcham Loktoun Hulle Wadham Pynchebek et Rikille dederunt aurum scilicet cras conversionis sancti Pauli etc." [4]

Even this was probably not the first group call. The names in the 1388 note correspond almost exactly with the conjectural list which Professor Arnold has calculated from the sudden appearance of the new serjeants' names in the Year Books.[5] The coincidence of these lists makes it almost certain that Professor Arnold is correct in supposing, by similar calculation, two earlier calls in 1372 and 1376. We must hope that these will in time be confirmed by manuscript evidence, but search has not so far proved fruitful.

The 1388 note also shows that all the serjeants of that call came from inns which we know as Inns of Court. Although in 1396 a serjeant was called from Clifford's Inn, we have already guessed that this was exceptional: so exceptional, indeed, as to warrant a commemorative inscription in the hall window.[6] The ascendancy of the major inns may explain the Chancery ordinance of 1388 which attempted to set the Inns of Chancery (not yet a generic term for all the lesser inns) above, or at least apart from, the inns of the apprentices.[7] Fortescue's clear demarcation between the Inns of Court and Chancery had probably not yet emerged; the distinction was rather between the inns of the men of court (the apprentices of the Bench) and the inns of the Chancery clerks. But it now seems established that in practice certain major inns were, by 1388, identifiable as superior to the other inns, at least in the sense that they alone provided the leaders of the Bar.

An obvious omission from the note is Lincoln's Inn. Even in 1425, Lincoln's Inn provided only one new serjeant,[8] and references to the Inn as a legal society may be sought in vain before the Black

---

[4] Lincoln's Inn, MS. Hale 77, f. 194.
[5] M. S. Arnold (ed.), *Year Books 2 Richard II* (1975), p. xxxiii. The only divergence is that Clay does not appear in the Year Book; he was summoned in 1382–3, but defaulted.
[6] Brit.Lib., MS. Harley 980, f. 261; *infra*, p. 117.
[7] G. W. Sanders, *Orders of the High Court of Chancery* (1845), i, 1, at pp. 2–5; T. F. Tout, *Chapters in the Administrative History of Medieval England* (1928), iii, 446–447.
[8] John Weston, who owned St Mary's Inn: will dated 1419, proved 1427, P.C.C. 8 Luffenham.

Books commence in 1422.[9] Although a sample of eight lawyers is not sufficiently large to enable any firm conclusions to be drawn, the omission must strengthen the doubt whether Lincoln's Inn existed as an Inn of Court as early as 1388.

As far as the other three Inns are concerned, the note furnishes the earliest known reference to each of them as distinct societies, showing in particular that the Temple was already divided into two. Hitherto the earliest known reference to the Middle Temple was in a will of 1404, while Professor Simpson's discovery itself contained the earliest mention of the other two. The known history of all three societies is therefore carried back a generation. By the same token, we now have the names of the first eight men known to have belonged to particular Inns of Court. All are known from other sources; five became judges, and we still have portraits of three of them.[10]

The biographical aspect of the discovery leads still further. The clear statement that Gascoigne C.J. was from the Inner Temple—a fact which Fuller stated long ago, but without giving his source [11]— finally discredits the earlier portion of the Segar chronicle of members of Gray's Inn, which has been the foundation for some speculation about the early history of the Inn.[12] Segar's work has already proved unreliable. He seems to have confused two Markhams, and his claim on Starkey C.B. conflicts with another Year-Book note of a serjeants' call.[13] It has been persuasively contended that he took the names from sixteenth-century windows in the hall or chapel, or failed to distinguish different generations of lawyers with the same surname.[14] Now that the only contemporary evidence proves Segar wrong about Gascoigne as well, the doubts previously felt about his authority become certainties. His statements about the readerships in the fourteenth century can no longer be taken seriously.

Inner Templars may well rejoice at finding the great Gascoigne among their alumni. They will also have noticed that no less than five of the eight new serjeants were drawn from that society, as against one from the Middle Temple. We must repeat the caution that this is a limited sample,[15] but it strongly suggests that the Inner Temple may have been the largest inn in 1388. This would hardly be

---

[9] See R. F. Roxburgh, *Black Books of Lincoln's Inn*, V (1968), at p. 465. There is a valuable survey of what is known about the early inns, *ibid.*, pp. 448–476.
[10] Huls J. (brass at Watford, Hertfordshire); Gascoigne C.J. (effigy at Harewood, Yorkshire); and Cassy C.B. (brass at Deerhurst, Gloucestershire).
[11] T. Fuller, *History of the Worthies of England* (1662), p. 199.
[12] Brit.Lib., MS. Harley 1912. The list is printed in W. R. Douthwaite, *Gray's Inn* (1886), pp. 45–76; it is substantially reliable from Tudor times onwards.
[13] T.18 Edw. 4, 10, pl. 29: again the Inner Temple wins.
[14] A. W. B. Simpson, " The Early Constitution of Gray's Inn " [1975] *Cambridge Law Journal* 131 at pp. 135–138.
[15] In 1425 the proportions were: Gray's Inn (3), Inner Temple (2), Middle Temple (1), Outer Temple (1), Lincoln's Inn (1). Gray's Inn held sway in the Order of the Coif for most of the 15th century.

surprising, since it occupied the core of the old military establishment; the Inner Temple hall stands where the ill-starred knights who preceded the lawyers kept their refectory. It appears that the Temple housed the principal, if not the first, nucleus of lawyers in the suburbs of London. There was an old tradition that lawyers were there by 1346, and reasonable evidence that apprentices of the Bench lived there in 1356. Chaucer—who may himself have been a fellow of the Inner Temple[16]—mentions " a Temple" as a society of expert lawyers, and we hear from chroniclers of the havoc wrought there among the *apprenticii nobiliores* by the insurgents of 1381.[17] It may be mere chance, but we do not yet find literary allusions to the other societies by name. The Temple, whether or not an undivided Temple, seemed the archetypal inn of court as soon as such a thing was recognisable. It would not be too fanciful to suppose that, the lawyers having first moved into the apartments of the knights around the hall and church, the Middle Temple (and, to judge from the 1425 note, the Outer Temple) represented extensions necessitated by the increase in their numbers.

NOTE

For an agreement to maintain a student among the apprentices of the king's court as early as 1323, see M. J. Bennett, "Provincial Gentlefolk and Legal Education" (1984) 57 B.I.H.R. 203-208. For learning exercises around 1340, see below, pp. 13-14. There is a useful survey of what is now known about the early history of the inns of court and chancery in N. L. Ramsay, "The English Legal Profession *c.* 1340-*c.* 1450" (Cambridge Ph. D. thesis, 1985), Appendix 5, pp. xv-xlii.

---

[16] E. Rickert, " Was Chaucer a Student at the Inner Temple?" in *Manly Anniversary Studies in Language and Literature* (1923), pp. 20-31; J. M. Manly, *Some New Light on Chaucer* (1926), pp. 7-45. Tout had reservations, but they now seem less well-founded: see " Literature and Learning in the English Civil Service " (1929) 4 *Speculum* 365 at pp. 383-384.

[17] R. F. Roxburgh, " Lawyers in the New Temple " (1972) 88 L.Q.R. 414.

2

LEARNING EXERCISES IN THE MEDIEVAL INNS OF COURT AND CHANCERY*

Sir Edward Coke, describing the inns of court and chancery in 1602, said they "altogether do make the most famous university for profession of law only, or of any human science, that is in the world, and advanceth itself above all others".[1] This legal university, which Sir George Buc a few years later named "The Third Universitie of England",[2] was not a university in the technical sense; it had no *studium generale*, its masters did not possess the *jus ubique docendi*, its regulation was independent of the Church, its members were unincorporated and there was no charter of foundation. Not only was there no central structure or constitution, but the individual societies were not in the legal sense colleges; they were unincorporated associations of lawyers living together in hostels. Yet it would be misleading to regard the inns, except perhaps in their earliest stages, as purely private societies. They constituted one of the foremost institutions of medieval England, an institution which in the later middle ages and beyond served much the same function with respect to the lay administrators and governors of England as the two universities did for the Church.

Of the origins of the inns nothing is known, but we do know that they acquired most of their principal characteristics by the end of the fourteenth century. Already by 1388 the societies of the Inner and Middle Temple and Gray's Inn seem to have attained a superior status,[3] and either by that time or soon afterwards Lincoln's Inn joined them as the fourth of the inns which in the fifteenth century were distinguished as the inns "of court".[4] The lesser inns fluctuated in number and size, but little is yet known of their history before Tudor times. They came to be called inns "of chancery" because some of them had originated as hostels kept by Chancery clerks; but by no means all of them began in that way. By the end of the fifteenth century the number had settled at nine,[5] and no more were subsequently founded. The inns as a whole were

---

* Extended version of an unpublished lecture.

[1] *Le tierce part*... [The Third Part of Coke's *Reports*] (1602), preface.
[2] Appendix to J. Stow, *Annales* (1615).
[3] See above, pp. 3–6.
[4] R. F. Roxburgh, "Lincoln's Inns of the Fourteenth Century" (1978) 94 L.Q.R. 363–382. See also his "Lawyers in the New Temple" (1972) 88 L.Q.R. 414–430. For a thesis as to the origins of the inns, see S. E. Thorne, "The early History of the Inns of Court" (1959) 50 *Graya* 79–96; *Essays in English Legal History*, pp. 137–154.
[5] Barnard's Inn, Clement's Inn, Clifford's Inn, Davies (later Thavies) Inn, Furnival's Inn, Lyon's Inn, New Inn, Staple Inn and Strand Inn.

not much smaller than the University of Cambridge in the mid-fifteenth century, numbering between them about a thousand residents.[6] Sir John Fortescue, a governor of Lincoln's Inn in the time of Henry VI, foreshadowed Coke's sentiments when he described them as comprising a *studium publicum* more suitable for the study of the common law than any university, by virtue of its proximity to the king's courts.[7]

The men who flocked to this law school were not necessarily seeking legal careers in the narrow sense. The best intellects, particularly if fired by ambition or need, might well stay the course and become eminent practitioners and perhaps eventually judges; or they might enter the higher ranks of the civil service, which by 1450 was more than half lay. The less well able or well placed found employment as attorneys or court officials, or as financial or general advisers, or in local government. The vast majority returned to the country to follow their fathers as country gentlemen, making use of their brief acquaintance with legal scholarship when acting as justices of the peace or when discussing their own affairs with their counsel. All, however, were in some measure exposed to the learning exercises in the inns, and it is likely that these tests of skill and industry helped to sort out the men of destiny from the men of more modest abilities. The inns therefore fulfilled one of the roles of a university in discovering the relative abilities of the young and setting them on appropriate careers. But this object was attained through the study and exercise of one severe discipline only, and it was normally achieved (so far as we can tell) with minimal tutorial coddling.[8] Students were expected largely to teach themselves or at best to teach each other. Much could be learned by attending Westminster Hall in term-time and discussing afterwards what one had observed. There was an obscure institution known as the *pecunes* or *pekenes* which apparently facilitated such discussion; the etymology of this word has so far eluded the grasp of the few who have turned their mind to it, though it appears to have denoted the wooden gallery at the side of the court.[9] To this kind of self-help the learning exercises added a more ordered framework for study and a measure of individual prowess. Attending the exercises, together with attending the courts, was the principal method of learning legal

---

[6] The figures for both institutions are somewhat uncertain. The problem is discussed below, pp. 75–98.
[7] S. B. Chrimes (ed.), *Sir John Fortescue De Laudibus Legum Angliae* (Cambridge, 1942), ch. 48, p. 116.
[8] There are occasional references to supervision. In 1432 an orphan was sent to Gray's Inn to be instructed under the care of Richard Hungate: R. R. Sharpe (ed.), *Calendar of Letter Books of the City of London*, Book K (1911), p. 143. And in the Paston letters is a request of about 1478 for a young kinsman to be placed "for hys lernyng" with a member of Lincoln's Inn, "and to be occupied under a drede of displeser undre subjection, wyth erly rysyng accustomed, for slouth ys the moder and noryssher of all vice": N. Davis (ed.), *Paston Letters and Papers*, Vol. II (1976), p. 423, no. 780. Probably sharing chambers with an older relative was the usual way of ensuring supervision.
[9] Below, pp. 171–175.

skills when books were few. Performing in them, and surviving, was the only legal examination which mattered.

Graduation by performing exercises

These latter remarks might equally be made of the medieval universities. The modern conception of graduation, as a combination of examination success and presentation ceremony, does not readily fit the medieval picture. The formalities of graduation which survived in the older universities were not so much graduation ceremonies as vestigial survivals of the various stages in the old system of exercises. Graduation under that system was a beginning rather than an ending of each stage in the course of disputations (or *quaestiones*) and lectures; and the graduation occurred, not by the incantation of a Latin formula, but by the actual performance of the appropriate exercises. Thus a Cambridge bachelor of arts was not admitted, as now, *ad gradum baccalaurei in artibus*; he was admitted *ad respondendum quaestioni*, and only became a complete bachelor by "determination" in the schools.[10] Bachelors in the higher faculties were admitted *ad intrandum*, while masters and doctors were admitted *ad incipiendum* in their respective faculties. At first glance this system might seem very remote from the inns of court and chancery. It would have been strange, however, if the educational notions of Paris, Oxford and Cambridge, which were taken for granted in university circles, had no influence in London. And we believe that in truth the obvious differences are outweighed by the similarities.

In the classical inns of court system, as established by the midfifteenth century, the student progressed through actual participation in the exercises. At first he was involved solely in basic reading and rote learning, and in disputations or moots at an elementary level. When he was of standing to dispute at or outside the "bar" of his inn, he became an utter-barrister simply by so doing. Later he might be chosen to deliver lectures, and in the capacity of *lector* or "reader" he also presided over disputations, propounding and determining questions. After reading he became a senior member of his inn, sitting on the bench at moots. It is unlikely that these advancements were at first accompanied by much ceremony or formality. We may well imagine that the first "calls" to the bar were merely invitations to take the place

---

[10] For the last survivals, see H. Gunning (ed.), *The Ceremonies observed in the Senate House of the University of Cambridge* (Cambridge, 1828). These may be compared with the lengthier exercises described in the 16th century by Matthew Stokes: printed in G. Peacock, *Observations on the Statutes of the University of Cambridge* (Cambridge, 1841) appendix A. The determination became the "tripos", a word derived from the seat on which an "old bachelor" sat to dispute with the determiners: cf. bench and bar in the inns. The words of creation (or inauguration) were pronounced collectively by the proctors, and not (as Rashdall says) by the vice-chancellor: it was thus a faculty matter, part of the exercise, rather than a university matter.

of barristers at moots. No doubt promotion soon came to be regulated by customs and orders as to standing, but in the inns (as in the universities) the rules were easily varied or dispensed with to suit particular individuals who provided sufficient consideration; and the fifteenth-century "Black Books" of Lincoln's Inn, like the coeval proctors' grace books of Cambridge and Oxford, are full of these *ad hominem* arrangements. The degrees of barrister and bencher are first mentioned in the Black Books in 1466, in the first of a series of orders which make it clear that call to either status carried with it educational obligations during the learning vacations.[11] As late as 1475 the older concept of graduation is apparent in a dispute about whether men who had been called to sit on the bench at moots during the vacation, for want of other benchers, were caught by the regulations requiring new benchers to keep six learning vacations;[12] evidently it was argued that by presiding over moots they had ipso facto become benchers, just as presumably anyone who once argued from without the bar was automatically an utter-barrister. By the end of that century calls to the bar and bench were becoming more solemn, and in 1494 it was ordered in Lincoln's Inn that they should not take place without the advice of the governors and all the benchers given in term-time.[13] Still it was not thought necessary to record calls to the bar in any permanent form. Lincoln's Inn began to do so in 1518, but the other inns did not follow suit until the time of Elizabeth I. It was during this period that calling to the bar came to be seen as a public graduation which carried with it a minimum qualification for practice in the central courts.[14] From this period also, and for the same reason, the inns introduced some uniformity into their regulations. It was only at that stage that someone thought to describe the system in writing: in about 1540 a report was prepared for King Henry VIII explaining it in some detail, and there survives from the inquiry a description of the constitution and customs of the Middle Temple.[15]

By 1540 the system had reached its final form. The two main types of exercise, readings and moots, took place in the learning vacations during Lent (in February or March) and during August. Some moots also took place in term-time. Those who had delivered readings were

---

[11] J. D. Walker (ed.), *The Records of Lincoln's Inn. The Black Books*, Vol. I (1897), pp. 41–42.
[12] *Ibid.*, p. 59.
[13] *Ibid.*, p. 100.
[14] J. H. Baker, *The Reports of Sir John Spelman*, Vol. II (Selden Soc., Vol. XCIV, 1978), introduction, p. *129*; and the references in note 5 there.
[15] Report by T. Denton, N. Bacon and R. Cary, printed in E. Waterhous, *Fortescutus Illustratus* (1663), pp. 543–546, and reprinted by D. S. Bland, "Henry VIII's Royal Commission on the Inns of Court" (1969) 10 Jo. Soc. Public Teachers of Law 178–194. The Middle Temple report in Brit. Lib. Cotton MS Vitellius C. IX, ff. 319-323, is edited by R. M. Fisher, "Thomas Cromwell, the Dissolution of the Monasteries, and the Inns of Court" (1977) 14 Jo. Soc. Public Teachers of Law 111–117.

thereafter accounted benchers, and sat on the bench at moots. The "bench" was evidently the high table occupied to this day by the benchers in the hall of each inn. Set before them, in the middle of the hall, were forms "which they call the bar". The "inner barristers", or youngest students, sat on the inside of the forms, and the "utter barristers" on the outside. The latter were those who "for their learning and continuance are called by the said readers to plead and argue in the said house doubtful cases and questions which amongst them are called moots". From the utter barristers of the inns of court were appointed the readers of the inns of chancery, and from more senior utter barristers were elected the readers in court. We may supplement the information in the 1540 report from the records of the inns themselves. It is known that the inns of chancery also had inner and utter barristers, but the readers were sent down from the inns of court and the "grand" moots in the learning vacations were attended by members of different inns.[16] The statutes of Clifford's Inn and Clement's Inn both mention two additional exercises, the "report" and the reading of a writ.[17] The precise manner of mooting, and the different kinds of moot and case-putting, varied from one inn to another, but the minutiae of procedure are not readily discernible before the later sixteenth century and we shall not pursue them here.[18] The system was kept up in all essentials until continuity was broken by the Civil War in 1642. Some of the exercises were later revived, and a few survived as perfunctory recitations, but the inns of court never really recovered as academic institutions and the inns of chancery began their slide into total oblivion. Historians have written of this decline, but the purpose of the present paper is to provide a sketch of the system at its peak and to speculate on the development of the system described in 1540.

Medieval origins of the exercises

It is as difficult to trace the origins of the learning exercises as of the inns themselves, but it is possible to perceive traces of an educational system at a period long before there is any evidence to show that lawyers had organised themselves into learned societies. The clearest traces are in the manuals of the 1250s which have been given the generic title *Casus Placitorum*, but which seem more often to have been called *Cas e Demaundes* and are in one manuscript *Casus Eruditionum*. These seem to be based largely on actual cases in court, but it seems that the "casus" of the title is intended rather to denote a put case or a set of facts for

---

[16] *Spelman's Reports*, Vol. II, pp. *127–129*.
[17] Below, pp. 18–19.
[18] For their later history, see C. I. Hammer, "Bolts and Chapel Moots at Lincoln's Inn in the 16th Century" (1970) 11 Jo. Soc. Public Teachers of Law 24–28; W. R. Prest, *The Inns of Court 1590–1640* (1972), pp. 115–136; W. C. Richardson, *A History of the Inns of Court* (Baton Rouge, c. 1978), pp. 128–210; below, pp. 25–30.

discussion[19] and that the "demaundes" are likewise *quaestiones* in the academic sense. Their modern editor felt them to belong in a context of teaching and learning:

> A few of the notes are written in a rhetorical style, which gives them a pedagogical tone ... At a time when questions and answers, readings and arguments formed the prevailing method of instruction, the *Demaundes* with their answers and *Aprises* may have served as lecture-notes for a teacher; and *les cas*, surely, belong to the long tradition of legal education which lies behind the modern 'case' method of instruction in the law. Often a question in the Casus begins with the familiar medieval expression, *ore est a saver*, and then the answer starts with *les uns dient*, continues with *mes les autres dient*, and, sometimes, concludes with a *mes jo di*. The phrases *ausi jo di, jeo di par jugement*, and *jo vous di* which begin some of the answers to the questions exude the authoritative ego of the pedagogue. At other times the question itself is in the first person singular—*jo vous demande*—and the note concludes with a single *nent* or *nanil* in reply ... The putting of the question *Jeo vous demande par quel bref* ... and the translation of the writ into the spoken language are good reasons for believing that this matter was read aloud to students by their teachers.[20]

Professor Dunham also pointed out that the "some say—but others say—and I say" type of report recurs in the fifteenth-century treatise on conveyancing by Simon of Oxford, which is thought to be derived from a university course.[21] To this we may add that the phrases *ascuns diont, semble a auters*, and *moy semble*, are to be found as late as the 1550s in a collection of Inner temple moots.[22] They clearly indicate disputations, the identity of the speakers having been suppressed as immaterial. Another eminent commentator on the *Casus Placitorum* concluded that it "positively reeks of chalk and duster and ink":

> There is no other work on English law which gives us so strong an impression of being in a medieval class-room. It is much to be hoped that it will catch the eye of some expert in teaching methods during the Middle ages, for he may be able to give a more precise meaning to some of the technical words of the teacher's art which frequently appear in it.[23]

This hope has not yet been realised, though it could be that words such as *demaunde* and *aprise* were not "technical" in the sense of having a specialised meaning. Moreover, neither Dunham nor Plucknett nor any subsequent writer has been able to establish what kind of law school

---

[19] Cf. J. H. Baker, *Manual of Law French* (1979), p. 65, s.v. *cas*.
[20] W. H. Dunham (ed.), *Casus Placitorum* (Selden Soc., Vol. LXIX, 1952), introduction, pp. xxxi–xxxii. There is no clear evidence as to authorship: Dunham suggested "apprentices or clerks, or both" (p. xxxv). Several more cognate texts have been found since 1952, and there is room for further work.
[21] *Ibid.*, p. xxxii, n. 1.
[22] Cambridge Univ. Lib. MS Dd. 13. 24, ff. 12–48.
[23] T. F. T. Plucknett, *Early English Legal Literature* (Cambridge, 1958), p. 90.

Learning Exercises in the Medieval Inns of Court 13

might have generated such writing. Almost certainly they are too early to represent the work of a particular inn. It is therefore possible that there was a law school or *studium* for the apprentices of the king's court[24] before the rise of the quasi-collegiate system which eclipsed it in the fourteenth century. If that is so, there is another parallel with the universities, where there was a general tendency for the teaching initiative to pass from the faculties to the colleges. But in the common-law scheme there was no corporate university or faculty system to continue as a central focus; and its highest graduates, the serjeants at law, though often compared with doctors, retained no doctoral functions save those of disputing in open court in real cases before the assembled learners.

Since the origins of the inns are still so obscure, the manner in which the learning system devolved on these voluntary associations can only be a matter of guesswork. The *Casus Placitorum* did not develop as a distinct genre of legal literature, but was overtaken by the reports of discussions in the Common Pleas—the " year books "— which began in the 1280s. Maitland did his best to bridge the gap. The year books themselves showed that:

> Vigorous intellectual effort was to be found outside the monasteries and the universities. These lawyers are worldly men, not men of the sterile cast; they marry and found families, some of which become as noble as any in the land; but they are in their way learned, cultivated men, linguists, logicians, tenacious disputants, true lovers of the nice case and the moot-point. They are gregarious, clubable men, grouping themselves in hospices, which become schools of law, multiplying manuscripts, arguing, learning and teaching, the great mediators between life and logic, a reasoning, reasonable element in the English nation.[25]

The first reference to these inns occurs in the year books themselves, and appropriately it refers to the learning exercises which had become established there. In a case of 1346, when counsel moved to abate a writ, Justice Willoughby and Serjeant Skipwyth answered that the point " was never an exception in this Place, but we have often heard it among the apprentices in the *hostels* ".[26] This chance remark shows that arguing about writs was a regular exercise in the inns by the 1340s, though no manuscript notes of moots have survived before Tudor times. Another form of exercise is preserved by two texts in the University Library,

---

[24] A law school in London was closed by royal edict in 1234, but it is generally thought not to have been a school for students of the common law of the king's courts: T. F. T. Plucknett, *Concise History of the Common Law* (1956 ed.), p. 219.

[25] F. W. Maitland, *The Year Books of Edward II* (Selden Soc., Vol. XVII, 1903), introduction, p. lxxxi.

[26] Y.B. Mich. 29 Edw. III, fo. 47 (translated). William Skipwyth has been claimed, on unreliable evidence, as a member of Gray's Inn; he became a serjeant in 1344. Richard Willoughby had been a serjeant since 1324. See J. H. Baker, *The Order of Serjeants at Law* (1984), pp. 154, 157.

Cambridge. The title *Hae sunt quaestiones compilatae de statutis* adequately indicates the contents, which are short questions and answers concerning points of statute law, apparently arranged in statute order from Magna Carta to the legislation of Edward I.[27] The form of each paragraph is " Quaestio . . . dicitur quod sic [*vel*] non ", sometimes followed by a reason and occasionally by a case citation. For example:

> If an heir who is ravished marries without the ravisher's assent, can the ravisher afterwards when the wardship is recovered make agreement with the true lord in respect of this marriage? *Dicitur per* Swayn *quod sic*, as appears in Trinity term *anno octavo Regis nunc.*

All the cases cited appear to date from the first eight years of Edward III, and the date of the text could be around 1340. Eight of the named speakers became serjeants (four in 1342, one in 1344 and three in 1354) and two were probably judges already; but seven (Braunscombe, Bretton, Delves, Kikeby or Kyrkeby, Swayn, and Wakeb' or Wakel') were never serjeants or judges, and this circumstance leads us to speculate that the forum may have been one of the inns at a time not long before the serjeants' call of 1342. Here we see learning exercises centred on the thirteenth-century statutes, and since the readings of the fifteenth century were invariably on the same texts it is a reasonable conjecture that there was some kind of evolution from the one to the other. The readings were not merely lectures, but involved cases being put by and to the reader which related more or less to the subject-matter. Even the name *quaestiones* suggests a university parallel; but the form of the *quaestiones* in the Cambridge texts also provides a tenuous link between the *demaundes* of the thirteenth century and the readers' cases of the fifteenth and sixteenth centuries.

The earliest text resembling a reading, in the later sense, is perhaps that in the Bodleian Library, MS. Lat. hist. d. 3, ff. 302–333v, headed "Magna Carta". It is a string of notes on the statute, each beginning "Item dictum est . . ." or "Item si . . ." or "Item nota que . . ." . There are references to cases down to 1374 at the latest, not all of which can be found in the printed year books. Very few names are mentioned, and it is not always clear whether they were speakers in the exercise or in the cases cited; but two names (Fyncham on fo. 302v, and Newnam on fo. 313v) are of men who did not become serjeants and who seem therefore to be speaking as members of an inn. A similar collection of notes, chiefly on tenures, in British Library, MS. Add. 22552, ff. 19–30, also features Newnham (ff. 28, 29v); and in the same volume (ff. 51v–54v) is a

---

[27] MS Hh. 2. 8, ff. 115–120v; MS Ll. 4. 17, ff. 219–222v. (The writer has enjoyed a valuable correspondence on the subject of these texts with Professor S. E. Thorne.) A text worth comparing with these is Brit. Lib. MS Add. 5924, ff. 27–51v, in which paraphrases of 13th-century statutes are accompanied by occasional *quaestiones* (e.g. on fo. 45, under the heading *Exceptiones brevium*).

Learning Exercises in the Medieval Inns of Court 15

Tractatus super statutum Westmonasterii secundi which may well be a reading of the same period. This fashion of stringing together notes on statutes certainly typifies the first identifiable readings, which Professor Thorne has tentatively assigned to the early years of King Henry VI.[28] In these texts each statute is taken clause by clause; the reader "rehearses" the common law prior to the statute, explains the effect of the legislation, and explores its applications by putting cases. Occasionally the reader is interrupted with opposing questions, but very few names are preserved in the texts and the identity of the reader is rarely ascertainable. Professor Thorne has established relationships between texts which indicate that readings from different inns could influence each other, presumably through the circulation of written copies or "reports".[29] The early readers were not expected to give a wholly original performance, but to expound and develop the traditional learning surrounding their texts. By the later fifteenth century it can be shown that the statutes were expounded in a chronological cycle, the reader having no choice of text. New readers were assigned to lecture in August, while the Lent vacation was usually occupied by a "double" or second reading. Since the cycle of statutes was the same as that in the older *quaestiones*, it may have been a continuous tradition to expound legislation in that way. Why readings were always on statutes, rather than the common law, has remained something of a mystery; but it could simply have been an ingrained notion that one could not lecture without a written text. In practice readers could treat of the common law by selecting suitable key words in the statute. By the end of Henry VIII's reign, however, the old course had been abandoned and readers had a choice of statute. Some chose new statutes, and some gave new subjects an individualistic treatment which earned them a fleeting place in legal literature.[30]

The development of disputations in the inns of court between the *quaestiones* of the 1340s and the first surviving texts of cases in the 1480s and 1490s is impossible to trace. The word "moot" was in use by 1428, when a member of Lincoln's Inn was expelled for some default in mooting;[31] and in 1430 Chief Justice Babington is reported in the year

---

[28] S. E. Thorne, *Readings and Moots in the Inns of Court in the 15th Century*, Vol. I [readings only] (Selden Soc., Vol. LXXI, 1954), introduction. The readings can sometimes be dated approximately from exchanges between named speakers. At least five manuscripts have discussions involving "Neuton", presumably the Richard Newton of the Middle Temple who became a serjeant in 1425: Brit. Lib. MS Lansdowne 465, fo. 61; Cambridge Univ. Lib. MS Ee. 5. 22, fo. 291; MS Hh. 2. 8, fo. 38v; Bodleian Lib. MS Rawlinson C. 294, fo. 154; Univ. Coll. Oxford MS 163, ff. 162v, 198; Baker, *Serjeants at Law*, pp. 162, 260.

[29] For reports of readings, see Thorne in Selden Soc., Vol. LXXI, p. xxiii; *Spelman's Reports*, Vol. I (Selden Soc., Vol. XCIII, 1977), p. 105. The word was also used in the universities: e.g., in All Souls' College, Oxford (MS 53), are some 15th-century lectures on the decretals, called *reportata*.

[30] *Spelman's Reports*, Vol. II, pp. *133–135*.

[31] *Black Books*, Vol. I, p. 3.

books as referring to a question which had been the point of a moot-case.³² But there is reason to think that the fourteenth-century exercises were the direct ancestors of the reader's case rather than of the moot in the classical sense. To this distinction we shall return after considering the development of exercises in the lesser inns.

Exercises in the inns of chancery

No written notes have yet been found of disputations in the inns of chancery before the 1490s. No readings have been found before the middle of the sixteenth century. Nevertheless, we know that the readings began much earlier, for as it happens the earliest references to readings in chancery are earlier than the evidence for readings in court. First, there are some rough accounts kept by a member of an inn of chancery in the time of Richard II or Henry IV which include a payment of 2s. "lectori nostro."³³ Then, the seventeenth-century abstract of the lost records of Furnival's Inn says that in 1408, "The Reader *tempore Autumnali* had allowed him from everie one of the house in commons iiij$^{d.}$"³⁴ This probably does not mean that there were then autumn and Lent readers, as in the inns of court, but rather that the payment for the reader was raised in the autumn. An entry of about 1452 in the same records shows that then, as in the sixteenth century, the reader held office for one year.³⁵ Both these references to readers show that the members of the lesser inns had to pay somewhat for their instruction, and a likely explanation is that they had to induce members of the superior inns to come and perform the task. By the sixteenth century the system had become regularised, so that each inn of chancery had a "parent" inn of court which was supposed to send down a reader each year. There is insufficient evidence to establish when these links were forged.³⁶

Of disputations in the inns of chancery we also have early evidence. The first allusion in the year books is ambiguous. In a case of 1400 an attorney asked a question and Justice Rikhill told him to go and ask it of his fellows in his inn.³⁷ Of course, this does not necessarily imply a formal means of putting cases as opposed to a discussion at the dinner-table. Neither can we safely assume that an attorney would in 1400 have been a member of an inn of chancery rather than an inn of court. But the

---

[32] Y.B. Trin. 9 Hen. VI, fo. 24, pl. 19 ("il ad este un point dun case dun mote").
[33] Brit. Lib. MS Add. 5666, fo. 17. The writer is grateful to Mr. N. L. Ramsay for drawing his attention to this volume.
[34] D. S. Bland (ed.), *Early Records of Furnival's Inn* (Newcastle upon Tyne, 1957), p. 23.
[35] *Ibid.*, p. 28 ("pro feodo lectori ut de tertia parte feodi quinquaginta solidorum per annum – xvj$^{s.}$ viij$^{d.}$").
[36] The question is discussed by Dr. D. S. Bland, "Learning Exercises and Readers at the Inns of Chancery in the 15th and 16th Centuries" (1979) 95 L.Q.R. 244–252.
[37] Y.B. Mich. 2 Hen. IV, fo. 6, pl. 24 ("Demaundes ceo de vostre compaignons en vostre hostel").

next reference, in 1458, is plain enough, because it speaks expressly of the "form of pleading in the inns of chancery."[38] The only way in which pleading could have been a matter of form in the inns of chancery was through the exercises there. It is not unreasonable to guess that the exercise here alluded to was of the kind mentioned in the Furnival's Inn records for 1465, where two members of the inn *protulerunt placitum* and two others defended.[39]

Most of the surviving texts of moots in the inns of chancery from the time of Henry VII and Henry VIII are of moots in the usual sense of disputations. These were evidently the vacation "grand moots" attended by students from other inns, and sometimes by readers of the inns of court and their assistants.[40] Those texts usually mix cases from several inns, and do not always state where the discussion occurred: it is as if one single law school was holding classes in different halls. But there is at least one surviving text which indicates the character of the domestic and more elementary pleading exercise mentioned above. In the John Rylands Library, MS. Eng. 288, ff. 171-174, is a brief series of pleadings in law French, bound up with notes of moots and readings and an early Littleton. The first case (fo. 171) is a writ of waste by John Hill against Thomas Denys; the second (fo. 172) an assize of novel disseisin by John Frice against John K.; the third (fo. 172v) an action of covenant by Alice, wife of William Bree, against Charles Hoppyng; and the last (fo. 173v) an action of *nuper obiit* by Alice S. against Joan S. There is no accompanying discussion. The date 1 August in the fifth year occurs in one of the pleadings, and this (assuming the reign to be Henry VII's) fixes the date as 1490 or soon afterwards. Now, four of the men named (William Bree, John Frice, John Hill and Charles Hoppyng) can be shown to have been members of Lyon's Inn in the 1490s; and it is very likely that Denys was also of that house before he joined the Inner Temple. We shall have occasion to mention later some Gray's Inn exercises from the following decade in which the students used each other's names, and there seems little doubt that we have here a glimpse inside Lyon's Inn in the 1490s. We see an exercise in which six men from the west country—the principal catchment area for Lyon's Inn—learned the forms of counts and pleadings by making them up in imaginary actions and reciting them in French. Since we have the names, it is also worth noticing that with the exception of Denys these were not men who proceeded to an inn of court afterwards. Most of them became attorneys of the Common Pleas and remained members of Lyon's Inn till death.

---

[38] Y.B. Hil. 37 Hen. VI, fo. 14, pl. 4 (" cest la forme de pleding en innes de chauncerie mes la fourme nest bon").
[39] Bland, *Early Records of Furnival's Inn*, p. 29.
[40] *Spelman's Reports*, Vol. II, p. 133.

Further details of the exercises in the inns of chancery are provided by surviving tables of statutes promulgated by the governing bodies of two of them. The statutes of Clifford's Inn, apparently rewritten in the early sixteenth century from an older text, ordained:

> If any common pensioner being in commons and lying within the same inn be absent from a writ-reading he shall lose a farthing (and for a lecture a halfpenny, a moot one penny, and a report a halfpenny) to the use of the company. And also if any learning, to wit a writ-reading, moot or report, be lost by their default, he who is in default shall pay for a writ 6d., for a moot in term-time 20d., for a report 6d., and for a moot in vacation-time 3s. 4d.

This shows the paramount importance of the vacation moots, and introduces us to two exercises not found in the inns of court, the writ-reading and the report. The manner of exercise is not prescribed, but it is further ordained that common pensioners of six months' standing should be bound to bring in " all manner of learnings of the same inn which belong to an inner barrister", and after a year and a day should likewise perform the learnings of an utter barrister; and that none should be passed over, although each companion could appoint a deputy at his peril.[41] The "learnings" of an utter barrister in Clifford's Inn cannot have been as demanding as those of an utter barrister in the inns of court, since they were performed prior to becoming an inner barrister in the latter and there was no provision for admission *ad eundem gradum* from the lesser to the greater inns. The statutes of Clement's Inn survive in a seventeenth-century copy which does not clearly distinguish the older from the newer orders; but some of the statutes appear to date from the fifteenth century. They mention the same exercises as in Clifford's Inn and are more explicit about their conduct. The youngest of the first mess of every table was to put a case each working day, on pain of 4d. Exercises in the learning vacations were to be performed in the same order as the chambers were occupied in the inn. The principal was empowered "to call to the bar to moot" such of the fellows as seemed to him able to do it, and everyone who refused to moot " at the outer bar" was to be fined 20d. or discommoned. The fine for defaulting at moots was 6s. 8d. for an utter barrister and 3s. 4d. for an inner barrister. The fine for refusing to "report," an exercise apparently for utter barristers, was 6d. Not attending a moot cost 4d., and not attending a reading 2d., but attorneys and clerks of the courts and others of twelve years' standing were excused. Everyone under two years' standing was obliged, on pain of one penny a time, to be present on every working day in term and vacation when the principal read a writ in the

---

[41] Inner Temple MS Misc. 189, par. 40 (translated), 46.

Learning Exercises in the Medieval Inns of Court 19

Natura Brevium.[42] The exercises of moot and report were to be done "perfectly without book," which suggests they were primarily tests of memory.[43] The system was thus—as we have already supposed—designed to teach young students the forms of writs and pleadings, the rudiments without which they could not profit from the more demanding exercises in the inns of court.[44] To these matters we may now return.

Inns of court disputations 1490–1540

The earliest written report of cases in an identifiable inn seems to be the Inner Temple collection of the 1480s which was printed together with Keilwey's reports in 1602.[45] There are other Inner Temple cases from the 1490s in the British Library, MS. Harley 1691 and MS. Hargrave 87, and in the recently discovered notebook of Sir John Port. A few Gray's Inn cases from the same period occur in other manuscripts. After 1550 there is a substantial body of unpublished notes of all kinds of exercise in the inns of court and chancery. It is not always easy for an outsider to tell what is going on, since the purpose of the notes is not to recreate the moot proceedings so much as to record memorable pronouncements and the common learning which emerged from discussion. For a general description of the exercises, therefore, we must again turn to the 1540 report.

In connection with readings, the report mentions an exercise whereby:

> one of the younger utter barristers rehearseth one question propounded by the reader and doth by way of argument labour to prove the reader's opinion to be against the law, and after him the rest of the utter barristers and readers one after another in their ancienties do declare their opinions and judgments in the same, and then the reader who did put the case endeavoureth himself to confute objections laid against him and to confirm his own opinion, after whom the judges and serjeants, if any be present, declare their opinions.[46]

---

[42] In *Spelman's Reports*, Vol. II, p. 129, n. 1, the writer suggested that this denoted a lecture on a writ; but on reflection it seems more likely to have been a mere recital of the formula. Either the writ-reading or the report may be intended in the entry of 1422 when fellows of Furnival's Inn were fined *pro brevibus importandis* (Bland, *Early Records of Furnival's Inn*, p. 26). The Harvard Law School possesses a copiously annotated 1537 edition of Fitzherbert's *Natura Brevium* which belonged successively to Thomas Rolleston and Anthony Gell, both of whom are known to have been principals of Clement's Inn.

[43] C. Carr (ed.), *Pension Book of Clement's Inn* (Selden Soc., Vol. LXXVIII, 1960), pp. 219–220, par. 10–15. See also p. 224, par. 36, which requires the principal to read the statutes twice a year in hall, during the Easter and Michaelmas terms, on pain of 40s.; but this may be later in date than the rest. Par. 38–39 seem to be later statutes about mooting, since the fine for refusing to moot has been reduced to 12d.; attendance at a moot was required to last for one hour.

[44] *Spelman's Reports*, Vol. II, p. 128.

[45] *Relationes quorundam casuum* (1602), ff. 102–136.

[46] Waterhous, *Fortescutus Illustratus*, pp. 544–545 (modernised).

The Inner Temple moots of the late fifteenth century seem to be of this nature, but the earliest collection in which the theme of the reading can be clearly followed from case to case is that associated with John Spelman's reading in Gray's Inn in 1519.[47] In some inns a similar exercise was conducted after dinner, the cases being propounded by the readers at their own table.

These reader's cases are possibly direct descendants of the *quaestiones de statutis* of Edward III's time. Indeed, in a text containing " lez casez arguez en le lecture Mr. Henley " at Gray's Inn in 1530 there is a running headline " Questiones ".[48] They are not, however, what the report describes as mooting. Mooting, at any rate by 1540, was conducted in imitation of real cases at Westminster, the arguments being addressed to formal pleadings upon a writ:

> In these Lent and Summer vacations every night after supper, and every fasting-day immediately after six of the clock, boyer ended (festival-days and their evens only excepted), the reader, with two benchers or one at least, cometh into the Hall . . . and after arguing a case at the cupboard they . . . sit down on the bench in the end of the Hall whereof they take their name; and on a form toward the midst of the Hall sitteth down two inner barristers, and of the other side of them on the same form two utter barristers; and the inner barristers do in French openly declare unto the benchers (even as the serjeants do at the bar in the king's courts to the judges) some kind of action, the one being as it were retained with the plaintiff in the action, and the other with the defendant; after which things be done, the utter barristers argue such questions as be disputable within the case (as there must be always one at least) and this ended the benchers do likewise declare their opinions how they think the law to be in the same questions; and this manner of exercise of mooting is daily used during the said vacations.[49]

The report does not make clear how the disputable questions were selected. It seems that in Lincoln's Inn they were assigned by the utter barristers and " written " by the inner barristers; there, as at Clement's Inn, the disputants were chosen in the order of their chambers.[50] But how were the questions formulated? It is now clear that by 1500 there existed in some inns a traditional body of mootable cases which were collected in moot-books. What appears to be the old Lincoln's Inn moot-book, on vellum and with a calendar of saints, has recently been identified in Cambridge.[51] An Inner Temple moot-book is preserved in

---

[47] Brit. Lib. MS Harley 5625, ff. 112–128v; Bodleian Lib. MS Rawlinson C. 705, ff. 128–139. Another Gray's Inn series is in Lincoln's Inn MS Misc. 486.
[48] Brit. Lib. MS Harley 5103, ff. 24–31.
[49] Waterhous, *Fortescutus Illustratus*, p. 545 (modernised). The report goes on to say that speakers always argued in reverse order of seniority, and that barristers argued in French while benchers used English. The Middle Temple followed the same practice (op. cit. in note 15).
[50] *Black Books*, Vol. I, pp. 126–127, 201, 215, 257.
[51] Below, pp. 25–30.

Learning Exercises in the Medieval Inns of Court 21

the Harvard Law School.[52] In the Inner Temple the cases were given mnemonic names, such as Isaac and Jacob, Jacob and Esau, Hobbe and John, Le Verge, Corona, Rosa inter spinas, Cat in the Pan, Lesperver, and Parva rosa; and moots with these names recur in different manuscripts.[53] Even so, it is probable that new cases were invented from time to time, for it was not uncommon for the benchers to rule that a case was not mootable.[54] The cases were in the form of set problems, not unlike examination questions in English law schools today, but usually ending with the occult question " Ceux que droit?" Some may have been based on real cases, as in the *Casus Placitorum*, but many of them were self-evidently devised purely as academic tests of ingenuity and analytical skill. This extreme example is from Gray's Inn in the 1510s:

> A lease is made to one J.M. for term of years at the will of R.N., remainder to R.N. for term of the life of J.M.; and the lessor confirms their estates *habendum* in fee; and they are jointly possessed of a horse with a stranger; and they grant a rent-charge to a husband and wife to the use of the husband for term of life, remainder of the moiety of the rent to the wife in fee; and then they confirm their estates to the husband in tail; and they have issue; and a stranger comes by the rent and the deed; and the husband and J.M. (who is his brother) release to him with warranty and die seised of an advowson; then the mother dies; the issue in tail distrain the same horse, and the stranger makes rescue, and he brings a writ of rescue. *Ceux que droit?*

If we are mystified by the case, we may take some comfort from the fact that it provoked a complaint when it was set: " it is an unreasonable case to be mooted at one time for there are twenty-eight points in it if it be well scanned: so seek them out well and study them diligently."[55] That might have been a practicable assignment for the studious then, but there is probably no one alive today who could confidently identify all the 28 points in the case. Law school was no easy option in Henry VIII's time.

When the case had been assigned, the inner barristers responsible for

---

[52] J. H. Baker, *English Legal Manuscripts*, Vol. I (Zug, 1975), p. 63, and plate VIII on p. 100.
[53] *Ibid.*; *Spelman's Reports*, Vol. II, p. *133*. See also Brit. Lib. MS Hargrave 87, fo. 6: " Memorandum quod in vacatione in anno xix H. VIII, Barons adtunc lector, casus que appellatur *Le Verge* fuit motatus per Only et Moyn barestarios exteriores et per Capell et Tame barestarios interiores per totam vacationem, que quidem casus devidebatur in duabus actionibus . . .".
[54] *Spelman's Reports*, Vol. II, p. *132*. But on one occasion it was suspected that the benchers of Gray's Inn were too tired to argue: Bodleian Lib. MS Rawlinson C. 705, fo. 43 (" Et quant il venust al bank, T. Nevyll dit que toutz nouz sount agrees que cest clere case . . . et sic surrexerunt etc. Mez Hendley credit que le cause fuit pur ceo que le temps fuit passez et ne fueront desposez de arguer, quar est un auncien mote cas "). The next year full justice was done to the same case before other benchers.
[55] Bodleian Lib. MS Rawlinson C. 705, fo. 20v; Harvard Law School MS 125, no. 82 (translated). In 1557 it was ordered that in the inns of *chancery* the moot-cases should not contain more than two points: *Black Books*, Vol. I, p. 320.

it set to work drawing up pleadings designed to raise the point for argument, following exactly the forms used in the royal courts. Some of these pleadings survive from Gray's Inn in the first decade of the sixteenth century. As in the Lyon's Inn example noticed above, the members made free with each other's names. One day Anthony Fitzherbert is defendant in a writ of entry, another day William Coke is plaintiff in an assize, and another day Alys Hales brings ejectment against Christopher Hales.[56] The moot itself began with the recital of these pleadings, in law French, by the inner barristers. It then proceeded, like a real case in the Common Pleas, with objections to the form of the pleading before arguments were addressed to the substance. It was even permissible to attack the writ.[57] In arguing the speakers did not have to speak their own minds, but might oppose for the sake of argument.[58] On the other hand, it seems they were not compelled to take sides and on one occasion it was noted that " all argued on one side."[59] Speakers doubtless indicated when they were not expressing their own view, so that solemn pronouncements, especially by the benchers, could be regarded as evidence of the law.[60] Decisions at previous moots were sometimes cited, and we need hardly doubt that the copious notes of these exercises were taken to serve as guides to law as well as to clever arguments. Some students, indeed, digested dicta at moots and readers' cases into alphabetical or topical collections, thus severing the legal conclusions altogether from the process by which they had been arrived at.[61]

Conclusion

As a system of education, the learning exercises in the inns suffered from some of the defects which Rashdall identified in medieval scholastic education in general; it was dogmatic and disputatious and treated facts with indifference. Yet, as a form of practical training, it was severely effective; it "trained pure intellect, encouraged habits of laborious subtlety, heroic industry, and intense application" and gave the student practice in readiness and facility of expression.[62] These were qualities of

---

[56] Bodleian Lib. MS Rawlinson C. 705, ff. 54v, 65, 89v. Hales became attorney-general; the other two became Common Pleas judges.
[57] *Ibid.*, fo 37v (" Et auxi X. Halys dit que le brefe nest bon... quod fuit concessum ") and fo. 95v.
[58] *Ibid.*, fo. 55 (" Hunston encontre son volunte semble le contrary "); Harvard Law School MS 125, nos. 37 (" Knightle dit que il voile luy mesme conforme al ley, et agree que le ley est tiell, mes *gratia argumenti* il argue all contrarie "), 80 (" Dodeley pur son pleasure semble le contrarie "), 94 (same case).
[59] Bodleian Lib. MS Rawlinson C. 705, fo. 91v (" et sic toutz argueront a un syde ").
[60] *Spelman's Reports*, Vol. II, pp. *132–133*.
[61] E.g., Harvard Law School MS 47 (perhaps by William Porter of Gray's Inn); Brit. Lib. MS Hargrave 388, ff. 211–272, and other texts (Roger Yorke of Gray's Inn); H. E. Huntington Lib. MS HM 46980 (John Port of the Inner Temple).
[62] H. Rashdall, *Universities of Europe in the Middle Ages* (Oxford, 1936 ed.), Vol. III, pp. 453–454.

Learning Exercises in the Medieval Inns of Court 23

value in law and government. And so, while the universities stood as gateways to the Church, the inns of court and chancery trained and selected the ruling and administrative classes of secular England. No doubt the learning exercises were over the heads of many of the students, but that was their strength; most of the students did not become lawyers. The system was highly praised by Renaissance writers, who looked to the inns rather than the universities for models of effective education.[63] Sir Thomas Elyot, himself a product of the Middle Temple, considered the exercises to be perfect if unconscious revivals of classical rhetoric.[64] Even the universities, while disdaining the use of vulgar languages such as law-French and English, could not match the high standards of Holborn and the Temple: Sir Thomas Smith, in his inaugural lecture as Regius Professor of Civil Law at Cambridge, expressed his admiration for that other law school and its methods of argument.[65]

Historians in general have tended to remember the inns chiefly for their cultural contributions to English life, the music and the drama. It is right that such things should be remembered. But their greatest gift to England was their contribution to the common law, both by exploring refinements of doctrine in advance of the courts where it was applied[66] and by training a small cadre of advocates to a high level of expertise. In the centuries to come the law nurtured in this little academy was to cover a third of the globe. Well might the Third University of England justify Coke's claim that it should occupy a prominent place in the history of the world.

---

[63] See R. M. Fisher, "Thomas Cromwell, Humanism and Educational Reform" (1977) 50 B.I.H.R. 151–163.
[64] *The Boke named the Governour* (1531), fo. 56.
[65] Cited in F. W. Maitland, *English Law and the Renaissance* (Cambridge, 1901), pp. 89–90.
[66] *Spelman's Reports*, Vol. II, pp. *123–125, 132–135, 155, 302–303.*

1 The Lincoln's Inn moot book

Cambridge University Library MS Ll. 1. 11, fo. 25

THE OLD MOOT BOOK OF LINCOLN'S INN

It is often said that little can be discovered about the inns of court before Elizabethan times, but information is slowly being excavated from the many legal manuscripts and records which have so far escaped examination. Work on the early learning exercises has been pioneered by Professor Thorne, who has shown how the fifteenth-century readings in Gray's Inn and the Inner Temple followed a cycle of statutory texts.[1] More recently it has become possible to suggest that moots also followed a cycle, though perhaps of a less regular kind, following the set problems which circulated within each inn.[2] This is easiest to demonstrate for the Inner Temple, where the most familiar cases were known by cryptic names and recur in different manuscripts. Robert Keilwey's moot book, now in the Harvard Law School,[3] contains 139 cases, some of them with names such as *Jacob et Esau, Le Verge, Hobbe et John, Rosa inter spinas, Corona, Cat in Pan, Lesperver* and *Parva rosa*. John Caryll, junior, reported a moot on the case *Isake et Jacobe* in the Inner Temple in 1533, and *Le Verge* occurs in an earlier manuscript.[4] And as late as Elizabethan times we find *Fitz John, Kate in the Panne, Case de la Rose*, and *Esperver*, in another Inner Temple moot collection.[5] There are other pre-1550 collections of moot cases, the distinguishing mark of which is the occult phrase *Ceux que droit*, or *Ceux*, at the end of each problem.[6] The only printed example of this genre, *Les Cases de Greys-Inn* (1680), was published as mooting itself was verging on extinction; the date of the text is not known. Most later manuscripts report discussion of the cases, often by named speakers, but the existence of problem collections such as Keilwey's points to official or semi-official cycles from which cases were assigned to the mooters.

The printed records of the inns provide only oblique clues as to the way the mooting system operated. We know that in Gray's Inn and the Middle Temple, and perhaps in the Inner Temple also, the assignment of moots was controlled by the puisne butler, who kept a

---

[1] S. E. Thorne, *Readings and Moots in the Inns of Court in the 15th Century*, I (1954), 71 Seld.Soc. introd. For the cessation of the cycles, see *The Reports of Sir John Spelman* II (1978), 94 Seld.Soc. introd. at pp. *134–135*.

[2] 94 Seld.Soc. at p. *133*.

[3] See *English Legal Manuscripts*, I (Zug, 1975), p. 63, and plate VIII on p. 100. It is inscribed on the fly, " Iste liber pertinet ad Robertum Kaylway Teste Thoma Coke Thoma Gaude et multis aliis." Keilwey († 1580) was a bencher of the Inner Temple from 1547.

[4] Brit.Lib., MS. Harley 1691, f. 194v; MS. Hargrave 87, f. 6.

[5] Camb.Univ.Lib., MS. Dd. 13. 24, ff. 99v–100v. The volume contains (at ff. 12–48) imparlance exercises from the 1550s to 1562.

[6] Brit.Lib., MS. Sloane 775, ff. 9, 41v–42, 44–52 (15th century); Camb.Univ.Lib., MS. Gg. 5. 2 (Middle Temple). For the meaning of *Ceux que droit*, which is apparently a question, see 94 Seld.Soc. at p. *133*, n. 6.

"moot book" for the purpose.⁷ It is possible that some of these books were registers of mooters rather than collections of set cases, but it seems very likely that the butlers also had moot books in this second sense. The earliest relevant record is from Lincoln's Inn, where on January 30, 1528, the benchers ordered, " that the Utter Barresters and Inner Barresters gyffe ther attenduance for to assygne the mote and tymes accustumyd, and the Butlers to wayte upon them with the Booke and candell." ⁸ If this " Booke " was a moot book of the second type, it appears to have survived the candle by 450 years. MS. Ll. 1. 11 in the University Library, Cambridge, has been in Cambridge since 1715 when it was presented by King George I, but its true character seems to have eluded previous cataloguers. While in the possession of Bishop Moore it had been described as, " An old Law book in French, containing Cases in Law, beginning with a Calendar." 150 years later Professor Abdy, with characteristic inattentiveness, described it as, " A collection of cases illustrating the law of Descents." ⁹ It is a thin parchment volume, of 33 leaves, badly affected at the edges by damp and excessively trimmed by the eighteenth-century binder, who labelled it " Law Cases M.S." On folios 9–31 there is a collection of 143 moot cases, each ending *Ceux*, in a hand of the time of Henry VII. Prefixed to this collection (ff. 2–7) is a pre-Reformation calendar of saints, with red and blue rubrication; and before that (f. 1) a single leaf with an " Almanack " from 1588 to 1620. At the end (ff. 32–33) are notes and tables relating to corn measures and the London assize of bread, and some insertions to which we shall return when we have established the provenance. There is no express mention of Lincoln's Inn, but the association can be deduced from various clues. To begin with the calendar contains a number of interpolations: January 13, " Hillarii "; March 9, " Dedicatio ecclesie sancti Andree in Holborn "; June 25, " Nativitas sancti Launceloti et sancte Milburge " ¹⁰; July 7, " Translatio sancti Thome Martiris "; July 14, " Dies caniculares incipiunt "; December 29, " Sancti Thome Martiris." There appear also to be references to

---

⁷ See J. B. Williamson, *History of the Temple* (1924), p. 185 (order of 1594); *Master Worsley's Book* (1910 ed.), p. 189 (practice in 1734); *The Pension Book of Gray's Inn*, I (1901), pp. 243 (order of 1621), 309 (order of 1631). In 1590 two Inner Temple barristers were fined 20s. for mooting a case which was " not warranted by the general case of the House "; *Calendar of Inner Temple Records*, I (1896), p. 367. In 1681 the " book of exercise " was kept in that inn by the Exercise Butler: *ibid.*, III (1901), p. 178.

⁸ *Records of the Honorable Society of Lincoln's Inn, The Black Books*, I (1897), p. 219.

⁹ E. Barnard, *Catalogi Librorum Manuscriptorum Angliae et Hiberniae in unum Collecti* (Oxford, 1697), II, p. 365, no. 193; *A Catalogue of the Manuscripts preserved in the Library of the University of Cambridge*, IV (1861), p. 6.

¹⁰ According to D. H. Farmer, *The Oxford Dictionary of Saints* (Oxford, 1978), p. 279, this day was kept as the translation of St. Milburga, whose cult was centred on Shropshire. St. Lancelot has not been traced.

readings in March and August. Some of these insertions suggest a legal provenance, and if we consider also the unique circumstance of a collection of moots written on parchment rather than paper and preceded by a calendar, we might already guess that this was the official moot book of one of the six inns situated in the parish of St. Andrew, Holborn. The particular inn is indicated by the names written, perhaps in autograph, on folio 33v. They include " Richard Lyndesell," " Peeter Warburton " and Frances Knyvett." [11] Lyndesell († 1540) was admitted to Lincoln's Inn in 1520, having previously served as butler,[12] and it is a reasonable conjecture that he possessed the book in that capacity; the moots, and the tables, were his special concern. The book was probably still used in the inn after the Reformation, because the calendar is annotated " non modo " throughout. It was perhaps still in official custody when Peter Warburton († 1621) became Treasurer of Lincoln's Inn in 1589; indeed, he may well have added the almanack on folio 1. A Frances Knyvett, son of Sir Thomas, was admitted to the inn in 1611; if he was an owner, then presumably the book had by that time lost its official status. How it came into Bishop Moore's library is not known, but it is pertinent to note that in the same library there was a fourteenth-century book of *Narrationes* which belonged to another butler of Lincoln's Inn in Henry VIII's time and may have been used in connection with pleadings at moots.[13]

The problems assigned for exercise to the young barristers of Lincoln's Inn—doubtless the very problems mooted by Sir Thomas More and his father, and perhaps even by Fortescue—were quite as demanding as any modern Bar examination. One would like to meet a Bar student, or even a law professor, capable of attempting them unseen at the present day. Here are two typical specimens, translated from the law French:

> 88. A man seised of a manor to which several villeins are regardant has a [right of] action to demand the moiety of one carucate of land by formedon in the descender; he has issue a daughter, and dies; a stranger enters; the daughter takes a husband; the husband manumits one of the villeins and confirms his estate in fee which he had in the land which he holds in villeinage, yielding to him and his heirs a certain rent by deed

---

[11] The other names, which have not been certainly identified, are " William Broune " (possibly earlier than Lyndesell), " Johannes Dalton " (16th century) and " John Harvie " (17th century). There are also the notes "Genney per Potter " and " P. [?] Saunderson charged."
[12] *Black Books*, I, pp. 195, 196. A copy of his will is in the Public Record Office, P.C.C. 5 Alenger.
[13] MS. Dd. 6. 85, which is inscribed on f. 68r, " Ricardus Rusburgh pincerna de Lyncoln' Inne." It was no. 414 in Moore's library. On f. 67v are some tables for calculating multiples of sums of money, probably for use by the butler.

indented with a distress clause; the villein purchases land in ancient demesne; the tenant who holds the entailed land grants common of pasture to the villein in the whole carucate of land, in return for which grant the villein grants to him and to all those who should be terre-tenants of the same land a certain rent from all his land, with a distress clause, upon condition that if ever he should be disturbed in respect of the common the rent should cease; the husband and wife have issue a daughter, and die; the daughter brings formedon for the moiety of the land and recovers, and brings a writ of aiel for the manor and recovers, and disturbs the villein in respect of the common; and she purchases the other moiety, and suffers him to use his common, and then disturbs him; the rent falls behind; she distrains; he brings replevin. *Ceux?*

119. Two coparceners, seised of a manor by descent, have a tenant who holds the manor by homage and fealty and by the services of 20s. a year, repairing the mill and roofing the hall of the manor; the tenant grants part of the manor to a stranger, to hold of the chief lord of the fee by the services due; one of the parceners commits felony, for which she is attainted; the lord enters as in his escheat; and then they make partition between themselves, so that the mill is allotted to the lord and they hold the hall and the other services in common; and then they grant the hall to a man *pur terme d'auter vie*, during whose time the hall is unroofed; he for whose life the hall was leased dies; they enter as in their reversion; the lord makes a recognizance to a stranger to pay certain money at a certain day, at which day he does not pay, and so the other sues execution and has execution in respect of the mill; and during that time the mill falls down; the money is paid; the lord enters and distrains them; the tenants make replevin. *Ceux?*

The medieval system must have been highly effective in weeding out the inferior intellects.

Some scribbles at the end of the Lincoln's Inn moot book may be of wider interest. It is well known that the late-medieval inns of court and chancery promoted musical and dramatic activities, to such an extent that they are now regarded as having been a focus of English cultural tradition. Lawyers being conservative spirits, the oldest forms of entertainment were kept up long after ordinary folk had moved on to newer fashions; and in the solemn revels, with the old measures and songs performed on such occasions,[14] we see vestiges of medieval court life. John Spelman set down in detail the Christmas customs of Gray's Inn as he witnessed them in the time of Henry VII.[15] They

---

[14] " The Old Songs of the Inns of Court " (1974) 90 L.Q.R. 187–190; 94 Seld.Soc. at pp. *130–131*, and the works cited there.
[15] *Reports of Sir John Spelman,* I (1977) 93 Seld.Soc. at pp. 233–234.

included the election of a "king" and his court, processions, singing, dancing and playing games. At Gray's Inn there seems to have been a cycle of carols, including the song "Round about the fire," which presumably accompanied the measures trodden around the fireplace in the centre of the hall.[16] Only one of the Gray's Inn carols has been traced elsewhere, the Epiphany carol "Fare well and have good day." On Twelfth Night the marshal and steward of Christmas bade farewell to the company assembled by torchlight in hall:

> Now fare ye well, all in fere
> Now fare ye well, for all this yere
> Yet for my sake make ye gud cher
> Now have gud day.[17]

With this, the marshal and steward broke their wands of office and Christmas was over for another year. The Lincoln's Inn book, which is coeval with Spelman's account, affords new evidence of the carolling tradition in the inns, for on folio 32^r are the words and music of a polyphonic carol. The music has been published in modern notation, with the words in modern English,[18] but the inns of court context has not hitherto been noticed. This Lincoln's Inn carol, "Nowell, nowell, out of your slepe," is also to be found—with a different musical setting and three more verses—in an earlier manuscript from John Selden's library.[19] The Selden text seems not to be of legal provenance, though another of the carols in it is strongly reminiscent of the burden from the "old song of myrth and solace" which continued to accompany the ring-dance in Lincoln's Inn and the Inner Temple until the eighteenth century:

> Alle manner of merthes we wole make
> and solas to our hertys take
> my semely lorde for your sake
> Good day.[20]

---

[16] 90 L.Q.R. at pp. 187–188. For the association of carolling with the medieval *carole* or ring-dance, see R. L. Greene, *The Early English Carols* (2nd ed., Oxford, 1977), chapter II. Musical commentators have generally overlooked the long survival of this association in the inns of court.

[17] 93 Seld.Soc. at p. 234, n. 3; R. L. Greene, *The Early English Carols* (1935), pp. 96–97; text (without music) in Balliol College, Oxford, MS. 354.

[18] J. Stevens, *Musica Britannica*, IV, *Mediaeval Carols* (2nd ed., 1958), p. 114, no. 14A, and p. 124. The words are repeated, almost illegibly, on f. 33v of the moot book. The text is printed verbatim in Greene, *op. cit.* (2nd ed.), p. 17, No. 30B.

[19] Bodl.Lib., MS. Arch. Selden b. 26, f. 14v, reproduced in facsimile in J. Stainer (ed.), *Early Bodleian Music Sacred and Secular Songs*, I (Oxford, 1901), pl. LX; transcribed in Stevens, *op. cit.*, pp. 18–19, no. 25; Greene, *op. cit.* (2nd ed.), pp. 16–17, no. 30A. Several carols printed by Greene are from legal MSS.: *e.g.* Brit.Lib., MS. Harley 1317 (abridgment of Statutes); Royal MS. 17 B. XLVII (legal commonplace); Lincoln's Inn, MS. Hale 135 (Thornton's Bracton, with an early carol); H.E. Huntington Library, MS. Ellesmere 1160 (Old and New Tenures). Brit.Lib. MS. Add. 5666, which contains several carols with music, also has the accounts of John Whyte's expenses at an inn in the 1390s and 1400s.

[20] Selden MS., f. 8; Stainer, *op. cit.* pl. XLVII; Stevens, *op. cit.* pp. 12–13, no. 18; Greene, *op. cit.* (2nd ed.), p. 3, no. 5. *Cf.* 90 L.Q.R. at pp. 188–189.

There is a further musical treasure in the Lincoln's Inn moot book. On folio 33ʳ, probably in the hand of one of the butlers of the inn around the time of Henry VII or VIII, is "The howe of the howse." The word "howe" is not in the dictionaries, and a seventeenth-century hand has glossed it " or the old meas[ure]." But it is surely the courtly hove-dance (or *hof dans*), as mentioned by John Gower in *Confessio Amantis*:

> Wher as I moste daunce and singe
> The hovedance and carolinge.[21]

Gower († 1408) was possibly, like Chaucer and Hoccleve, a member of an inn; and his words, though not written in a legal context, conjure up a faint vision of the men of court at their leisure. The notes of the Lincoln's Inn measure bring this hove-dance to life, and may well provide the only authentic account of this ancient dance form[22]:

> The howe of the howse
> Fyrst half turn and undo yt agayn, flower, iij forth, the fyrst man and the second folowe, flower and roll into other placys, hole turn, flower, and then roll into other placys.

Such scraps as these—and we may be sure there are others awaiting discovery—encourage us to believe that a picture of life in the medieval inns of court is not wholly beyond reconstruction.

---

[21] G. C. Macaulay (ed.), *The English Works of John Gower*, II (1901) 82 E.E.T.S. (Extra Ser.), p. 171, lib. VI, line 144. See also p. 459, lib. VIII, line 2680: "The hovedance and the carole. . . . A softe pas thei dance and trede."

[22] For the old measures as set down about a century later, see the appendices to J. P. Cunningham, *Dancing in the Inns of Court* (1965).

4
READINGS IN GRAY'S INN, THEIR DECLINE AND DISAPPEARANCE*

OVER four hundred readings are known to have been given in the hall of Gray's Inn over the course of two and a half centuries, though only a small proportion have survived in writing or in lecture-notes. By chance, however, both the earliest and the latest surviving readings in the inns of court are from Gray's Inn, and this evidence casts some light on the history of readings in general.

Professor Thorne has produced a conjectural list of readers of the inn from 1435 to 1470, and has shown how their lectures were given on a cycle of statutes from Magna Carta down to the legislation of Edward I and the undated "statute" *Prerogativa regis*.[1] A few texts from this period are yet extant, and Professor Thorne has printed those of Henry Spelman (*c*. 1452) and Thomas Brugge (*c*. 1469). That of Miles Metcalfe (*d*. 1486), a future recorder of York, is the earliest which can be dated, since the reader puts a case concerning a bond payable in three years' time at Christmas 1462;[2] and this date of 1459 helps towards the assignment of conjectural dates to several of the others. Another interesting reading is that of John Baldwin (*d*. 1469), who became common serjeant of London in 1463: it includes what may be the fullest account since the thirteenth century of English criminal law.[3]

From 1470 to 1513 an almost complete list of readers has been compiled from a multitude of sources, though it is difficult to marshal them in exact chronological order, and in all but a few cases the subjects of the lectures remain undiscoverable. The earliest name in this extension of Thorne's list is that of John Brewode (*d*. 1500), whose reading in the 1470s is mentioned in a Harleian manuscript.[4] Brewode has never before been noticed as a reader of Gray's Inn, and there are probably a few others whose names are lost. The most important extant readings from this period are those of Edmund Dudley on *Quo warranto*

---

* Edited version of a lecture given in Gray's Inn hall, 20 Nov. 1979.

[1] S. E. Thorne, *Readings and Moots in the Inns of Court in the 15th Century*, Vol. 1 (Selden Soc., Vol. LXXI, 1954). The list is at p. xxxi–xxxiii.
[2] Cambridge Univ. Lib. MS Hh. 2. 6, at fo. 219v.
[3] *Ibid.*, ff. 59–68v. His membership of Gray's Inn was mentioned on his tomb, formerly in the Greyfriars: Brit. Lib. MS Harley 544, fo. 58v.
[4] Brit. Lib. MS Harley 2051, fo. 97 (" per Brerewod lectorem tempore xl "). The reading was apparently attended by " Hussy lattourney le roy ", which dates it between 1471 and 1478. "Brewod" spoke at a Gray's Inn moot in the 1490s: Bodleian Lib. MS Rawlinson C. 705, fo. 105v. He also speaks in the Y.B. Mich. 21 Edw. IV, fo. 65, pl. 42. He was a J.P. (Cambs.) from 1470, and counsel to the bishop of Ely from 1476.

32   *The Legal Profession and the Common Law*

(1496) and Anthony Fitzherbert on *Beau pleader* (c. 1507). John Chaloner's reading on Westminster II in the Autumn of 1493 is preserved in Gray's Inn library in a manuscript which belonged to Fitzherbert himself.[5] Thomas Thatcher's reading of c. 1500, on an unknown subject, has the distinction of being the only reading mentioned in the year books.[6] Some of the readings in the period 1505–1513 were noted by John Spelman in his reports.[7]

From 1514 there is a complete list of readers in Sir William Dugdale's *Origines Juridiciales*, and another in Simon Segar's manuscript in the British Library.[8] The list as far as 1569 is taken from the lost first pension book of Gray's Inn, but unfortunately Dugdale and Segar differ—sometimes by two or three years—in their interpretations of the manuscript. From 1569 we have the pension books themselves; but the record of an election to the office of reader does not prove that the man actually read, because readings were sometimes deferred on account of plague and sometimes readers simply defaulted. The only satisfactory evidence is a dated manuscript note by someone who heard the lectures; and we have assembled corroborative evidence of this nature for nearly one third of the readings between 1514 and 1674.

By Henry VIII's reign the old cycle of statutes had been abandoned, and readers seem to have had a free choice of text. More modern statutes were often selected, and readers did not shun controversy: for instance, the chronicler Edward Halle read in 1540 on *Seint eglise*,[9] and in 1669 the recorder of Brecknock (Edmund Jones) read on the Statute of Wales 1536 and discussed the current controversy over the jurisdiction of the King's Bench in Wales.[10] Some readers selected brand new statutes, which was not always wise: John Boys is said to have expounded the Statute of Uses 1536 in the year it was passed, and to have subjected himself to some ridicule by completely misunderstanding it.[11] Alternatively, a reader could choose a text which enabled him in effect to lecture on the common law. For instance, the only reading yet found (from any inn) on the important subject of actions on the case is that delivered by James Hales in Gray's Inn in 1537 on the Statute of Costs 1531.[12] This

---

[5] MS 25, ff. 263–276; J. H. Baker, *English Legal Manuscripts*, Vol. II (Zug, 1978), p. 195.
[6] Y.B. Trin. 15 Hen. VII, fo. 11, pl. 21 ("En lectura Thatcher cest cas fuit dit pur ley per Fineux Chiefe Justice...").
[7] *Reports of Sir John Spelman*, Vol. I (Selden Soc., Vol. XCIII), pp. 213 (Richard Hesketh), 64 (John Goring), 17 (Richard Covert).
[8] W. Dugdale, *Origines Juridiciales* (1680 ed.), pp. 292–297; "Succession of readers" (by S. Segar), Brit. Lib. MS Harley 1912, ff. 172–187v, printed in W. R. Douthwaite, *Gray's Inn* (1886), pp. 43–76.
[9] Brit. Lib. MS Hargrave 88, ff. 74–78; MS Hargrave 92, ff. 57–62v. Both texts are incomplete, and the reading may have been stopped.
[10] Bodleian Lib. MS Rawlinson C. 824, pp. 401–425; Brit. Lib. MS Add. 50116, fo. 155.
[11] F. Bacon, *The Learned Reading ... upon the Statute of Uses* (1642), p. 34. Boys nevertheless became attorney of the duchy of Lancaster in 1540.
[12] Brit. Lib. MS Hargrave 92, ff. 21–40. The statute only mentioned actions on the case in passing.

technique was sometimes criticised in the seventeenth century, and it was for some readers a matter of pride to avoid " common-law points " and stick to the statute.[13] Nevertheless, a reader had to bear in mind the capacities and interests of his audience. John Brograve, who selected the jointure provisions of the Statute of Uses for his 1576 reading, was frank about the reasons for his choice.:

> In the conclusion of his first reading he showed the cause why he made election of this statute, and of this branch of the statute, before all other statutes. He assigned two reasons for this. First, for the " necessariness " and the use of matters of jointures, worthy to be known. The other, for the " familiarness " thereof; in which he had a greater regard for the company dwelling here in vacation time, which for the greater part consists of " innes studentes ". And if he had treated of counterpleas of vouchers, or of such difficult matters, too few of the company would have attained the intelligence thereof. For the same reason also, and for want of sufficient learning and ingenuity for such difficult and excellent points as uses are, he avoided the handling and treating of them, contenting himself with this branch . . .[14]

The readings usually occupied about seven to twelve days, spread over three of four weeks, though the period was later reduced to one or two weeks. After a prefatory speech, and presumably a full reading of the statute, the reader proceeded to analyse the text clause by clause, expatiating on the points that most interested him, and putting difficult cases arising from the text—which at the end of each morning were discussed by the old readers present. In earlier times even the judges—those who had belonged to the inn—came along to join in the disputation, so that (for instance) Dudley's reading of 1496 was graced by the presence of both chief justices, Thomas Bryan and John Fyneux, both former readers of Gray's Inn and very distinguished lawyers. The readers' cases could stray some distance from the text: further even, it seems, than the readings themselves. Thus, in Peter Dillon's 1516 reading on the Statute of Ireland *De coheredibus* there was an interesting discussion of *assumpsit* and nonfeasance.[15]

The manuscript copies which survive are as variable in quality as the readings must have been, and since many of them are merely students' jottings of headings or salient points it is not easy to evaluate the performances or even to imagine what they sounded like. Something of the eloquence, or occasional grandiloquence, of the original efforts comes over in the full texts which circulated of some of the more famous readings. Spelman (1519) on *Quo warranto* begins:

---

[13] See W. R. Prest, *The Inns of Court 1590–1640* (1972), p. 128.
[14] Brit. Lib. MS Harley 829, fo. 40.
[15] *Spelman's Reports*, Vol. II, p. 272.

> The body politic of this realm of England, which is composed of the king as the head and the lords and commons as members, is only preserved by justice; for wherever justice is not well administered, there is decay of princes. For it well appears in divers chronicles that the Romans, for so long as they did justice, had dominion over the whole world . . . .[16]

Sir Francis Bacon (1600) on uses began even more memorably:

> I have chosen to read upon the law of uses made 27 Hen. VIII, a law whereupon the inheritances of this realm are tossed at this day like a ship upon the sea, in such sort that it is hard to say which bark will sink and which will get to the haven . . .[17]

The nautical metaphor was pushed further by Robert Callis (1622) in his celebrated reading on sewers:

> My most worthy fellows and companions of this noble and renowned society, the hour-glass of my puisne time is run, and I am now come to take possession of your reader's place; wherein I must hazard to your censures the fortunes of my inability. These twenty-six years complete I have had continuance here, and in that time I have only taken the measure and length of your hall. And herein I acknowledge Gray's Inn to be the patron of my best fortunes, and yourselves the best companions of my forepast and present life. Twenty years likewise of my past time I have in the practice of my profession spent . . . In which time I launched forth my ship *in profundum maris* for a voyage to the sea, and now she is returned to your shores, furnished and ballast with merchandise of several estimates . . . Marvel not, I pray you, at these my sea-like salutations, for this day I am become God Neptune's orator, and I mean to display the power of his empire: for my statute, my cases, my argument, will all depend upon the element of water, over which (as poets feign) Neptune hath chief predominance . . .[18]

Those were men who relished the chance to read, and excelled in the performance. Most were less enthusiastic, and were motivated chiefly by the need to avoid the heavy fine which fell on those who disobeyed the call. Some were open about their shortcomings, like Edmund Pelham (1588):

> Besides the want of good gifts, some causes may be alleged as impediments why I cannot so effectually explain the intent of that statute I intend to read on: as, that it comes sooner than I expected . . . Neither did I till I tasted this kind of travail think it so laborious to read as I now find it . . . Again, this short time hath not been so quiet as importing me and others as it might. This I speak not to justify my negligence but to admonish them that succeed to have more circumspect care and take longer deliberation to discharge so weighty a burden than my self have done.

[16] For the texts, see *Spelman's Reports*, Vol. I, p. xi, n. 7.
[17] *The Learned Reading*, p. 1.
[18] Printed in 1647, 1685 and 1686.

He seems only to have managed three days, and then grumbled that time had cut him off. Nevertheless, Bacon made a kind and eloquent speech of thanks.[19]

The usual method of the lectures themselves was merely to provide a disjointed catalogue of isolated legal propositions, with little more analysis or comment than was found in an abridgment. Although some readers tried to show off, they rarely rose above the case-method at its most pedestrian. This may explain the apparent decline in the circulation of texts after the fifteenth century. Coke certainly thought they had lost their former clarity and authority. Whereas Littleton had rightly treated readings as a source of law,

> now the cases are long, obscure and intricate, full of new conceits, liker rather to riddles than lectures, which when they are opened they vanish away like smoke; and the readers are like to lapwings, who seem to be nearest their nests when they are farthest from them, and all their study is to find nice evasions out of the statute.[20]

The system came to an abrupt end in 1642 with the Civil War.[21] The inns went on electing benchers, but their reading was excused and the two ranks of bencher and reader became finally separated. During the interregnum, John Cooke of Gray's Inn—the self-styled solicitor-general who prosecuted Charles I—proposed a reconstruction of the learning exercises on more rational principles, with readings not on statutes but on " the present law of the times ", dealing with matters of most practical value, and with the appointment of professors in each inn to direct studies.[22] This radical suggestion fell on stony ground, and the vision was not fulfilled until modern times. Had action been taken, the later history of the inns might have been very different. But in 1650 there was no prospect of raising funds to pay professors, nor any persuasive reason why senior members of the bar should make things easier for new entrants than it had been for themselves. Furthermore, an understandable aversion to some of the excesses of the period swept the good ideas away with the bad in 1660. Back came law French, Latin and court-hand, and all the legal formalities which proved that England was again free. In 1661 the old system of readings and moots was revived in its ancient form, against considerable resistance and without lasting success. It was one of the more serious errors in the history of legal education.

Only for Gray's Inn do we have a tolerably complete record of the readings given after 1661. They are in two notebooks—one at Oxford,

---

[19] Brit. Lib. MS Hargrave 398, fo. 149v.
[20] Co. Litt. 280b.
[21] Prest, *The Inns of Court*, pp. 135-136, 237. There was, however, a partial revival of moots after 1647.
[22] *A Vindication of the Professors of the Law* (1646); Prest, *The Inns of Court*, pp. 170-173.

written by the reporter Joseph Keble,[23] and the other in the British Library with the signature "Raymond".[24] It appears from the speeches found in these notebooks that one of the main difficulties attending the revival was that, since the list of potential readers had been left to lengthen for nineteen years, the men called upon to read were a generation older than in times past and regarded themselves as too senior to take on the burden. Francis Bacon—the third of that name to read in Gray's Inn—complained rather gruffly in 1662:

> that he was forty-four years' standing in Gray's Inn, admitted in Sir John Finch's time; and in those days they used to read at forty, and not sixty years of age. That he was descended of a family which for one hundred years had been of this house. That he chose this statute [of simony] because the students were ignorant of it . . .[25]

His successor, Thomas Edgar, also complained:

> that he had been forty-two years of this house . . . he said that Justice Godbold was but twenty-four years' standing when he read, and he wished that thirty years' standing in commons might be a discharge from reading . . .

He then emphasised his point by reminiscing about the great benchers of Gray's Inn in the 1620s.[26] The next reader, William Ellis, started by saying, "I know it rather your wonder than expectation to see one here having passed the meridian of my age and fortune. . .".[27] And after him Thomas Hardres, the Exchequer reporter, complained of his age and "numerous progeny, his want of practice and decimation in the late times". Keble, who recorded the speech, also noted that Hardres (having been elected in the Michaelmas term) on the first Sunday of the Lent vacation 1664 "took his place in the chapel in his tufted gown" with two men in livery.[28] Clearly expenses were being cut: earlier readers had had a dozen servants in livery. The tufted gown was still a mark of the reader's rank, but it was soon to be appropriated by king's counsel.[29] Reading had ceased to be a necessary qualification for the coif,[30] and it never was necessary for king's counsel. It was therefore no longer relevant to professional advancement.

Despite their reluctance, the last readers of Gray's Inn chose some interesting subjects: usury, simony, merchants, mortmain, marine

---

[23] Bodleian Lib MS Rawlinson C. 824; *English Legal Manuscripts*, Vol. II, pp. 177–178.
[24] Brit. Lib. MS Add. 50116, ff. 144–157v. Raymond may have been Thomas Raymond, who became a serjeant from Gray's Inn in 1677.
[25] *Ibid.*, ff. 147–148.
[26] *Ibid.*, fo. 149.
[27] Bodleian Lib. MS Rawlinson C. 824, p. 2.
[28] *Ibid.*, p. 56.
[29] See "History of the Gowns worn at the English Bar" (1975) 9 *Costume* 15, at pp. 16–17. Francis North was the first K.C. to wear it (1668), and not without controversy.
[30] J. H. Baker, *The Order of Serjeants at Law* (1984), pp. 40–41.

insurance, and the constitutional position of Wales. But evidently it was difficult to maintain interest. Edmund Jones's reading (1669) ended early " by reason other houses concluded now, and some disturbance happened on his grand day in the hall ".[31] Keble reported no readings beyond that of William Lane in 1671. He was not quite the last. Two copies exist of the 1674 reading by Sir William Jones, then solicitor-general, on the law of replevin and distress;[32] and it is thought that Robert Baldock delivered the very last reading three years after that.[33] Readings ceased around the same time in the other three inns of court.

From this time the inns began to decline in numbers and vitality, and in the case of Gray's Inn the decline persisted until the turn of the present century. The inns went on electing readers—as some of them still do three centuries later—but they were not expected to give any manner of instruction. When, in 1740, pension made an order concerning readers, it was recited that reading had " for many years been discontinued, being found not only very expensive but useless and not fit to be revived ".[34] No doubt the benchers of 1740 would have been puzzled by Coke's claim in 1604 that the inns of court were a university: another of his quaint misconceptions. In Coke's time the description still made sense,[35] though (as we have noticed) he remarked in his *Institutes* on the decline since the golden days of Littleton in the fifteenth century. Neither he nor the Gray's Inn benchers of 1740 thought of any change beyond a reversion to the past: something which Coke seemed to want, but his obscure Georgian successors (looking back to a different past) did not.

In 1753, to their immense credit, the benchers of Gray's Inn initiated a bold experiment in legal education by appointing Danby Pickering, a barrister of twelve years' standing, to deliver a course of lectures and to " moderate " debates in hall. It would be valuable to know more about this enterprise, which began in the same year as Blackstone's experiment at Oxford. We do know that what succeeded at Oxford failed in Holborn. And we may hazard a guess that the result might have been the same if Blackstone and Pickering had changed places. Pickering was well remunerated and apparently gave good lectures, but the students in general did not trouble to attend them. After sixteen years—ironically, on the occasion of Pickering's call to the bench—they were discontinued.[36] In the metropolis there was no longer a framework for scholastic discipline,[37] and even the working students were slaves to the

---

[31] Bodleian Lib. MS Rawlinson C. 824, p. 425.
[32] Harvard Law School MS Ac. 704770 (English text); Brit. Lib. MS Add. 50116, fo. 158v.
[33] R. J. Fletcher (ed.), *The Pension Book of Gray's Inn*, Vol. II (1910), p. 46.
[34] *Ibid.*, p. 235.
[35] Not, of course, in a technical sense: cf. below, pp. 45–46.
[36] Fletcher, *Pension Book*, Vol. II, p. xxiv.
[37] Blackstone referred to this in his inaugural lecture. See also an anonymous review of Cunningham's *Inns of Court* in *Monthly Review* (1781), p. 74: ". . . the idea of keeping

minutiae of practice. The inns of court had ceased to be academic institutions, and were learning the painful lesson that the extinction of tradition, intellectual spirit and morale is almost as irreversible as death itself.

Coke is often justly accused of historical—or rather unhistorical—romanticism. But in this instance his picture of a golden age carries conviction. Through our sparse and opaque sources we see a more vigorous and influential Gray's Inn in (say) 1496, when two renowned chief justices came to sit in hall and reason with Edmund Dudley, soon to be a principal minister of the crown; or in 1499, when one of those chief justices made a statement in hall which seems in retrospect to mark the beginning of the modern law of contract;[38] or a few years after that, when the erudite Fitzherbert laid aside his toil on the great abridgement to teach the gentlemen of Gray's Inn the mysteries of pleading.[39] The glory and the vitality could still be felt in the days of Nicholas Bacon (d. 1579) and his son Francis. It would have been no exaggeration then to praise the inns of court as "the most famous university . . . of any humane science that is in the world".[40]

---

up anything like academical discipline in the heart of this opulent and licentious metropolis, is too wild and chimerical. It is found sufficiently difficult in our two universities, though at the distance of fifty or sixty miles from the grand seat of dissipation."
[38] *Spelman's Reports*, Vol. II, pp. *269–270*.
[39] *Ibid.*, p. *143*.
[40] Coke's words, in the preface to the third part of his *Reports*.

5

THE OLD CONSTITUTION OF GRAY'S INN

Although the origins of the Inns of Court and Chancery are lost in mystery, and likely to remain so, more information is now being found in the public records than might have been foreseen a few years ago. Among the treasures in store are some 15th century lists of members of Gray's Inn; but the present note is concerned with formal structure rather than with biography.

When the first extant Pension Book begins (in 1569), the Society is found to be governed not by benchers but by readers. The style of Pensions was *coram lectoribus,* and decisions were often expressed to have been made by the readers, never by the masters of the bench. There are, it is true, references to benchers even in Henry VIII's reign;[1] but these refer to the fellows of the Inn appointed to preside at moots, and even in Elizabeth I's time there were some learning exercises (the library moots) at which relatively junior fellows occupied the bench. There is no evidence of calls to the bench in a formal, permanent sense before Francis Bacon was admitted to the high table ("where non ar but reders") in 1586[2]. There are also references to barristers, and by the 1570s there were clearly defined qualifications for election to the utter bar.[3] It is clear, however, from the Pension Book—and from the earlier lost records extracted by Segar—that election as a barrister had far less significance than election to the grand company (*magna societas*). The "ancients" elected to the grand company ranked next after the readers, and as late as 1623 had authority to give rule in hall and house when the readers were absent from commons.[4] Professor Simpson has recently argued, from this evidence, that the peculiar position of the readers and ancients in Gray's Inn probably represented an earlier constitution which was slowly eroded as the Society was assimilated to the other three Inns of Court.[5]

Clear evidence has now come to light in support of Professor Simpson's thesis. In 1585 the two Treasurers of Gray's Inn brought an action of debt in the Common Pleas against an ancient who had failed to keep the nine learning vacations imposed on members of the grand company by a Pension order of 26th January 1569, and had refused to pay the fine attendant upon such failures. The declaration is printed below. The order of Pension, paraphrased in the declaration, was made just a few months before the first surviving Pension Book

---

[1] Selden Society, Vol. 93, p. 41, case 4; Vol. 94, p. 132, note 7.
[2] *Pension Book,* i, 72n. Cf. the clearer example on p. 110 (1595).
[3] Ibid. 9, 27, 49. The requirements were: two moots without the bar in hall, two grand moots in the Inns of Chancery, and two library moots.
[4] Ibid. 26 (rank), 261 (authority).
[5] A. W. B. Simpson, "The Early Constitution of Gray's Inn" [1975] *Cambridge Law Journal,* 131-50.

began. But breach of the order was not in itself a sufficient cause of action, and so the Treasurers had to set out the authority by which it had been made. Gray's Inn, they said, was *"antiqua domus curiae et societas generosorum studentium leges communes"*, and enjoyed certain immemorial usages. The society was divided into two: the "grand company" (consisting of the readers and ancients), and the "company of masters and clerks" (consisting of the students and "other gentlemen"). Of these, it was the readers who had the prescriptive right to make orders in Pension and to enforce them by pecuniary fines. The outcome of the suit is not known, because the record ends with an imparlance; the record is not, therefore, a conclusive authority on the vexed question whether the Inns of Court are prescriptive societies or corporations. The declaration, nevertheless, is a remarkable statement of the traditions of Gray's Inn as understood by its officers in 1585. It is particularly noteworthy that the constitution of the Inn was defined without reference to benchers or barristers, and that the grand company included the readers as well as the ancients.

Several reasons might be suggested for the decline and disappearance of the old constitution. The Privy Council had already begun to issue orders for the four Inns of Court, designed to introduce uniformity of practice with respect to learning exercises and degrees. The establishment of a class of benchers who were not readers may in part have been linked with the increase in size of the profession, as a result of which the old practice of electing two readers a year did not provide advancement for all those with sufficient expectations. And, perhaps most important in its ultimate consequences, the status of utter barrister was coming to be regarded as a public degree. Even in 1585 it did not carry a right of audience at the bar, and the process by which the degree became a necessary prerequisite to exercising that privilege was probably not quite complete.[6] That it was a degree, however, had been recognised by the Act of Supremacy 1563, which required the oath of supremacy to be taken by all persons "that have taken or hereafter shall take any degree of learning in or at the common lawes of this realme, aswell utter barresters as benchers, readers [and] auncientes, in any howse or howses of courte".[7] This applied to all four Inns of Court, and in Gray's Inn new utter barristers were sworn at the "cupboard" in hall.[8] The new status of the barrister may also be traced in the plea rolls in the two forms of action in which professional status was a material fact: maintenance, and slander by way of profession.[9] In the 15th century a man of court could justify maintenance merely by pleading that he was *eruditus in commune lege,* perhaps adding that he was a fellow of an Inn of Court; his status within a particular society was legally

---

[6] See below, pp. 127-135.
[7] 5 Eliz. I, c. 1, s.4.
[8] *Pension Book*, i, 19 (1574).
[9] See below, pp. 109-112.

immaterial. Thus, in 1454, one Richard Alfray pleaded to an action of maintenance that he was *de hospicio de Greys In et homo in lege terre eruditus*.[10] Similar formulae are found in slander declarations in the first half of the 16th century.[11] Shortly before 1600, however, it became usual to plead specifically a call to the bar. There is a Gray's Inn precedent of 1598, in which Thomas Mildmay pleaded that

> he had been for the space of twelve years last past a fellow of the honourable society (*honorabilis consorcii*) of the Inn called "Greys Inne" in the county of Middlesex, and had been brought up during all that time in the laws of this realm of England, and had for all that time been reputed and noted as of upright living and conversation, and by reason of his sincere conversation and upright living and of his long approved learning and knowledge in the laws of this realm of England, and of the good opinion conceived of the same Thomas by the readers and ancients of the said Society of the aforesaid Inn, he was six years since called, made and constituted one of the counsellors (in English) a "barryster" at law.[12]

The emergence of call to the bar as a decisive and significant act was thus demonstrably complete by 1598, but it is interesting still to find a reference to the readers and ancients: in other words, the grand company. The process by which the government of the Inn finally passed from the grand company to the masters of the bench is beyond the scope of the present note, but it should be possible to trace the story in the Pension Books.

TREASURERS OF GRAY'S INN v. GARGRAVE (1585)[13]

Middlesex. Cotton Gargrave, late[14] of Gray's Inn in the aforesaid county esquire, was summoned to answer John Brograve, esquire, and Thomas Colbye, Treasurers of Gray's Inn aforesaid, in a plea that he render unto them £27 which he owes them and unjustly detains etc. And thereupon the same John and Thomas, in their own

---

[10] *Forster v. Alfray* (1454) CP 40/774, m.313.

[11] E.g. *Rowley* v. *Roberdys* (1538) KB 27/1109, m.68v, where the plaintiff described himself as *in lege terre Anglie eruditus unusque sociorum de hospicio de Greys Inne*. He recovered £20 damages for an accusation that he had stolen swans.

[12] *Myldemaye v. Starlynge* (1598) KB 27/1347, m.616 (translated). He was accused of ambidextry in a Chancery suit, and recovered £33 6s. 8d. damages. Cf. *Sayntpole v. Norton* (1545) KB 27/1136, m.153, where George St. Paul described himself as *unus sociorum Lincolniensis hospicii per multos iam retroactos annos non minime diligencia audiendo leges domini Regis regni sui Anglie versatus est et sese exercuit exinde* and in that manner was *doctus et eruditus* in the laws of the realm. It is likely that the first declaration in the new form, setting out the degree, was that used by John Hele of the Inner Temple in 1591: [1969] *Cambridge Law Journal*, at pp. 217-8. The Gray's Inn form is different. For a Gray's Inn precedent of 1642, see J. Hansard, *Book of Entries* (1685), p. 61.

[13] CP 40/1447, m.2428d (translated): the plea roll for Trinity Term 27 Elizabeth I. The writer is indebted to Dr. R. H. Helmholz for bringing this record to his attention.

[14] This word does not imply subsequent expulsion, but was standard form in expressing an addition. Gargrave was admitted to Gray's Inn in 1563: J. Foster, *Register of Admissions to Gray's Inn* (1889), col. 32.

persons, say that Gray's Inn aforesaid is an ancient house of court and a society of gentlemen studying the common laws of this realm of England; and within the house there are, and have been from time immemorial, two degrees of the society: that is to say, the grand company (which consists of the readers and ancients of the same house), and the company of the masters and clerks (which consists of the students and other gentlemen of the house). And that the readers for the time being of the same house are accustomed, and have been accustomed from time immemorial, to hold common councils (commonly called "pensions") within the same house, and in the same pensions to make and constitute decrees, laws and ordinances for the good rule and governance of the said ancients, masters and clerks [and the] officers and ministers of the same house, and for the exercise and continuance of the study of the common laws of this realm of England within the same house; and in the same pensions to impose pecuniary penalties on the ancients, masters, clerks, officers and ministers of the house, according to their wholesome discretions, to the use of the aforesaid house and society, for not observing such decrees and ordinances as should be made and constituted by them the said readers in form aforesaid. And that the same readers are accustomed, and have been accustomed from time immemorial, at the will of them the said readers, to elect two or one of the company of them the said readers to the office of Treasurers of the aforesaid house; and that the Treasurer or Treasurers so elected are accustomed, and have been accustomed from the time aforesaid, to seek, receive and accept all the sums of money which should be paid to the use of the house and society aforesaid by any ancients, masters, clerks, officers or ministers whatsoever of the aforesaid house in respect of all manner of amercements, fines or forfeitures forfeited by them the said ancients, masters, clerks, officers, and ministers, or any of them, and being in arrear unpaid, as well during the time that the same Treasurer or Treasurers so elected should continue in that office as at any time previously. And the same John and Thomas further say that it is the usual custom, and has been the usual custom since time immemorial, to keep in the aforesaid house two vacations, whereof one begins, and has from time immemorial begun, on the Monday in the first week of Lent (except in those years in which Hilary term is not ended by that Monday, and then on the morrow of the end of Hilary term) and continues for six weeks then next following, and the other begins, and has from the time aforesaid begun, on the first Monday in August (except in those years in which the first day of August happens to be a Tuesday, and then on the morrow of that Tuesday) and continues for seven weeks then next following. And the same John and Thomas further say that on 26 January in the eleventh year of the reign of the present lady queen [1569] a pension was held in Gray's Inn aforesaid before Thomas Seckford, Gilbert Gerrard, Ralph Barton, John Kitchen, Robert Alcocke, Thomas Colby and Robert Shirborne, then readers of the same house; and in the same pension it was ordered by the same readers, for the exercise and continuance of the study of the common laws of this realm of England, that every fellow of the same house elected into the grand company of the house should be attendant upon the reader for the autumn and lent vacations throughout the nine vacations next following his election, on pain that every of them should pay £3 for each default.[15] And the same John and Thomas further say that the aforesaid Cotton was a fellow of the aforesaid house at the time when the aforesaid pension was held; and that afterwards, to wit, on 29 May in the twenty-first year of the reign of the present lady queen [1579] another pension was held, before Ralph Barton, Richard Aunger, William Whiskins, Christopher Yelverton, Thomas Snagg, William Cardinall, John Brograve, Richard Kempe and Humfrey Purefay, then readers of the same house, and the aforesaid Cotton (then being a fellow of the house) was elected by the same then readers in the same pension into the grand company of the aforesaid house; and that, after the election of him the said Cotton into the aforesaid grand company and before the day when the original writ of them the said John and Thomas was purchased (to wit, the [   ][16] day of September in the twenty-sixth year of the reign of the present lady queen [1584)], the nine vacations next and immediately following the election of the aforesaid Cotton into the aforesaid grand company were kept in Gray's Inn aforesaid; and the same Cotton, being throughout that time a fellow of the aforesaid grand company in the aforesaid house, was not attendant at any of the same nine vacations thus to be kept next after his election into the aforesaid grand company, and so he forfeited for each default of his attendance as aforesaid £3 to be paid to the use of the house and society aforesaid: which several sums amount in total to the aforesaid £27. And the same John and Thomas further say that, before the day when the aforesaid original writ was purchased, to wit, on 5 February in the twenty-sixth year of the reign of the present lady queen [1584], the same John and Thomas (then being of the company of readers of Gray's Inn aforesaid) were duly elected by the readers of the same house into the office of Treasurers,[17] and still are the Treasurers of the house; so that action has accrued to the same John and Thomas to demand and have from the aforesaid Cotton the aforesaid £27; nevertheless the aforesaid Cotton, though often requested, has not yet rendered the aforesaid £27 to the same John and Thomas, but has until now refused to render it to them and still refuses; whereby they say they are the worse, and have damage to the value of £40; and thereof they produce suit etc.

[Gargrave imparls through five terms, to the octave of Michaelmas 1586.]

---

[15] For earlier and later promulgations of this rule, see Simpson, *op. cit.*, p. 144.
[16] Blank.
[17] *Pension Book,* i, 60. Brograve was Attorney of the Duchy of Lancaster.

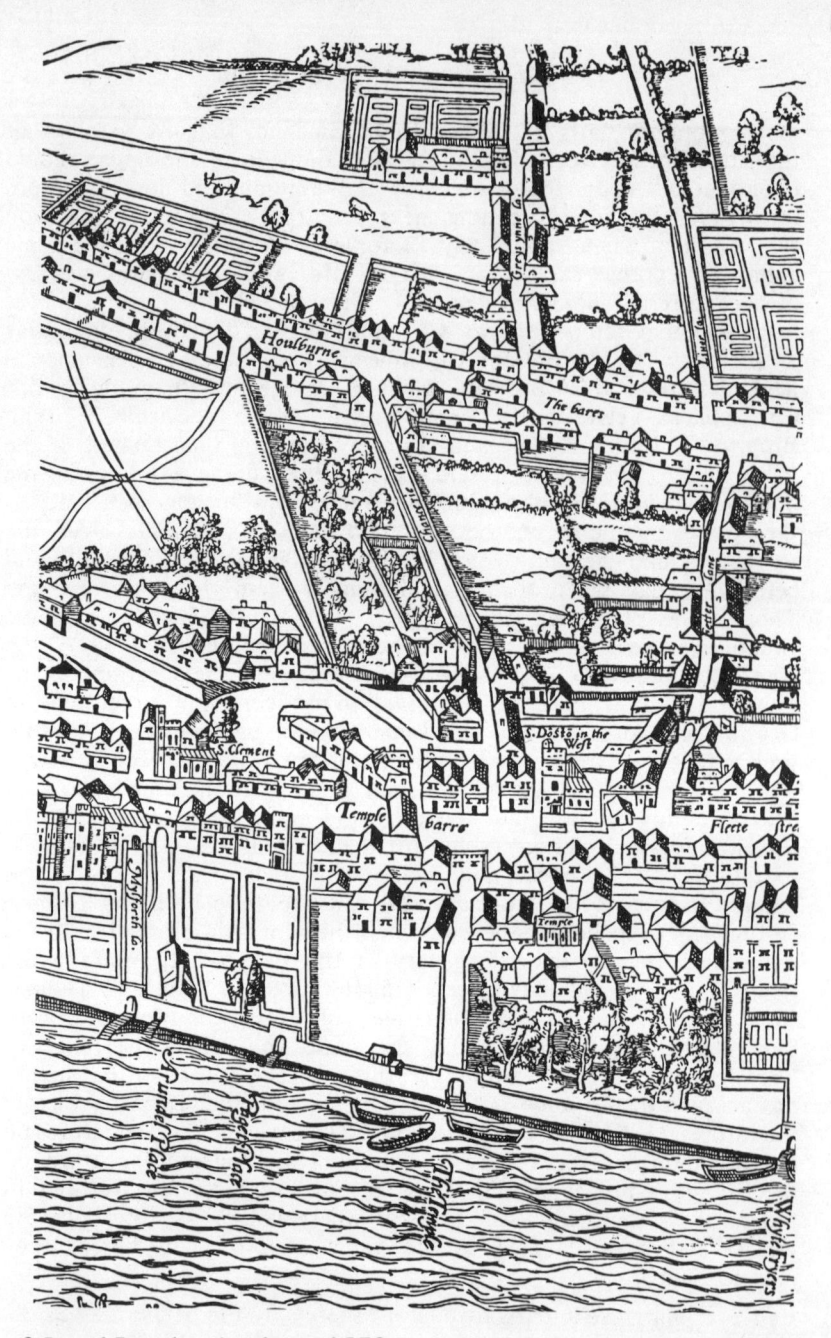

2 Legal London in about 1570

At the top is Gray's Inn, with its gardens neatly laid out. In the centre, west of Chancery Lane, is Lincoln's Inn. Towards the bottom the 'round' of Temple Church is marked, and below it the Inner Temple gardens stretch down to the river. Eight inns of chancery were also situated in the area shown.

From an engraving by Ralph Agas. *Guildhall Library*

6

THE INNS OF COURT AND CHANCERY
AS VOLUNTARY ASSOCIATIONS

It seems almost a contradiction in terms nowadays to speak of an unincorporated university, yet some of our best lawyers used to refer to the inns of court and chancery as the 'Third University of England' ([1]). The word 'university' in this context was not being used as a legal term of art, but was intended to convey the same sentiment as Fortescue intended when he wrote (in about 1470) that the inns formed a *studium publicum* more suited to the study of English law than any university ([2]). For this lawyers' university or *studium* was unusual, if not unique, in having virtually no existence as a body. Its constituent colleges were autonomous and formed a university only in the sense that they performed similar functions, in close geographical proximity, under the general supervision of the king's council or the judges ([3]). The inns had no recorded foundations or written constitutions, and were never incorporated, either individually

---

([1]) 3 Co. Rep. pref.; 1 Bl. Comm. 24-25; and see W. R. PREST, *The Inns of Court 1590-1640* (1972), 115. The committee of inquiry into the inns of court (1855) recommended that the inns be 'united in a University' in the legal sense (p. 17).

([2]) J. FORTESCUE, *De Laudibus Legum Anglie* (S. B. Chrimes ed., 1942), 116-117.

([3]) In 1974 the inns of court came together to form a Senate of the Inns of Court and the Bar, with power 'to consider and lay down general policy with regard to all matters affecting the profession (other than matters within the exclusive jurisdiction of the Bar Council or the Inns)'. This was a culmination of earlier developments in the centralisation of educational and disciplinary matters.

or collectively. Most writers on corporate personality have treated them as awkward anomalies, to be mentioned in asides or footnotes as exceptions to the usual course of things. Even the more practical law books treat the legal status of these societies as a matter of speculation ([4]). Yet why should lawyers, of all people, have been a law unto themselves? Their inns have played a prominent part in the history of the nation. Can we believe that they were denied privileges granted not only to academics and merchants but even to scriveners and parish clerks? It is inconceivable. As Maitland reminded us, ' Our lawyers were rich and influential people. They could easily have obtained incorporation had they desired it. They did not desire it ' ([5]). The purpose of this paper is to examine how and why the common lawyers managed their societies without recourse to legal incorporation.

It would be anachronistic to assume that there has always been a clear distinction between corporate bodies and the other species of company, fellowship or voluntary association. Even under present English law the distinctions are not always sharp ([6]). The many words used in medieval times to describe groups of people seem all to have been capable of bearing different senses. The lack of any precise distinction in terminology may indicate the absence of any perception of corporateness, but this cannot be assumed. It is a matter of fact rather than of law that coherent groups are seen as something different from their individual

---

([4]) So also in Scotland, where it has been suggested that the Faculty of Advocates is a common-law corporation ' by long recognition ': D. M. WALKER, *Principles of Scottish Law*, I (1970), 376. The faculty considered formal incorporation in 1701, when a new library and premises were acquired, but did not pursue it: J. M. PINKERTON, *The Minute Book of the Faculty of Advocates*, I (Stair Soc., 1976), xiii, 227.

([5]) F. W. MAITLAND, *Trust and Corporation*, reprinted in H. D. HAZELTINE et al., *Maitland: Selected Essays* (1936), 141 at p. 191.

([6]) Thus, a statute of 1970 defines ' company ' for the purposes of corporation tax as including any unincorporated association. Yet it has been held that the Conservative Party, which claims a continuous existence since the 17th century, is not a voluntary association for this purpose: *Conservative Central Office* v. *Burrell*, [1982] 2 All E.R. 1.

members. That fact has always been reflected in language. We have collective names for a flock of sheep, or a swarm of bees, because the groups are seen to have an identity distinct from that of the individual animals, both in appearance and behaviour. Corporateness, however, is a legal concept. It involves treating the group for legal purposes as having a personality distinct from that of its members, so that the group itself can own property or engage in litigation. It is not to be taken for granted that this legal notion would, from the beginning, require a distinct vocabulary. Indeed, the words used to describe corporate bodies were the same collective words (college, company, fellowship, society and the like) as were used for unincorporated associations. It follows that the history of the legal idea cannot be traced through nomenclature as such. It can be seen more clearly in the language of royal charters. Express grants of perpetual corporate status began because it proved more convenient and precise to confer privileges on defined bodies with perpetual succession than on vague groups of people living in a certain place or following a certain trade. Before we consider why the inns of court and chancery disdained to seek such grants, it is appropriate to survey briefly the spread of charters of incorporation among other professional and learned bodies.

Mercantile and academic bodies (c. 1450-1600)

From the time of Henry VI many of the London livery companies were incorporated by royal charter, and in the sixteenth century the practice was extended to merchant trading companies. The purpose was partly to facilitate or regularise the ownership of land, and partly to confirm their powers of self-regulation and their monopolistic control of particular trades. Moreover, in the case of trading companies, the acquisition of corporate status might enable them to trade in a joint stock which was free from claims by the private creditors of members [7].

---

[7] C. T. CARR, *Select Charters of Trading Companies 1530-1707* (Selden Soc., 1913), xiv-xix.

Grants of incorporation to academic colleges are not found before the fifteenth century at Oxford or Cambridge. But when Henry VI founded King's College, Cambridge, in 1441 he made it ' quoddam collegium perpetuum ... perpetuis extunc futuris temporibus duraturum', with a name, a common seal, and the capacity to acquire land and to sue and be sued by the corporate name. Seven years later, the same king granted that the president and fellows of the queen's foundation of St Bernard and St Margaret (now Queens' College, Cambridge) 'sint unum corpus in se, in re et in nomine et perpetuam habeant successionem'. And in 1475 Edward IV granted that Catharine Hall, Cambridge, ' sit unum collegium perpetuum et una societas et comitiva perpetua per se, in re et in nomine ... incorporatum, unitum, firmum et stabilitum pro perpetuo permansurum', with the capacity to purchase, sue and be sued, and a common seal [8]. The universities of Oxford and Cambridge themselves were not expressly granted corporate status until as late as 1571 [9].

In all these instances, however, the grant of incorporation seems to have been designed to ratify and confirm an existing, if legally unclear, state of affairs rather than to innovate. The livery companies had not only existed but had enjoyed some of the characteristics of corporate bodies long before they were expressly incorporated by royal charter [10], and as late as the mid-fifteenth century we find formal grants of armorial bearings being made to fellowships which (in the eyes of later lawyers) were not yet corporations [11]. There had been colleges in Oxford

---

[8] Letters patent of 12 Feb. 1441, 10 July 1443, 30 March 1448 and 16 Aug. 1475, printed in *Documents relating to the University and Colleges of Cambridge* (1852), vols II, III.

[9] 13 Eliz. I, c. 29.

[10] See C. GROSS, *The Gild Merchant* (1890), I, 93-105.

[11] E.g., to the Haberdashers in 1446 (granted to the ' churche wardeyns of the craft of habacdasshers '), and to the Ironmongers in 1455 (granted to the ' crafte and felasship '). See J. BROMLEY, *Armorial Bearings of the Guilds of London* (1960). (The inns did not obtain grants at this period, but assumed arms by about 1600. Under present theory they could not receive grants. But in 1700 Lincoln's Inn had its arms certified by Lancaster Herald: *Black Books* [*of Lincoln's Inn*], III, 207-209. And in 1949 the Middle Temple had its

The Inns of Court and Chancery

and Cambridge since the thirteenth century, and successive kings had recognised their perpetual nature by granting them privileges with words of succession instead of words of inheritance. Thus, Edward II in 1326 licensed the university of Cambridge to establish Clare College in two messuages, to have and to hold them unto the scholars of the college and their successors for ever. Similar grants were made on the foundation of Pembroke College in 1347, Gonville Hall in 1348, Trinity Hall in 1350 and Corpus Christi College in 1352. But when Gonville Hall was refounded in 1557 (as Gonville and Caius College), the charter recited that it had been used, received and accepted as a *collegium perpetuum* for two hundred years: a virtual recognition that by sixteenth-century criteria it had not before been formally incorporated ([12]). The universities, like the colleges, had received numerous grants from successive kings on the basis that they were perpetual bodies. And they had always had proctors. Proctors enabled a university to sue as a body for its privileges, and the recognition of a right to be represented by proctors was perhaps the first indication that the universities of Paris, Oxford and Cambridge had corporate personality ([13]).

It was in this middle period, when corporate status was beginning to find a place in the conceptual framework of English law, but was not yet reflected in express grants from the crown, that the inns of court and chancery sprang up in the suburbs of London. In the fifteenth century all the usual collective words were applied to them — fellowship (*societas*) ([14]), company (*comi-*

---

arms registered by Richmond Herald: *Coat of Arms*, IV, 305. The Inner Temple has followed suit).

([12]) Letters patent of 20 Feb. 1326, 23 Dec. 1347, 28 Jan. 1348, 23 Feb. 1350, 7 Nov. 1352 and 4 Sep. 1557, printed in *Documents relating to Cambridge*, vol. II.

([13]) See G. POST, *The Parisian Masters as a Corporation*, in *Speculum*, IX (1934), 421-445. The proctors did not represent the universities in the English royal courts.

([14]) E.g., *Black Books*, I, 2 (society, 1427), 4 ('felawschip', 1431), 41 ('consortes societatis et hospicii', 1466), 63 ('societas curie nostre', 1476); below, p. 110.

tiva) (¹⁵), college (¹⁶), and so forth. Yet they never took what seems in other contexts to have been the natural step of securing royal charters to settle their status. It is, therefore, not so much in their origins as in their choosing to remain unincorporated that their anomalous position rests.

Professional and learned bodies (1518-1752)

Perhaps the earliest example of an incorporated professional body, apart from the universities and livery companies, is Henry VIII's College of Physicians in London (1518). Avowedly based on an Italian model, it has been described as standing on the line between college and gild (¹⁷). The charter granted that all men practising medicine in London should be 'unum corpus et communitas perpetua, sive collegium perpetuum', with an elected president; and that the president and college should have perpetual succession, a common seal, capacity to acquire property and to sue and be sued by their corporate name, the privilege of meeting and making statutes, the right to license medical practitioners and to punish those who practised without licence, and the exemption of its members from jury service. The charter was confirmed by act of parliament, which in addition gave the college power to examine physicians throughout England, other than graduates of Oxford and Cambridge (¹⁸). These major privileges sufficiently explain the grant of incorporation. In the kindred faculty of surgery, the Mystery and Commonalty of Barbers and Surgeons (1540) — which was a union of the Barbers' Company (1462) with the unincorporated Sur-

---

(¹⁵) W. RASTELL, *Collection of Entrees* (1596), f. 431v ('comitiva novi hospicii', 1457); CP 40/743, m. 124 ('comitiva in hospicio vocato Lyncolne is Inne', 1446); *Furnival's Inn* v. *Leycrofte* (c. 1487), C1/93/66 ('pensions due to the said company'); 'thanswere of the company of Stronde In' (c. 1505), STAC 2/26/354 ('felowe of the ryght honorable company of Gray's Inne').

(¹⁶) Letter to John Paston, in N. Davis ed., *Paston Letters*, II (1976), 22, no. 439 ('your college the Inner Temple', 1440); brass of William Crofton at Trottescliffe, Kent ('legis peritus ac collega de Greysyn', 1483).

(¹⁷) CARR, *Charters of Trading Companies*, cxxxiv.

(¹⁸) Charter of 23 Sep. 1518; 14 & 15 Hen. VIII, c. 5.

geons' Company — was incorporated by the same king partly in order to confer privileges upon it, including the macabre right to claim four dead felons' bodies a year for anatomical dissection [19].

Among non-vocational learned societies the historians were perhaps the first to consider incorporation. In 1603 three members of the Elizabethan society of antiquaries drew a petition to Elizabeth I seeking the incorporation of a proposed Academy for the Study of Antiquity and History. The academy was never founded, though it is not certain that the petition was ever presented. Its interest in the present context is that two of the petitioners (James Ley of Lincoln's Inn and John Dodderidge of the Middle Temple) were benchers of their inns of court. The main purpose of the scheme was the foundation of a 'Library of Queen Elizabeth', which was to have been something like a combined British Library and Public Record Office. The petitioners claimed that such an academy would not encroach on the universities, since the latter did not regard history as one of the liberal arts, but it has been suggested that objections by the universities may have killed the project [20]. In this case the request for a charter was a matter of securing royal patronage for a magnificent new library which had yet to be assembled and financed. The present Society of Antiquaries of London (1752) had a separate history, and its incorporation by George II may have followed the precedent set by the Royal Society (1662). The Royal Society was founded under the patronage of Charles II himself, and so a charter was the natural instrument of foundation. Its charter was also necessary to confer various privileges upon the society, including the same right as the Surgeons to claim bodies for anatomising [21]. Despite these notable precedents, it remained the exception for learned societies to seek charters. Even the Royal Academy (1768) was not a body corporate.

---

[19] 32 Hen. VIII, c. 42.

[20] M. McKISACK, *Medieval History in the Tudor Age* (1971), 167-168.

[21] The first charter is printed in C. R. WELD, *History of the Royal Society* (1848), II, 480-493.

Societies of lawyers (1539-1833)

The first societies of lawyers to receive royal charters were two companies of Chancery clerks in the sixteenth century. The Six Clerks were incorporated by charter and private act of parliament in 1539, chiefly to enable them to acquire the freehold of Harflew Inn in Chancery Lane (which they had previously occupied as tenants) and also to endow them with land in Lincolnshire ([22]). The Company of Cursitors was set up by Sir Nicholas Bacon in 1573 and incorporated by charter, partly to establish their title to the site on which they proposed to build their inn and partly to fix their number, with the monopoly of the privilege of writing original writs ([23]).

The civilian advocates, who had formed a society in Doctors' Commons by the 1490s, remained unincorporated until 1768 and provide a close analogy to the inns of court. Until 1568 their premises had been let to nominees, in trust for the society, but since 1568 the head lease of their new college was held by Trinity Hall, Cambridge, and the occupants of chambers held sub-leases from that college. There was a long dispute as to whether Trinity Hall were trustees for the doctors, and eventually by a Chancery decree of 1767 the doctors were 'deprived of any beneficial interest in their building'. It was after this that they incurred the 'very considerable expense' of a charter. The charter recited that the College of Doctors of Law exercent in the Ecclesiastical and Admiralty Courts had 'for centuries past been formed into a voluntary society' and that they desired incorporation 'for the better support of the said society and for securing to themselves a fixed place of residence for the future'. It embodied

---

([22]) Patent of 28 April 1539 (31 Hen. VIII, pt. 7, m. 12); 31 Hen. VIII, c. 27 (omitted from *Statutes of the Realm* and *Statutes at Large*). They received a new patent in 1637, but on complaint by the master of the rolls they waived it: Privy Council Register, PC 2/48, f. 434; 3 Ves. Jun. at p. 590.

([23]) Patent of 4 Sep. 1573 (*Calendar of Patent Rolls 1572-75*, 96, no. 416); orders of Sir N. Bacon, 26 Oct. 1573, printed in G. W. SANDERS, *Orders of the High Court of Chancery* (1845), I, 41-42 (company to make rules and to elect a principal and assistants); *Black Books*, I, 388.

various constitutional regulations, but it has been shown that these merely codified the existing state of affairs. The purpose was to enable the society to take a direct lease of their premises without the interposition of trustees. Afterwards (in 1782) the college was granted a royal bounty from the droits of admiralty to enable it to purchase the freehold, and the agreement between the corporation and the vendors was confirmed by private act of parliament in 1783. The doctors sold the freehold in 1861, but the corporation continued to exist until the death of Dr Tristram in 1912 ([24]).

What is now the Law Society was incorporated in 1831 by the unwieldy title of ' The Society of Attorneys, Solicitors, Proctors and others not being Barristers practising in the Courts of Law and Equity of the United Kingdom '. The society had already purchased a site in Chancery Lane (including the former Harflew Inn) under an elaborate deed of settlement, and many of the provisions of the deed were repeated in the charter. The main purpose of incorporation was to enable the society to raise money on a joint-stock share basis (soon abandoned), and to enable it to make bye-laws ([25]).

Finally, we may notice the Honourable Society of Judges and Serjeants at Law, which was incorporated by private act of parliament in 1833 to enable the freehold of Serjeants' Inn in Chancery Lane to be purchased from the bishop of Ely. The statute provided for a perpetual rentcharge payable to the see, and annual payments to the churchwardens of St Dunstan's in lieu of rates, with provisions for apportioning the payments on the occupants of chambers ([26]). The society had been tenants of the see of Ely since the 1420s, the leases being made to trustees, but the purchase of the freehold was a prudent preliminary to the extensive rebuilding and enlarging of the inn for public pur-

---

([24]) G. D. SQUIBB, *Doctors' Commons* (1977), 53-55, 75, 210-214; *London Topographical Record*, XV (1931), 83-84; 23 Geo. III, c. xxx.

([25]) Charter of 22 Dec. 1831; ' History of the Society ' in *Law Society Handbook* (1938), 1-6.

([26]) 3 & 4 Wm IV, c. cx (private act, but ' deemed and taken to be a Public Act ').

poses (27). The corporation sold the freehold in 1877 and ceased to exist on the death of Lord Lindley in 1921. The other serjeants' inn, in Fleet Street, was occupied under a series of tenancy agreements with the dean and chapter of York. It was never incorporated, and was dissolved in 1733 after a dispute which prevented the renewal of the lease (28).

THE POSITION OF THE INNS OF COURT AND CHANCERY

The examples given above illustrate the principal reasons why corporate status was desired by various kinds of professional or learned body. First, it enabled a body to own property in perpetual succession. Without such a privilege, the occupation of premises might be precarious (as the judges and serjeants discovered when they were evicted from the Fleet Street inn in 1730), and major building work a risky speculation. As an incidental right, the body was enabled to make and accept grants authenticated by its common seal. Secondly, incorporation enabled the crown to grant to the body privileges which could not easily be acquired by usage. Thirdly, it enabled the body to bring actions at law by its name of incorporation, without the need to join all the individual members for the time being. Fourthly, it gave the body a constitution and, in appropriate cases, the authority to make regulations or byelaws for a particular trade or profession. And, finally, it enabled the body to make contracts binding the common stock, without charging the private property of the members.

If there were no corresponding disadvantages, the inns of court might well have purchased some or all of these privileges for themselves. But corporate status had its awkward side. Best

---

(27) Rebuilding was completed in 1839 and included judges' chambers and Common Pleas offices. Government involvement had been discussed in 1830: Serjeants' Inn 'Gesta', PRO 30/23/1/2, p. 300. The additional property was acquired from the Rolls by the statute 6 & 7 Wm IV, c. 49.

(28) The story is fully related in H C. KING, *Records and Documents concerning Serjeants' Inn, Fleet Street* (1928).

known of the problems was the effect of the mortmain legislation, which prevented corporations from acquiring land without licence from the crown. Although many charters granted dispensations from the legislation, the operation of such clauses was often unclear, and the muniment rooms of colleges and companies are stuffed with expensive licences under the great seal [29]. Perhaps the principal drawback, however, was that a corporate body was tied rigidly to the constitution given it at the time of birth. If the details spelt out in the charter proved unworkable or unsuitable, the only remedy was a new charter. An early academic example is that of King's College, Cambridge, which was founded in 1441 as the rector and scholars of the King's College of St Nicholas, only to be refounded two years later with an amended constitution as the provost and scholars of the King's College of St Mary and St Nicholas. The Royal Society required two new charters within seven years of its foundation in 1662, in order to iron out constitutional difficulties, even though the first charter had been drawn with all the skill of Sir Heneage Finch. If, on the other hand, the charter omitted such details, the gap could not be supplied by prescription, because a body with a definite date of foundation could not be immemorial. Usually the void was filled by the founder's statutes, but these could be more difficult to alter than the charters themselves. The universities and their colleges, for instance, found themselves considerably hampered in the nineteenth century by ancient statutes, and the position was only remedied by Victorian acts of parliament.

These difficulties might well inhibit sensible bodies from seeking charters, if they could possibly manage without. With that in mind, we can turn to consider how the inns of court and chancery managed to avoid the disadvantages of being unincorporated.

---

[29] In 1531 parliament extended the mortmain legislation to trusts in favour of companies and brotherhoods made 'without any corporation': 23 Hen. VIII, c. 10. But this was never applied to the inns, and was construed by the courts to extend only to superstitious uses.

1. *Ownership of property*

At present the freehold property of each of the four inns of court is vested in trustees, appointed from the benchers, in trust for the societies. But it was only by degrees that the inns came to acquire their freeholds. The medieval position in all the inns of court and chancery was that the land and buildings were let to lawyers acting on behalf of their societies. Since very few leases have survived, precise details of the arrangements are not known. A lease to four nominees of Clifford's Inn in 1461 is recorded [30] and we know of leases to members of Serjeants' Inn, Chancery Lane, in the fifteenth century [31]. In other cases it is possible that the tenancy agreements were unwritten. Thus, in 1467 the landlord of New Inn sued two successive principals of the society for arrears of rent on the basis that they were tenants at will [32]. And in two cases from the time of Henry VIII, involving Furnival's Inn and Staple Inn respectively, the landlords sued for rent in Chancery on the grounds that an inn of chancery, being an unincorporated body, could not be sued at law [33]. These actions show that the three inns last mentioned were not even leased to nominees for a term of years.

In the sixteenth century some of the freeholds of the inns of chancery were acquired by the inns of court. Thus, Gray's Inn bought Staple Inn in 1528, the conveyance being made to the ancients of the former inn at the time. The title seems thereafter to have been vested in trustees. In 1582 a further portion of Staple Inn was conveyed to the then readers of Gray's Inn (by name) and their heirs, to their own use [34], but presumably

---

[30] *Calendar of Fine Rolls 1461-71*, 20. The first two lessees were probably joint principals of Clifford's Inn.

[31] W. DUGDALE, *Origines Juridiciales* (1680 ed.), 333.

[32] *Turnaunt v. Clerk* (1467), CP 40/822, m. 412; *Turnaunt v. Bastard* (1467), CP 40/823, m. 127. A Chancery suit was also commenced: C1/55/35.

[33] *Earl of Shrewsbury v. Principal of Furnival's Inn* (c. 1508), C1/364/93; *Copwode v. Principal of Staple Inn* (c. 1527), C1/401/9. See also *Dean and Chapter of Lincoln v. Principal of Barnard's Inn* (1502), DL 5/2, f. 28 (a suit for rent before the council learned).

[34] *Pension Book of Gray's Inn*, I, 58.

on undisclosed trusts. The appointment of trustees seems subsequently to have lapsed, for in 1811 the grand company of Staple Inn themselves conveyed the inn to trustees in trust for their own society ([35]). Lincoln's Inn bought the site of Furnival's Inn in 1548, and of Thavies Inn in 1551. The former was conveyed by Lord Talbot and Furnival to three benchers, to their own use ([36]), whereas the latter was conveyed to the use of the fellowship ([37]). The Inner Temple bought Lyon's Inn in 1583 ([38]), and the Middle Temple bought New Inn in 1608 ([39]).

The first inn of chancery to acquire its own freehold was Clifford's Inn. Lord Clifford in 1618 conveyed the fee simple to the principal of the inn and another trustee, in consideration of £ 100 paid by the society, so that the inn should ' for ever hereafter be continued and employed as an inn of chancery for the good of the gentlemen of the society and for the benefit of the commonwealth '. This conveyance was held in 1900 to have created a charitable trust, and therefore on the dissolution of the society the proceeds of the sale of the inn were to be applied *cy près* ([40]). Clement's Inn also acquired its own freehold, but in a rather odd way. In 1544 the landlord had agreed with the principal and ancients that they and their successors should pay £ 4. 6s. 8d. rent for the inn for evermore. There was some doubt as to the legal effect of this agreement, and leases for years continued to be made from time to time. In 1629 the earl of Clare, claiming the freehold, refused to renew the lease, and Lord Keeper Coventry decreed that the inn should remain to

---

([35]) *Report of Inns of Court Inquiry* (1855), 91, shows that it was still vested in trustees in 1854.

([36]) *Black Books*, I, 286-287. Lincoln's Inn sold it in 1888.

([37]) Ibid., 297. The title was thereafter a matter of long dispute, and even litigation, between the two inns. Lincoln's Inn sold it in 1772.

([38]) [*Calendar of*] *Inner Temple Records*, I, 467.

([39]) The conveyance was by common recovery in favour of the benchers: *Report of Inns of Court Inquiry*, 74-75. The title was litigated in Chancery between the two inns at the end of the century: *Calendar of Middle Temple Records*, 87. There was further litigation in 1740, compromised on terms in 1744. The inn was compulsorily purchased in 1899.

([40]) *Smith* v. *Kerr*, [1900] 2 Ch. 511; [1902] 1 Ch. 774.

the professors of the law for ever at the customary rent. This decree was apparently forgotten in 1678 when another dispute arose, but again the Chancery decreed possession to the principal and ancients for ever (⁴¹). It might be tempting to read into these decrees a recognition that in equity an inn of chancery had corporate status, but the reasoning was in fact rooted in the law of charities and proprietary estoppel, the society having spent large sums on building in the belief that it was entitled to occupy the premises in perpetuity under the 1544 agreement. After 1678 the legal title was vested in trustees.

Only one inn of chancery continued its medieval arrangements until the end. The members of Barnard's Inn continued in occupation as tenants of the dean and chapter of Lincoln for over four centuries, and only at the end of their society's existence (in 1892) bought the freehold with a view to sale.

The title to the four inns of court was in medieval times vested in various religious corporations. Lincoln's Inn belonged to the see of Chichester. In 1536 it was conveyed by the bishop to William and Eustace Sulyard, who as members were probably acting as nominees but nevertheless received rent from the inn. In 1580 their heir, Edward Sulyard, conveyed the fee simple to the then benchers (by name) and their heirs (not successors). Since then the title has been similarly vested in trustees. Gray's Inn apparently purchased their freehold from the crown around 1539, though no conveyance has ever been discovered. By 1687 at the latest the title was held by trustees ' to and for the common profit, benefit and utility of the society of Gray's Inn and the members of the same for the time being, for ever, according to the true, ancient and laudable government thereof '. A quit rent was payable to the crown or the crown's grantees until 1733, when the latter sold it to the then treasurer of Gray's Inn in trust for the society (⁴²). The Temple came to the crown on the dissolution of the order of knights hospitaller, and the crown took rent from the two inns there until 1608. By a royal charter

---

(⁴¹) C. T. CARR, *Pension Book of Clement's Inn* (Selden Soc., 1960), li; C78/1022 (not mentioned by Carr, but giving more details).

(⁴²) *Report of Inns of Court Inquiry*, 76-77.

of 13 August 1608, the Temple was granted to the benchers of the Inner Temple and Middle Temple (named individually), their heirs and assigns, to their own use, but with the command that it be used for the accommodation and education of students and professors of the law for ever ([43]). In 1732, after a dispute between the two societies, a partition agreement was embodied in a deed made by the benchers of each inn ([44]).

Thus, although occasional uncertainties arose as to ancient titles, it is clear that the inns of court and chancery occupied their premises securely, and with enough confidence to erect costly buildings, since the middle of the fifteenth century. With one exception ([45]), the inns did not receive endowments of land beyond their collegiate sites. Nor did they invest in real property. The lack of common seals was therefore no disadvantage. The seals which the inns use ([46]) are not common seals, because there are no standing orders or votes on sealings, but merely office seals used for authenticating certificates.

2. *Privileges*

The only privileges which the inns are likely to have wanted confirmed are those connected with their professional functions. But there was never any doubt about such things. The right to teach law, the right to give degrees in the common law and thereby to control the membership of the bar, freedom from disturbance or outside interference: all these things the inns had without the need for charters. Historians no longer believe that the inns of court originated in the royal writ of 1292 touching the apprentices who followed the king's court, but lawyers may

---

([43]) Printed in *Inner Temple Records*, II, 337.

([44]) Ibid., IV, 109; deed printed in *Report of Inns of Court Inquiry*.

([45]) The Rainbow Tavern in Newgate Street was left to Lincoln's Inn by Sir Roger Cholmeley in 1565, and retained as an investment until 1927: *Black Books*, I, 348; V, 1.

([46]) C. T. CARR, *Law of Corporations* (1905), 55; D. LLOYD, *Unincorporated Associations* (1938), 51. The Inner Temple had a seal engraved 'for the office' in 1777: *Inner Temple Records*, V, 362.

once have believed it, and it was true that the men of court (from whom the inns of court took their name) were a fellowship by virtue of their calling and needed no other warrant for assembling together. By the 1450s at least, membership of an inn of court or chancery was ipso facto evidence that a man was learned in the law and exempt from the laws against maintenance ([47]). Then, or soon afterwards, both the discipline and the education in the inns came under the direct supervision of the king's council, and this would have cured any misgivings as to their legitimacy. The teaching was not exempt from political interference if it was thought subversive of government interests ([48]), but no charter would have made it freer. The degrees of barrister and reader originated in the internal educational routines of each inn, and at first had no public significance. The recognition of these degrees as qualifications for practice was convenient and sensible, but it resulted from the judges' inherent authority to control the bar rather than from any claim of privilege by the inns. It is only in relatively recent times that the inns have used their powers in order to regulate professional conduct at the bar, as opposed to domestic discipline ([49]). That function was performed in earlier times by the courts themselves, or by the king's council.

The judges were inclined to recognise that the inns possessed other privileges of an academic character. There is a precedent

---

([47]) See the pleas in bar of maintenance in *Kyrryell* v. *Pettillesdene* (1446), CP 40/743, m. 124 (' in comitiva in eadem lege eruditorum in hospicio vocato Lyncolne is Inne communicans et conversans '); *Michell* v. *Cloutesham* (1453), CP 40/771, m. 114 (' commorans et conversans in quodam hospicio vocato le Stronde in comitatu Midd. per diversos et plures annos et dies ad discendum legem terre Anglie '); *Forster* v. *Alfray* (1454), CP 40/774, m. 313 (' de hospicio vocato Greys In '); *Clou* v. *Kellowe* (1457), (' de hospicio de Stapull Inne '); Rastell, *Entrees*, ff. 431v (' homo in lege terre eruditus comitive novi hospicii ', 1457), 432 (' unus sociorum de Lincolnes Inne ', undated).

([48]) E.g., J. H. BAKER, *The Reports of Sir John Spelman*, II (Selden Soc., 1977), 351 (Star Chamber, 1540).

([49]) The authority is recognised in *Report of Inns of Court Inquiry*, 14; *Seymour* v. *Butterworth* (1862), 3 F. & F. 372, at pp. 381-382. In 1830 Lincoln's Inn expelled a conveyancer who appeared to be a public auctioneer: *Black Books*, IV, 179.

The Inns of Court and Chancery

of 1632 for a writ to prohibit building near an inn of chancery, 'if it would happen that the students of the inn, incumbent in the same in the study of our laws, would be so much disturbed with the clamours and noise of men resorting to that place that they could not follow their studies' ([50]). And in 1697 the court of King's Bench declared that, although the Temple was not a place privileged from the making of arrests, it would not countenance arrests being made in term-time and would set offending bailiffs by the heels ([51]). The Templars claimed, sometimes rather fiercely, to be exempt from any civic jurisdiction, and to this day the Temple enjoys many constitutional peculiarities both ecclesiastical and civil ([52]). The other inns claimed in later times, with almost complete success, to be extraparochial and therefore exempt from parish rates ([53]). In later times various forms of public taxation were laid upon the inns, as indeed they were upon colleges, but they generally avoided poll-taxes and aids until the end of the seventeenth century ([54]) on the grounds that

---

([50]) *Clement's Inn* v. *Ford* (1632), in *Pension Book of Clement's Inn*, 230-231; R. MOYLE, *Exact Book of Entries*, 70-71. Cf. *Black Books*, II, 85 (Chancery suit for nuisance in building near Lincoln's Inn, 1604).

([51]) *Brown* v. *Borlace* (1697), Skin. 684.

([52]) See Lord SILSOE, *The Peculiarities of the Temple* (1972). Under the London Government Act 1963 (c. 33), s. 82, the Sub-Treasurer of the Inner Temple and the Under-Treasurer of the Middle Temple exercise some of the functions of the council of a London borough and may levy rates in the Temple. The act commits the solecism of referring to the two inns in the Temple as 'the Temples'.

([53]) *Wakelin* v. *Coles* (1739), in KING, *Records and Documents*, 258 (Serjeants' Inn, Fleet Street, extraparochial); *Pension Book of Gray's Inn*, II, 318 (Gray's Inn found extraparochial in 1774 and 1830); *Treasurer of Serjeants' Inn, Chancery Lane* v. *Brown* (1824), 1 C. & P. 224 (found extraparochial); *Bryerley* v. *Principal and Ancients of Staple Inn* (1826), 5 B. & C. 1 (found extraparochial); *Baker* v. *Bains* (1826), ibid. 24n (Barnard's Inn found extraparochial); *R.* v. *Butterworth* (1826), 2 C. & P. 391 (Serjeants' Inn, Fleet Street, again found extraparochial); *Marsden* v. *Waithman* (1826), ibid. at p. 397n (Thavies Inn found extraparochial). Lincoln's Inn lost a dispute with St Clement's parish in 1774 (*Annual Register*, p. 169), but most of the inn was made extraparochial by a private act of parliament, 14 May 1829.

([54]) See complaints about the 1690 tax in *Black Books*, III, 171; *Inner Temple Records*, III, 267-268. The 1523 poll-tax (*Inner Temple Records*, I, 455)

those of the members worth taxing all had country residences and contributed there ([55]). When the inns were taxed, on the other hand, they claimed to be assessed as separate bodies so that they could apportion the total sum themselves ([56]). It would require laborious research to uncover all the details, but appearances suggest that the inns of court were treated much like other academic bodies.

3. Right to sue

The inability of an inn of court or chancery to sue as a body did not deter the inns from litigation, especially with their own members. From the fifteenth century numerous actions of debt may be found in the plea rolls of the Common Pleas and the files of the Chancery and Requests, in which the plaintiff is an officer suing on behalf of an inn to recover dues. The earliest known to mention an inn is a Common Pleas suit by John Ingoldesby as 'pensionarius de Lyncolnesyn' in 1454, and the earliest on behalf of a named inn of chancery is by Alexander Dykes as 'principalis de Furnyvale In' in 1461 ([57]). But there are similar actions throughout the century which seem to be brought on behalf of unnamed inns. For example, Robert Wyllenhale sued 24 gentlemen of Holborn in 1448, the year in which he was pensioner of Lincoln's Inn, and nearly all the defendants occur in the *Black Books* as members of the inn ([58]). And the following year an action was brought against five London gentlemen, for 40s. each, by John Catte, who is known from other sources to have been principal of Barnard's Inn ([59]). The writer has studied the entries of over a hundred such debt actions before

---

is unique in including members of the inns, but only the wealthiest inhabitants were affected.

([55]) Cf. *Black Books*, III, 84, which also gives as the reason, 'that wee are noe corporation'.

([56]) Petition to parliament (1774), *Black Books*, III, 474.

([57]) CP 40/773, m. 276d (1454); CP 40/801, m. 293 (1461).

([58]) CP 40/749, m. 398d.

([59]) CP 40/754, m. 240.

1500, and after 1500 they become still more frequent ([60]). The official title of the plaintiff in these actions varied from inn to inn. In the case of the inns of chancery it was almost always the principal, though Lyon's Inn sometimes sued by its pensioner (1484, 1502) and sometimes by its treasurer (1486, 1488, 1493, 1495). Lincoln's Inn usually sued by its pensioner, though sometimes the steward (without being named as such) and from 1505 actions by the treasurer are found. In the fifteenth century the Inner Temple always sued by its governors, or treasurer and governors, though in 1502 an action by the steward was enrolled. The Middle Temple was the first inn of court to sue expressly by its treasurer (1486), but in 1500 there is an action by its steward. Gray's Inn, down to at least 1525, was never mentioned in actions against its members, which were nevertheless brought by a permanent official (probably the steward). The variations in title reflect not only constitutional differences between the inns, but also the different kinds of contract which members might make with their inn. Moreover, some of the debts seem to have been pursued over the years by successive officers. It would be interesting to know how such successors would have framed their claims in law, but unfortunately there are very few declarations ([61]).

The earliest declaration to have been found is in an action which does not mention an inn, but which was almost certainly brought by the principal of Staple Inn. One of the eight defendants appeared, and the plaintiff declared on an accounting together in Holborn on 10 June 1454 ([62]). The device of *insimul computaverunt* was well chosen, because it avoided the need to specify the nature of the member's contract and would have

---

([60]) The printed records of the inns mention such actions in the 17th century. E.g., in 1629 the steward of Lincoln's Inn was given leave to sue for £ 450 in unpaid commons: *Black Books*, II, 290.

([61]) Most actions proceeded as far as exigent. Others were withdrawn before appearance.

([62]) *Gresham* v. *Tufold* (1462), CP 40/805, m. 349d. The action against eight London gentlemen, including Tufold, is in CP 40/802, m. 434d; CP 40/803, m. 182d; CP 40/805, m. 190.

enabled dues in the time of former principals to be brought in. An action of 1499 resulted in a declaration by the principal of Furnival's Inn against a member for the rent of his chamber, which had been leased from year to year by the plaintiff's predecessor at a rent or pension of 6s. a year. The plaintiff recited his own election as principal, and concluded that the arrears of rent for thirteen years were due to him ([63]). This comes very close to assuming a corporate succession, and it would be interesting to know how the court would have reacted to such an assumption. But the action ends with an imparlance. In Elizabeth I's time we have an elaborate declaration on behalf of Gray's Inn, setting out the immemorial constitution of the inn and its claim to exact fines for non-residence during the learning vacations ([64]). And in 1700 we find a different custom set out by Gray's Inn in claiming commons from a member ([65]). This last is the first such case in the law reports, but it confirmed the usage of 150 years. If the member's contract for dues is with the treasurer, then the treasurer may sue in his own name ([66]). Only two years later there was a reported case where the principal of Furnival's Inn declared against a member on an accounting together for money due to the principal and ancients. This proved to be a mistake, because if the money was due to them all as members of an unincorporated society, then they should all have joined in their natural capacities ([67]). We may be sure that no action was ever brought in that form. The defect was one which could have been cured by more careful pleading, by alleging a contract with the principal, or a custom that the principal should sue; but the decision was a reminder that the inns could not regard themselves in the same light as corporations.

([63]) *Principal of Furnival's Inn* v. *Pottyer and Spencer* (1499), CP 40/949, m. 484.

([64]) *Treasurers of Gray's Inn* v. *Gargrave* (1585), CP 40/1447, m. 2428d; quoted below.

([65]) *Levinz* v. *Randolph* (1700), 1 Ld Raym. 594, 12 Mod. 413.

([66]) Serjeant Levinz was suing as a former treasurer, to whom the defendant's bond was made on call to the bar. But the claim included dues in the time of a later treasurer.

([67]) *Principal of Furnival's Inn* v. *Hardesty* (1702), 7 Mod. 116.

Even this last difficulty may not have arisen in the equity courts, where from the fifteenth century it was possible for an inn to sue collectively by what would later be called a representative action. In the 1480s, for instance, an action was brought in Chancery by the principal and fellowship of Furnival's Inn against a pensioner who was alleged to have embezzled pension moneys [68]. And in about 1530 the treasurer and fellows of Lyon's Inn complained in Chancery of a nuisance with dung and filth, which had allegedly caused fatal illnesses among the company [69]. Similar actions were brought in later centuries, though there are few traces in the law reports. The later practice, however, was for the action to be brought by named representatives of the inn rather than in the name of the whole society [70]. The first reported judicial recognition of this practice seems to be Lord Eldon's observation, in a case on representative actions in 1802: ' Suppose Mr Worseley's cup was taken away from the Middle Temple: the society must some way or other be permitted to sue ' [71]. It has been suggested that this was the first decision to allow representative actions on behalf of voluntary associations, and that Lord Eldon's conclusion was influenced by his reflecting on the security of the silver of his own inn [72]. But, whether or not Lord Eldon was aware of it, such actions already had three centuries of precedents behind them.

It seems likely that a suit in equity could, conversely, be brought against the head of an inn as representative of the so-

---

[68] *Principal and Fellowship of Furnival's Inn* v. *Leycrofte* (c. 1487), C1/93/66. The plaintiff said that ' the rule and governance of all courte ' belonged to the chancellor.

[69] *Treasurer and Fellows of Lyon's Inn* v. *Proctour and Cokey* (temp. More C.), C1/606/15.

[70] Cf. *Lincoln's Inn* v. *Bond* (1770), where a committee of benchers reported that the inn could not sue at law for certain dues on chambers in Serle Court, but that a representative action should be brought in Chancery by six benchers: *Black Books*, III, 403.

[71] *Lloyd* v. *Loaring* (1802), 6 Ves. Jun. 773 at p. 779. He was referring to the richly chased cup given by Charles Worsley in 1739.

[72] H. J. LASKI, *The Personality of Associations*, in *Harvard Law Review*, XXIX (1916), 404 at pp. 421-422.

ciety. At any rate, we have already noted two cases in the early sixteenth century in which the landlords of Furnival's Inn and Staple Inn claimed rent in Chancery on the express ground that they could not sue an unincorporated body at common law.

4. *Constitutional regularity*

The inns of court did not legislate jointly for the profession until modern times, but even in the fifteenth century membership of an inn was in fact, if not by law, a sine qua non of practice at common law. Admission and expulsion were therefore grave decisions. Moreover, Fortescue tells us that expulsion by one inn would prevent admission to another [73]. Yet, despite the possession of this immense authority the inns remained (and perhaps still remain) free from judicial review in its exercise. Here was a major difference from corporations. For, whereas in the seventeenth and eighteenth centuries the King's Bench developed an extensive and much-used jurisdiction to control elections to and expulsions from all manner of corporations, the jurisdiction was never extended to the inns. In 1641 the King's Bench refused to grant a writ of *mandamus* to the Middle Temple to restore an expelled member, because they were 'no body corporate, but only a voluntary society and submission to government' [74]. And in 1663 the King's Bench judges said *obiter* that *mandamus* would not lie to compel an inn to call a person to the bar, because 'there is no person to whom the writ should be directed' [75]. In the 1820s and 1830s attempts were made to use *mandamus* to compel inns to admit applicants, but again the court would not interfere [76]. The proper remedy of an

---

[73] *De Laudibus*, 119.

[74] *Booreman* v. *Middle Temple* (1641), March N. R. 177; cit. Style 457, *per* Wilde J. Thomas Burman, called to the bar in 1639, was expelled from the inn in 1641 for not paying commons, but later readmitted: *Middle Temple Records*, II, 914.

[75] *Townsend* v. *Mayor of Oxford* (1663), T. Raym. 69, 1 Keb. 458. The point was expressly determined in *R.* v. *Gray's Inn* (1780), 1 Doug. K. B. 353.

[76] *R.* v. *Lincoln's Inn* (1825), 4 B. & C. 855; *R.* v. *Barnard's Inn* (1836), 5 Ad. & El. 17.

aggrieved person, it was said, was to appeal to the twelve judges as visitors of the inns of court ([77]). The visitatorial jurisdiction of the judges is not mentioned in the law reports before 1641, although it was then said to be 'ancient and usual' ([78]).

As for their internal arrangements, the inns of court were not governed by statutes. Some, perhaps all, of the inns of chancery had statutes, but these seem to have been simply codifications of the regulations made by the society from time to time rather than fixed constitutions. A modern lawyer would probably analyse the constitution of the inns, as of other voluntary societies, in terms of a contract between the members. The possibility of a contract between a member of an inn and all his fellows was contemplated as early as 1436, when a member of Lincoln's Inn made a covenant with the fellowship ([79]), and in 1474 two members of Furnival's Inn entered into recognizances for good behaviour 'erga societatem hospicii ... et eorum quemlibet' ([80]). These, however, were specific contracts. The contract created on admission was perhaps more conveniently viewed as being an agreement with the appropriate officer or officers. This seems to have been the approach of Clifford's Inn in an early Jacobean action for commons. The declaration asserted that the defendant had put himself in commons with the principal, paying 3s. a year for the common pension and such weekly sum as be-

---

([77]) The inns of chancery did not have visitors, though the chancellor may have exercised a supervisory role. In the 1520s Wolsey C. and the common-law judges made a decree concerning readings in Lyon's Inn: *Inner Temple Records*, I, 95. In the time of Charles II's time, however, it was settled that appeal lay from an inn of chancery to its parent inn of court, from thence to the lord chief justice, and from him to the lord chancellor: *Benchers of the Inner Temple* v. *Ince* (1677), 3 Keb. 835; *Clement's Inn* v. *Kellett* (1678), C78/1022. In the *Case of Clement's Inn* (1661), 1 Keb. 135, an appeal is said to have gone from Clement's Inn to the Inner Temple and thence to the 'judges', but this may be loose reporting.

([78]) *Booreman* v. *Middle Temple* (1641), March N.R. 177.

([79]) *Black Books*, I, 6.

([80]) C244/119/25, 26. For bonds made to the principal and fellowship of the same inn in the 1490s, see D. S. BLAND, *Records of Furnival's Inn* (1957), 36.

came due for commons ([81]). Either kind of contract might have been intended by the King's Bench in 1641, when it spoke of a 'submission to government', or by Dr Chamberlayne in 1671:

> The societies are no corporations, nor have any judicial power over their members, but have certain orders among themselves, which have, by consent, the force of laws: for lighter offences, they are only excommoned, or put out of commons, not to eat with the rest; and for greater offences they lose their chambers, and are expelled the colledge; and being once expelled they are never received by any of the three other societies ([82]).

This system in itself, of course, gave the inns a measure of self-help which avoided recourse to litigation. But when the inns were obliged to sue their members they seem to have rested their authority to make levies on immemorial usage rather than contract alone. We can be sure that the inns of court did not exist in 1189, but the absence of any dates of foundation prevented any objection being taken to prescriptive claims on that ground. In fifteenth- and sixteenth-century pleadings the inns of court were said to be immemorial ([83]), and in 1519 a dispute between successive principals of New Inn resulted from an audit held according to the alleged immemorial custom of the inn ([84]). Even when these 'immemorial' customs were on record they

---

([81]) *N. S.* v. *W. P.* (c. 1606), in R. BROWNLOW, *Latine Redivivus*: A Book of Entries (1693), 219-220, no. 58.

([82]) E. CHAMBERLAYNE, *Angliae Notitia* (1671 ed.), II, 236. This is probably derived from Fortescue's passage *delinquentes non alia poena*, which is glossed in E. WATERHOUS, *Fortescutus Illustratus* (1663), 538: 'This is introduced to shew that these societies are no corporations, or have any judicial power over their members, but onely administer prudential cures to emergent grievances, which being submitted to by the society have (by consent) the honour and effect of lawes'.

([83]) Rastell, *Entrees*, f. 108 (Clement's Inn alleged to have been for a long time 'quoddam hospicium hominum curie legis temporalis necnon hominum consiliariorum ejusdem legis', 1479), and f. 432 (Lincoln's Inn alleged to have been from time immemorial 'quoddam hospicium hominum de curia legis temporalis et hominum consiliariorum legis predicte'); *Gray's Inn* v. *Gargrave* (1585), below.

([84]) *Barton* v. *Kyrkeby* (1519), CP 40/1028, m. 682.

did not bind the inns, because they were only *res judicata* between the parties. The possibility of setting up quite different immemorial constitutions for the same inn is well illustrated by two cases involving Gray's Inn. The first was an action in 1585 by the joint treasurers of the inn to recover a fine payable for breach of an order of pension. The plaintiffs recited that

> Gray's Inn is an ancient house of court and a society of gentlemen studying the common laws of this realm of England, and within the house there are (and have been from time immemorial) two degrees of the society, that is to say, the grand company (which consists of the readers and ancients of the same house) and the company of the masters and clerks (which consists of the students and other gentlemen of the house); and that the readers of the same house for the time being are accustomed (and have been since time immemorial) to hold common councils (commonly called ' pensions ') within the same house, and in the same pensions to make and constitute decrees, laws and orders for the good rule and governance of the said ancients, masters and clerks, and the officers and ministers of the same house ... ([85]).

No plea was entered by the defendant, and so the custom here alleged was never tried. It is, nevertheless, a little surprising to see that as late as 1585 the presiding members of Gray's Inn set out their understanding of the constitution without reference to benchers or barristers. By 1700, however, the immemorial constitution of Gray's Inn had changed, in imitation of the other societies. In an action on a bond to secure payment of dues, a former treasurer of the inn recited that

> Gray's Inn is (and from far remote times was) an ancient *hospicium curiale* and an ancient, praiseworthy and honourable society of gentlemen studying the laws of this realm of England, commonly called an ' inn of court ', and one of the four societies or inns of court of this realm of England, in which (and in each one of which) all and singular the gentlemen and persons studying the laws of England in order to be called to the bar and allowed as counsellors at law are admitted, educated and

---

([85]) *Treasurers of Gray's Inn* v. *Gargrave* (1585), CP 40/1447, m. 2428d (translated); printed in translation above 41-43.

> approved ... in which inn and society of Gray's Inn there are (and for all the aforesaid time were) several degrees of gentlemen of that society, and the first and principal degree among them consists of the readers and their assistants (called 'benchers'), which readers and benchers are called *socii de banco* (in English 'benchers'), and these benchers for the time being are (and for all the aforesaid time were) governors and rulers of that society and inn, having the care amongst other things of examining the students and members of the said society for call to the bar ... ([86]).

Although the benchers here claim an apostolic succession from the readers, the constitution seems to have changed and it seems now to be assumed that the inns of court are themselves a prescriptive body of four similar societies. This constitutional flexibility illustrates one of the main advantages of avoiding incorporation, and contrasts strikingly with the position of Oxford and Cambridge colleges, whose constitutional wrangles were constantly being taken to court. There is reason to think the constitutions of the individual inns diverged even more considerably in earlier times ([87]).

The visitatorial jurisdiction of the judges has also remained remarkably flexible and ill-defined down to the present day. Before the Judicature Act of 1873 the jurisdiction was exercised by the twelve (or so) judges of the coif: that is, the judges of the King's Bench and Common Pleas and the barons of the Exchequer. Under the Judicature Acts, their authority vested in the judges of the High Court, to be exercised 'in the same manner as formerly' ([88]). But the number of High Court judges is now such that it is unthinkable that even a majority of them

---

[86] *Levinz* v. *Randolph* (1700), 1 Ld Raym. 594, 3 Ld Raym. 317. Cf. Lincoln's Inn's petition to parliament in 1774: *Black Books*, III, 474 ('Lincoln's Inn is one of the four inns of court, and hath been for time immemorial and now is a society intrusted with the education of young gentlemen studying rhe law and with the power of admitting them to practise the same, and hath accordingly been always governed and regulated by the benchers of the said society').

[87] See A. W. B. SIMPSON, *The early Constitution of the Inns of Court*, in [1970] *Cambridge Law Journal* 241-256.

[88] Supreme Court of Judicature (Consolidation) Act 1925, s. 34.

should all sit on one case, and besides many of them would be benchers of the inn appealed from. It has therefore become the practice for appeals from the benchers of an inn of court to be heard by a panel of High Court judges drawn from the other inns. In a case of 1969 five judges sat as visitors of Gray's Inn ([89]). In the last few years, however, the number of visitors has been reduced to three ([90]). There has been no authority for these changes other than the common consent of the judges and benchers. There could be no question of changing college visitatorial jurisdiction in that informal way. Here, then, is another example of the greater constitutional freedom allowed to voluntary societies than to corporations.

5. *Contract and personal property*

The capacity of the inns to make contracts does not seem to have occasioned any legal difficulty in six centuries. Major contracts, such as building agreements, were sometimes signed by all the governing members ([91]). But most contracts, for goods supplied and work done, were probably made informally by the officers. The records of the inns show that disputes with tradesmen were rarely taken as far as the courts. But there can have been no legal difficulty in suing an officer. There is mention of an action by a brewer against the treasurer of Lincoln's Inn in 1685 ([92]). The costs of lawsuits, mostly actions against members for debts, were regularly allowed in the accounts of each inn, and so it need not be supposed that the officer bore any personal liability. It was said in 1854 that the fear of personal liability may have inhibited benchers from authorising substantial rebuil-

---

([89]) *Re S.*, [1969] 1 All E.R. 949.

([90]) *Re H.*, [1981] 1 W.L.R. 1257 (Gray's Inn); *Re T.*, [1981] 1 W.L.R. 653 (Lincoln's Inn).

([91]) E.g., *Black Books*, II, 469 (contract with ten benchers ' nominated in trust for the sayd society ', 1657); III, 458 (benchers of Lincoln's Inn make contract, 1682); *Pension Book of Clement's Inn*, 66-67 (usage of inn with respect to building contracts).

([92]) *Black Books*, III, 150.

ding work ([93]), but there is no evidence that benchers ever did suffer personally and much building was done in every century.

The inns do not appear to have built up substantial assets in money or investments until the eighteenth century. Money was raised chiefly by pensions and similar payments, and extraordinary expenses were raised as and when necessary by levies on the members. Yet they always had movable property. By 1500 each of the inns probably had a library, and the books were conceived of as belonging to the fellowship ([94]). In the seventeenth century they began to build up collections of silver, for use in hall and chapel, and the inscriptions indicate that the silver belonged to the societies ([95]). The way in which this property could be said to belong to the societies is a legal conundrum of some nicety. Personalty cannot be settled at common law on a succession of owners, and the 'use and occupation' could only be settled if the legal title was vested in someone else ([96]). On the other hand, it is hard to see how the property could belong jointly to all the members of a fluctuating body. Nevertheless, the problem seems never to have given trouble in practice. The question arose from time to time in framing indictments for

---

([93]) *Report of Inns of Court Inquiry,* 75. He was expressing a personal opinion, not that of the inn.

([94]) *Reports of Sir John Spelman,* II, *131-132*. There is record of a 15th-century inscription 'Iste liber pertinet societati de Greysynn' in Brit. Lib. MS. Add. 34901, but it is no longer there. Sir David Brooke left books 'to the worshipfull companye of the Inner Temple' in 1559: PCC 10 Mellershe, PROB 11/43, f. 70. Serjeant Cholmeley left various books in 1563 'to the companie of Linckolnes Inne': PCC 23 Chayre, PROB 11/46, f. 184. There are many examples of similar bequests.

([95]) E.g. the Wandesford basin of 1652 'presented to the Honorable Society of Lincoln's Inn'; the Greene cup of 1661 inscribed 'hospicio Lincolniensi'; the Middle Temple chalice inscribed 'Henricus Barker Armiger Adsocius de Banco Medii Templi hanc Calicem eidem Societati dedit Anno 1663'; and many others of later date.

([96]) *Reports of Sir John Spelman,* II, *218-220*. A further problem was that a gift could not be made to a fluctuating body. In an Inner Temple moot of c. 1492 it was argued that, whereas a gift to parishioners was good, a gift 'to the company of the Temple [*comitive dell Temple*] is not, because they have no corporation ... but a gift to all those in the pension roll, or to the twenty men standing by the fire, is good ...': Brit. Lib., MS. Hargrave 87, f. 64 (translated).

the theft of property belonging to an inn, but the clerks of the crown do not seem to have bothered unduly. Thus, in 1552 a man was indicted for stealing 60 pewter vessels of the goods and chattels of the fellows of Clement's Inn, in the custody of the principal; and in 1788 a man was convicted of stealing window fittings in Elm Court, the property of the benchers of the Middle Temple ([97]). The problem had also been turned over in the mind of Lord Eldon, and as we have seen he thought the plate was vested (presumably in equity) in the society as a whole, who could protect it by means of a representative action. During the eighteenth century, also, the inns began to invest regularly in stocks ([98]), with no obvious legal difficulties. Whatever theoretical doubts may linger over some of these questions, there is no evidence that the inns of court were in this respect ever at a disadvantage compared with colleges and other corporate bodies.

CONCLUSION

Whether the inns of court ever consciously weighed the factors we have discussed, in deciding to remain unincorporated, is not recorded. Incorporation must surely have been contemplated from time to time. It was expressly proposed for the new inn of court planned in about 1540 ([99]). It must have been discussed when the Temple charter was obtained in 1608. It was certainly discussed during the inquiry into the Inns of Court in 1854.

([97]) J. C. Jeaffreson ed., *Middlesex County Records*, I, 9; *R. v. Senior* (1788), 1 Leach 496 (upheld by all the judges).

([98]) The first investment entries in the printed records are for South Sea bonds in the 1720s. Later in the century consols were more common. Gray's Inn deposited £500 with the Bank of England in 1695: *Pension Book*, I, 118, 123. For the 18th-century bank accounts of the inns, see CARR, *Pension Book of Clement's Inn*, xxxv.

([99]) The report by Denton, Bacon and Cary to the king started by pointing out that 'none of the four houses of court have any corporation whereby they are enabled to purchase, receive or take lands or tenements'. But the King's House was to be a corporation by patent and by act of parliament. See WATERHOUS, *Fortescutus Illustratus*, 540, 544.

The then treasurer of the Middle Temple thought incorporation would be an advantage to the inns, for instance in making building contracts without incurring personal liability. The commission themselves recommended that the four inns be incorporated as ' The chancellor, barristers at law and masters of law ', to be governed by a senate and to have power to award not only the vocational degree of barrister but also the academic degree of master. The senate came, a century and more later, but without the corporation or the power to award degrees. The advantages of corporateness were never sufficiently overwhelming to induce the lawyers to give up the freedom they possessed in managing their own affairs. Just as the use (or trust) had enabled landowners paradoxically to become more absolute owners of their land by conveying it out of their hands, and just as the merchants by using instruments not recognised by the common law were able to achieve greater flexibility in their affairs, so also the lawyers by avoiding the formalities of incorporation achieved all or most of the benefits without any of the concomitant restrictions. Maitland, in considering the peculiar legal position of the inns of court, laid stress on the ' thoroughly English machinery of the trust ' ([100]). He was thinking of the trust in its later technical sense, which (as we have seen) was only one of several techniques employed. In all the affairs of the inns, however, we see the older notion of a trust: an arrangement which is expected to work through general consent, even though it is not clothed in a form recognised by law. By a combination of trust, agency, contract and custom, and also — perhaps most important — by endeavouring to prevent awkward questions from coming to the fore, the inns of court have for over six centuries preserved the medieval concept of a fellowship or company without recourse to incorporation.

---

[100] F. W. MAITLAND, *History of English Law* (from *Encyclopaedia Britannica* for 1902), reprinted in H.M. Cam ed., *Selected Historical Essays of F. W. Maitland* (1957), at p. 108. See also CARR, *Pension Book of Clement's Inn*, xv.

7

THE ENGLISH LEGAL PROFESSION, 1450-1550

The legal profession was a significant element in late-medieval English society, both by reason of its intellectual contribution to the development of England's characteristic institutions and traditions and by reason of the opportunities which it provided for the gifted individual to rise and prosper. Given its importance, it has not yet received anything like its fair share of attention from historians. Among the reasons for this neglect the most obvious are the dearth of internal professional records and the forbidding vastness of the public and private archives from which less accessible information may be pieced together. Work on the latter is beginning to show that lawyers at all levels left more traces in the records than has been supposed. With a combination of local and central records, such as wills and subsidy rolls, the accounts of civic, noble and ecclesiastical clients, and above all the records of courts, it would be possible to produce thumbnail sketches of thousands of lawyers in the late-medieval period and to place each man in a social category. The labour would be immense, but not technically difficult, given a list of names to work with and perhaps a computer to help with the sorting and indexing. Since that has not yet been done, it is possible here to attempt no more than a preliminary sketch of the profession, with a view to solving some of the initial difficulties inherent in producing the working list of names.

The first difficulty for the historian lies in his understanding of the concept of a legal profession. That there were, by the fifteenth century, a considerable number of men who earned their living from the law in one way or another is beyond contradiction. Contemporaries, indeed, were wont to think the supply excessive:

> I suppose that in all Christendom are not so many pleaders, attorneys and men of the law as be in England only, for if they were numbered all that belong to the courts of the Chancery, King's Bench, Common Pleas, Exchequer, Receipt and Hell, and the bag-bearers of the same, it should amount to a great multitude. And how all these live, and of whom, if it should be uttered and told it should not be believed.[1]

1. W. Caxton, *Game and Playe of the Chesse* (1474) [1883 reprint], p. 95 (modernised). This was an English version of the book by J. de Cessolis. 'Hell' was a record repository in Westminster Hall. It was not a large department but is doubtless mentioned for literary effect.

The problem is to reconstruct a complete picture of this multitude. Most pieces of research are limited by the classes of evidence upon which they rest, and concentrate on particular courts or particular kinds of lawyer. When we contemplate lawyers as a whole, we are bound to wonder whether these diverse men of law can properly be regarded as constituting a single profession. Some lived from the profits of public office, others from private practice; many combined both. Some were in the permanent employ of great magnates or religious houses, others grubbed for work of a more *ad hoc* character among lesser folk; many had mixed practices, serving high and low as occasion offered. Some specialised in advocacy and the intellectual functions associated with the advocate or 'counsellor', including skilled draftsmanship, advice, and acting in arbitrations.[2] Others kept to the more menial tasks associated with attorneyship, clerkship and auditorship. Some followed both callings at once, and may even have combined them with other occupations. This was no straightforward social or economic hierarchy. Some clerks amassed small fortunes, while mediocre counsellors might end their days in poverty and obscurity or quit the law for other pursuits. It is difficult even to define the classes in professional terms. The expressions 'barrister' and 'solicitor' made their appearance in our period,[3] but had still not by the end of it come to denote two separate branches as we know them; they were not titles which in themselves indicated a qualification for practice.[4] Yet, if the whole number of lawyers and legal clerks lacked a comprehensive professional structure, there was one common factor which linked them together in their several stations. The unifying element was the great legal university situated in the western suburbs of London. From learned counsel to pettifogging clerks, most were associated in some way with the inns of court and chancery.[5]

Membership of an inn was probably conceived, by 1450, as being the clearest indicator of professional status and as a warrant for claiming the vague qualification 'learned in the law' which afforded

---

2. For the distinct character of the counselling function, see below, pp. 99 et seq.

3. J.H. Baker, *Manual of Law French* (London, 1979), pp. 57, 186, and the texts cited there.

4. The origins of the division between barristers and solicitors are explored below, pp. 125-149.

5. From this statement (and from the present study) must be excepted the lawyers who practised in and presided over the ecclesiastical and admiralty courts, whose focal point was the university. The English civilians and canonists have not received much attention in our period, but the origins of Doctors' Commons have now been traced to the late fifteenth century: see G.D. Squibb, *Doctors' Commons* (Oxford, 1977).

The English Legal Profession, 1450-1550

protection against the stringent laws of maintenance.[6] In 1450 this was still not an exclusive prerogative of the four inns of court,[7] because a member of an inn of chancery could assert the same status as *homo in lege terrae eruditus* (a man learned in the law of the land), even when acting as an attorney.[8] Although pleas justifying maintenance did not always expressly allege membership of an inn, it is inconceivable that anyone would lay claim to be learned in the laws of the land if he had not spent some time performing the exercises of learning in such a society. Our study of the legal profession as a whole must therefore, to a large extent, be part of the history of the inns of court and chancery. Nevertheless the subjects do not coincide, because membership of an inn would not in itself provide a sufficient definition of a professional lawyer. The reason is that the majority of members were not in any acceptable sense lawyers. The sons of gentlemen and even noblemen attended the inns for social purposes and in order to acquire a general education, without any intention of practising law.[9] How, then, are we to distinguish the professional members of the inns from the rest? The best answer at present is that there was no precise distinction, but a scale of professional commitment related to the length of residence and the extent to which a member became involved in the academic discipline of his society. These factors were measured at two stages of membership by the degrees of barrister and reader. But here the records fail us, since records of these degrees are gravely defective in our period. For the inns of court there are no records of calls to the bar in this period, except for Lincoln's Inn after 1518; while for the inns of

6. For the justification of maintenance (the wrong of maintaining or supporting litigants), by reason of professional status, see below, pp. 109-113, 135 et. seq.

7. The classic precedent is the undated entry in W. Rastell, *A Collection of Entrees* (London, 1566), fo. 396, pl. 16, where a defendant justified maintenance as 'homo consiliarius de et in lege eruditus' and explained that he was one of the fellows of Lincoln's Inn: see below, chapter 8, p. 110. See also *Forster* v. *Alfray* (1454), CP 40/774, m. 313, where the defendant pleaded that he was 'de hospicio vocato Greys In et homo in lege terre eruditus'.

8. There are no express decisions, any more than for the inns of court, but three precedents have been found from the 1450s. In *Mitchell* v. *Cloutesham* (1453), CP 40/771, m. 114, the defendant pleaded that he had been 'commorans et conversans in quodam hospicio vocato le Stronde in com. Midd. per diversos et plures annos et dies ad discendum legem terre regni Anglie et sic [note the consequential implication] dicit quod ipse . . . fuit homo in lege terre eruditus'. Less detailed pleas are found in *Anon.* (1457), in Rastell, *Entrees*, fo. 396, pl. 17 ('fuit homo in lege terre eruditus comitive novi hospitii' and acted as an attorney); *Clon* v. *Kellowe, attorney C.P.* (1457), CP 40/786, m. 403 ('fuit homo in lege terre eruditus et de hospicio de Stapull Inne' and retained as counsel). See also *Dynham* v. *Gylbert* (1478), CP 40/866, m. 158 (says 'erudivit legem terre Anglie' in St Dunstan's parish (i.e. Clifford's Inn) and 'fuit et adhuc existit sufficienter eruditus in lege Anglie ad ligeos domini Regis in materiis suis prosequentes et defendentes consulendos').

9. See pp. 92, 95-6 below.

chancery there are no records of barristers,[10] and very little evidence relating to senior membership, throughout the period. It follows that, although the profession can only be understood in the context of the inns and the facilities they provided, any attempt to distinguish the professional members of the inns before their records near completeness must be based on a study of what individuals were doing outside these societies. For this purpose we have divided the profession into six fairly distinct classes.

The Six Classes of Common Lawyer

Serjeants and Judges

The most clearly identifiable and best documented branch of the English legal profession was the order or fraternity of serjeants-at-law. The serjeants formed the bar of the the Court of Common Pleas (or Common Bench), the principal common-law court in Westminster Hall, and had become an exclusive guild or brotherhood around the time of Edward II. There were usually fewer than ten in practice, excluding those who had been raised to the bench; and every ten years or so, when numbers had fallen through death and promotion, there would be a group call of six to eight new serjeants, chosen from the double readers in the inns of court. They were 'created' — a word reserved for degrees of dignity[11] — with much ancient ceremony, the focal point of which was the new serjeant's first 'count'[12] at the bar of the Common Pleas. These were the men whose arguments were reported in the year books, and who in that way were responsible for fashioning the common law. Their exclusive right of audience in their own court made them, according to Chief Justice Fortescue in the fifteenth century, the wealthiest advocates in the world.[13] In the whole of our period only one hundred were created. They were the cream of the profession. They stood apart from their lesser colleagues not only by their social prestige and exclusiveness, which was represented outwardly by their colourful monkish habit and white linen coifs, but also by the custom which required them to leave their inns of court upon graduation. The reason for this rule was doubtless the same as that which forbade Chancery clerks to live with the other apprentices; serjeants, like the clerical masters in Chancery, were deemed to have

---

10. The degree existed in these inns, though it never became a public degree. The statutes of Clifford's Inn (Inner Temple, Add. MS 189) mention both inner-barristers and utter-barristers around 1500; for this distinction, see p. 91, below.

11. The serjeant's writ, ordering him to prepare for the creation, used the phrase 'statum et gradum servientis ad legem'.

12. The oral recitation, in law French, of the plaintiff's declaration (opening pleading) in a 'real' action brought to recover specific property. In earlier times serjeants had been called 'countors' (*narratores* in Latin).

13. *De Laudibus Legum Anglie*, p. 124, lines 14-15.

The English Legal Profession, 1450-1550

passed beyond the communal life of students and teachers. By 1550 all or most of the serjeants belonged to one of the two serjeants' inns (in Chancery Lane and Fleet Street respectively), both of which were in existence on a smaller scale in 1450; but in 1450 most serjeants and judges probably kept their own households in London or its suburbs. The serjeants' inns differed from the others in that they had no educational functions and conferred no status on their members; they existed purely for social convenience, though in course of time they became a venue for public transactions such as judicial conferences and chambers business.[14] The serjeants maintained links with their old inns of court, to which they were expected to return for the readings in order to join in the discussions. The old serjeants of Lincoln's Inn sometimes acted as governors.

Only serjeants could be appointed judges of the Common Pleas and King's Bench. This was another privilege they had enjoyed since the fourteenth century. Sixty of the hundred serjeants called between 1450 and 1550 became judges of the superior courts, one of them (Audley) being Lord Chancellor. The judicial element in the order of the coif was numerically stronger than the practising element, and the brotherhood between judges and serjeants enhanced the prestige of the order still further. Some of the serjeants who did not receive full-time appointments served as commissioners of assize, an office which could only be held by a member of the order. Just under half the serjeants created in the period also served the crown as king's serjeants, an office to which they were appointed by patent at a small salary and which amounted to a general retainer on behalf of the crown without otherwise restricting private practice. There were three or four king's serjeants at any one time, and they were the leaders of the English bar; most of them became judges in due course.

In Tudor times the crown appointments of attorney-general and solicitor-general, already by the end of the fifteenth century appropriated to readers in court, began to be regarded as more important in practice than that of king's serjeant, though they were not given technical precedence until well after our period.[15] No one could have foreseen in 1550, when the rank of king's counsel extraordinary had not been invented, that the rise of the crown law officers would be one of the main factors in the decline and eventual extinction of the serjeants. But already the law officers effectively shared with serjeants the claim to judicial appointments, because the expedient was adopted of making

14. 'The Serjeants' Inns' in Baker, *Spelman's Reports,* introduction, pp. *135-7.*

15. After 1623 the attorney- and solicitor-general had precedence before all but the two senior king's serjeants, and after 1813 before the entire bar. The changes were effected by royal warrant. For a list of office-holders under Henry VII and Henry VIII see Baker, *Spelman's Reports*, pp. *390-2.*

them serjeants immediately prior to appointment. This happened twice before 1550. In 1519 John Erneley of Gray's Inn, the Attorney-General, was chosen in preference to all the serjeants to be Chief Justice of the Common Pleas; he was created serjeant a few days before his judicial patent was sealed, and was probably the first serjeant since the time of Edward II to have been created singly. The precedent was followed in 1546, when Richard Lyster, a former Solicitor-General who had remained a bencher of the Middle Temple whilst serving as Chief Baron of the Exchequer, was translated to the King's Bench.[16]

The bench of the Court of Exchequer had been dominated by clergy until Henry VI's reign, and therefore never became the exclusive property of the serjeants. By 1450 the barons of the Exchequer were laymen, most of whom seem to have been trained up on the clerical side of the Exchequer. Some are known to have been members of inns of court, but it is hard to say whether they were all readers in the ordinary course before appointment. The chief barons, however, were either serjeants-at-law or full readers in court throughout the period. It was not until 1579 that a serjeant was appointed to the office of junior baron.

The Court of Chancery remained a clerical preserve much longer than the Exchequer. Until the appointment of Wolsey in 1515, the chancellors were all clerks in orders having degrees in Civil or Canon law. The masters of the court were also clerical, until a few lay doctors were appointed after the Reformation. The inns of court did not begin to infiltrate the Chancery bench until the middle of Henry VIII's reign. From 1529 to 1544 two common lawyers (More and Audley) held the great seal, and from 1534 until after 1550 laymen filled the office of master of the rolls.

Judicial appointments outside Westminster Hall, such as the chancellorship of the Duchy of Lancaster, recorderships of boroughs, stewardships of manors and leets, and membership of commissions of the peace and of gaol delivery, cannot be considered to represent separate branches of the profession. The acquisition of such appointments was of much significance to a rising advocate, and they might be heavy burdens; but they were of a part-time nature and did not preclude private practice. They could, moreover, be held in plurality. In assessing the size of the several classes of lawyer, we should therefore reckon only the twelve or so judges of the three common-law courts and the twelve or so masters in Chancery as having permanent judicial appointments. There were no appellate judges above them, nor anything akin to the full-time circuit judgeships of the present day.

16. Ibid., pp. *395-6.*

Clerks and Officers of the Central Courts

Next to the judges among the permanent legal officials were the principal administrative officers who controlled the proceedings in the courts at Westminster. Tables of office-holders can be reconstructed with reasonable precision at the upper levels, but the secondaries and under-clerks in the various offices leave little trace in the records and are such shadowy figures that it is difficult even to estimate the size of the clerical staff belonging to particular judicial departments.[17]

In the King's Bench the senior officers were the King's Coroner and Attorney (or Clerk of the Crown), the Chief Clerk (or Prothonotary), the Clerk of the Papers, the Custos Brevium (who was also Clerk of the Warrants), and the thirteen filazers.[18] In the Common Pleas the Custos Brevium claimed to be Chief Clerk, but there were in addition three prothonotaries; and the other principal officers were the four exigenters, the Chirographer, the Clerk of the Outlawries, the Clerk of the Juries, the Clerk of the Warrants, the Clerk of the Essoins, the Clerk of the Treasury (or of 'Hell'), and the thirteen filazers. The Exchequer had more officers even than the Common Pleas, though most belonged to the revenue side and were not directly concerned with litigation. There was only one chief clerk on the plea side, the Clerk of the Pleas. But many of the revenue officials, from the Lord Treasurer of England down to the tellers and auditors, were men of the inns of court and chancery. The King's Remembrancer and Lord Treasurer's Remembrancer were invariably lawyers bred in the course of the Exchequer and frequently rose to be barons of the Exchequer. All the officials mentioned in this paragraph probably had under-clerks.

The Chancery had a large complement of clerks beneath the masters, but they were members of the chancellor's household and unlike the clerks of the other central courts were in 1450 invariably ordained clergy. Only the Clerk of the Crown seems throughout our period to have been a layman. Laymen infiltrated the Chancery offices before they reached the Chancery bench. In 1468 Piers Pekham, gentleman, is described in a pardon roll as one of the clerks of the Chancery and also a mercer of London; and another gentleman clerk of the Chancery was pardoned in 1484.[19] Several Chancery clerks from this period were admitted to Lincoln's Inn, which suggests (but by no means proves)

---

17. For the King's Bench and Common Pleas in Henry VIII's reign, see ibid., pp. *352-82*.
18. See 'Clerks of the King's Bench 1399-1547' in *LRH*, pp. 128-39, which includes a list of filazers from the notes of the late C.A.F. Meekings.
19. C 67/46/37 (Pekham); C 67/51/27 (William Heed, 1484). Pekham is also described, in a 1484 pardon, as an usher of the chamber to Edward IV: C 67/51/35. Heed was a JP in Kent and probably a member of the Inner Temple.

that they were laymen.[20] The plea rolls contain numerous claims by laymen to privilege on the grounds that they were servants of Chancery clerks, but the claims were usually disputed and often seemingly tenuous.

These were the major courts. Other central and local courts had their own officers; usually one clerk sufficed. Each county had a clerk of the peace, and each assize circuit had a clerk of assize; both offices were vital to the administration of criminal justice. Clerks of the peace were often clerks of the central courts, and much of the clerical work of the circuits seems to have been done by the prothonotaries. Since the courts at Westminster sat only about one hundred days in the year, these vacation employments did not interfere with the greater offices. One cannot confidently assume that any of these local offices were full-time, and therefore they ought not to be counted when estimating the size of this class of the profession.

Very few officials received a salary, and their income was derived from fees they were entitled to charge for each item of business transacted. Approved scales of fees show that even in the two Benches most fees amounted only to a few pence or shillings,[21] but it is obvious that for some officers the total amounted to a respectable or even large income. Many officers augmented their income by practising as attorneys in the central courts, and when they did so they were usually among the busiest attorneys. Some acquired outside offices: thus Edward Cheseman (d. 1510), a filazer of the King's Bench, was also Cofferer of the Household to Henry VII.[22] Several filazers acted as clerks of the peace. Some were even members of guilds,[23] but this may mean no more than that they acted as clerks or legal advisers to the companies. Robert Maycote (d. 1533) of Lincoln's Inn, the first known Clerk of the Papers in the King's Bench, left a collection of books on surgery to his son Richard, an attorney, which may be evidence that his Kent practice took in surgical patients as well.[24]

The senior clerks were usually members of the inns of court, but

20. E.g. William Curteys (1478), William Nanson (1481), Christopher Hanyngton (1482) and John Trewynian (1494).
21. See M. Hastings, *The Court of Common Pleas in Fifteenth-Century England* (Ithaca, 1947), pp. 247-55; M. Blatcher, *The Court of King's Bench 1450-1550* (1978), Ch. 3, pp. 34-46.
22. He described himself as an esquire and was clearly of some substance: P.C.C. 33 Bennett (will); C 1/302/82 (inventory of goods).
23. Robert Brystall, Clerk of the Pleas of the Exchequer, was described in 1509 in his own roll as being also a London fishmonger: E 13/186, m. 30. Another fishmonger was Oliver Southworth, filazer of the King's Bench, who began his career as servant to Edward Cheseman: Baker, *Spelman's Reports*, p. 356. Richard Bolton, filazer of the Common Pleas, was a merchant in Lincoln in the 1460s. Piers Pekham, Chancery clerk and mercer, has been mentioned above: note 19.
24. P.C.C. 8 Hogen. For the Maycotes, see Baker, *Spelman's Reports*, p. 364.

more often than not gained admission by virtue of their office, having spent their previous career in an inn of chancery. Such a career might well begin in the office before admission to an inn at all. John Lucas (d. 1525), who rose to be Secondary of the King's Bench, noted in an autobiographical memorandum that he went to his 'master' in the King's Bench on 6 November 1492 but was not admitted to New Inn until 1 August 1501; he was specially admitted to Lincoln's Inn in 1508, after serving five years as a filazer, at the behest of John Roper, then reader of the Inn and Chief Clerk of the court.[25] The majority of clerks belonged to the lower economic level of the legal profession, but promotion within a department was the usual way of filling vacancies and therefore men of ability (like Lucas) could hope for advancement. The judges felt so strongly about the need for training that in 1465 they rejected the king's nominee for the office of Clerk of the Crown on the ground that he had not been brought up in the Crown Office; after full debate, the king approved the appointment of the Under-Clerk of the Crown instead.[26] Those fortunate enough to ascend to the higher clerkships prospered noticeably. The way in which the Roper family fortunes were founded on the chief clerkship of the King's Bench is well known. The first founder of those fortunes, John Roper (d. 1525), possessed more movable wealth than any other lawyer in the land, and his son married the Lord Chancellor's daughter.[27] Both he and his predecessor, Reynold Sonde (d. 1491), were armigerous.[28] His colleagues on the crown side, Henry Harman (d. 1502) and William Fermour (d. 1552), also bore arms.[29] The like status was attained by the chief officers in the other courts. William Porter (d. 1521), Clerk of the Crown in Chancery, was armigerous.[30] Robert Blagge of the Inner Temple was probably granted arms while he was still King's Remembrancer; and his Secondary, John Copwode (owner of Staple Inn), also received a grant of arms in Henry VIII's reign.[31] Even some of the

25. Baker, *Spelman's Reports*, p. 365. Another King's Bench filazer spent 28 years in Clement's Inn before being admitted to the Inner Temple in 1522: ibid., p. *128*, n. 2.

26. *Re Vynter* (1465), KB 27/818, m. 66; Rastell, *Entrees*, fo. 443; Y.B. Pas. 9 Edw. IV, fo. 5, pl. 20; *Calendar of Patent Rolls 1467-77*, p. 11; Baker, *Spelman's Reports*, p. *361*; Blatcher, *King's Bench*, p. 37. The precedent was twice followed by the Common Pleas in later times: see J.H. Baker, 'Sir Thomas Robinson (1618-83), Chief Prothonotary of the Common Pleas', below, pp. 253-255.

27. Baker, *Spelman's Reports*, pp. *55, 363*; Blatcher, *King's Bench*, pp. 145-6.

28. Sonde's arms: *Archaeologia Cantiana*, vol. 40, p. 931. Roper's (emblazoned in 1518): KB 27/1028, m. 1.

29. Harman's arms: *Archaeologia Cantiana*, vol. 40, p. 100. Fermour's appear on his wife's brass (1510) at Hornchurch, Essex; he became Clerk of the Crown in 1509: Baker, *Spelman's Reports*, p. *362*.

30. The arms were displayed on his monument in St Michael Paternoster, London: B.L. MS Harley 6072, fo. 57^v.

31. B.L., Add. MS 45133, fo. 28^v (both arms).

filazers and lesser clerks achieved armigerous status.[32] The senior clerks were men of moment within the profession as well as outside it. Judges consulted them on points of practice and pleading, and future leaders of the bar and judges studied under them; for example, Mr Prothonotary Jenour (d. 1542) was pupil-master to four chief justices in the time of Henry VIII.[33]

It will have been noted from this brief survey that the superior common-law courts at Westminster alone had over fifty senior legal officials, and if each of them had on average one or two under-clerks there must have been well over one hundred men earning a living from the clerical side of those courts. There must have been at least that number in secretarial and administrative posts in the central bureaucracy, and possibly as many again, though not necessarily full-time, in the provinces. One estimate has put the size of this officialdom, in the century or so before the Civil War, at over a thousand persons.[34] This larger group cannot strictly be reckoned part of the legal profession, but it is emerging that many of them were members of the inns.

Attorneys

The largest single group of lawyers were the attorneys. Every formal step in litigation, unless the litigant was personally present in court, had to be authorised by a duly appointed attorney; and long before 1450 the exercise of this function had given rise to the professional attorney. Attorneys also acted as general practitioners, retaining counsel and giving it. Since the thirteenth century their appointment had been supervised by the judges, and in 1292 the judges had been directed to limit the number to 140.[35] The judges were supposed to examine candidates for admission, who were then sworn in and their names were added to the 'roll'. This process could be reversed, so that an attorney guilty of gross misconduct could be put from the roll and physically 'cast over the bar'.[36] No rolls of admission have survived for our period; but the names of the active attorneys can be ascertained from the memoranda of warrants of attorney enrolled by the Clerks of the Warrants at the end of the plea rolls for each term (KB 27 and CP 40), and,

    32. E.g. Oliver Southworth (d. 1537) — see note 23 above — a filazer and a member of Clement's Inn, who directed his arms to be placed on his tomb: P.C.C. 1 Dyngeley. Thomas Jakes (d. 1514) of the Inner Temple, Clerk of Hell and Clerk of the Warrants, married the widow of Chief Justice Fyneux and directed that their arms be placed on his tomb in the Blackfriars, London: P.C.C. 2 Holder. See also note 87 below.
    33. Baker, *Spelman's Reports*, pp. *129-30*.
    34. L. Stone, 'Social Mobility in England 1500-1700', *P & P*, vol. 33 (1966), p. 25.
    35. *Rotuli Parliamentorum* [1783], vol. 1, p. 84.
    36. 4 Henry IV, c. 18; Y.B. Trin. 20 Hen. VI, fo. 37, pl. 6, *per* Newton C.J. (attorney may be 'trait hors del roll dattorneys' and forbidden to practise in the king's courts); below, p. 126.

The English Legal Profession, 1450-1550

where they are available, from the files of warrants.[37]

For the purposes of this chapter, the writer sampled the rolls of the three common-law courts for the four terms of 1480. The warrants of attorney showed that about 130 attorneys were active in the Common Pleas, 100 in the King's Bench, and 30 in the Exchequer. The Exchequer attorneys, with very few exceptions, kept themselves exclusively to that court. About half the King's Bench attorneys also practised in the Common Pleas, and about thirty of the attorneys in those courts also occupied major clerical offices in one of them. The total number of attorneys active in 1480, besides officers of the courts, is therefore around 180. It is clear, however, that the number of attorneys alive in 1480 exceeded that figure. Sampling a few rolls before and after 1480 suggests that there may have been at least 30 attorneys still in practice but by chance not appearing in the warrants for that year. Others may have been following a purely country practice, employing London agents as in later times, or they may have retired from active practice as attorneys either on grounds of age or by reason of other employment. These latter categories escape notice in the records and are therefore virtually beyond investigation. There is reason to think that the number of attorneys in 1550 was still much the same as in 1480, although a massive increase was to begin soon afterwards.[38]

The number of attorneys active in the central courts in 1480 does not greatly exceed the ideal maximum fixed in 1292, and yet laymen frequently complained of the number of attorneys in some parts of the country. Norfolk and Suffolk were particularly well provided for, as were the south-western counties, but the higher proportion of attorneys in those parts probably reflects the greater litigiousness of the inhabitants.[39] Contemporaries were more inclined to attribute the volume of litigation in these regions to the excess of attorneys. A bill presented through the Commons in 1455 complained that the number of attorneys in Norfolk and Suffolk had risen from six or eight to 24 and more,

---

37. Separate files of King's Bench warrants (KB 150) have been found back to 1463, but few have survived from our period. Common Pleas warrants were filed at the beginning of each *Brevia* file. See C.A.F. Meekings, 'King's Bench Files in *LRH*, p. 112. Admissions were later noted informally by the Chief Prothonotary on his remembrances (CP 45). The docket rolls (IND 1-) contain reckonings of attorneys' dues to the officers and may provide a convenient guide to their engagements: Baker, *Spelman's Reports*, p. *101*. None of these records have yet been properly investigated.

38. The 1480 sample is published in 'The Attorneys and Officers of the Common Law in 1480', *Jo. Legal Hist.*, i (1980). For a 1560 estimate (excluding the Exchequer), see C.W. Brooks, 'Litigants and Attorneys in the King's Bench and Common Pleas 1560-1640' in *LRH*, p. 53. The writer counted over 160 in 1495.

39. Dr Franz Metzger has informed the writer that during Wolsey's chancellorship (1515-29) the most litigious counties in England from the Chancery point of view were Devon (9 per cent of all cases) and Norfolk (6 per cent).

the most part of them not having any other living but only their winning by their said attorneyship, and the most part also of them not being of sufficient cunning [i.e. learning] to be any attorney; which go to every fair, market and other places where congregation of people is, and stir, procure, move and excite the people to take untrue suits, foreign suits, and suits for light trespasses, light offences and small sums of debt, the actions of whom be triable and determinable in court baron . . .

and also vexed their clients with actions for fees before such suits were concluded. The Commons prayed that the number of attorneys in those counties should be fixed at six for Norfolk, six for Suffolk, and two for the city of Norwich, and that appointments beyond that number should be void. The king assented, 'if it be thought to the judges reasonable', but the judges probably did not approve and the bill did not become law.[40] The 1480 sample included at least nineteen Norfolk attorneys and twelve Suffolk attorneys, which suggests that even the two dozen complained of in 1455 had been surpassed. And many of them were indeed men of small account, though we can no longer assess their ethical standards. As members of inns they would have claimed the title 'gentleman', but we may wonder how many of them could have maintained the claim on grounds of birth or substance or would have had any living apart from their attorneyship. One we find described in a bill of privilege the year before as 'William Crowche of Wetherden, Suffolk, *husbandman*, attorney of the Common Bench'.[41] At the other end of the scale, however, we must also notice among the attorneys William Eyre (d. 1509), a country gentleman and Treasurer of the Inner Temple, depicted on his brass at Great Cressingham, Norfolk, in a long gown and described on the inscription as *legis peritus*.

Eyre's example reminds us that no rigid separation existed between the classes of practitioner. Another attorney who became treasurer of an inn was Walter Roudon of Lincoln's Inn. Two Inner Temple benchers who began as attorneys rose to become judges: John Salter (d. 1513), a Welsh judge, and Humfrey Coningsby (d. 1535), a King's Bench judge. Some of these may have gained entry to their inns of court by virtue of their clerical appointments — Roudon was a clerk of the parcels in the Exchequer, Salter a clerk of the peace, and Coningsby a prothonotary of the Common Pleas — but Salter delivered a reading, Coningsby (if he did not read) certainly participated in learning exer-

---

40. *Rotuli Parliamentorum* [1783], vol. 5, pp. 326-7, no. 57 (modernised). The figure 24 is printed |XX/iiii|, which has sometimes been interpreted as fourscore; but that is an impossibly high figure in view of the reform proposed.

41. CP 40/869, m. 325 (9 February 1479). In 1491 he is described as being of Wetherden, Suffolk, gentleman: CP 40/917, m. 245.

cises as a bencher, and Roudon is known to have been called to the bar, so they may all be said to have qualified themselves in the customary manner for the upper reaches of the profession. The majority of attorneys, however, held no clerical offices and remained in the inns of chancery. About a third of the attorneys in the 1480 sample can be assigned to particular inns of court and chancery; and, given the poor survival-rate of membership records, this is quite consistent with their having all been members. Perhaps the usual condition for an attorney in this period, as in later times, was that of 'ancient' in one of the inns of chancery. There are few lists of ancients in this period, and so this hypothesis cannot be proved; but we know that several attorneys served as principals of their inns in the second half of the fifteenth century, and the rest, by remaining in residence, must presumably have become governing members by reason of seniority. Although the inns of chancery were regarded as inferior to the inns of court, both in size and in terms of the quality of the members and the learning exercises, members were almost invariably described in records as gentlemen; and, as we have suggested, membership was held (at least by some) to confer that professional status as 'learned in the law' which was later appropriated solely to inns of court men. Pleas in bar of maintenance sometimes refer to the retainer of a named person, known to have been an attorney, as a person *in lege terrae eruditus;*[42] and we have seen a record of 1522 in which an attorney described himself as *eruditus in lege domini Regis communi.*[43] Some of these men, however, were members of inns of court; the attorneys were not yet excluded from the greater inns.

Besides the two hundred or so Westminster attorneys, whose identities may be ascertained with reasonable precision, were an indeterminate number of lesser 'practitioners' whom we prefer to exclude from the class of professional attorneys until more is known about them. Attorneys in local courts were usually not Westminster attorneys, but it is possible that they were not lawyers at all — that is, not members of the inns of court or chancery. For a similar reason, we should exclude courtholders, scriveners and notaries. The addition 'courtholder' is sometimes found in records, but seems not to have been applied to men recognisable as lawyers; a lawyer might indeed hold

---

42. E.g. *Benet* v. *Kyng* (1472), CP 40/844, m. 435 (John Polstede 'in lege terre eruditus' retained as counsel); *Gere* v. *Mone* (1473), CP 40/848, m. 562 (John Whyte 'in lege terre eruditus' retained as attorney); *Hadley* v. *Weymer* (1500), KB 27/955, m. 38d (William Fyssher 'in lege terre eruditus'). See also *Maydeford* v. *Love* (1495), KB 27/937, m. 64d (Thomas Glantham and John Heyron named as men learned in the law whose approval was required for a common recovery). Whyte was of Lincoln's Inn, Fyssher and Heyron of the Middle Temple, and Polstede of Clement's Inn.

43. Baker, *Spelman's Reports*, p. 248, n. 1 (John Colyns).

many courts as steward, but would prefer the title 'gentleman'.[44] Notaries had no place in the English legal system, though they had employment in ecclesiastical and mercantile affairs and some may even have belonged to inns.[45] Scriveners, or professional writers, drew contracts and conveyances and therefore must not be overlooked in a study of the history of solicitors; but drawing documents was not a peculiarly legal role and so even the most ambitious scrivener ought not to be classed as a lawyer.[46] Little or no work has been done on these lowly men of affairs; until it is, we can do no more than guess at their social and intellectual characteristics.

Apprentices

The most difficult class to define is that of the apprentices-at-law. The word 'apprentice' is usually in other contexts suggestive of student status, but in the legal profession it was used for members of the upper branch who were already thoroughly learned: that is, for fully-fledged advocates below the degree of serjeant. Fortescue, for instance, writing around 1470, divided English advocates into only two classes, serjeants and apprentices.[47] The year books sometimes report the arguments of such counsel in the Exchequer Chamber, King's Bench and Chancery, and upon adjourned assizes, and if they add any description to the surname it is invariably that of 'apprentice'.[48] Apprentice was not, however, a degree to which graduands were expressly called by the king or by the inns of court. It is therefore not immediately apparent whether contemporaries used the term to define a qualification for practice at the bar or merely to describe those who so practised. Some seventeenth-century writers anachronistically equated apprentices with barristers. Coke, more vaguely but also more historically, observed that apprentices-at-law were described in pleading as 'homines consiliarii et in lege periti' (counsellors and men learned

---

44. See further Ives, 'Reputation of the Common Lawyer', p. 161; *idem*, 'The Common Lawyers in Pre-Reformation England', *TRHS*, 5th ser., vol. 18 (1968), pp. 147 ff.

45. E.g. Nicholas Colles, admitted to Lincoln's Inn in 1479. In 1475 he was 'notarius' and a servant to a Chancery clerk: *supersedeas* of privilege in *Markys v. Collys* (1475), CP 40/856, m. 340.

46. The range of a fifteenth-century scrivener's practice is admirably illustrated in A.E.B. Owen, 'A Scrivener's Notebook from Bury St Edmund's', *Archives*, vol. 14 (1979), pp. 16-22.

47. *De Laudibus Legum Anglie*, p. 22 ('et aliis iuris peritis quos apprenticios vulgus denominat', which rightly implies that *apprenticius* was not a recognised legal term).

48. There is one apparent reference to barristers, but it may be a printers' extension of *le barr*, meaning the bar (i.e. the advocates at the bar): below, 'Counsellors and Barristers', p. 109, n. 65. The first reference to an 'utter-barrister' in law reports seems to be in Gell's Ms Reports (Library of Congress), Mich. 36 Henry VIII, fo. 25^v and 33 (1544): 'Forster utter barester'.

in the law),[49] but we have seen that the like description was used even for attorney members of the inns of chancery: 'learned in the law' was the genus comprising apprentices as one of its species. Sir Henry Spelman compared the degree of barrister with the university degree of bachelor, apprentice with that of master, and serjeant with that of doctor;[50] and, although the equivalence might have been disputable,[51] the hierarchy seems correct. Most seventeenth-century writers treated the title 'apprentice' as denoting a readership in the inns of court. The office of reader was only of internal significance in the inns, but it carried with it a public status for which the other title was more appropriate.[52] Many of the apprentices so named in the year books are known to have been readers, and the rest were of such standing that they were probably readers in the inns for which no records survive.

During the sixteenth century, rights of audience seem to have been extended by reference to the lesser degree of utter-barrister, and in a proclamation of 1547 it was asserted to have been always the practice to admit utter-barristers 'and other students of the four houses of court' as advocates in the royal courts. It is possible, therefore, that even before the end of our period the vagueness of the term 'apprentice' had given the judges a wide discretion in deciding whom to receive as advocates. Yet in practice audience in the superior courts, save perhaps for routine practice motions, appears from the evidence to have been confined to the more senior practitioners. An earlier proclamation, of 1546, gave only readers the right of audience, with power for a committee to select others.[53] The earliest piece of evidence so far dis-

49. *Institutes of the Laws of England*, vol. 2, p. 564. Sir Henry Spelman equated apprentices with barristers when he defined them as 'Hi quod post septene (vel id circiter) studium, cancellos fori (quos barros vocant) salutare, atque illic causas agere permitterentur': *Archaeologus* (1626), p. 43. Likewise T. Blount, *Glossographia* (1670), p. 42.

50. *Glossarium Archaiologicum* (1687), p. 512.

51. William Noy in 1632 argued that the degree of apprentice was superior to the 'specious and swelling titles' of masters and doctors, because it was given to readers after about 27 years' study: T. Gibbon, *Commonplace*, B.L., MS Harley 980, fo. 153.

52. In *Giles* v. *Coulshill* (1576), Harvard Law School, MS 2071, fo. 58^v, a graduate who had taken the LLD by grace (without keeping his acts) was likened to 'one who is chosen reader in an inn of court and never reads; and one who is so chosen and never reads is not an apprentice in law nor a reader, but if he had read he would have been a reader and also an apprentice in the law' (translated). Robert Brerewood, in the next century, said that a reader 'having a degree as apprentice of the law takes precedence of all utter-barristers even outside his own house': MS cited in A.R. Ingpen (ed.), *Middle Temple Bench Book* (London, 1912), p. 14. See also E. Coke, *The Tenth Part of the Reports*, preface; G. Buc, *The Third Universitie*, appended to Stow's *Annales* (1615) at p. 1074; E. Waterhous, *Fortescutus Illustratus* (1663), p. 138; W. Dugdale, *Origines Juridiciales* (1680 edn), pp. 143, 197. According to Brerewood and Dugdale, the title was sometimes reserved for double readers.

53. Below, p. 127.

covered is a list of 'the pleaders or apprentices of the king's courts' drawn up in 1518 for Cardinal Wolsey.[54] There were 37 apprentices 'supposed now to be present at this term' and 12 'supposed now to be absent from this term', thus giving a total bar of about fifty. All but five of the men listed as apprentices were readers in court. Three of the five (John Baker, John Pakyngton and Richard Wye) had recently been elected benchers of the Inner Temple before reading; another (Francis Mountford) read in 1519 and his name appears to have been added to the original list. Only one name, that of Edmund Knightley (who did not read until 1523), is difficult to account for; but he may have been another bencher elected prior to reading. The list shows very clearly that in 1518 the practising bar, the apprentices of the king's courts, were simply the benchers of the inns of court. Barristers and others were not included.

This conclusion provides a convenient basis for definition and analysis, but it so happens that almost half the elections of readers in the period 1450 to 1550 are not recorded.[55] The records of elections begin as follows: Lincoln's Inn in 1465, Middle Temple in 1502, Inner Temple in 1506, Gray's Inn in 1514. The identities of most Gray's Inn readers since 1435 have been discovered from other sources, and the same may be done for the Inner Temple from the 1480s and for the Middle Temple from the 1490s. If the missing names from the fifteenth century could be found, they would almost certainly be names already well known from other evidence but which cannot at present be linked with particular inns. All those we know of were established practitioners, great officers of state, or major office-holders at Westminster. Of 188 readers in the four inns of court between 1500 and 1540, one-quarter became serjeants-at-law, and about the same proportion became judges (including barons of the Exchequer), while at least another quarter held major offices in law or government. Most served as justices of the peace in their home counties..Sixteen per cent of the group became knights, more than half by virtue of judicial appointments. The group includes statesmen such as Dudley, More, Audley and Rich; writers such as Fitzherbert, More and the chronicler Hall; and law reporters such as Spelman, Yorke and Pollard.

---

54. C 82/474/36. The date must be before 26 January 1519, when Erneley became Attorney-General.

55. We have well over half the names, but for many the date of reading is not known. Approximate dates can sometimes be worked out from appearances in the year books and mention in manuscript copies of learning exercises: see S.E. Thorne, *Readings and Moots in the Inns of Court in the Fifteenth Century, vol. 1* (Selden Society, vol. 71, 1954).

Utter-barristers[56]

For several centuries now barristers-at-law[57] have formed a distinct branch of the English legal profession, but there are two reasons why they cannot be so regarded in the period 1450 to 1550. There are no recorded calls to the bar in this period except for Lincoln's Inn, and then only from 1518. Call to the bar occurred during a moot and involved no more than calling upon a student who had served his time as a mootman or inner-barrister to perform the part of an utter-barrister at the moot. It was a commencement, in the academic sense. But commencement in the common law was only slowly becoming a graduation, because the position of barrister in an inn was not at first a public degree.[58] Barristers were certainly professed lawyers, in the sense that they had taken part in the requisite learning exercises for the prescribed length of time, which in Lincoln's Inn was evidently not less than five years and on average about six.[59] Moreover, call to the bar was an essential prerequisite of call to the bench, for which further learning exercises were required, including (usually) a readership at one of the inns of chancery.[60] The average standing of readers on election was 17.6 years from admission in Lincoln's Inn and 16.5 years in the Middle Temple,[61] whence it seems that election to read came after about ten years as an utter-barrister. It cannot be assumed, however, that all barristers stayed on the ladder of promotion by remaining in residence for this period. We have noted that they were not regarded as full advocates, or apprentices, until they became benchers. For about ten years, therefore, they had to support themselves by soliciting causes, or undertaking non-contentious work, or by acquiring an office. Some who settled for careers other than advocacy obtained exemption from reading. Some who were in a position to do so may have returned to the life of country gentlemen. Of the 89 barristers

---

56. The term 'utter-bar' is now used differently, to distinguish junior counsel from queen's counsel. But in our period an utter-barrister, who argued from outside the 'bar' of the inn, was superior to an inner-barrister. The title was in use by 1466.

57. The Bar Council recently sanctioned the omission of the suffix 'at law', which dates from the sixteenth century and distinguished the utter-barristers of the inns of court (who were deemed to have a public degree) from the inner-barristers and from the barristers in the inns of chancery.

58. Below, pp. 128ff.

59. This average is based on the standing at call of 84 barristers called between 1518 and 1550. Thirty-three per cent were of five years standing, 27 per cent of six years standing, 21 per cent of seven years standing, and 19 per cent of longer standing.

60. Exact dates of readership in chancery are rarely preserved. Thomas Atkins (d. 1551), Common Serjeant of London, may be a typical example: he was admitted to Lincoln's Inn in 1524, called to the bar in 1529, elected reader of Furnival's Inn in 1535, and of Lincoln's Inn in 1542.

61. This is based on the records for the period 1500-40, save that admissions to the Middle Temple are only available for the period 1502-24.

92   *The Legal Profession and the Common Law*

called by Lincoln's Inn between 1518 and 1550, only 35 became benchers, of whom one in five became serjeants.[62] The majority did not appear again in the records of the Inn and were not practitioners of any note at Westminster. For these, as for the non-practising barrister of today, call to the bar was a mark of intellectual attainment and of gentle (or professional) status, but not an occupational description.

Solicitors and Accountants

The least established members of the legal profession were those who performed the miscellaneous functions associated with the term 'solicitor'. In strictness, soliciting applied only to lawsuits, and meant the prosecution of causes in a court where the 'solicitor' was not an officer or attorney. But men who ran such errands usually had the other clerical skills needed by a general adviser. A job description compiled by a Gray's Inn solicitor in the 1520s listed among his capabilities the writing of common-law entries, court-keeping, auditing, and acting as bailiff, receiver, steward of a household, clerk of the kitchen, clerk of works, comptroller and paymaster, all of which he had done under his father as servant to the Duchess of Norfolk.[63] Persons possessing such skills were likely, in the words of this solicitor, to have 'had the speculative' (learned the theory) in one of the inns of court or chancery. But how far these practitioners should be counted as members of the legal profession must be a rather arbitrary matter. An illustration of the difficulty is provided by the vocation of an 'auditor', which corresponds with that of an accountant today. Accountancy may require some legal training, but it is not a legal exercise as such. In our period many auditors were also legal practitioners, and perhaps most were members of inns. Walter Gorphyn of Clifford's Inn was auditor to the Duke of Buckingham in 1484 and had an appointment in the office of chancellor of the Exchequer.[64] John Knyght (d. 1496), of Holborn (doubtless one of the inns), had permanent retainers as an auditor with the Dukes of Norfolk and Buckingham, the Earls of Nottingham and Derby, Lord Dacre, Lord Fitzwaren, Lord Strange and the Prior of Lewes; he bequeathed to his son-in-law John Maxey, of Furnival's Inn, all his books 'that belong to an auditor'.[65] William Vowell, a

---

62. The same proportions are found in the earliest possible Inner Temple sample. Of the 24 barristers called from 1567 to January 1571, eight became benchers, of whom two became serjeants; but the standing at call was on average eleven years.

63. Letter from John Fairechild to Wolsey, SP 1/10, fo. 50-2, printed in Ives, 'The Common Lawyers', p. 152.

64. E 13/165, m. 18d (bill of privilege, 22 June 1480); CP 40/883, m. 407 (of Barking, Essex, gentleman, 1483); C. Rawcliffe, *The Staffords*, (Cambridge, 1978), p. 199. He was sued for dues by Clifford's Inn in 1464.

65. P.C.C. 1 Horne (listing his clients' papers). See also Rawcliffe, *The Staffords*, p. 199.

bencher of the Middle Temple, was auditor to the Dean and Chapter of Wells and the Prior of Bridgewater.[66] Guthlac Overton (d. 1537), of Lincoln's Inn, was auditor to the Duchy of Cornwall and the Prior of St John's; in an interesting Chancery suit he claimed solicitor's fees and also his expenses in teaching the defendant's nephew 'in the faculty of auditorship'.[67] Not only were such men members of the inns, sometimes even quite senior members, but their profession was on the fringes of the law and is certainly one of the lineal ancestors of the present solicitors' profession as well as the present profession of accountancy. It is not at all improbable that there was a greater overlap between this class and the utter-barristers than between this class and the attorneys. Even in later times, utter-barristers were expected to fill in the time before election to the bench by practising as solicitors.[68] The elusiveness, for the historian, of the practitioners in this category is perhaps the greatest obstacle to producing a numerical analysis of the legal profession in the late-medieval and Tudor periods.

The Inns of Court and Chancery

From the foregoing it may be calculated that the active practising membership of the inns at any one time in our period must have numbered at least four hundred: fifty benchers, one hundred or so continuing barristers, fifty senior legal officials, and two hundred attorneys. Most of these would have had servants and clerks, some of whom were at 'clerks' commons' in the inns or even members of higher standing. To this number must be added the inner-barristers and other students, including the many who did not intend to follow legal careers. Obviously the figure of four hundred falls far short of the total membership, and it is to the missing larger figure that we now turn.

Fortescue, at the beginning of our period, reckoned at least two hundred men to each of the four inns of court, and at least one hundred each to the ten or so inns of chancery;[69] though he added that they did not always gather in them at the same time.[70] His figures would give a total membership of 1,800, slightly larger than the resi-

---

66. Ives, 'The Common Lawyers', p. 161.
67. Baker, *Spelman's Reports*, p. *263*, n. 2 (modernised).
68. Baker, 'Counsellors and Barristers', pp. 221-2; *idem*, 'Solicitors and the
69. He says there were ten or more, but only nine are definitely known from contemporary records: Barnard's, Clement's, Clifford's, Davies (or Thavies), Furnival's, Lyons's, New, Staple and Strand Inns.
70. *De Laudibus Legum Anglie*, p. 116.

dent membership of either university at that period.[71] Fortescue was not, however, speaking of the numbers in residence but of the names on the books. Thus, Lincoln's Inn had 245 names on the books in 1455, but they cannot all have lived in the inn because even in 1574 there were only 92 sets of chambers for 160 men.[72] Furnival's Inn had 139 names on its pension roll in 1451, but never more than 80 in residence throughout our period.[73] Few nominal rolls have survived, but the inns used to possess records extending back many years. In 1607 Gray's Inn produced an enormous list of over 2,000 members, which must have represented over thirty years' admissions and greatly exceeded the number resident in chambers.[74] Even in our period we find actions being brought in the Common Pleas to recover dues against lists of members stretching back over two or three decades. In the case of Furnival's Inn, over 190 names occur in such actions between 1461 and 1500, while in 1523 the Inn sued 101 members in one action. These records constitute the principal source for reconstructing the early membership of the inns, and they are still being studied. They confirm that Fortescue's figures are distinctly on the low side for total membership. The resident membership, on the other hand, is hardly likely to have exceeded the 1,100 reckoned as possessing places in chambers in 1574.[75] The available scraps of evidence suggest that the inns of court and chancery were slightly smaller than the University of Cambridge, with perhaps 120 as the average size of an inn of court, and 60 for an inn of chancery, at any one time. Obviously these figures could be exceeded in particular cases. Furnival's Inn, we have seen, went up to 80; but it may have been larger than average. The Inner Temple in 1521 is said to have turned out 160 members to accom-

71. The most recent estimate for fifteenth-century Oxford is around 1,600: T.H. Aston, 'Oxford's Medieval Alumni', *P & P*, vol. 74 (1977), pp. 1-40. Cambridge was smaller; even in 1564, when the Queen visited the university, there were only 1,267 members in residence: C.H. Cooper, *Annals of Cambridge*, vol. 2 (Cambridge, 1843), p. 207.

72. *LIBB*, vol. 1, p. 52 (list of 245 fellows in 33 Henry VI); *ITR*, vol. 1, p. 468.

73. D.S. Bland, *Early Records of Furnival's Inn* (Newcastle-upon-Tyne, 1957), p. 28 (pension roll quoted). Figures in residence are given at various dates throughout the fifteenth century; the highest was 78 in Lent Term 1412, followed by 73 in the autumn vacation 1451. In a disputed election, around 1504, 76 votes were cast: ibid., p. 39. As late as 1586 the numbers resident in term were reckoned about 80: *LIBB*, vol. 1, p. 460.

74. This is a chance survival in the Exchequer Miscellanea, E 163/17/7. Gray's Inn had increased its admissions by a remarkable proportion since 1530, overtaking the other inns by a wide margin: see the figures in Prest, *Inns of Court*, p. 11.

75. A survey in that year showed 627 resident in the inns of court: *ITR*, vol. 1, p. 468. The figures for the inns of chancery were about 75 per cent of the inns of court total in 1586: *LIBB*, vol. 1, p. 460. There had perhaps been a relative decline in the inns of chancery, because Fortescue's figures give them 125 per cent compared with the inns of court.

pany the new serjeants to Westminster;[76] but that also seems an unusually high figure. If these figures were representative of the inns of court and chancery, the total would have been around 1,400; but it seems inconceivable that 300 places in chambers could have been lost before 1574, during a period of expansion and rebuilding. Either there were more people to each set of chambers before Elizabethan times or we must adhere to about two-thirds of Fortescue's figures as the best estimate for the period 1450 to 1550.

It is rather easier to estimate the total admissions than the number of residents at any one time. For Lincoln's Inn we have a continuous and nearly complete record of admissions throughout our period; and comparison with the other inns in the sixteenth century shows a similar pattern. About twelve to fifteen admissions a year was usual in all the inns except Gray's Inn, which after 1530 was admitting over twenty a year. The total inns of court admissions between 1450 and 1550 probably stood somewhere between 5,000 and 6,000. The total for the inns of chancery may well have been higher, since the length of stay for most students was probably shorter, but we have no definite records.[77] Even if we were to assume a figure of the same order, say 5,000, we have no sure way of guessing what proportion of those 5,000 went on to inns of court. In estimating the total number of persons, the figures may also be inflated by migrations, which the Common Pleas records suggest were not uncommon. Even so, it is clear that between 6,000 and 10,000 men at least went through the inns of court and chancery in our period, of whom probably less than one-third followed legal careers.[78]

If we take Lincoln's Inn from 1450 to 1500, we find that of 576 admissions as many as 53 per cent of the names make no further appearance in the Inn's records; only 10 per cent became apprentices at law (that is, benchers), and about the same proportion were attorneys or court officials, so that only one in five are clearly identifiable as professional lawyers. Of the scores of young men joining the inns of court and chancery every year, therefore, only a few can seriously have contemplated legal careers. The majority were sons of the gentry, very often eldest sons, who returned to the country after their sojourn in London. The Common Pleas records show this to have been as true of the fifteenth-century inns of chancery as of the inns of court.

76. *ITR*, vol. 1, p. 63.
77. Only three dates of admission have been discovered for the entire period, all in manuscript autobiographical memoranda: Baker, *Spelman's Reports*, pp. *128*, nn. 1-2, *365*.
78. We have seen (from estimates of the size of the profession) that at least one-third of the residents of the inns as a whole must have been professional lawyers, but since they remained in residence longer than the rest they represent much less than one-third of the total number admitted.

Some of these *nobilium filii*, as Fortescue termed them, may have felt a calling towards the law, and some indeed reached superior positions. Most, however, must have gone there to mix with their peers and to acquire a grounding in law, general knowledge and manners to fit them for life. Some bought exemption from the learning exercises; others followed as best they could without intending to proceed further. The less well-born student must have been more likely to take the exercises seriously in the hope of professional success. For all comers, however, the system helped the young to discover their aptitudes. The exercises were tough and sorted out the able from the average intellects as effectively as any modern examination. The student's prowess in hall and library doubtless made clear to him and to his contemporaries whether he was suited to the law.

A third important factor, besides aptitude and motivation, was financial support. The average age on admission to an inn of court seems to have been 20 or 21,[79] and so if prior attendance at an inn of chancery was usual[80] the student would have gone to the latter at 17 or 18. Without long-term maintenance no progress could be made. Fortescue said that only the sons of gentry could afford the inns of court, because an allowance of at least £13 6s 8d a year would be needed.[81] Some had more than that. Serjeant Constable in 1501 provided for his son to attend Cambridge at 15, and at 18 to go to an inn of chancery for three years with £25 a year.[82] Serjeant Caryll, however, in 1523 left his son £10 a year to study in the Inner Temple, saying he knew it would suffice 'if he live and use himself well and honestly and wisely like a learner and student';[83] the son became Attorney of the Duchy, and a bencher of the Inn. Caryll's estimate seems to have been widely accepted,[84] but some had to make do with still less. Anthony

---

79. This is based on 39 admissions between 1470 and 1530 where dates of birth are known from paternal inquisitions *post mortem*; it is therefore confined to eldest sons of men of property. The youngest so far discovered was Walter Hobart, son of Sir James (a bencher), who appears to have been 14 on admission to Lincoln's Inn in 1490: C 142/32/15 (aged 40 in 1517).

80. See Baker, *Spelman's Reports*, p. *127*. It is not known how easy it was to make the transition. One accepted means of admission to an inn of court, apparently as of right, was to become principal of an inn of chancery; but that would not account for more than a few admissions a year.

81. *De Laudibus Legum Anglie*, p. 118.

82. P.C.C. 5 Blamyr; *Surtees Society*, vol. 53, p. 195.

83. P.C.C. 10 Bodfelde (modernised).

84. Sir John Erneley spent ten marks a year finding one Culpeper at an inn of chancery before 1518, under the terms of a marriage agreement recited in P.C.C. 3 Maynwaryng. Sir Richard Basset left his son £12 a year to study in Gray's Inn: *Testamenta Eboracensia*, vol. 5, p. 147 (1522). John Williamson left his son ten marks to study at an inn of court on leaving university at the age of 20: ibid., p. 279 (1529). James Hadley left his sons ten marks a year each while they were at Strand Inn, and then £10 a year at an inn of court: P.C.C. 3 Dyngeley (1537). Brian Rouclyff, baron of the Exchequer, left his nephew Guy Palmes £20 a year for his exhibition at the Middle Temple: *Testamenta Eboracensia*, vol. 4, p. 105 (1494).

The English Legal Profession, 1450-1550

Fitzherbert's mother left him only five marks a year to keep him at an inn of court,[85] though he may have had other sources of income. Richard Wye, a bencher of the Inner Temple, had been sent to the Inn with only six marks a year under his father's will of 1504.[86] Even small sums such as these would have put the inns beyond the reach of the majority of the population. But the inns were not exclusive to the gentry and nobility. Although the title of gentleman was bestowed on all entrants to the inns, and therefore confuses social origins for the historian, it is known that yeomen could gain admission. Thus Thomas Underhill, yeoman, went from his inn of chancery to Lincoln's Inn on becoming Clerk of the Juries in 1474; and either he or his son was armigerous.[87] Luke Langland, formerly of Clifford's Inn, yeoman, was admitted to the Inner Temple in 1510 as a servant of the new Earl of Wiltshire.[88] Many names in the records suggest an obscure background. Some found they could not manage to live at all. One Leonard Perpoint was expelled from the Inner Temple in 1547 because 'he lacketh exhibition and is not able to pay his dues'; but he was a member of Furnival's Inn when he died in 1566.[89] Such drastic action was probably unusual. Many were outlawed (or at least put in exigent) for non-payment of dues, but there are reasons for doubting the effectiveness of such action. The inns appear rather to have shown considerable forbearance with respect to debts; so that, although no evidence has come to light of endowed exhibitions as in Oxford and Cambridge, it is possible that communal charity enabled talent to prevail over adversity. An express instance occurs in the Black Books in 1482, when William Lancaster, a member of six years' standing, was pardoned various debts on account of poverty.[90] The proportion of poor students making careers in the law is difficult to estimate, but Dr Ives has shown that of the 53 serjeants called between 1463 and 1510 only half came from a social background of any consequence, and that all the serjeants called in 1486 were of obscure origin.[91]

The Place of the Inns of Court and Chancery

The inns of court and chancery had a deeper influence on English society and culture than is, even now, generally acknowledged by his-

---

85. Baker, *Spelman's Reports*, p. *143*, n. 2.
86. P.C.C. 21 Holgrave.
87. Pardon of 1471, C 67/48/24 (described as of St Clement Dane's, London, and Haverhill, Suffolk, gentleman *alias* yeoman); *LIAdmR*, vol. 1, p. 19; arms on brass at Great Thurlow, Suffolk (1508).
88. *Calendar of Patent Rolls 1494-1509*, p. 343; *ITR*, vol. 1. p. 21.
89. *ITR*, vol. 1, p. 146; P.C.C. 29 Crymes.
90. *LIBB*, vol. 1, p. 75.
91. The writer is obliged to Dr Ives for this information. For his analysis of the 1495 call, see Ives, 'The Common Lawyers', p. 157. Cf. *BIHR*, vol. 31 (1958), p. 100.

torians of this period. They were, in Fortescue's words, a *studium publicum* having some practical advantages over the universities by virtue of their proximity both to the law courts and to the nation's capital city. Perhaps as many as one-third of the gentry of England passed through them, something which can by no means be confidently asserted of the universities in this period.

The inns contributed much to the development of the common law, by exploring doctrine ahead of Westminster Hall,[92] and by training a small cadre of advocates to a high level of expertise. But they also helped in a broader way to form the character of English society. They were, already by 1450, the third university of England, a university which may have had more influence on the gentry than Oxford or Cambridge. Here the future statesmen, members of parliament, sheriffs, country magistrates, and official classes, joined together in work and play. They learned the names which would matter to them, dined and prayed together, displayed their wealth or their talents (whichever was more conspicuous), talked of law and much else, drank, diced and misbehaved. The experience coloured one's whole life: well might Justice Shallow's mind dwell in his closing years on the days he had spent in Clement's Inn. If English society between 1450 and 1550 possessed any common characteristics, a community of attitudes and aspirations, it was in no small measure the inns of court and chancery which (almost without design) brought it about. And the chief representatives of the inns were their graduates and governors, the members of the legal profession. Small wonder if this profession embodied the opinions and feelings of the English gentry, who loved to chase in the courts as much as they loved to chase in the field, whose very lives seem to have been mapped out in parchment and wax. Erasmus was a poor judge of the qualities of the common law, but he perceived that those who succeeded in it were highly regarded: 'there is no better to way to eminence [in England], for the nobility are mostly recruited from the law'.[93]

---

92. Baker, *Spelman's Reports*, pp. *123-5, 132-5, 155, 302-3*.
93. P.S. and H.M. Allen (eds.), *Opus Epistolarum Des. Erasmi Roterdami* (1906), vol. 4, p. 17, no. 999; cited in R.W. Chambers, *Thomas More* (1938), p. 85.

8

COUNSELLORS AND BARRISTERS

It is rather surprising that no one has yet written a history of the English Bar in its modern form. Although much valuable work has been done on the history of the legal profession, particularly in its earlier stages,[1] and although the history of attorneys and solicitors has been written,[2] little is known about the development of barristers as a branch of the profession and their relations with the other branches. The present article can hardly supply this deficiency, which is a very large one, but it may lay open some aspects of the subject in the hope that more research will follow.

There has been a divided legal profession in this country, as in the civil law system, ever since there has been a " profession." Indeed the distinction between attorney and pleader is older than the profession itself, and an effort must be made to avoid confusing the name of a function with the name of the profession which later came to enjoy its sole exercise. In the absence of a professional organisation, anyone might perform the functions of attorney or pleader, for reward or otherwise, and therefore anyone might combine the functions. The fact that the same man might have been an attorney one day and a pleader the next does not mean that there was no clear distinction between the two characters, but that there was no organisation which could enforce a monopoly. As it happened, steps were taken within

---

* The writer is most grateful to Mr. D. E. C. Yale, Mr. M. J. Prichard and Mr. Gareth Jones for reading the first draft of this article and making suggestions for improvement.

[1] Full length works include H. Cohen, *History of the English Bar and Attornatus to 1450* (1929); E. W. Ives, *Some Aspects of the Legal Profession in the late fifteenth and early sixteenth Centuries* (1955) Univ. London Ph.D. Thesis; J. H. Baker, *History of the Order of Serjeants at Law* (1968) Univ. London Ph.D. Thesis. Important recent articles are E. W. Ives, " The Reputation of the Common Lawyers in English Society 1450–1550 " (1960) 7 *University of Birmingham Historical Journal* 130; P. Lucas, " Blackstone and the Reform of the Legal Profession " (1962) 77 *English Historical Review* 456; W. R. Prest, " Learning Exercises at the Inns of Court 1590–1640 " (1967) 9 *Journal of the Society of Public Teachers of Law* (New Series) 301; E. W. Ives, " The Common Lawyers in pre-Reformation England " (1968) 18 *Transactions of the Royal Historical Society* (5th Series) 145.

[2] E. B. V. Christian, *Short History of Solicitors* (1896); R. Robson, *The Attorney in Eighteenth Century England* (1959); M. Birks, *Gentlemen of the Law* (1960).

a generation or so of the emergence of professional attorneys and *narratores* in the thirteenth century to separate the two classes.[3] The exact method by which this was effected in the royal courts is no longer known,[4] but it had been accomplished by the time the year books began. The result was the establishment of a select intellectual Bar practising in the Common Bench, which in the fourteenth century became a sort of gild or society, the order of serjeants at law.

Chaucer selected a serjeant to exemplify his " man of law." [5] He was well versed in the law, possessed a law library, and was retained by many clients as a pleader and as a conveyancer. Chaucer's serjeant would probably not have heard of a " barrister " or a " solicitor," nor of the rules of etiquette now associated with those professions. Fortescue, nearly a century later, would have heard of both but could not have foreseen their later importance; having briefly described the Inns of Court as educational institutions he discoursed only of the serjeants and judges.[6]

THE COUNSELLOR

The distinction between the pleader and the attorney represents the difference between the intellectual or scientific function and the mechanical or ministerial function. A closely analogous division was made in the medical profession between the physicians, learned in medicine and physic, and the surgeons and apothecaries.

The attorney was retained *ad prosequendum et defendendum*, to follow and defend causes mechanically, continuing a suit by issuing the process and making the necessary entries. The *narrator* was originally employed *ad narrandum,* to recite the count or declaration before the judges. By the time of the first year books his principal concern had become pleading and the juristic problems which special pleading raised. His task therefore came to be that of argument at the bar, and as a natural consequence the judges came to be chosen from his class. But the prosecution and pleading of law suits were not the only functions requiring professional discharge.[7] A layman

---

[3] In 1280 the City of London made regulations for keeping separate the countors, attorneys and essoiners in the Mayor's Court: *Liber Custumarum* (Rolls Series), f. 205.

[4] Maitland presumed that some ordinance similar to that in the City must have been made in the Common Bench in the 13th century: F. Pollock and F. W. Maitland, *History of English Law* (1898), i. 194. This is a reasonable inference from later history. As to the 1292 ordinance concerning attorneys (Rot.Parl. i. 84) see 85 L.Q.R. at p. 336.

[5] G. Chaucer, *Canterbury Tales* (written *c.* 1390), prologue. The attorney, though a minister of the law, was not regarded as a " lawyer " even in the 17th century: see R. North, *Autobiography* (1882) ed.), p. 141.

[6] J. Fortescue, *De Laudibus Legum Angliae* (written *c.* 1470), ed. by Chrimes (1949), Chaps. 49–51. Fortescue nowhere uses the words, but they were current by his time.   [7] See Ives, *op. cit.,* 7 Univ.Birm.Hist.Jo. at pp. 159–160.

needed advice on his legal rights, on transactions not yet made, on conveyancing and drawing technical documents, on the desirability of litigation, on the conduct of a jury trial in the country, on the choice and retainer of counsel, and so on. The sum of these functions may be termed "counselling" in its widest sense, and the subject of the present study must be what the plea rolls call *homo consiliarius*, the counsellor. Even this compendious name can mislead. It eventually became synonymous with " barrister," [8] in the sense of " jurisconsult," while some of the counselling came in fact to be done by attorneys and solicitors.

The retainer of counsellors

The contract of retainer is that which distinguishes professional employment from gratuitous service, and its use enabled lawyers to escape the legal prohibition of maintenance.[9] There is no doubt that in medieval times the retainer of men of law was a binding covenant or contract, and it will be as well to dwell on this point for a moment in view of the later doctrine of contractual incapacity.

Retainers might be by parol or by deed. Religious houses and other great landowners frequently retained attorneys and counsellors on an annual or periodic basis at a fixed salary or fee, and sometimes a livery of clothing.[10] Such an arrangement was normally contained in a sealed document operating as a grant of the fee or annuity. But a counsellor might also be retained by the mere payment of a suitable reward,[11] and a good deal of a lawyer's business must have been acquired in this way, just as today a barrister is usually retained by the payment of a fee, or rather by the delivery of a brief with the fee marked on it.[12] In such cases communication with the client was direct. A serjeant could be found in the morning in Westminster Hall, and it is supposed that in the afternoon the serjeants resorted

---

[8] *e.g.*, 2 *Inst.* 564; *R.* v. *Mayor of Bath* (1671) Tremaine P.C. 542: " *conciliarius in lege anglice* ' an utter barrester at law ' "; T. Wood, *An Institute of the Laws of England* (1722 ed.), p. 448. On monumental brasses the commonest description of barristers before 1660 is " counsellor at law ": Mill Stephenson, *List of Monumental Brasses* (1926), pp. 76, 120, 180, 222, 523, 535, 550, 565.

[9] *Articuli super Cartas* 1300, 28 Edw. 1, c. 11, exempted countors and learned men who gave counsel " *pur du son donant*." This exemption was omitted from the later statutes, but remained valid.

[10] See Ives, *op. cit.*, 7 Univ.Birm.Hist.Jo. at pp. 158–159. The giving of liveries to men of law was permitted by the 7 Hen. 4, c. 14, 8 Hen 6, c. 4 and 8 Edw. 4, c. 2.

[11] The word " fee " (*feodum*) is suggestive of a grant, and so " reward " seems the better term for a single payment although the two became synonymous. From the 15th century the King's serjeants were granted by patent their customary " *vadia feoda vesturam et regarda*," and in slander actions a counsellor averred the receipt of annuities, fees and rewards (*Co.Entr.* 22) or something similar.

[12] For the introduction of briefs drawn by solicitors, *vide infra*, p. 116.

to St. Paul's [13] or the Guildhall [14] for the purpose of being consulted directly by City clients. Both Chaucer and Fortescue referred to serjeants being at the " parvise," [15] the meaning of which is still controverted [16] but which is generally taken as the parvise of Paul's, the general meeting place of London. By the middle of the sixteenth century pressure of business had put an end to this convenience, and clients had to find their counsel in chambers.[17] An eminent lawyer might have to employ a porter to keep the queue of suitors away from his study,[18] and Sir Roger Owen could not believe that the serjeants had once demeaned themselves by plying for hire.[19]

Formal retainers

In the middle ages the retainer of men of law by documents under seal was common. The many " fees and robes " of the pilgrim serjeant were probably annuities,[20] for it is more likely that Chaucer meant he had many permanent clients than that he hoarded money and clothing. The retainer might be for life, or a term of years, or for a particular purpose such as an assize.[21] An advantage of the permanent retainer was that a person of substance could secure to himself the counsel of his choice and prevent future adversaries from obtaining their services against him.

The grant of the fee or annuity was usually expressed to be "*pro*

---

[13] W. Harrison, *A Description of England* (1587), ii. Chap. 9; ed. by Furnivall (1877), i. 204: " Our lawiers did sit in Powles upon stooles against the pillers and walles to get clients." In 1603 the Masters in Chancery argued their superiority to the serjeants because the latter "aunciently stood by certaine pillars in St. Paules church, to bee caried by anie client for a slender fee, whether soever the occasion should lead " (Brit.Mus.MS. Sloane 1710, f. 133). And see W. Dugdale, *Origines Juridiciales* (1666), p. 142a. New serjeants were each assigned a pillar here at their creation (Bodl.Lib.MS.Ashm. 1147, f. 26 (1521); Dugdale, *op. cit.*, p. 124b), but Sir Roger Owen suggested this was a devotional observance later mistaken for a survival of the old tradition (*Of the Common Law*, Brit.Mus.MS. Harl. 1572, f. 493).
[14] Dugdale, *op. cit.*, p. 142a: " St. Paul's Church, where each lawyer and serjeant at his pillar heard his client's cause, and took notes thereof upon his knee; as they do in Guild Hall at this day " (1666). *Cf.* Harrison, *loc. cit.* (1587): " now some of them will not come from their chambers to the Guildhall in London under ten pounds."
[15] G. Chaucer, *Canterbury Tales*, prol.; Fortescue, *op. cit.*, Chap. 51 (the litigants in the afternoon "*se devertunt ad pervisam et alibi consulentes cum servientibus ad legem et aliis consiliariis suis*").
[16] See J. Selden's edition of Fortescue, *op. cit.* (1672 ed.), p. 50; J. Manly, *Canterbury Tales* (1928), p. 518; H. Cohen, *op. cit.*, p. 489; G. L. Frost, " Chaucer's Man of Law at the Parvis " (1929) 44 *Modern Language Notes* 496–501; S. B. Chrimes, *Sir John Fortescue* (1949), pp. 129, 205.
[17] Harrison, *loc. cit.* in note 13, *supra*. Thereafter clients began to go in the first place to solicitors, who would instruct counsel for them: *infra*.
[18] R. Hutton, *Diary*, Univ.Lib.Camb.MS.Add. 6863, f. 60v (speech to Sir Robert Heath on being made a serjeant in 1631).
[19] *Of the Common Law*, Brit.Mus.MS.Harl. 1572, f. 492.
[20] *Cf.* H.21 E.3, 7, *pl.* 20.
[21] *e.g.*, Serjeant Yaxley's retainer (1501): *Plumpton Correspondence*, Camden Society 1839, p. 152.

consilio impendendo," but the actual words used are of limited assistance in studying the work of counsellors because they were more or less stereotyped and, in the counsellor's interests, did not specify his duties in detail. The words "*pro consilio*" were in any case narrowly construed in favour of the grantee. If the counsellor brought an action, he did not have to aver the giving of counsel because it was for the client to plead any defeasance of his grant.[22] The right to the annuity was not lost by refusing to travel to court at the client's request, for that would have involved more than giving counsel and the counsellor might have incurred expenditure which he had no claim to recover.[23] On the same principle it was held that the annuity granted to the infamous Richard Empson for his counsel was not determined by his confinement in the Tower because it did not appear that he was thereby prevented from giving counsel.[24] The same lenience of interpretation was shown a century later, when it was held no plea for the client to say that the grantee had refused to sign a bill, because he was merely bound to give counsel.[25] The latter case is said to have decided that it is not the office of a counsellor to sign bills and pleadings,[26] but this is to take the decision out of its artificial context.

The counsellor would only fail to recover his annuity if the client could show a refusal to give counsel or the breach of some positive condition in the retainer. In 1430 when an advocate of the canon law was permitted to enforce an annuity *pro servicio impendendo,* even though he had refused to attend the consistory court for his client, Strangeways J. said the outcome might have been different if he had bound himself to attend.[27] Even this tentative argument was later denied by Broke, on the ground that such a clause would not have amounted to a condition,[28] a position which was at least tenable

---

[22] M.39 H.6, 21, 22, *per* Prisot C.J.; 1 Plowd. 32, *per* Hinde J.; *Poutrel's Case,* Cro.Eliz. 547. But where an abbot was sued on a retainer by his predecessor, the plaintiff had to aver that counsel was given to the use of the house: *Bruin v. Abbot of Chester* (1460) M.39 H.6, 21, *pl.* 31. *Cf.* H.9 E.4, 48, *pl.* 3, and f. 53, *pl.* 17.

[23] H.21 E.3, 7, *pl.* 20; M.41 E.3, 19, *pl.* 3; H.8 H.6, 23, *pl.* 9. *Cf.* T.10 E.3, 24, *pl.* 23. In *Cantok v. De Wyche* (1294) 42 Seld.Soc. 199, the grantee sought to justify his refusal to act though he was present in Westminster Hall at the time of the request. A physician, however, might be obliged to give personal attendance by virtue of a retainer "*pro consilio*": M.41 E.3, 19, *pl.* 3.

[24] *Oliver v. Emsonne* (1514) Dyer 1, Plowd. 382. *Cf.* F. Bacon, *Maximes of the Common Lawes* (1630 ed.), reg. 1.

[25] *Mingay v. Hammond* (1618) Cro.Jac. 482, Popham 135. Lilly seemed to think something turned on the fact that it was "but a small annuity of 40s. per annum": *Practical Register* (1719), pp. 76, 356.

[26] *Mounson v. Dawson* (1630) Brit.Mus.MS.Harg. 25, f. 31 at f. 33. Counsel relied on *Mingay's Case* as showing that "*n'est l'office d'un counsellor . . . de transcribe ascun bill ou declaration, mes solement adviser . . .*"

[27] *Stile v. Prior of Hailes* (1430) H.8 H.6, 23, *pl.* 9. *Accord.* T.32 E.3, Fitzh.Abr. *Annuitie pl.* 30.

[28] Bro.Abr. *Annuitie pl.* 18.

where the grant was in the common form "*pro consilio impenso et impendendo*," because the counsel given in the past made the grant absolute.[29]

Where the counsellor expressly bound himself to particular services, it was considered that he could be sued in covenant for his failure to perform them,[30] regardless of whether the grant itself was determined. There was no hint of immunity in medieval times. Reported cases suggest that express covenants were uncommon, but this cannot be finally accepted until an examination is made of extant deeds of retainer reposing in local and family archives. An interesting early example has survived in the *Letter Book* of William of Hoo, sacrist of the monastery at Bury St. Edmund's. It is a covenant between William of Hoo and Robert of Leicester "*iuris professor.*"[31] Robert promised faithfully to support William in all causes and law suits whenever asked to do so, in perpetuity, and not to give counsel to any of William's adversaries, and further that if William should be undefended in any matter through his failure or neglect ("*insolentia in curia vel desidia*") he would restore any damage by the arbitration of lawful men.[32]

The permanent retainer system went into decline in the post-medieval period, though it has survived in the form of offices such as that of Queen's counsel and law officers of the Crown and corporations.

Parol retainers

Parol retainers may be divided into two classes: first, the periodic retainer for which a deed was not made, and secondly, the retainer *pro re nata* by the payment of a fee.

No litigation arose out of the latter situation until the action on the case was developed, because the lawyer's promise was *nudum pactum*,[33] and while in theory the lawyer could sue in debt for his fee he would rarely need to do so because of the invariable practice of requiring the payment of fees in advance. The origin of this custom is unknown, but it is a safe guess that it was introduced to protect the profession, especially the serjeants at law. Paston J. said in 1436 that a serjeant was liable for nonfeasance,[34] possibly because

---

[29] *Anon.*, Rolle Abr. i. 435, *Condition* (B.10).
[30] H.21 E.3, 7, *pl.* 20, *per* Sharshulle J.; T.32 E.3, Fitz.Abr. *Annuitie pl.* 30; H.8 H.6, 23, *pl.* 9.
[31] He was a royal clerk and sometime keeper of the writs and rolls of the justices in eyre in Surrey: *Cal.Patent Rolls* 1272–1281, p. 329. A *Roger* of Leicester was a justice of the Bench at this period.
[32] *Suffolk Records Society Publications* v. 86, *no.* 166 (1280–1294). The original is in Brit.Mus.MS.Harl. 230, f. 37.
[33] H.21 E.3, 7, *pl.* 20, *semble*; H.11 H.6, 18, *pl.* 10, *per* Babington C.J.
[34] 14 H.6, 18, *pl.* 58. *Cf. Doige's Case* (1442) T. 20 H.6, 34, *pl.* 4; 51 Seld.Soc. p. 97, *per* Stokes (probably John Stokes, King's Notary of the Chancery).

of his calling. He took an oath at his creation to serve the King's people,[35] and at least by 1425 this imposed on him the obligation to plead for any person who instructed him.[36] As late as 1605, Williams and Fenner JJ. opined that a serjeant, like an innkeeper, might be sued for refusing his services to anyone who requested them.[37] The benefit thus conferred on the public was enhanced by the fact that the old serjeant's fee was fixed by usage as half an angel or a multiple thereof.[38] Anyone could approach a serjeant, whose identity was advertised by his coif and habit,[39] proffer the accustomed gold coin, and expect the usual services. It was therefore reasonable that the serjeants should safeguard themselves by demanding prepayment, for if they brought a defaulting client to justice they would be met by wager of law. The rule was under constant criticism from the public for over four centuries. Langland wrote that one might as well try to move the mist from the Malvern Hills as open the mouth of a countor without a fee.[40] Later the serjeant was likened to Balaam's ass, which did not speak until it had seen an angel.[41] The practice was certainly abused by some lawyers, who took several fees before the case began to make sense to them,[42] although this was only a counteraction to inflation. By the middle of the sixteenth century many lawyers would not accept

[35] The earliest precedent of the oath yet found is of late 15th century date: Brit.Mus.MS.Harl. 1859, f. 1.
[36] M.21 H.6, 4, pl. 6, note of *Pole's Case* (1425), *infra* note 52: "*Un serjeant del ley est compelable per ley estre de counsel de ascun person.*" Accord. Bro.Abr. *Ley gager pl.* 45.
[37] *Brooke York Herald* v. *Mountague* (1605) Brit.Mus.MS.Harl. 1679, f. 134: "*Si sergeant al ley refuse d'estre de counsel que est demand, accion sur le case gist come si hostler refuse al harbage traveller, etc.*" This passage is not reported by Croke.
[38] The angel was 6s. 8d. (the older demi-mark or noble) from the time of Edward IV to 1526. The sum of 3s. 4d. and its multiples are found as the fee of serjeants and counsel in medieval bills of costs: see Ives, *op. cit.*, 7 Univ.Birm. Hist.Jo. at pp. 152–153. In 1603 it was said to be the "ancient fee" of a serjeant: Brit.Mus.MS.Add. 12497, f. 114v. It was also the usual fee for counting at the bar in fines and recoveries: Lincoln's Inn, MS. of Prothonotary Moyle, f. 40; Inner Temple, Petyt MS. 511/13, f. 102.
[39] *Paston* v. *Genny* (1471) 64 Seld.Soc. 190, *per* Catesby sjt.: "*l'abit n'est forsque un puplishment et notice a le peple issint qu'ilz poient conustre queux sont ables de pleder.*" The serjeants had worn a distinctive dress since at least the time of Richard II.
[40] W. Langland, *The Vision of Piers the Plowman*, ed. Kane (1960), p. 183.
[41] See *Numbers*, xxii. 27–30. Puns of this nature abounded, *e.g.*, S. Brant, *Ship of Fools* (1509), xvi: "Aungels worke wonders in Westmynster hall"; J. Willock, *Legal Facetiae*, p. 354: "My lawyer said the case was plaine for mee, The angell told him so hee tooke for fee"; R. Tisdale, *The Lawyer's Philosophy* (1622), sig. A7: "Nor that, whose golden fees makes the tongue flow with arguments of wit, and troll apace in Angell-rethorick," and so on.
[42] W. Harrison, *Description of England* (1587), ed. Furnivall (1877), i. 204. An Elizabethan serjeant might earn £400 in one term: *ibidem*.

fees under ten shillings,[43] and eventually a guinea or half-guinea became the minimum fee for counsel.[44]

Retainers were not necessarily by cash payment. The periodic retainer by an annual livery of robes or other valuables has already been mentioned; single retainers might be effected in the same way. Counsel were often treated to dinner by their clients, and the bill was part of the legal costs. In a plea of 1555, the defendant alleged that he had retained Roger Manwood (later Chief Baron) to be of his counsel in devising a conveyance, by personally giving him, at the Inner Temple, twenty shillings, an ell of taffeta to be made into a doublet and a cypress chest.[45]

The fear of speaking *gratis* may have been connected with the prohibition of maintenance. The counsel who spoke *pur son donant* [46] was plainly acting in the course of his profession, but he who spoke for nothing might be accused of barratry or maintaining quarrels. An exception was made in favour of paupers, whom the serjeants at least were in honour bound to advise gratuitously.[47] The serjeants assembled in court have been likened to a debating society, for it seems that any of them might join in an argument though not retained.[48] Thus when Cardinal Wolsey brought an action in the Bench he expected the serjeants to argue it, but because he was out of favour they refused to do so on the ground that they were not retained.[49] When the serjeants were discussing academic points they were acting as *amici curiae,* but the same could not be said of counsel

---

[43] This may have been justified by the revaluation of the angel. Ives, *op. cit.*, 7 Univ.Birm.Hist.Jo. at p. 153, gives examples of 7s. 6d. fees (the new angel) in 1540.

[44] A full study has not been undertaken here. *Nisi prius* costs in 1623 included " for your counsailes fee—at least 10s.": T. Powell, *The Attorney's Academy*, p. 141. North said one guinea fees were the " gage of my practice ": *Autobiography* (1887 ed.), p. 168. A pamphleteer of 1707 complained of " golden counsellors that hardly in a year have a fee in anything but gold, that would throw a 10s fee at a man's head, should he offer it 'em ": *Proposals for remedying the great Charge and Delay of Suits at Law and in Equity*, pp. 17–18. Later it was thought unprofessional to take a fee in silver: story of Serjeant Davy (d. 1780) in Polson, *Law and Lawyers*, i. 124.

[45] *Manwood* v. *Worland* (Trin. 3 & 4 Phil. & Mar.) K.B. 27/1183, m. 190. *Cf. Vavasour* v. *Puttenham, infra,* note 59: loan for seven years.

[46] The words of 28 Edw. 1, c. 11.

[47] *e.g.,* speeches to new serjeants: " Be as glad to tel the poure man the truth of the law for God's sake as the riche man for his monye " (16th century) Brit.Mus. MS.Harl. 160, f. 192v; " As you should have one tongue for the rich for your fee, as a reward for your long studies and labours, so should you also have another tongue as ready without reward to defend the poor and oppressed " (1594) Popham 45. It was not maintenance to give financial aid to paupers. There were also special statutes and rules of court governing proceedings *in forma pauperis.*

[48] P. Winfield, *Chief Sources of English Legal History* (1925), p. 158. The year books sometimes give the opinion of all the serjeants (*e.g.,* P. 15 E.2, 464: " *tout la serjaunte d'engleterre* "). In one case a judge asks the serjeants for their opinion (M.2 H.6, 5, pl. 3).

[49] *The Cardinal's Case* (1523) *Spelman's Reports*, Brit.Mus.MS.Harg. 388, f. 52.

Counsellors and Barristers

who sought to plead or move on behalf of a party. A seventeenth-century story illustrates the strictness of the rules of etiquette in this connection. William Noy is said to have made his début in a case in which he intervened spontaneously with an argument of great ingenuity. Judgment was ready to be given against the defendant, " when Mr. Noy, being a stranger, *wisheth her to give him a fee, because he could not plead else*: and then moves in arrest of judgment, that he was retained by the defendant. . . ."[50] His " touting "[51] may perhaps be defended in that the trial had already taken place and the intervention prevented a miscarriage of justice.

Obviously cases would occasionally arise where a counsellor accepted a promise of a fee instead of a cash payment and then wished to sue the client for non-payment. In the principal reported case on this point, Serjeant William Pole brought an action of debt on a parol retainer for two years at £10 per annum. It was considered that the action lay, but that the defendant could wage his law.[52] It was later suggested that mere willingness to give counsel would be *quid pro quo*,[53] and also that a serjeant could bring debt even if no fee were fixed, because he was entitled to 3s. 4d. as of common right.[54] The books of entries confirm that debt could be brought by a counsellor upon a parol retainer,[55] but there are few if any reported cases.

An unreported Chancery case of the early Elizabethan period affords an interesting example of an action on a parol retainer. Andrew Vavasour, an ancient barrister of the Middle Temple,[56] was retained by the father in law of one Elizabeth Windsor as counsel to recover lands as heir to her brother. He alleged in his petition that he was promised £100 " for his travall and costes susteyned " or a loan of £200 for seven years, if Elizabeth should recover any lands as heir.[57] The respondent, George Puttenham, a member of the Middle Temple and an habitual litigant,[58] denied the alleged promise

---

[50] *Life of the Author*, prefaced to W. Noy, *Compleat Lawyer* (1665 ed.).
[51] *Cf.* Hutton, *op. cit.*, Univ.Lib.Camb.MS.Add. 6863, f. 85 (1636): " Men must not thrust themselves into cases wherin they are not reteyned," *per* Bramston C.J. Even in the 18th century this was considered a matter of pride rather than ethics, and it is said that Wedderburn solicited City causes when making his way: L. F. Powell, *Boswell's Life of Johnson* (1934) ed.), ii. 430.
[52] *Serjeant Pole's Case* (1425) H.3 H.6, 33, *pl.* 26; 50 Seld.Soc., pref. p. xviii. See also P.3 H.6, 42, *pl.* 14, *per* Martin J.; M.21 H.6, 4, *pl.* 6, note.
[53] P.37 H.6, 8, *pl.* 18, *per* Prisot C.J.
[54] *Tailour* v. *Jeretrude* (1452) M.31 H.6, 9, *pl.* 1, *per* Moyle sjt.
[55] *Intrationum Liber* (1546), p. xxiii (b); R. Brownlow, *Declarations and Pleadings in English* (1652), p. 80; *Latine Redivivus* (1693), p. 172.
[56] *Middle Temple Records* (1904), i. 79, 136, 140 (reader elect in 1563).
[57] A century later contingent fees were held illegal: *infra*, n. 39.
[58] *M. T. Rec.*, i. 106; *Banks' Dormant and Extinct Baronage* (1808), ii. 614; *The Complete Peerage* (1959), xii. 795–797; *Victoria County History of Hampshire*, iii. 367; *Cal. State Papers Dom.* (1547–1550), pp. 363, 364, 602. More of the Puttenham saga may be learned from another Chancery suit in which he and his solicitor accused each other of lewdness and misconduct: *Hartilpoole* v. *Puttenham* (*c.* 1567), petition to Sir Nicholas Bacon L.K., C.3/90/84.

and retorted with an attack on Vavasour's reputation. The action was brought in Chancery because the petitioner "haythe nott anye specyaltie of the sayd promys wiche is contrarye to all lawe equyte and good conscience."[59] Further research in the public records will no doubt reveal much more information about such cases.[60]

THE OLD AND NEW PROFESSIONS

In the foregoing case study little attempt was made to identify the professional class to which each counsellor belonged. Such an attempt would be very difficult because of the dearth of records, and is in any case beyond the scope of the present investigation. It will suffice to assume that the counsellors might as well be serjeants, attorneys or other *legis periti*. The nebulous category of *legis periti* or apprentices of the law (the meaning is the same) is the source from which the new profession developed. Yet "apprentice" was an informal[61] and ambiguous word which conveys little information about the person it describes, and by 1600 had been artificially confined to readers in the Inns of Court.[62] Once again, the safest course is to study the function and not the name.

Pleading and advocacy

When argument at the bar was closely associated with oral pleading, and when the Common Bench was the principal royal court for actions between subjects, most of the important work of the Bar naturally belonged to the serjeants at law. In other courts the apprentices acted as advocates, hoping some day perhaps to be rewarded with the coif themselves. But when attention came to be focused on the trial and motions *in banc* after verdict, and common pleas strayed across Westminster Hall to the King's Bench and Exchequer, the serjeants' privileged position was challenged and the apprentices began to share the more important work. How or when

---

[59] *Vavasour* v. *Puttenham* (c. 1558–1574), petition to Sir Nicholas Bacon L.K., C.3/185/74. The object was probably to avoid wager of law.

[60] See, for instance, *Babham* v. *Hampden* (c. 1545), petition to Sir Thomas Wriothesley L.C., C.1/1106/1. This was a suit to recover arrears of and to enforce an annuity *pro consilio impenso et impendendo*, which was originally granted to one John Cheyne for life. In 1531 the annuity had been assigned by parol to John Babham in consideration of marriage and "in the name of one yerely fee for the counsell aswell of the said John Cheyn as of your said supplyaunt."

[61] Fortescue, *op. cit.*, Chap. 8: "*aliis iuris peritis quos apprenticios vulgus denominat.*"

[62] 10 Rep., pref. p. xxxvii; E. Waterhouse, *Fortescutus Illustratus* (1663), p. 138; Dugdale, *op. cit.*, p. 143. Noy in 1632 compared the Inns to the Universities and suggested that the humble title "apprentice to the law" was superior to the "specious and swelling titles" of masters and doctors, being given to readers after about 27 years' study: T. Gibbon, *Commonplace Book*, Brit.Mus.MS.Harl. 980, f. 153.

this work came to be appropriated exclusively to the barristers of the Inns of Court is still very obscure. The title " barrister " probably originated to denote the position occupied at moots,[63] and had no direct connection with the bar of any court.[64] Until the sixteenth century it was a word used only within the Inns, probably because it was a new word,[65] and in the courts and for formal purposes lawyers preferred the older word " apprentice." Of course these words were not synonyms, and it must also be remembered that because an advocate is described in the year books as an apprentice, it by no means follows that all apprentices could appear as advocates. The same difficulty attaches to the name " barrister," for even today the majority of barristers have no rights of audience because they are not in chambers and " practising " as etiquette requires. As late as 1632 it could be said that the title of barrister was " a word of contempt " even though it corresponded to the degree of master of arts in the Universities.[66]

The recognition of barristers may be traced through the occasional entry in the plea rolls. Until 1967 the ancient crime and tort of maintenance confined the conduct of litigation, as a matter of law, to a professional class. A layman who meddled in a law suit could be sued, and punished by the court. Thus in 1549 a man who appeared at the bar to argue on behalf of his servant was committed to the Fleet prison, on the prayer of the King's serjeants. Mountague C.J. warned him, " What you do here is apparent maintenance which we will not suffer for example to others." [67] An examination of pleas in bar of maintenance should therefore give some indication of who might claim to practise the law. In some cases the defendant simply pleaded that he was " *homo eruditus in communi lege terre*," [68]

[63] Hence " inner " and " utter " barristers. See *Report to King Henry VIII*, printed in E. Waterhouse, *Fortescutus Illustratus* (1663), p. 544; J. D. Walker, *Black Books of Lincoln's Inn*, I, pref. p. x; W. R. Prest, " Learning Exercises in the Inns of Court 1590–1640 " (1967) 9 J.S.P.T.L. (New Series) 301, 311.

[64] H. H. L. Bellot, " Some early Law Courts and the English Bar " (1922) 38 L.Q.R. 168 *et seq.*

[65] The first known use is in 1466: *Black Books*, I, 41. *Cf. ibid.*, p. 26 (1455): " *duo de optimis barrer.*" Benchers are mentioned in 1442: *ibid.*, p. 11. The expression " Bench and Bar " is used in older year books, and the reference to barristers in the printed year book of 1489 (P.4 H.7, 7, *pl.* 4: " *fuit argue per les barresters*") may originally have been to the " Bar " (same case, Brit.Mus. MS.Harg. 105, f. 129v: " *fuit argue per le barr'* . . ."). The full title " barrister at law " dates from at least the 16th century: *e.g.*, " practiser and utter barryster at lawe " (*Chabnor* v. *Dyke* (1589) Req.Proc. 2/186/23), and see note 86, *infra*.

[66] T. Gibbon, *Commonplace Book*, Brit.Mus.MS.Harl. 980, f. 153, *per* Noy Att.-Gen. at Atkyns' reading in Lincoln's Inn.

[67] *Rudston's Case* (1549) *Dalison's Reports*, Brit.Mus.MS.Harg. 4, f. 102; Moore K.B. 6, *pl.* 20 (different report). A century later a petition by two soldiers to plead at the bar in the Upper Bench was rejected " as against law being maintenance for such to plead ": J. Clayton, *Reports at Yorke* (1651), ep.ded. Maintenance was abolished by the Criminal Law Act 1967, s. 13, Sched. IV.

[68] *e.g.*, *G. and A.* v. *T.* (1520) Brit.Mus.MS.Harl. 1715, f. 144v.

the plantiff traversed, and of course nothing is known of the evidence given on the trial of the issue. One or two known entries are a little more helpful, though it is apprehended that important evidence is still dormant in rolls which have not been searched.

In a case of 1457 a defendant pleaded in maintenance that he was learned in the law and of New Inn, and as the party's attorney had retained T.Y., learned in the law, as his counsel at a fee of 6s. 8d.[69] The maintenance here was the retainer of counsel, which was justified as attorney, but it is significant that the attorney described himself as learned in the law and a member of an Inn.

Even more explicit and illuminating is the plea from an unidentified roll printed by Rastell. The defendant justified as "*unus sociorum hospicii de Lincolnes Inne*" which from time immemorial had been and still was "*quoddam hospicium hominum de curia legis temporalis et hominum consiliariorum legis predicte*," and as "*homo consiliarius de et in lege predicta eruditus*." The plaintiff traversed this by replying "*quod fuit homo laicus et non homo consiliarius de et in lege predicta eruditus.*"[70] The right to maintain is here linked with membership of an Inn of Court, though it seems from the traverse that the material part was the averment that he was a learned counsellor. It is to be noted that the defendant did not say that he was a barrister, but that he was a fellow of an Inn of men of court. The explanation may be, of course, that he had not been called to the bar, but it seems more likely that the degree was not then thought to carry any privileges outside the Inn. In funerary inscriptions of the fifteenth and sixteenth centuries members of Inns were nearly always described as *socii* and not as barristers or readers.[71] It is suggested that this supports the proposition that the Inns derived their status from being the *hospicia* where the men of court chose to dwell, rather than that the lawyers at first derived any status by virtue of their degrees within the Inns.[72] This suggestion

---

[69] W. H. v. W. C. (1457) W. Rastell, *A Collection of Entrees* (1596 ed.), p. 431v, Maintenance pl. 17. It was not essential for a general attorney to justify as one learned in the law: H.34 H.6, 26, *pl.* 3, per Moile J., semble.

[70] Rastell, *op. cit.*, p. 432, Maintenance pl. 18. The date is not given, though it is probably later than *c.* 1500. *Cf. ibid.*, p. 357, Forger de faits pl. 6: averment of retainer as "*unus sociorum de Greis Inne.*"

[71] *e.g.*, five inscriptions to *socii de Grays Inn* (Greyfriars, 1469–1516): J. Stow, *Notebook*, Brit.Mus.MS.Harl. 544, ff. 48v. 54, 58, 60v, 63v. "*Jacobus Bayle medio templo sociatus*" (Temple Church, 1470): J. Weever, *Funerall Monuments* (1767 ed.), p. 225. "*Ricardus Wye socius commitivi Interioris Templi*" (Temple Church, 1519): Dugdale, *op. cit.*, p. 173. All these are now destroyed. Extant inscriptions on brasses rarely mention Inns before the 17th century. Unique in the 15th century is William Crofton "*legis peritus ac collega de Greysyn*" (Trottecliffe, Kent, 1483). The first to mention a degree seems to be the brass of Heigham C.B., reader of Lincoln's Inn (Barrow, Suffolk, 1570).

[72] See J. H. Baker, "The Status of Barristers" (1969) 85 L.Q.R. 334 at pp. 336–337. (A documented modern parallel is the establishment of the Inn of Court of Northern Ireland in 1921 by the common act and assent of the Bench and Bar

would explain why Clement's Inn was claimed in the fifteenth century to be an Inn of men of court.[73] Once the Inns acquired their status, the degree of barrister took on a wider significance and became a qualification for practice. Unfortunately, no plea in bar of maintenance as a " barrister " has yet come to light, though in one obscure case the issue was raised in reverse where a person, not being a barrister, had been licensed to plead at the bar by letters patent. The nature of this unique privilege is not clear and the case is not very informative.[74]

There is another group of cases, however, in which the formal recognition of the barrister may be traced more closely. In an action on the case for defaming a counsellor in his profession an averment that the plaintiff was a practising counsellor was necessary and material.[75] It was therefore legally necessary to set out the authority by which he practised. The earliest known case of this kind, discovered by Professor Milsom, was an action by Richard Elyot as " *serviens domini Regis ad legem et eruditus in lege regni Anglie* " in 1513.[76] But whereas a serjeant and law officer could plead his degree in this way, the barrister did not do so until the end of the century. The form used in the earlier declarations was the time-honoured " *eruditus in legibus terre.*" [77] The change took place, apparently, in 1591 when John Hele brought an action for slander as a reader of the Inner Temple. He showed at some length that he had studied the law assiduously for twenty-nine years as a fellow of the Inner Temple [78] and by reason of his skill was called to the place and degree of utter barrister in that Inn,[79] and later made a

---

there.) It is evident that the Inns " of Court " were so named after the " men of court " and not *vice versa*; for this expression see *Cal. Patent Rolls* 1436–1441, p. 195, and 46 L.Q.R. 150n.

[73] *J. v. W. P.* (1479) Rastell, *op. cit.*, p. 108, *Plee al Briefe per misnomer pl.* 7: " *et dicit quod ipse tempore impetracionis brevis fuit de hospitio de Clements Inne . . . quod quidem hospitium est . . . quoddam hospitium hominum curie legis temporalis necnon hominum consiliariorum eiusdem legis.*" *Cf.* note 70, *supra*: Lincoln's Inn.

[74] *Prince's Case*, cited in W. Hudson, *Treatise of the Star Chamber* (c. 1635) *Collectanea Juridica* ii. 93. *Cf. Boughton's Case*, cit. Popham 207, discussed more fully in Bodl.Lib.MS.Rawl. c. 720, f. 28v.

[75] *Cary's Case* (1626) Popham 207; *Gibs v. Price* (1650) Style 231. The action lay for an attorney, but the form of pleading was different.

[76] *Elyot v. Tofte* (Hil. 4 Hen. VIII) K.B. 27/1006, m. 62. See S. F. C. Milsom, *Historical Foundations of the Common Law* (1969), pp. 339, 424.

[77] *Manwood v. Worland* (1557) K.B. 27/1183, m. 190 (Manwood was described as " *unus scociorum interioris Templi,*" but only by way of addition); *Snagg v. Gray* (1571) K.B. 27/1238, m. 114 (*Co.Entr.* 22, *pl.* 19; *cf.* Dalis. 97, Rolle Abr. i. 55); *Stanhope v. Blythe* (1586) *Co.Entr.* 21, *pl.* 8. In *Broughton's Case*, *supra*, this form was held bad because the jurors could not determine a man's learning.

[78] " *Ut socius venerabilis consorcii generosorum hospicii interioris Templi.*"

[79] " *Ad locum et gradum fore de exteriore barra vocatus* ' an utter barrester ' *in hospicio predicto . . . evocatus electus et assignatus fuit.*"

112   *The Legal Profession and the Common Law*

bencher [80] and reader,[81] and thus gave counsel to many great men and earned his living.[82] After this date it was usual [83] to plead the degree of barrister specially in this type of action, though the choice of words was not always uniform.[84] For instance, in 1634 a member of the Middle Temple pleaded that in 1611 he had, for his proficiency and learning in the study of English law, been called to the degree and office of an utter barrister, and thus became " *licentiatus iuris.*" [85] By the second half of the seventeenth century, being a barrister could be pleaded with less verbiage,[86] a sign that it was a degree fully recognised by the law. The degree was recognised as a judicial qualification by a statute of 1623.[87]

Soliciting causes

The general prosecution of litigation, by instructing counsel, paying fees to officials, and so on, was similarly caught by the laws against maintenance.[88] But the law necessarily permitted servants

---

[80] " *Evocatus et electus fuit ad dignitatem locum et preheminens fore unum de banco hospicii predicti vocatus* ' a bencher in court.' "

[81] " *Evocatus electus et assignatus fuit fore lector legis et statutibus regni Anglie anglice* ' a reader in courte ' *in hospicio predicto.*"

[82] *Hele* v. *Gyddy* (Trin. 33 Eliz. I) K.B. 27/1318, m. 682 (reported Moore K.B. 695, 2 Anders. 40, 269). The record was not printed, but a similar declaration by an utter barrister of Gray's Inn in *Clifford* v. *Astrye* (1642) was printed in J. Hansard, *Book of Entries* (1685), p. 61.

[83] In the *Liber Placitandi* (1674), p. 53, *pl.* 76, is a late example of the " *homo eruditus in legibus huius regni.*" The even more anachronistic " *legis apprenticius* " is found in an indictment for ambidextry printed by J. Tremaine, *Placita Coronae* (1723), p. 261.

[84] See the following cases subsequent to *Hele's Case*, the records of which have not been examined: *Palmer* v. *Boyer* (1594) Cro.Eliz. 342, Golds. 126, Owen 17; *Rich* v. *Holt* (1609) Cro.Jac. 267; *Bestley* v. *Dixon* (1610) 13 Rep. 71, Noy 98, Rolle Abr. i. 55, *pl.* 22; *Bankes* v. *Allen* (1615) Rolle Abr. i. 54, *pl.* 14; *Powell's Case* (1618) Popham 139; *Cary's Case* (1627) Popham 207; *Peare* v. *Jones* (1634) Cro.Car. 382, Rolle Abr. i. 55, *pl.* 16; *Francis Cory's Case* (n.d.) cited in *Cory's Reports*, Brit.Mus.MS.Harg. 23, f. 117; *Gibs* v. *Price* (1650) Style 231.

[85] *Franklyn* v. *Boteler* (Mich. 10 Car. I) K.B. 27/1611, m. 463 (reported in Brit.Mus.MS.Add. 35968, f. 502, but not in print): " *Ad gradum et officium causidici anglice* ' an utterbarrister' *in eadem societate debito modo electus et vocatus fuit et licentiatus iuris in eadem hospicio . . . factus et allocatus fuit.*" He was later made " *unus gubernatorum anglice* ' bencher' *et lector legum anglice* ' a reader' *hospicii predicti per consensum omnium aliorum gubernatorum anglice* ' benchers' *eiusdem hospicii.*"

[86] e.g., *The Clerk's Manual* (1678), p. 166: " *in legibus communibus Angliae existens inde graduatus videlicet* ' a barrester at law '."

[87] 21 Jac. 1, c. 23, s. 6; *Clapham's Case* (1627) Cro.Car. 97. In *mandamus* proceedings to restore to the recordership of Bath in 1671, it was returned that the Borough were by charter to have " *unum probum hominum discretum in legibus Anglie eruditum* " as recorder, and that the applicant " *non fuit neque adhuc est conciliarius in lege anglice* ' an utter barrester at law' *neque aliquo modo eruditus in legibus terre huius Regni Anglie* ": *Ex parte Hawley*, J. Tremaine, *Placita Coronae* (1723), pp. 541–543.

[88] e.g., *Anon.* (1515) *Spelman's Reports*, Brit.Mus.MS.Harg. 388, f. 25: held maintenance where defendant went to Serjeant Broke at request of a stranger and asked him to be of counsel for the stranger. Cited and approved by Coke

to run errands for their masters, such as to retain counsel,[89] and counsel themselves could lawfully solicit causes as part of their profession. Andrew Vavasour, the Elizabethan barrister, " toke greate paynes ... as well in rydyng iorneys att his owne costes to seke evydens as also in his lying att London of his owne charge abowte the pennyng of replicacions intergatores and copying other wrytynges." [90]

Once it was clear that only barristers in the Inns of Court could be *legis periti* it was necessary to consider the legal standing of solicitors who were not of this class. As land agents or general advisers there could be little objection to them, but in fact many of them practised the law.[91] In the first reported case in which the legality of solicitors was challenged, Dyer C.J. said their services were lawful so long as no suits were depending in a court of law.[92] It was many years, however, before their right to maintain causes was established. Coke and Ellesmere were united in their attacks on " general " solicitors. In a case of 1600 the latter said that a general solicitor " had noe warrant but is punishable of mayntenance." [93] A few years later Coke C.J. said that only a counsellor or attorney could justify maintenance, and " to be a solicitor to another, he cannot for this justifie, *if it bee not for his master*; for none can be a solicitor-general in all courts, but onely for the King." [94] By the time William Hudson wrote his well-known invective against the " new sort of people called solicitors," [95] the common law had begun to recognise them and to allow them to recover their fees.[96] As

Att.-Gen. in *Wortley* v. *Savill*, Brit.Mus.MS.Add. 25212, f. 15. *Cf.* M.21 H.6, 15, *pl.* 30, *per* Markham J.; H.34 H.6, 26, *pl.* 3, *per* Prisot C.J.

[89] See *Hull* v. *Daucomb* (1425) T.3 H.6, 53, *pl.* 24; M.11 H.6, 10, *pl.* 24; M.19 H.6, 30, *pl.* 56; M.39 H.6, 5, *pl.* 8; *J. H.* v. *T. W.* (1500) Rastell, *op. cit.*, p. 428v, *Maintenance pl.* 8. Conversely, a master might maintain his servant: *Pomeroy* v. *Abbot of Buckfast* (1442) M.21 H.6, 15, *pl.* 30; *Clement Tailour's Case* (1450) T.28 H.6, 12, *pl.* 28; *Robert Horn's Case* (1456) H.34 H.6, 25, *pl.* 3; M.19 E.4, 3, *pl.* 9; M.21 H.7, 40, *pl.* 62; Rastell, *loc. cit., pl.* 9.

[90] C.3/185/74, *ut supra*, note 59. In the time of Henry VIII a Gray's Inn man might act as " a generall attorney or solissitour to the commone law ": Ives, *op. cit.* (1968) T.R.H.S. at p. 152. An attorney could act as a solicitor, and might recover his fees on a retainer " *ad negotia solicitandum* ": Rastell, *op. cit.*, p. 202v, *Dette sur reteiner pl.* 9.

[91] George Puttenham's solicitor had the " charge of all his doinges aswell of receiptes and paymentes in London as all his causes in the lawe and other secrete and weightie affaires ": note 58, *supra*. And see M. Birks, *Gentlemen of the Law* (1960), Chap. 5.

[92] *Onely* v. *Earl of Kent* (1577) Dyer 355. *Cf.* P.5 H.7, 20, *pl.* 1, *per* Keble sjt. And see *Worthington* v. *Garstone* (1580) Hob. 67.

[93] *Heydon* v. *Good* (1600) Brit.Mus.MS.Add. 25212, f. 7v. See also W. J. Jones, *The Elizabethan Court of Chancery* (1967), pp. 317-320. In 1601 Anderson C.J. said solicitors were illegal by statute: *Anon.*, Bodl.Lib.MS.Rawl. c. 720, f. 65v.

[94] *Note* (1614) 2 Bulst. 230 (no italics in original). The office of King's Solicitor-General was instituted in 1461.

[95] *Treatise of the Star Chamber* (c. 1635) *Collectanea Juridica* ii. 94.

[96] *Rolls* v. *Germine* (1596) Cro.Eliz. 459, Moore K.B. 366; *Osbourn* v. *Eden* (1600) Cro.Eliz. 760; *Leach* v. *Penton* (1614) Viner Abr. *Maintenance* (E.6); *Bradford* v. *Woodhouse* (1619) Cro.Jac. 520; *Gage* v. *Johnson* (1622) Winch

they had no immediate antecedents, nor any professional organisation, it is difficult to define their functions with precision. They did not do the work of the pleaders or attorneys, but solicited causes in the Chancery and prerogative courts, and " being learned in the lawes and instructed in theire maisters cause [did] informe the sergeantes and councellors at lawe in the same." [97] By the middle of the seventeenth century the solicitor was chiefly employed in Chancery affairs, as all he had to do in the common law courts was " to be able to breviate his clyent's cause fit to instruct counsel; for in all other things he is but a servant to the attorney." [98]

Conveyancing

Non-litigious professional activities, such as conveyancing, were not prohibited by law and were not therefore appropriated to any particular class of practitioners. Chaucer's serjeant, it will be remembered, was renowned for his "writing," and two centuries later it was still considered part of a serjeant's duty to advise on conveyancing matters.[99] But the work was shared with other specialists, including attorneys and scriveners, and even laymen.

Functions of the Bar restricted

The vast increase of legal work in the sixteenth century affected not only the serjeants and attorneys but also the barristers. There was an enormous growth in the number of students in the Inns,[1] and in the number of barristers. Sir Christopher Hatton C. said in 1586, " I finde that there are now more at the barre in one howse than was in all the Innes of the Courte when I was a younge man. And I finde theis places are bestowed manye times upon unmeete men verie rawe and younge men which are negligent and careles." [2] The diversification of jurisdictions and the increase of business led to barristers taking on more work than they could manage, a matter of constant complaint. The serjeants called in 1577 were exhorted " not

---

53; *Thursby* v. *Warren* (1629) Cro.Car. 159, W. Jones 208; *Kelloway* v. *Mere* (1629) Brit.Mus.MS.Harg. 25, f. 54v, MS.Add. 25222, f. 188; *Sands* v. *Trevilian* (1630) Cro.Car. 107, 193; *Herne* v. *Roth* (1634) Brit.Mus.MS.Add. 35967, f. 22v.

[97] *Addendum* (c. 1574–1582) to T. Smith, *De Republica Anglorum* (1906 ed.), p. 153. Solicitors were not usually described as "learned in the law."

[98] T. M., *The Sollicitor* (1662 ed.), pp. 23, 102. See also W. S. Holdsworth, *History of English Law* (1924), vi. 449 *et seq.*

[99] *e.g.*, speech to new serjeants (1577): " The first [part of your service is] to councell in matters of assurance " (Chancery Decrees and Orders 1577 " A," C. 33/55, f. 4). Other speeches *similiter.* As to conveyancing, see Holdsworth, *op. cit.*, pp. 447–448; M. Birks, *Gentlemen of the Law* (1960), Chap. 4.

[1] See Ives, *op. cit.*, 7 Univ.Birm.Hist.Jo. at pp. 146–147; (1968) T.R.H.S. at pp. 146–147.

[2] G. W. Sanders, *Orders of the High Court of Chancery* (1845), i. 1036. W. R. Prest has considered these changes in relation to the supposed decline of the learning exercises in the Inns: 9 J.S.P.T.L. 301.

to embrace more matters than you can well and throughlie consider of which thinge I note doth oftenest happen unto those which trust to moche tò the presentnes of there wittes and thereby answere theire clientes causes upon a sodayne to the losse and overthrowe (as yt often happenethe) of theire clientes causes." [3] Ley C.J. said that this type of misbehaviour was "a kind of theevery or robery." [4] The stream of criticism suggests that the Bar did not fully reform this abuse,[5] but it seems that one result of the pressure was that barristers abandoned a good deal of their "counselling" work in order to concentrate on advocacy in court.

Pleading at the bar had already been superseded, except for the formalities of fines and recoveries, by written pleadings, and argument took place on demurrers and motions *in banc*. A relic of the old practice was the rule which required the "hand" of a barrister (or serjeant, in the Common Pleas) to demurrers and special pleas.[6] But the signature was, or became in the seventeenth century, a mere formality and the actual drawing of pleadings fell to lesser practitioners. A pamphleteer of 1652 complained that the serjeants were "for the most part taken up in moving and arguing at the bars of the severall courts, and pleading at tryalls at the common law, and hearing in Chancery, whereby few or none can procure them to contrive any [special pleas] . . . by occasion whereof suiters in these latter times have been constrained to goe to clerks or attornies to have such things contrived or drawn, whereof some have been very ignorant." [7] Roger North confirms this, and relates that he did not much apply himself to "records and drawing pleadings . . . being taken up into a higher form." [8]

More significant than this, in the long run, counsel began to abandon direct consultation with their clients and to lean on the lower ministers of the law to "inform" them. Although it is now an important rule of etiquette that counsel must be approached through a solicitor, at any rate in respect of civil litigation, this seems to have begun as a time-saving device contrary to the best opinion of

---

[3] Chancery Decrees and Orders 1577 "A," C 33/55, f. 4. *Cf.* Sanders, *op. cit.*, p. 1034: "it is all one not to come as either to come unprepared or depart before it be ended" (speech of 1580).
[4] Hutton, *op. cit.*, Univ.Lib.Camb.MS.Add. 6863, f. 8v (speech of 1623).
[5] A proposal was made, though nothing came of it, to "sort" the bars of each court and restrict them to named barristers (Brit.Mus.MS.Lansd. 106, f. 103v). In theory the serjeants were expected to put their Common Pleas business first, but they practised in the other courts as well.
[6] T. Powell, *The Attorney's Academy* (1623), pp. 114–116. See also *Barret's Case* (1619) Hobart 249.
[7] E. Leach, *Down-fall of the Unjust Lawyers* (1652), p. (5).
[8] R. North, *Autobiography* (1882 ed.), p. 126. *Cf. Discourse on the Study of Laws* (1824 ed.), p. 39: "the gown has derelicted the practice of forms, so that all is now left to [the attornies]." The gown, of course, derived some material advantage from the greater number of jeofails to be exploited.

what was correct. The decaying standards of the old school may once more be discerned from the speeches to new serjeants. The sixteenth-century speeches give guidance to the serjeants in their chambers practice, and show that it was then still normal for counsel to advise directly. The serjeant counsellor was to do his best to encourage settlements, and to deter groundless or false actions.[9] By the early seventeenth century there are signs that counsel were becoming less attentive. Ley C.J. warned the 1623 call, " You must be carefull to be fully instructed, and lett your clyents informe you att large."[10] The serjeants created in 1640 were told by Lord Keeper Littleton not to " betray " their clients' causes by neglect but to instruct themselves, "*and to that purpose take not briefes of ordinary solicitors, but drawe the breifes yourselves.*"[11] Serjeant Maynard was one of the last to observe the old system regularly,[12] on the Western Circuit, when " no attorney made breviate of more than the pleadings, but the counsel themselves perused and noted the evidences; if deeds, by perusing them in his chamber, if witnesses, by examining them there also before the trial." [13] North attributed the change to laziness, " or rather superciliousness, whereby the practice of law forms is slighted by counsel, [and] the business, of course, falls to the attorneys." [14]

In his *Autobiography* he wrote:

> The gentlemen of the law, having left the mechanic part of their practice, that is to speak with the client at the first instance to state his business and to advise the action . . . hath been the cause that the attorneys carry all from them . . . and if young gentlemen will ever think to secure a practice to themselves they must set pen to paper and be mechanics and operators in the law as well as students and pleaders. Mere speculative law will help few into the world.[15]

OFFICIUM INGENII AND OFFICIUM LABORIS [16]

The process described by North was crucial to the preservation of the two present branches of the legal profession. The reason why the

---

[9] *e.g.*, Sanders, *op. cit.*, i. 1033–1036; Chancery Decrees and Orders, C. 33/55, ff. 4, 86. A barrister may even today give direct advice sometimes, as to friends or paupers, but not as a rule to " clients."
[10] Hutton, *op. cit.*, Univ.Lib.Camb.MS.Add. 6863, f. 8v.
[11] Brit.Mus.MS.Lansd. 211, f. 118 (no italics in original).
[12] There are instances at a later date (*e.g., Bawdes v. Amhurst* (1715) Prec.Cha. 402), but the passage cited in note 98, *supra*, shows that it was usual for solicitors to " breviate causes " by 1662.
[13] R. North, *Discourse on the Study of Laws* (1824 ed.), p. 39. Cf. *Autobiography* (1887) ed.), p. 141: " even the making of breviats at the assizes was done by the lawyers." [14] *Discourse*, p. 39.
[15] *Op. cit.*, p. 141. It is strange that he later refers to this sort of practice as " smut " and says he always rejected requests to undertake a whole cause: *ibid.*, pp. 168–169. For later instances, see *Doe* d. *Bennett* v. *Hales* (1850) 15 Q.B.D. 171. [16] This is Coke's distinction: 2 *Inst.* 514.

division was so strong and lasting seems principally to have lain in the efforts made by the Bar to assert their intellectual and social superiority over the " mechanics " of the law. The barristers stepped, in a sense, into the heritage of the serjeants, but their mode of so doing was the product of a conscious and deliberate policy in shaping the new profession. A similar attempt to preserve distinctions in the medical profession led eventually to litigation,[17] but less antagonism arose in the legal profession because the barristers in elevating their status were at the same time conferring additional business on the attorneys and solicitors. Thus in the legal profession the idea took root that he who had the humility to become a " ministerial person of an inferior nature "[18] would be assured of business, but he who sought the distinction of belonging to an élite profession might have to pay a considerable price in the insecurity of his practice.

The process may be traced back ultimately to the rise of the four Inns of Court and the depression of the Inns " of Chancery," some of them older and grander than the Inns of Court, into *hospicia minora*, mere satellites of the major Inns. This prevented the barristers and readers of the Inns of Chancery from acquiring any public status, whereas those of the *hospicia majora* became a profession. It is probable that after 1396 [19] the serjeants (and consequently the judges) were all Inns of Court men, though no one yet knows how or why the four particular Inns achieved their superior standing. One of the effects of this was that the Inns of Chancery came to be associated with the attorneys and lesser practitioners of the law. The next stage of the process was the attempted exclusion of attorneys and solicitors from the Inns of Court, or at any rate from the degree of barrister therein, in the sixteenth and seventeenth centuries. The story is well known,[20] and it is also well known that the motive behind the

---

[17] *College of Physicians* v. *Rose* (1703) 1 Bro.P.C. 78. See also B. Hamilton, " The Medical Profession in the Eighteenth Century " (1951) 4 *Economic History Review (2nd Series)* 141 *et seq.*; C. Wall, *History of the Worshipful Company of Apothecaries of London* (1963), Chaps. 4, 6. The surgeons were concerned only with outward cures, but the apothecaries (originally druggists) acquired the right to prescribe medicine by usage. The physicians argued that this encroachment would deprive the gentry of " one of the professions by which their younger sons might honourably subsist ": Wall, *op. cit.*, p. 399.

[18] *Infra*, note 21.

[19] In this year six serjeants were called to that degree (see *Cal. Patent Rolls* 1396–1399, p. 28), one of whom had been been a member of Clifford's Inn. In the window of the old Hall was the inscription: " *Will. Screen electus et vocatus ad statum et gradum servientis ad legem extra hospitium istud et non aliunde* . . ." (T. Gibbon, *Commonplace Book* (c. 1635) Brit.Mus.MS.Harl. 980, f. 300). The inscription was destroyed before 1851: E. Foss, *The Judges of England* (1851), v. 141. Skrene is the latest *known* example of such a call.

[20] See H. H. L. Bellot, " The Exclusion of Attorneys from the Inns of Court " (1910) 26 L.Q.R. 137 *et seq.*

campaign was to preserve the supposed inferiority of solicitors and attorneys.[21]

At the same period the Inns, encouraged by the judges, began to insist upon the gentility of their members,[22] and to aspire to the neo-classical ideal of a profession of gentlemen, detached from the pursuit of lucre and united in their devotion to a superior vocation.[23] The rules of etiquette prohibiting social contact between the two branches arose from the same cause, and at the same period. Lord Keeper Finch told the serjeants called in 1637 that they must not " hugg an attorney, nor make an attorneys' feast and soe drawe them by those base meanes to bringe them clyents." [24] Perhaps the most interesting, and familiar, result of this development was the appearance of the classical notion of the liberal arts and the *honorarium*. The lawyers adopted Ulpian's doctrine that the profession of the law was such a holy thing that it was not to be debased or evaluated in monetary terms, and that certain things could not with honour be sued for albeit they might with honour be accepted as presents.[25]

The honorarium doctrine

The introduction of the classical doctrine as a rule of law or binding custom has generally been attributed to Serjeant John Davies,

---

[21] *Judge's Orders* 1614: Dugdale, *op. cit.*, p 317. *Cf. ibid.*, p. 320 (*Orders* of 1630), in which " counsellor " becomes " utter-barristers, readers in court and apprentices at law." Repeated in 1661: *ibid.*, p. 322.

[22] See the valuable original studies of P. Lucas, " Blackstone and the Reform of the Legal Profession " (1962) 77 Eng.Hist.Rev. 456, 467 *et seq.*; and W. R. Prest, " Legal Education of the Gentry 1560–1640 " (1967) 38 *Past and Present* 20–39.

[23] *e.g.*, Anon., *The Institucion of a Gentleman* (1555), sig. D.iiii, which says lawyers of no great fortune " may resonablye take monye for their counsel, travail and paines, having alwais respect to the sayinge of Plato, that is *Homines hominis causa esse generatos* . . ." L. Humphrey, *The Nobles or Of Nobility* (1563), sig. Qvv, looks back to classical times when lawyers were always gentlemen. J. Ferne, *Blazon of Gentrie* (1586), p. 93: " One lawyer of gentle lineage is more frequented with the client of *Forma pauperis*, more vigilant to his client's cause, more easie in his fees . . . than tenne advocates of base and ungentle stocke." Speech of Hobart C.J. to new serjeants (1623): " Lett not your ends be to inrich yourselves and to wast and consume the clyent, for you make the law to serve you and you doe not serve the law" (Hutton, *op. cit.*, Univ.Lib.Camb.MS.Add. 6863, f. 4v).

[24] Hutton, *op. cit.*, Univ.Lib.Camb.MS.Add. 6863, f. 83v. *Cf. ibid.*, f. 85, per Bramston C.J.; Brit.Mus.MS.Lansd. 211, f. 118 (1640), per Littleton L.K.: " I hope yow all abhorr in shareing with sollicitors."

[25] D.50, 13, 1, 5: " *est quidem res sanctissima civilis sapientia, sed quae pretio nummario non sit aestimanda nec dehonestanda dum in iudicio honor petitur qui ingressu sacramenti offerri debuit, quaedam enim tametsi honeste accipiantur, inhoneste tamen petuntur.*" (Quoted in Brit.Mus.MS.Harg. 4, f. 21, *infra*.) *Cf.* Davies (next note): " That moral rule *Multa honeste accipi possunt quae honeste peti non possunt*." The *Lex Cincia* (c. 204 B.C.) forbade advocates to accept money for their services, and at no time could advocates or professors of law hire their services by *locatio conductio*. In later times advocates (but not professors) could recover fees by a *cognitio extraordinaria* (D.50, 13, 1, 9–10). See also J. A. C. Thomas, " Locatio and Operae " (1961) *Bulletino dell'Istituto di diritto romano*, lxiv. 231 at pp. 245–247.

since his is its earliest known exposition. In his essay in praise of the common law and lawyers, which was prefixed to his *Reports* (published in 1615), he said that the professors of the common law had not accumulated their wealth " by any illiberal meanes (as envie sometimes suggesteth) but in a most ingenious and worthy manner." Almost in the words of the *Digest* he explained:

> For the fees and rewards which they receave, are not of the nature of wages, or pay, or that which wee cal salerie, or hire, which are indeed duties certain, and grow due by contract for labour or service, but that which is given to a learned Councellor is called *honorarium*, and not *merces*, being indeed a gift which giveth honour as well to the Taker as to the Giver: neither is it certaine or contracted for; no price or rate can be set upon councel, which is unvaluable and inestimable. . . . Briefly, it is a gift of such a nature, and given and taken upon such tearmes, as albeit the able client may not neglect to give it without a note of ingratitude . . . yet the worthy councellor may not demand it without doing wrong to his reputation.[26]

It is not likely that Davies was the original instigator of the reception of this doctrine in England, though the above passage was very influential in securing its acceptance. The notion of *honorarium* had been applied in 1607 to the case of a barrister who had accepted payment for his services as a commissioner of bankrupts. Coke C.J. said that although a judge could not make a contract for his services, which would infringe his oath, it was reasonable to accept payment for travel and expenses as *honorarium*. To this Lord Ellesmere agreed, and added that the commissioner might have taken more than he did, for, as he said, " a lawyer *cessans lucrum damnum est*." [27] There is a suggestion that the principle had received judicial support in respect of barristers in 1610,[28] but there is no clear statement of it in print before Davies.

It may be observed that the Bar were hardly inconvenienced by the *honorarium* doctrine, as is sometimes supposed. For one thing it avoided champerty, since a lawyer could accept part of an estate recovered so long as he did not contract for it *pendente lite*.[29]

---

[26] J. Davies, *Le Primer Report des Cases en les Courts del Roy en Ireland* (Dublin, 1615), preface; A. B. Grosart ed. *Works of Sir John Davies* (1876), ii. 280–281. See also R. Roxburgh, " Rondel *v.* Worsley, etc." (1968) 84 L.Q.R. 178, 513.

[27] *Lewes* v. *Lany* (1607) Hawarde, *Reportes del cases in Camera Stellata* (1894 ed.), p. 342.

[28] W. Sheppard, *Grand Abridgment* (1675), i. 536: " It is said also that the counsellor shall have debt for his fees. 3 H.6, 33. But it seems the law is otherwise for a barrester for his counsel. *Trin.* 8 *Jac.* B.R." The second case has not yet been traced.

[29] *Penros' Case* (1412) H.13 H.4, 17, *pl.* 12, *per* Hankford C.J. The principle was still acceptable three centuries later (see Viner Abr. *Maintenance* (M)7), though Coke said " Hanckford imperfectly citeth it " (2 *Inst.* 564). Penros was a serjeant at law about the time of Richard II.

Furthermore, as fees were usually paid in advance it actually prevented a client from recovering back the fee for a failure of consideration. It was not unknown for unscrupulous lawyers to take several fees before making any progress with their client's cause,[30] and in 1616 the Court of Common Pleas promulgated a rule that if a serjeant or counsellor failed to attend a cause he should be ordered to return the fee,[31] which implies that there was a difficulty in recovering it back at law.[32]

Serjeant Pole's Case [33] was an obstacle to the acceptance of the new theory. Sheppard was prepared to treat serjeants as an exception,[34] though by his time there was little logic in so doing. Others regarded the new idea with scepticism or confusion,[35] and few books stated the rule as absolute. For instance, it was held that *assumpsit* lay to recover a fee promised for counsel already given.[36] If the past consideration in such a case were allowed to be good, it would have been difficult to treat the express promise as void. Where, on the other hand, the fee was paid in advance, there was no express promise and therefore the payment might well be treated as a gift.

In the first known judicial statement on the subject, Serjeant John Bridgman, Chief Justice of Chester, considered prepayment to be the essence of the matter. In the Court of the Marches of Wales in 1631 he said, according to Sheppard, " A barrester cannot have this action [debt] or any other for his fees, for giving of councel as a serjant or attorney may, and therefore he is not bound to give advice before he have his fees ";[37] alternatively, " A counsellor is not bound to

---

[30] W. Harrison, *Description of England* (1877 ed.), i. 204–205. A proposal to remedy this in 1653 came to nothing: F. A. Inderwick, *The Interregnum* (1891), p. 209.

[31] G. Cooke, *Rules and Orders of the Court of Common Pleas*, Hilary Term 14 Jac. 1, No. VI. Rule VII provided for the return of excessive fees.

[32] *Cf.* Turner v. Philipps (1791) Peake 166, *accord.* Likewise in the civil law: D.19, 2, 38, 1.

[33] *Supra*, note 52.

[34] W. Sheppard, *Faithful Councellor or the Marrow of the Law* (1651), p. 258: *infra*, note 37, *per* Bridgman C. J. Chester. In his *Grand Abridgment* (1675), i. 536 is the remarkable muddled passage: " It is said, *a serjeant at law* shall not have debt for his fees. But the law is otherwise for a serjeant at law."

[35] *e.g.*, W. Glisson and A. Gulston, *A Survey of the Law* (1659), pp. 165, 182. In attempting to clarify the 1659 text, Style made it even more confused: " Serjeant at law shall not have debt for his fees and is not bound to be retained without. *Q.* for he is [*sic*] bound to be of counsel till he receive his fee." (*The Common Law Epitomised* (1679 ed.), p. 219.) Style also questioned whether a counsellor could recover his fees, " for a counsellor's fee is not certain, and is rather *honorarium* than *mercenarium*": *ibid.*, p. 197.

[36] *Marsh* v. *Rainsford* (1588) 2 Leon. 111, *pl.* 146, *per* Anderson C.J.; *Anon.* (1629) Brit.Mus.MS.Add. 35329, f. 23, *per* Jones J.: " *Si homme promise a J.S. (esteant home erudite en le ley) 20 li. pur le bone counsell que il avoit a luy done (pro consilio impenso) que l'accion sur ceo promise gist bien.*"

[37] *Marrow*, p. 258: " So was the opinion of Mr. Justice Bridgman. *Et Curia in le Marches de Wales* 7 Car."

give counsell till he have his fee; for he hath no remedy for it." [38] This was not, of course, a rationalisation of the rule because the prepayment principle was much older than the inability to sue for fees. Five years later, Bramston C.J. in his address to the new serjeants expressed the rule, in relation to serjeants at any rate, as a rule of etiquette. " He tould them that they must not contract for their fees, nor take a case in hand to have soe much when it is done, or if he prevayle,[39] this is not the duty of an advocate, for the fee is *honorarium munus*." [40] The notion of *honorarium* was affirmed by Rolle J. in 1646.[41]

In the British Museum is an interesting collection of notes evidently made in connection with a reading in an Inn of Court or Chancery [42] on the statute 3 Jac. 1, c. 7. This statute provided, *inter alia*, that no attorney or solicitor should be allowed to recover from his client any fees " given " to any serjeant or counsellor at law unless he had a receipt signed by the serjeant or counsellor.[43] The notes, which date from about 1663,[44] include some jumbled material on legal fees. The reader said that the difference between the counsel and the attorney stood on the same footing as that between the advocate and the proctor in the civil law, and that while attorneys made contracts for their services (their office being " mean and mercenary "), counsel did not make contracts but were given *honoraria*.[45] Since counsellors could bring no action for their fees,

---

[38] *Grand Abridgment*, i. 536: " By *Justice Bridgman*. 7 *Car*. in *Curia de Marches of Wales*." Sheppard cited a number of west country cases in the *Marrow* and the *Abridgment*, which are quite possibly of his own reporting or recollection. He was called in 1629 and, like Bridgman, came from Gloucestershire.

[39] A contract for a contingent fee was held illegal in *Penrice* v. *Parker* (1673) Rep.*t*.Finch 75.

[40] Hutton, *op. cit*., Univ.Lib.Camb.MS.Add. 6863, ff. 84v–85 (1637).

[41] W. Style, *Regestum Practicale or Practical Register* (1657), p. 104: " An action of debt doth lie for a councellor or attorney for his fees against the party that retained them. Mich. 22 Car.B.R. Q. whether it lie for a councellor for his fee is *honorarium quiddam* and not *mercenarium*, a gratuity rather than wages or a salary. By *Rolle* Chief Justice." Same case, *ibid*., p. 152; Sheppard, *Grand Abridgment*, i. 527; J. Lilly, *Practical Register* (1719), i. 401. The case may well be *Evely* v. *Livermore* (Mich.22 Car.B.R.) Aleyn 4.

[42] Brit.Mus.MS.Harg. 491, ff. 1 *et seq*. At f. 23v: " those persons and places that beare a parte in this exercise, the Innes of Chancery where yourselfe and some of these gentlemen have been and other of them in due time may bee worthy readers."

[43] See *Evely* v. *Livermore* (1646) Aleyn 4, *Twisden's Reports*, Brit.Mus.MS.Add. 10619, f. 77v; *Brickwood* v. *Fanshaw* (1690) Carth. 147, 1 Salk. 86, 1 Show.K.B. 96.

[44] At f. 3 the *Judges' Orders* of 14 & 15 Car. 2 are cited, apparently as an addition to the first draft. The latest textbook cited is Wingate's *Maxims* (1658).

[45] *Op. cit*., f. 21: " Le difference inter le councell et le atturney al comon ley estoit sur mesme termes come inter le advocat et le proctor al Civil Ley . . . Le office de atturney est meane et mercenaria et certa et ex contractu tiel que le ley don luy action come al servant pur service chescun term. Mes le councell salaria ex nullo contractu sed ex clientulorum liberalitate tanquam honoraria (come nous appellons presents) advocatis dantur. Et per ceo Ulpian . . ." He then cites *D*.50, 13, 1, 5, *ut supra*, note 25.

their clients made them a present of the fee before they sought counsel, just as any person would who desired a favour of another: " And the common saying is, to take corn, to sell a horse, or to render counsel, cash in hand." [46] The reader also suggested that counsel might have a lien on evidences for his fee.[47] His most interesting statement, perhaps, for it preceded Blackstone by a century, was that counsel, unlike attorneys, were immune from suit for giving wrong advice: " *Un est quasi mechanicall, l'autre scientificall, et le disceit ou misdeam' in l'un est dishonest et actionable, mes le miscariage ou misadvice n'est issint quar touts homes sont subiect al error.*" [48]

The *honorarium* doctrine found general acceptance after this period, but like so many well-known rules of law was not directly put to the test in court. The old case of *Moor* v. *Row* (c. 1630) [49] did not decide the point, as is sometimes supposed, for the court gave judgment for the defendant " *nisi causa* " and no further proceedings are reported.[50] In 1714, Powys J. ruled that if gentlemen of the Bar would not take fees " after the usual manner " (in advance), they ought not to be allowed to recover them in an action at law,[51] and in 1742 Lord Hardwicke refused to allow a barrister to recover his fees in an indirect manner, because they were *quiddam honorarium*.[52] The rule was stated by Blackstone in 1765 [53] and has never since been in doubt.

[46] Ibid., f. 21: " *Et le common disant est frument prender chival vender counsell render deniers in poign.*" (Also quoted at f. 11v.)

[47] Ibid., f. 21: " *Et ieo ay oy que councell ayant evidence peruse pur doner councell sur eux poit detein eux tanques le party ad don luy son fee.*" Accord. Style's *Practical Register* (4th ed), p. 24. This is still not established, but it seems on principle that a lien could not be exercised over papers not actually drafted or worked on by the counsel: *Steadman* v. *Hockley* (1846) 15 M. & W. 553.

[48] Op. cit., f. 21. For the later history of the doctrine, see *Rondel* v. *Worsley* [1967] 1 Q.B. 443; [1967] 3 All E.R. 993 and R. Roxburgh, " Rondel *v.* Worsley: The Historical Background " (1968) 84 L.Q.R. 178; " Rondel *v.* Worsley: Immunity of the Bar," *ibid.* p. 513. Sir Ronald Roxburgh is quite correct to say that the rule was not *established* when Blackstone wrote: *ibid.* p. 181. The older cases where counsel was liable in an action on the case were cases of ambidextry: see cases collected by A. K. R. Kiralfy, *The Action on the Case* (1951), p. 219, and *Syms* v. *Newbury* (1629) Brit.Mus.MS.Add. 35329, f. 23v; Rastell, *op. cit.*, p. 2, *Action sur le case, etc., pl.* 2, 3. The dictum of Popham C.J. in *Brooke* v. *Mountague* (1605) Cro.Jac. 90 was based on a wide interpretation of Paston J. in 14 H.6, 18, *pl.* 58 (see the report in Brit.Mus. MS.Harl. 1679, f. 135), and applied only to a refusal to act.

[49] 1 Cha.Rep. 38.

[50] See 13 C.B.(N.S.) 706–707. The suit was brought against the solicitor, not the lay client, because it was alleged that the solicitor was to account with the counsel at the end of each term.

[51] *Dean's Case* (1714) Viner Abr. *Counsellor* (A) 22.

[52] *Thornhill* v. *Evans* (1742) 2 Atk. 330, 332. *Cf. Stupholm* v. *Hart* (1680) Rep.t.Finch 477; 79 Seld.Soc. 618 (reasonable fee allowed to counsellor's executors).

[53] W. Blackstone, *Commentaries on the Laws of England* (1765), iii. 28.

Counsellors and Barristers

For a long time lawyers distinguished *honoraria* from express retainers: there was no rule absolutely prohibiting a binding contract between counsel and client. The many old cases could not be disregarded, and the precedents of actions brought on retainers *pro consilio* were not expunged from the later books of entries.[54] Thus the presumption that a barrister's services were honorary was a rebuttable presumption. Lilly made this distinction in 1719,[55] and was followed by Wood,[56] Jacob[57] and Mallory[58] shortly afterwards. The special retainer was by this time a dying entity, but it was not until 1863 that it was finally laid to rest by the decision, contrary to the precedents, that counsel was incapable of making a special contract for his services.[59] The presumption thus became a rule of law. Since then, the periodical retainer has even been ruled unethical.[60]

Thus by the adoption of a very ancient distinction between liberal professions and ministerial occupations, the Bar achieved an aura of superiority over attorneys and solicitors[61] which, though fading, has lasted to the present day. As Coleridge said in 1833, the honorary character of the fees of physicians and barristers "contributes to preserve the idea of a profession, of a class which belongs to the public—in the employment and remuneration of which no law interferes, but the citizen acts as he likes *in foro conscientiae*."[62]

---

[54] *e.g.*, J. Hern, *The Pleader* (1657), p. 19; R. Brownlow, *Declarations and Pleadings in English* (1652), p. 112; *Latine Redivivus* (1693), p. 190; J. Mallory, *Modern Entries* (1735), ii. 404.

[55] J. Lilly, *Practical Register* (1719 ed.), i. 401; (1745 ed.), i. 547. He copied Style, *ut supra*, note 41, and added: "but if it be upon a special retainer, I conceive an action will without all doubt lie for a counsellor."

[56] T. Wood, *An Institute of the Laws of England* (1722 ed.), p. 449: "Certainly, if it is upon a special retainer, the action will lie." The passage appears to be based on *Lilly*.

[57] G. Jacob, *A New Law Dictionary* (1729), title "*Barraster*." This is based on *Wood*.

[58] J. Mallory, *Modern Entries* (1735), ii. 269: "An Attorney shall have an Action of Debt for his Fees . . . But *Quaere* of a Counsel. 3 H.6.3. *pl.* 26. 21 H.6.4. *pl.* 6. unless the Contract was made certain by a Promise to pay so much *pro Consilio Impendendo*, 37 Hen. 8."

[59] *Kennedy* v. *Broun* (1863) 13 C.B.(N.S.) 677. This result was not reached in the case of physicians: *Veitch* v. *Russell* (1842) 3 Q.B. 928. Physicians were formerly presumed to attend on an honorary basis, like barristers: *Chorley* v. *Bolcot* (1791) 4 T.R. 317. This presumption became obsolete as a result of legislation: *Gibbon* v. *Budd* (1863) 2 H. & C. 92. But fellows of the Royal College of Physicians are prevented by a by-law from suing for fees.

[60] See *Annual Statement of the Bar Council* (1951), p. 27.

[61] By the 18th century attorneys claimed to be gentlemen by office, but by then barristers claimed to be esquires, *armigeri*, which was a degree higher: *Messor* v. *Molyneux* (1741) cit. 1 Wils. 245.

[62] S. T. Coleridge, *Table Talk* (1836 ed.), p. 189 (January 2, 1833).

NOTE

The foregoing article was prompted by the case of *Rondel* v. *Worsley* [1969] 1 A.C. 191, concerning the legal relationship between barristers and their clients. The modern legal question inevitably led to a more historical question: how did barristers come to acquire a different legal status from solicitors? In trying to answer this, it became apparent just how little was known about the origins of the distinction between barristers and solicitors. The article was perhaps marred by having as its starting point a legal question, and an attempt was made in the article which follows to remedy the defect and fill some gaps. The two should be read in conjunction.

What is said on pp. 110-111 about the ways of pleading legal expertise has been augmented and confirmed by finds in the earlier plea rolls: see pp. 41, 60, and 77, above, for the 15th and earlier 16th centuries. Two yet earlier precedents were found by Sir Matthew Hale: *R.* v. *Hatton* (1354) KB 27/374, Rex m. 35 (Hatton, accused of maintenance, "dicit quod ipse est homo legis et quod erat de consilio... pro suo dando" and is discharged); *Lathebury* v. *Fitzherberd and Foljambe* (1410) KB 27/595, m. 16d (in conspiracy, Thomas Foljambe pleads that he is *apprenticius legis* and was retained as counsel, and as such gave information to the justices which led to the plaintiff's indictment). It seems, therefore, that the more elaborate plea mentioning membership of an inn was devised in the 15th century. The further development mentioning the degree of barrister at law still seems to be late Elizabethan.

The speeches to new serjeants at law (pp. 114-115, 118, 121), which contain numerous statements relating to professional ethics, have now been printed in full in *The Order of Serjeants at Law* (Selden Soc. Supp. Ser. vol. 5, 1984), part III.

Much more work is now being done on the social history of the early-modern bar. See, in particular: W. R. Prest, *The Inns of Court under Elizabeth I and the early Stuarts 1590-1640* (1972); W. C. Richardson, *A History of the Inns of Court* [c.1978]; W. Prest ed., *Lawyers in Early Modern Europe and America* (1981); E. W. Ives, *The Common Lawyers of pre-Reformation England* (1983).

9

SOLICITORS AND THE LAW OF MAINTENANCE 1590-1640

THE surviving image of the Elizabethan and Jacobean solicitor was created for us by the pamphleteers and playmongers, who could be sure of immediate applause or popular sympathy by introducing into their work a few caricatures drawn from the seamier recesses of the legal world. We are encouraged by these writers to imagine a London plagued by these vermin of the law, scurrying in and around the Temple and lurking in the shadows of Westminster Hall, waiting to pounce on the unsuspecting bumpkin who had the misfortune to wander near their reach. Whether and to what extent these portraits bear any relation to reality are questions which social historians have yet to answer. Legal historians have made but a slight contribution to the history of solicitors during the period which, for them, was the most critical of all.[1] To this period may be assigned the beginning of a process of demarcation between the functions of barristers and solicitors, and when we understand how this came about we shall have traced for the first time the origin of the solicitors' branch of the profession.[2]

It will be necessary in tackling these questions to search through classes of material which are unfamiliar to legal historians, and to undertake individual biographical studies covering as wide a range of legal practitioners as is possible. Such investigations are already being undertaken by those who are trained to use information of this kind. But one factor which has been consistently overlooked by previous writers, and which the legal historian is the best equipped to explore, is the attitude of the judges during the critical period before solicitors were fully recognised by the law. It would be idle to pretend that this evidence is impartial, for the judges are known to have been actively involved in the struggle to elevate the social standing of the legal profession by excluding the lower orders.[3] Yet the statements from the

---

[1] E. B. V. Christian, *A Short History of Solicitors* (1896), pp. 70–110 (where he misinterprets the early legal position); *Solicitors: An Outline of their History* (1925), pp. 73 *et seq.* (a survey of contemporary literature); W. S. Holdsworth, " The Solicitors " in *History of English Law*, Vol. VI, pp. 448–457; M. Birks, *Gentlemen of the Law* (1960), p. 98.
[2] An approach to this question was outlined in " Counsellors and Barristers ", above, pp. 108-118.
[3] As to this, see P. Lucas, " Blackstone and the Reform of the Legal Profession " (1962), 77 *English Historical Review* 456; W. R. Prest, *The Inns of Court 1590-1640* (1972), Chap. II.

bench are significant as attempts to formulate in reasoned (and presumably well-informed) terms the objections to the new branch of the profession, and also as a partial explanation for the difficulty which the solicitors experienced in establishing themselves as a profession.

The modern solicitor is an officer of the Supreme Court and his office is regulated by Act of Parliament; he also inherited the character of the attorney when that office was extinguished by the Judicature Acts. But it is necessary to remember that in earlier times solicitors and attorneys were by no means necessarily the same people, and that the names described different activities. Of the two the attorney is much easier to define, at any rate if we take the attorney of the Common Pleas as the archetype. He belonged to a long-established profession which had grown up alongside and apart from that of the serjeant-at-law. He was admitted to practise after an (admittedly somewhat superficial) examination by the judges, sworn to good behaviour, and his name entered on the rolls of the court, whereupon he became an officer or minister of the court and enjoyed the privileges incident to such a position. He was also subject to disciplinary supervision by the court, and for infamous conduct might have his name extracted from the roll and suffer the indignity of being physically " pitched over the bar " into the outside world.[4] His work was different from that of the advocate in that he actually took his client's place in litigation and conducted proceedings in his client's name. He took out process and kept the prothonotaries and other officers properly informed so that all the necessary entries might be made upon the roll. None but a duly constituted attorney might do this—at least in theory—and the names of those who were permitted so to act were enrolled of record. There is, alas, no such clarity with regard to the solicitor. The name originally described not a class of persons but one of the activities which fell within the province of the " apprentice at law." Under the old order, dominated by the Common Pleas, the only important distinction in the profession was that between the advocate (the serjeant-at-law) and the attorney. The other lawyers, whether they were engaged as fully-fledged practitioners in lesser courts or in the country or in chambers, or whether they were still engaged in study, were subject to little if any formal regulation because they did not for legal purposes " represent " their clients and did not regularly (except perhaps on procedural matters) seek the ear

[4] This undignified ceremony is referred to as early as 17 Hen. 8 in a slander case cited by Coke, B.M. MS Lansd. 1076, f. 146. See also *Aldridge & al.* v. *Woolridge & al.* (1597) Hawarde, *Cases in Camera Stellata*, p. 70. There are numerous references to it in the 17th century and it must have been a not infrequent entertainment. The statutes regulating attorneys are listed in the works referred to in n. 1, *supra*.

of the Common Pleas judges *in banc*. The lack of regulation left them, as a class, ill-defined. It may be a fair assumption that most of them were members of the inns of court or chancery, but before 1550 at least their degree within such an inn seems to have been of no significance for public purposes.[5] An apprentice of any degree might advise or represent or solicit the causes of anyone who chose to retain him. Only in the Common Pleas, so far as is known, was he excluded from appearing as an advocate, because the counsel there had been formed into the closed Order of the Coif.[6] He might, if he wished, become an attorney of one of the courts, but it is far from clear whether the acceptance of an attorneyship disabled the holder, except for practical reasons, from accepting any of the other types of business undertaken by apprentices. The name " apprentice " was itself too vague for it to be exclusive of more particular functions.

This situation changed radically in the sixteenth century. Increases in wealth and population brought more law-suits, more law courts, and more lawyers. Since much of the new work came the way of gentlemen not of the coif, this section of the profession achieved a status which demanded professional regulation. The first regulation of which anything is known is contained in a proclamation of 1546, which restricted the privilege of being a pleader in any of the courts at Westminster to readers in court and such others as were appointed by the Lord Chancellor and two Chief Justices with the advice of two benchers from each inn of court.[7] The proclamation is valuable as showing that the right to practise at the bar was not yet associated with the degree of utter barrister, but it was the nearest England came to direct judicial control of the Bar. The proclamation was never printed, the king died soon after it was issued, and it was superseded by another proclamation made in November 1547. The second proclamation recited that:

> always heretofore the utter barristers *and other students* of the four houses of court for the time being have been from time to time admitted and allowed to be pleaders and setters forth of the causes and suits of the king's majesty's highness' subjects, in all and every his courts, the Court of Common Pleas at Westminster only excepted. . . .

---

[5] See above, pp. 109-111; A.W.B. Simpson, "The early Constitution of the Inns of Court" [1970] C.L.J. 241 at pp. 251-253.

[6] The ecclesiastical courts also had an exclusive bar, but they are outside the scope of this article since they were beyond the purview of the statutes of maintenance and in many respects were a law unto themselves: see *Constantine's Case*, n. 52, *infra*; *Tisdall* v. *Bevington*, Noy 68.

[7] P. L. Hughes and J. F. Larkin (ed.), *Tudor Royal Proclamations*, Vol. I (1964), pp. 371-372, no. 270; abstracted in *Letters and Papers of Henry VIII*, Vol. XXI (i), pp. 560-561, no. 1145.

It went on to provide that, previous proclamations notwithstanding, such barristers and students might lawfully " plead and be counsellors and pleaders " provided that they had been members of an inn of court for at least eight years.[8] Still the rights of audience were not limited to barristers *eo nomine*, but were defined in terms of seniority by admittance to an inn. It is, nevertheless, difficult to assess how many men of eight years' standing in the inns would not, in 1547, have been utter-barristers. In 1559 the eight-year period was lengthened to ten years by command of the judges; the new regulation was in the form of an exhortation to the " Utter Barre," which suggests that they were the class primarily affected.[9]

Thus at the beginning of Elizabeth's reign it would not have seemed incongruous (though it was probably unusual) for a fellow of an inn who had not become an utter-barrister to practise at the bar of a court.[10] On the other hand, the regulations against admitting solicitors to the inns did not at this date require the expulsion of members who became solicitors, and there was nothing to prevent a barrister soliciting causes so long as he did not neglect the learning exercises expected of him.[11] In 1574 an Order of the Council was promulgated in the inns of court restricting practice at the Bar to readers, benchers, barristers of five years' standing, and readers in Chancery of two years' standing.[12] By this time it was clearly not contemplated that anyone but barristers or readers should practise at Westminster or at assizes; and the degree of utter-barrister had come to be recognised by law as a " degree of learning in the common laws." [13] These orders were domestic regulations which reflected the standards which had come to be accepted, but which probably did not have any legal force. The first public regulations were the orders of court requiring the signature of counsel to special pleas; these were promulgated in Michaelmas Term 1573,[14] but unfortunately no attempt was made to define " counsel " for the purpose. The most important development

---

[8] *Tudor Royal Proclamations*, pp. 408–409, no. 294. I am indebted to Dr. W. R. Prest for drawing my attention to these proclamations.
[9] *Black Books of Lincoln's Inn*, Vol. I (1897), p. 328; W. Dugdale, *Origines Juridiciales* (1680 ed.), p. 311.
[10] Thus a fellow of an inn could justify maintenance without showing that he had been called to the bar: W. Rastell, *Collection of Entrees* (1596 ed.), p. 432, *Maintenance pl.* 18.
[11] See the orders issued in 1555 and 1574; *Black Books*, Vol. I, pp. 315, 391; J. B. Williamson, *History of the Temple* (1924), pp. 157, 226; *Calendar of Inner Temple Records*, Vol. I (1896), p. 277; *Middle Temple Records*, Vol. I (1904), p. 200; *Acts of the Privy Council*, Vol. VIII (1894), p. 246; Dugdale, *op. cit.* p. 312.
[12] Order cited in last note. This was renewed in 1584: *Pension Book of Gray's Inn*, Vol. I (1901), p. 62.
[13] 5 Eliz. 1, c. 1, s. 4; Stat.Reg. iv, 403.
[14] See M. Hastings, *The Court of Common Pleas in 15th Century England* (1947), p. 114. Dr. W. H. Bryson informs me that the Exchequer Order is of the same date.

of all, however, was the limitation of the right to practise at the Bar, for the purposes of the law of maintenance, to utter-barristers. This was completed in the important case [15] of *Broughton* v. *Prince* in 1590.

Richard Prince's case

Richard Prince (or Prynce), the son of a Shrewsbury shoemaker,[16] was specially admitted to the Inner Temple in April 1554 at the instance of the Lent Reader, William Symmonds.[17] He spent six or seven years in residence,[18] but was never called to the bar. On his return to Wales he became clerk to a Mr. Aylesbury and also a " counsel at the Barre " in the Council in the Marches of Wales.[19] By 1562 he was also feodary of Shropshire.[20] His legal ability must have been considerable, for he built up a large practice and his success enabled the Prince family to become established among the principal gentry of the county. In 1578 he built a magnificent house in the Abbey Foregate, Shrewsbury, which excited the admiration of contemporaries [21]; and in 1584 he took out a grant of arms.[22] Two of his sons were knighted; one of them, also a lawyer, became sheriff of Shropshire.[23] Richard Prince died in 1598 and was buried in the Abbey church, Shrewsbury.[24]

Prince's generation included the last few " apprentices at law " (in the old sense) who had earned their fortune at the Bar without

[15] In chapter 8 above, p. 111, I said this case was obscure and not very informative. Now that the case is not quite as obscure, I have reversed this opinion.
[16] *Shrewsbury Burgess Roll* (H. E. Forrest, ed., 1924), p. 244, records Richard's admission as a burgess in 1551 by the description of " scholar," son of John Prynce " corvisor." " Scholar " is a misleading translation of *literatus*, which rather suggests self-education. Richard does not appear to have attended either university.
[17] *Calendar of Inner Temple Records*, Vol. I (1896), p. 173. In a manuscript article on the Prynce family by H. E. Forrest (Shropshire Record Office MS 224/6) it is stated (p. 19) that Richard was called to the bar in 1554; but this is obviously a misunderstanding of the special admittance. Forrest had little to say about Richard's legal career. I am indebted to Miss Mary Hill, County Archivist of Shropshire, for bringing this article to my attention.
[18] According to his plea in *Broughton* v. *Prince* (*infra*), he stayed in the Inner Temple from 1 Mary 1 (1554) until 3 Eliz. 1 (1560–1561).
[19] T. F. Dukes, *Antiquities of Shropshire* (1844), p. 296, notes in a Council suit of 1563: " Richard Prince of Foriat Monacher (Abbey Foregate, Shrewsbury) examined as to the conveyances he had drawn: he is styled ' counsel at the Barre ' in the court of the Marches: he had been clerk to Mr. Aylesbury when he drew this conveyance."
[20] *Calendar of Patent Rolls 1560–1563* (1948), p. 449.
[21] See T. Churchyard, *The Worthines of Wales* (1587), sig. K3 (Spenser Society facsimile reprint, 1876); MS Chronicle of Shrewsbury, cited in H. Owen and J. B. Blakeway, *A History of Shrewsbury* (1825), Vol. I, p. 562. The house is now called the Whitehall, and is used for local government offices.
[22] *The Visitation of Shropshire 1623, Part II* (Harleian Society, 1889), p. 409.
[23] J. B. Blakeway, *The Sheriffs of Shropshire* (1831), p. 109.
[24] Abbey Register, October 5th, cited in H. E. Forrest's MS at p. 27.

possessing the degree of utter-barrister.[25] He may have been typical of the practitioners of a former age, but by the middle of Elizabeth's reign his kind was becoming anomalous. It is uncertain whether the provincial courts were less strict than the royal courts in controlling those who practised before them, although numerous complaints were made about the behaviour of the counsellors-at-the-bar in the Marches.[26] As it happens, we know more about the process of regulation in the Marches than we know about developments at Westminster, because the Council there (unlike the central royal courts) was controlled by written instructions of which numerous copies survive. These instructions perhaps codify for the provinces rules which had already been unofficially formulated at Westminster, or they may represent an experiment which preceded central regulation; the dates suggest, however, that there were more or less contemporaneous measures both in Westminster Hall and in the provinces. The first regulation for the Marches was made in 1570, when it was ordered that:

> the said Lord President and Council shall not admit any person to plead any matter at the bar, nor to subscribe any bill of pleading as counsellor learned in the law, except the same be first known and allowed as an utter-barrister of the inns of court. . . .
> Provided nevertheless, that if at this present there be some few that be pleaders there, and be not utter-barristers, the same being of good experience and honest behaviour shall be suffered to remain by special allowance of the Council, so as from henceforth none be hereafter admitted but of the quality of an utter-barrister.[27]

In 1575 a suggestion was made for tightening this rule further, to bring it into line (presumably) with the 1574 orders of the Council, by imposing a minimum qualification of five years' standing as an utter-barrister.[28] In the ensuing instructions for the Marches there was no express saving for non-barristers such as Prince, and as a result Prince

---

[25] A second example is David Baker of the Inner Temple, who described himself as a solicitor but seems to have practised as a counsellor before taking the monastic habit in 1605: see *Memorials of Father Augustine Baker O.B.* (J. McCann and H. Connolly, ed., 1933), pp. 67, 71. Another is Richard Broughton of the Inner Temple (*infra*), who eventually became a Welsh judge.

[26] See P. Williams, *The Council in the Marches of Wales* (1958), p. 173. Most of the instructions referred to below are cited, but not quoted, in Dr. Williams' valuable monograph.

[27] Historical Manuscripts Commission, *Report on the MSS of Lord De L'Isle and Dudley*, Vol. I (1925), p. 334 (and p. 351, paraphrased); R. Flenley (ed.), *A Calendar of the Register of the Council in Wales and the Marches 1569–1591* (1916), p. 81 (a paraphrase of Bodl.MS 904, f. 29v). The quotation is from the 1574 reissue, printed in R. H. C[live], *Documents connected with the History of Ludlow* (1841), pp. 323–324.

[28] William Gerard, " Discourse on the Council in the Marches " (1575), printed in 13 *Y Cymmrodor* (1900), p. 137 at p. 157; Clive, *op. cit.* p. 342. See also the 1579 instructions: B.M. MS Eg. 2882, f. 25, and Cotton MS Vitell. C. i, f. 58v.

seems to have been temporarily displaced.[29] In 1577, however, he was restored by order of the Privy Council.[30]

In 1586 fresh instructions were drawn up for the Council in the Marches. These contained the clause:

> And further her Majesty being informed that presently there be a number of discreet persons learned in the laws of this realm who for divers years past have practised in that court as counsellors at the bar, and now the most part of them being well stepped into years and using little practice in other courts, it seemeth inconvenient that every man towards the law should be permitted at his pleasure to come to the court to use practice to the hindrance of such as have had so long continuance in the service of the Court, her Majesty doth therefore appoint that the said Lord President and Council shall not from henceforth permit above the number of eight persons to be counsellors at the bar in that Court. And none to be so allowed except he be *qualified with the degree of an utter-barrister.* Provided nevertheless that *Richard Prince* in respect of his long service in the Court *and her Majesty's special licence* shall be continued according to her Highness' said licence. And the rest that now exceed the number of eight of usual practisers there, being of long continuance, to be likewise tolerated.[31]

Four years later the maximum permissible number of counsellors was increased to ten, " whereof the said Richard Prince to be one." [32]

The fact that Prince was not a barrister of his inn does not, therefore, seem to have cost him any business in the Marches, but it was to be a fact of some moment in the history of the profession. In the 1580s he became involved in a quarrel with Richard Broughton, another Shropshire member of the Inner Temple who acquired a comfortable practice at the bar without being an utter-barrister.[33] The outcome of the squabble was that Broughton in 1589 preferred three bills of *quominus* against Prince in the Exchequer of Pleas. The first was an action for having libelled the plaintiff (for subtraction of tithes) out of the diocese where the plaintiff resided. The second was an action of trespass *quare clausum fregit* at Hurdley, Montgomeryshire. And the third, reciting the statute of maintenance, declared that Prince had maintained a suit brought by Rhys (*Riceus*) Forde against the plaintiff before the President and Council in the Marches of Wales

---

[29] Williams, *op. cit.* pp. 173-174, citing Clive, *op. cit.* p. 349, and Gerard's report (12 *Y Cymmrodor* 55). Both references seem rather to refer to John Price, Queen's Attorney in the Marches. But see the next note.

[30] *Acts of the Privy Council 1575-1577* (J. B. Dasent, ed., 1894), p. 379.

[31] Instruction no. 17: B.M. MS Lansd. 49, ff. 200v, 211v; MS Eg. 2882, f. 3v; Cotton MS Vitell. C. i, f. 88. (Orthography modernised, emphasis added.)

[32] " Dyreccons to the Clerk of the Counsaill in the Marches of Wales " (1590) B.M. MS Lansd. 63, f. 94.

[33] For a short biography see W. R. Williams, *History of the Great Sessions in Wales 1542-1830* (1899), p. 90. Broughton later became Vice-Justice of Chester; he died in 1604.

at Hurdley in June 1586.³⁴ To this last action Prince later pleaded a justification. Relying, it would seem, on the precedent in *Rastell*,³⁵ Prince said that:

> diu ante predictum tempus quo supponitur levacio querele predicte fieri, scilicet in anno primo regni Domine Marie nuper Regine Anglie, ipse idem Ricardus Prynce fuit unus sociorum hospicii de Interiori Templo London' in parochia sancti Dunstani in le West in Warda de Faringdon extra, quod quidem hospicium est, et a tempore cuius contrarii memoria non existit fuit, quoddam hospicium hominum de curia legis temporalis et hominum consiliariorum legis predicte; Idemque Ricardus a predicto anno primo dicte nuper Regine Marie usque in annum domine Regine nunc tercium in hospicio illo moram suam traxit ac leges temporales predictas per idem tempus studebat; Quodque ipse tempore manutencionis predicte fuit et adhuc est homo consiliarius et in lege predicta eruditus. . . .

and as such was retained by Rhys Forde at Ludlow, and by virtue of that retainer he was of counsel in the said matter. This plea the plaintiff traversed, following closely the printed precedent:

> Et predictus Ricardus Broughton dicit quod ipse per aliqua preallegata ab accione sua predicta habenda precludi non debet, quia dicit quod tempore manutencionis predicte predictus Ricardus Prince fuit laicus homo et non homo consiliarius in lege predicta eruditus prout predictus Ricardus Prince superius allegavit. Et hoc petit quod inquiratur per patriam.³⁶

Precisely what happened next is unclear, because the only contemporary report so far discovered is difficult to reconcile with the record. According to the report in Leonard's collection,³⁷ Broughton (apparently in person) submitted that Prince had joined issue on this replication and that there could be no further legal discussion until the verdict had been given. But Atkinson, a barrister of the Inner Temple appearing for Prince, sought to offer several points of law " now to the jury." The report then goes on to say that unless Prince would demur to the replication, the issue would proceed to trial. Evidently Prince wished to avoid a trial, and so he demurred. Whether this indicates that he was allowed to retract his acceptance of the issue, or whether issue had not in fact been joined, perhaps does not matter too much; at any rate, the record only reveals the demurrer.

The main ground of Prince's demurrer to the replication was that it should not have concluded *per patriam*:

---

[34] *Placita de Scaccario*, Trin. 31 Eliz. 1 (E. 13/373), m. 25. All the entries end with imparlances. For yet another action, a prohibition, noted in Hilary Term 1590, see B.M. MS Harl. 1633, f. 78.
[35] *Collection of Entrees* (1596 ed.), p. 432, *Maintenance pl.* 18. (First edition 1566.)
[36] *Placita de Scaccario*, Mich. 32 & 33 Eliz. (E. 13/378), m. 4. (Punctuation added.) [37] 3 Leo. 237.

Solicitors and the Law of Maintenance 1590-1640   133

for that cannot be tryed by the country, but by the judges: for here is a question of the learning of the defendant, and that is to be tryed: and his sufficiency in this learning is to be discerned by those who are skilful in the laws of the land; for if a matter of law is to be tryed by the judges, *a multo fortiori*, the learning of the law is to be tryed by them; for that is more difficult to be judged.

Prince may well have felt qualms about submitting his qualifications to a common jury; but his demurrer might be interpreted as a tactical manoeuvre, designed to ensure that Prince's professional status was not impeached. For, if the demurrer succeeded, there would presumably be no enquiry by the judges; and if it failed, there would be no trial of the issue by jury. A demurrer in law precluded any issue of fact. But the decision would determine the course of future actions of this kind. Whether a jury in the Year Book period had ever been required to try a lawyer's learning is not recorded, but if Prince lost his demurrer such a task might well in subsequent cases fall to twelve Elizabethan laymen.

The record of the case does not contain any judgment, and it may be that none was given. But Manwood C.B. is reported as having said that the issue could be tried by the country.[38] The printed report—not printed, incidentally, until 1663—does not enlarge upon this statement. It is almost certain, however, that there had been some discussion as to the way such a question could be put to a jury. It is hardly credible that Manwood C.B. really expected laymen to subject lawyers to some kind of examination to find out if they were *in lege periti*. They could only be expected to enquire into known facts, such as whether the lawyer had been called to the bar by the benchers of his inn. This, it is submitted, was the import of the case for contemporaries. Perhaps Manwood C.B. had gone so far as to say that lawyers who wished in future to plead their qualification to practise would have to allege some issuable fact such as call to the bar. That was certainly how the decision was remembered when it was vouched in 1599: " he should have said that he was called to the bar, *etc.*, and so learned in the law, so that issue might be taken here upon the calling to the bar." [39] This interpretation was later corroborated by Sir William Jones,[40] who was

---

[38] *Ibid.* p. 238. *Cf.* the recollection of the case in *Clegatt* v. *Hammersly* (1636) B.M. MS Harl. 1330, f. 47: " *Tr. 33 Eliz. en lexchequer Broughton et Princes case. Traverse, non consiliarius neque lege peritus, cest bon ple et issuable.*"

[39] *Lane* v. *Cotton* (1599) Univ.Coll.Lond. MS Ogden 29, f. 337 (translated). *Cf.* Owen 128; B.M. MS Harg. 12, f. 153v; Bodl.Lib. MS Rawl. C. 728, f. 28v (" *il duist aver allege que il fuit student per certeine temps et come il fuit elect per le Benchers destre un Barrister* "); Cro.Eliz. 728 (" he ought to have pleaded, that he had been a student in such an inn of court, and called to be an utter barrister.")

[40] *Carye's Case* (1626) Poph. 207, *per* Jones J.: " in maintenance against [*sic*] Broughton it came in question upon evidence to a jury [*sic*] whether one who is [not] a Barrister may give advice, and it was ruled that he could not, albeit he had Letters Patent to inable him as fully as if he had been called to the Bar." This garbled version makes no sense without the " not."

a member of Lincoln's Inn when the case was heard, and by William Hudson.[41]

Jones and Hudson both confuse the story by introducing the remarkable assertion that Prince had been granted by letters patent the privilege of pleading at the bar.[42] There is no mention of such a unique privilege [43] in the pleadings, and search in the indices to the patent rolls has uncovered no trace of such a grant. Maybe there was a patent which was not enrolled, but more likely there was a misunderstanding of the " special licence " referred to in the instructions of 1586. Whether or not there was a patent does not affect the decision in *Broughton* v. *Prince* because no special privilege was pleaded and so it could not come into issue.

That the profession understood the decision to mean that the degree of barrister was an essential qualification for practise at the bar may be inferred from the change in the form of declaration for slandering a counsellor in his profession. Until 1590 the barrister plaintiff had said nothing of his degree, but had used the customary formula that he was *in lege terre eruditus* and as such was retained by many clients, and so on. After 1590 it was regarded as essential to plead specifically that the plaintiff had been a member of an inn of court and had then been called to the bar and (where appropriate) to the bench of that inn.[44] The first reported case in the new form was *Heale* v. *Giddye* in 1591, after which it became standard practice.[45] A few precedents of the earlier form persisted after 1591, which must

[41] *Treatise on the Star Chamber*, printed (from MS Harl. 1226) in F. Hargrave (ed.), *Collectanea Juridica* (1792), Vol. II, p. 94. Hudson was not admitted to Gray's Inn until 1601.

[42] *Loc. cit.* in last two notes. From Jones' remark it might be thought that the letters patent were put in a hypothetical case during argument, but Hudson specifically states that Prince was "the only man in his age that was allowed to practise at the bar by letters patent under the broad seal, and never called to [the bar of ?] any inn of court, which I suppose was a reason of the traverse." In J. Manning, *Serviens ad Legem* (1840), p. 279, is an extract from B.M. MS Harl. 980 concerning a "Mr. Finch of Shrewsbury" who had a similar right; but this is merely an error for "Prince." Prince's name occurs as "Finch" in several manuscript versions of Hudson's text: e.g. Camb.Univ.Lib. MS Add. 3106, ff. 45v–46.

[43] A similar right seems to be referred to in W. H. Turner (ed.), *Calendar of Charters and Rolls preserved in the Bodleian Library* (1878), p. 153, summarising Middlesex Ch. 42, as granting to John Greene, Recorder of London (1659), the privilege and freedom of practising at the bars of the courts of Westminster. In fact the privilege was that of practising *within* the bars, Greene being already a bencher of Lincoln's Inn.

[44] See above, chapter 8, p. 111. Further cases are *Hugh Hare* (I.T.) v. *Browne* (1586) B.M. MS Lansd. 1076, f. 146, MS Harl. 1624, f. 159v; *Stone* v. *Mounford* (1587) MS Lansd. 1076, f. 125; *Nicholas Vaus* (M.T.) v. *Serle* (1589) MS Harl. 664, f. 36; *Nicholas Kinnersley* (I.T.) v. *Coper* (c. 1589) Camb.Univ.Lib., MS Gg. v. 4, f. 119v.

[45] See above, ch. 8, pp. 111-112. (The fact was observed before the significance of the date was appreciated.) Further cases are *Nethersall's Case* (1596) B.M. MS Add. 25232, f. 26; *Cuthbert Reynold's* Case (I.T.) (1597) MS Harl. 4552, f. 131v; *Preston's Case* (1627) Noy 98; *Nurse* (G.I.) v. *Pounford* (1631) Hetley 161.

be ascribed either to ignorance of the reason for the change, or to the inability of the plaintiffs to meet the new requirement.[46] But when in 1637 Andrew Burton of Gray's Inn brought an action for defamation as "*vir eruditus in legibus Anglie*" the judgment was arrested because:

> it is not slander in his profession, for it does not appear that he is a lawyer authorised to give counsel and to profess it; for *eruditus in lege* does not import that he has authority to give counsel, for everyone must be cognisant of the law *quia ignorantia legis non excusat* [!]; but he must lay that he was of the inns of court, and for his learning and honesty called to the bar to profess according to the orders of the house.[47]

Another reason was that " he must by statute be sworn, and there are many learned in the law who may not practise." [48]

The legal status of solicitors after 1590

The nebulous class of apprentices of the law, of *legis periti*, had been too vaguely defined to permit of regulation through the law of maintenance. If a closer definition were required, it was a natural consequence of the developments of the previous three or four decades that the new qualification should have been linked to a degree in the inns of court. But the effect of the development was to split apprentices into two distinct groups: the barristers and attorneys, and the rest. Intentionally or otherwise, the decision of 1590, or at least the reasoning believed to have accompanied it, disabled from practice in litigation the man who was neither a barrister nor an attorney. This was soon seized upon by the judges and the senior members of the inns as a new means of curtailing the rise of the inferior ranks of legal practitioners. Maintenance was a criminal offence and an actionable wrong, and it was an offence easily committed by anyone who meddled without justification in litigation: for instance, by paying fees to counsel.[49]

---

[46] E.g. *Nicholas Halsequell* ("*unus sociorum interioris Templi . . . in lege terre valde eruditus*") v. *Valance* (1592) MS Harl. 664, f. 37. No such name is to be found in the *Calendar of Inner Temple Records*, nor in *Students Admitted to the Inner Temple 1547–1660* (1877).

[47] Univ.Lib.Camb., MS Ii. v. 23, f. 220. (translated).

[48] Univ.Lib.Camb., MS Gg. ii. 20, ff. 1117v–1118, per Jones and Berkley JJ. (translated). The oath of allegiance was required by the 5 Eliz. 1, c. 1, s. 4, to be taken by all " persons that have taken or hereafter shall take any Degree of Learning in or at the Common Lawes of this Realme, aswell utter Barresters as Benchers Readers Auncientes in any Howse or Howses of Courts." *Quaere* whether the oath was necessary for an advocate without such a degree; the statement seems to assume that call to the bar was an indispensable prerequisite to practice, which by 1637 it no doubt was.

[49] See *Pomeroy* v. *Abbot of Buckfast* (1442) M. 21 Hen. 16, 15, pl. 30; *Horne's Case* (1456) H. 34 Hen. 6, 26, *pl.* 3; *Anon.* (1479) M. 19 Edw. 4, 3, *pl.* 9; *Anon.* (1515) *Spilman's Reports*, copy in MS Harg. 388, f. 25; *Anon.* (1549) Moo. 6, *pl.* 20. An exception was made where the person paying the fees used money which he owed to the party. *Cf. John Doket's Case* (1454)) H. 32 Hen. 6, 24, *pl.* 11.

The majority of the members of the inns of court and chancery in the period 1590–1640 were below the degree of utter-barrister. Indeed, of all those admitted to the inns of *court* in this period, only about one in six was called to the bar; and in Gray's Inn the barristers were outnumbered ten to one.[50] In the inns of chancery there were, by definition, no utter-barristers " in court " who were qualified for practice. But the undergraduate majority of the inns of court were by no means equivalent to the young students of today. Many were gentlemen finishing their general education, men who had no intention of earning a living from the law or of continuing long enough in residence to qualify for call to the bar. There were others who professed the law but could not, for reasons of conscience, take the oath of allegiance required by statute upon call to the bar or bench of an inn. Many more, however, were the less fortunate practising lawyers who lacked the influence or the ability to attain the degree of barrister. For, although the population of the inns steadily increased until the last decade of the period under review, the benchers were persuaded by the Council to endeavour to limit the number of calls each year to a number well below the number of qualified applicants for call. Had the policy emanated from the inns, one might have inferred that the benchers—like the old practitioners at Ludlow—had begun to fear the competition of younger men. The reasons behind the policy were more likely a genuine belief that more would mean worse, and a sense of uneasiness at the prospect of too much social mobility.[51] Whatever the motive, and however reluctantly and weakly the policy may have been pursued, otherwise deserving candidates must have been thereby prevented from acquiring the qualification which was coming to be insisted upon for practice as counsellors at the bar. The unfortunates had longer to wait, and less to do while waiting. Some of them might become attorneys or clerks in the courts, and as such they could justify assisting litigants within the sphere of practice to which their office qualified them. But if they prosecuted causes in other courts, they were in no better position than laymen[52]; and by becoming attorneys they might well diminish or lose their prospects of call to the bar. *A fortiori* those who did not become attorneys were not entitled to be regarded as qualified lawyers, and it no longer made any difference that they were fellows of an inn. Since

[50] W. R. Prest, *The Inns of Court 1590–1640* (1972), p. 52.
[51] *Ibid.* Chaps. I–III; Lucas, *op. cit.* in n. 1, *supra*.
[52] *Lord Lincoln's Case (temp.* Eliz. 1), cited in following: *Constantine* v. *Barnes* (1595) Rolle Abr., Vol. II, p. 114, line 44, *Maintenance* (E. 4), also reported in Univ.Lib.Camb. MS Ee. iii. 2, f. 55v, and cited in Noy 68; *Germyn* v. *Rolls* (1596), *infra*. Many of the cases concerning "solicitors" involved attorneys retained to solicit causes in other courts.

Solicitors and the Law of Maintenance 1590-1640   137

it was not difficult to become an attorney,[53] those who did not do so may be presumed to have been either wholly without merit or substance,[54] or (more likely) were biding their time until they could be called. It may be that this latter class formed a considerable proportion of the solicitors; we do not yet know. It is a reasonable possibility that if such men lacked private means they would wish to engage in those aspects of legal practice which did not involve advocacy in court: for instance, advising clients, drawing documents, and instructing counsel. In the earliest reference to solicitors in the law reports, it seems to be assumed that they were "*apprise en ley*."[55] The same assumption seems to underlie the statement in a treatise on the courts which was written in the 1580s:

> solicitors are or should be learned in the lawes of the Realme, who being rightly instructed of the suitors cause do more skilfully enforme the serieants and Counsellors at Lawe in the same.[56]

Although the passage distinguishes solicitors and counsellors, it assigns to solicitors functions more appropriate to men learned in the law than to ministerial officers such as attorneys. Nevertheless, a solicitor of the type which has just been postulated was unqualified and as such inferior in status to the members of the Bar. Already by 1594 it could be seriously argued that it was an actionable slander to say of a counsellor (presumably an utter-barrister) that he was an attorney or a solicitor.[57] Moreover, the unqualified class would include the dishonest and the dim-witted as well as the meritorious candidate for call whose only disqualification was lack of means or friends. It was the absence of regulation and definition which opened the whole class to abuse and attack; and, although in the debates which follow it may well be important to establish the type of "solicitor" under discussion, the debates themselves do little to distinguish one type from another.

Before the 1590s the law had not objected strenuously to solicitors. According to Serjeant Keble, they were allowed to disburse money for their clients,[58] and their expenses and disbursements were later held

---

[53] The total number of attorneys of the Common Bench is said to have risen from 313 in 1578 to 1,383 in 1633: E. B. V. Christian, *Solicitors: An Outline of their History* (1925), pp. 114–115.

[54] *Cf.* T. M., *The Sollicitor* (1662 ed.), pp. 22–23; "every idle fellow, whose prodigality and ill husbandry hath forced him out of his Trade or Employment, takes upon him to be a sollicitor."

[55] P. 5 Hen. 7, 20, *pl.* 1, *per* Keble serjeant.

[56] 83 Camd.Soc. (3rd ser.), p. 2 *Cf.* the slightly different version printed as an addendum to T. Smith, *De Republica Anglorum* (1906 ed.), p. 153. *Cf.* also H. Spelman, *Glossarium Archaiologicum* (1687 ed.), p. 518.

[57] *Brooke* v. *Harrald* (1594) Univ.Lib.Camb., MS Ll. iii. 9, f. 412v, *per* Hele serjeant. The contention was unsuccessful.

[58] Note 55, *supra*.

to be recoverable in *assumpsit*.[59] Rastell's *Entrees* also contained a precedent for an action to recover fees by an attorney retained *ad solicitandum*.[60] In 1577 a member of Gray's Inn sued the Countess of Kent on a promise to pay the expenses he had incurred in attending, at her request, to "*diversa negotia, sectas, et querelas dependentia*" before her marriage with the Earl in 1574. The objection that the consideration was unlawful, being maintenance in the plaintiff, was overruled on the ground that "*negotia, sectas et querelas dependentia*" did not necessarily imply suits depending in a court of law.[61] But Dyer C.J. made it clear that "if the word had been dependent *in aliqua curia vel in lege*, then it had been clearly maintenance and the consideration void."[62] It was further laid down in 1580 that to be a solicitor was a lawful consideration to maintain *assumpsit*, so long as there was no maintenance and that no money was laid out for maintenance.[63] No contemporary report of the decision has been found, but the record[64] shows that the plaintiff was probably not an attorney—his only addition is *generosus*—and that the consideration for the defendant's promise was that the plaintiff had, at the defendant's special instance and request, solicited two specified actions of trespass in the King's Bench "*pro esiamento utilitate et comoditate predicti Johannis* [the defendant]." Thus the case fell within Dyer's condition, in so far as the soliciting was in a court of law; but it was not a case of a general retainer to solicit. The plaintiff had been specially retained to solicit two cases at the request of the promisor, and there was no suggestion that the sum promised was a reimbursement of money laid out. The decisions of 1577 and 1580 were both later relied on by the solicitors, but the first did not take the matter very far—indeed the reasoning worked against the solicitors—and the second avoided the two most controversial questions of the soliciting of counsel and the retainer of a "general" solicitor. Both these questions were discussed by the Court of King's Bench in 1596.

Germyn, an attorney of the Common Pleas, recovered in an action of debt in that court against Rolls, the executor of his client, moneys

---

[59] *Fisher and Browne* v. *Sadler* (1589) B.M. MS Harl. 4562, f. 104v. Contra: *Anon.* (c. 1600) ibid. folio ultima.
[60] *Collection of Entrees* (1596 ed.), f. 202v.
[61] *Edward Onley's Case*, Dyer 355, 356. The pleadings are printed in Old Benloes 297, pl. 292, citing T. 18 Eliz. rot. 934. In 1506 a jilted fiancé recovered his expenses in soliciting the law-suits of his betrothed: *Lewes* v. *Style*, K.B. 27/979, m. 71v.
[62] Exeter College, Oxford, MS 119, f. 73 at f. 77. This report is superior to that in Dyer. A third good report may be found in W. Shuger's Collection, Gray's Inn MS 27, ff. 101–104, taken (apparently) from the book of "Ashton."
[63] *Worthington* v. *Garstone* (1580) collected in Hob. 67, and noted in Rolle Abr., Vol. I, p. 17, lines 14–20, Cf. *Anon.* (1580) cited in Cro.Eliz. 760.
[64] *William Worthington* v. *John Garsten*, clerk (1580), Coram Rege Mich. 22 & 23 Eliz. 1. K.B. 27/1275, m. 378. The declaration is lengthened by the allegation of a forbearance to sue, the main contract being laid in the preter tense.

disbursed by him in suing a licence of alienation in the Chancery. The judgment was removed before the King's Bench on a writ of error, and the main ground for the proceedings in error was that debt was an inappropriate form of action against executors. It was arguable that debt lay against executors for attorneys' fees, since the attorney was compellable by law to execute his office for his fee, and therefore wager of law was not available to the defendant. But an attorney was not compellable to solicit cases in other courts, and it was arguable that it was maintenance for him to do so. Popham C.J. seems to have first raised this latter point, on the argument in Hilary Term:

> There is another matter in this case which troubles me, for he demands 3s. 4d. for suing a licence of alienation in the Chancery upon recovery in the Common Bench, and so he demands part of the debt as solicitor. And it seems to me that debt does not lie for a solicitor, for the law does not take any regard or notice of such people....[65]
>
> If a solicitor disburse money without special warrant about the cause of his client, no action lies for [*i.e.* to recover] this, because it was agreed that solicitors are unnecessary in the common wealth and make confusion in the law. So, if an attorney disburse money for counsellors' fees, no action lies, because he is not compellable to disburse, since although the cause should go against his client for default of counsel by reason of the not disbursing, the attorney is excused....[66]

This seems at first sight a rather draconian point of view, since the client would be left without adequate means of securing representation. But the essence of the objection lay in the phrase "without special warrant", as Popham C.J. himself explained:

> If one retains J. S. to solicit such a cause in this Court, or in the Chancery, and he in the same cause retains counsel and disburses money therefor, the solicitor exceeds his authority and therefore his client is not bound by the law to repay this. It is otherwise if the solicitor has a special commandment to lay out money. And I know that by such means counsellors as well as clients are notably abused....[67]

If the reason for the distinction still eludes us, the clue is perhaps to be found in the last sentence. A major complaint was that solicitors surprised their clients with bills they had never anticipated: a genuine case of an agent exceeding his authority. The point was more explicitly made in Easter Term, when the case was fully reargued:

---

[65] Sir John Neale's MS (now in Univ.Coll. London), f. 85 (translated). A slightly abridged copy is B.M. MS Harl. 4552, f. 43v. The point is briefly reported in Cro. Eliz. 459.

[66] Univ.Lib.Camb. MS Gg. vi. 29, f. 113v (translated).

[67] *Were's Reports*, MS Harg. 7, Part II, f. 159 (translated); also in Lincoln's Inn MS Misc. 490, f. 600.

> This disbursing of moneys by the solicitors and attorneys spoils the practice of the law, for by such means the counsellor is defrauded and the subject charged. And the benefit redounds solely to the solicitors, for they will make large bills of charges to the client of fees for serjeants and counsellors, *when they owe few or none.* And therefore it is not reason to give them actions for such expenses, but for their own fees where they are compellable to serve.[68]

It seems rather hard to deny a remedy to honest solicitors because others were rogues, but in fact the question which so troubled Popham C.J.—while explaining his attitude to solicitors—was not directly in issue in *Germyn's Case*, because the money had not been disbursed to counsel.

On the main issue, Fenner J. ventured to suggest that "an attorney of one court may follow causes in other courts, and it is neither unlawful nor maintenance (otherwise of a solicitor); and by consequence debt lies for his fees in other courts."[69] Popham C.J., however, denied that the office of attorney protected its holder from the sin of being a solicitor: "an attorney in one court is nothing but a solicitor in other courts," and "a solicitor deserves no favour."[70] Gawdy J. intervened with the suggestion that although an attorney could not bring debt for his fees in another court, yet it was not unlawful for him to follow causes there. Popham C.J. would not even accept this compromise, replying, "I doubt that, because in another court he is nothing but a common solicitor of causes, *quod est omnium genus hominum pessimum.*"[71] Judgment was therefore reversed. It might well be argued that the narrow ground for the decision was simply that debt only lay for an attorney against executors in respect of situations in which he was compellable by law to act, and that soliciting causes was obviously not such a situation. But the legal world could not help but notice how the judges "all inveighed greatly against solicitors."[72] "This," concluded Fenner J., "is a bad precedent for solicitors."[73]

The King's Bench was not the only source of bad precedents for solicitors. In the same term as these pronouncements were made, a solicitor was severely punished for *scandalum magnatum*, and the new

---

[68] *Were's Reports*, f. 186v (translated and emphasis added); Lincoln's Inn MS Misc. 490, f. 677v.
[69] Univ.Lib.Camb., MS Gg. vi. 29, f. 115v. (translated).
[70] *Ibid.* (translated). *Cf. ibid.*, f. 114v (*Trussell* v. *Mounslowe*), in which the defendant was a solicitor, and the court could not forbear to observe that "solicitor ... is not a profession or place tolerable in law, and by consequence [it is] maintenance in him."
[71] *Ibid.* (translated).
[72] MS Harl. 4552, f. 43v (translated).
[73] MS Harg. 7, Part II, f. 186v; Lincoln's Inn MS Misc. 490, f. 677v (translated). A wise suggestion is made in this report that the solicitor could avoid the legal difficulty by taking his money in advance.

Lord Keeper (Egerton)—who thought the punishment was too lenient —took advantage of the occasion to deliver "his conceit for solicitors":

> He had not learned any lawe to allowe or to warrant them, and they are caterpillars of the common weal. And maintenance would lie against them. For at all times the laws and Acts of Parliament give authority in cases necessary to make attornies, and therefore solicitors are not warrantable by any law, and therefore they should be punished and a remedy should be provided against them. And he promised that he would advise as to punishment against them, and to abolish and extirpate all solicitors.[74]

The threat had little apparent effect, and the caterpillars thrived to such an extent that in 1599 a notorious solicitor (before he was put down) took out as many as 300 original writs in one term alone.[75] The campaign nevertheless continued to be waged in the Star Chamber during the later years of Elizabeth.[76]

The Court of Common Pleas, though generally a very conservative tribunal at this period, seems to have been the least energetic in attacking solicitors. In 1600 it allowed an action of *assumpsit* for solicitor's fees, perhaps because there was no allegation that money had been disbursed by way of maintenance.[77] But in the same year Serjeant Spurling demurred to a similar action on the ground that the consideration was illegal: "for the attorneys ought to bestow this and not other strangers [solicitors] which is an unusual and upstart name." Serjeant Heron (or Herne), for the plaintiff, sought to defend the upstarts:

> The name of a solicitor is not a new name, nor such a strange word, for we read of it in 5 Hen. 7. And we are to consider the times in which we live and shall hereafter live, that a solicitor is necessary enough. For suppose one same cause is commenced in each court of England or in divers of them, and thus it is requisite to have a solicitor to put the attorneys in remembrance

[74] *Att.-Gen.* v. *Kinge* (21 May 1596) in J. Hawarde, *Reports del Cases in Camera Stellata* (W. P. Baildon ed., 1894), p. 44 at p. 45 (repunctuated). *Cf.* MS Harg. 26, f. 58, to the same effect (perhaps the same case): "In all his reading he had not read that a solicitor has any calling in our law, but only counsellors, serjeants, and attorneys. For attorneys were not allowed by the common law, but by statute. For [at common law] everyone must prosecute his own cause." (Translated.)

[75] "In 41 Eliz. Sprouse que fuit famous sollicitor que en un terme purchase 300 originalls, et le court ne voile suffer luy de practize, et puis fuit admitt household servant al Count de Hertford": recollection by the court in *Herne* v. *Rolfe* (1634) B.M. MS Add. 35967, f. 24.

[76] Speech to the judges (June 1600) referred to by Chamberlain, *Cal. State Papers Dom.*, vii, 441; *Heydon* v. *Good* (1600) MS Lansd. 1074, f. 365, and B.M. MS Add. 25212, f. 7v; *Wortley* v. *Savill* (1600) MS Lansd. 1074, f. 369, and MS Add. 25212, ff. 13, 14v. In *Wilson* v. *Pecke* (1629) MS Lansd. 1094, f. 66, are listed six cases in which litigants were fined by the Star Chamber for soliciting. See also W. J. Jones, *The Elizabethan Court of Chancery* (1967), p. 318.

[77] *Osbourn* v. *Eden* (1600) Cro.Eliz. 760; the report is less than helpful.

of their business and to pay them, without the doing of which things they would not look to the cause. For which reason such consideration is good and lawful.

The court were inclined to uphold the demurrer, but "departed without giving any certain resolution."[78] By the following year, however, Anderson C.J. had been persuaded that solicitors were prohibited by the statute of maintenance.[79] And in 1602 both the Chief Justices concurred with Egerton L.K. in holding clearly that:

> A clerk or attorney in one court may not solicit a cause in another court, although it be for the same matter as the cause which is in his proper court. And also that no one may justify maintenance in the soliciting of suits, unless he be a servant to the party for whom he solicits, or of his fee in the law, or a son or brother, or has particular interest in right or in reversion or remainder of the land.[80]

On this occasion a clerk of Mr. Prothonotary Brownlow of the Common Pleas was fined £100 for soliciting causes in the Exchequer, Exchequer Chamber, and Court of Requests. Moore had argued in defence of attorneys that such practices were "usual and common"; but the Lord Keeper retorted that a multitude of sinners took away the shame but not the guilt: *multitudo peccantium pudorem tollit non peccatum*.[81] If attorneys were not permitted to solicit causes, *a fortiori* the prohibition extended to persons who were not members of the inns of court or chancery.[82]

The evidence which has just been collected, and in particular the attitude of Egerton, provides ample corroboration for Hudson's invective, which was probably the best-known formulation of the case against solicitors:

> In our age are stepped up a new sort of people called solicitors, unknown to the records of the law, who, like the grasshoppers of Egypt, devour the whole land; and these I dare say (being authorised by the opinion of the most reverend and learned lord chancellor that ever was before him) were express maintainers and could not justify their maintenance upon any action brought: I mean not where a lord or gentleman employed his servant to solicit his cause, for he may justify his doing thereof, but I mean those which are common solicitors of causes, and set up a new profession, not being allowed in any court, or at least not in this

---

[78] *Anon.* (1600) Inner Temple, MS Barrington 6, f. 32 (translated).
[79] *Anon.* (1601) Bodl.Lib., MS Rawl.C. 720, f. 65v.
[80] *Postern's Case* (1602 or 1603) Moo.K.B. 656, *pl.* 898 (translated); also in W. Hudson, *Treatise on the Star Chamber*, printed in F. Hargrave (ed.), *Collectanea Juridica* (1792), Vol. II, p. 94.
[81] J. Bruce (ed.), *The Diary of John Manningham*, 99 *Camden Society* (Old Ser.) (1868), p. 81, quoting MS Harl. 5353, f. 59 (November 1602). This may be a reference to *Postern's Case*.
[82] *Att.-Gen. ex rel. Nicholas* v. *Hichecoke* (1605) in J. Hawarde, *Cases in Camera Stellata*, p. 244.

court, where they follow causes; and these are the retainers of causes, and devourers of men's estates by contention, and prolonging suits to make them without end.[83]

The Statute of 1606

The onslaughts from the Bench did not succeed in extirpating solicitors, and so it became increasingly necessary to control them. The principal complaints against them had been that they stirred up unnecessary suits and prolonged suits unnecessarily, that they concocted false bills of costs, and simply that there had become too many of them. The increasing numbers of lawyers at all levels had given cause for concern, in 1596 the judges ordered the inns to call no more than four men to the bar each year. In the inns, however, the resistance was overcome by financial considerations and patronage, and by 1602 Ellesmere was complaining of " calls by the dozens or scores." [84] Whether the grievances voiced by the politicians and judges about the solicitors were as substantial as the grouses about the inns is a question which might well attract the attention of social historians. For the moment we must confine our attention to the law.

Besides the deterrent warfare which had been waged in Westminster Hall, the preventive medicine of the reformers had been fermenting in Parliament and elsewhere. In 1580 a bill had been read to reduce the " excessive multitude " of attorneys in the Common Pleas. It does not seem to have proceeded very far.[85] In 1601 another bill was brought forward " to repress the greate number of comon sollicitors," which was joined with a bill against frivolous suits to form " A Bill for avoyding of multitude of sutes for trifling cawses and for suppressing of pettifoggers and unlawfull sollicitors and stirrers up of unnecessary sutes." The bill was referred to a committee full of lawyer members (including Hobart, Moore, Jones and Tanfield), but again it was dropped.[86] In 1606, however, Parliament did pass " An Acte to reforme the Multitudes and Misdemeanours of Attorneys and Sollicitors at Lawe." The preamble related how excessive or fictitious fees had been charged, " whereby the subiectes growe to be overmuch burthened, and the practise of the juste and honest sergeant and counsellor at lawe greatly slandered." It therefore provided that an attorney or solicitor should not be allowed to recover any fee which he had given to a serjeant or counsellor unless he had a ticket signed by the counsellor or his clerk, and that their own bills

---

[83] Op.cit. from the text printed in Collectanea Juridica (1792), Vol. II, at pp. 94–95.
[84] W. R. Prest, The Inns of Court 1590–1640 (1972), pp. 53, 54–58.
[85] 1 H.C.J. 124, 127, 128, 130. The Committee met in " the New Hall in the Temple " and so it probably included a preponderance of lawyers.
[86] S.P. 12/282/52, f. 125 (list of the committee, dated 12 November 1601); S.P. 12/282/73, f. 168 (title of bill in " Notes for the parliament ").

of costs should be true and signed with their own names. Furthermore, if any attorney or solicitor should "willingly delay his clients suites to worke his own gaine," or demand more than he had laid out, he was to be liable to an action for treble damages and to be discharged from being an attorney or solicitor. In the second section it was provided:

> And to avoide the infinite number of Sollicitors and Attorneys, Be it enacted by authoritie of the present Parliament, That none shall from henceforth be admitted Attorneyes in any of the Kinges Courtes of Recorde aforesaide, but such as have been brought up in the same Courtes, or otherwise well practised in Solliciting of Causes, and have beene found by their Dealinges to be skilful, and of honest Disposition; and that none to be suffered to sollicite any Cause or Causes in any of the Courtes aforesaide, but onely such as are knowen to be Men of sufficient and honeste Disposition.[87]

This statute was passed at the height of the campaign to enhance the standing of the Bar, and its language was calculated throughout to visit the sins of the blackguards on the whole race of the practitioners under the Bar. Yet the statute did, for the first time, confer legal recognition upon solicitors. It was implicit that, provided they were honest, solicitors were permissible; indeed practice as a solicitor was now among the statutory qualifications for attorneys. A statute intended to humiliate and depress the ministerial classes of lawyer therefore proved to be, ironically, the solicitors' charter.

Within two years of the statute solicitors were apparently succeeding in actions brought at common law for their fees.[88] Nevertheless, the attacks on "general" solicitors in the Star Chamber—the usual forum for complaints of maintenance—continued with little abatement. "If any man doe sollicite generally in all courtes and stirr up old titles upon noe ground this is contrary to the law and noe man can be a generall solliciter but in the Kinge's case." [89] Even when an attorney was acquitted of maintenance, a stern lecture was considered appropriate because he had solicited a cause in another court:

---

[87] 3 Jac. 1, c. 7; text from Stat.Reg. iv, 1083–1084. The history of the enactment is obscure, and it is not referred to in W. Notestein, *The House of Commons 1604–1610* (1971). For the formal stages, see 2 H.L.J. 380, 382, 390, 391, 429; 1 H.C.J. 282, 286, 290, 307. (The bill was introduced in the House of Lords in February 1605/6, sent to the Commons in March and passed in May.)

A reader on this statute said it was intended "to retrench and obviate the occasion of those imputations that ly upon the law—it were to bee wisht they were onely slanders—multitude of atturneys and solliciters, traffiquing in causes and delaying them, more for private gaine then their clyents' (their masters') good": B.M. MS Harg. 491, f. 3v (anonymous and undated).

[88] See J. Herne, *The Pleader* (1657), pp. 163, 195: two cases of 1607 in which attorneys of the Common Bench were retained to solicit causes in Chancery.

[89] *Snigg* v. *Chambers* (1607) Univ.Lib.Camb., MS Add. 3105, f. 137v. Accord. 2 Buls. 230 (1614), *per* Coke C.J.

> No man can be a generall sollicitor, and the lawe takes knowledge of none to intermeddle with law busynesses but *homo consiliarius et in lege peritus, et attornatus sive procurator*; and they must doe it for there Fees; neyther can they disburse monie for Fees or Copies, but in there owne Cawses; and therefore that Atturnie Sayd well, which was old Crowe, when his Clyentes would have him paye Fees and disburse monie for them, " I doe not love," quothe he, " that any man shoulde goe to lawe with my monie." Which was commended for a good and honeste aunsweare, and the man ys yet lyvinge, and hathe 500 li. lande by the yeare. Yet yf a man wryte unto an attornie to instructe or reteyne counsell, or take out proces for him, it is so common and necessary for the poore of the countrye that, albeit yt be an offence againste the lawe, yet this Courte will not sentence yt.[90]

Perhaps this should be interpreted, in the light of the foregoing, as a generous gesture towards the attorneys. At least it recognised what had become common practice, and confirmed that soliciting was tolerable provided the solicitor did not exceed the scope of his authority by laying out his own money without the client's approval. For laying out money, however, the Star Chamber continued to fine solicitors heavily.[91]

The Court of Common Pleas relented still further in *Solomon Leech's Case* (1614). It is worth remarking that, although this was a leading case in the history of solicitors, it does not appear in any of the printed volumes of reports. It was an action of *assumpsit* brought by an attorney of the Court on a promise to pay his fee of 3s. 4d. a term for soliciting causes in Chancery. It was admitted on all sides that an attorney could lawfully solicit an individual case in another court, this having been the purport of the Star Chamber decisions [92]; the question now was whether a retainer by the term was lawful. Warburton J. thought it was:

> It has been adjudged in the King's Bench that an attorney of this Court may pursue a suit there. And in 5 Hen. 7 you will find general solicitors. And, admitting that a general solicitor is lawful, an attorney may solicit generally: to which Hubbart [C.J.] agreed. We in Cheshire have but two attorneys; now if one man retains both is it not reasonable that an ignorant man shall retain an attorney to solicit his cause? [93]

Nevertheless, the consideration in the present case was held to be unlawful and so the action failed.[94]

---

[90] *Att.-Gen. ex rel. Stafforde* v. *Parmeter* (1607) in J. Hawarde, *Cases in Camera Stellata*, p. 331.
[91] *Quelch's Case* (c. 1610) Univ.Lib.Camb., MS Add. 3105, f. 146.
[92] MS Harl. 1692, f. 37v, per Nicholls J.: " *il ad estre tenus en camera stellata que un attorney del un court poit sollicite un suite pur un speciall home en auter court.*" [93] *Ibid.* (translated). The last sentence is obscure.
[94] Rolle Abr., Vol. I, p. 17, line 33, *Accion sur le Case* (T) 10; Exeter College, Oxford, MS 151, f. 30v; 1 Bro. & Golds. 73; Hetley 129, *per* Richardson C.J. Followed in *Gage* v. *Johnson* (1622) Winch 53.

Five years later an attorney of the same court brought an action of debt for his fees as a solicitor in the King's Bench, and counsel did not trouble to pursue the question whether the contract was lawful; the argument turned only on whether debt was the appropriate remedy.[95] Yet another action by an attorney of the Common Pleas, in 1629, resulted in further confirmation of the principle that an attorney of one Bench might follow causes in one of the other superior courts as a solicitor; and this was upheld by the King's Bench on a writ of error.[96] The court on this latter occasion distinguished the offence of maintenance by a person of substance—which was surely the mischief contemplated by parliament—from the case where a " solicitor of inferior rank " took money to maintain a cause.[97] This marked another improvement in the legal status of solicitors, even if the victory was diluted by the reasoning that soliciting was lawful only if done by inferior persons. The position had therefore come to be that an *attorney* could justify soliciting causes in other courts provided he had express instructions, and could bring an action on the case to recover his fees and expenses if he had incurred them with his client's authority.

In 1629 the more interesting question came into debate whether a man who was not an attorney could bring an action on a promise made in consideration of soliciting. Serjeant Henden contended that the consideration was lawful, relying on the Year Book case of 1490, *Onely's Case*, and the statute of 1606.[98] Richardson C.J. seems to have been persuaded by the argument:

> Solicitor is a person known in the law: 5 Hen. 7, 20b. And there was one Snowden's case: one brought an action against him for slander of his title, and he justified that such a one made title to the land and that he was his solicitor in the suit, and ruled that it was a good justification, whereby it appears that solicitor is a person known in law. And the statute of 3 Jac. much prevails with me for this opinion. And it would be a miserable case if you would allow no solicitors except attorneys in the Star Chamber and Chancery, for there the attorneys will not move out of their chambers. And it is inconvenient that an attorney in this court should follow business in the King's Bench.[99]

[95] *Bradford* v. *Woodhouse* (1619) Cro.Jac. 520; Shepp.Abr., Vol. II, p. 407; 2 Rolle Rep. 76. Croke later said that he had been of counsel in this case and that the maintenance point was not argued: *Sands* v. *Trevilian* (1630) Univ.Lib.Camb., MS, Ii. v. 23, p. 66.
[96] *Thursby* v. *Warren* (1629) Cro.Car. 159, W. Jones 208. The same point was made in *Kelloway* v. *Mere*, argued on the same day: Univ.Lib.Camb., MS Ii. v. 23, p. 8; B.M. MS Add. 25222, f. 188; MS Harg. 25, f. 55v; MS Harg. 24, f. 97; MS Harg. 47, f. 7; MS Harg. 111, f. 13v. [97] W. Jones 208.
[98] *Wilson* v. *Peck*, Hetley 129. The printed report is taken from a very bad copy, and omits half a sentence from Henden's argument. Other copies of the text of this case are: Univ.Lib.Camb., MS Dd. iii. 46, f. 34; MS Ii. v. 35, f. 233v; B.M., MS Add. 35957, f. 218v; MS Add. 35962, f. 252; MS Lansd. 1085, f. 273; MS Harg. 362, f. 210v. The reports are probably by Humphrey Mackworth.
[99] Hetley 129, corrected from the MSS.

> He shall have his salary for he deserves it for his pains, and it is not maintenance to solicit, for solicitors are for the benefit of the subjects who are remote. And the statute of 3 Jac. c. 7 mentions solicitors with attorneys, and therefore they are allowable.[1]

Harvey J. is also said to have agreed with the Chief Justice, but he drew attention to a similar case:

> now depending in the King's Bench, and there the opinion is that an attorney or counsellor who has a profession toward the law may solicit any suit in any court, and it is not maintenance. *But another person may not.*[2]

Hutton and Yelverton JJ., however, differed from the view of Richardson C.J. They remembered the teachings of Lord Ellesmere, and also *Leech's Case*.[3] Fortunately their speech was taken down in some detail by James Ravenscroft (whose reports have never been published), and it tells more about the state of the profession than most of the printed reports together:

> A solicitor shall not have wages for soliciting, for this is maintenance in him to meddle in causes. For he is no man of the law, nor does the court take any notice of him as solicitor, nor is he attendant at the court. And it is more convenient and also beneficial to the common weal that those who have business should retain young barristers to be of counsel with them and to advise them in their business and to take care of it. And it is more fitting for them [i.e. young barristers] to see to the business of men and to prepare business for the great counsel. And they may send their clerks to the offices and other places in their clients' business. And also they are of more credit and fitter to be trusted with business of men than an ignorant and vagrant solicitor. And it is fitting that such young counsellors be trained up in business below the great counsel for enabling them the better. Also they are dispersed in every county, so that men may easily [4] repair to them; and by this means £1,000 would accrue every term to the young counsellors for their encouragement. So if anyone other than those who are professors of the law will solicit in other men's business, be it at their peril, for it is maintenance in such a solicitor.[5]

Whatever the merits of this point of view, here, perhaps for the first time in the reports, is a convincing reason for what at times looks like a very artificial interpretation of the law of maintenance. It was not

---

[1] *James Ravenscroft's Reports* (see n. 4, *infra*), MS Lansd. 1094, f. 43v, per Richardson C.J. and Harvey J. (translated).
[2] Hetley 129, corrected from the MSS. The case referred to is *Thursby v. Warren* (n. 96, *supra*).
[3] Hetley 129.
[4] The MS says "*ousterment*" (utterly), which does not make sense.
[5] MS Lansd. 1094, f. 43v (translated). On f. 135 the writer records the death of his father Thomas Ravenscroft, and signs himself James Ravenscroft. The writer was called to the Bar by the Inner Temple in 1626: *Calendar of Inner Temple Records*, Vol. II (1898), p. 155. The fact that he was himself a "young counsellor" in 1629 probably accounts for his interest in the speech. The volume belonged to Edward Umfreville and was purchased by Lord Lansdowne after the 1758 sale.

just that "solicitor" was a word unknown to the vocabulary of the law, although novelty was always a powerful argument. It was a matter of professional ethics and of what is now called "demarcation" of roles. Solicitors who were neither attorneys nor members of the Inns of Court were subject to no direct control over their education, dress, or manners: they were (at least, potentially) "ignorant and vagrant." The young barristers, on the other hand, needed encouragement and assistance to maintain themselves during the years before they were considered fit to practise at the Bar. What better training than that they should help the senior barristers, a form of education which was much later to develop into the pupillage system? Moreover, during this state of pupillage the young barristers were to be able to practise as solicitors in order to gain experience. The objection was not to the function of solicitors but to the kind of men who exercised it. It will be recalled that it was still considered ethical, indeed desirable, for counsel to deal directly with their lay clients and to prepare their own briefs. Young barristers practised as solicitors until after the Restoration, and some observers felt it was a sign of sloth that the Bar abandoned the humbler aspects of its work to the vagrant and unqualified solicitor.[6] The judges in *Wilson* v. *Pecke* seem never to have reached agreement on the collateral question whether an attorney was entitled to act as a solicitor [7]; but in fact the propriety of an attorney so acting does seem to have been questioned again.[8]

The last full discussion of the lawfulness of a "layman" acting as a solicitor seems to have taken place in the Common Pleas in 1634. An *assumpsit* upon a promise to pay him for his services was brought by a servant who had solicited the defendant's causes for thirty-five years and had served him as a household servant for two years. The main objection raised to the consideration was that it was past, but Serjeant Thynne took a final stand against solicitors: "Solicitor is a novel trade, and when the law took notice of them it would extirpate them. . . ." Serjeant Hitcham's reply was predictable:

> At first the law took no notice of solicitors, but the recent [*darrein*] law took notice of them. In former times there were few suits, and therefore every man might solicit his own business. But now multitude of business has induced the necessity of solicitors . . . and the statute of 3 Jacobi [9] takes notice of solicitors and explains what manner of men they should be and what shall be their fees.

Finch C.J. and the rest of the court agreed:

> that a *common* solicitor, according to the decree in the Star

---

[6] Above, pp. 115-116; W.R. Prest, *The Inns of Court 1590-1640* (1972), p. 27.
[7] See the reargument in Hilary Term 1635, MS Lansd. 1094, f. 65v.
[8] *Cf. Eveleigh* v. *Parker* (1640) MS Harg. 42, f. 20v; Rolle Abr., Vol. I, p. 53, Action sur le Case (S) 3.   [9] "Caroli" in the MS is clearly wrong.

Solicitors and the Law of Maintenance 1590-1640   149

Chamber, is a common barrator, and in all ages the judges have suppressed them. . . . And they all admitted that a clerk or attorney or gentleman of the Inns of Court, who are in relation to the law, may solicit business. But they said that here he is not a common solicitor but may be taken as a servant, for he has said that for two years he was his household servant and for thirty-five years had solicited his business; and this does not exclude but that he might thus continue, and then it is no question but that he may solicit his business just as [he may] do any service for him.[10]

This was as far as the common law was to go. The solicitor was to be tolerated provided he was either a barrister or an attorney of one of the superior courts, or a household servant. The technical problem whether a solicitor could bring debt for his fees rumbled on into the Interregnum,[11] but the constitution of the profession was becoming clearer and it was codified by the courts of King's Bench and Common Pleas in the well-known order of 1654:

That for the future common solicitors be not admitted to practise in this court unless they are admitted attorneys of either bench; provided that it extend not to the managing of evidence at a trial, nor to private solicitors or servants of corporations, or other persons in the cases of their masters.[12]

It will be as obvious to the reader of this article as it has been to the writer that there is still much to be learned about the history of the legal profession in the sixteenth and seventeenth centuries. Previous attempts to deal with the subject seem for the most part to have been based on the unquestioned assumption that the distinction between barristers and solicitors has always been the same as it now is. The manuscript evidence tempts us to the conclusion that the apparent continuity is an illusion. It is now for the social historians to tell us about the men who practised as solicitors in this early period: who they were, where they came from, what were their qualifications, what they did for a living, and for whom. The story may surprise or even upset some of us. But it is a story which must be told before anyone can confidently begin—as some day someone must—to write the history of the English Bar.*

---

[10] *Herne* v. *Rolfe*, B.M., MS Add. 35967, ff. 23-24 (translated). Also noted in Rolle Abr., Vol. I, p. 13, *Action sur le Case* (R) 18. Cited and followed in *Blowlewell* v. *Turnwill* (1637) Univ.Lib.Camb., MS Gg. ii. 20, f. 976. A " common " solicitor was one who solicited causes generally for a living, as opposed to a private servant.

[11] See *Utber* v. *Cooper* (1654), *Pratt* v. *Banks* (1654-55), Bodl.Lib. MS Brasenose College 69, ff. 135v, 137, 142.

[12] R. Peacock (ed.), *Rules and Orders of the Court of Common Pleas* (1811), p. 2; *Rules and Orders of the Court of King's Bench* (1811), p. 20. Whether and to what extent this order was observed in the years following are questions which for the time being we must defer.

* I am most grateful to Mr. M. J. Prichard for reading a draft of this paper and for his valuable comments.

NOTE

The foregoing article was not concerned with the earlier history of solicitors, about which very little is known (cf. pp. 92-93, above). Winchester College employed a *sollicitator in curiis domini regis* as early as 1410 (1 *Notes & Queries,* 12th Ser., p. 362). But the earliest references to solicitors which have so far been found in the plea rolls are to actions brought for solicitors' fees in the reigns of Edward IV and Henry VII. They are all actions by Common Pleas attorneys retained *ad negocia solicitanda:* John Whyte in 1478 (CP 40/868, m. 412) sues on a retainer of 1469 to be the defendant's attorney in the King's Bench and Common Pleas *ac ad negocia sua in eisdem curiis solicitanda* as his attorney and *solicitarius;* John Samuell in 1490 (CP 40/913, m. 429) on a retainer as attorney and *solicitarius* in all the king's courts; William Denne in 1494 (CP 40/928, m. 367) on a retainer as attorney and *solicitator,* having subsequently solicited causes in Chancery; and John Grote in 1496 (CP 40/935, m. 379) on a retainer as attorney and *solicitarius.* (Cf. Rastell's precedent, p. 138, above.) The lack of a settled Latin word is suggestive of novelty. A third form *(solicitor)* is used in Andrew Dymmok's patent as solicitor-general in 1485 (patent roll, C66/561).

Actions in Chancery for solicitors' fees are met with in the time of Henry VIII: e.g., Guthlac Overton, "solyciter" (C1/551/49), Thomas Hatche, "solyster" (C1/674/19), and Henry Ryshton (C1/668/20).

II

LEGAL INSTITUTIONS AND LITERATURE

3 The Courts of King's Bench and Chancery, c. 1620

This view towards the south end of Westminster Hall shows the King's Bench on the left, overlooked by a two-tiered wooden gallery, and the Chancery on the right. Litigants and lawyers mingle in the foreground.

British Museum

10

THE CHANGING CONCEPT OF A COURT*

WHAT IS A COURT? If that seems a naive question, so much the better: for my theme is that the concept of a court is too often taken for granted. We think we know what a court is, because the numerous different courts with which we are familiar today all have distinctive characteristics in common. Indeed, our age is so sure it knows what a court is that many decision-making bodies which do not fit our assumptions about courts have been given other names, such as "councils", "boards" and "tribunals". In order to find a way of subjecting such bodies to judicial review, public lawyers were once driven to invent the awkward notion of a "quasi-judicial" body, rather than admit that such institutions actually were courts. If lawyers are so sure what courts are, it is perhaps not surprising if historians sometimes project their assumptions about courts onto earlier institutions. When an institution has been labelled a "court", it is easy to assume that this has somehow fixed its character, whereas in truth courts have not always shared the same characteristics. The fact is that the councils, boards and tribunals of today might well in former times have been called courts. So would parliament; so, perhaps, would a medieval village meeting; and so, in rather later times, would a board of directors of a chartered company. Our present image of a "court" is the outcome of history, not the reflection of some constant truth which transcends history. Can we assume that our medieval ancestors would have been so clear about the nature of a court? The twelfth-century courtier Walter Map, at the beginning of his book *De Nugis Curialium*, wrote of the royal court, " De curia loquor et nescio, Deus scit, quod sit curia ": which might be freely translated, " I am speaking of the court, but God knows I have no idea what a court is ".[1]

It would be injurious to the purposes of this paper to try to supply a definition. That is a task I am pleased to leave to the judges and writers on administrative law. I think it might be appropriate, nevertheless, to reverse the usual procedure of historians and begin with the present day, in order to establish that even now the legal concept of a court is far from

---

* Extended version of a lecture delivered to the Citadel Inn of Court, Charleston, South Carolina, on 21 March 1983.

[1] W. Map, *De Nugis Curialium* (M. R. James ed., Anecdota Oxoniensia, 1914), p. 1.

being as tidy as lawyers are wont to imagine.[2] The Supreme Court of Judicature Acts 1873-1875 and the Courts Act 1971 have considerably confused the notion of a court in England. For one thing, the courts have been partly divorced from their judges. The lord chancellor has the power to authorise almost any judge to sit in a court to which he does not belong by the terms of his appointment. This judicial mobility has led to some refined distinctions. Since 1875 there has been provision for High Court judges to sit in the Court of Appeal (which is not part of the High Court); but such judges, while having all the jurisdiction and powers of the Court of Appeal, are not to be deemed to be judges of the Court of Appeal. The Crown Court introduced in 1971 is not part of the High Court, but a High Court judge sitting in the Crown Court is a judge of the Crown Court; and (rather more remarkably) a judge of the Court of Appeal sitting in the Crown Court is to be regarded as a judge of the High Court.[3] The court is therefore an entity distinct from the judges who sit in it. Moreover, the court is no longer a meeting of the judges who are appointed to sit in it. In that sense, the superior courts in England never meet at all, except for ceremonial purposes or to discuss rules of court. Then again, a court, although in name a single body, has become capable of manifesting itself in different places at the same time, even in different parts of the same building. It may take on the character of another court if it sits in special places: for instance, the Crown Court becomes the Central Criminal Court whenever it—that is, not the whole, but some particular manifestation of it—sits in the city of London. Judges of the Crown Court have the power "to sit simultaneously, to take any number of different cases in the same or in different places", and those places may be anywhere in England or Wales. It has been possible since 1873 for High Court judges to sit anywhere, in open court or in chambers, and in all such cases "any Judge sitting in Court shall be deemed to constitute a Court".[4] If this puzzling provision is not a tautology, "Court" is here used in three different senses at once: for the court which the judge is deemed to constitute is presumably not the court in which he is already sitting, nor yet the High Court itself. What, then, does "sitting in Court" mean? The High Court has been known to sit in a village hall, on Brighton pier, in an orchard, in a judge's bedroom, in a taxi-cab, and (it seems) even on a mass of solidified bird-droppings in the Pacific Ocean.[5] Were the

[2] See F. Pollock and F. W. Maitland, *History of English Law before the time of Edward I* (1968 ed.), Vol. I, p. 190. In *Att.-Gen.* v. *B.B.C.* [1980] 3 W.L.R.109, the House of Lords considered the nature of a "court in law." Lord Scarman concluded that a body which parliament calls a "court" and which has a duty to act judicially is nevertheless not necessarily a court.
[3] Supreme Court of Judicature (1873) Amendment Act 1875, 38 & 39 Vict., c. 77, s. 4; Courts Act 1971 (c. 23), s. 4 (2, 3).
[4] Supreme Court of Judicature Act 1873, 36 & 37 Vict., c. 66, s. 39.
[5] W. G. Thorpe, *The Still Life of the Middle Temple* (1892), pp. 302-304 (Stephen J. in a

judges in those cases sitting in court? And, if they were not, in what capacity were they functioning? Courts which can sit in several places at once have another very strange feature. The single judge of the High Court, or the two or three judges in a sitting of the Court of Appeal, act judicially as if they were the High Court or the Court of Appeal, and their decisions are the decisions of those courts. Since each manifestation of such courts governs itself by a small majority, in most cases a majority of one, the decision of the court is made by a tiny proportion of the judges who belong to it or can sit in it. The present convention that the Civil Division of the Court of Appeal is bound by its own decisions therefore leads to the odd result that a decision by two judges in a particular appeal will be binding on the other hundred judges qualified to sit in the Court of Appeal, even if nearly all of them disagree with the decision. We shall have occasion to return to the majority principle later. When we do, we should recall that the superior courts in England now govern themselves by a *minority*, because there is no ordinary machinery for ascertaining the majority view.

So much for the oddities of our English legal system in 1985. If we now make the effort to see back to the time of the Norman conquest, we cannot hope to achieve more than a hazy picture of judicial institutions in England, but we can at least perceive that the various bodies which historians are accustomed to call courts have little or nothing in common with our courts. Not only are there no wigs and gowns and panelled courtrooms: there are no judges, no juries, no lawyers and no legal argument. The Latin word *curia*, which always translates " court ", seems then to have had only a physical connotation. It was a lord's house or, perhaps more strictly, the courtyard around which it was built.[6] This sense was embodied in the name of the writ *de curia claudenda*, which had nothing to do with shutting down law-courts, but lay to enforce a duty to fence or enclose a courtyard or close. The French and English word "court", found in the twelfth century, was not derived from *curia* but from *cohors* (acc. *cohortem*), in its classical sense of a garden (cf. *hortus*) or yard. We still use "court" in this sense at Cambridge, in preference to the Oxonian quadrangle; and a tennis court is the same sort of thing. The names and physical layout of great houses such as Hampton Court preserve the pristine sense of a lord's palace built around a courtyard.

---

cab, Hawkins J. on Brighton pier); *The Times*, 15 Aug. 1968, letter from D. N. Pritt, Q.C. (Rowlatt J. in his orchard); *St Edmundsbury Diocesan Board* v. *Clark* [1973] 2 All E.R. at p. 1161 (Evans P. in his bedroom, Megarry J. in a village hall); *Tito* v. *Waddell* [1975] 3 All E.R. 997, [1977] 3 All E.R. 129 (Megarry V.-C. on Ocean Island, which is covered with rich phosphorous deposits of uncertain but possibly avian origin). Two of these cases arose from holding a "view", and it is not clear whether a view *is* a sitting of the court. Thorpe also recounts an occasion when Shadwell V.-C. made an order while swimming in the River Thames; but that was before the Judicature Acts.

[6] F. W. Maitland, *Domesday Book and Beyond* (1897), p. 94.

Within a century of the conquest, the word *curia* had become pregnant with subtle differences of meaning. It had come to denote the entourage who are found in a great man's court, the body of *curiales* or courtiers. This sense also survives. Ambassadors are still accredited to the Court of St. James's. And English judges, at any rate until Victorian times, wore different robes *at* court from those which they wore *in* court. The word had also come to denote an event, a meeting of the courtiers. Just as a host might now be " at home " on a certain day, so a king or lord might transact business or receive visitors " at a court " held on a certain day. Then again, it could mean a place where " legal " business is transacted *in curia*. This is the closest to our notions. But we cannot assume that the senses were clearly distinct. *Curia* could mean a place, a body of men, an institution, or a jurisdiction: and perhaps all four at once. Let us look at the last three senses in turn.

1. The Court as Jurisdiction

In some of the earliest references to courts in a legal context they are treated as a species of property, to which words of ownership are appropriate. A writ of 1101 confirms to an abbot *curiam suam*, another of slightly later date contains a proviso that a lord is not to lose his court.[7] Every court belongs to someone. The feudal principle that every free man has a court for his tenants was thought worthy of protection in Magna Carta: the writ *praecipe* was not to issue for any tenant whereby a free man might lose his court. If a *praecipe* was brought in the king's court, it was open to the lord either to come and pray his court and have it given back to him, or to bring a writ *de non intromittendo* to achieve the same end.[8] Of course the lord did not lose his court in any permanent sense by reason of a writ of right. His jurisdiction over his other tenants remained intact: what he had lost was control of the case in question. And the concern was not so much with judicature, for it was not the lord's function to make or declare law, but rather a concern that lords' courts should be entitled to control claims to be tenants.[9] The lord himself did not decide the claims, and the court (as Glanvill tells us) might be constrained by customs, which varied from one court to another. The same could be said of other courts, for there was no coherent system of courts or of jurisdictions, either in terms of geography or of subject-matter, in the twelfth century. What mattered was who had authority over whom, and whether that authority could be interfered with from outside. Whether the authority consisted in judicature, legislation or administration would have been a question in

---

[7] R. C. van Caenegem, *Royal Writs in England from the Conquest to Magna Carta* (1959), Selden Soc. Vol. 77, p. 429, no. 34; p. 432, no. 42. See also p. 434, no. 45 (" *curia mea* ").
[8] M. Clanchy, 79 Eng. Hist. Rev. 542.
[9] Maitland, *Domesday Book and Beyond*, pp. 101–102; S. F. C. Milsom, *The Legal Framework of English Feudalism* (1977), p. 71.

The Changing Concept of a Court

advance of the time.[10] Nor was the distinction quick to emerge. In later times, the lack of differentiation between these functions is most obvious in the highest courts—parliament, the council and the Tudor revenue courts—since they were least interfered with. Hale, indeed, was of the opinion in the seventeenth century that the highest court of law and the supreme legislature were necessarily the same body.[11] But a similar lack of differentiation may be seen in lowlier bodies, such as the quarter sessions, which continued to exercise local government functions until Victorian times.

To return to our point: in the twelfth century, a court seems to be simply lawful authority, and the machinery whereby it is exercised—the outward manifestation of authority. There were no jurisdictional boundaries as we understand them. Lords' courts heard all manner of pleas (according to their usages), save those which the king took to himself, and there was no classification of seignorial courts. In the *quo warranto* enquiries, the question was not what courts a lord had but what powers the lord exercised in his court.[12] The hundred, the county and the king's court likewise had seemingly unlimited powers, subject always to their customs. The learning on courts in Glanvill is not about their spheres of competence, but about how cases can be removed from one to another: Glanvill teaches us not only that cases might move around from one court to another, but that in cases of difficulty a lord could actually adjourn his court into the king's court.[13] This was not a slip of the pen. It was not uncommon for one court to attend another, as when hundreds attended the county; and when the king's justices in eyre sat in the county they were not a *curia regis* separate from the county, but were by their presence making the county a *curia regis*. All this emphasises the absence of a modern conception of jurisdiction as something delimiting the competence of particular courts.

A failure to appreciate this led to considerable difficulties and even controversies over the origins of the central royal courts. It is now accepted that *curia regis* is a generic term denoting a number of different phenomena. There was not a single *Curia Regis* which split into three distinct courts. In whatever manner the king's justices sat, they were *curia regis* and enjoyed whatever authority belonged to the king's court. Maitland, of course, knew this: " the form which [the king's] court shall take, the mode in which it shall do justice, these are matters for the king; he is very free to decide them from day to day as he pleases, and this by a

---

[10] Professor Tierney has recently found the earliest trace of this threefold division of government in the work of Hervaeus Natalis (*c.* 1315): *Religion, Law and Morality* (1982), p. 45.
[11] J. H. Baker, *An Introduction to English Legal History* (2nd ed., 1979), pp. 180–181.
[12] F. W. Maitland, *Select Pleas in Manorial Courts* (1888), Selden Soc., Vol. 2, pp. xvi–xvii, liii.
[13] Glanvill, VIII.11 (" potest dominus . . . curiam suam ponere in curiam domini regis ").

few spoken words".[14] Moreover, the Court of Exchequer, the court *coram rege*, the bench, the justices in eyre, were not in the twelfth century separate jurisdictions or distinct courts: they were merely different manifestations of the king's authority, different ways of deploying the king's judicial resources. If the justices of the bench adjourned a matter *coram rege*, they were not sending it to another court, but putting it off until the king was at hand. If the bench was "suspended", to use the modern expression, no court had disappeared: it was simply that no judges were being spared from other duties to remain at Westminster. If the justices were convened at the Exchequer, they were not establishing a distinct revenue court but merely making use of a conveniently large room in the palace for their sitting. There was thus no jurisdictional distinction between the various forms of *curia regis* before Magna Carta. Clause 18 was to change the system, by its provision that common pleas should not follow the king but should be held in a certain place. Yet it is doubtful whether anyone in 1215 intended to create jurisdictionally separate courts, and indeed no courts were mentioned at the time. It is true that a separation soon occurred, in terms of records, judges, and clerical staff, and that Bracton wrote of the king having several courts.[15] For some time, nevertheless, the courts were regarded in the old way: the judges often changed places, cases were easily transferred from one to the other, and it was even possible for process to be made returnable alternatively in one or the other.[16] It was long after 1215 that the clause was construed to exclude common pleas from the Exchequer, on the ground that the latter met notionally *coram rege*. The Court of Exchequer became a separate institution for administrative reasons; but even then the Exchequer Chamber was to remain a meeting place for judges and courts unconnected with revenue until the nineteenth century.

Had Magna Carta been filed with the lost legislation of the twelfth century rather than with the parliamentary legislation to come, clause 18 would have been just another ad hoc expedient to improve the conduct of business. There had been a similar enactment in 1178, which misled earlier generations precisely because they put it on a level with Magna Carta. It was the longevity of Magna Carta, and its repeated confirmation by parliament, which brought about entrenched constitutional distinctions between royal courts. Similar long-term consequences flowed from other constitutional enactments, beginning with Magna Carta, concerning due process. This legislation would later be seen as setting bounds on conciliar and irregular courts, and as justifying in 1641 the abolition of the Star Chamber because it did not

---

[14] Pollock & Maitland, *History of English Law*, Vol. I, p. 153.
[15] E.g. at fo. 105v ("Habent enim plures curias ...").
[16] See G. O. Sayles in Selden Soc., Vol. 57, p. xxxix; vol. 74, pp. xxvi, xxxiv.

follow common-law procedure. Somehow or other the king had limited his judicial sovereignty by the mere fact of exercising it, much as God had committed himself to a particular kind of universe by the act of creation. That metaphor was used by a Jacobean serjeant:

> All kingdoms in their constitution are furnished with the power of justice both according to the rule of law and equity, both [of] which being in the king as sovereign were after settled in several courts, as the light being first made by God was settled in the great bodies of the sun and moon.[17]

The central royal courts of King's Bench and Common Pleas, the moon and sun of the common law system, became by the end of the middle ages a fundamental feature of that system, without which the common law had little meaning, for their " course " was itself common law.[18] The demarcations between inferior courts came about in a similar way, by the introduction of those very constitutional limits and controls which reduced them to the status of "inferior" tribunals. No one seems to have intended to put down communal and seignorial institutions in order to advance royal justice, but the inescapable result of constant tinkering with inferior authority was the emergence of a single constitutional theory to embrace what was coming to be seen as an English legal system.

The effects of this change in the concept of a court were deep and lasting. Lawyers tidied the haphazard miscellany of disparate tribunals into a hierarchical structure. All judicial authority had to derive from the Crown—so that even the prehistoric county court became a royal court— and mistakes in any one court could be corrected in a higher. The sixteenth and seventeenth centuries brought several books about the judicial system, which in modern fashion list the various courts and their jurisdictions as species of the same genus.[19] Thus, in Coke's *Fourth Institute* we find no less than seventy-six species of jurisdiction displayed in all their beautiful complexity. Since all jurisdiction was derived from the king, the chain of delegation had to be precise or the proceedings would be *coram non judice*. Courts which went too far were prohibitable. Inferior courts which strayed outside their charters or prescriptive customs, or ignored the requirements of due process, were liable to have their decisions reversed. A lord needed a writ of right to deal with freehold. A sheriff needed a *justicies*, in all but minor cases. A borough needed a royal charter or immemorial usage. Even a royal judge, except

---

[17] *Martin* v. *Marshall and Key* (c. 1615), Hob. 63, *per* Hitcham Sjt. See also Baker, *Introduction to English Legal History*, pp. 83–84.
[18] *Long quinto*, fo. 109v; Y.B. Trin. 11 Edw. IV, fo. 2, pl. 4; Mich. 2 Ric. III, fo. 18, pl. 45, *per* Fairfax J.; St. German's *Doctor and Student*, ed. T. F. T. Plucknett and J. L. Barton (1974), Selden Soc., Vol. 91, pp. 46–48; *Lane's Case* (1586), 2 Co. Rep. 16; *Lord Mounson* v. *Bourne* (1627), Cro. Car. 527.
[19] *Diversité de courtes* (1526); *Articuli ad narrationes novas* (1539); R. Crompton, *Lauthoritie et jurisdiction des courts* (1594); E. Coke, *Fourth Part of the Institutes* (1644).

in certain cases before the king himself, could only proceed if he had specific delegated authority in the form of a writ or commission. That is why the remedies which constituted the law were then conceived principally in terms of jurisdiction. The original writs—the little slips of parchment which began as tickets of admission to a particular court—came inadvertently to provide the conceptual framework for the whole common law.[20]

2. The Court as an Institution

In those early references where *curia* is not used in a proprietary sense, it is frequently used in a temporary sense to describe a single historical event. Besides meaning authority, and the machinery for exercising authority, it could denote the actual meeting held to decide how to exercise it. The earliest definition of a court I have found, in *L'Ancienne Coutume de Normandie* (c. 1300), treats it as " an assembly of wise men in a certain place at a certain day by whom right is to be done in a dispute to those who plead ".[21] A court, be it noted, is something that happens on a certain day. Again and again the familiar captions of local courts begin: *Curia tenta ibidem tali die.* . . . At the end of the day, the court—that court—was no more. Some courts could only be held on certain days and at certain intervals. All courts were tied to the day or days specified in the process. *Jour*, the day in court, was an important heading in the books. If a court could adjourn—and the ability to do so was sometimes a vexed question—it probably needed the help of a fiction in recording the proceedings as being on the same day.[22] The link between a court and its " day " was most evident in the case of a commission: before the commission was read, and after it had been executed, the justices had no judicial authority whatever. In the case of a trial by peers, the great office of Lord High Steward was brought into being for the day only (*pro hac vice tantum*), and his lordship bore a white wand symbolising his authority. This wand he broke solemnly in two as soon as judgment was delivered, to signify the dissolution of the commission. In that ancient ceremony, last performed (with some physical difficulty) in 1935, the court was seen to end as sharply as it had come into existence.

The difference between that concept of a court (as a once-and-for-all event) and the more continuous entity which the regular courts became is indicated in the English language by the definite article. *A* court held

---

[20] See S. F. C. Milsom, *Historical Foundations of the Common Law* (2nd ed., 1981), pp. 33–36.
[21] *L'Ancienne Coutume de Normandie*, ed. W. L. de Gruchy (Jersey, 1881), p. 133, ch. 53 (" Court laye est une assemblee de saiges hommes en certain lieu et a certain jour par lesquels droict doibt estre faict des contends a ceulx qui pledent . . ."). It goes on to explain that the duke of Normandy has a court, that freeholders have a court for their tenants, and that elder brothers have a court in certain cases for their younger brothers.
[22] E.g., *The Reports of Sir John Spelman*; ed. J. H. Baker (1977), Selden Soc., Vol. 93, p. 155, s.v. " Jour ".

on a specific day is distinct from *the* court which meets from time to time without losing its continuous identity. This means of distinction is lacking in Latin, but the distinction itself probably existed at quite an early date. It may have owed something to the locative sense of *curia*: a court had been a place before it had acquired judicial connotations, and a twelfth-century judicial court was still, in the natural sense, a place. Glanvill tells of the things which took place *in curia*,[23] and the plea rolls constantly refer to comings and goings and doings *hic in curia* or *in curia domini regis*. Three centuries later the treatise *Diversité de Courtes* defined courts as " the places where the justices sit to do justice ", and as late as the 1630s Coke defined a court as " a place where justice is judicially ministered ".[24] In this sense *curia* was analogous to *aula*, the hall of justice,[25] and synonymous with *placea*, the space marked out by bars in front of the judges' bench.[26] Some major courts, such as the Star Chamber and Exchequer Chamber, were even named after the rooms where they met.

The court as a geographical location was clearly continuous, even if the place and the personnel were not fixed. The *curia regis* in which the judges were ordered to remain by the 1178 ordinance[27] was presumably a location, perhaps the king's palace; for the king's justices were in a sense *curia regis* wherever they sat. It is but a short step, however, to regard the changeable personnel who inhabit the court as themselves constituting a continuous institution. Walter Map reflected on this when exploring his difficulties in defining the royal court:

> The court is indeed temporal, changeable and various, stationary and wandering, never continuing in one stay. When I leave it I know it perfectly, but when I come back to it I find nothing or but little of what I left . . . yet the court is not changed; it remains always the same.[28]

It is easy to see how a court came to be regarded as not merely a place, or an isolated meeting, but a continuous body with a collective mind of its own.

One of the chief functions of the human mind is memory, and there is no distinction between mind and memory in law French or Latin.[29] What helped more than anything else to give courts a continuous

---

[23] Glanvill, I.7, 21, 23, 26.
[24] *Diversité de courtes* ("1523" ed., probably 1532), sig. Alv ("Et les lieux ou les justices seount pur faire justice sount appelles courtes, les queux sont de divers natures "); Co. Litt. 58.
[25] 4 Co. Inst 268.
[26] Selden Soc., Vol. 94, p. 62, n. 1.
[27] W. Stubbs, *Select Charters and other Illustrations of Constitutional History* (8th ed., 1900), p. 131.
[28] Map, *De Nugis Curialium*, tr. M. R. James, p. 1.
[29] In English we still use the expression " time out of mind " to mean beyond the reach of human memory (in law French, *hors de memorie*). Unsound mind in law French was *non sane memorie*.

character was the employment of written rolls to give them a memory.[30] The court, by recording its orders and decisions permanently on parchment, gave them a new significance. Soon they would be more than mere remembrances of things done: they would be precedents, a guide to the future and a source of law. This was so even before the birth of law reports. The origins of the common law owed almost as much to sheep as to men.

The creation and preservation of this written memory required staffs of officials, whose very being demonstrated that the courts were permanent organisations. These officials were not members of the court, nor were they appointed by the court, in its corporate sense; but they were *homines de curia*, men of the court, whose attendance on the court entitled them to privileges and whose work was regulated by rules of court. Eventually the expression " men of court " came to include also the advocates—the "apprentices of the king's court"[31]—and other court-followers, whose societies were known in the fifteenth century as the inns "of court".[32] By that time, over a hundred officers were employed in the central royal courts, besides the attendant counsel and more than two hundred attorneys. The courts had become major departments of state, and our inns were needed to supply them with trained men at all levels.

The transition from " court as meeting " to " court as institution " begat another, more subtle, change. Since the court remembered the past and governed the future through its record, which was incontrovertible, it was possible for business to be transacted outside the physical confines of the court and outside the hours of sitting, and yet to be recorded as having been done in court, and therefore in law—that is, by legal fiction—to be deemed to have been done in court. Coke resisted this undermining of the "open court" principle by attempting to remove the distinction we have just drawn. Commenting on the first chapter of the Statute of Marlborough (1267), *quod tam majores quam minores justiciam habeant et recipiant in curia domini regis*, Coke wrote:

> These words [*in curia domini regis*] are of great importance, for all causes ought to be heard, ordered and determined before the judges of the king's courts openly in the king's courts, whither all persons may resort; and in no chambers or other private places: for the judges are not judges of chambers but of courts . . .[33]

---

[30] Pollock & Maitland, *History of English Law*, Vol. I, p. 190. For the broader context of this development, see M. T. Clanchy, *From Memory to Written Record* (1979).
[31] Rot. Parl., Vol. II, p. 96 (1337).
[32] The original phrase may have been "inns of the men of court" (*hospicia hominum curiae*), which is found in an undated entry (probably 15th century) in W. Rastell, *A Collection of Entrees* (1574 ed.), fo. 396. Cf. *Benet's Chronicle*, in Camden Soc. (4th series), Vol. 9, p. 222 ("insurrexerunt curiales de omnibus hospiciis super Flette strete").
[33] 2 Co. Inst. 103.

The Changing Concept of a Court

In this instance, as in others, Coke was trying to overrule history. It had been established practice before he was born for *ex parte* business to be transacted when convenient in chambers, so that a plaintiff could "appear" and judicial writs could issue without troubling the court sitting in Westminster Hall, and for the parties by consent to exchange pleadings in the office.[34] Whatever an officer did in the course of his duty was an act of the court, even if the judges knew nothing of it, and the doctrine was pressed so far as to make sheriffs' returns incontrovertible on the ground that sheriffs were "officers deputed by the law to the king's courts".[35]

In the seventeenth century, if not before, it even became possible for judgment to be entered in the vacation, so long as the record said it had been given in term.[36] By then it was also usual for attorneys to exchange pleadings privately, although in theory it was still their filing in the office which made them effective,[37] and even though the entry on the roll said they were spoken by the parties in court. Moreover, certain acts of the court were being delegated to single judges in chambers.[38] In a sense, therefore, the court was not located only in the public "place" in Westminster Hall, but also in its offices in the inns of court and chancery and in the judges' chambers in Serjeants' Inn. A remarkable illustration of this geographical extension is afforded by a case as early as 1318. A clerk of the king's court had the unfortunate experience of being urinated on in Fleet Street on his way to Westminster, in the company of other men of the court. This was made out to be a contempt of court, and the *venire facias* (to summon men of court to try it) recited that the trespass was done *in presencia curiae*.[39]

With the development of the offices, the role of the public court came to be increasingly supervisory, exercised through hearing motions to make or discharge rules (which were entered in the officers' remembrances and books), and decreasingly the actual participation in what the plea rolls minuted fictitiously as having occurred in court. This change, too, had a profound effect on legal development.[40]

The change was neatly recognised in a rather pedantic resolution of 1650. Judgment had been entered "*ideo consideratum est* ad *eandem curiam*" instead of "*Ideo consideratum est* per *eandem curiam*". The court reversed the judgment, "for it might be considered at the court,

---

[34] See Selden Soc., Vol. 94, pp. *90, 96, 136–137*.
[35] Diversité de courtes, sig. Blv.
[36] *Anon.* (1646), Style Pr. Reg. (1694 ed.), p. 302; *Mason* v. *White* (1699), 1 Ld Raym. 485.
[37] *Anon.*(1648), Style Pr. Reg. 303.
[38] The history of this change remains to be traced. It does not seem to have required legislation. It was held in the 19th century that when a statute conferred any power on "the court" it could be exercised by a judge in chambers, unless a contrary intention appeared: *Smeeton* v. *Collier* (1847) 1 Exch. 457.
[39] *Thorp* v. *Makerel* (1318), Selden Soc., Vol. 74, p. 79, pl. 31.
[40] Milsom, *Historical Foundations of the Common Law*, pp. 60–81; Baker, *Introduction to English Legal History*, pp. 71–82.

which may be meant only the place where the court is held, and yet not be the act of the court, viz. of the judges of the court ".[41] To this we might add the gloss that something could be done *per curiam* without being considered *ad curiam* and without the judges having actual knowledge of it.

These processes should not be regarded as irreversible. Indeed, in relatively recent times the constitutional principle of due process, having hindered reform, has been laid to rest in England. Parchment, once one of the hallmarks of a court of record, has become too expensive to use. The courts' memory is now supported by electronic means, and the "record" has come to mean everything said in court and caught on tape.[42] The contrast between the record and what happened in court therefore no longer has any meaning. Moreover, in 1875 all the supposedly "fundamental" courts were abolished. Courts are once more as changeable as the law itself.

3. *The Court as a Corporate Body*

The third approach is for a court to be regarded not merely as a group of judges and staff but as a body with a juristic personality of its own. By placing it third, I do not mean to imply any chronological progression, for already in the Constitutions of Clarendon (1164) and Glanvill (*c.* 1189) we read that a court—*curia*, in the singular—may "see" and "consider" and "decide" things. And Map's conundrum, that the court is the same although the courtiers change, clearly points to a notion of corporate personality.

That notion is strongest in relation to the communal assemblies. Indeed, there is a sense in which every distinguishable community *is* a court, or can become one when required. The county and the hundred were courts for many purposes, and yet the "courts" were not very distinct from the communities at large. Maitland even found a reference to *curia villae*, the court of a vill.[43] The earliest plea rolls show that these courts and bodies had many characteristics of juristic persons.[44] In 1200, a writ of false judgment was brought against a county, and in 1201 another was brought against a lord's *curia*.[45] A court could be vouched to warranty, and summoned to appear in the king's court.[46] The court could appoint representatives, so that a vouched court could come by envoys (*missi*),[47] and a county would wage battle by

---

[41] *Anon.* (1650), Style Pr. Reg. 318.
[42] *R.* v. *Knightsbridge Crown Court*, ex. p. *International Sporting Club (London) Ltd* [1981] 3 All E.R. 417.
[43] *Collected Papers*, Vol. II, p. 364.
[44] See W. S. Holdsworth, *History of English Law*, Vol. I, p. 69.
[45] *Curia Regis Rolls* [hereafter *CRR*] I.276; II.80.
[46] *CRR* II.19, 272 (1201–03). This was later common.
[47] *CRR* III.29, 79.

The Changing Concept of a Court

its champion.[48] (The prospect of a county fighting in person could not have been a pleasant one.) It was not unknown for a seignorial court, according to its own roll, to speak, or to give a verdict.[49] A court could be punished, in which case the penalty fell on the suitors, or at least those who were known to have been present.[50] These courts were perhaps the earliest lay corporations. It is arguable that, as time went on, the court was seen as something different from the community, if only because the suitors of the court were a more select body than the inhabitants at large. In later times, therefore, we hear of communities more often than courts. But no such distinction is discernible at first. The community in its corporate capacity was only visible in its meeting, or court, and had no corporate existence outside its regular meetings. Corporateness is closely linked with constitutional formality, because, although a real person can break rules, a fictitious person only exists when he conforms to the constitution. If the suitors meet on the wrong day they are not the county and their doings are of no legal validity. Perhaps the point of most significance to our present enquiry is that these early courts do not seem to have evolved from mere meetings into corporate entities: rather, the community *was* a corporate entity whenever it assembled in court.

The central royal courts were never communities in that sense. They were not summoned to appear in other courts. They were not fined. False judgment or error could be brought against royal justices, but such proceedings were directed against the justices rather than the court,[51] and the writ of error was simply an order to the chief justice to transmit the record to the superior court. Writs were never addressed to the court as such, but to the justices: either anonymously,[52] or to the chief justice. Nevertheless, at a very early date the justices of the king's court were regarded as a society or fellowship. In 1208, a court adjourned because Simon de Pateshall had no fellow (*nullum socium habuit*); while four years later there is a reference to Pateshall *et socii sui, justiciarii de curia*.[53] Again and again thereafter royal courts are referred to in formal records as having been held before the chief justice " and his fellows " (*et sociis suis*). And before the necessity of appointing judges by patent was settled, the method of appointment was by a writ directing the chief

---

[48] *CRR* VIII.223, 389.
[49] E.g., Selden Soc., Vol. 2, pp. 22, 35 (" dicit curia "); 29, 67 (" veredictum curiae ").
[50] *Hengham Magna*, ed. W. H. Dunham in *Radulphi de Hengham Summae* (1932), p. 13. Cf. *CRR* III.133, where a lord's court was amerced for false judgment and the names of those present set out. Much later it was held that such proceedings only bound the suitors whose names appeared in the sheriff's return, even if others had been present: *Case of the Court of Godmanchester* (1567), Dyer 262.
[51] See *CRR* XIV.314, no. 1474, for an early example (1237) of false judgment against assize justices, who were amerced.
[52] For early examples, see *CRR* III.273 (writ to "justiciariis de curia), 274 (to "justiciariis de banco "), both in 1205.
[53] *CRR* V.151; VI. 322.

justice to admit the new judge into the fellowship (*in societatem*).[54]

Now, *societas* is a word which commonly denoted a corporate entity. The judicial *societas* was a single body, with a common seal, which could only act as a body and in so acting was distinct from its individual members. This was proved by the fact that a judge could sue or be sued in his own court, on the assumption that the court could proceed without him.[55] The position of assize commissioners seems on the face of it to contradict this. They were *socii*, as the writ of association makes explicit, but unless they had a special writ (*si non omnes*) entered of record they were all obliged to be present or the proceedings would be void.[56] The reason, however, was that the commissioners were individually named, whereas the process of the two benches was in general terms: *coram rege* or *coram justiciariis de Banco*. Even on assizes, it required no legislation to introduce the practice whereby one judge took the crown side and the other sat at *nisi prius*: both were present at the appointed place, and could consult each other if need be. The record of a trial at assizes did not indicate which judge presided; and likewise the record of proceedings in banc did not identify judges by name.[57] The rolls spoke only of what appeared to or was decided by "the court" or "the justices here".[58] The year books sometimes lift the veil and show that only one judge was on the bench,[59] though it is doubtful whether at that period a single judge was regarded as a "court". No doubt in a sense he represented his companions in their absence, but it is unlikely that he could give judgment without consulting them[60] and certain that he could not sit independently. Whatever its quorum, the court was a unity.

Whether unity imported unanimity is a difficult question to tackle.

---

[54] E.g. Selden Soc., Vol. 74, p. xxii (also in Vol. 82, p. xx): "mandetur Willelmo de Bereford quod eos in societatem admittat" (1309).

[55] Y.B. Trin. 11 Hen. VI, fo. 49, pl. 7; *Case of the Bailiffs of Newcastle* (1607), 2 Rolle Abr. 93; J. H. Baker, *The Order of Serjeants at Law* (1984), p. 46.

[56] *Prior of St Mary Overy* v. *Culpeper* (1523), in Spelman's *Reports*, Selden Soc., Vol. 93, p. 109, pl. 4.

[57] The judges were only named in final concords. These were genuine lists of those present, and if a judge himself levied a fine his name had to be omitted: Y.B. Hil. 8 Hen. VI, fo. 19, pl. 6; Trin. 11 Hen. VI, fo. 49, pl. 7. The first membrane of each term was tested by the chief justice, or (if his office was vacant) by the secondary justice. If the chief justice was a party, the process and record of that case had to be tested by the secondary: Hil. 8 Hen. VI, fo. 19, pl. 6, *per* Babington C. J.; Bro. Abr., *Judges*, pl. 6; Rolle Abr., *Judges*, A: Viner Abr., *Judges*, A6.

[58] Judgment was entered simply as *Consideratum est* ..., or *Consideratum est per curiam*.... Where a question of law had been raised by demurrer or writ of error, this was preceded by a vague recital that the question had been looked into and fully understood *per justiciarios domini regis hic*, or (more commonly) *per curiam hic*.

[59] E.g., Y.B. Pas. 6 Hen. VII, fo. 1, pl. 1; Mich. 10 Hen. VII, fo. 8, pl. 15; Pas. 22 Hen. VIII in Brit. Lib MS. Harley 1691, fo. 239; Hil. 26 Hen. VIII, fo. 9, pl. 1.

[60] See *CRR* V.151 (court adjourned in 1208 because Pateshall J. had no fellow); Y.B. Mich. 10 Hen. VII, fo. 8, pl. 15 (court adjourned in 1494 because Huse C. J. alone); Hil. 26 Hen. VIII, fo. 9, pl. 1 (Fitzherbert J., being alone, said he would give judgment when his companions came). Cf. adjournments of inferior courts "pro tenuitate curiae": Selden Soc., Vol. 2, pp. 60, 67. It required a statute of 1576 to enable the chief justice alone, or two puisne justices, to conduct Middlesex *nisi prius* trials in banc: 18 Eliz. I, c. 12.

The Changing Concept of a Court 167

The record omitted voting figures, and so phrases such as *videtur justiciariis hic* or *consideratum est per curiam* are potentially misleading. They are not actually fictitious, because the views of individual judges are not the views of the court, and the views of dissentient judges are not those of "the justices" as a body. What the record prevents us from knowing is whether dissentients could be overruled or ignored. It effectively conceals the history of judicial majoritarianism. Maitland, addressing himself primarily to political institutions, regretted that the History of the Majority was one of the great books no one had yet written. He pointed out that in earlier times

> it is unanimity that is wanted; it is unanimity that is chronicled; it is unanimity that is after a sort obtained . . . until men will say plainly that a vote carried by a majority of one is for certain purposes every whit as effectual as an unanimous vote, one main contrast between corporate ownership and mere community escapes them.[61]

In the papal Rota and in the conciliar courts it inspired on the continent, majority decisions seem to have been acceptable at any early date: the lawyers, indeed, preferred to dispute whether a minority could prevail if it was the *sanior pars*. But we know that in England, by 1367, the royal judges had insisted on the unanimity principle for trial juries, perhaps to save themselves the embarrassment of having to act as umpires when juries divided.[62] And there were analogous arguments in favour of judicial unanimity on those relatively few occasions when the court was required to decide a matter peremptorily. There was no appeal, the judgment would be a precedent for the future, and so the judges felt no obligation to decide demurrers unless the law was abundantly clear.[63] In case of doubt or disagreement they were supposed to stay judgment so that the matter could be considered in council[64] or in the Exchequer Chamber[65] or so that the parties, recognising the balanced merits, could be induced to settle.[66] This policy suggests that unanimity was the goal; and we know that the judges often left cases undetermined for years in the hope of attaining it. We also know that in a politically sensitive case such as *Lord Dacre's Case* (1535), where a speedy decision was required despite substantial judicial disagreement, the minority were persuaded to give way in the sense that the decision was

---

[61] *Township and Borough* (1898), pp. 34–35.
[62] Y.B. Mich. 41 Edw. III, fo. 31, pl. 36. This had not always been the law: see Fitz. Abr., *Verdit*, pl. 40 (1329); Mich. 20 Edw. III (Roll Series), Vol. II, p. 555, pl. 110. (It never was extended to trial by peers, or to accusations by grand juries.) For the explanation, see Pollock & Maitland, *History of English Law*, Vol. II, p. 627; Baker, *Introduction to English Legal History*, p. 66.
[63] Selden Soc., Vol. 94, pp. 156–157.
[64] See *Oklond v. Danvers* (1311), Selden Soc., Vol. 63, at p. 171, *per* Bereford C. J.
[65] See M. Hemmant, *Select Cases in the Exchequer Chamber* (1933), Selden Soc., Vol. 51, introduction, for the preconditions of such an adjournment.
[66] Selden Soc., Vol. 94, pp. *92, 157.*

published as if it had been unanimous.[67] Even so, unanimity was not always obligatory. In a case of 1484 we find Bryan C. J. giving judgment against his own opinion because he felt constrained by " le plus party des judges " in the Exchequer Chamber;[68] but this was after verdict, and it may be that the judges' moral right to procrastinate was generally confined to cases where the parties had mutually agreed to stick on a point of law.

It is possible to perceive a change of attitude in the sixteenth century, when the courts were called upon more frequently than in the past to lay down the law definitively upon demurrer, or special verdict, or motion in arrest of judgment. In a famous case of 1535, Fitzherbert J. advised the profession to take a year-book case of 1520 out of their books because it had been decided by two judges of the King's Bench " without any advice, but only according to their opinions ".[69] These two judges (in a three-man court) were acting in a manner which today is commonplace, though in Henry VIII's reign it still gave offence to a conservative such as Fitzherbert—at any rate when he disagreed with the previous decision. By the end of the century, however, it was common for judgment to be given on the strength of a majority opinion,[70] even on demurrer.[71] It was possible for two judges to give judgment in the absence of their fellows,[72] where by themselves they were not a majority of the full court; and in one case of 1593, where the four judges of the Queen's Bench were evenly divided, two judges one day seized the opportunity to give judgment themselves when Popham C. J. was absent.[73] Yet it was still the normal practice to adjourn if one judge was dissatisfied,[74] and it seems that the dissentient judge or judges still had to be persuaded to abide by the majority.[75] This may be why *Slade's Case* (1602), decided by a bare majority of all the judges, stuck in the gullet of the dissentients and was not immediately accepted by the minority.[76]

The newer and harsher form of the majority principle represented the

---

[67] Spelman's *Reports*, Selden Soc. vol. 93, pp. 228–230; vol. 94, p. *140*.
[68] Selden Soc. vol. 64, p. 62. See also vol. 51, p. xxxvi.
[69] Y.B. Trin. 27 Hen. VIII, fo. 23, pl. 21, referring to *Cleymond* v. *Vincent* (1520), Mich. 12 Hen. VIII, fo. 11, pl. 3; KB 27/1037, m. 40.
[70] E.g., Cro. Eliz. 132 (1589), 147 (1589), 191 (1590), 210 (1590), 249 (1591), 258 (1591), etc. For some curious learning on majority decisions where the court was divided into more than two sides, see *Earl of Shrewsbury's Case* (1610), 1 Buls. 11; *Rudyard's Case* (1670), 2 Vent. 22, 24.
[71] E.g., Cro. Eliz. 217 (Common Pleas, 1591), 266 (Exchequer, 1591), 342 (Queen's Bench, 1594).
[72] E.g., Cro. Eliz. 66 (1587), 256 (1591).
[73] Cro. Eliz. 300.
[74] E.g., Cro. Eliz. 193 (1590), 314 (1594), 448 (1595).
[75] This seems to be explicit in Cro. Eliz. 420 (1595): ". . . because three of them agreed against the plaintiff but upon several reasons, Gawdy [who differed] consented unto them that judgment should be given against the plaintiff."
[76] Baker, *Introduction to English Legal History*, pp. 286, 289.

triumph of judicial (or rather " curial ") authority over the older notion that law was " common learning ", the better opinion of the profession as a whole.[77] The ultimate test for the new approach came in proceedings in error; for a decision by a bare majority in a court of error could result in a minority of all the judges of England prevailing over the majority. This possibility does not seem to have attracted any comment before 1600, no doubt because it was simply unthinkable.[78] In 1602, however, a law student noted with dismay that if the Queen's Bench by a majority overturned a unanimous Common Pleas decision, three judges would prevail over five;[79] and in 1611 Coke C. J. complained that one third of the judiciary could defeat the majority if five unanimous King's bench judges were reversed 4:3 in the Exchequer Chamber.[80] It would be good to know a little more about this seemingly momentous change in the philosophy of judicial authority, which prepared the way for our present practice that two judges may bind a hundred.

Conclusion

I have been raising questions rather than answering them, and since they are questions which have not received much airing in the past it would be premature to suggest any general thesis concerning the development of the idea of a court. The present purpose is merely to show that the idea is not the changeless notion we so often assume, and that it has an intellectual and legal history of its own. The subject may seem a little narrow and recondite. Nevertheless, since the common law has for some long time been equated with the words and deeds of courts, I suspect that the history of the common law, and the nature of the characteristics which distinguish it from other legal systems, will remain beyond our full understanding unless we first recognise that the concept of a court is complex and changeable.

---

[77] See Selden Soc. vol. 94, pp. 159–163; below, pp. 482–483.
[78] In a case of 1599 a majority judgment (2:1) was reversed by another majority (4:3), so that the judges of both courts were evenly divided (5:5): Cro. Eliz. 696.
[79] *The Diary of John Manningham of the Middle Temple*, ed. R. P. Sorlien (1976), p. 149.
[80] *Maine* v. *Peacher* (1611), MS. in Middle Temple, fo. 124v; Cambridge Univ. Lib. MS. Gg. 4. 9, fo. 38.

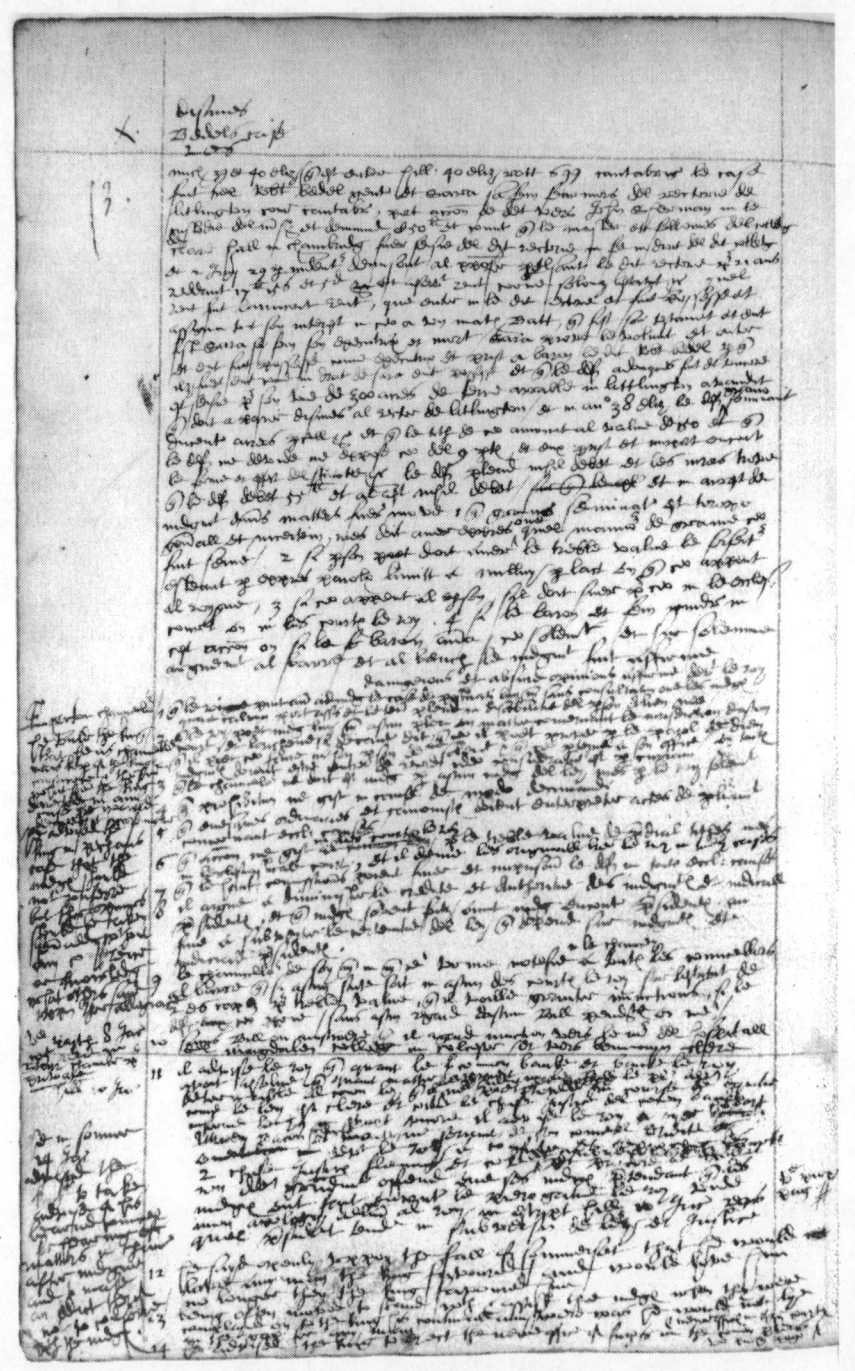

4 "Daungerous et absurd opinons affirme devant le roy"

A page from Coke's fifth notebook *(E)*, with his notes criticising Lord Chancellor Egerton. *Cambridge Univ. Lib., MS. Ii.5.21². fo. 47ᵛ.*

11

THE PECUNES

ACCORDING to the Black Books of Lincoln's Inn, the governors of the inn in 1483 or 1484 ordered the payment of 40s. for the "pekynnes" newly made.[1] Baildon, with some justification, felt puzzled by this strange word. He suggested that it might be a variant of "piggins," which were small wooden barrels.[2] In fact it is the latest example yet found of a word which occasionally appears in the year books. It must be one of the most mysterious words lurking in those arcane volumes, since it has almost entirely[3] escaped the notice of philologists and lexicographers and has no recorded meaning or etymology. The latest instance of the word in the year books seems to be in Trinity term 1467: "*Et Vavisor dit a ces compaignions que en les pecōns que deins les namz presedentz que cel addicion servant fuit debate en lescheker chambre....*"[4] Unfortunately, the passage does not make sense as it

---

[1] MS. Black Books, II, f. 57v (now 49v): "*Et xl*ˢ· *solut' Hunt per mandatum gubernatorum pur lez pekynnes noviter fact'*." Hunt is perhaps Thomas Hunt, an attorney of the Common Pleas (and clerk of the peace for Derbyshire), specially admitted to Lincoln's Inn in 1470.

[2] J. D. Walker [and W. P. Baildon] ed., *Records of the Honorable Society of Lincoln's Inn. The Black Books*, I (1897), p. 80n.

[3] There is a brief note in J. H. Baker, *Manual of Law French* (1979), p. 158.

[4] Trin. 7 Edw. IV, f. 10, pl. 1, from Pynson's edition (c. 1520), C[ambridge] U[niversity] L[ibrary], Syn. 4. 52. 6. The text is substantially the same in later editions, including the spelling of pecōns (with the tittle). A suggested translation is: "And Vavisor said to his fellows [who were] in the *pecouns* that within the last two years this addition 'servant' had been discussed in the Exchequer Chamber...."

stands in print, and there is no surviving manuscript text. Almost certainly "namz," which is faithfully reproduced in all the editions down to 1680, is a misreading of "ii anz," the reference being to a case decided two years earlier.[5] Still there is something wrong; perhaps the first and third "que" should be omitted. The sense seems to be that Vavisor cited the recent case to his fellows in the *pecons* or *pecouns*, as having some bearing on the case currently before the court. That the word denoted some place where lawyers commented on cases is confirmed beyond doubt by three year-book passages from the 1450s. In Hilary term 1454, after a joinder in demurrer by Serjeant Moyle, the reporter noted a comment on the point of pleading, made in the *pekons*, and there is then a reference to an earlier case.[6] A year later, while reporting another argument by Moyle (now a judge), the reporter interpolated a comment made in the *pecunes*.[7] And in Michaelmas term 1450, when Serjeant Choke dared not demur to a tender of law in debt on an account, the reporter noted a stir of general astonishment: "*quod nota, car touts queux fueront en le pekenes marvailent a ceo....*" Prisot C.J. added his own expression of surprise: "*Modico fidei, quare dubitastis?*"[8] Only two earlier references have been found in the year books, both in Michaelmas term 1430.[9] The second of them is not unlike the 1459 example, because it records an opinion held by everyone in the *pecunes* contrary to that followed by a serjeant pleading at the bar.[10] The first attributes a remark in the *pecouns* or *pecunes* to a named individual: "*Porteman dit en le pecouns que le matier [que] Caundish ad allege serra plede 'et issint nient son fait'....*"[11] Once again, therefore, the subject of discussion is a point of pleading which has just arisen in court.

The *pecunes*, or *pekynnes*, thus have nothing to do with barrels. But what and where were they, and why did Lincoln's Inn contribute towards some new ones? Since neither Portman nor Vavisor were members of Lincoln's Inn, the pecunes cannot have been an institution peculiar to one inn of court. Walter Portman († 1451) was a Somerset lawyer, the first of a long legal dynasty, whose grandson and great-grandson were both readers of the Middle

---

[5] *Long Quinto*, f. 320.
[6] Hil. 32 Hen. VI, f. 33, pl. 28 ("*Et nota fuit dit en les pekons que...*").
[7] Hil. 33 Hen. VI, f. 8, pl. 23 ("*mes fuit dit en les pecunes que...*").
[8] Mich. 38 Hen. VI, f. 6, pl. 14. Prisot C.J.'s quotation is from St. Matthew, 14, 31 ("O ye of little faith, why did ye doubt?").
[9] I am grateful to Mr. Nicholas le Poidevin for bringing these to my notice.
[10] Mich. 9 Hen. VI, f. 55, pl. 41 ("*et touts en les pecunes teignent que le ple en barre fuit matter a contrarye de briefe*"). The text in C.U.L., MS. Gg. 5. 8, reads: "*Et toutz en lez pecunez teignent que cest plee en barr est merement contrarie al brefe.*"
[11] C.U.L., MS. Gg. 5. 8, passage corresponding to Mich. 9 Hen. VI, f. 37, pl. 12 ("*Portmain dit en le pecunes...*").

Temple.[12] He himself was a Member of Parliament, and by 1430 may have reached the position of reader. "Vavisor" in the 1467 text is probably John Vavasour († 1506), who was admitted to the Inner Temple in the 1450s and became a serjeant in 1478; but it could conceivably be his brother William († 1500)[13] or his father John († 1482).[14] So it seems likely that members of each inn might be found in the pecunes. It must have been a single, and presumably central, institution. Was it, then, some kind of law class held after court hours? The 1459 case suggests a rather more immediate reaction than would be expected in a law school. Prisot C.J.'s biblical exclamation appears actually to have been prompted by the gasp of amazement. We seem, therefore, to be present in court.

It is at this point that we may recall a parallel problem which puzzled, and defeated, Maitland. In a manuscript year book he noticed that a pleading was said to have caused amazement in court, and that the reporter noted a comment afterwards made in the *cribbe*: "*Et postea dictum fuit en le Cribbe.*..."[15] Two speakers, apparently in the *cribbe*, are named as Richard de Aldeburgh and John de Trevanion, both of whom we now know became serjeants around 1313. Maitland challenged legal historians to identify the place referred to: "What the Crib was we fain would know."[16] The puzzle was solved by Turner, who discovered a petition to King Edward II by "*ses emprentis de sun comun banke*" in which they begged permission to make "*une crubbe pur lour esteer a lour aprise*" like the one on the other side of the court.[17] The *cribbe* or *crubbe* was therefore some kind of enclosure at the side of the court where the apprentices stood to learn the law. Turner did not speculate as to the form of this enclosure or structure, but Bolland plausibly supposed it to have been the wooden box or stand

---

[12] He was member for Taunton 1417–35, and the patent rolls show that he was a feoffee for the abbot of Glastonbury in 1426, a commissioner of gaol delivery from 1432 to 1451, and a justice of the peace from 1442 to 1451. His son and heir John († 23 Nov. 1486) was a justice of the peace 1483–84, and was described as of Orchard, Somerset, and London, gentleman, which suggests membership of an inn. This John's son and heir, John († 5 July 1521) was a double reader of the Middle Temple (1509, 1515) and was buried in Temple Church. John II's son and heir, William († 2 Feb. 1557), was also a double reader of the inn (1532, 1540) and became Chief Justice of the King's Bench.

[13] William Vavasour († 26 March or 24 May 1500) was described in 1471 as of Spaldington, Yorkshire, and London, gentleman, which suggests he may have belonged to an inn. He is probably the William Vavasour who was sued by Clifford's Inn in 1481 for unpaid dues.

[14] This John Vavasour was of Spaldington. He served on commissions from 1452, and was justice of the peace for the east riding of Yorkshire 1455–82. He may be the same John Vavasour who was clerk of the warrants in the Common Pleas from the 1430s to the 1450s. A John Vavasour was sued by Staple Inn in 1461 for unpaid dues.

[15] British Library, MS. Add. 35116, f. 170v.

[16] Selden Soc., vol. XIX, p. xvi.

[17] Selden Soc., vol. XXII, p. xli.

which is mentioned in later times.[18] The etymology of *cribbe* is as obscure as that of *pecunes*. Some have supposed it to refer humorously to the youth of the apprentices, but more likely there is a separate sense denoting a pen or scaffolding.[19] Even at the end of James I's reign the galleries in Westminster Hall seem to have been rather ramshackle wooden constructions on stilts.[20] Their physical details may yet emerge from documents in the unsorted files of the court.

It is an irresistible speculation that the *cribbe*, or *cribbes* (if the second was built), somehow came to be called the "pecunes." But the change of name we are at a loss to explain. There is hardly a satisfactory etymology save by way of *pecunia*, but if that is the case here the word must be a legal colloquialism. Maybe the apprentices had to pay money to go up into the stalls. It will not be long before an expression such as "in the three and sixes" will require a learned explanatory gloss for future generations. A connection between the pecunes and *pecunia* was indeed made, if only for the sake of a pun, as early as the 1370s. The meaning of the allusion to the pecunes has not hitherto been discerned by modern commentators. The passage occurs in John Gower's poem *Mirour de l'Omme*, probably written between 1376 and 1378:

" Cest la coustumme a Westmoustier,
  Qui voet aprendre le mestier
  Du loy, lors falt en un estage
  De les peccunes halt monter,
  Cest un estage pour conter:
  Bien accordant a celle usage
  Sur les peccunes devient sage,
  Quil du peccune lavantage
  En temps suiant sache amasser
  Pour son prou et lautry damage
  Sur les peccunes son corage
  Attorne a la peccune amer...." [21]

---

[18] W. C. Bolland, *The Year Books* (1921), p. 3; *Manual of Year Book Studies* (1925), pp. 10–11.

[19] See *Oxford English Dictionary*, s.v. "crib" and "curb," which does not have any early examples in this sense. "Cradle" was also used in the same sense. The year-book reporters knew the French for crib or cradle in the usual sense: Selden Soc., vol. XXXI, p. 161 (" berz "); Hil. 2 Edw. III, f. 5, pl. 4 (" berche ").

[20] A sketch of the Hall taken in ink around 1620, now in the British Museum, shows the galleries in the Chancery and King's Bench. The latter has two tiers, with planks at the sides. A wooden gallery in the Common Pleas is shown, albeit crudely, in Gravelot's drawing "The First Day of Term" (c. 1739), engraved by C. Mosley in 1740.

[21] C.U.L., MS. Add. 3035, f. 133. This is the only known text. It is accurately printed, but without translation, in G. C. Macaulay ed., *Complete Works of John Gower*, II (1899), p. 269, lines 24350–24361. In the glossary (at p. 536) Macaulay translates " peccune " as " money," without attempting to explain the plural form.

Now that we know the double meaning of *peccunes,* we can venture a prose translation:

> "It is the custom at Westminster that he who wants to learn the mystery of the law must climb up high on a platform [22] of the *peccunes*. This is a stand for counting.[23] It is a very appropriate custom that he should become wise on the *peccunes*, that he might know how to amass a pecuniary advantage in time to come, for his own profit and the disadvantage of others: upon the *peccunes* his heart turns to the love of *pecunia*."

As thus interpreted, the passage therefore takes us back a century before the Lincoln's Inn entry and incidentally confirms that the apprentices were not merely penned in on the ground but had to climb up to a gallery.

The discovery of a new word for the dictionaries is satisfying; but the identification of the pecunes is not without its significance for legal history. It shows that the gallery was a place not merely for passive observation but also for assessing and commenting on the moves in court. It might be argued that Portman and Vavasour were uttering *sotto voce* asides which the reporter happened to catch. But it seems more likely that the lawyers in the pecunes had an opportunity to discuss what they had seen, and even to cite earlier cases to each other. Such discussion occurred in the hearing of the year-book reporters, who must themselves have been in the pecunes. Perhaps, then, it was in the pecunes—rather than at learning exercises in the inns of court or chancery—that the year books were formed. On any view of the matter, the modest contribution by Lincoln's Inn in the 1480s was an investment of the utmost importance for its members.

---

[22] For the possible shades of meaning of *estage,* see *Oxford English Dictionary,* s.v. "stage."

[23] The exact meaning of this line is not clear, unless Gower intends another pun: between counting money and counting in the technical sense of reciting a count or declaration.

5 Sir Edward Coke

Chief Justice of the King's Bench. Painted between 1606 and 1616.

The Earl of Leicester, Holkham Hall

12

COKE'S NOTE-BOOKS AND THE SOURCES OF HIS REPORTS

FOUR hundred years ago this April, Edward Coke of Trinity College, Cambridge, was admitted to the Inner Temple, an event momentous not merely in the history of the Inn but also in the history of the common law. For it was in 1572 that young Coke began to attend the courts and to observe the decisions there,[1] to listen to Bendlowes and Plowden and Dyer as they opened for him the secrets of jurisprudence. He was to continue his attendance at Westminster Hall for forty-four years, and from 1579 to record all the important cases which came to his notice. It is, therefore, an auspicious moment to remember Coke's achievement as a reporter of cases, a matter of particular interest in " that famous University of Cambridge, *alma mea mater*," to whose legal offspring Coke's literary works were especially addressed.[2]

It is unnecessary to sing the praises of Coke's *Reports* as sources of law and history. For all their quaint defects they " will last to be admired by the judicious posterity whilst fame hath a trumpet left her, and any breath to blow therein." [3] In view of their undiminished importance, the almost complete absence of original textual studies is somewhat remarkable. In the latest edition of the *Reports*, published as long ago as 1826,[4] Mr. J. H. Thomas attempted to sever the personal comment and digression from the actual resolutions of the courts; but his only guide was his own instinct, corroborated where possible from other contemporary reports. Then, exactly thirty years ago, Professor Plucknett set himself the task of trying to discover the sources of, and the plan behind, the *Reports*.[5] He brought to the

---

[1] In Co.Litt. 384, 385, is cited a Common Pleas case of 1572 which Coke himself " heard and observed." The earliest case he reports at length in print is *Vernon's Case* (1572) 4 Rep. 1. For other observations between 1572 and 1579, see note 49, *infra*. Coke was twenty years old in 1572.
[2] Co.Litt., preface. Coke was admitted to Trinity College in September 1567, and went down at the end of 1570. He was admitted to Clifford's Inn on 21 January 1571, and to the Inner Temple on 24 April 1572. (Memoranda in MS.Harl. 6687.) There is no record of his taking the B.A. degree. An Edward Coke of the Inner Temple graduated B.A. in 1600 from St. Catharine's Hall, but this was Sir Edward's eldest son. Sir Edward proceeded M.A. in 1597 by special grace, and was elected High Steward of the University in 1614. (*Ibid.*; *Venn*.)
[3] T. Fuller, *History of the Worthies of England* (1662), p. 251.
[4] By J. H. Thomas and J. F. Fraser, in six volumes. Citations below are from this edition, always referring to the old foliation.
[5] " The Genesis of Coke's Reports " (1942) 27 *Cornell Law Quarterly* 190.

problem his usual insight and attention to detail, but confessed that the irregularity in composition was "deeply puzzling" and concluded that the reports had not been taken in the customary manner:

> The first glance at Coke is enough to show that the set of reports as a whole does not come from a chronologically arranged register like Plowden's, and does not reproduce a single series of cases noted down as they occurred. Indeed, no single series of any sort, chronological or systematical, seems to explain the present arrangement of the reports.

To solve the puzzle, Plucknett postulated that some of the cases had been taken from a commonplace book arranged by subject, and others from "collections made by other hands than his." He also posed, but left unanswered, the question whether the reports were contemporary, or were written up from memory, or from the writings of others, at the time of publication. Plucknett squeezed the last drop of evidence from the printed volumes themselves, but could not find the answer therein. He omitted to take into account the many short reports to be found in the *Institutes*, and because of war-time conditions he made no attempt to trace relevant manuscripts.[6] Further investigation was inhibited by the fact that no manuscripts of Coke's reports remained in his library at Holkham Hall, Norfolk; and it was thought that as a result of the confiscation of Coke's papers the original reports had long been lost.[7]

The new evidence began to emerge when the writer's attention was caught by MS.Harl. 6686 in the British Museum. It soon became apparent that, although no one seemed to have noticed the fact since 1715, the volume contained an extensive and valuable collection of reports in Coke's own hand, including not only early versions of reports which were later printed,[8] but also many cases not in print at all. Comparison with MS.Harl. 6687, which bears Coke's signature, confirmed the authorship; and Dr. W. O. Hassall's edition of Coke's own library catalogue (compiled *c.* 1634) revealed that both volumes had once belonged to Coke. The discovery at Cambridge of a further volume of reports in Coke's hand (MS.Ii.v. 21²), which answered to the description of another volume in the Holkham catalogue, confirmed the suspicion that the anonymous chronological series of reports listed there was Coke's own personal collection. It appears from the descriptions made *c.* 1634 that the complete series occupied seven

---

[6] *Ibid.*, esp. pp. 200, 203, 208, 212.
[7] See W. O. Hassall, *A Catalogue of the Library of Sir Edward Coke* (1950), pp. vi–vii: "The manuscripts of Coke's own *Reports* apparently already were lost in 1634, for they do not appear." It can now be shown that they do appear, but anonymously. The MSS. were probably confiscated in 1634, and they never returned to Holkham: see pp. 196-198, *infra*.
[8] See below, pp. 208-209, 402.

notebooks. Of these seven, four are still lost. Fortunately they are the least important volumes in the series; but it would be valuable to find them, and for this reason descriptions will now be given of all seven. To avoid confusion with the numbered parts of the printed *Reports*, the notebooks have here been lettered in chronological sequence from A to G.

Manuscript A : 1579-88

The first manuscript in the series is now part of MS.Harl. 6687.[9] The careless script in which the volume is written, and the mass of corrections, additions, interlineations and annotations which cover its pages, are consistent only with its being a private notebook, and the autograph work of its author. The identity of that author is revealed by the signature " Edward Coke " and sixteen leaves of autobiographical memoranda at the front of the volume. Included in the volume is an interleaved copy of Littleton's *Tenures*, and this naturally led observers to the conclusion that the manuscript insertions contained the draft of *Coke upon Littleton*. Mr. R. Nares described the manuscript in 1804 as " the original observations and enlargements of the L.C. Justice Coke [on *Littleton*] in his own hand-writing," and pointed out that " this very curious and valuable book has till lately escaped the notice of the editors and commentators upon Lord Coke's writings."[10] The volume is now labelled *Coke upon Littleton Autograph*.

In spite of Nares' comments, advertised to the learned world in the printed catalogue of the Harleian collection, the only part of the volume which has attracted any further attention (and that over a century ago) is the autobiographical section at the beginning. The Commissioners on the Public Records drew attention to this part in 1812,[11] and an anonymous contributor to the *Penny Cyclopaedia* hailed it as the long lost *Vade Mecum* mentioned in Fuller's *Worthies*.[12] It was published in 1840 in an antiquarian journal.[13] The editor, John Bruce, described the remainder as comprising " the germ and substance of Coke's celebrated commentary " on *Littleton*.

---

[9] For its provenance, see p. 198, *infra*.
[10] *Catalogue of the Harleian Manuscripts*, Vol. III (1808), p. 384.
[11] *Report from the Commissioners etc.*, 8 June 1812, p. 78.
[12] Fuller, *op. cit.*, note 1, *supra*, p. 251; copied *verbatim* in D. Lloyd, *State-Worthies* (1670 ed.). p. 824; *Penny Cyclopaedia*, Vol. VII, p. 332. Isaac Disraeli had hoped that the *Vade Mecum* might be recovered (*Curiosities of Literature* (1st ed., 1817), Vol. III, p. 170), but either he was unaware of or unconvinced by this identification when he wrote in 1849 that " this precious memorial may still be disinterred ": *Curiosities etc.* (14th ed.), Vol. II, p. 576. For Fuller's description, see p. 198, *infra*.
[13] J.B., " Sir Edward Coke's Vade Mecum " (1840) VI *Collectanea Topographica et Genealogica*, 108-122. For the identification of J.B. as Bruce, see E. Foss, *Judges of England* (1870), p. 179.

He had obviously not read it. Such descriptions deterred anyone from deciphering the difficult script in which the greater part of the volume is written. Since the printed *Coke upon Littleton* was prepared for the press by the author, there seemed little value in poring over the preliminary draft from which it was supposedly printed.

In fact the manuscript bears no resemblance to the printed *Commentary upon Littleton*. It has all the appearance of having been Coke's constant companion in his legal studies, and is more like a commonplace book than a continuous text or comment. As a work of reference its usefulness expired with its author. The printed *Commentary*, on the other hand, was the fruit of the author's retirement and truly his *magnum opus*. Its publication during Coke's lifetime removed the contemporary value of the manuscript, and it is uncertain whether it survived.[14]

When it was presented to Harley the volume had been a massive octavo of over 900 leaves, which by 1800 were in danger of falling apart. Shortly after that date the librarian of the British Museum caused the book to be disbound and rebound in four separate volumes. In this process the original order seems to have been lost. The volumes are now foliated continuously throughout in red ink, but the original foliation in black ink enables the constituent parts to be reconstructed from the confusion. It appears that, besides the printed *Littleton*, there are no less than five separately foliated items. It is not improbable that originally these had been separate, or in smaller volumes. Apart from the separate foliation, the signs of constant use suggest that they would not have held together as a unit while Coke was active. They were, however, bound together before Coke's death, perhaps when he had finished with them, or at the beginning of his retirement. They were "covered with a rich embroidery wrought by his own daughter," [15] and were thus described in the library catalogue prepared shortly before Coke's death:

> Littleton mixed not onely with booke cases and many titles of the lawe intermixed therewith, but with many reports of cases in the raigne of Queene Eliza: before the 32. yeare of the same Q: with a Cover of Crimson Sattine curiouslie imbrodred with gold silver and silke and over that a Cover of Crimson damaske. in 8°.[16]

---

[14] Sir Thomas Phillipps owned a manuscript (MS.Phill. 2628) described as "Coke's comments on Lyttleton." This was sold at Sotheby's in 1903 for one shilling (Phillipps sale, 29 April, lot 599). It is not described in the catalogue, and the purchaser, Dobell, was a bookseller. The present Mr. Dobell has no record of its resale. I am grateful to Dr. A. L. Munby, Librarian of King's College, for tracing this sale for me.

[15] R. Nares, *op. cit.*, note 10, supra. The embroidered covers were thrown away when the volume was rebound.

[16] *Catalogue of the Library of Sir Edward Coke* (W. O. Hassall, ed., 1950), p. 29, no. 369. (Hereinafter cited as the *Holkham Catalogue*.) The original is Holkham MS. 748B, and is signed by Coke in several places.

If only this description had been more widely known in the nineteenth century, the truth would have been revealed before now. The component parts are as follows [17]:

(i) Littleton's *Tenures* in French (1572 ed.—note the date): S.T.C. 15741. With some marginal notes by Coke. (Begins in Vol. *A*, f. *187*, and continues in Vols. *B* and *C*.)

(ii) Commonplace book, prefaced by personal memoranda; with Coke's signature. 121 ff. (Vol. *A*, ff. *17–186*.)

(iii) Another commonplace book; including the "booke cases" (Year Books), and a long section on uses. Probably an early study companion. 145 ff. (Vol. *D*, ff. *756–906*.)

(iv) A third commonplace book; begins with notes on estates, and includes extracts from *Plowden* and other reports. 284 ff. (Vol. *A*, ff. *189–243*; Vol. *B*, ff. *245–291, 340–496*; Vol. *D*, ff. *498–704*).

(v) Reports of cases, 21 Eliz.1–Mich. 26 & 27 Eliz.1. (Hil. 27 Eliz.1 missing). The first cases are from *Bendlowes*, but by f. *304* Coke has begun his own series. 55 ff. Eight leaves now missing near the end. (Vol. *B*, ff. *293–339*; table at f. *339*.)

(vi) Reports of cases, Pas. 27 Eliz.1–Mich. 30 & 31 Eliz.1. A continuation of the last. 48 ff. (Vol. *D*, ff. *708–755*.)

The last two parts are those which we have together designated MS.A. Although separately foliated, they were continuous; the missing term is matched by eight missing leaves at the end of the book numbered (v). Their identification as the first part of Coke's original manuscript reports is corroborated by Coke's own statement that he began reporting in the twenty-second year of the Queen,[18] which is where the more substantial reports begin.

Manuscript B : 1588–91

The series continued in a smaller volume, which has become separated from its partners and apparently lost. It may have been with MSS.A and C when these were presented to Lord Harley in 1715,[19] but it has not been traced in the Harleian collection. Coke

---

[17] References are to the modern foliation in red.
[18] 1 Rep., preface, p. xxviii.
[19] Wanley, the librarian, noted the receipt of the gift on 6 August 1715, and said " Those *three* which are in covers of velvet etc. are supposed to be of the Hand of the Lord Chief Justice Sir Edward Coke ": *The Diary of Humfrey Wanley* (C. E. and R. C. Wright, eds., 1966), p. 13. (My italics.) The third book ought to be MS.B, unless either MS.Harl. 6686 or 6687 was then in two parts; but there is no other reference to their being divided in this way.

referred to this as his "*petit livre de reports*,"[20] and it was thus described in his lifetime:

> A little booke covered with blewe velvett cont: reports of 31. 32. and 33 Eliza: cont' alsoe a table to the reports of the Cheife Justice, and lastlie a table or repertorie of records and acts of parliament, which the Cheife Justice called his Vade Mecum. in 8°.[21]

The volume presumably started in the latter part of Michaelmas Term 1588, and began with a "*fort bon case.*"[20] It contained a report of the great case of *Finch* v. *Throgmorton* (1591) on f. 34.[22] The reports probably occupied little more than fifty leaves.[23] Its main contents could be reconstructed from the printed reports, but it is almost certain that (like MSS.A and C) it contained cases never printed, and it would be useful to find it.

Manuscript C : 1591–1606

The next manuscript, which continues the chronological series from Michaelmas Term 33 & 34 Eliz. 1 to Trinity Term 4 Jac. 1, was presented to Harley with MS.A, and is now MS.Harl. 6686. Although it was attributed to Coke in 1715, this had been forgotten by the end of the century, when it was described as " A thick octavo, containing precedents and cases in law from the 33 Eliz. until 5 [*sic*] James 1. 713 leaves, very closely written in a small hand."[24] The "small hand" is clearly Coke's, and the volume answers to the description in Coke's library catalogue: "One booke of reports covered with black velvett in 8°. beginning with Pasche 33 Eliz: and ending Tr: 4° Jac: regis and cont' 713. leaves."[25] The velvet covers were lost when the book was rebound *c.* 1805; the new binding is labelled "Law Precedents."

The manuscript is inscribed by Coke "*liber primus.*" The inference is that Coke regarded the earlier reports as youthful experiments, and that he had now taken seriously to reporting as a public service.

---

[20] MS.C, f. 567v: "*vide fort bone case in mes reportes Mich. 30 et 31 Eliz. regine fol. 1 in le petit livre de reportes.*" This does not refer to MS.A, so Michaelmas Term must have been divided between MSS.A and B.
[21] *Holkham Catalogue*, p. 27, no. 336. It is there listed separately from MSS.C–G.
[22] Cited in MS.C, f. 99. There should also be a report of *Herlakenden's case* under Trin. 31 Eliz. (cited MS.C, f. 22v); of *Thetford's case* on f. 22v (cited MS.C, f. 20); of *Daubeney* v. *Gore* on f. 25 (cited MS.A, f. 306v); and a case of slander on f. 27 (cited MS.A, f. 325v).
[23] There was a case of Pas. 33 Eliz. on f. 44 (cited MS.A, f. 331), and there was only one later term (Trin. 33 Eliz.).
[24] *Loc. cit.*, note 10, *supra*. " 5 " is an error for " 4."
[25] *Holkham Catalogue*, p. 22, no. 293. The volume begins with a single case entered in Easter Term 33 Eliz. I (*Elmer* v. *Thacker*: see Co.Litt. 355b), and this would account for the date here. The "*liber primus*" commences, however, on f. 7 (originally f. 1), in Michaelmas Term.

Perhaps by now he had publication in mind. His report of *Shelley's Case* had already enjoyed a wide circulation in manuscript,[26] and by the time he had filled up MS.C he had published the first five parts of the *Reports*. The volume is far more substantial than its predecessors. Whereas MS.A covered ten years in about one hundred leaves, MS.C covers fifteen years in over seven hundred leaves. It contains the core of the *Reports*—more than one half of all the printed cases—and many more besides.

Manuscript D : 1606–1608

The manuscript here designated D, which Coke would have called his *liber secundus*, was described in 1634 as: " Another booke of reports beginnings Pasche 4° Jac: regis and endinge Mich: 6° Jac: regis and cont' 81 leaves, with a redd guilded closure in 4°." [27] Clearly it was nowhere near so substantial a volume as MS.C. It probably contained *Calvin's Case*, the last six cases in Part VI (ff. 56–80), and the last five in Part VII (ff. 38–45). The residue was separated after Coke's death and later published from a copy as ff. 1–65 of Part XII. Since this volume passed into circulation after Coke's death, it is doubtful whether the original manuscript would contain any cases not already to be found in the collections associated with Part XII. But it would be satisfying to find it, and to have Coke's original and private versions of the important cases which he himself published from it.

Manuscript E : 1608–11

The fifth volume in the series (or the third, counting MS.C as *liber primus*) was described as: " Another booke of reports beginninge Mich. 6° Jacobi regis and ending Pasche 8° eiusdem regis, and cont' 111. leaves, bound in redd leather in fol: " [28]

In 1658 this very volume was displayed to the profession by Henry Twyford the law publisher, at his shop in the Temple.[29] At some time in the next forty years it came into the possession of John Moore, Bishop of Norwich and later of Ely; by which time its identity had been forgotten.[30] Moore's library, fortunately, was purchased by King George I and presented to Cambridge University in 1715. (It seems to be pure coincidence that MSS.A and C were acquired by

---

[26] See p. 189, *infra*.
[27] *Holkham Catalogue*, p. 22, no. 294.
[28] *Ibid.*, no. 295.
[29] See p. 200, *infra*.
[30] It was described by Bernard as " Reports in the reign of King James 1. fol.": *Librorum MSS. D.D. Johannis Mori Episcopi Norvicensis Catalogus*, p. 375, no. 542, in E. Bernard, *Catalogi MSS. Angliae* (1697).

Harley in the same year.) The oblivion into which MS.E had fallen was not dispelled when Professor Abdy carelessly described it, in the 1858 printed catalogue, as "Law Reports ... some of the cases are in Coke, Croke, Ley, and Moore." [31] The volume has now lost its red leather binding, and has been bound behind another work with which it has no connection. But it is in the same distinctive hand as MSS.A and C, with all the author's interlineations and corrections. The reports collate exactly with the printed cases in Part XIII, and the number of leaves and the period covered are exactly as described in the *Holkham Catalogue*. Moreover, the book is inscribed "*Liber tertius*" on f. 1, and is dated 4 November 1608, presumably the date of commencement. This date alone is inconsistent with the volume being anything but Coke's contemporary notebook, and it shows that the Michaelmas Term was divided between MSS.D and E at the beginning of November.

The volume is slender beside MS.C, although it is written on larger paper and contains nearly ninety entries, including such famous cases as *Crogate's, Dr. Bancroft's,* and *Dr. Bonham's*.[32] It accounts for all the printed cases from the period covered, except for a few cases of Michaelmas Term 1608 which were presumably noted (in MS.D) before 4 November. It is the source of nearly every case in Part VIII, and of the whole of Part XIII.

Manuscripts F and G: 1611–16

The series was completed by two notebooks, overlapping in date, which are both lost. One of them (MS.G) was a mere twenty-six leaves, with cases between Hilary Term 1614 and Hilary Term 1616. The other must have contained most of the remaining cases used by Coke in his later volumes, and the residue which appeared in Part XII: in other words, Part VIII, ff. 144–end, Part IX, ff. 242–end, the whole of Part X, Part XI (excepting three earlier cases),[33] and Part XII, ff. 65–end. This latter volume contained 222 leaves, and was bound in vellum.[34]

Coke's Method

Coke began his long series of reports in the traditional manner by collecting cases out of the reports of his immediate predecessors: in his case, from Plowden, Dyer, Broke, and from the manuscript

---

[31] *Catalogue of Manuscripts in the Library of the University of Cambridge*, Vol. III (1858), p. 486. The shelf-mark is Ii.v.21².
[32] At ff. 9v–10, 42, 90v–95v.
[33] *The Case of Monopolies*, MS.C, ff. 571v–574; *Auditor Curle's Case*, MS.E, f. 84; *Earl of Devonshire's Case*, which was probably in MS.D.
[34] *Holkham Catalogue*, p. 22, nos. 296 and 297.

reports of Serjeant Bendlowes which Coke borrowed about the time he was called to the Bar in 1578.[35] Soon after this date he was himself noting down decisions which he had heard given at Westminster or which he heard about in the Temple. He had soon caught the eyes of the older lawyers, and so it is no surprise to find him noting what he had been told by old Plowden,[36] or the Solicitor-General,[37] or a friendly serjeant,[38] or by Wray C.J. "*veniendo de* Westminster." [39] The chronological arrangement of the notes, with a flourish of red ink at the start of each new term (in MS.A), and continuous headlines indicating the term and year, show that Coke wrote all this down contemporaneously. The notebooks were also used as a commonplace, in which Coke would write personal memoranda,[40] obituaries,[41] notes on the royal prerogative and on administrative practices,[42] historical notes from ancient records,[43] notes on the meaning of statutes,[44] particularly of recusants,[45] and numerous notes of things Popham C.J. had told him.[46]

Nevertheless, a significant number of reports do not appear in their proper chronological places. This is because Coke continued

---

[35] MS.A, f. 292: *Ex libro Bendlowes servientis ad legem.* It is not known how widely these circulated before the serjeant's death in 1584. Coke later had two copies at Holkham: *Holkham Catalogue*, p. 26, no. 330, and p. 28, no. 349.

[36] MS.A, f. 327v: " *Nota in mesme cestui terme* [M. 1583] *Plowden dit a moy....*" Plowden died the following year. *Cf.* 3 Rep. 79.

[37] MS.A, f. 318 (H. 1583): " *Egerton Sollicitor dit a moy....*"

[38] *Ibid.*, ff. 317v ("*Nota que Gawdy serieant dit a moy veniendo de Westminster...*"), 725 ("*Nota Serieant Walmesley dit a moy...*").

[39] *Ibid.*, f. 712 (M. 1585).

[40] MS.C, ff. 34–35 (appointed Solicitor-General), ff. 86–87v (appointed Attorney-General). On the flyleaf of MS.A is a note, presumably scribbled when Coke was made Chief Justice: " Choller of SS. con' 53 SS. and knotes, foure percullis & two roses."

[41] MS.C, f. 54 (Manwood, different from 3 Rep. 26): *cf.* 6 Rep. 75 (Popham); 9 Rep. 14–15 (Dyer), 121–122 (Lord Sanchar); 10 Rep. 34 (Fleming).

[42] See MS.C, ff. 57v–58 (tithes), 69v (fees of the Clerk of the Market, 1 July 1593), 88v (letters patent), 112 (debt to the Crown), 257v (" Concerning the mynte "), 261 (" Concerning the stalling of debts due to her majestie "), 327v (forests), 461v (fines on original writs), 503v (Green Wax). Notes on Parliament: *ibid.*, ff. 56, 209–210, 576v. Notes on purveyance: *ibid.*, ff. 606v–609, 649v–651v, 682v–686, 688–694v.

[43] See MS.C, ff. 69v (fine before eight justices, 1453), 118v (ancient Welsh custom that females did not inherit, 1430), 119 (Rolls Chapel, and attorneys), 123 (grant of swan-mark), 123v (Priory of St. John's, 1352), 124 (London customs concerning widows), 124v (record of 1229 showing that younger sons inherited before daughters of elder sons), 143–144 and 147–148v (record of 1298 proving that lands held by grand serjeanty were forfeited for alienation without licence), 207v (*Cobb v. Nore*, 1465), 271v (degradation of duke, 1477), 373 (creation of Prince of Wales by Edward I), 446 (removal of Swillington A.-G. for misdemeanours, *c.* 1526). Some of the records were copied by a secretary.

[44] See MS.C, ff. 57, 65, 81, 89, 145v, 255, 284v, 320v, 403v, 418, 459v–461v, 505, 554v, 562, 609v.

[45] See MS.C, ff. 68v, 81v–82, 84v–85, 99, 125v.

[46] *e.g.*, MS.C, ff. 93, 109, 135v, 158, 159, 171, 203, 274, 306, 307, 308, 317v, 396v, 446, 563. *Cf.* ff. 81, 82v (Egerton), 135 (Anderson).

throughout his career to enter into his notebooks details of earlier cases which he had come across in writing or which he had heard cited in court. He entered such cases under the term in which he learned of them, usually citing the plea roll. This fact provides a touchstone for separating the cases written down as they were decided from those which were probably collected by hearsay. No such indication is given in the printed versions. Thus *Thoroughgood's Case*, decided in 1584, appears under Trinity Term 1598 with the explanation: " In this same term I saw a record in the Common Bench, Trin. 26 Eliz., Filmer, Essex. . . ." [47] This case is followed by notes of *Manser's Case*, *Goddard's Case*, and *Wiseman's Case*, all apparently extracted from the rolls of 26 and 27 Eliz. 1, with notes of the argument added. Coke later printed these cases at the beginning of Part II, though in a different order, giving no indication that they were other than his own report. It is possible, of course, that Coke recalled having been present; but the fact that he made no note for fifteen years suggests otherwise. His interest may have been aroused by research in the plea rolls, after which he made enquiries of the counsel and judges involved, or borrowed a report. Sometimes Coke noted that he had " seen " an earlier case, which probably meant he had seen a report or record.[48] Sometimes, especially in the *Institutes*, he mentioned cases which he had " heard " or " observed " [49]; most of these date from the period 1572–79, and probably Coke was using another report of a case which he remembered from his student days but which he had not himself reported.

Reports cited by Coke

Plucknett suggested that Coke had taken some of his cases from Sir Christopher Wray's reports, citing a passage in Part IV where a reference is made to something which was " said and reported by Wray C.J." [50] It is submitted that this plainly refers to an oral report by Wray, and not a written report. Elsewhere Coke relates what he

---

[47] *Ibid.*, f. 300v. See 2 Rep. 1–16.
[48] *e.g.*, MS.A, f. 732v (T. 1584, seen M. 1587); MS.C, ff. 29v (M. 1588, seen H. 1592), 40v (H. 1591, seen M. 1592), 68 (H. 1590, seen P. 1593), 112 (M. 1576, seen H. 1595), 133v (1583, seen H. 1596), 192 (T. 1562, seen P. 1597), 230 (H. 1593, seen M. 1597), 266 (T. 1585, seen H. 1598), 268 (M. 1588, seen H. 1598), 300 (T. 1584, seen T. 1598), 348 (M. 1594, seen T. 1599), 355v (M. 1590, seen T. 1599), 558v (M. 1574, seen P. 1603). Several of these appear in the printed *Reports* without any indication that they were second-hand. Most of them were decided in Coke's own time.
[49] MS.C, f. 21; 11 Rep. 48, 60; Co.Litt. 31v, 59v, 77, 210, 211, 221v, 249, 269, 270v, 311, 317, 318v, 365v, 384, 385; 2 Inst. 313 (" in my time "), 502. Only two of these fall outside the period 14–21 Eliz., and they are both in the notebooks (Co.Litt. 210=MS.A, f. 308; Co.Litt. 270v=MS.C, f. 239v).
[50] 27 *Cornell Law Quarterly* at p. 212; 4 Rep. 63.

heard Wray " report " in the King's Bench,[51] and the word " report " often indicated citations in open court.

To what extent Coke did draw upon other identifiable reports is not easy to judge from the notebooks themselves, because Coke did not always state his source. He possessed, and frequently cited from, Serjeant Bendlowes' reports.[52] He owned a copy of part of Justice Spilman's reports, and sometimes cited from it.[53] He had access to a manuscript of " Keilwey " before it was published in 1602.[54] He had access to some of Justice Dalison's reports which were not in print.[55] He had seen a manuscript by Plowden, in which there was a report of *Sir John Baker's Case* superior to that in *Dyer*.[56] By 1610 at least he had acquired a manuscript said to be in Dyer's handwriting,[57] containing numerous cases not in print, from which Coke often made citations.[58] Coke also cited " Periam," by folio, presumably reports by Chief Baron Peryam (d. 1604)[59]; and also " Wyndam," presumably by Francis Wyndham J. (d. 1592).[60] His library catalogue lists three books of reports by " Thurston," and three anonymous volumes of reports.[61] Apart from the allegation that he

---

[51] 4 Inst. 324. Apparently Wray did compile reports, which appear to be cited in MS.Lansd. 1084, ff. 36v, 81 (*cf.* f. 93 : " *come Wrai dit a moy* ").

[52] Note 35, *supra*; cited in MS.A, f. 292, MS.C, ff. 38, 177, 192v, 1 Rep. 26, 96, 176, 2 Rep. 49, 3 Rep. 91, 4 Rep. 51, 88, 95. (Later citations may be from the printed edition of 1602.) Many MS. versions are known.

[53] *Holkham Catalogue*, p. 26, no. 326; cited in MS.C, f. 568, 6 Rep. 62, 63, Co.Litt. 130, 146, 229v, 2 Inst. 49, 50, 493, 636, 3 Inst. 9, 17, 30, 126, 4 Inst. 59, Cro.Jac. 152. Spilman's original MS. was still in the possession of his family in Coke's time, but it is now lost; the best copy, though it contains many errors, is in MS.Hargr. 388.

[54] See MS.C, ff. 138 (" *extra librum Keylwey* "), 245v (" *ex libro Kelywaye* "). John Croke, who published the reports in 1602, was a bencher of the Inner Temple; it is likely that Coke saw his manuscript.

[55] See Golds. 153.

[56] MS.C, f. 170; " *Nota in mesme cestui terme ieo viewe le case . . . report per mounsieur Plowden.*" It is not in the printed book. Coke cites the same case in 7 Rep. 8 " as I myself have seen."

[57] Exeter Coll. Oxford MS. 128, f. 149v (cited by G. D. G. Hall, 69 L.Q.R. 208n) : " This cause is found in a manuscript written altogether with the hand of my Lord Dyer remayninge in the Custody of my lord Cooke." *Cf.* 10 Rep.pref., p. xxxiv : " the very original whereof, written with his own hand, I have." See *Holkham Catalogue*, p. 23, no. 302: " Foure bookes of the Collection of cases by the Lord Dier in fol : whereof two are written with his owne proper hand." See also 9 Rep. 15, 11 Rep. 77, 3 Buls. 49. The MSS. are no longer at Holkham. *Cf.* Inner Temple MS.Petyt 511.13, ff. 34–70; MS.Hargr. 26, ff. 166v–174.

[58] See Co.Litt. 9, 13, 58v, 148v; 2 Inst. 61, 657, 682; 3 Inst. 17, 24, 61, 112, 126, 127, 172, 182; 4 Inst. 61, 240.

[59] MS.C, ff. 81, 124. Peryam was alive at the time of the citations, so Coke must have borrowed them from the author.

[60] MS.A, ff. 305v, 711v, 722, 741v.

[61] *Holkham Catalogue*, p. 28, nos. 347–348 : " Thurstone 3 books of reports in fol : and one other . . . Two other Ms : of reports in fol :" Thurston is probably John Thurston, Reader of the Inner Temple in 1560. Coke may have been referring to his reports when he showed in court a report of the serjeants' case of 1555 " reported by an ancient and learned bencher of the Inner Temple " (10 Rep. 128).

used the reports of Bridgeman in composing some of his own printed reports,[62] which it is difficult as yet to check, there is little reason to think that Coke actually borrowed many primary reports from these sources. Most of the sources were too old. When he did refer to them he did so by name, and he was more meticulous than most writers in noting references to his authorities. The fact that the unattributed reports are scattered throughout the notebooks suggests that they came from a variety of sources, probably verbal as well as literary. It should not be thought, in any case, that these reports are numerous in relation to the collection as a whole; and there is certainly no doubt as to the authorship of the longer reports, where all the argument is noted in detail.

One obvious contrast between the notebooks and the printed reports is that the former are more intimate and personal, and less polished. They are full of "*ieo argue*" and "*moy semble*": a continuous record of Coke's professional career. In MS.A he usually noted when he was retained of counsel, and it seems he was engaged in most of the important cases noted. Even when all else escaped Coke's notice, he would record his own argument: as he did with *Slade's Case*.[63] It was only natural that a reporter who himself played a leading role in the cases reported should remember his own arguments and citations more clearly than those of the other side. Of the one-sidedness of Coke's reports there is contemporary, if biased, corroboration by at least two sources.[64] Moreover, once Coke was in busy practice he could hardly have been present throughout the hearing of many cases in which he was not personally engaged; this fact alone divides the reports into those in which Coke was involved, and therefore probably had a formed opinion, and those which he presumably heard about by the relation of friends. Most of the "*graund*" cases, however, attracted Coke's personal attendance.

The change in character of the reports in the notebooks suggests that most of the later reports were original. In his earlier years, before he was at the centre of legal life, Coke was more dependent on hear-

---

[62] Lost MS. report of *Lloyd* v. *Gregory*, cited by Ellis J. in 1 Mod. 205, in which: " Jones . . . denied the case of *Hunt* v. *Singleton* [3 Rep. 60]. He said, that himself and Sir Rowland Wainscott [Wandesford] reported it, and that nothing was said of that point, but that Lord Coke followed the report of Bridgeman, who was three or four years their puisne, and that he mistook the case." There is no reference to Bridgeman's reports in Coke's manuscript: MS.C, f. 349v.

[63] See below, pp. 394-395.

[64] Bacon and Ellesmere. See J. Spedding (ed.), *Letters and Life of Bacon*, Vol. V (1869), pp. 86 (" too much *de proprio* "), 399 (" many exorbitant and extravagant opinions "); Vol. VI (1872), pp. 65 (" some peremptory and extrajudicial resolutions more than are warranted "), 87 (" scattering and sowing his own conceits "). See also Brit.Mus.MS.Add. 14030, f. 91; MS.Harg. 254. Anderson C.J. said of the report of *Shelley's Case*: " rien de ceo fuit parle en le Court ne la monstre " (1 And. 71).

say; though he took care to note what was not his own. In 1583 he wrote in the margin against cases cited in court: "*ex auditu.*"[65] Elsewhere he copied a report shown to him and ended: "*Quod nota ex relatione aliorum, ideo vide recorda in banco communi*"[66]; a mere report was not enough without checking the record. Towards 1600, and even more so after, it becomes clear that Coke's personal experience was sufficient to account for most of the material. By this time he had publication in mind and "*nota lecteur*" is frequently found in the manuscript. The majority of cases in MS.C, and the great majority in MS.E, are contemporary. The evidence confirms that Coke was unwilling to trust to memory, and regarded an "orderly observation in writing" as the most essential requisite to the knowledge of the common law.[67]

The Published Reports

Coke tells us that he had lent his reports to friends before they were printed, and in this way they had become partly public in the last decade of the sixteenth century.[68] No complete copy of the earlier reports is known, and only a few partial copies have been discovered. The first general publication by Coke was his *Report of Shelley's Case*, completed in January 1582 and dedicated to Lord Buckhurst. This enjoyed a wide circulation in manuscript.[69] It was the case in which Coke made his name, only two years after his call to the Bar, and the report was primarily a record of his own speech for the plaintiff. Of immense value to the profession, it was not without value as publicity for Coke, although in the manuscript version he tactfully attributed his speech to "an utter barrister of the Inner Temple." The report was evidently written in order to be published; it is not in MS.A, and all the known versions are in English.

By 1600 Coke had covered over one thousand pages of his *Vade Mecum* with reports, and in that year he published his first selection

---

[65] MS.A, f. 327. *Cf. ibid.*, f. 714v: "*come fuit dit a moy.*"
[66] *Ibid.*, f. 732 (1587).
[67] See 1 Rep.pref., p. xxvii: "I allow not of those that make memory their storehouse, for at their greatest need they shall want of their store. . . ." See also 7 Rep.pref., p. iv, quoted below.
[68] *Ibid.*, p. xxviii. In MS.Lansd. 1084, f. 42v, are two cases "*report per Cooke*," which must refer to the MS; one is in MS.A, f. 308, the other in MS.C, f. 119v. The most extensive copy discovered so far is Camb.U.L.MS.Gg.v. 4, ff. 37–50, 63v–68v, which begins "*Cases escrie ex Libro Cooke que il mesme collect 22 et 23 Eliz. in Bancke le roy.*" It contains a selection of over fifty cases from MS.A, ff. 305–332 (1580–84). The copy was certainly made in Coke's lifetime, but it cannot be accurately dated since the Cambridge MS. is itself a copy of the copy.
[69] *A Report of the Judgment and Part of the Arguments of Shelleys Case* (2 Jan. 1581/82), Holkham MS. 251; MS.Lansd. 1072, ff. 107–120; MS.Harl. 443, ff. 1–9; MS.Hargr. 373, f. 56; Camb.U.L.MS.Dd.xiii. 24, ff. 52v–58: Lincoln's Inn MS. Misc. 361, ff. (i), 1–11; MS. at Longleat House. The dedication is signed by Coke, and the signature is copied in each case by the transcriber.

190   *The Legal Profession and the Common Law*

in print.[70] This first volume contained, naturally, the cream of his collection, including the report of *Shelley's Case* translated into French. The preface to that case was adapted and extended to form the " Preface to the Reader." All the cases in the volume are from MS.C, except *Pelham's Case* (which was probably in MS.B), *Corbet's*, *Albany's*, and *Chudleigh's Cases*.[71] Coke expressly states that his report of *Corbet's Case* was " a summary report only of the principal reasons and causes of their judgment." A good proportion of it was taken up with reports of two other cases, cited by Anderson C.J., both of which were fully reported in MS.C.[72] Coke himself was of counsel in *Chudleigh's Case*, though he admits that he did not hear some of the arguments of counsel.[73] Of his report he says:

> All which arguments of the judges and barons I heard, except only that of Justice Beamond, and therefore what I shall say of that, I shall say by credible relation of others; but my intent is not to report any of their arguments at large, and in the same form as they were delivered by them, but to make such a summary collection of the effect and substance of them all, as the matter (it being the first case which was adjudged, and being of great importance), will permit.[74]

Clearly this report was not typical of the collection as a whole.

The *Second Part*, published in 1602, is more typical, and is more nearly contemporaneous with the cases it contains. Coke now abandoned the division according to the courts in which the cases were decided, and put them in more or less chronological order. Nearly all of them were either decided or shown to Coke between 1594 and 1601, and noted in MS.C. And of the many cases cited within cases, over half were from MS.C. Two principal cases have not been traced, but they were probably in MS.B. The *Third Part*, published the same year, follows the same scheme. Apart from *Cuppledike's Case*, on f. 5,[75] the cases are in strict chronological order, beginning with four

---

[70] S.T.C. 5493. The publisher was Thomas Wight.
[71] The references in MS.C are: f. 271v (*Buckhurst's Case*), ff. 42v–45 (*Porter's Case*), ff. 384–400 (*Alton Woods' Case*), ff. 41–42 (*Capel's Case*), ff. 236v–237 (*Archer's Case*), f. 237 (*Bredon's Case*), f. 90v (*Mayowe's Case*), ff. 323v–327 (*Rector of Chedington's Case*), ff. 400v–402 (*Digges's Case*), ff. 298–300 (*Mildmay's Case*). There is not the space to give references to the cases in the later parts discussed below.
[72] *Germin* v. *Arscot* (ff. 128v–133), *Cholmley* v. *Humble* (ff. 228v–230).
[73] 1 Rep. 121. See Wallace's comment: *The Reporters* (1882 ed.), p. 176.
[74] 1 Rep. 132. Coke's version may profitably be compared with other good MS. reports: *e.g.* MS.Harg. 26, ff. 176v–186, MS.Lansd. 1072, f. 201, Camb.U.L. MS.Hh.ii. 1, ff. 102v–106, MS.Ii.v. 12, ff. 81–85. Coke's must have been one of the best, for a contemporary collector wrote " *Icy fuit le case Chudley que ieo aie interlesse quia est report per Mr. Attorney coment soit icy excellment report* " (MS.Ee.iii. 2, f. 34v). And another wrote " *Vide cest case in Mounser Cokes Reportes en print en un excellent manner* " (MS.Harg. 26, f. 176v). See also 1 And. 309, Poph. 70.
[75] From MS.C, ff. 486v–489.

from MS.A. Again, over half the " cases within cases " are from the *Vade Mecum*.

After an interval of two years, the *Fourth Part* appeared. The plan this time was different. Most of Coke's longer cases had already been printed, and Coke now began to distil from his *Vade Mecum* the less substantial cases. The volume was longer, and there were more cases in it than there had been in all the first three parts. Instead of arranging it wholly in chronological order, Coke divided the first part by subjects. After f. 48 the order is chronological, with a few cases from MSS.A and B, and sixteen cases drawn strictly in order from MS.C. The cases grouped by subject were taken from the same collections, and not from any other book arranged by subject as Plucknett guessed. A similar pattern was reproduced in the *Fifth Part* (1605). Of nearly the same length, it contained 120 cases. All but a small handful of the cases reported have been traced in MSS.A and C. It begins with a separately foliated report of *Cawdrey's Case*, which originated in MS.C; then follows a subject arrangement, which fades as the number of cases on each subject reduces, until f. 70, after which the chronological order is resumed in two sequences. The first sequence ends with *Semayne's Case*, Michaelmas Term, 1604, and the second with a case of Easter Term, 1605. It looks as though Coke had made a selection late in 1604, and had then been through his notebook again the next year to extend the collection by some forty folios.

The *Sixth Part* (1607) was the first to contain cases of later date than MS.C. This may account for some of the pre-1605 cases which have not been found in MS.C; they might have been shown to Coke after 1605, and recorded in MS.D. In ff. 1–56 are forty-one cases, of which all but six are from MS.C and none from MS.A. The remaining eleven cases must have been in MS.D. With three exceptions, the arrangement after f. 11 is chronological.

The following year was published the *Seventh Part*, prompted, according to its author, by the determination of *Calvin's Case*: " the greatest case that ever was argued in the hall of Westminster." [76] Coke's original note of this case was probably in MS.D, though it is evident from the following significant passage that he entirely rewrote the case for the press:

> This great case (for that memory is *infida et labilis*) while the matter was recent and fresh in mind, and almost yet sounding in the ear, I set down in writing, out of my short observations which I had taken of the effect of every argument (as my manner is, and ever hath been), a summary memorial of the principal

[76] 7 Rep.pref., p. iv.

authorities and reasons of the resolutions of that case, for my own private solace and instruction. . . . Now when I had ended it for my private use, I was by commandment to begin again (a matter of no small labour and difficulty) for the public. For certainly, that succinct method and collection that will serve for the private memorial or repertory, especially of him that knew and heard all, will nothing become a public report for the present and all posterity.[77]

The report of this case occupies over one third of the volume, which is the shortest of all eleven parts. The remainder is in roughly chronological order, beginning with a case from MS.A and ending (ff. 38–45) with cases presumably from MS.D.

The *Eighth Part* was printed in 1611, by which time Coke's notes had reached MS.F. He felt it "more painful than any of the other have been to me."[78] It began with the great *Prince's Case*, which is not in MS.C where it belongs. All the cases (except three) between ff. 32 and 138 are from MS.E, including the Elizabethan cases. The remaining cases were presumably from MS.F, except for four of the cases in the final section of cases in the Court of Wards.

The *Ninth Part* (1613) is almost entirely based on the lost MS.F, and so little can be said of its construction. It appears on its face to contain far more comment and digression than the earlier volumes. The *Tenth Part* (1614) contained one case from MS.C, three cases on sewers from MS.E, and the remainder (8–11 James 1) must have come from MS.F. In the preface, Coke explained his reasons for publishing each case; a novel departure, perhaps occasioned by criticisms which were being levelled at him.

Coke published his eleventh and last volume of cases "in the tempest of many other important and pressing business"[79] in the latter part of 1615. It contains eighteen cases between Trinity Term 10 James 1 and Trinity Term 13 James 1, presumably from MS.F, with the addition of the *Case of Monopolies* from MS.C, and two others.

Of the manuscript versions which Coke prepared for the press, and the very useful and entertaining prefaces, no trace seems to have remained. The absence of any reference to them among Coke's papers at the time of his death suggests that they may not have been preserved.

---

[77] *Ibid.*, pp. iv–v. There is a short note in MS.C, f. 570v (H. 1603) on the status of *post-nati*.
[78] 8 Rep.pref., p. xxxi.
[79] 11 Rep.pref., p. x. He "therefore could not polish them as [he] desired": *ibid.*, p. xi.

Changes made before publication

Coke took a good deal of trouble preparing his reports for publication.[80] He distinguished between private and public reports, and pressed on with the eleven volumes for fear that if he left the material unedited at his death someone would publish them in their imperfect state.[81] He considered it his duty to select for publication only such cases as were " leading cases for the public quiet " [82] and to pass over arguments which were " not worthy to be moved at the bar, nor remembered at the bench." [83] He also claimed as the right of every reporter " to reduce the sum and effect of all to such a method, as, upon consideration had of all the arguments, the reporter himself thinketh to be fittest and clearest for the right understanding of the true reasons and causes of the judgments and resolutions of the case in question." [84] Yet most of the comment which it might have been thought that Coke added while editing a case for the press is to be found in the *Vade Mecum*. A detailed textual study will be necessary before it can be said how far Coke altered his reports for the press, and why.

The most obvious interpolations in the printed volumes are the transcripts from the records, which in the earlier parts occupy much space. The records in the first volume were considered so important that in 1601 they were analysed and digested in a small book by Richard Cary.[85] The extent to which Coke relied on the plea rolls as sources of law is evident from all his writings, and particularly from his *Booke of Entries* (1614). Coke included a few reports in the *Booke of Entries*,[86] some of which were taken from the *Vade Mecum*. He also printed a remarkable report of two cases of 1579, written in law French and enrolled in the Exchequer at the command of the barons to avoid erroneous interpretations by posterity of the differing judgments they had given.[87] It seems impossible that Coke could have done all this work in person, but, with or without clerical assistance, he clearly had a command of the contents of all the plea rolls of the reign of Elizabeth 1 and the first fourteen years of James 1.

---

[80] See 10 Rep.pref., pp. iv, xxii; 11 Rep.pref., p. xi.
[81] 8 Rep.pref., p. xxxii. The fear was perhaps aroused by the posthumous publication of Dyer's notebook in 1585: see 10 Rep.pref., p. xxxiv.
[82] 9 Rep.pref., p. xi. See also the apologies in 10 Rep.pref.
[83] *Case of Sutton's Hospital*, 10 Rep. at p. 24.
[84] *Calvin's Case*, 8 Rep. at p. 4.
[85] *Le necessarie vse & fruit de les Pleadings conteine en le lieur de le tresreuerend Edward Coke* (1601): S.T.C. 4719. Cary did the work in the " last sommers vacation " and dedicated it to Anderson C.J.
[86] Preface, sig. *Av*: " Here shall you find Presidents adjudged upon Demurrer ... which being never reported, here is for thy better Light (Studious Reader) a short touch given of the reasons and causes whereupon they were adjudged." There are about 22 such reports.
[87] *Imber* v. *Wilking, op. cit.*, ff. 380–381, 383–384v.

It would be interesting to know how Coke acquired his mastery of these cumbrous records.

The smaller textual alterations to the reports themselves are not unworthy of the legal historian's attention. Not only is the first person abandoned—*ieo* becomes "Coke"—but, either to enhance his own authority or to avoid embarrassment to others, Coke omitted many personal details in the printed reports. He does not say that he was told about a case by Anderson C.J.[88] or Popham C.J.[89] or that he was "shown a report." [90] He does not always say when he was of counsel, as he does in the notebook, and does not always make it clear that what he reports is his own speech. Sometimes judicial identities are obscured. Thus the sole dissentient in *Shelley's Case*, anonymous in the printed book, is named in the manuscript as Mead J. It was no secret that Walmsley J. was an habitual dissenter,[91] and Coke records his dissent in *Chudleigh's Case*[92]; but he omits to tell us that he dissented in *Pinnel's Case*,[93] and thereby perhaps unwittingly anticipated modern criticisms of that decision. We also find that the famous "Mischief Rule," related by Coke as the resolution of the Court of Exchequer in *Heydon's Case*, began life in a dictum of Manwood C.B.:

> And he said that he did not take any certain ground for the construction of statutes, be they penal or beneficial, restrictive or enlarging of the common law, but only to consider the mischief which was before the statute and the remedy which the parliament intended to provide, and upon this to make construction to repress the mischief and to advance the remedy according to the intent of parliament.[94]

Presumably the contemporary note, written by Coke in 1584, is more historically accurate than the revised version of 1602; but it is easy to sympathise with Coke's desire to present such an attractive statement as a "resolution." Of course, Manwood C.B. may have been speaking on behalf of the court; but, if this were a resolution of the

---

[88] *Case of Market-Overt* (1596) 5 Rep. 83, MS.C, f. 35. Anderson reported the case himself: 1 And. 344.
[89] e.g., *Wild's Case* (1599) 6 Rep. 16, MS.C, f. 328; *Vaughan's Case* (1596) 10 Rep. 114, MS.C, f. 157v. Cf. 4 Inst. 240, 297: "Of the report of Popham". (Was this a written report?)
[90] e.g., *Thoroughgood's Case*, 2 Rep. 9, MS.C, f. 300v; *Beckwith's Case*, 2 Rep. 56, MS.C, f. 266; *Henstead's Case*, 5 Rep. 10, MS.C, f. 348; *Knight's Case*, 5 Rep. 54, MS.C, f. 268; *Chamberlain of London's Case*, 5 Rep. 62, MS.C, f. 355v.
[91] See below, p. 412.
[92] 1 Rep. 132.
[93] 5 Rep. 117, MS.C, f. 548v. Coke also omits to mention that Walmsley J. dissented in *Calvin's Case*.
[94] MS.A, f. 333 (translated). Cf. 3 Rep. 7, 11 Rep. 73. The sentiment was not entirely new: see Camb.U.L.MS.Gg.v. 2, f. 132, per Periam J. (1582): "Cest statute coment que soit penal serra prise liberally pur restrain' le mischief que les fesors intend de restrainer."

court, one would not expect other reporters of the case to miss it altogether.[95]

This is not the place to multiply examples; these few instances should be sufficient to demonstrate the value of comparing the note-books with the printed cases.[96]

The Cases Not Printed in Parts I–XI of the Reports

It is well known that the *Reports* were prominent among the works and doings of Coke which were attacked at the time of his downfall in 1616, and that as a result Coke never published a further volume of reports after that date.[97] But he took with him in his retirement all that "formerly he had written, even thirty books with his own hand, most pleasing himself with a Manual, which he called his *Vade mecum*, from whence at one view he took a prospect of his life pass'd, having noted therein most remarkables."[98] We may now with reasonable confidence identify this "Manual" or *Vade Mecum* with the seven volumes described above,[99] and discard the nineteenth century interpretation which supposed the "remarkables" to have been purely personal autobiography.[1] It was truly the most extensive collection of reports written since the Year Books, covering nearly thirty years without intermission and occupying over 2,500 pages[2] of closely written notes. From it Coke had already filled eleven printed volumes, surpassing in number and influence, if not in length, all the collected editions of the Year Books. There was still a plentiful store remaining.

The extent to which Coke continued to use this material in his writings after 1616 has been overlooked. Plucknett even said that the whole of Coke's intellectual equipment was to be found in the Year Books.[3] But Coke drew heavily on all the recent material he could lay his hands on, particularly on the later plea rolls and his own manual. In the *Institutes*, written for the most part before

---

[95] 1 Leo. 4, 4 Leo. 117, Sav. 66, Moo. 128.
[96] Anyone who wishes to find the original of the renowned statement on judicial review in *Dr. Bonham's Case* will find it in MS.E, f. 93v. But he will be disappointed. No substantial alterations were made.
[97] See note 64, *supra*. Even in 1633 the Council had the *Reports* under scrutiny: see memoranda of Council business, S.P.16/248/15, f. 52v: "In March 1632/33 Mr. Attor: was ordered to examin Sr Edw: Cokes reportes." Dr. Louis Knafla of the University of Calgary is editing Ellesmere's criticisms of the *Reports* for publication.
[98] T. Fuller, *The Worthies of England* (1662), p. 251.
[99] This is confirmed by Tourneur, who copied reports from "Lo. Cokes vade mecum": Univ.Coll. London, MS.Ogden 29, f. 569. See note 25, *infra*.
[1] See note 12, *supra*.
[2] MSS.A, C, D, E and F contained 1,241 leaves. MS.B probably contained about 50 leaves: note 23, *supra*. Only one term (T. 1593) is intermitted in the extant MSS.
[3] *Concise History of the Common Law* (5th ed., 1956), p. 282.

1628,[4] over three hundred references may be found to cases decided in Coke's time, for which no report is cited. A preliminary search shows that about half of these are reported in the extant volumes of the *Vade Mecum*.[5] The remainder may be accounted for as having come from the lost volumes, or as having been taken directly from the records. Clearly by the time of his death in 1634 Coke had put his laborious collections to good use. Whether he would have continued with his published reports, if given the opportunity, is a matter for speculation; certainly there was enough material. Many of the leading cases relied on in the *Institutes* were never published in full, though Coke probably set out in the text most of what he considered worth recording. No doubt he preferred the institutional medium, since he could digress more freely and indulge his passion for giving instruction without the risk of censure for exceeding the duties of a reporter. The most substantial omissions were the great cases of state and matters touching the prerogative, which for various reasons Coke kept to himself. It was well known before Coke's death that he had an unequalled store of such material, and Charles 1 was worried that it might be put to bad use. In 1631 the King ordered enquiries to be made after Coke's health:

> and if hee bee in any present danger that care may bee taken to seal upe his study (if hee dies) where such papers are as use may bee made of them (haveing passed thourow so many great places in the state) for his majesties service and som supressed that may disserve him.[6]

Months before Coke's death a commission issued under the royal Sign Manual to Sir Francis Windebank authorising him " to repair to the house or place of abode of the said Sir Edward Coke, and there to seize and take into your charge, and bring away all such papers and manuscripts as yow shall think fitt."[7] This commission was executed a few days before Coke's death in September 1634. A

---

[4] Co.Litt. (1st ed., 1628), preface. In 3 Inst. 47 is reference to a case of 1630 " since these Institutes." The last part was completed between 1631, when it was in progress (see note 6, *infra*), and April 1633, when the MS. had been seized and the original notes sent to Pepys for safe keeping (see note 8, *infra*). It was suppressed by the King.

[5] *Cf.* 4 Inst. *proeme*: " I have published nothing herein but that which is grounded . . . especially upon the resolution of the Judges of later times upon mature deliberation in many cases never published before; wherewith I was well acquainted, and which I observed and set down in writing, while it was fresh in memory."

[6] S.P.16/183/18, f. 29: letter from the Earl of Holland to Lord Dorchester, the King's Principal Secretary, 24 Jan. 1630/31. The recipient was to write to the Lord Keeper that the book which Coke was working on should not " come forth." *Cf.* letter of Thomas Barrington (1631 ?), cited H.M.C. VII Rep., p. 548: " Sir Edw. Coke hath his papers seized by reason of a report that he is about a book concerning Magna Charta, and is likely to incur some trouble."

[7] S.P.16/272/62, f. 121: 26 July.

large trunk was taken from John Pepys, Coke's private secretary, and brought to the King at Bagshot. The King " poked and stirred in the dusty relics of a life," and found, *inter alia*, a smaller trunk sent to Pepys on 17 April 1633 containing:

> One greate book of statutes called the buckskin book. three other books composed by him vizt. the pleas of the Crowne. the Jurisdiction of Courtes & the exposicion upon Magna Carta & other ancient statutes, which last is imperfect for that which was finished was taken away.[8]

Windebank also found a collection of state papers, with Coke's notes on all the great treason trials in which he had been engaged, in buckram bags.[9] Then, in December, Windebank authorised a clerk of the Council, called Nicholas, to break into Coke's study in the Inner Temple and to seize any papers " as you shall conceave in any sort to concerne his majesties service, or as may in any wise be behoofull or prejudiciall to the same." [10] The remainder of the books and papers were to be delivered to Sir Robert Coke, son and heir of Sir Edward.[11] The books seized by Nicholas included " A booke *in folio* intitled with Sir Edward Coke's own hand a Booke of Notes of my Arguments at the Barre, when I was Solicitor Attornie and before." [12] This precious volume has not been recovered; it would be of the utmost value if it could be identified.

None of the inventories mention the *Vade Mecum*, but Roger Coke (Sir Edward's grandson), who must have had further information, said that among the papers seized were:

> Sir Edward Coke's Comment upon Littleton, and the History of his Life before it, written with his own Hand, his Comment upon Magna Charta &c. the Pleas of the Crown, and Jurisdiction of Courts, and his 11th and 12th Reports in Manuscript, and I think 51 other Manuscripts.[13]

---

[8] " A note of such thinges as were found in a Trunk of Sr. Edw: Coke taken from Pepys his servant. This trunk was brought to Bagshot by his Majesties comandment, & there broken up by his Majesty: 9: Septem: 1634:" Lambeth Palace MS. 943, ff. 369, 375. Most of the papers were of little consequence. The quotation is from C. D. Bowen, *The Lion and the Throne* (1957), p. 461.

[9] *Ibid.*, f. 371: " A catalogue of Sr. Edward Cookes papers that by warrant from the Councell were brought to Whitehall. . . ." They included " a great buckrom bagg of the pouder treason." Mrs Bowen presumed these came from the Temple: *The Lion and the Throne* (1957), p. 460.

[10] S.P. 16/278/10: 4 December. The study had apparently been sealed on Windebank's orders. The same study had been ransacked 14 years earlier by Sir Robert Cotton and Sir Thomas Wilson, while Coke was in the Tower: Holkham MS. 727, Biography of Coke, cited H.M.C. IX Rep., p. 373.

[11] S.P. 16/278/28: 9 December.

[12] " A Note of the bookes & papers brought out of Sr. Edward Coke study from ye Temple remayning in ye Box ": S.P. 16/278/35 (my italics). The books were delivered to Windebank on 10 December. The only other reports were " A Manuscript in folio intitled Le Case de Proxis " and " Another Manuscript in folio intitled Reports of Cases in Ireland " (Davies ?).

[13] *A Detection of the Court and State of England* (1697 ed.), p. 253.

The first item is obviously MS.A, and the distorted mention of the reports probably refers to the remainder of the manual. It is almost certain that these were among the papers seized, because if they had been handed to Sir Robert Coke in 1634 they would have returned to Holkham. The precise fate of the collection after this is unclear. Some of the manuscripts came into the hands of Coke's executors.[14] Others (probably including the third and fourth *Institutes*) came into the hands of Finch C.J., who passed them on to his successor, Littleton C.J.[15] Others were apparently dispersed. The *Vade Mecum* probably passed into private hands at this time, because it was not recognised for what it was. Towards the end of 1640 Sir Robert Coke petitioned the House of Commons for the return of the papers, hoping to make some profit by their publication. By 1641 the three remaining parts of the *Institutes* had been returned, and the heir was desired to publish them with the protection of copyright granted by Parliament.[16] They were published in 1642 and 1644.[17] None of the volumes of the *Vade Mecum* was returned to Sir Robert.

The Twelfth and Thirteenth Parts

The exact history of the manual will probably never be known. It is safe to assume, however, that at an early stage MSS.A–C were separated from the later volumes. They may well have fallen into the possession of the Wyndhams of Norfolk and Somerset. Ann Wyndham, sister of Sir Hugh (Justice of the Common Pleas, d. 1684) and Sir Wadham (Justice of the King's Bench, d. 1668), was the mother of Sir George Strode, serjeant at law, whose daughter presented the volumes to Harley in 1715.[18] The Wyndhams were closely connected with the Cokes, and Sir Hugh had married a daughter of Coke's friend Fleming C.J.

The later volumes, however, passed into general circulation and were avidly copied by legal collectors. This explains all the mystery

---

[14] H.C.J., Vol. II, p. 85: 13 February 1640/41.
[15] *Ibid.*, p. 69: 18 January 1640/41. In C.U.L.MS.Ee.iv. 7, a commonplace book of Parliamentary matters written by Edward Littleton, there are several references to "Coke MS. pl Cor." (ff. 13–15), and a reference to "Coke MS. jurisdn. of Courtes" (f. 9).
[16] *Ibid.*, pp. 45, 80, 470, 554; 2 Inst. (1642), f. 745v; Roger Coke, *op. cit.*, pp. 253, 279.
[17] The history of the printing of the *Third Institute* in 1644 is now known from an important document discovered by W. A. Atkinson: "The Printing of Coke's Institutes" (1926) 162 *Law Times* 435.
[18] *The Diary of Humfrey Wanley* (C. E. & R. C. Wright, eds., 1966), Vol. I, pp. 13–14. The identification of the donor, Madam Thynne, seems beyond dispute. She was by 1715 the widow of Thomas Thynne, Viscount Weymouth, the owner of Longleat; but it is unlikely that the volumes were removed from Serjeant Thynne's collection, which is still preserved at Longleat. She was, however, the *heir* of Serjeant Strode, who died in 1701: see H. W. Woolrych, *Lives of Eminent Serjeants at Law* (1869), Vol. I, pp. 436–440.

which has hitherto surrounded the texts of the two posthumous parts of Coke's reports. None of the manuscript copies collates exactly with any other, because each copyist made different omissions and took his copies in different sequences. Some of the copies were taken directly from Coke's manual, others at second or third hand. One common feature, however, is that the cases usually fall into chronological groups which correspond exactly to the periods covered by each of the volumes of the *Vade Mecum*. None of the copies contains a single case from MSS.A–C.

A copy in the Hargrave collection, said to be taken from the autograph,[19] contains cases solely from MS.F. Another, in the University Library Cambridge, is taken solely from MS.D.[20] Two extant copies contain cases from MSS.D and F only.[21] The copy which belonged to Sir Matthew Hale was taken from MSS.D and F, with only ten cases from MS.E.[22] Most of the copies, however, combine material from all three (or four) volumes.[23] In Serjeant Maynard's copy the cases are arranged in chronological order throughout[24]; but in the other copies the notebooks were used out of order. Thus Timothy Tourneur's copy begins with MS.F, continues with MS.D, and ends with MS.E.[25] John Bradshaw's copy, in the Inner Temple library, was formerly attributed to Coke himself on the basis of comparison with MS.Harl. 6687; but the hand is quite different, and some of the marginal notes (in a second hand) were written after

[19] MS.Harg. 34, ff. 108–130: "*Ceux Reportes et cases ensuant sont escrie hors del Reportes Sir Edw: Cooke que sont escrie ove son maine demesne.*" It is 12 Rep. 69–110, with omissions.

[20] MS.Ll.iv. 9, ff. 1–111: "Lo. Cookes Reportes" It is 12 Rep. 6–64, with some variations. See also the four small leaves bound in MS.Ll.iii. 10, ff. 178–181, with copies of the *Case of Prohibitions* (12 Rep. 76), *Ashley's Case* (12 Rep. 90), and the *Case of Proclamations* (12 Rep. 74). These seem to be from an early copy, and are bound with readings given in the summer of 1634.

[21] (1) Brit.Mus.MS.Add. 35956: "*Decisiones Judiciales.*" Corresponds roughly with 12 Rep. 71–84, 88–end, with omissions. (2) Lincoln's Inn, MS.Misc. 162. Corresponds with 12 Rep. 69–end, 1–15, 65–68.

[22] MS.Lansd. 601, signed "Math.Hale" on f. 3. Umfreville said that Hale had entitled the volume "*Collectanea Edwardi Coke.*" He noted that the last ten cases were not in Part XII, but did not look as far as Part XIII, where they are all to be found. The cases from MS.D correspond with 12 Rep. 6–35.

[23] This information is deduced from a knowledge of the contents of MS.E, and of the periods covered by MSS.D and F. It is not possible to take MS.G into account since it overlapped with MS.F. There are probably more MS. copies which we have overlooked. The Harvard Law School has a copy, apparently from MSS.D, E and F, corresponding to 12 Rep. 6 *et seq.*

[24] Lincoln's Inn, MS.Mayn. 80: "The Lord Cookes 12th Reportes," 103 ff. Note at f. (97): "*Le Senr. Coke eit reporte que cest terme il veyast . . . ceux recordes.*" The volume also contains eight cases of prohibition from the "Reporte del Mr. Rolls" (Rolle ?).

[25] Univ.Coll. London, MS.Ogden 29, ff. 439–569. Note at f. 569: "Soe farre of Lo. Cokes *vade mecum hoc libro: le residue vous troveres al fine de mes Reports del Eschequer in auter liver commenceant ove Widdrington Reports et finiant ove Reports del Eschequer 5 Car.*" Tourneur's is probably a direct copy, including the "*Poyntes dangerous et absurd . . .*" from MS.E, f. 47v.

Coke's death.[26] It begins with MS.E, continues with MS.F, and ends with MS.D. The same order is observed in the copy which Serjeant Pheasant transcribed in 1644 from the exemplar lent to him by Bramston C.J.[27] Yet another copy, from the library of Robert Paynell of Gray's Inn, begins with cases from MSS.D and F, some of them transposed, and ends with MS.E, including some cases not printed.[28]

Until the discovery of MS.E the textual problem raised by these widely divergent copies was insoluble. It is now quite easy to see how the copies derive from Coke's original, which was in form quite different from any of them. The copyists naturally left out what Coke himself had printed, and they also left out in varying degrees what they did not consider useful. When the *Twelfth Part* was published in 1658,[29] one of the incomplete copies was followed, containing cases from MSS.D and F only. Hence the jump at f. 65 from 6 James 1 to 8 James 1. Lawyers possessing more complete copies realised at once that the stock was not exhausted, and in the following year one J.G. published " some remains of [Coke's], under his own hand-writing, which have not yet appeared to the world "; known ever since as the *Thirteenth Part*.[30] All the cases in this book are in MS.E, and none are from elsewhere; it is possible, therefore, that Coke's original was used, as the publishers keenly asserted.[31] There are, however, a few omissions in the printed version. There is nothing " spurious " about the volume, as Winfield suggested[32]; it is an accurate copy by the standards of the day, and fairly typical of Coke's unpolished and

[26] MS.Add. 21, presented in 1898 by H. D. Greene K.C. The marginal notes refer to "*Le Snr. Coke*" whereas Coke himself used the first person. On f. 140 is a note dated 1635, and on ff. 104v–105 are notes from a parchment register in the Tower lent to the writer by Mr. Collett on 30 January 1635/36. The annotator was probably Bradshaw, who was called to the Bar in 1627; his signature appears near the front of the book. The dates seem to indicate an early copy. Dr. Conway Davies attributed the notes to Coke himself: see Esther S. Cope, " Sir Edward Coke and Proclamations: a New Manuscript " (1971) 15 A.J.L.H. 317. This cannot be accepted.
[27] MS.Lansd. 1079, ff. 1–123: "*Reports per Snr. Coke. 12a. pars. Liber Justice Phesant.*" Corresponds roughly to 13 Rep. 1–71, 12 Rep. 69–135, 1–63. At the end the copyist wrote: "*Touts les cases devant fueront de Reports Snr. Coke, et jeo eux ay hors de un copy, que Sir John Brampstone, jades Cheif Justice d'Bank le Roy, lende a moy. Anno 1644. Pet: Phesaunt.*"
[28] MS.Harl. 4815: "*La Douzieme Part des Reports de Sir Edward Coke . . . Ne unques Publie in Printe.*" This seems to derive from more than one copy, since there are several sequences and some duplication. For Paynell's ownership, see *The Diary of Humfrey Wanley* (C. E. & R. C. Wright, eds., 1966), Vol. I, p. 122.
[29] *The Twelfth Part of the Reports of Sir Edward Coke, Kt., of divers resolutions and judgments . . . most of them very famous, being of the King's especiall reference, from the Council Table, concerning the prerogative . . .* (1658).
[30] *Certain Select Cases in Law, reported by Sir Edward Coke . . . Translated out of a Manuscript written with his own Hand* (1659), sig. A.2.
[31] *Ibid.,* sig. A.2v: " If any should doubt of the truth of these reports of Sir Edward Coke, they may see the originall Manuscript in French, written with his own hand, at Henry Twyford's shop in Vine-Court Middle Temple."
[32] *Chief Sources of English Legal History* (1925), p. 189.

unsorted notes. Both the posthumous parts, being published after the statute of 1649, were translated from the manuscripts into English.

The unpublished residue

The two posthumous volumes published in 1658 and 1659 exhausted the greater part of the residue of MSS.D–F which Coke had not printed himself. Perhaps a dozen cases could be found which were not published, but none of them seems to be of great interest. The one item of value in MS.E which escaped the press is the roughly scribbled " *Poyntes Dangerous et Absurd affirme devant le Roy per Egerton Chancellor*," [33] which throws some additional light on the dispute between Coke and Ellesmere.

It has been generally, and no doubt correctly, assumed that the reason why Coke did not himself publish the constitutional cases in MSS.D–F was that it would have been impossible, or at least impolitic, for him to have done so. Certainly he left a rich residue to be culled over after his death and published when the political climate was appropriate. The same is true, though to a lesser degree, of the earlier volumes of the *Vade Mecum*. But, because of the accident that these were separated and hidden soon after Coke's death, this part of the residue never saw the light of day.

The treason cases cited in the *Third Institute* have aroused not a little interest, since they appear inconsistent with Coke's traditional image as a persecutor of suspected traitors.[34] We now have the source of these cases, and can read Coke's original accounts of *Ninian Menville's*, the *Earl of Devonshire's*, *Francis Dacre's*, *Dr. Lopes'*, *O'Cullen's*, *Da Gama's*, *Bradhaw's*, and *Lord Cobham's* cases.[35] More important than these is an extensive account of the Earl of Essex's failure to put down the rebels and end the " *lingering guerres* " in Northern Ireland, and of his trial and sentence at York House for disobeying instructions and returning to England without permission. Coke makes some critical comments, and notes in particular that he was sentenced for contempt of the Council notwithstanding that his original commission was the widest and most absolute ever issued in war or peace.[36] There is also a full account of the trial of Essex, with the Earl of Southampton, for treason in 1601. This ends with a note of his decapitation on Tower Green and a remembrance of the recent " wofull examples " of traitors: " so that six dukes, two

---

[33] MS.E, f. 47v. Also occurs in the Tourneur and Bradshaw copies.
[34] See G. P. Bodet, " Sir Edward Coke's Third Institute: A Primer for Treason Defendants " (1970) 20 Univ. Toronto L.J. 469.
[35] MS.A, f. 336; MS.C, ff. 75v–78, 78v–79, 82v–85v, 127, 153, 194–195v, 246–248 (notes on treason), 562v–568v. There is also a brief note on Mary, Queen of Scots at ff. 82v–83, *in margine*.
[36] MS.C, ff. 408v–410.

marquesses, ten earls and seven lords have been attainted of treason within our memory." [37] The same volume contains brief notes on the trial of Thomas Wynter, Guy Faux and others for the gunpowder treason, and on the trial of Abbingdon for receiving Henry Garnet, the jesuit, one of the gunpowder conspirators.[38] The notes are not concerned with the evidence, but with the legal problems of venue. Another interesting treason case is virtually unknown. Some apprentices had been whipped and pilloried by order of the Star Chamber, and afterwards (in 1595) a band of their fellow apprentices conspired to release them, to whip the Lord Mayor of London to death, and to sack the City. This was held to be treason within the statute of 13 Eliz. 1, c. 1, as an intent to levy war.[39]

Also of constitutional interest are the substantial reports of the suit against the executors of Sir Walter Mildmay, Chancellor of the Exchequer, concerning the royal treasure [40]; the *Earl of Derby's Case* concerning the Isle of Man [41]; *Sir Moyle Finch's Case* concerning the jurisdiction of the Chancery [42]; *Lord Zouch's Case* concerning the authority of the President and Council of Wales, following a conflict with the King's Bench over Magna Carta c. 29 and the liberty of the subject [43]; *Blofield* v. *Havers*, a case of *non procedendo rege inconsulto* [44]; and several notes on Parliament, the prerogative, and of the licence given to Sir Walter Ralegh.[45] The report of *Doughtey's Case*, concerning the offices of Constable and Marshal, reveals that the appeal was brought against Sir Francis Drake himself for the death of Doughtey " *in son grand voiage per la mere*," and that the Queen refused to create the officers " *considerant le veritie et circumstances de ceo*." [46] The details of this remarkable interference with the course of justice do not, needless to say, appear in the *Institutes*.

The emotional element which one expects in Coke's writings is furnished by the full accounts of his elevation by Queen Elizabeth to the two law offices. He relates how on 14 June 1592 he was summoned to Greenwich and rebuked by the Queen for being of counsel in *Paget's*, *Englefield's*, and other cases, to defraud her of her escheats. Coke writes that he was

---

[37] *Ibid.*, ff. 438v–441v (translated).
[38] *Ibid.*, ff. 682, 686v–688.
[39] *Ibid.*, ff. 114–115v.
[40] *R.* v. *Cary and Doddington* (1597), *ibid.*, ff. 214v–222.
[41] *Ibid.*, ff. 274, 279–284. *Cf.* 4 Inst. 284.
[42] *Throckmorton* v. *Finch* (1598) MS.C, ff. 222v–227. See 4 Inst. 86; "The Common Lawyers and the Chancery" (1969) 4 *Irish Jurist* (N.S.) 368 at pp. 371–372. See also *Hyde* v. *Cormet* (1594) MS.C, ff. 104v–105, on the jurisdiction of the Star Chamber.
[43] MS.C, ff. 600–605, 617. *Cf.* 4 Inst. 242.
[44] MS.C, ff. 47v–49. *Cf.* 2 Inst. 269; Vin.Abr. *Rege Inconsulto* (A) 9.
[45] MS.C, ff. 55v–56v, 75, 95, 209–210, 376v, 629v.
[46] MS.A, ff. 311v, 330. *Cf.* 3 Inst. 48.

so wholly appalled and dismayed (and being surprised with an incomparable greife that so gracious a prince should in any sort suspect my loialtye and inward duty and allegiance to her highnes, and feling a wonderfull naturall feare and love which god hath grafted in a subjectes hart towardes his naturell soveraigne) that my harte shaked within my body and all the partes of my body trembled so as I neyther could marke the conclusion of her speeche nor make any aunswere at all, nor untill myne eyes gushed out with teares could be reduced to perfect memory. . . .

The Queen, perceiving Coke's "exceading griefe and anguish of mynde" then spoke gently to him, and after he had made a "sobbing" and "trobled" speech, informed him that she had appointed him to be her Solicitor-General. The tone of Coke's reply may be imagined.[47] When Coke succeeded Egerton as Attorney-General, he was also unable to control his emotions, and his "chekes were watered with teares" at the Queen's kindness.[48]

The more colourful material is only a small part of the unpublished residue of MSS.A and C, which mostly concerns private law. Many of the cases were woven into the fabric of the *Reports* and *Institutes*, and many of them are reported elsewhere. It is, nevertheless, valuable to have Coke's own selections and comments; and particularly valuable to have his unpolished, but full, accounts of such cases as *Collard* v. *Collard*,[49] *Germin* v. *Arscott*,[50] *Harvye* v. *Facye*,[51] *John Littleton's Case*,[52] *Atkyns* v. *Longvile*,[53] and so on. If these names are unfamiliar, it is only because Coke did not publish their cases at length. There are also dozens of cases, more briefly reported, of which no other printed report exists. That the notebooks are a mine worth working there can be no doubt.

It is difficult to resist the comparison of Coke with his eminent contemporaries Bacon and Shakespeare; what they were to philosophy and literature, Coke was to the common law.[54] Yet his works have received less editorial attention than a minor poet can usually expect, and his unpublished works have been completely forgotten. It is

---

[47] MS.C, ff. 34–35.
[48] *Ibid.*, ff. 86–87v.
[49] *Ibid.*, ff. 102v–104, 186. For other reports, see Vin.Abr. *Uses* (O.2) 1.
[50] MS.C, ff. 128v–133. Coke summarised the case at 1 Rep. 85, and it was fully reported in 1 And. 186. See also Vin.Abr. *Condition* (Z) 26.
[51] MS.C, ff. 173v–178: "*Nota cest case duit aver estre report.*" Coke noted the case briefly in 3 Rep. 91. See also 2 And. 109; Poph. 61; Univ.Lib.Camb. MS.Ee.iii. 45, ff. 54v–68v.
[52] MS.C, ff. 508v–525v. Coke noted the case at 9 Rep. 15. The only printed report is the brief note in Moo. 746.
[53] MS.C, ff. 620–625v. The only printed reports are very brief: Moo. 934, Cro.Jac. 50.
[54] So says W. S. Holdsworth, *Some Makers of English Law* (1938), p. 132. *Cf.* J. M. Gest, "The Writings of Sir Edward Coke" (1909) 18 *Yale Law Journal* 504.

more than three centuries since the *Thirteenth Part* of the *Reports* was published. The time must now be ripe for the *Fourteenth*.

Note

To save others from repeating fruitless enquiries, a brief mention must be made of two spurious " Coke " manuscripts.

(1) G. P. Macdonnell, at the end of his biography of Coke in the *Dictionary of National Biography*, refers to " a law commonplace book, 2 vols., supposed to be by Coke, in the Bishop's Library, Norwich, No. 462." This very misleading citation is presumably a careless allusion to the catalogue of the library of John Moore, Bishop of Norwich, printed by Bernard in 1697: " A Law Common-place Book believ'd to be made by the Lord Chief Justice Cooke and to be written with his own hand. 4to. 2 vols." [55] The volumes were in the Bishop's personal library, not in the Library of the Bishops of Norwich, and they are now in the University Library Cambridge: shelf-marks Hh.iv. 4–5. They contain abridged Year Book cases in a neat law hand, inscribed in a later hand on f. 1 " MSS. Edwardi Coke Mil' &c. 2 Voll." They belonged to Anthony Ireby (of Lincoln's Inn) in 1694. They are certainly not in Coke's handwriting, and they are in no way remarkable. The note on f. 1 is probably a bookseller's puff.

(2) Mrs. C. D. Bowen includes in her bibliography of Coke's works: " Autograph MS., *Reports in the King's Bench, 15th–19th Years of the Reign of James I*. Carson Collection on Growth of the Common Law, Philadelphia Free Library. Folio, 97 leaves, in the handwriting of Sir Edward Coke." [56] These dates are, of course, inconsistent with the account given above. But the manuscript (shelf-mark LC. 14/48) is not in Coke's handwriting and has no connection with his *Reports*. The false identification was probably made by a bookseller.[57]

---

[55] *Librorum MSS. D.D. Johannis Mori Episcopi Norvicensis Catalogus*, p. 373, no. 461 (not 462).
[56] *The Lion and the Throne* (1957), p. 483. The reference further down the page to MS.Harl. 1572 should be to MS.Harl. 6687.
[57] The writer is grateful to Mr. Howard J. Heaney, Librarian of the Rare Book Department, Free Library of Philadelphia, for the latter suggestion and for sending photocopies of specimen leaves.

THE COMMON LAWYERS
AND THE CHANCERY: 1616

1616 was a catastrophic year in the history of the English judicial system: a year, wrote Bacon (1), "consecrate to justice". The story of the political, legal and personal controversies which reached a climax in that year is well known, for in some ways those controversies formed the first phase of the seventeenth century constitutional revolution (2). But the story of the dispute between the common lawyers and the Chancery will bear telling in detail (3). The viewpoint of Coke and his supporters has been glossed over by most writers on the subject, who have tended to accept Gardiner's statement that on the Chancery question "it has been universally admitted that Coke was in the wrong" (4). Yet it is clear that Coke's fears about the rule of law were shared by many of his brethren and his profession. The common law, because of its appearance of antiquity and continuity, commanded some popular support, whereas the newer systems, most of them worked by Civil lawyers, were often associated with unlimited royal prerogative and tyranny. In the first decade of his reign, King James I had evinced little sympathy for the common law in spite of his outward affirmations (5), and it was widely rumoured that he wished to replace it with the Civil Law (6); the arguments over prohibitions and prerogative courts were at least partly caused by the fear of Civil Law encroachments (7). When barristers could be imprisoned for impugning the prerogative at the bar (8), and the superior judges

---

(1) "A Memorial for his Majesty": J. Spedding, *Letters and Life of Francis Bacon* (1869), vol. 5, p. 349.
(2) C. H. McIlwain, *Political Works of James I* (1918), p. xl.
(3) This is not intended as a criticism of the article by J. P. Dawson, "Coke and Ellesmere disinterred: The Attack on the Chancery in 1616" (1941) 36 *Illinois Law Review* 127. The aim of the present study is to examine in greater detail the events as they happened, and contemporary reactions to them.
(4) S. R. Gardiner, *History of England* (1883), vol. 3, p. 24.
(5) See J. P. Kenyon, *The Stuart Constitution* (1966), p. 91.
(6) James strongly denied the rumours on several occasions: *e.g.* speech in Parliament, 21 March, 1609, *Political Works* (ed. McIlwain), p. 310; *His Majesties Speach in the Starre Chamber the xx of June 1616*, sig. B4; *Cal. State Papers* (Dom. 1611-1618), p. 375. Evidently the rumour persisted.
(7) See McIlwain, *op. cit.*, pp. xl-xli, lxxxvii-lxxxix; J. Simon, "Dr. Cowell" [1968] *Cambridge Law Journal* 260; R. Usher, *The Rise and Fall of the High Commission* (1968 Repr.), pp. 149-221.
(8) *E.g.* Nicholas Fuller (1607) and James Whitelocke (1613). Taswell-Langmead said of these cases, "James was careful to do what he could to repress the independence of the Bar": *English Constitutional History* (1880 ed.), p. 515 n. *Cf.* Plucknett's 11th ed. (1960), p. 352. James declared in 1616 that it was blasphemy to question his prerogative at the bar: speech in Council on 6 June, *Acts of the Privy Council 1615-1616* (1925), p 602; *His Majesties Speach etc.*, sig. Dv, D3.

coerced into extra-judicial consultations with the King (9), there was some cause for anxiety about the independence of the common law.

The difficulty in making a balanced judgment in hindsight arises largely from the fact that the Bacon-Ellesmere material is superabundant, whereas anti-prerogative opinions were safer in the mind than on paper. This imbalance is reflected in Spedding's biased account of Bacon's part in the events of 1616. In restoring the balance, one manuscript in particular has been heavily drawn upon here: a volume of law reports written by Timothy Tourneur, a barrister of Gray's Inn (10). In 1616 he was thirty years old and of five years' standing at the Bar, and although some of his views are strong they deserve respect because of his position. Tourneur was a Welsh judge under Charles I, out of office during the Interregnum, and near the end of his days, in 1669, one of the oldest serjeants at law ever created (11).

The general background

The story has been told in several ways. It is one aspect of the fall of Coke through his opposition to James I and the absolute prerogative (12). Coke came into frequent conflict with the King over the extent of the residuary or extraordinary jurisdiction of the Crown, and in 1608 he is supposed to have provoked James to physical anger by denying the authority of the High Commission and asserting that the King, being unlearned in the law, ought not to decide cases in person (13). To Coke, the King was under God and the law, which the King construed to mean under God and the common law judges. The King believed himself answerable to God alone, and that all judicial authority was received through himself as God's vicegerent on Earth. The dispute came to a head in 1616 after several attempts by the King to stay argument in cases touching his prerogative rights until the judges had consulted him. Coke resolutely resisted such attempts to

---

(9) *Infra*, note 14.
(10) Brit. Mus. MS. Add. 35957, from the Hardwicke collection. At the top of f. 1 the book claims to be *Liber Timothei Tourneur de Gr. Inne appr. in lege*, and there is internal evidence confirming that he was its author and not merely an owner. At f.124v he records the birth of his daughter Susan Tourneur on 1 November, 1622, and he also reports events at Chester (f.77v) and Ludlow (f.124v), which was his home country. There is also some Gray's Inn material. The manuscript may be compared with a collection by Tourneur, MS. Ogden 29 in the library of University College, London. The latter includes an autobiographical memorandum (f.116) and both have references to Branlingham's reports, which the writer has not met with elsewhere.
(11) W. R. Williams, *Lives of the Welsh Judges* (1899), p. 38. He took the coif at 85, and was excused the procession on foot to Westminster: Edward Ward, *Notebook 1668-1678*, Lincoln's Inn MS. Misc. 500, f.53v. He died in 1677.
(12) E.g. S.R. Gardiner, *History of England* (1883), vol. 3, pp. 1 *et seq.*
(13) See R. G. Usher, "James I and Sir Edward Coke" (1903) 18 *English Historical Review* 664. On one occasion the King said that the judges deserved to be hanged for disobeying his instruction, and that he could question any of their judgments in person: *ibid.*, p. 673.

interfere with the judiciary (14), and his conduct in the Privy Council on June 6, 1616 (15) resulted in his dismissal later in the year.

Alternatively, the story has been told as the culmination of a long-standing conflict between the common lawyers and the jurisdictions based on discretion, Civil Law, and prerogative (16). Coke was ever vigilant to keep extraordinary jurisdictions within their bounds, and while he was on the bench prohibitions issued daily to the ecclesiastical courts, the Admiralty, Requests, and provincial conciliar or equity courts. His enemies represented his surveillance as an encroachment on the prerogative itself (17), though in fact the King stated openly that he wished to preserve the jurisdictional *status quo* (18). The Chancery was the supreme "prerogative court", and its conflicts with the common law the most serious of all.

Thirdly, the events of 1616 are represented as the climax of the personal antagonism between Coke, conservative defender of the old common law, and Lord Ellesmere, personification of the King in judgment and stout defender of the royal pregrogative. Coke's fall is seen to have been stage-managed by Francis Bacon, the Attorney-General, anxious to take the Great Seal from the moribund Ellesmere. There is some evidence that Bacon's advancement to be a Privy Councillor in 1616 (19) was upon condition that he "exercise his power to disgrace the Lord Coke" (20), a task which he discharged successfully. With these great guns aimed at Coke, questions of principle lost much of their significance.

Ellesmere and the Common Law

The dispute between Coke and Ellesmere was not about the need for equity in suitable cases, but about the finality of judgments at

(14) *Peacham's Case* (1614) Spedding, *op. cit.*, vol. 5, pp. 90-128; *Case of Rege Inconsulto (Brownlow v. Michel and Cox)* (1615) *Works of Bacon* (1859 ed.), vol. 7, pp. 683-725; 1 Rolle Rep. 188, 206, 228; 3 Bulstrode 32; Moore K.B. 842; *Somerset's Case* (1616) Spedding, *op. cit.*, vol. 5, p. 269, note.
(15) *Case of Commendams* (1616) *Acts of the Privy Council 1615-1616* (1925), pp. 595-609. There are many copies of this in manuscript. For the proceedings at law see *Colt and Glover v. Bishop of Lichfield and Coventry* (1614-1616) 1 Rolle Rep. 451, Hobart 140, Moore K.B. 1262.
(16) E.g. Dawson, *op. cit.*, pp. 128-132.
(17) See Bacon's list of "Innovations introduced into the Laws and Government" (1616) Spedding, *op. cit.*, vol. 6, pp. 90-93.
(18) Speech in Parliament 21 March, 1609, *Political Works* (ed. McIlwain), p. 312; *His Majesties Speach in the Starre Chamber the xx of June 1616*, sig. D2.
(19) He was sworn on 9 June, having obtained the favour through Villiers: Spedding, *op. cit.*, vol. 5, pp. 255, 260, 347-349. After this date he ceased to practice at the Bar: *ibid.*, p. 348; R. Hutton, *Diary vol. I*, Univ. Lib. Camb. MS. Add. 6862, f. 98.
(20) MS. Add. 35957, f. 55: "*Et ceo advancement de Bacon ut audivi fuit sur certen purposes et condicions (come Shileton dit a moy) q'il exercisera son power a disgracer le Seignor Coke ...*" His informant was probably Richard Shilton of the Inner Temple, a favourite of Villiers, who became Attorney-General in 1625 (D.N.B.; Brit. Mus. MS. Lansd. 1118, f. 166). Coke had fallen foul of Villiers over a patent office in the King's Bench: see Gardiner, *op cit.*, vol. 3, pp. 27-35. Bacon regarded Coke as a rival contender for the Seal: Spedding, *op. cit.*, p. 242.

common law and the enlargement of Chancery jurisdiction at the expense of the law courts (*21*). Coke never denied the need for a system of equity, though he sometimes adopted a restrictive view of its scope. He believed that the King's Bench was bound to watch all other courts to ensure that they did not exceed their powers; this was an established attitude long before Coke came to office (*22*).

Interference with common law judgments had been a source of complaint for over a century (*23*). One of the Lords' articles against Wolsey had charged that "the said Lord Cardinall hath examined divers and many matters in the Chancery after judgment thereof given at the common law, in subversion of your lawes" (*24*). There were two basic objections to such interference. Firstly, parties would try their luck at common law, and if unsuccessful could re-open the whole case in Chancery (*25*). This was, in effect, an appeal from a judgment at law, a procedure regarded by many as unconstitutional. Secondly, and as a consequence, the value and finality of the judgment was lessened, and the law itself might have been subverted because litigants would bypass the law and commence their suits in Chancery (*26*).

The answer of the Chancellor was that the suit in equity was not an appeal to correct the legal decision, but a means of correcting the corrupt conscience of a party who sought to avail himself of a judgment contrary to equity (*27*). Whether or not the suit was an abuse of the Chancery or the law courts was a matter of conscience for the Chancellor, and not the King's Bench, to decide (*28*).

In 1598 this question, having caused some bad feeling, was referred to all the judges of England assembled in the Exchequer Chamber (*29*). Coke participated in the arguments, which went over all the grounds

(*21*) The struggle has therefore been interpreted as a competition for judicial remuneration: D. E. C. Yale, *Lord Nottingham's Treatises* (1965), pp. 9-10; J. Simon, "Dr. Cowell" [1968] Camb. L.J. at p. 265.
(*22*) W. J. Jones, *The Elizabethan Court of Chancery* (1967), pp. 463 *et seq.*
(*23*) An early example is M.22 E.4, 37, *pl.* 6, *per* Hussey C.J.
(*24*) Articles of 1 December, 1529, 4 *Inst.* 91, no. 20. *Cf.* no. 26. Coke had seen the original document (3 *Inst.* 124), which is now lost: A. F. Pollard, *Wolsey* (1929), p. 261, note 3.
(*25*) MS. Add. 35957, f. 55v: "*Et ceo est ore usuall que quant le defendant al comon ley ad try son fortunes la et* stood out all the course of the law and in the end the matter adjudged against him then will he exhibite his bill in Chauncery and grownd yt upon poinctes of equitie for which he might have preferred his suite in Chauncery before the judgment *et issint dowble et infinite vexacion*".
(*26*) 3 *Inst.* 124-125. See also S. F. C. Milsom, *Historical Foundations of the Common Law* (1969), p. 84.
(*27*) *Earl of Oxford's Case* (1615) 1 Cha. Rep., pt. i, pp. 1-16. In *Throgmorton's Case* (note 29, *infra*), counsel argued "*que l'entention del plaintiff ne fuit a impeacher les ditz iudgmentes mes ore confessant les iudgmentes d'estre relieve pur matter in equitie*".
(*28*) W. J. Jones, *op. cit.*, pp. 484-485.
(*29*) *Finch v. Throgmorton* cited 3 *Inst.* 124, 4 *Inst.* 86, 3 Buls. 118, Cro. Jac. 344. A full report, in Coke's own hand, is to be found in Brit. Mus. MS. Harl. 6686, ff. 226v-229. The matter was referred to the judges because it was "*de graunde consequence, et semblable d'estre president a multes auters*" (*ibid.*, f. 227). Dawson traced the case in the Chancery Order Book, which confirms that Egerton consulted the judges; *op. cit.*, pp. 134-135.

which were to be raised in 1616, and according to his report all the judges except Walmsley J. held that Chancery could not re-examine matters after judgment at law:

> It would be perilous to permit men after judgment and trial in law to surmise matter in equity and by this to put him who recovered to excessive charges. And by these means suits would be infinite and no one could be in peace for anything that the law had given him by judgment. But a contentious person, who had an unquiet spirit, might continually surmise matter in equity and so vex him who recovered endlessly; which would be a great inconvenience. And it is absurd that a court, which as to equity is not a court of record, should control judgments which are of record (30).

The judges also ruled, according to Coke, that such a suit in Chancery was prohibited by the statutes of 4 Hen. 4, c. 23 and 27 Edw. 3, c. 1. The resolution was communicated to Lord Keeper Egerton by Popham C.J., who evidently made no protest at that time. Whether Coke's report is trustworthy is an open question since no independent report has so far come to light. Neither is it certain why Walmsley J. dissented from the resolution, because in 1600 he said of the Court of Requests:

> We have been informed that they assume to call our judgments in question and to annihilate them and to order that the party release the judgments, or to imprison him. To which it was said by the whole court that it is good to lay informations on the statute of Edward III for calling the judgments in question where they have nothing to do with them (31).

In 1606, in another case concerning the Court of Requests, Popham C.J. apparently asserted that a bill in equity might be preferred after a judgment at law, and Coke, standing at the bar, protested:

> If this were the law then the statute of 4 H. 4, c. 23 would serve for little or nothing ... And then also it would seem that all injunctions out of these courts of equity are idle, if they may as well decree it after judgment. And he said that it had been resolved accordingly by all the judges in a case in which he had been of counsel (32).

Coke was appointed Chief Justice of the Common Pleas in June 1606, and as he began his crusade to uphold the supremacy of the common

---

(30) *Ibid.*, f. 228 (translated). For Coke's attack on the Chancery on the ground that it was not a court of record see S. E. Thorne in 2 *Toronto Law Journal* at p. 47.
(31) *Smith's Case* (1600) Inner Temple MS. Barrington 6, f. 43v (translated). The reference to the statute of *praemunire* is interesting in the light of the events to come in 1616.
(32) *Cardinall v. De la Broke* (1606) Inner Temple MS. Barrington 7, ff. 209v-210 (translated). The reporter ended "*Quere de cest matter*". It would seem strange if Popham C.J. had forgotten the decision of 1598, but he died a year later and may have been amnesic.

law, Egerton (created Lord Ellesmere in 1603) began to assert the supremacy of the Chancery over the courts of law in a dogmatic fashion. As Ellesmere grew older he became more obstinate and difficult and opposed to the common law (33). He regarded himself as outside and above the rest of the judiciary (34). In 1613, Fleming C.J. had written to the King complaining that the Chancellor was hearing suits which were determinable at law, and Ellesmere caused the King to be greatly offended, and persuaded him to hear his law officers "confute and reproach" the Chief Justices (35), a humiliating technique to which he was to resort again in 1616. Serjeant Hutton witnessed that Ellesmere became more choleric and "in many things laboured to derogate from the common law and the judges" (36), and Tourneur described him as "*acerrimus propugnator* of the Chauncerye and Starchamber, in a worde the bane of the law, yet not for any hate he bare yt but for the love he bare to his owne honor to greaten himself by the fall of others (37). One lawyer went so far as to say he was "the greatest enemye to the common law that ever did bear office of state in this kingdome" (38).

The Proceedings of 1614-1616

Coke was translated to the King's Bench in October 1613 and was thus given more power to attack the prerogative courts. By this time the excesses of Ellesmere's Chancery were becoming intolerable to common lawyers. Ellesmere himself was a good lawyer and judge, but he was growing very old and relying more and more on his subordinates, and less and less on the judges assistant. The appointment of Sir Julius Caesar as Master of the Rolls in 1614 on the death of Sir

(33) Chamberlain to Carleton, 29 June, 1615, *Letters of John Chamberlain* (ed. McClure, 1939), vol. 1, p. 604 (ascribes defects to sourness of age). In an obituary letter Chamberlain says he "left but an indifferent name beeing accounted too sowre, severe and implacable, an ennemie to parlements and the common law, only to maintain his owne greatnes, and the exorbitant jurisdiction of his court of chauncerie": *ibid.*, vol. 2, p. 65.
(34) E. Coke, "Poyntes dangerous et absurd affirme devant le Roy per Egerton Chancellor", copied (from Coke's *vade mecum*) in U.C.L. MS. Ogden 29 (*supra*, note 10), f. 569, no. 13.
(35) *Ibid.*, no. 11. Coke, then Chief Justice of the Common Pleas, also submitted a written opinion that this precedent "*tend al subvercion del ley et justice*". Egerton had promised the King not to exceed his jurisdiction (*infra*, note 10), and soon after receiving the Seal in 1596 had promised not to give "*ascun reliefe in equitie contrary a ascun positive ground in ley*" nor aid in any case "*ou ascun bon remedy d'estre ew per comon ley*": Note, Inner Temple MS. Petyt 561/5, f. 58v.
(36) R. Hutton, *Diary vol. 1*, Univ. Lib. Camb. MS. Add. 6862 f. 126 (obituary): "*il fuit un home de grand et profound judgment, un eloquent speaker, et uncore in son daren temps il deveigne plus chollerick et oppose le jurisdiction del common ley et inlarge le jurisdiction del Chancery, et il in plusors choses a derogate del common ley et del judges.*"
(37) M.S. Add. 35957, f. 81v. (obituary). He has some good things to say; like Hutton he acknowledges his profound judgment and pleasing tone of voice.
(38) J. Whitelock, *Liber Famelicus*, Camden Soc. (O.S.), vol. 70, p. 53. Whitelocke, a barrister of the Middle Temple, had been badly treated by Ellesmere for defending the Chancery jurisdiction against the Commissioners for the Office of Earl Marshal; *ibid.*, pp. 34-40; *supra*, note 8.

6 Thomas Egerton, Lord Ellesmere

This portrait shows Ellesmere in parliamentary robes, with the purse of the great seal. It seems to reflect the choleric disposition referred to in Hutton's notebook.

Lincoln's Inn

7 Francis Bacon, Baron Verulam

This portrait shows Bacon with the purse of the great seal, which was delivered to him as Lord Keeper after Ellesmere's death. He became Lord Chancellor and Baron Verulam in 1618, Viscount St Albans in 1621.

National Portrait Gallery

Edward Phillips (39) exacerbated the lawyers. He was a Civil lawyer by training, ignorant of Chancery procedure, unwilling to accept advice, and unable to dispatch business efficiently (40). The constitutional questions were approaching a climax, and the Chancery was, under Ellesmere, a bastion of the prerogative. In 1614 the House of Commons heard a bill to prevent judgments at common law from being questioned in other courts, "for the peace of the King's subjects", though it proceeded no further than its first reading (41). In the same year Coke refused to obey a Chancery injunction to stay execution of a judgment in the King's Bench (42), and also considered the possibility of sending prohibitions to the Chancery (43). However, the vehicle of interference was not to be the prohibition, but the writ of *habeas corpus*. The use of this writ to examine the lawfulness of a committal by the Chancellor was established before Coke's time (44). Some of the cases which came before the King's Bench were most unmeritorious, but a judge cannot prearrange cases on which to make a point of principle. Coke's duty, as he saw it, was to see that the law had been observed in cases which came before him, regardless of their merits.

Glanvill's Case

The first case in the series was, indeed, singularly lacking in merit. Richard Glanvill, an unscrupulous London jeweller, had in 1606 sold Francis Courtney a topaz which he misrepresented as a diamond, and thereby obtained an unduly high price. Glanvill's accomplice, Davies, pretended to be the servant of a goldsmith, Hampton, and took an obligation in Hampton's name for the price. Glanvill recovered this sum by using Hampton's name. Apparently judgment had been obtained without the privity of Courtney or the judges by the fraudulent method of paying an attorney to confess judgment out of term on Courtney's behalf. The judgment was affirmed on error, but pending the writ of error Courtney had preferred a bill in Chancery. Notwith-

---

(39) Phillips was a serjeant at law and respected by the lawyers. In *Wraynham's case* (1618) a man was punished by the Star Chamber for defaming Phillips (though dead) and Coke praised his memory very highly: Univ. Lib. Camb. MS. Dd. iii. 87, art. 7, f. 13.

(40) Hutton, *op. cit.*, f. 89, wrote of his appointment "*pur le quel [office] in l'opinion de plusors sages dit ley il fuit grandment unapt,*" Tourneur, *op. cit.* f. 79v., says he was "*trop ignorant in le course del Chancery et nient hable a faire ascun despatch*". See also E. Foss, *The Judges of England* (1857), vol. 6, p. 270.

(41) Draft Bill, 3 June, 1614, in the House of Lords Library: H.M.C. *Third Report*, Appendix p. 15.

(42) *Heath v. Ridley* (1614) 2 Bulstrode 194, Cro. Jac. 335.

(43) *Wright's Case* (1614) Moore K.B. 836, 1 Rolle Rep. 71. There was some authority for this: Fitz. Abr. *Prohibition*, pl. 11 (13 Edw. 3); R. Compton, *L'Authoritie et Jurisdiction des Courts* (1594), pp. 56-57; *Note*, Cary 3.

(44) M.22 E.4, 37, pl. 6, per Hussey C.J.; *Astwick's Case* (1567) Moore K.B. 839; *Humfrey v. Humfrey* (1577) Dalison 81, 3 Leonard 18, per Bendlowes sjt.; *Michell's Case* (1577) Moore K.B. 839; *Addis' Case* (1609) Cro. Jac. 219; *Anon.* (no date) Moore K.B. 916.

standing the judgment in error, the Master of the Rolls decreed a rescission of the sale, fixing a proper price for the stone, and ordered that Hampton should be procured to release the judgment at law (45). It was the last part of the decree which became the basis of complaint, because the Chancery had not previously claimed the power to interfere with the judgment itself (46).

Glanvill refused to obey the decree and was committed, in 1613. In Michaelmas Term 1614 he was removed into the King's Bench by *habeas corpus*, and his counsel prayed his discharge. The court of equity, said counsel, had imprisoned him for a matter of which he had two judgments at law. Coke exclaimed "So long as I have this coif on my head I will not allow this" (47), and expressed his surprise that the Chancellor had gone back on his promise not to interfere with judgments at law. Glanvill was bailed until Hilary Term when, because the return gave no cause for the commitment, he was released (48).

Lord Ellesmere joined battle by committing Glanvill again, on 7 May, 1615. A new *habeas corpus* was sued out in Trinity Term, and this time the return was: *quod commissus fuit prisone per mandatum Thome Domini Ellesmere Cancellarii Anglie.* The judges, following the precedents, held the return bad for its generality (49). According to Coke, this decision was the result of a conference with all the judges of England (50). There one may leave Glanvill for the moment, but it was by no means the end of his story.

It may have been unfortunate that the issue was raised in a case so devoid of merit. Yet the question at issue was the validity of the return, and according to all the judges at that time the King's Bench were entitled to ask not merely *who* committed the prisoner but *why*. For this purpose, no judicial notice could be taken of the merits.

Apsley and Ruswell

Two cases less deficient in merit were debated at the same time as *Glanvill's Case*. Michael Apsley had been in the Fleet for seven years for contempt of Chancery. Ruswell, who had refused to obey an illegal decree (51) had been committed on 30 May, 1614, *per*

---

(45) See "Richard Glanvill's Case 4° Jacobi", Brit. Mus. MS. Harl. 1767, f. 37; MS. Harl. 4265, f. 75v; "The state of the cause between Richard Glanvill citizen and goldsmith of London and Francis Courtney Esquire", Brit. Mus. MS. Lansd. 163, f. 122; and the law reports cited below.
(46) *Cobb v. Nore* (1465) a very similar case, was relied on: the problem had then been referred to a special commission of the Chancellor and some judges. This, according to Coke, showed that the Chancellor could not deal with it of his own authority. The case had been discovered by Coke as counsel in *Throgmorton's Case*: Brit. Mus. MS. Harl 6686, ff. 212v, 227v. Cf. 3 *Inst.* 124, 4 *Inst.* 86.
(47) 1 Rolle Rep. 111.
(48) *Ibid.*, 2 Bulstrode 302, Moore K.B. 838, Cro. Jac. 343.
(49) 2 Bulstrode 302, 1 Rolle Rep. 218. Cf. the cases cited in note 42, *supra*.
(50) MS. Add. 35957, f. 2v.
(51) The decree was contrary to the Statute of Wills and was later reversed by Bacon: Rolle Abr. *Chancerie* (S) 5. Yelverton, Att.-Gen., spoke strongly against the decree: MS. Add. 35957, f. 82.

consideratione curie Cancellarie Domini Regis pro contemptu eidem Curie. These two cases, and others (52), came before the King's Bench in Easter Term 1615. In each case the return was general. After an adjournment until Trinity Term, and several debates, privately in Coke's house and in open court, Coke delivered the unanimous opinion of the judges that the returns were bad. Ruswell's return was altered later in the Term so as to set out the decree in detail. George Croke, who complained that his conduct was being watched(53), argued that the matter was outside the Chancellor's jurisdiction. The case was adjourned because of a doubt (54), and no more was heard of it until 1617 when hostilities were over.

Allen's Case

The line was drawn in the case of Allen, the archetype inhumane creditor. The matter arose out of the bankruptcy of one Edwards, whose lands were sold at a low price to Allen. Later the creditors entered into a composition agreement whereby Allen was to convey the land to two of the creditors, Smith and Wood, who would bind themselves to pay out ten shillings in the pound to all the others. Allen then repudiated the agreement and sued in Chancery for possession, which was decreed to him. He evicted Edwards' children "in frost and snowe" despite the undersheriff's tearful plea for compassion. When the parents died of plague *pendente lite* Lord Ellesmere re-opened the case, out of humanity, and assigned Serjeant Francis Moore to be of counsel for the children *in forma pauperis*. A new, and more just, decree was made and for refusing to perform it Allen was committed on 13 November, 1613. Apparently he had two judgments at law relating to the debts, but he had instituted the Chancery suit himself and had previously assented to the composition agreement (55). It was difficult to find any ground for his *habeas corpus* application, and the King's Bench refused to deliver him (56). These facts have been related because Allen re-appears a little later in the dispute.

These cases opened the way for the collision between Coke and Ellesmere. This collision occurred, but with less impact than might have been expected, in Michaelmas Term 1615 in an important case involving the Master of Magdalene College, Cambridge.

(52) 1 Rolle Rep. 193.
(53) Brit. Mus. MS. Harl. 1691, f. 55v: "*del commencement que il parle en cest cause il ad estre watche: mes hors del son duty al court il voile parler.*" In the case of *Commendams*, the Bishop of Winchester had been watching for the Crown: *Acts of the Privy Council 1615-1616*, p. 596. And in the case of *Rege Inconsulto*, Secretary Winwood had sat below the judges in the King's Bench "*et come fuit report in le Sale le Secretary fuit enioyne per le Roy d'estre present al argument*": MS. Add. 35957, f. 37.
(54) 1 Rolle Rep. 219. Coke is reported to have said, "*Cest returne induce nous al tryer le bill et answer et pur ceo portes ceux en court*": MS. Harl. 1691, f. 55v.
(55) "Allen's Case in Chancery", Brit. Mus. MS. Harl. 1767, f. 39; MS. Harl. 4265, f. 78.
(56) Moore, K.B. 840.

The Earl of Oxford's Case

The Chancellor was well aware of the preceding events and in September had set the King's counsel to investigate precedents for him by delivering them a treatise with his own reasons in it (57). The test case was to be *The Earl of Oxford's Case,* the last of the *habeas corpus* applications before 1616. Legal historians have attached much significance to this case. Perhaps they have given it too much significance, because it did not result in a final decision of the question.

The case concerned the power of the Chancery to interfere with the legal title to land, contrary to statute, on the basis that a person who built houses on another person's land ought to be compensated in equity. In 1613 an action of ejectment had been brought in the King's Bench to try the Earl's title to a lease of Covent Garden by Magdalene College. The title, which depended on certain statutes, was discussed by the judges with a great deal of erudition and in 1615 they decided against the plaintiff (58). The plaintiff then preferred a bill in Chancery, and the defendant demurred on the ground that he had had judgment at law. Sir John Tindal, Master in Chancery, ordered him to make answer, and for refusing to do so he was in October 1615 committed to the Fleet. The plaintiff was allowed to proceed in default of answer. Lord Ellesmere took the opportunity to explain the nature of his jurisdiction and its relationship with the law in a judgment familiar to generations of law students (59). The Chancery did not meddle with the judgment, said Lord Ellesmere, but with the "hard conscience of the party".

No doubt this was intended as a challenge to Coke. Coke was forced to accept it when the defendants, Dr. Googe (60) and the lessee Smith, came before the King's Bench on *habeas corpus.* The return stated that they had been committed to the Fleet by order of the Chancery for refusing to answer the bill, which was specified. Serjeant Bawtrey moved for their release, because the matter in the bill had already been determined at law and the Chancery suit was contrary to the statute of 1403. Coke answered that if the matter did appear

---

(57) This had a wide circulation in manuscript. In the British Museum are at least nine copies. It was printed in 1641 as *The Privileges and Prerogatives of the High Court of Chancery.*

(58) *The Case of Magdalene College (Warren v. Smith)* (1615) 11 Rep. 66, Cro. Jac. 364, 1 Rolle Rep. 151 Dodderidge J. later stated, "There never was any learned man (if he were an honest man) that was of another opinion than we were of, in the giving of this judgment (unless he was a time-server)": 3 Bulstrode 116.

(59) *The Earl of Oxford's Case (Oxford and Smith v. Googe and Wood)* (1615) 1 Cha. Rep., pt. i, 1; White and Tudor, *Leading Cases in Equity* (1928 ed.) vol. 1, pp. 615-621. The date of committal is variously given as 22 October (*ibid.*), 31 October (1 Rolle Rep. 277) and 21 October (Brit. Mus. MS. Harl. 1767, f. 30v; MS. Harl. 4265, f. 68v; Univ. Lib. Camb. MS. Mm. i. 43, f. 466).

(60) Barnaby Googe or Gouch, M.A., LL.D., Master of Magdalene College, Cambridge 1604-1626.

to be the same, the court would deliver the prisoners, because their committal would be contrary to statute and common law. Dodderidge J. agreed with Coke that "It would tend to the downfall of the common law, if judgments here given should be suffered to be called in question in courts of equity". There followed a debate as to whether the matter did appear to be the same, and the argument ended inconclusively. Coke told counsel, "It is better for you that we hear no more of it". The prisoners were bailed until the next term on sureties to attend *de die in diem*, but nothing more was done *(61)*.

The impression given by the reports is that Coke was unwilling to take a stand against Ellesmere on *habeas corpus* *(62)*. For one thing, the King had personally intervened to remonstrate with his two principal judges about their "disgraceful" disputes, and told them to refer cases of difficulty to himself *(63)*. And then the state trial of Somerset distracted both Coke and Ellesmere from pursuing their personal rivalries *(64)*. Possibly Coke would have preferred that the question were raised in such a way that it could be tried by jury, so that the judges took no personal responsibility for the result. Whatever the reason, no more was heard of *habeas corpus* to examine Chancery decrees.

The dispute began to move into the sphere of the criminal law. In *Dr. Googe's Case* Coke referred to the two statutes which were to figure largely in the arguments which followed, the 27 Edw. 3, st. 1, c. 1 and the 4 Hen. 4, c. 23. Both had been relied on in 1598 in *Throgmorton's Case*. Back in 1614 Coke had remarked, "It is much to be wondered that none will inform upon these laws in such cases against the party that procures such injunctions after judgments at common law . . . " *(65)*, and he had dropped the same hint on other occasions *(66)*. The statute of 1403, though directed primarily at the Council, could be interpreted to support Coke's proposition in relation to the Chancery *(67)*. St. Germain, nearly a century earlier, had construed it to include the Chancery, for it was better, he said, that an individual should occasionally suffer than that "great vexations and

---

(61) *Dr. Googe's Case* (1615) 1 Rolle Rep. 277, 3 Bulstrode 115.
(62) Glanvill, whose word is not gospel, later said of the *habeas corpus* that "Lord Coke misliked it": *loc. cit.* in note 74, *infra*.
(63) Winwood to Carleton, 13 July, 1616, *Cal. State Papers* (Dom. 1611-1618), p. 381.
(64) Bacon to the King, 27 January 1616, Spedding, *op. cit.*, vol. 5, p. 236: "they will not square while those matters are in hand, so that there is *altum silencium* of that matter."
(65) *Heath v. Rydley* (1614) 2 Bulstrode 194.
(66) See *Trobervil v. Brent* (1611) 2 Brownlow & Golds. 97; *Wright v. Fowler* (1614) Moore K.B. 836, 1 Rolle Rep. 71, 2 Bulstrode 284; *Glanvill's Case* (1615) Moore K.B. 838.
(67) The statute (4 Hen. 4, ch. 23) recited how parties had been brought before the King or his Council in subversion of the common law, and ordained "q'apres juggement rendu en les courtes nostre seignur le Roy les parties et leur heirs soient en pees tanqe le juggement soit anientiz par atteinte ou par errour . . ."

unjust expenses" should be incurred if the law had no end (68). The statute of Edward III did not cover the case so clearly, for it was designed to restrain appeals to Rome (69). But Ellesmere and Bacon both conceded that it included ecclesiastical courts since the Reformation, and stood upon the point that the Chancery did not meddle with judgments directly. In 1614 Sir Anthony Mildmay was convicted of *praemunire* for committing a party by authority of his office as a Commissioner of Sewers, contrary to a judgment at law (70). Coke believed the same could be done with the Chancery, and he was not the first to hold this belief. In 1588 John Hele, a bencher of the Inner Temple, had been indicted on the statute for counselling a Chancery suit after a judgment at law. The indictment had been quashed for misnomer, but the judges endorsed it that the matter was good (71). No doubt reliance was placed on the more doubtful statute because of the penalties contained in it, and the absence of a specific sanction in the statute of 1403. It could not be long before someone would take Coke's hint, and to the undoing of the common lawyers' case it was taken up by the least deserving characters.

The indictments for praemunire

The rogue Glanvill after his release by the King's Bench had incubated an enthusiasm for the common law which manifested itself in an irresponsible scheme to overthrow the Chancery. Fired with this nefarious ardour, he visited the Fleet prison and spread the news to the prisoners that they might all be freed if they brought *habeas corpus* as he had done (72). He calumniated Ellesmere, saying that he lived on bribes and was in league with the Devil (73). Worst of all, he fixed his attentions on the statute of *praemunire*. Why should he not indict the Chancellor and everyone who had persecuted him? The King would surely be grateful for the forfeiture of Ellesmere's estates, and there might be something in that for Glanvill. An indictment was drawn accordingly, but on reflection Glanvill decided it would be

(68) *Doctor and Student*, book 1, ch. 18. *Accord.* R. Crompton, *L'Authoritie et Jurisdiction des Courts* (1594), pp. 41, 66, 67.
(69) The relevant words of the 27 Edw. 3, st. 1, ch. 1, imposed the penalties of praemunire on all lieges of the King who "*suent en autri court a deffaire ou empescher les juggements renduz en la Court le Roi.*" "Autri court" means "the court of another" and not "any other court". Chancery and King's Bench were both courts of the King.
(70) *Mildmay's Case* (1614) 2 Bulstrode 197, Cro. Jac. 336.
(71) *Hele's Case* (1588) 2 Leonard 115, 3 *Inst.* 124, Crompton, *op. cit.*, pp. 57-58. The Chancellor committed the counsel who drew the indictment to the Fleet and expressed his wonder at such a proceeding "to blemish and deface the authority of the court": C. Monro, *Acta Cancellariae* (1847), p. 5-8.
(72) "The Breviate of the Cause in the Starchamber between the King's Atturney pl. against Allen and Glanvill and Levesay def. 1616": Brit. Mus. MS. Add. 11574, at f. 43. This hitherto unnoticed document in the Caesar papers has been used in the present account, though it must be remembered that it is taken from the prosecutor's brief.
(73) *Ibid.*, art. 2 This was the standard complaint of the aggrieved Chancery litigant, and cannot be taken seriously.

politic to proceed, at first, against lesser persons. He enlisted the help of Crown Office lawyers in drawing an indictment, according to Mildmay's precedent, by pretending that he had directions from Coke (74). The defendants were Courtney, and his counsel and attorney. The bill was preferred in Michaelmas Term 1615, but the grand jury of Middlesex returned it *ignoramus*.

Undaunted, Glanvill enlisted the support of the infamous Allen, and a dishonest scrivener called Levesay. Perhaps he also made representations to the judges, for when the Middlesex grand jury appeared at the bar in Hilary Term 1616 a new article was given in charge by Sir John Croke: "If any man, after a judgment given, had drawn the said judgment to a new examination in any other court" (75). One of the grand jurors was Levesay, and on the last day of term (13 February) he delivered the bills of indictment to his fellows. This time Allen had also preferred a bill, against his Chancery opponents (76), Serjeant Moore (77), and Master Sir John Tindal (78). The accounts of what took place in court are biased, but sufficient evidence was collected to indicate that Coke's behaviour was decidedly partial (79). Though pressed by Levesay, the jurors were unwilling to find the bills true. Coke grew angry. He remanded them two or three times and threatened to commit them, but they were adamant. The foreman insisted on returning *ignoramus*, at which Levesay protested that it was not a unanimous verdict. Coke therefore examined the jurors by the poll, one by one, and counted seventeen against two. The verdict of *ignoramus* was therefore accepted. Coke warned the sheriff to produce a wiser jury the next term, and is said to have told Glanvill and Allen to prepare themselves. Later the same day Coke threatened to foreclose any barrister from practice in the King's Bench if he put his hand to a bill after a judgment at law (80).

Glanvill and Allen employed themselves in the Lent Vacation following to petition the Privy Council, stating that they had preferred bills of indictment for the King, and if the prosecutions had been successful the King's coffers would be greatly filled (81). This appeal

(74) *Ibid.*, f. 44, art. 5. Glanvil confessed the indictment drawn against Ellesmere, but it was never preferred.
(75) Bacon to the King, 21 February, 1616, Spedding, *op. cit.*, vol. 5, p. 251.
(76) Smith and Wood. Bacon adds Alderman Bowles (Edwards' mortgagee), but he is not named in the Caesar MS.
(77) Moore was "*un graund favorite de Egerton*" (MS. Add. 35957, f. 54v). One of the Chancellor's last acts was to try to secure for the serjeant a place as Baron of the Exchequer in 1617: Whitelock, *Liber Famelicus*, p. 54.
(78) Tindal was shot in November by an unbalanced litigant.
(79) The prosecution brief, preserved among the Ellesmere papers in the Huntingdon Library, California, (MSS. EL. 5971, 5973), has been published by Professor Thorne: "Praemunire and Sir Edward Coke" (1938) 2 *Huntington Library Quarterly* 85-88. This is presumably the document cited by Lord Campbell in his *Lives of the Lord Chancellors* (1848), vol. 2, pp. 257-258. There is a different summary in the Caesar Papers: MS. Add. 11574, f. 47. See also MS. Add. 35957, f. 54v; Spedding, *op. cit.*, vol. 5, p. 251.
(80) *Goodwyn v. Gouldsmithe*, cited 2 *Huntington L.Q.* at p. 88.
(81) Copies of both petitions in MS. Add. 11574, ff. 44, 46.

to the royal avarice was hardly tactful, and the two petitioners before long faced prosecution themselves. Glanvill's last fling was an action of false imprisonment against the Warden of the Fleet and his gaolers. The Warden was actually arrested by a serjeant-at-mace, but of course was promptly discharged by a *supersedeas* from the Chancery. Glanvill's campaign was not allowed to proceed any further (82).

The retaliation of Bacon and Ellesmere

These circumstances provided Bacon and Ellesmere with the opportunity they had been waiting for to settle the dispute, and perchance to disgrace Coke at the same time. Bacon complained to James of the "great and public affront" not only to the Chancellor himself ("at a time when he was thought to lie on dying, which was barbarous") but to the Court of Chancery, the court of the King's absolute power (83). Though Bacon accounted the affair to be "a kind of sickness of my Lord Coke's", he confessed he could not implicate Coke in the prosecutions, and suggested that the real blame lay with the puisne judges (84). He recommended the disgrace of any judge whose implication could be proved, the removal (but without disgrace) of Coke, and the reproof of all the judges on their knees in Council. The suggestion that an unfair advantage had been taken of a dying man was ludicrous. Ellesmere was very senile and prone to constant bouts of sickness, and many believed that he was apt to feign illness when it suited him (85). If he could not defend his own actions, he was unfit to continue in office (86). In any case, Bacon privately wrote that the matter would enliven the old Chancellor and "raise his spirits" (87).

Ellesmere made his own "greevous complaint" to the King, blaming Coke (88), and asking for James' personal resolution of the following case:

> Whether upon apparent matter of equity, which the judges of the law by their place and oath cannot meddle with or relieve, (if a judgment be once passed at common law) the subject shall

(82) *Ibid.*, f. 45, art. 7.
(83) Bacon to the King, 21 February 1616, Spedding, *op. cit.*, vol. 5, pp. 249-254.
(84) His caution seems to be political rather than genuine, since Coke's disgrace would have been dangerous in view of his popularity. The Ellesmere Papers reveal a clear attempt to implicate Coke. It was to be shown that he had browbeaten the jury, told them that Ellesmere was dead, and that he had been overheard saying to the other judges "wee must seeme to knowe nothing of this matter": 2 *Huntington Lib. Q.* 85, 87.
(85) W. J. Jones, *op. cit.*, p. 93 When he absented himself at the time of Coke's removal, the rumour was that he was pretending to be ill: MS. Add. 35957, f 62v; *Chamberlain Letters*, vol. 2, p. 35.
(86) See below, note 34.
(87) Bacon to Villiers, 19 February, 1616, Spedding, *op. cit.*, vol. 5, p. 248.
(88) MS. Add. 35957, f. 54v: "Le Chancelor esteant a ceo temps (come le mond pense) in graund favour ove le Roy fait greevous complaint de ceo attempt al Roy. Et le matter fuit mult aggravate, ut audivi, vers Coke Chief Justice entant que le Court de Chauncery (come fuit urge) fuit le very Treasury del ancient prerogative del Corone et le mynte de novels prerogatives. Ee que (come fuit auxi urge ut audivi) le Seignior Coke in ceo matter affront principallment le prerogative."

perish, or that the Chancery shall relieve him; and whether there be any statute of *praemunire* or other, to restrain this power in the Chancellor (89).

The matter being thus presented to him, the King's course was inevitable. He decided to take advice. But whereas his predecessor would have taken the advice of her judges, James was prevailed upon to consult his own law officers, who had in any case been briefed by Ellesmere the previous year. Coke must have found this as galling as anything that happened in 1616—that the King should have acted on the advice of his counsel without conferring with the judges (90). The King also ordered Glanvill and Allen to be prosecuted in the Star Chamber, which was done in Easter Term (91). They were tortured, or rather clogged with irons (92), to persuade them to answer interrogatories (93), but Bacon failed to fix the authorship of the indictments on any particular judge. The Archbishop of Canterbury and others were appointed to take evidence concerning the *praemunire* (94), probably with a view to inculpating Coke, but it seems that little they collected could be used against him (95).

The King's counsel, acting on two commissions (96), duly collected their precedents and arguments, and consulted other members of the Bar such as William Hakewill (97). The content of the official report of the King's counsel is well known (98). But in some ways more interesting is the florid dissertation by Anthony Ben of the Middle Temple (99), preserved among the Caesar papers (1). In his opinion on the *praemunire* proceedings he expatiated in wide terms on the need for equity as an adjunct to a legal system. "God forbid", he

(89) Spedding, *op. cit.*, vol. 5, p. 350. *Cf.* alternative form of the question, *ibid.*, p. 389. Both forms were, of course, "leading" questions.
(90) See his "Poyntes dangerous et absurd etc.", cited in note 32, *supra*, at f. 569. Coke complained openly about this practice in the *Case of Commendams*: *Acts of the Privy Council 1615-1616*, at p. 606.
(91) Att.-Gen. v. Glanvill, Allen and Levesey (1616), copy of Star Chamber bill in MS. Add. 11574, f. 49.
(92) See Yale, *op. cit.*, p. 26n. This was the *peine fort et dure* which was designed to induce accused persons to answer the charges against them.
(93) Att.-Gen. v. Glanvill et als. (1616) Hobart 115. Their refusal was held tantamount to refusing to answer the bill.
(94) *Calendar of State Papers* (1611-1618), p. 370 (4 June).
(95) Spedding (*op. cit.*, vol. 5, p. 380) could not find any report. But the paper cited in note 79, *supra*, may have been their work. It was certainly used in the charges against Coke: *Acts of the P.C. 1616*, at pp. 645-646.
(96) Dated 19 March and 27 March and transmitted through Ellesmere: see Spedding, *op. cit.*, vol. 5, pp. 386, 388.
(97) Brit. Mus. MS. Lansd. 174, f. 226. Hakewill was a legal antiquary and Member of Parliament. (*D.N.B.*)
(98) It is printed in Carey 117-133; 1 Cha. Rep. iii, 20-48; Spedding, *op. cit.*, vol. 5, pp. 385-395; *Collectanea Juridica*, vol. 1, pp. 35-53.
(99) Ben was favoured by Buckingham and the King. See Whitelocke, *Liber Famelicus*, p. 54; *Chamberlain Letters*, vol. 2, p. 134. He was made Recorder of London in 1617 and died in 1618.
(1) "Mr. Antony Ben his discourse touching the premunire brought against Serjeant More and others for prosecution of a cause in Chancery after judgment given thereof at common lawe": Brit. Mus. MS. Lansd. 174 ff, 205-215.

wrote (2), "that we should think all justice is tyed to the common law, or that all that is done in equity is done against justice, because it is done in a diverse manner from law ... " Equity served the same end as law:

> Justice is her plain song, as it is the plaine song of the lawe; the descant is manyfold, yet no other then such as the law also makes her musick of ... Justice is the soule of the law and equity is the life of justice ... why then should law and equity become now of a sodaine incompitible who have so long time bene found proffitable servauntes to the state, why should they now be presented to the world like Essau and Jacob wrestling for birthright?(3).

This is how posterity has tended to view the dispute, but the dispute was not about theory. Ben did not discuss the defects of the Chancery or of the Chancellor, for he was not retained to do so. The judges were not given the opportunity to state their case openly, and it may be that King James was not fully apprised of all the facts. Howbeit, the object was achieved, the reasons were collected, and a public decision was to be given.

The King's speech in the Star Chamber

James conceived it his divine duty to terminate the conflict between his courts, and he resolved to do so in the Star Chamber. It was the first time he had sat there. He had, he explained, spent seven years studying the law, and another seven waiting for a suitable opportunity (4). So on 20 June, 1616 the Star Chamber was prepared with "great magnificence" and the King was escorted thither by the peers and judges, from King's Bridge, and made his entry, with Prince Charles and the officers of state, to deliver a speech to the assembly (5).

He was there, he said, to perform his coronation oath concerning justice, and to discharge his duty as God's vicegerent: "As Kings are to accompt to God, so Judges unto God and Kings" (6). He proclaimed his respect for the common law and denied the rumours that he intended to introduce the Civil Law from Scotland (7). Then he turned to address the judges. He wished to purge the law from two corruptions, uncertainty and novelty. The judicial office was *ius dicere*, not *ius dare* (8). They might not encroach on the King's prerogative, nor invade other jurisdictions, "which is unfit, and an unlawfull

(2) *Ibid.*, f. 210v.
(3) *Ibid.*, ff. 211v, 214v-215.
(4) *His Majesties Speach in the Starre Chamber the xx of June Anno 1616*. sig. B2. The speech is reproduced in C. H. McIlwain, *Political Works of James I* (1918), pp. 326-345.
(5) W. Camden, *Annals of James I*, in *A Complete History of England* (1706), vol. 2. p. 646; MS. Add. 35957, f. 55.
(6) *His Majesties Speach etc.*, sig. B1v.
(7) *Ibid.*, sig. B4. See note 6, *supra*.
(8) *Ibid.*, sig. C4. (The very words with which Bacon began his 56th essay. *Of Judicature*).

thing" (9). The King was careful to explain that he expected all the courts, including the Chancery, to keep their ancient bounds. The Chancellor had no warrant but to proceed according to precedents: "these were the limits I gave unto him; beyond the same limits hee hath promised me he will never goe" (10). So far the King had been strictly impartial, but on the question of the *praemunire* he was firm and specific:

> I thought it an odious and inept speach, and it grieved me very much, that it should bee said in Westminster Hall, that a *premunire* lay against the Court of the Chancery and the officers there: how can the King grant a *premunire* against himself? It was a foolish, inept and presumptuous attempt, and fitter for the time of some unworthie King: understand me aright; I meane not, the Chancerie should exceede his limite; but on the other part, the King onely is to correct it, and none else. And therefore sitting here in seate of judgement, I declare and command, that no man hereafter presume to sue a *premunire* against the Chancery (11).

The King then turned to the audience and charged them to be acquiescent in judgments, for "it is better for a King to maintain an unjust decree, than to question every decree and judgment, after the giving of sentence; for then suites shall never ende" (12). A clever twist, to make the faults of the Chancellor those of the litigants. Even so, these words were a weak royal confirmation of the spirit of the statute of 1403. The rest of the speech was given in the manner of the annual charge to the circuit judges.

To the moderate ear this speech was tolerant and balanced, not intended to introduce any novelty into the legal system, but to put a stop to the *praemunire* prosecutions. Serjeant Hutton thought it "a most gracious speech, full of religion and justice" (13). There was no public disgrace to the judges, as had been widely expected (14), and the King's words were in no way derogatory of the law. The only part of the speech which might have given offence was the assertion that the Chancery was not subject to review by any other court. Tourneur, however, perceived another ominous evil creeping into the constitution, and noted a very angry reaction to the affair. Although his words were extempore he evidently intended them to be read and used by later generations (15). "God forbid," were his feelings, "that the irregular power of Chancellors who respect nothing but their private ends should turn the common law of the land into contempt by making decrees

(9) *Ibid.*, sig. D2.
(10) *Ibid.*, sig. D4.
(11) *Ibid.*, sig. D4-D4v.
(12) *Ibid.*, sig. E4. He added, "Make not changes from court to court: for hee that changeth courts, shewes to mistrust the justnesse of the cause. Goe to the right place, and the court that is proper for your cause; change not thence, and submit yourselves to the judgment given there."

after judgments at common law, against statute law and common law, upon causes of equity in being long before the judgment at law obtained . . . "

> And this is maintained by the high power of the Chancellors who persuade the King that they are solely the instruments of his prerogative, and insinuate with the King that his prerogative is transcendant to the common law. And thus in a short time they will enthral the common law (which yields all due prerogative), and by consequence the liberty of the subjects of England will be taken away, and no law practised on them but prerogative, which will be such that no one will know the extent thereof. And thus the government in a little time will lie in the hands of a small number of favourites who will flatter the King to obtain their private ends, and notwithstanding the King shall be ever indigent. And if these breeding mischiefs are not redressed by Parliament the body will in a short time die in all the parts. But some say that no Parliament will be held again in England, *et tunc valeat antiqua libertas Anglie* (16).

The decree of 18 July, 1616

The royal pronouncement of 20 June did not end the matter. Perhaps it was thought that the Chancellor's authority was left in some doubt, and it seems Ellesmere wanted a specific direction in writing—"some formal manifesto with the reasons" (17)—which could be enrolled in the Chancery. A decree was drawn up accordingly, under the privy seal, which set out the complaints of the Chancellor and the opinions of the King's counsel, and ordered that:

> Our Chancellor or Keeper of the Great Seal for the time being shall not hereafter desist to give unto our subjects upon their several complaints now or hereafter to be made such relief in equity (notwithstanding any former proceedings at the common law against them) as shall stand with the true merits and justice of their cases, and with the former ancient and continued practice and precedency of our Chancery (18).

---

(13) *Op. cit.*, f. 98. Camden said "he made a very fine speech . . . and gave the judges a gentle touch": *loc. cit.*, note 5, *supra*.

(14) M.S. Add. 35957, f. 55v: "*Nul particuler disgrace fuit fait a ceo temps al ascun des judges come le common people a ceo temps expect, nec come spero unquam serra, car lour disgrace est tort al ley mesme.*" In the margin is added, "Disgrace of the judges and professors of lawes done to the lawe itself for without them the law is but a dead letter."

(15) See *ibid.*, memorandum at end.

(16) *Ibid.* (translated). Possibly this was written after the issue of the decree of 18 July (*infra*).

(17) Spedding, *op. cit.*, vol. 5, p. 385.

(18) *Ibid.*, pp 385-395; Pat. 14 Jac. p. 6, m. 25: *Cal. State. Papers* (Dom. 1611-18), p. 384; Carey 186. The decree was widely circulated in manuscript. In the British Museum see MS. Harl. 1767, f. 49; MS. Harl. 4265, f. 83; MS. Lansd. 174, f. 119; MS. Lansd. 613, f. 47; MS. Lansd. 826, f. 2; MS. Stowe 298, f. 217v; MS. Stowe 415, f. 63; MS. Harg. 227, f. 583; MS. Harg. 249, f. 159; MS. Harg. 269, art. 6.

This had the appearance of finality, and the victorious Chancery treated the decree as its charter of independence (19). Yet the matter in it remained contentious. The judges had not been consulted and the King could not change the law spontaneously. Coke was in no position at the time to remonstrate since he was about to be suspended from the Council and from sitting as a judge. In his private papers he wrote that the decree had been "obtained by the importunity of the then Lord Chancellor being vehemently afraid: *sed judicandum est legibus,* and no president can prevail against an act of parliament" (20).

The decree certainly put a stop to *praemunire,* and *habeas corpus,* against the Chancery. But it was confined to the Chancery and was not extended to the other courts of equity (21). And the judges continued to assert that the Chancellor could not meddle with a judgment at law as his proceedings were *in personam* (22). By the time of the Interregnum the royal decree itself would be disputed (23).

The decree was also a theoretical success for the prerogative notion of Chancery jurisdiction: the "precedency of our Chancery." But in practice it was detrimental, if not nearly disastrous, to the already overburdened equity jurisdiction. The Chancery was overloaded, and the pressure on the Chancellor far greater than Ellesmere could bear. It was observed that the Chancery was generally complained of at the time of the decree because its jurisdiction was "inlarged out of measure, and so suits become as yt were immortall" (24). Tourneur of course, was highly critical:

> Note that this term [Hilary 1617] I heard a Clerk of the Chancery affirm that there were 8,000 suits depending in court there, of which without doubt 7,900 are thrust into chambers and corners by reference to the Masters of the Court, and to the merchants and others in the country to arbitrate them or to make report of their opinions. Which shuffling of causes arose by reason of the great age of Egerton Chancellor who is now so decrepit that he cannot expedite business as in time past, and yet will not voluntarily resign to any other who might better order the Chancery (25).

(19) See Yale, *op. cit.,* p. 14, note (2).
(20) 3 *Inst.* 125. This was published posthumously.
(21) *Calmady's Case* (1640) Cro. Car. 595.
(22) Anon. (1627) Litt. Rep. 37: "*si judgment soit done in un accion al common ley, le Chancellour ne poet alter ou medle ove le judgment, mes il poet proceede versus le person pur corrupt conscience quia il prend advantage del ley encounter conscience.*" *Tompson v. Hollingsworth* (1641) March N.R. 83; *Anon.* (1647) Style 27.
(23) See W. S. Holdsworth, *History of English Law,* vol. 1 (1956 ed.), pp. 463-465, which is based on Hargrave's learned note to Swanston 22, in 36 E.R. at p. 542-544. Serjeant Rolle wrote that "*un cause ne serra examine sur equitie en le court de Requestes Chancerie ou auter court de equitie apres judgment at common ley*": *Abridgment de plusieurs Cases* (1668), vol. 1, p. 381, *Chancerie* (Y) 2.
(24) Chamberlain to Carleton, 14 November, 1616, *Letters of Chamberlain,* vol. 2, p. 36.
(25) MS. Add. 35957, f. 79v. He also said that the realm was greatly vexed by the inability of Ellesmere and Caesar to manage their places.

Exeunt Coke and Ellesmere

The lasting effect of these events could not be ascertained until the two principal characters left the stage. Fate arranged this to happen within the year. The story of the removal of Coke and its significance in English constitutional history is familiar. After Coke's censure, his dismissal was postponed by James until Michaelmas Term, possibly because of Coke's great popularity (26). When Bacon and Ellesmere jogged the royal memory in October, they suggested summary dismissal rather than a hearing in Council to which the rules of natural justice would apply (27). Montague, the King's Serjeant, was to be the new Chief. If the King were tired of a Chief Justice who put the rule of law first, he would choose one who would put the King first. Anyway, it was thought Montague would pay more than the other contenders (28). Coke's *supersedeas* was sent in November by Sir George Coppin, Clerk of the Crown, and Coke received it "with dejection and tears". Montague added to the injury by asking Coke for his collar of SS., but Coke declined to part with it (29). On 18 November Montague was made Chief Justice and the whole affair was calculated to humiliate Coke as much as possible. Ellesmere, now Viscount Brackley, dragged himself from his sick bed to relish the opportunity of railing against his defeated enemy in public. In addressing Montague he denounced his predecessor by way of example, saying that it had been God's pleasure to cut down Coke and set up Montague (30). When the Chancellor rose to leave, the new Chief Justice bowed obsequiously and

> required to be defended by his lordship, promising to attempt nothing rashly. Which submissive petition was noted as unworthy to proceed from a Chief Justice. Also the chorus censured my Lord Chancellor of over much presumption thus taking upon him to schoole a Lord Chief Justice, which I heard some of the graver sort say had nott bin used in former tymes. This solempnity performed the old deathgreeved Chancellor departed, his deepe rooted malyce against the Lord Coke little satisfied with his breakefast (31).

The next day Montague went in grand procession to Westminster Hall in his new robes, which was the final affront. It was obvious

---

(26) See *Chamberlain Letters*, vol. 2, p. 11. Serjeant Hutton wrote, *"Dieu grant que il poit estre restore"*: *op. cit.*, f. 105.
(27) Spedding, *op. cit.*, vol. 6, pp. 76-82.
(28) Sherburn to Carleton, 5 October, 1616, *Calendar of State Papers* (Dom. 1611-1618), p. 397.
(29) C. D. Bowen, *The Lion and the Throne* (1957), pp. 325-336. The requisite warrants were sent to the King by Bacon on 13 November: Spedding, *op. cit.*, vol, 6, p. 97. In his private papers Coke noted his complaint that the discharge was worded in general terms *"pro diversis causis"*, whereas in fact there was no cause: Brit. Mus. MS. Harl. 6687, f. 15v.
(30) Moore K.B. 826; *Buccleuch Papers* (H.M.C. 1926), vol. 3, p. 196; Hutton, *op. cit.*, f. 112; MS. Add. 35957, f. 62v; S.P. 14/89, nos. 26-28; S.P.Misc. 12, f. 117; Brit. Mus. MS. Harl. 39, f. 281; Bodl. Lib. MS. Ashm. 781, f. 119.
(31) MS. Add. 35957, f. 63, Cf. *Buccleuch Papers, loc. cit.*

that the robes had been prepared before Coke's discharge, and all the ceremonies betrayed an indecent haste (*32*).

At the time of this unsavoury exhibition Brackley himself was growing into disfavour with the King, partly because his son had not been made Lord President of Wales (*33*). The Chancellor was mentally ill, or senile, as well as bodily infirm (*34*), and it was thought he was reluctant to give up the Great Seal (*35*). One of Dudley Carleton's correspondents wrote that if the Chancellor recovered from his sickness there would be more bills preferred against him in the Star Chamber than had been preferred against Coke (*36*).

As he lay dying he kept the Seal near him, and he wrote to the King that he was "an old man and did not use to putt off his cloathes before he went to bed" (*37*). Finally, after the Chancellor had refused to put the Seal to certain patents, the King paid him a visit on 3 March and personally relieved him of it (*38*). Tourneur cynically wrote that this hastened Brackley's death "for wanting the smell of yellow waxe" (*39*). His retirement was indeed short-lived, and he departed this life on 15 March.

The Significance of the 1616 Decree

Montague was obviously not disposed to step into Coke's shoes and continue the opposition to Chancery, and he had publicly promised Brackley that he would not do so. Soon after his appointment he stayed execution in a King's Bench case because a suit had been commenced in Chancery after judgment at law (*40*). Yet the King was desirous of avoiding a repetition of the personal clashes, and when he gave the Great Seal to Bacon he charged him not to repeat the faults of his predecessor. He was to "contain the jurisdiction of the court [of Chancery] within the true and due dimits, without swelling or excess" (*41*), and not to extend the royal prerogative too far (*42*).

(*32*) Hutton, *op. cit.*, f. 122: "*Et fuit mult marvailed at que il voet vaer al Westminster le prochein jour cy hastement, intant que per common probability s'il n'ad provide ses robes devant main, il ne puissoit estre ready, et ne fuit politiquely handled*".
(*33*) Hutton, *op. cit.*, f. 126; MS. Add. 35957, f. 81v; Tate to Montague, 27 February, 1617, *Beaulieu Papers* (H.M.C. 1900), p. 93.
(*34*) S.P. 14/87, no. 17; S.P. 14/90, no. 135.
(*35*) He had earlier petitioned to be allowed to resign. Perhaps senility had made him unpredictable. See S.P. 14/87, nos. 17, 67; S.P. 14/90, nos. 105, 135; MS. Add. 35957, ff. 79v, 81v.
(*36*) S.P. 14/90, no. 113.
(*37*) Hutton, *op. cit.*, f. 126. Cf. *Letters of Chamberlain*, vol. 2, p. 9.
(*38*) Camden wrote that the giving up of the seal had been voluntary and that the King took it with tears: *Annals of James I*, in *A Complete History of England*, (1706), vol. 2, p. 647. It is difficult to judge between the conflicting accounts.
(*39*) MS. Add. 35957, f. 63, margin.
(*40*) Anon. (Mich. 1616) Brit. Mus. MS. Harl. 1692, f. 61; cf. *Huet v. Conquest* (Mich. 1616) MS. Add. 35957, f. 66. Tourneur wrote in the margin "When Coke was gone they began to make Chancery orders" (in the King's Bench).
(*41*) Spedding, *op. cit.*, vol. 6, p. 184. He had given the like direction to Egerton: *supra*, note 6.
(*42*) Camden, *loc. cit.*, in note 33, *supra*. This report is not very explicit.

When Bacon took his seat in Chancery on 7 May, 1617 he made an announcement, emulating the Roman praetors, of the principles he would observe in exercising his judicial office (*43*).

Firstly, he would supply, but not subvert, the law, and would try demurrers or pleas to the jurisdiction in person. Secondly, as to suing in Chancery after judgment at law, he referred to the King's decision of the previous year. But to meet the criticisms of the practice he would require such complainants to enter into good bonds to prove their suggestions (*44*), "so that if he will be relieved against a judgment at common law upon matter of equity, he shall do it *tanquam in vinculis,* at his peril" (*45*). In drawing up regulations to give effect to this he was careful to acknowledge the spirit of the 1403 statute: "Decrees upon suites brought after judgment shall containe no words to make voyd or weaken the judgment, but shall onely correct the corrupt conscience of the party . . . " (*46*). Thirdly, he would not grant injunctions to stay proceedings at law merely upon priority of suit (*47*), or upon a mere complaint without evidence, nor would he alter possessions *pendente lite.* Fourthly, he would not act upon the report of a Master in Chancery without giving the party time to show cause against it. Finally, he said he would never be "so sovereign or abundant in mine own sense" as to neglect the assistance of the common law judges in cases of difficulty.

The last promise was not made idly. Bacon, having achieved the ambition which was the cause of all his scheming, was genuinely anxious to restore peace. The day after his speech in Chancery he invited the judges to dinner and told them to account him one of their number—as their "foreman". Sitting with them after the meal he said

> He was firmly persuaded that the former discords and differences between the Chancery and other courts was but flesh and blood; and now the men were gone, the matter was gone; and for his part, as he would not suffer any the least diminution or derogation from the ancient and due power of the Chancery, so if any thing should be brought to them at any time touching the proceedings of the Chancery which did seem to them

---

(43) "The Effect of that which was spoken by the Lord Keeper . . . at the Taking of his Place in Chancery in Performance of the Charge his Majesty had given him when he Received the Seal": Spedding, *op. cit.*, vol. 6, pp. 182-193. This was widely circulated in manuscript.
(44) This was the suggestion of the lawyers. Tourneur had the same year written that if this were done "*les subiectes trovera mult ease et les officiers de Chauncery meyns profit*": MS. Add. 35957, f. 79v. See 15 Hen. 6, ch. 4 and 17 Ric. 2, ch. 6.
(45) Cf. *Ordinances made by Bacon* (pr. 1642), no. 33.
(46) *Ibid.*, no. 34. Cf. note 18, *supra.*
(47) This had been the practice at the end of the 16th century: *e.g. Bill v. Body* (1560) Cary 50, Dick. 1; *Crowder v. Robinson* (1577) Cha. Cas. 115. Bacon said "I do not mean to make it a horse-race who shall be first at Westminster Hall"; *loc. cit.*

exorbitant or inordinate, that they should freely and friendly acquaint him with it, and they should soon agree.
At these words, Bacon saw "cheer and comfort in their faces" (48).

One of Bacon's first acts was to re-open the case of *Ruswell*, and to appoint Dodderidge and Hutton JJ. as assistants. In the course of argument the judges, with Bacon's assent, laid down some general principles governing the relations between law and equity. Equity could not operate against a maxim of the law, which would be to make a new law, but could only relieve in cases of particular mischief (49). And while equity could in particular instances relieve against a statute (50), it would not directly "cross" a statute, as had been done in the case at bar (51). Accordingly, Lord Ellesmere's decree was reversed. These deliberations were comforting to the common lawyers, but they also demonstrated that error in Chancery could only be tried in the Chancery itself, on a bill of review (52). This may have been the point at which the judges amicably, for the time being, gave up the struggle to control the Chancellor's decisions. For the rest of Bacon's tenure of the Great Seal little is heard of the older wrangles.

Bacon's successor, the last clerical custodian of the Seal, was wise enough to preserve the good relations with the law. Bishop Williams in his praetorian address of 1621 announced:

> I will never make any decree, that shall cross the grounds of the common or statute laws, for I hold by my place the custody not of mine own, but of the King's conscience; and it were most absurd to let the King's conscience be at enmity and opposition with his laws and statutes. This Court (as I conceive it) may be often occasion'd to open and confirm, but never to thwart, and oppose, the grounds of the laws. I will therefore omit no pains of mine own nor conference with the learned judges, to furnish myself with competency of knowledge, to keep my resolution in this point firm and inviolable (53).

Thomas Coventry, who followed Williams as Lord Keeper, was a judge's son and a barrister, and he made efforts to continue the reforms of the Chancery. In his first year of office he cleared a backlog of two hundred cases, and earned the reputation of being a helpful and

---

(48) Spedding, *op. cit.*, vol. 6, p. 198. The quotation has been transposed from the first to the third person here.
(49) H. Rolle, *Abridgment de Plusieurs Cases* (1668), vol. 1, pp. 375-377, *Chancerie* (R) 1, 5, 8, 10, 11, 12, 13.
(50) *Ibid.*, (S) 1, 3, 5, 6, 8. This had been at issue in the *Earl of Oxford's Case*, *supra*.
(51) *Ibid.*, p. 379, (S) 5. Ellesmere's decree had been contrary to the Statute of Wills.
(52) *Ibid.*, p. 382, *Chancerie* (Z) 1. Cf. *Sir George Reynell's Case* (1617), *ibid.*, (Z) 2.
(53) J. Hackett, *Scrinia Reserata* (1693), part 1, p. 73. The same biographer affirms that "the counsel at the Bar were greatly contented with him"; *ibid.*, p. 76.

intelligent judge in equity (54). An anonymous biographer commented on this good reputation:

> Where it falls into observation that this high place [Lord Keeper] is rarely well served but my men of law and persons of deepest judgment in the statute and common lawes of the land; whereby they may distinguish of cases whether they lye proper in that court to be relieved in equitie without intrenching on the jurisdiction of the kingdome, which is the inheritance of the subject (55).

Bacon, Williams and Coventry succeeded in banishing that part of the rivalry which was governed by envy and the clash of forceful personalities. The remaining defects of the Chancery, and the reforms proposed during the Revolution, form the subject of another story which cannot be recounted here.

Conclusion

Maitland wrote of the affairs of 1616: "The victory of the Chancery was final and complete—and if we were to have a Court of equity at all, it was a necessary victory" (56). It is submitted that this is an exaggeration (57). For one thing, it is doubtful whether the decree had any effect other than prohibiting the common law courts from reviewing Chancery decisions. And if Bacon, Williams and Coventry genuinely attempted to remedy the defects and seek the advice of judges assistant as in the past, the common law courts had no need for such a revisory power. In so far as the dispute was about interference with judgments, Bacon made it clear that he would not "subvert" the law, but only correct the conscience, and so the bone of contention was buried. To the minds of such contemporaries as Tourneur, the decree had greater political than juridical significance. This is certainly true of the events of 1616 as a whole. Pollock found in the wider implications of these occurrences the motivation of Selden's famous aphorism that "equity is a roguish thing" (58): "It is so because the measure of the Chancellor's foot may go too near to follow the measure of Charles I's foot, peradventure even Archbishop Laud's" (59). Another writer has proposed that but for the other

---

(54) Anon., *The Character of Lord Keeper Coventry*, Brit. Mus. MS. Stowe 619, ff. 50v, 52; MS. Sloane 3075, f. 7. The latter copy seems to be nearer the original.
(55) MS. Sloane 3075, f. 7v.
(56) F. W. Maitland, *Constitutional History of England* (1908), p. 270, Potter went so far as to say that the decree "determined the continued right of the Chancery to exist": *Historical Introduction to English Law* (1958 ed.), p. 160.
(57) Later writers have tended to make less of the decree: e.g. W. S. Holdsworth, *History of English Law* (1924), vol. 5, p. 236; Yale, *op. cit.*, p. 14; Jones, *op. cit.*, p. 473.
(58) J. Selden, *Table Talk* (1927 ed.), p. 43.
(59) F. Pollock, *Essays in Legal History* (1913), pp. 294-295.

events of that eventful year, the Chancery dispute would have been no more than a storm in a tea cup [60].

It is easy to see a connection between the decree of 1616 and s. 25 of the Judicature Act, 1873 [61]. There is more than a hint in some books that the common lawyers lost in the end. Sir Jocelyn Simon has conjured up the murmur of Coke turning in his grave as the clause was passed by the House of Commons without debate [62], but it is doubtful whether Coke's remains would have been so exercised. Equity by its very nature prevails over law in appropriate circumstances, but the difficulties which had troubled Coke and his contemporaries had been practical problems of judicial comity and personality, rather than theoretical problems of conflicting notions of justice. The battle had been fought not so much between equity and law, as between the Chancellor and the common lawyers. As Bacon himself said, "When the men were gone, the matter was gone". The Judicature Acts in fact prevented the possibility of such troubles recurring, by fusing the administration of law and equity and abolishing common injunctions. Equity is now administered by the same judges who administer the common law, and the Lord Chancellor rarely, if ever, sits in equity. One is therefore tempted to conclude that in 1873 it was Coke's victory which became final and complete.

NOTE

Since the foregoing article was published, several further writings have appeared: G. W. Thomas, "James I, Equity and Lord Keeper Williams" (1976) 91 Eng. Hist. Rev. 506-528; C. M. Gray, "The Boundaries of the Equitable Function" (1976) 20 A.J.L.H. 192-226; L. A. Knafla, *Law and Politics in Jacobean England: the tracts of Lord Chancellor Ellesmere* (1977), esp. pp. 123-181. These do not detract from the thesis advanced above. The title, however, is potentially misleading: it was not meant to imply that the confict was with Civil lawyers, or that there was in 1616 a distinct Chancery bar.

---

[60] Jones, *op. cit.*, p. 473.
[61] 36 & 37 Vict., c. 66, s. 25 (11); now the Judicature Act 1925, s. 44. Maitland said the provision had little effect because there was no conflict between law and equity before the Act was passed: *Lectures on Equity* (1969 repr.), pp. 16-17. For the connection, see generally White and Tudor, *op. cit.*; Yale, *op. cit.*, p. 14; G. W. Keeton, *An Introduction to Equity* (1965 ed.), p. 43; J. Tiley, *Casebook on Equity and Succession* (1968) p. 20.
[62] [1968] Cambridge Law Journal at p. 272.

8 Edward Littleton, Baron Lyttelton of Munslow

This portrait shows Littleton in his robes as Chief Justice of the Common Pleas (1640-41).

National Portrait Gallery

14

THE NEWE LITTLETON

No account of the history of English legal literature can omit the name of Littleton. Sir Thomas Littleton's treatise on tenures made the family name almost synonymous with the common law itself.[1] But it is not generally known that another member of that illustrious family left unfinished a work which, had it been completed and published, would have earned him a position of importance in the history, not only of English, but of universal jurisprudence. In so far as the will ought to be taken for the deed, perhaps some measure of recognition may justifiably be afforded to his work even after three centuries of oblivion. The author was Edward Littleton (1589–1645), Baron Littleton of Munslow, a direct descendant of Sir Thomas.[2] Educated at Christ Church College, Oxford, he entered the Inner Temple in 1608; and there, like his near-contemporary John Selden (1584–1654),[3] he developed a taste for comparative jurisprudence, legal history, and the study of records. His reputation for learning brought him in 1640 to the seat of Chief Justice of the Common Pleas, and within a year he was made Lord Keeper. The transition to high office was a personal disaster, since Littleton's nature did not suit him for a position of political delicacy, and his brief tenure of the Seal was scarcely less miserable than that of his predecessor Finch—who had fled to Holland in 1640. Among Littleton's first tasks was to preside over the preliminaries to the proposed impeachments of Finch and the ship-money judges, and the lengthy preparations for the trial of Strafford. Within months he became ill, and from February until August 1641 he absented himself from the House of Lords. The following year, either from fear or high-mindedness, he quit London, following the King to York and thence to Oxford. In his hurried flight he apparently left behind some of his goods and papers in the " Black Lodgings " in the Inner Temple.[4] His health continued to deteriorate, and he died (aged 56) on 27 August 1645.[5]

[1] W. Fulbecke, *Direction or Preparative to the Study of the Law* (1600), f. 27v. Sir Thomas was, in fact, the son of Thomas Westcote; his mother was the heiress of Thomas de Littleton, and her name was assumed by her eldest son (Thomas) at the time of his christening.
[2] Biographical details are taken from the preface to *Les Reports des Seigneur Littleton* (1683), sig. B; A. Wood, *Athenae Oxonienses*, iii, 175; E. Foss, *Judges of England*, vi, 343–352; *Dictionary of National Biography*.
[3] Selden was admitted to the Inner Temple, from Oxford, in 1603.
[4] There was some question whether these belonged to Lord Littleton or his brother, Serjeant (later Baron) Timothy Littleton: *HLJ*, vi, 265 (21 October 1643).
[5] Monumental inscription, Christ Church Cathedral, Oxford.

Within weeks of his death, the House of Commons issued a writ for the seizure of his books and papers and ordered that they be bestowed upon Bulstrode Whitelocke.[6] Whitelocke noted:

> I undertook this business, as I had done others of the like kind, to preserve those books and manuscripts from being sold, which the sequestrators would have done: but I saved them to have the present use of them, and resolving, if God gave us a happy accommodation, to restore them to the owner, or to some of his family.[7]

Whitelocke does not say why the papers were worth saving, nor whether he did make use of them; but the inference is that they were important, and the transaction is reminiscent of the scramble for Coke's papers after his death.[8] It is possible that Whitelocke restored the papers to Sir Timothy Littleton, one of the barons of the Exchequer. A volume of reports, said to have been found in just such a collection,[9] was published in 1683 with the name of Lord Littleton on the title-page. (The volume no doubt belonged to the Lord Keeper, but it is unlikely that he was the author; despite the publisher's contrary assertion, there is some textual overlapping with other contemporary reports such as "Hetley."[10]) The only other writings which have been generally noticed are the reports of his 1628 speeches on the liberty of the subject, and his Inner Temple reading of 1632 on the statute of merchant strangers.[11] The printed sources leave the matter thus. Whatever there may have been in the Black Lodgings, or in the study at Christ Church, was long ago forgotten.

In the Treasure Room of the Harvard Law School there is a folio manuscript volume with the title: *An Enterviewe betweene the lawes and customes of England and those of other nations, or, The newe Littleton. The first parte.*[12] It was acquired by the Law School in 1904, for £2 8s., from a bookseller.[13] Its provenance was the library of Lieutenant-Colonel Carew at Crowcombe Court, near Taunton, a

---

[6] *HCJ*, iv, 274 (16 September 1645). The House also disposed of his embroidered purse and gowns: *ibid.* 330.
[7] B. Whitelocke, *Memorials of the English Affairs* (1853 ed.), i, 513.
[8] As to which, see above, pp. 196-198.
[9] *Les Reports des Seigneur Littleton* (1683), epistle, sig. B^v: "The Reason why these Reports came out so long after the Author's death, is that his Papers rested till within these few years in the hands of his Brother, and Executor, Sir Timothy Littleton . . . who kept them for his own private use." Littleton B. died in 1679.
[10] It seems that these were partly by a Mr. Allestree and partly by Humfrey Mackworth: note by Edward Umfreville, Brit.Lib., MS.Harg. 362, f. 3v.
[11] Brit.Lib.. MS.Harg. 372 (3), f. 90; MS.Add. 42117, f. 1; Salk. 46, pl. 2. The statute is 27 Edw. 3, cap. 17.
[12] Harvard Law School, MS. 2106. The writer is indebted to Dr. Edith G. Henderson, Curator of the Treasure Room, for allowing him to examine the entire collection of manuscripts, few of which have been noticed in print.
[13] Unidentified cutting, item 814, which incorrectly (and inexplicably) gives the date as 1580. [The bookseller was William Ridler. *Add.*]

portion of which (including *The Newe Littleton*) had been sold at auction in 1903.[14] The record commissioners had visited Crowcombe Court, but there is no mention of this manuscript in their report.[15] Both the bookseller and the auctioneers dated the manuscript to the wrong century, and neither gave any indication of its contents or authorship. It is written in a shaky scrawl, mostly in English, but with a few passages in what is more like contemporary French than law-French; there are numerous untidy annotations and interlineations. Internal evidence identifies it as the work of the Lord Keeper,[16] and it was evidently written at Oxford between 1643 and his death.[17] During his forced retirement to his old College, Littleton was obviously fighting against time, war and illness, to gather his life's work into a compilation of considerable magnitude. Exile had already made possible two classics of English law. But Lord Littleton, unlike Fortescue and Coke, did not survive to bring his work to fruition. Some indication of his intentions may be gathered from the following note scribbled on the fly:

> Selected Tracts of the lawes and Customes of England.
> The newe L.
> My directions for the publishing of those tracts of the lawe contained in this booke and in another of mine of tracts beginning with the letter A. with additions out of my blewe booke as made at Oxford § Abate Abiuration Abeyance other titles there and in my Forest booke and in my notes of coment upon the two first bookes of Littleton. 1. if I live to perfect them with the title in Page following [*An Enterviewe* . . .] otherwise with this above here to be drawne into Alphabeticall order . . . there are materiall things in my blewe booke made at Oxford fit to be added.

The other books here referred to have not been found, but it is clear from this note that Littleton wanted to work the contents of his notebooks into an alphabetical encyclopedia, and that, given time, he would have developed the collection into a comparative treatise. The Harvard volume is arranged alphabetically, but it contains only the thirty-seven titles beginning with the letter A.[18] It is described as

---

[14] *Catalogue of a selected portion of the Crowcombe Court Library* [sold by Messrs. Sotheby, Wilkinson and Hodge on 6 May 1903], p. 23, lot 201, where it is wrongly dated to the eighteenth century.

[15] *HMC*, IV, Appendix, pp. 368 *et seq.*

[16] See the Preface, and also various references throughout to his own decisions as Chief Justice and Lord Keeper. Plucknett identified it in 1927 (note inside the volume), but seems to have thought it of no particular importance.

[17] He cites several cases decided between 1640 and 1643, and also two recent works: H. Grotius, *Florum Sparsio ad Ius Iustineanum* (Paris, 1642; or Amsterdam, 1643); C. B. Morisot, *Orbis Maritimi Generalis Historia* (Dijon, 1643).

[18] In this table the number of pages is given in parentheses; the volume is unpaginated. Abbot (4). Abeyance (3). Abjuration (3). Abbreviation (1) [" The rules of the laws of England for Interpretation of abbreviated words."] Abridgment

"The first parte," and one can only guess at the number of later parts now missing or perhaps not completed. It is quite different in character from the numerous alphabetical commonplace books to be found in all legal libraries of the time, which are usually merely keys to the work of others. Littleton's work is original, scientific, comparative and lucidly written. Many of his titles are unconventional for a common lawyer, emphasising ecclesiastical and introducing international law. Lord Keeper Littleton had become not only Colonel Littleton,[19] but also Doctor Littleton [20]; an industrious law don, whose attempt to fuse Inns of Court law with university learning during those last two years of his life at Oxford resulted in a work which, even in its fragmentary state, is so unusual that it encourages further attention.

In so far as Littleton treated of the common law and English affairs, he ranged far beyond the Year Books and abridgments and technical authors. He refers to plea rolls, to Domesday Book, to a book on maritime matters in Sir Robert Cotton's library,[21] to a book in the College of Arms, to the Forest Eyre of Dean 1634, to the Dialogue of the Exchequer; and—most important of all—to the unprinted autograph copies of Coke's *Second, Third,* and *Fourth Institutes,* which had passed into Littleton's possession from his predecessor Finch.[22] There are interesting notes of cases in which Littleton had been involved personally, including: two cases of 1638 and 1643 concerning the Admiralty; a case tried before himself at Norwich in 1640 in which damages for adultery were recovered in trespass *vi et armis*[23]; *Lady Sandys' Case* (1640); the case of the disputed election of the Master of Sidney Sussex College, Cambridge (1642)[24]; and a detailed account, in French, of the advice he gave in November 1643 on the question of adjourning Parliament. Amongst other manuscripts in his own library he cites[25]: a charter of Sir Thomas Littleton, found

---

of Demaundes and Plaintes (4). Abuttals (1). Accessories (11). Accounts (9). Acquittance (4). Aire (3) [Eyre]. Acra (1). Action (12). Adjournement (20). Admirall (14). Adulterie and Fornication (20). Advouson (15). Age (7). Agistment (2). Aides (10). Alderman (2). Alien (4). Ambassadors (10). Annates (6). Apostates (5). Apostle (3). Appeales (5). Apprentice (6). Appropriations (13). Arbiterment (10). Arrerages (1). Arrest (1). Assaut (6). Assise (2). Assurance (3). Atturney (5). Auncient Demesne (10). Avoury (1).

[19] He took command of the Inns of Court Regiment in 1643.
[20] He proceeded Doctor of Civil Law in 1643.
[21] S.v. Admirall. Probably Brit.Lib., Cotton MS. Otho E. ix.
[22] *HCJ,* ii, 69; chapter 12, p. 198, *supra;* Cambridge University Library, MS. Ee. iv.7, ff. 9, 13 (*infra*).
[23] S.v. Adulterie. It was held that the adultery fell within the *et alia enormia ei intulit* clause of the general writ: a good example of the artificial extension of an old writ to provide a new remedy. (The action on the case for criminal conversation was invented later.)
[24] S.v. Appeals. This confirmed the principle that, in default of a visitor appointed by the founder, appeal lay to the King in Chancery. The earlier decision had been forgotten when the principle was laid down in *R.* v. *Master and Fellows of St. Catharine's Hall* (1791) 4 T.R. 233.
[25] S.v. Abbot, Action, Age, Admirall, Aids.

in the Littleton muniments by Dugdale; his own notes on the Statute of Limitations; his own notes on *Pigot's Case* and *Prince's Case*; " my booke of shipping "; and " my records noted in the margent of F[itzherbert] N[atura] B[revium] *procedendo ad iudicium.* This wilbe fit to be made a complete tract if opportunitie be offered after regaining of my books and notes." He also cited manuscript chronicles, and Leland's manuscripts in the Bodleian Library.[26] Among the other English writers, of whose works it is unnecessary here to give details, are mentioned Francis Bacon, John Bale, Bede, William Camden, Geoffrey Chaucer, John Cowell, Henry of Huntingdon, William Lambarde, Matthew Paris, Ralph of Chichester, John Selden, Thomas Smith, Henry Spelman, Thomas Walsingham, and Richard Zouche. There is also a reference to John Skene's *Regiam Majetstatem.*

Still more impressive is the display of familiarity with foreign authors, beginning with those of antiquity,[27] continuing with various medieval authors,[28] and with the jurists of the Renaissance period, right down to the latest works of Grotius [29]—who was an almost exact contemporary and died in the same month as Littleton. Seven titles are devoted to ecclesiastical matters, and in most of them Littleton relies not only on the texts of the Canon Law but on medieval Canonists such as William Lyndwood (*c. 1375–1446*), George Codin (fl. 1430),[30] and Mathieu Nicolas de Clamenges, Archdeacon of Bayeux (*c. 1360–1440*),[31] and on contemporary writers such as the Swiss Jean-Rodolphe Fabri (1580–1650). There are references to the Civil Law in many of the titles—to the *Corpus Juris Civilis*, the barbarian codes, and the Renaissance commentators. Littleton reveals a wide knowledge of Renaissance jurisprudence, history, philosophy, and philology.[32] From Italy we find: Giovanni Battista da Sambiagio (1425–92),[33] Giovanni Antonio da San Giorgio (1439–1509),[34] and

---

[26] Probably Bodl.Lib., MS.Top.Gen. c. 4. For Leland and his manuscripts, see M. McKisack, *Medieval History in the Tudor Age* (1971), pp. 1–7.

[27] Authors include Aristotle, Cicero, Columella, Philoxenus, Plautus, Pliny, Suetonius, Terence, Tertullian, Tully, Valerius Maximus, and Xenophon.

[28] St. Anselm, Hector Boethius, St. Gregory of Tours, Marculfus monachus, Bartolomeo Platina, and Jean Zonaras.

[29] *De Iure Belli ac Pacis* (1st ed., Paris, 1625); *Appendix ad Commentationem de Anti-Christo* (Amsterdam, 1641); *Annotationes in Libros Evangeliorum* (Amsterdam, 1641); *Florum Sparsio ad Ius Iustineanum* (Paris, 1642).

[30] Codinus, *De Officiis* (Lyon, 1588).

[31] Clamengius, *De Annatis non Solvendis* (Cologne, 1535).

[32] The notes which follow give the citation as in the manuscript, and then (in square brackets) an attempt to identify the work. Where there is more than one edition, the earliest has been given. Perhaps the very books which Littleton used are still at Oxford?

[33] " Jo. Baptista de Arbitriis." [1st ed., Venice, 1481. And in *Tractatus Universi Iuris* (Venice, 1584).]

[34] " J. de St. Georgio tract. de homagiis." [*De feudis et homagiis* (Lyon, 1544).]

Vincent de Franchis.[35] From Germany and the Low Countries: Jean de Beka (fourteenth century),[36] Andreas von Gaill (1526-87),[37] Daniel Heinsius (1580-1655),[38] Andreas Rauchbar,[39] Matthew Wesenbeck (1531-86), and Ulrich Zasius (1461-1535). But it is Littleton's acquaintance with French law and literature which is the most remarkable, over twenty French authors being mentioned at various places throughout the book. These include: Bertrand d'Argentré (1519-90),[40] Pierre Ayrault (1536-1601),[41] Claude de Battandier (fl. 1560),[42] François Baudouin (1520-73), [43] Josias Bérault (1563-1640),[44] Laurent Bouchel (1559-1629),[45] Jules-César Boulenger (1558-1628),[46] Guillaume Budé (1468-1540),[47] Barthélemi de Chasseneux (1480-1541),[48] René Chopin (1537-1606),[49] Jean de Coras (1513-72),[50] Jacques Cujas (1522-90),[51] Estienne Forcadel (1534-73),[52] Denis Godefroy (1549-1622),[53] François Hotman (1524-90),[54] Claude-Barthélemy Morisot (1592-1661),[55] Guy de la Pape (d. 1487),[56] Estienne Pasquier (1529-

[35] " Vincent de Franchis decis." [*Decisiones sacri regii Consilii Neapolitani* (Venice; 1580).]
[36] " Jo. Beka in Chron. Ultraj. et Cons. Hollandiae." [*Chronicon continens res gestas Ultrajectinae et comitum Hollandiae* (1611).]
[37] " Gaile de arrestis Imperii." [*De manum iniectionibus, impedimentis, sive arrestis Imperii* (1578).]
[38] " Heinsius exercitationes sacr." [*Exercitationes sacrae ad novum Testamentum* (Leyden, 1639). *Cf. Sacrarum Exercitationum Libri XII* (Cambridge, 1640), STC 13040.]
[39] " And. Rawchbar 50 quaest. insign. ad iuris saxonici."
[40] " Argentrius in consuetudines Britannie." [The first complete edition appeared in 1608, but d'Argentré began publishing the customs of Brittany in 1568.]
[41] " P. Erod. Pandect." [*Rerum iudicatarum pandectae* (Paris, 1588).]
[42] " Claudius de Battandier in pract. crim. Regula." [*Cf. Praxis causarum criminalium* (1567).]
[43] " Balduinus in institut." [*In quatuor libros institutionum Iuris Civilis Commentarii* (Lyon, 1583).]
[44] " Josias Berault coment." [*La coustume reformée du pays et duché de Normandie . . . avec les commentaires . . . par M. Josias Berault* (Rouen, 1612).]
[45] " Bochellus in thesauro iuris Gallicani." [*Cf. La bibliotheque ou thesor du droict Francois* (Paris, 1615).]
[46] " Bulenger. imperii Romani." [*De Imperatore et Imperio Romano* (Lyon, 1618).]
[47] " Budaeus . . . philologiae." [*De Philologia* (Paris, 1532).] " Bude greeke Commentarie." [*Commentarii Linguae Graecae* (Paris, 1529).]
[48] " Cassaneus de consuetud. Burgund." [*Commentarii in consuetudinibus ducatus Burgundie* (Lyon, 1528). This author was known to Coke: see 5 *Irish Jurist* (N.S.) at p. 397.]
[49] " Renatus Chopinus de Domanio Franc." [*De Domanio Franciae* (Paris, 1574).]
[50] " Corasius Paraph. ad sacerdot. materiam." [*In universam sacerdotium materiam Paraphrasis*, in *Tractatus Universi Iuris* (Venice, 1584).]
[51] " Cuiacius . . . Paratitles." [*Paratitla in libros IX Codicis* (Lyon, 1606).]
[52] " Forcatulus de Gallorum moribus." [*Cf. De Gallorum Imperio et Philosophia* (Paris, 1580).]
[53] " Gothofred." [*Corpus Iuris Civilis cum notis Gothofredi* (Lyon, 1583).]
[54] " Hotoman Coment." [*Commentarius de verbis iuris* (Basle, 1558); or *Commentarius in Institutionem* (Basle, 1560); or *Commentationum Iuris Civilis Libri XXII* (Basle, 1576).]
[55] " Morisotus orbis maritimi historia." [Dijon, 1643.]
[56] " Guido Papaeus Decis." [*Decisiones Parliamenti Delphinatus* (Lyon, 1562).]

1615),[57] François Rageuau (d. 1605),[58] Jean du Tillet jun. (d. 1570),[59] Andrée Tiraqeau (1488–1558),[60] and Lancelot-Voisin de la Popelinière (d. 1608).[61]

Littleton's interest in international law is evident in the title *Ambassadors*, which occupies ten pages. This seems to be the first treatise on international law by a common lawyer.[62] Besides sources as diverse as Julius Caesar, Valerius Maximus, Philoxenus, Domesday Book, Matthew Paris, William Camden, and Sir Edward Coke, the author drew upon the work of thirteen identifiable international jurists[63]: Jean Bruneau (fifteenth century),[64] Jean a Chokier (1571–1656),[65] Alberico Gentili (1552–1608),[66] Anastasio Germoni (1551–1627),[67] Hugo Grotius (1583–1645),[68] Jean Hotman (1552–1636),[69] Friedrich Lindenbrog (1573–1648),[70] Frederik van Marselaer (1584–1670),[71] Ottaviano Maggi (fl. 1560?),[72] Carlo Pasquale (1547–1623),[73] Claude de Saumaise (1588–1658),[74] Gundisalvus de Villadiego (fifteenth century),[75] and Krysztof Warszewicki (1543–1603).[76] There is also Littleton's personal recollection of the visit of the French and Venetian ambassadors to Oxford in 1643.

[57] " Pasquier recherches." [*Des recherches de la France* (Paris, 1560).]
[58] " Rageau Indice des Droits." [*Indice des droits royaux et seigneuriaux* (Paris, 1585).]
[59] " Jo. Tilius de rebus Gallicis." [*Commentariorum de rebus gallicis libri duo* (Frankfurt, 1579).]
[60] " Tiraquel. de utroque retractu." [*Commentarii de utroque retractu* (Paris, 1543).]
[61] " *Popelliniere Amiral de France*." [*L'Amiral de France* (Paris, 1584).]
[62] *Cf.* 4 Inst., c. 26, which is cited by Littleton; but Coke's sources are almost entirely English, and Coke is only concerned with the municipal law relating to ambassadors.
[63] For further details of these authors and their works, see: V. E. Hrabar, *De Legatis et Legationibus Tractatus Varii* (1905); E. R. Adair, *The Extraterritoriality of Ambassadors in the 16th and 17th Centuries* (1929); B. E. Behrens, " Treatises on the Ambassador written in the 15th and early 16th Centuries " (1936) 51 *English Historical Review* 616; K. R. Simmonds, " Pierre Ayrault et le Droit d'Ambassade " (1960) 64 Rev.Gen.Droit Intern. Publ. 753; D. E. Queller, *The Office of Ambassador in the Middle Ages* (1967); S. E. Nahlik, *Narodziny Nowozytnej Dyplomacji* (1971), pp. 240–250. (The writer is grateful to Dr. W. E. Butler for bringing the last work to his notice.)
[64] " Brunellus de Legationibus." [*Tractatus de dignitate et potestate legati* (Paris, 1519).] [65] " Jo. a Chokier Tr. de legato. [Cologne, 1624.]
[66] " Alberic. Gentilis de legat." [*De legationibus libri tres* (London, 1585), *STC* 11737.]
[67] " Anastasius Germonius de legatis." [Rome, 1617.]
[68] " Grotius in Evangel."; " Grotius de bell. et P."; " Grotius florum sparsio." [*Supra*, note 29.]
[69] " Hotman." [*The Ambassador* (London, 1603), *STC* 13848.]
[70] " Lindenbr. annales ste. . ." [His major work was the *Codex Legum Antiquarum* (Frankfurt, 1613), which may be Littleton's source for the barbaric laws.]
[71] " Frid. de Marselare legatus." [Antwerp, 1618.]
[72] " Octav. Magius de legato Ven. 1566." [This is the first edition.]
[73] " Car. Paschalius de legationibus." [Rouen, 1598.]
[74] " Salmasius ad hist. August." [*Historiae Augustae Scriptores* (Paris, 1620).]
[75] " Gundisalvus de villa Diega de legato." [In *Tractatus Universi Iuris* (Venice, 1584). First edition, 1549.]
[76] " Christ. Warsevicius de legato et legat." [Cracow, 1595.]

238   *The Legal Profession and the Common Law*

There is thus a formidable display of erudition even in the one remaining volume, and an indication that there were at least seven other volumes of various kinds by Littleton's own hand which were available for incorporation in *The Newe Littleton*: a volume of tracts, the "blewe booke made at Oxford," a book on forest law,[77] another on maritime law, a commentary on the first two books of Littleton's *Tenures*, notes on cases, and an annotated *Natura Brevium* containing sufficient material for a separate tract. The last of these, and probably some of the others, were evidently left in London with the rest of Littleton's library. None of the volumes mentioned has come to light, but it is not beyond hope that some of them may be recovered now that a specimen of Littleton's hand is available for comparison. The present writer has in fact succeeded in tracing three more volumes in Littleton's distinctive scrawl and odd French, all in the University Library, Cambridge. The most useful of the three[78] contains, at one end, some moot cases of 1611–12, perhaps from Littleton's student days, but not positively identifiable as in his hand; and, at the other end, thirty-three leaves of notes on Parliament extending to March 1643. This latter collection is not so well polished as the Harvard volume, but shows signs of arrangement by titles.[79] Since Littleton used this book to note points touching the laws and customs of Parliament, there is not the comparative treatment found in the other; nevertheless the material is from an extensive range of sources. He cites the Coke manuscripts, as in the other, and also works by Prynne and Selden published in 1642 and 1643.[80] He refers to manuscript journals of both Houses, to the "Liber Parliam." in the Tower, and to manuscript reports (including Parliamentary notes by Serjeant Glanvill,[81] Maynard, Walter, Selden, and Rolle[82]). The most interesting parts of the volume are the notes from Littleton's own experience as Lord Keeper. There are two notes on the election of speakers of

---

[77] Cf. University Library Cambridge, MS. Mm.6.62, f. 68: "Vide mon forest law."
[78] University Library Cambridge, MS. Ee.iv.7. It is now bound up with other pieces, the original binding (with any preliminaries) having been destroyed.
[79] The main titles are: Privilege (ff. 2–3, 6), Subsidies (f. 3), Punition pur enfreindre des privileges (f. 4), Droit d'Elections (f. 4v), Impositions (f. 5), Elections (ff. 7–8), Assent (f. 9), Adjournments (f. 9), Procurators du clerge en Parliament (f. 9v), Judicature non limite per les loix ordinaires (ff. 10–15), Parliament en general (f. 26). On f. 27 is a memorandum of the introduction of Finch as Lord Keeper, and on f. 29 of an "introduction de novel Baron a la maison" in 1640.
[80] *Supra*, note. 22; J. Selden, *Priviledges of the Baronage* (1642), Wing S.2434; W. Prynne, *The Soveraigne Power of Parliaments* (1643), Wing P.4088.
[81] At f. 4v: "Voyez les reports de Glanvill qui estoit a la chaire pur elections 21° Jacobi il en a fait de reports." There was perhaps a tradition of keeping law reports of Parliamentary proceedings. Serjeant Richardson (Speaker 1620–1623) made a similar compilation, a copy of which by Trevor M.R. was sold at the Bromley-Davenport sale, Sotheby, Wilkinson and Hodge, 8 May 1903, lot 375.
[82] Margin of f. 4v: "Vide chez Glanvill Maynard et al. leurs reports;" f. 5: "See in the Parliament 21 et 22 Jacobi chez Walter, Selden, Roll, et al." *Cf.* MS. Mm.6.62, f. 22: "Serjeant Glanvill's reports of Priviledges."

the House of Lords to serve in the absence of the Lord Keeper—a common occurrence during the tenure of Finch and Littleton. In one of these he writes:

> 17° Caroli, le iour en August que le roy alla en Escosse, la maison des seigneurs declara qu'ils avoient droit d'eslire leur Parleur et qu'il ne deust departir la maison, le roy aiant envoie pur luy, sans conge de la maison—soit il peere ou autre. Et 27° Octobris quand i'allois a la roine, et 13° et 15° Novembris quand ie suis malade, ils appointerent le seigneur privie seale en ma place en pursuance de l'ordre, combien que Bankes chief Justice avoit commission d'estre Parleur en mon absence. Et ils dirent qu'ils peuvent appointer un de leur corps sans l'approbation du roy, mais non pas Juge qui n'est de leur corps.[83]

These rulings do not clearly appear in the Lords' Journals. There are also several notes on the preparation for the trial of Lord Strafford: for instance, a decision that the King might sit but not vote.[84] According to Littleton, he and other judges held the Statute of Treason inapplicable to peers, but Bramston C.J. protested that there was no precedent of an attainder in Parliament for treason without indictment or appeal, and that to proceed in such a way would be against the *iudicium parium* clause of Magna Carta.[85]

The other two volumes at Cambridge are also devoted to the subject of Parliament and the constitution. One contains abridged notes in Littleton's hand from the rolls of Parliament, interspersed with transcripts made by a clerk and annotated by Littleton.[86] The other is an extensive collection of brief notes and references relating to parliamentary and constitutional history, theory and law.[87] It is valuable principally for the notes of decisions by Littleton himself as Lord Keeper, 1640–1642, and of conversations with Selden and other friends during the same period. But it also affords further proof of Littleton's remarkably extensive reading, and of his interest in history and comparative constitutional theory. Camden, Dodderidge, Selden, Speed, and other historians feature throughout. Among foreign authors referred to,[88] besides Grotius, Hotman, and Pasquier

---

[83] From f. 26v, with added punctuation. See also *HLJ*, iv. 437a, 633b, 634a.

[84] At f. 11: "Feb. 16 Caroli tenus per moy, Bankes chief Justice de C.B., Herbert Attorney, et Selden, que le roy peut estre present au trial entre les seigneurs, come les precedens sont, mais les seigneurs sont les Juges."

[85] At f. 13. See also ff. 10, 12v, 14, 15v, 26v. These notes are first-hand sources, though they do not throw much new light on the matter. *Cf.* C. Russell, "The Theory of Treason in the Trial of Strafford" (1965) 80 *English Historical Review* 30.

[86] MS. Mm.6.68 (3). The notes on ff. 50–54, 82–104, are in Littleton's hand. At f. 88v he mentions records "au libraire d'Oxford."

[87] MS. Mm.6.62. The notes on ff. 22–28, 33–37, 40v–43v, 56–57, 63v–70, 74, 77–83, 114–124, 127v–138, 143, 145, 146, 148v–155, 158v, are in Littleton's hand. Other items in the volume are annotated by him. At ff. 156–157 is a note addressed to "Mr. Littleton at his chamber in the Inner Temple."

[88] Some of these were available in English editions: see *STC* 3185, 3193, 5051–5,

(mentioned above), are: Henning Arnisoeus (*c. 1580*–1636), Traiano Boccalini (1556–1613), Jean Bodin (1530–1596), Pierre Charron (1541–1603), Antonio de Guevara (1490–1545), Bernard de Girard, sieur du Haillan (1535–1610),[89] Vincent de la Loupe (sixteenth century), Niccolò Machiavelli (1469–1527), Diego Pérez de Salamanca (sixteenth century),[90] Pedro de Ribadeneira (1527–1611),[91] Jean Savaron (1550–1622), Jean de Serres (*c. 1540*–1598), Louis Servin (*c. 1555*–1626), Claude de Seyssel (*c. 1450*–1520),[92] Marco Antonio, Archbishop of Split (1566–1624), Jacques-Auguste de Thou (1553–1617), and Nicolas de Neufville, sieur de Villeroy (1542–1617). There are also references to manuscripts not previously mentioned: " all my notes upon Couel and others . . . liber specialis Noye . . . liber miscellaneorum Caroli Jones . . . mon livre fait per Hackewell . . . the case of W. Long in camera stellata entre mes records." [93] A reference to " my notes v. Abbot " is probably to *The Newe Littleton*, or to notes on which it was based.

It must be considered a serious loss to jurisprudence that Lord Littleton was not spared to complete *The Newe Littleton* or to arrange his remarkable collections in publishable form, that neither Whitelocke nor Sir Timothy Littleton took steps to edit or preserve what he left, and that the collection has been broken up and probably (for the most part) lost. The two books which remain are impressive and instructive, if a little hieroglyphic. Whether they should be published even now is a question worth consideration by scholars more familiar than the present writer with the subject matter. At least they should be looked into by historians of constitutional, international, comparative, and ecclesiastical law. And Lord Keeper Littleton should be given the honoured place in comparative jurisprudence which is his belated due.

NOTE

The writer has so far identified the following manuscripts as being in Littleton's autograph:

1. Harvard Law School, MS. 2106. *The Newe Littleton*, written *c.* 1643–1645.

12432–5, 17159, 17161, 17167, 22244–6. They include most of the founders of a school of institutional historians: see D. R. Kelley, *Foundations of Modern Historical Scholarship* (1970), esp. at pp. 212–214.

[89] *Lestat des affaires de France*. [Paris, 1570.]

[90] *Commentaria in . . . libros ordinationum Castellae*. [Salamanca, 1574–5. 1st ed., 1560. Glossed edition of Dr. Montalvo's ordinances of 1485.]

[91] *Las virtudes del Principe Christiano*. [Madrid, 1595; Antwerp, 1597. A criticism of Machiavelli.]

[92] *De republica Galliae*. [Argentorati, 1562.]

[93] William Noy (1577–1634), William Hakewill (1574–1655), and Charles Jones (barrister 1619, bencher 1636), were all members of Lincoln's Inn. Hakewill wrote *The Manner how Statutes are enacted in Parliament* (1641).

2. University Library Cambridge, MS. Ee.4.7. Notes on the law and privileges of Parliament, including memoranda 1640–1642 and earlier.
3. *Ibid.*, MS. Mm.6.62. Notes on the law and privileges of Parliament, written *c.* 1640–1642, perhaps a continuation of (2). Consists mainly of references to source material, with memoranda of events, decisions, and dicta, and copies (in a clerical hand) of documents and tracts with notes by Littleton. 60 ff. (of 158 ff.) are in Littleton's hand.
4. *Ibid.*, MS. Mm.6.63(2). Annotated draft of argument on ship-money (1637?). 21 ff., titled *Shipmoney.*
5. *Ibid.*, MS. Mm.6.63(4). Annotated draft of argument in *Selden's Case* (1629). 28 ff. On back page: " P. et T. 5 Caroli B.R. Sedition. Le grand cas de Jo: Selden. Habeas corpus. Voyez les arguments de Mason et Aske chez eux et auxi chez Mr. Gardiner. . ."
6. *Ibid.*, MS. Mm.6.63(7). Report of *The Five Knights' Case* (1627). 18 ff., titled *Habeas corpus for ye loanes B.R.* Another hand has added: " Mr. Littleton's copyes of the arguments in B.R. in the habeas corpus for the prisoners touching the loanes."
7. *Ibid.*, MS. Mm.6.68(3). Notes abridged from the Rolls of Parliament, Edw.3-Hen.4, with miscellaneous copies in another hand. 26 ff. (of 62 ff.) are in Littleton's hand.

The following lost manuscripts by Littleton are cited in the above works:

8. A volume of tracts.
9. Blue book made at Oxford.
10. Book on Forest Law.
11. Book on Shipping Law. [Ship-money?]
12. Commentary on Littleton's *Tenures*, books I–II.
13. Annotations to Fitzherbert's *Natura Brevium.*
14. Notes on Cowell and others.
15. Book of records.
16. Reports of cases. [There are some in 1, 2, and 3 above.]

NOTE

Since the foregoing was written, the following further Littleton manuscripts have been identified in Cambridge University Library:

17 MS. Dd.3.64. Miscellaneous drafts and notes in Littleton's hand, including (fo. 128v) notes on Stannaries, Staffe, Statio, Stallions, Stall, Stadles. These last are perhaps for the "S" section of *The Newe Littleton.*
18 MS. Dd.3.84(14). Copy of *Nobility according to Law*, attributed to Sir John Dodderidge or William Bird, copiously annotated by Littleton. Includes a report in his hand of the earl of Lincoln's case (1627) in the Star Chamber, and (pp. 12, 34) conversations with John Walter, Henry Rolle and John Selden.
19 MS. Mm.6.57. Miscellaneous notes, possibly in part (ff. 16-25v) for *The Newe Littleton*, s.v. "Marshal", concerning the marshal of the Exchequer and the earl marshal. Includes references to Noy's notes, "Coke MS. Pl. Cor. f. 30" (fo. 25v), and Sir Thomas Cotton (fo. 34). On fo. 109 an account in English of the negotiations between Britain and the States in 1629-30.

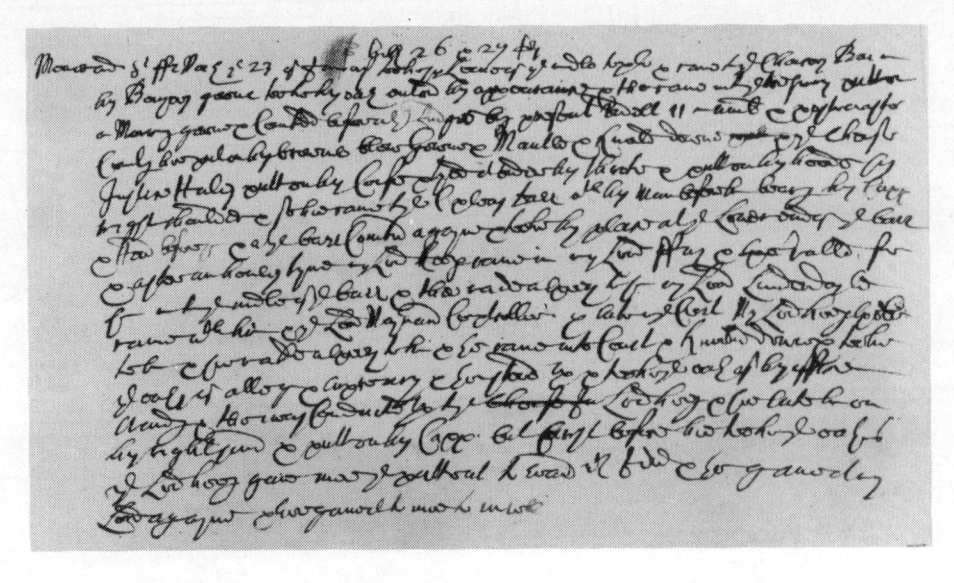

9 Thomas Robinson's notebook

The passage illustrated records the creation of Sir Francis North as a serjeant at law on 23 January 1675 and his installation as Chief Justice of the Common Pleas. Robinson refers to himself in the last line.

Bodleian Library, Oxford, MS Eng. Misc. f. 504, fo. 109[r]

15

SIR THOMAS ROBINSON (1618-83) CHIEF PROTHONOTARY OF THE COMMON PLEAS

THE acquisition by the Library of eight legal notebooks[2] associated with the name of Thomas Robinson is the occasion for the following note about them, their author, and his office.

With the exception of two volumes of precedents,[3] the Robinson notebooks constitute the surviving portion of a series of brief reports of cases in the Common Pleas from 1657 to 1678. The first (MS. Eng. misc. f. 500), marked AAA on the vellum cover, is inscribed on the fly: *Liber Thome Robinson de Staple Inne 1650, Note Booke upon passages in Court.* The 'passages' referred

---

[1] I wish to thank Miss D. M. Barratt and Mr. D. G. Vaisey for their helpful criticism of an earlier draft and for suggestions which have been incorporated in the following.

[2] MSS. Eng. misc. d. 912-13, and f. 500-5. These were almost certainly in the library of Kentwell Hall, Long Melford, Suffolk, formerly Robinson's home. In 1960 Mrs. C. D. B. Starkie Bence of Kentwell Hall was in possession of '3 note books of legal precedents, etc. of Thomas Robinson of Staple Inn, *c.* 1649–59': National Register of Archives report no. 6826, p. 2. Mrs. Bence's books and manuscripts were sold on 7–9 September 1970 by Messrs Boardman and Hill of Sudbury; lot 572 in that sale was described in the printed catalogue as 'Various manuscripts and note books, mostly 17th century, on legal matters of Suffolk (9)'. Although neither description quite fits, it is believed that the purchaser of lot 572 sold the Robinson notebooks to the Frognal Bookshop, London, from whom they were acquired by the Bodleian Library in 1974.

[3] MS. Eng. misc. d. 912 contains conveyancing precedents of Charles I's time. MS. Eng. misc. d. 913 contains entries from the period of the Interregnum.

to in this title begin at the back of the volume on f. 139 rev.[1] and are not reports, but 'special memoranda' or notes of events affecting the practice of an attorney. They begin in Michaelmas term 1641, and include adjournments of the term by proclamation, alterations in the process of the court after Charles I's execution, the change to English and secretary hand after the quindene of Easter 1651, the appointment of Cromwell as Lord Protector, the elevation of Hale and other serjeants and judges in 1653/54, the death of Oliver Cromwell and a brief history of his son's Parliament, and finally the Restoration. There are ten leaves of notes of cases from 1650 to 1654 (ff. 1–10), but the main series of reports begins (fol. 137 rev.) in Hilary term 1657 and continues until Hilary term 1659. This was the beginning of Robinson's tenure as Chief Prothonotary, which explains the title added on the outside cover: *Notes taken in Court per Prothon'* 1657 & 1658. The second volume (MS. Eng. misc. f. 501) seems to have been started as a register of appearances by attorney in cases in which Robinson was concerned between Trinity term 1646 and Michaelmas term 1655. Its principal contents, however, are a continuation of the reports from Michaelmas term 1658 until Hilary term 1660. This volume is signed 'T. Robinson' on fol. 1, and is lettered GGG on the cover. (It is not clear what volumes B to F would have contained, but the lettering may not be consecutive as regards the reports.) The third volume (MS. Eng. misc. f. 502) is lettered H, but the reports begin in 1662 and continue to Michaelmas term 1663, so that there seem to be about two volumes missing. It also contains memoranda of appearances (1649–1657), and this earlier use of the notebooks may account for the erratic lettering. The fourth volume (MS. Eng. misc. f. 503) is lettered NN, and contains reports from Michaelmas term 1668 to Hilary term 1671; which would be consistent with the loss of volumes I, K, L, and M, each containing one year's reports. There is another volume or two missing before the fifth (MS. Eng. misc. f. 504), which runs from 30 May 1673 to Hilary term 1677; but the sixth (MS. Eng. misc. f. 505) follows from that consecutively, from Easter term 1677 to 1678. The last two are not lettered. Although Robinson's

---

[1] The foliation proceeds 1–54 (44–51 being an index, and 52–4 blank), 139^v rev.–55^v rev.

name occurs only in the first two, the reports are all in the same crabbed and difficult handwriting. There is conclusive internal evidence that the author was Chief Prothonotary, for in describing the appointment of Chief Justice North in 1675 he says 'the Lord Keeper gave mee the pattent to read, which I did, and hee gave it to me to inroll'.[1]

Robinson's career provides an impressive illustration of the way in which a humble attorney could in the seventeenth century advance himself to a position of wealth and influence. Social mobility through success at the Bar was familiar enough; but Robinson, who was not bred to the science of the law as a barrister,[2] rose on the clerical side of the profession through mastery of the mechanics of legal procedure. Little is known of his origin, save that he was probably born in Westminster in 1618.[3] As his notebook shows, he was a member of Staple Inn and a practising attorney of the Common Pleas by 1650, and had probably been so in the 1640s (when the memoranda begin). By 1648 he had made a match which suggests that he was already beginning to establish himself respectably.[4] Doubtless he secured office as one of the sworn clerks of the court: this was the usual preliminary to higher office, and Robinson's Staple Inn contemporary George Townesend so describes the course of promotion in his entertaining guide for young clerks, *A Preparative to pleading* (1675).

Robinson became Chief Prothonotary of the Common Pleas in Hilary term 1657 after the death of Thomas Cory. It was the highest clerical office in the common law, and its acquisition

---

[1] MS. Eng. misc. f. 504, fol. 109. Robinson noted the event in his remembrance: P.R.O., CP 45/493, m. 1. He also read Scroggs' patent as a judge in 1676: MS. Eng. misc. f. 504, fol. 200ᵛ.

[2] He was made an 'associate of the Bar', preparatory to becoming an associate of the Bench, in 1657 when he became Chief Prothonotary: p. 31 n. 1 below .Before then he had been a member of Staple Inn. The *Complete baronetage* (p. 32 n. 2 below) is therefore wrong to describe him as a barrister.

[3] A Thomas, son of John Robinson, was christened on 11 September 1618: A. M. Burke (ed.), *Memorials of St. Margaret's Westminster: the parish registers 1539–1660* (1914), p. 98. There are too many John Robinsons to permit certain identification of the father. Our Thomas was aged 65 when he died in August 1683.

[4] His wife was Jane, daughter of Lumley Dew, esquire. They were married for seventeen years before she died in 1665, in the house of Sir John Davis at Pangbourne, after an unsuccessful operation for breast-cancer: monumental inscription in Pangbourne church.

usually cost the grantee between £5,000 and £10,000;[1] that Robinson could pay such a price is a sufficient indication of his material success. There were three prothonotaries, who as chief clerks of the Court of Common Pleas were responsible for keeping the plea rolls, supervising the entries which their own clerks made in them, controlling the business of the court by making 'rules' to declare or plead or to enter judgment, and minuting the business in their dockets and remembrances. Mesne process was entered by the filazers; but, once the defendant appeared, the pleadings and all subsequent proceedings were normally entered by the prothonotaries. The latter also had the exclusive right to enter common recoveries, which brought them substantial fees. In ordinary litigation the standard fee was only a shilling or two for each entry; but there were several entries to be made in each case, and tens of thousands of entries each year. In theory the three were equal, though attempts to share profits by agreement had failed.[2] In practice their respective incomes depended on how many attorneys 'settled' with them, for each attorney took all his business to the same prothonotary.[3] The Chief Prothonotary was the first to be consulted by the court on matters of pleading or procedure, and he had a few special responsibilities, such as swearing in attorneys and officers and enrolling judges' patents.

Time had been when the opinions of the prothonotaries had been reported in the year books with some reverence. By the middle of the seventeenth century the status—though not the value—of the office had somewhat declined; but Robinson nevertheless enjoyed the respect of the court as an authority on

---

[1] His predecessor, Cory, paid £9,500 in 1638: below, p. 36. His successor paid £6,000: below, p. 39. In 1711 the price had dropped to £4,000: N. Luttrell, *A Brief historical relation of state affairs* (Oxford, 1857), VI. 695. The less lucrative office of Third Prothonotary fetched £4,000 in 1627 and again in 1638: *Diary of Sir Richard Hutton*, vol. II, Cambridge Univ. Lib., MS. Add. 6863, ff. 40, 91.

[2] A scheme of 1594 broke down in about 1620 because John Gulston, Second Prothonotary, refused to accept its terms: Lincoln's Inn, MS. Misc. 586, pp. 37–8.

[3] T. Cory, *Course and practice of the Court of Common Pleas at Westminster* (1672), pp. 21 et seq., 35 et seq.; which is also to be found in *Praxis utriusque banci* (1674). For details of the fees, compiled from a lost 'Black Book of the Common Pleas', see M. Hastings, *The Court of Common Pleas in fifteenth century England* (Ithaca, 1947), app. i, pp. 249–55; T. Powell, *The Attourney's academy* (1623), pp. 143 et seq.; Moyle's second patent (1636) in R. Sanderson (ed.), [*Rymer's*] *Foedera*, XX (1735), 87–92.

the forms of pleading. Chief Justice Vaughan, on signing the imprimatur for Browne's *Formule bene placitandi* (1671) on 14 December 1670, acknowledged that the book had been recommended by Robinson, as if that in itself were sufficient testimony to its worth. Similarly, Lord Keeper Finch consulted him about the publication of Winch's *Le Beau-pledeur* (1680). The editor of the latter added that some interpolations into Winch's text had been perused and approved by 'that most Eminent Gentleman for his Skill in Pleading Thomas Robinson, Esq; at present Chief Prothonotary'. Admittedly, these tributes may have been no more than the courtesy due to his office; but it was still an office which commanded such respect. It was also an office of immense profit. The Brownlow fortunes had been built on the profits from the same office earlier in the century, and Robinson bid fair to become a second Brownlow. According to custom, he had been made an associate of the Bench of the Inner Temple on becoming Chief Prothonotary;[1] and he was soon to become one of the Inn's principal figures, in social as well as in physical stature. After the Great Fire he contributed over £8,000 towards a new building on the south-east side of King's Bench Walk; it was completed in 1671, and was known as Sir Thomas Robinson's Building until the last century.[2] Six years later he was made a complete bencher, for which privilege he made the inn a gift of £200. From 1682 until his death he served as Treasurer, in which capacity he took some interest in the improvement of Temple Church and began the controversial negotiations over the new organ. He seems also to have been responsible for erecting a new screen in the Inner Temple hall (removed in 1866), which is said to have borne his initials.[3] Meanwhile, in 1676 or 1677, Robinson had purchased the attractive Elizabethan house in Long Melford, Suffolk, called Kentwell Hall: 'a very faire brick house with 12 wainscot rooms, the park stored with above 150 deere'. This he also proceeded to improve, and it is known that he planted an avenue of limes there in 1678; the interior of the

[1] F. A. Inderwick (ed.), *Calendar of Inner Temple records*, II (1898), 323, 324. The like had been done for William Nelson (1583–90), Richard Brownlow (1590–1638) and Thomas Cory (1638–57). The office had been in the Inn at least since John Forde (1575–83), and continued there in the eighteenth century under the Cooke family.

[2] *Calendar of Inner Temple records*, III (1901), 83–5; V (R. A. Roberts, ed., 1936), 658.

[3] E. A. P. Hart, *The Hall of the Inner Temple* (1952), p. 26.

house was gutted by fire in 1826.¹ In January 1682, presumably in return for a further considerable outlay, the king granted him a baronetcy.² His glory was short-lived.

In the early hours of 2 August 1683 a fire broke out by Whitefriars Gate in the Temple and spread through Robinson's Building to Serjeant Hampson's Building next to the river. Sir Thomas was sleeping in his chambers on the first floor, and 'he, to avoid the fury and violence of the Flames, adventured to leap out at his Chamber Window, and thereby (being a very corpulent Man) so bruised his body, that he soon expired.'³ An eye-witness wrote to Viscount Hatton:

> Wee have had a deplorable fire, whereby 2 staire cases were most suddainly burnt in ye Temple, and no deeds, moneys, clothes, or anything but ye lives of a few, could bee saved. Sr Thomas Robinson, our treasurer, leaping out of his window one paire of stayers, was bruised, being grosse; so y^t wthin an houre hee dyed, and was just now buryed. Hee had an iron chest now found, and ye gold and silver in it melted thought neere 10000¹, and his office Ld Pemberton [the Chief Justice] hath 6000¹ to take for it. One Glyde, at whose chamber, a grounde roome, it is thought to have begun, was burned. Mr Lloyd, ye B^p of Peterborough's brother, in ye next chamber, escaped in his shirt. Mr Williams and one lodging wth him for a night are both burnt. This was below ye Kings Bench buildings.⁴

Robinson was 65 years old when he died, and he was buried in the church which he had so recently been helping to restore.⁵

The year after his death there was published under his name *A Book of special entries*, in the preface to which the editor alluded to the manuscripts which had been collected in the Chief Prothonotary's office and continued by Robinson:

> These Papers were some Years since designed for the Press by the Judicious Sir Thomas Robinson Baronet, whose great abilities in this kind of Learning were

---

[1] W. Parker, *The History of Long Melford* (1873), pp. 182–6; W. A. Copinger, *The Manors of Suffolk* (1905), I. 143 et seq. The manuscripts evidently survived the fire.

[2] J. and J. B. Burke, *Extinct and dormant baronetcies* (1841 edn.), p. 448; G. E. C[okayne], *Complete baronetage*, IV (1904), 125. Both contain inaccuracies. The baronetcy expired in 1743.

[3] H. Philipps, *The Grandeur of the law* (1684), p. 136. See also N. Luttrell, *A Brief historical relation of state affairs* (Oxford, 1857), I. 273; *Calendar of Inner Temple records*, III. 192, 201.

[4] Letter of William Longueville, 7 Aug. 1683, in *Correspondence of the family of Hatton*, II (E. M. Thompson, ed., Camden Soc. 1878), 33.

[5] Tablet in Temple church: K. Esdaile, *Temple Church monuments* (1933), pp. 55, 78, and plate XV(*a*) fac. p. 153.

Sir Thomas Robinson (1618-83)

eminently Conspicuous in that he held the Place of Chief Prothonotary in the Court of Common-Pleas for well-nigh Thirty Years. During the Series of which long Tract of Time, with what Candour and Integrity he behaved himself, is well known to those Worthy Gentlemen who were Clerks and Attorneys in his Office (who have Reason to Deplore his Unfortunate, Untimely Death.) And with what Industry and Care he preserv'd all the Special Pleadings which from time to time were Entred in his Office whilst he continued Chief Prothonotary, is obvious from the Multitude of choice Manuscripts he left behind of his own Collection, so that nothing of Moment in Pleading was ever Pretermitted... From the vast Collections of this Many-Volum'd *Atlas* of Pleadings, Sir Thomas Robinson some Years before his Death, directed these Pleadings for the Press, intending it chiefly for the Benefit of the Clerks and Attorneys of his Office (which by misfortune proves to be his last Legacy to them).

It would be interesting to know what happened to this *Atlas* and other office collections.[1] The notebooks, by contrast, were probably private compilations, and they remained in Robinson's country house undisturbed for nearly three centuries.

Although prothonotaries were still responsible for entering pleadings, and controlled the practical side of pleading by means of 'rules', they no longer drew the pleadings themselves and were even losing the struggle to keep the rolls within the control of their clerks. The pleadings were now drawn by counsel, signed (in the case of special pleas) by serjeants-at-law, and engrossed by attorneys. But the prothonotaries were still regarded as repositories of the minute learning involved in pleading and making entries. No doubt they were still often consulted, both by the court and by parties. Robinson evidently took some care over this responsibility and maintained an elaborate indexing system. The present-day historian, who has to grope through the mountains of parchment without assistance, has reason to mourn the disappearance of Robinson's great *Atlas*.

When the Common Pleas was sitting, the prothonotaries sat in their places at the table below the judges. A picture of the court in Robinson's day shows two prothonotaries in their distinctive

---

[1] Lincoln's Inn, MS. Misc. 586, may be one of them; it contains reports by Brownlow, Cory, and Gouldsborough, and some notes on the office of prothonotary attributed to Robert Moyle (d. 1638). Moyle's book of entries (which, like the Lincoln's Inn volume, later belonged to Serjeant Henry Lloyd and Edward Umfreville) is Br. Lib., MS. Add. 37321; and his 'book of judgments' is MS. Hargrave 364. Cory's large book of entries is MS. Hargrave 123.

round bonnets, one writing in a book and the other on a roll (pl. II);[1] perhaps one of these figures is Robinson himself. By virtue of their attendance in court they were well able to keep reports of the proceedings in addition to annotating the remembrance rolls. It was once believed that the earlier year books were written by prothonotaries.[2] That thesis is now exploded,[3] but it is clear that there was a reporting tradition of at least two generations when Robinson took office.

The later tradition began, as far as we can now tell, with Richard Brownlow, who was Chief Prothonotary from 1590 until his death in 1638 at the age of 86. He had an oracular reputation, and was said to have attained the office by 'only Merit, meerly upon the score of his skill in clerkship'.[4] His precedents were printed (if not very accurately) and were much esteemed. A series of his reports, from 1606 to 1619, is preserved in manuscript; while a better series, confined to the period 1610–12, was printed in 1652 as the *Second part of Reports of diverse famous cases in law collected by Richard Brownlow Esq*. The *First part* of this volume (dated 1651) contains shorter, alphabetically arranged, reports from about 1606 to 1619, ascribed both to Brownlow and to John Gouldsborough (Second Prothonotary 1613–19). Gouldsborough's name is also associated with a collection of Elizabethan reports which do not seem to be of his own taking.[5] It would be difficult to separate Brownlow's work from Gouldsborough's, though most manuscript texts refer to the latter only,[6] and the period between Gouldsborough's death and Brownlow's (1619–38) seems not to be covered by any of the reports. Thomas Cory, who succeeded Brownlow in 1638, began reporting in 1636 and continued until 1654, two or three

---

[1] Engraved title-page to G. Billinghurst, *Arcana clericalia, or, The Mysteries of clarkship* (1674). [This is probably the King's Bench. J.H.B., 1985.]

[2] e.g. W. Blackstone, *Commentaries on the laws of England* (1765), I. 71–2; L. O. Pike in *Year Books 20 Edward III*, part ii (Rolls ser. 1911), li–lxv.

[3] See F. W. Maitland in *Year Books 1 & 2 Edward II* (1903), Seld. Soc. xvii, intr. For some reports by early Tudor prothonotaries see Seld. Soc. xciv, p. *175*, n. 7.

[4] Preface to T. Robinson, *Book of entries* (1684).

[5] *Reports of that learned and judicious Clerk J. Gouldsborough, Esq.* (1653): see the preface, by W. S.

[6] e.g. Lincoln's Inn, MS. Maynard 21, and part of MS. Misc. 586; Camb. U.L., MSS. Dd. 3.2, and Mm. 6.67, fol. 102; Br. Lib., MSS. Harley 6840, fol. 71, Hargrave 45, Add. 25232, fol. *59*, and Add. 38008.

years before his own death.[1] The reporting tradition may even have survived Robinson, for in 1742 was published a collection of practice cases by Chief Prothonotaries Sir George and George Cooke.[2]

It cannot be pretended that any of the prothonotaries' reports are of high quality, compared with the best of their contemporaries; but reporting in the Common Pleas was less regular than in the King's Bench, and they contain material not found elsewhere. Their main interest is that they provide a picture of the work of the court as it appeared from the officers' table. For anyone with the patience to conquer Robinson's frightful hand, and to collate the reports with the cumbersome plea rolls and minutely detailed remembrances, they provide the missing element necessary to reconstruct a picture of the workings of the court in the seventeenth century. It is rare for legal historians to have as many as three parallel 'official' sources: but it is admittedly unlikely that anyone will accept the daunting challenge they present.

The reports are not 'practice cases' in the narrow sense of the term, but they do emphasize practical matters at the expense of more intellectual problems. They are particularly informative on biographical matters. The Chief Prothonotary was involved in the swearing-in of judges and attorneys, and the creation of serjeants-at-law. Judicial appointments are therefore often noted, beginning with Brownlow's minute of the ceremony in 1605 when Chief Justice Gawdy was sworn standing on the table.[3] Cory faithfully records all such appointments in his time; Robinson is less systematic, but does mention the promotion of Mr. Justice Scroggs in 1676, who 'came with 50 coaches and Grayes Inn'.[4] Both Cory and Robinson record nearly all the serjeants' creations in their time, often with minute detail; Robinson gives the only known version of a speech by Chief Justice Rainsford to the 1677 call.[5] There are also instances of

[1] Lincoln's Inn, part of MS. Misc. 586; Br. Lib., MS. Hargrave 23.
[2] *Reports and cases of practice in the Court of Common Pleas by a late eminent Hand* (1742).
[3] Lincoln's Inn, MS. Misc. 586, fol. 29. And see fol. 50 (Winch J.). Both entries are also in Cory's collection, Br. Lib., MS. Hargrave 123, fol. 192^v.
[4] MS. Eng. misc. f. 504, fol. 201. Two days later the prothonotaries and serjeants attended the Lord Mayor's dinner: ibid.
[5] MS. Eng. misc. f. 505, ff. 34–5.

attorneys being thrown over the bar, as the usage was, for misbehaviour.[1] But the most interesting notes, for present purposes, are those concerning the office of prothonotary itself.

The offices lay in livery rather than in grant, and were conferred by an induction ceremony in open court. The first and third offices were in the gift of the Chief Justice, while the second belonged to the Custos Brevium, who presented his nominee to the Chief Justice for admission. So valuable were the offices that succession to them was often contested,[2] always a matter of gossip. Cory describes the ceremony of his own admission on 9 October 1638; he was sworn in by the Second Prothonotary, given the round cap of office, installed in his place, and then took seisin by receiving his first fee. A week later he swore in and capped the new Third Prothonotary, George Farmer.[3] The background to these two appointments, which were caught up in Charles I's short-lived schemes to acquire and sell the reversions of valuable offices, is revealed in a note by Sir Richard Hutton, one of the justices of the Common Pleas. Hutton noted the deaths of Brownlow and Moyle in the summer of 1638, observing significantly that the former had been worth £7,000 or more a year and the latter but £500, and continued:

Le primer Jour de cest Terme [Michaelmas 1638] un Mr Corye, un bon Clerk, fuit Jure prothonotarie in ceo Office que Mr Brownlowe ad. Et il paye 9,500 li. al Agents del Marques Hambleton a que le Roy ad grant ceo office 2 ou 3 ans devant.[4] Car il please le Roy sur le nominacion de Serjeant Heath que fuit l'atturney generall de reserve un power a doner del dits Offices quel fuit un noveltie ne unques fait devant. Car de temps dont memory le done de deux prothonotaries ad apperteine de droit al Chief Justice et que il poit vender deux offices sans le danger del statute de Edward le primer, car ceux offices esteant in le done del Chief Justice are excepted, et le dit Chief Justice est oblige de faire grantes et d'apointer tiels offices al tiels per-

---

[1] e.g. 1 Bro. & Goulds. 44 (1617); MS. Eng. misc. f. 500, fol. 32 (1657); MS. Eng. misc. f. 504, fol. 3 (1673).

[2] For earlier instances, see Seld. Soc. xciv, pp. 376–378.

[3] Lincoln's Inn, MS. Misc. 586, fol. 42. The distinctive round cap is seen in the engraving (plate II), and on the bust of Robert Moyle in West Twyford church, Middlesex. It was also shown on the brass of John Gouldsborough, formerly in Temple church: *Monumental Brass Soc., Trans.*, vii. 13–16.

[4] Not enrolled, or mentioned in Finch C.J.'s patent. Cf. *C.S.P.D. 1635–36*, p. 1. On 17 December 1636 the king ratified Anderson C.J.'s grant to Brownlow: C66/2745, m. 14. And on 3 April 1639 he ratified Finch C.J.'s grant to Cory: C66/2844, m. 6. The patents contain detailed schedules of fees.

sons que le Roy apointera. Et in mesme le manner le Segnior Chief Justice, sc. le Segnior Finch, agree que le Roy disposera et que il allowera et donera ceux offices al tiels persons que le Roy nosmera.

Memorandum que 14° die Octobris Mr Farmer, un bon Clerk et un que ad marry le soer del feme de Mr Moyle, fuit Jure et fait prothonotarie in le dit place que Mr Moyle ad. Nota que le Roy ad grant un patent in Revercion[1] que quant Mr Moile moriera que un avera ceo al use del fits de Mr Moyle que fuit infant. Et sur Agreement del Allowance d'ceo patent quel fuit void in ley, Mris Moyle et ses Amies voluntariment offer 4,000 li. pur l'allowance de ceo, et ceo fuit gratiousment accepted. Et issint per Agreement Mr Fermer est d'execute le office tanque ascun del Children d'Mr Moyle vendra al age de 21 ans, et d'estre accompt pur le profitt ouster 500 li. quel Mr Farmour est annualment d'aver pur l'execucion del office.[2]

Cory also relates how in 1644 John Glynn, the Custos Brevium, was able to make two nominations within four months.[3]

The first contest alluded to by Robinson occurred in 1668:

Memorandum that 23 *Octobris isto eodem termino* Mr Allan Lockhart of Grayes Inne gentleman, late Clerke to Mr Gardiner, Secondary to Mr Pynsent, late Second Prothonotary of the Court of Common Pleas, was sworne Second Prothonotary in full court *ex assensu omnium Justiciariorum* upon the presentation of Mr Thursby the Custos Brevium, *non obstante* great opposition by Mr H. Kempe[4] that made pretence [?] to the said place to be admitted and gayned a hearing by all the Judges at the Serjeants Inne in Chancery Lane, and there my Lord Cheife Justice Vaughan

---

[1] *Council Order Book 1636–37*, f. 277. See also *C.S.P.D. 1635–36*, p. 56; *C.S.P.D. 1637–38*, p. 76; SP 16/326, fol. 71. On 8 November 1636 the king ratified the grant to Moyle, reciting the covenant between the king and Finch C.J.: Rymer's *Foedera*, XX. 76–92. (As to the office of Second Prothonotary, see *C.S.P.D. 1636–37*, p. 268; Gulston's ratification of 22 July 1636, Pat. 12 Car. 1, pt. 22, no. 5.) On 21 July 1641 the House of Lords, with the advice of the judges, held all these grants illegal: *Journals of the House of Lords*, IV. 322–3.

[2] *Diary of Sir Richard Hutton*, vol. II, Camb.U.L., MS. Add. 6863, ff. 90ᵛ–91. See fol. 40 for the appointment of Moyle ('un bon Clerk . . . il ad ew bon experience et est fitt pur cest place') in succession to Waller ('un honest grave home et skillfull in son office et mult beloved'). Hutton had also noted Gulston's appointment in 1618, adding 'dieu done a luy successe': reports in Br. Lib., MS. Hargrave 46, fol. 29ᵛ.

[3] Lincoln's Inn, MS. Misc. 586, sub dat. 5 Feb., 9 Feb. and 31 May; *Journals, House of Lords*, VI. 415.

[4] Probably either Henry Kempe (d. 1685), called to the Bar by the Inner Temple in 1653: *Calendar of Inner Temple Records*, II. 308, III. 454; or Henry Kempe (d. 1680), admitted to the Middle Temple in 1673: ibid. III. 452; *Register of Admissions to the Middle Temple* (1949), I. 188.

did object [?] that hee that was to be presented must bee [as ix?] Ed. the 4th[1] *educatus a Juventute* in the learning and practice of the Court, and he ought to have *longam experienciam* and to bee *maxime litteratus*, which being fully answered by Mr Thursby hee was this day sworne.[2]

For the full story we may compare the more ample anonymous note in a manuscript now in Lincoln's Inn:

Le prime jour de cest terme Allen Lockhart, darrainment un Attorney de Bernards Inne, et a cest temps admitt de Graies Inne, esteant circa l'age de 32 ans, fuit admitt et Jure le Second Prothonotary del Comen Bench en liew del Pinsent que morust cest vacacion. Et un Martyn, attorney de cest Court (a que Sir Joseph Ash le Custos Brevium en quel disposicion l'office del Second preignotary est ad darrainment grant cest office de prothonotary pur tryer le title de ceo ove Pinsent, inter que un dispute pur cest office fuit) seant en le liew del dit prothonotary surge hors de ceo et resigne al Court per escript desouth son maine. Et apres William Thursby del melieu Temple, Barrister al ley, esteant le nominall Custos brevium et comunement see en Court come Custos brevium, present le dit Lockhart al Court per escript desouth son maine d'estre prothonotary en le liew de Pinsent, que presentee fuit allow et approve per le Chief Justice. Et apres Lockhart, kneeling en le Court en un student's toge, prist les serements d'allegiance et supremacy et Robinson le principall prothonotary de cest Court lye a lui le serement del office et apres cest Lockhart prist son liew et le Chief Justice pone le Capp sur le teste de Lockhart et apres ceo shake et baseroit le main de Chief Justice et shake les mains del touts auters Justices et les mains de tout le sergeants accordant a lour seniority et les mains de Thursby, Custos brevium, et les mains de Robinson, Chief Prothonotary, et Wyrley, Third Prothonotary. Et mesme le terme Lockhart fuit appell al Bench en Graies Inne et fuit pense que il done 8000 li. pur son office.[3]

The next dispute mentioned by Robinson was in 1678, when Thursby presented Thomas Winford to the same office. This time the objection came from the judges, particularly from Mr. Justice Atkins, who took exception to Winford being sworn in chambers by Chief Justice North. The event is fully corroborated by North's own account, where he says he had taken Robinson's

---

[1] This is probably a reference to *Vynter's Case* (1465) KB 27/818, m. 66, when the King's Bench judges refused to admit an unqualified person as Clerk of the Crown, 'pro eo quod ... impossibile est eciam alique officia predicta occupare et exercere sufficienter nisi fuerit *educatus in eisdem a Juventute* et magnam et *longam experienciam habuisset* in eisdem nec unquam videbatur quod aliquis admittetur in eadem Curia ad officia predicta occupanda nisi ipse qui in officiis illis educatus fuit aut in aliis officiis ejusdem Curie diu continuaverit' (emphasis added). Knowledge of this case was transmitted by P. 9 Edw. 4, 5, pl. 20; Dyer 150; 2 And. 118. See also CP 40/843, m. 494; N. Neilson (ed.), *Year Books 10 Edward IV* (1931), Seld. Soc. xlvii, pp. xviii–xix; T. 18 Edw. 4, 7, pl. 6.

[2] MS. Eng. misc. f. 503, fol. 1. 'Thursby' in the last line seems to be a slip for 'Lockhart'.

[3] Lincoln's Inn, MS. Misc. 499, p. 460.

Sir Thomas Robinson (1618-83)

advice. Eventually Winford was sworn a second time 'for solemnity', but North put on his cap and directed Robinson to record the admission as done by him alone. Roger North, the biographer, informs us that the reason for this little squabble was that the judges expected a small present on the swearing in. 'His lordship told his brother Atkins, *that he should know here was no republic*; and the other answered *no, nor monarchy*'.[1]

Finally we may note, necessarily from another source, the contest which arose after the death of Robinson himself. The account is by Edward Ward, later Chief Baron:

Nota cest vacacion Sir Thomas Robinson, Baronet, principall prothonotary del Common Bench, morust per reason de un fall que il receive en le fewe in le Inner Temple. Et le Chief Justice Pemberton dispose le liew al Mr Adderly mesme le vacacion pur 6000 li. come fuit communement dit. Et fuit jure eins le dit liew en le vacacion. Mes apres en mesme le vacacion devant, Pemberton esteant remove et Jones fait Chief Justice, objection fuit fait envers le sufficiency de Adderley, n'esteant educate come un practiser en cest court. Et pur ceo, per le grace del roy et pur avoider questions, Adderly resigne et John Cooke del Inner Temple, un attorney al ley et Secondary al Wyrley un del prothonotaries, fuit admitt et jure eins cest liew per Chief Justice Jones en le vacacion. Et Adderly ad son money restore et Cooke agree ove Pemberton come fuit dit pur 5000 li. preter un respect al Chief Justice Jones al value de [*blank*]. Et notandum est que coment que Sir Thomas Robinson vene al mort per occasion d'un fall a son chambre fenestre uncore nul Coroner's Enquest fuit prise et son Corps continualment jesque L'interment fuit en le Inner Temple.[2]

THE SEVENTEENTH-CENTURY PROTHONOTARIES

In the absence of a published list of prothonotaries,[3] the following may be of some use; it is based on sources too numerous to detail here.

Chief Prothonotary

RICHARD BROWNLOW [Inner Temple, form. Clement's Inn]: Mich. 1590 to 21 July 1638 [died]

THOMAS CORY [Inner Temple, form. Lyon's Inn]: 9 Oct. 1638 to 16 Dec. 1656 [died]

[SIR] THOMAS ROBINSON [Inner Temple, form. Staple Inn]: Hil. 1657 to 2 Aug. 1683 [died]

---

[1] MS. Eng. misc. f. 505, fol. 106ᵛ; R. North, *Life of Francis North* (2nd edn., 1808), I. 187; II. 46-8. North's note is wrongly dated 1680.

[2] Lincoln's Inn, MS. Misc. 557, p. 21.

[3] A list from the time of Henry VI to 1600 will be published in *The Reports of John Spelman*, II (Seld. Soc. xciv), pp. 375-8.

[Mr. Adderley for part of Long Vacation 1683 only][1]
JOHN COOKE [Inner Temple]: Mich. 1683 to 22 Feb. 1710 [surrendered]

Second Prothonotary

ZACHARY SCOTT [Lincoln's Inn, form. Staple Inn]: 9 Oct. 1585 to Hil. 1609
THOMAS CROMPTON [Middle Temple, form. Barnard's Inn]: 10 May 1609 to Hil. 1613
JOHN GOULDSBOROUGH [Middle Temple, form. Barnard's Inn]: Pas. 1613 to 9 Oct. 1618 [died]
JOHN GULSTON [Gray's Inn and Middle Temple, form. Barnard's Inn]: Mich. 1618 to early 1644 [died]
RICHARD BARNARD [Lincoln's Inn?]: 9 Feb. 1644 to 25 May 1644 [died]
JOHN PYNSENT [Lincoln's Inn]: 31 May 1644 to Long Vac. 1668 [died]
[Mr. Martyn for part of Long Vacation 1668 only][2]
ALAN LOCKHART [Gray's Inn, form. Barnard's Inn]: 23 Oct. 1668 to 1671 [died]
GEORGE TOWNSEND [Lincoln's Inn, form. Staple Inn]: 1671 or Hil. 1672 to 1678 [surrendered]
THOMAS WINFORD [Lincoln's Inn, form. Clement's Inn]: 23 Oct. 1678 to 1701 [surrendered]

Third Prothonotary

HUGH BROWKER [Inner Temple, form. Barnard's Inn]: 28 Nov. 1588 to 2 Jan. 1608 [died]
THOMAS WALLER [Gray's Inn, form. Barnard's Inn]: Hil. 1609 to 5 May 1627 [died]
ROBERT MOYLE [Inner Temple]: 7 May 1627 to 29 Aug. 1638 [died]
GEORGE FARMER [Inner Temple, form. Lyon's Inn]: 16 Oct. 1638 to Hil. 1668
HUMFREY WYRLEY [Inner Temple, form. Clement's Inn]: Pas. 1668 to 23 Dec. 1684 [surrendered]
ANTHONY BELBIN [Inner Temple]: 23 Dec. 1684 to late 1687 or Jan. 1688 [died]
WILLIAM TEMPEST [Inner Temple, form. Staple Inn]: Hil. 1688 to 1702 [died]

III

COMMON LAW AND PROCEDURE

16

CRIMINAL COURTS AND PROCEDURE, 1550-1800

There are two ways of describing a legal system. The first, favoured by lawyers, is to expound the theoretical conception, the abstract rules revealed by legal authorities. Lawyers are bred on textbooks so written, and it may well be the only practicable way to begin. To the extent that the theory is derived from precedent, it must mirror reality; but the precedent from which such descriptions are derived is of the single kind which makes law, not of the compound kind which makes statistics. The second manner of description, more favoured by sociologists, is based on factual observation. Recorded events are preferred to the theoretical explanations of the lawyer or the commands of the lawgiver. The same distinction governs historical descriptions, in which law flits uncomfortably between intellectual and social history. But it by no means necessarily follows that the two kinds of description must always be in conflict, for anyone who describes a legal system must consider and compare both theory and experience. A true understanding of a legal system, as of chess or cricket, is only to be had from experience of the variety of action and result which can occur within the rules. The rules do not prescribe who will win, and (at least in a legal system) they are not always followed; but they do explain what the participants are up to. The following outline of the processes of criminal justice between 1550 and 1800 has been compiled chiefly from the law books,[1] in an attempt to provide a general background against which details gleaned from original research may be set. Such a brief summary must confine itself not only to generalizations, but also to the main features of a system notable for its eccentricities.

I THE MODES OF PROSECUTION

The prosecution of criminal justice had in a remote past rested with the victim or his kin, but by Tudor times blood-feuds were decidedly outside the law. The drive for retribution had been channelled first into the solemn appeal of felony; and then royal justice, disliking the tendency in the private

---

1 To save space, no references are given in the notes to sources of elementary propositions which may readily be found in the principal textbooks. Law reports are cited by the abbreviations in general use among lawyers. A list of the latter may be found in *A Manual of Legal Citations* (Institute of Advanced Legal Studies 1959), I, pp.39-75; or in C.W. Ringrose, *Where to Look for Your Law* (1962), pp.187-237. References to state trials are to vols I-XXVII of *State Trials* (1809-20), ed F. Hargrave, W. Cobbett, T.B. Howell and T.J. Howell.

sector to compromise suits for money, had sought to discourage even judicialized self-help by placing the responsibility for prosecution on the public at large. The frankpledge system and the constabulary, the robbery and murder fines, the hue and cry, the coroner's inquest and, above all, the grand jury, were products of this transfer of responsibility. Each played its part in the sixteenth century, but none of them can be regarded as the primary source of prosecuting energy. Throughout the period under review there was no organized police force, no county prosecuting solicitors, no Director of Public Prosecutions and in most cases no prosecuting counsel; so the detective work, the administrative oversight of prosecutions, the preparation of the case, and the conduct of the trial, did not fall to professional prosecutors. The grand jury was involved in most prosecutions for felony, but we know that the preparatory work had usually been done by the time the case reached the grand jury. It is true that the constable had a police function at a local level, but his lowly office usually ended when he brought an arrested person before a justice of the peace. Was it, then, the justice who managed prosecutions? Plucknett thought the Marian bail and committal statutes had turned the justice into 'something between a detective and a juge d'instruction', a role he filled until the formation of a professional police force in the nineteenth century.[2] This view has recently been persuasively reargued, and it is clear that the justices' duty to see the peace kept included in theory a general supervision of criminal justice, from initial police inquiries down to the trial. Much of the diligent justices' time was spent receiving and investigating complaints, calling witnesses before them and binding them over to appear at trial, examining accused persons and committing them to gaol or releasing them on bail, and attending sessions. In form the justice did not prosecute: he simply coerced the private complainant to do his own prosecuting. What is not clear is whether the initiative remained with the justice to conduct the prosecution at quarter sessions or assizes. Dr Langbein has argued that the justice did indeed 'orchestrate' proceedings at the trial, taking the depositions with him as a kind of policeman's notebook to 'buttress [his] oral performance'.[3] This thesis has been challenged,[4] and it seems more likely that it was the court officers — headed by the clerk of the peace and the clerk of assize — who coordinated prosecution materials once the preliminary investigation was over. It was they who managed the courtroom proceedings by preparing calendars, drawing indictments, arraigning prisoners, calling witnesses and keeping records.

2 T.F.T. Plucknett, *Concise History of the Common Law* (5th edn 1956), p.432.
3 Langbein, *Prosecuting Crime*, p.35.
4 J.S. Cockburn, 'Trial by the Book? Fact and Theory in the Criminal Process 1558-1625': paper delivered at the Cambridge Legal History Conference, 8 July 1975.

Perhaps it is misleading to seek a single source of prosecuting energy. Certainly we should not expect the same situation in 1700 or 1800 as in 1600. There seems rather to have been a slow shifting of responsibility for preliminary investigation from the populace, as represented first by the victim's kin and then by the grand jury and coroner's jury, to the magistrates, and from them (but beyond our period) to the police force. Of course the old survived alongside the new, and the change was disguised by appearances, disguised perhaps even from contemporaries. As late as 1677 it was said that the grand jury was 'the great and grand spring, or *primum mobile* ... that gives motion to all the other wheels';[5] yet it must by then have been unrealistic to accredit that body with the initiative for the bulk of prosecutions. There is an exact parallel in our own time. The magistrates have taken over the function of the grand jury, and the police have taken over the preliminary work of the magistrates, with the result that the focus is gradually shifting from the formal institution (the 'committal proceedings') to the informal (the 'questioning of suspects' by the police).

As we turn to the mechanics of prosecution, it will be as well to stress that in England it was not for any court to initiate prosecutions, for at common law a court could only resolve disputes brought before it by others.[6] Criminal proceedings were initiated and prosecuted in the name either of a private person or of the king.[7] The type of proceeding depended largely on the difference between felonies and misdemeanours (or trespasses), a distinction which was settled long before 1550. Felony was the more serious and usually carried the death penalty; treason and (according to some writers) murder were higher than felony, but were generally dealt with on the same footing. 'Misdemeanour' is a vague, non-scientific, name for the residuary class. In the case of felony, the private prosecution was by appeal of felony and the Crown prosecution was by indictment. In other cases, prosecutions were either by indictment or information. With the exception of attachment for contempt in the face of the court,[8] and the obsolete procedure of arraignment *sur le mainour*, no other modes of prosecution were countenanced by the common law. And the minimum requirements of the common law were sanctified and protected by chapter 29 of Magna

---

5 Z. Babington, *Advice to Grand Jurors in Cases of Blood* (1677), p.6.
6 A judge could, however, direct others to initiate proceedings, or advise on the settling of an indictment: e.g. *R.* v *Page* (1633), Cro. Car. 332; Hale, *Pleas*, II, pp.159-61; 'Newgate Reports', below, pp. 335-36. He probably had no judicial authority to do so, and could not enforce his direction.
7 The only important exception was impeachment: see below p. 272.
8 These involve no prosecutor, no indictment and no jury: see Blackstone, *Commentaries* (1765), IV, pp.287-8 ('not agreeable to the genius of the common law'); J.C. Fox, *History of Contempt of Court* (Oxford 1927). For a well-known example see Cockburn, *Assizes*, p.110. For contempt out of the view see *R.* v *Alman* (1765), Wilm. 243.

Carta and its progeny, the fourteenth-century statutes of due process.

Appeal of felony

The appeal followed the same pattern as a civil suit. It was commenced by writ or bill, the appellant counted at the bar against the appellee, who pleaded and put himself on trial, and the proceedings were recorded on the plea side of the court. The disadvantages to the appellant were considerable. He had to sue in person and find real pledges of prosecution. If he lost, he might be punished and the appellee had a chance of recovering damages against him; moreover, since the appellee was allowed counsel throughout the proceedings, the possibilities of technical failure were alarming. Even if he won, he had to bear the expense of that which might have been done at the expense of the community. For these reasons the appeal became far less popular than once it had been. By 1550 it was still a regular proceeding, and of sufficient importance (or complexity) for Staunford to give it more attention than the indictment. Between 1550 and 1650 it very nearly went out of use altogether. The advantage of restitution in the appeal of robbery had been extended to proceedings on indictment in 1529,[9] and it was only the appeal of murder which made much appearance in the later books. The principal surviving advantage of the latter was that it gave the next-of-kin a recourse if the grand jury failed to indict,[10] or the trial jury failed to convict, or the defendant obtained an undeserved pardon. At common law an acquittal either on indictment or appeal barred any further proceedings for the same offence; but by a statute of 1487 it was ordained that acquittal or attaint on indictment was not to bar appeals of murder,[11] and this kept the latter alive during advancing senility and in the face of judicial hostility. As early as 1610, in an appeal which proved 'an angry case, and did very much trouble the Court', Fleming C.J. declared that 'an appeal is in law to be very strictly looked into'.[12] There was a brief revival under Holt C.J., who vigorously defended the appeal as 'a noble prosecution, and a true badge of English liberties'.[13] But the liberty was not often demanded in the eighteenth century, and there are only about a dozen reported cases during the entire century.[14] By 1800 the appeal was as obsolete as any institution can be which has not been formally abolished.

---

9 21 Hen. VIII, c. 11.
10 Babington, *Advice to Grand Jurors*, pp.90-91.
11 3 Hen. VII, c.1. For the prior position see A. Fitzherbert, *La Graunde Abridgement* (1577 edn), tit. 'Corone', pl.44.
12 *Egerton* v *Morgan* (1610), 1 Bulst. 69-88.
13 *Stout* v *Cowper* (1699), 12 Mod. 375.
14 The latest are *Bigby* v *Kennedy* (1770), 5 Burr. 2643; *Smith* v *Taylor* (1771), ibid., 2793. In 1771 Eden described appeals as 'an old branch of the law, which by possibility may become an essential safeguard of the rights of the people': *Principles*, p.184. See also n.42 below.

Indictment

In the normal case, where no appeal had been commenced,[15] the prosecution for felony in the king's name could only be by indictment. An indictment was an accusation made by twelve or more laymen sworn to inquire in the king's behalf and recorded before a court of record. The need for an indictment was a constitutional principle of some importance, because it meant that the king and his ministers could not of their own motion put a man on trial for felony. A man could only be tried for his life upon either the appeal of an interested subject or the presentment of at least twelve of his peers. The supporting theory was that as the king had no personal knowledge of his subjects' affairs, he had no ground for proceeding against the subject without a presentment 'of record'.[16] Lord Treasurer Burghley, in a memorable speech in Star Chamber, said that

> it was the liberty of the subject of England more than of all other nations that he cannot be molested or imprisoned without indictment. Other nations have an accusation, which is verbal and at the promotion of a party, but this is by the presentment of his neighbours and peers with their oath, and made of record. And this liberty was purchased for the subjects of England with the blood of many people, noble and ignoble, and was the cause of the Barons' War, and it is the noblest accusation that may be.[17]

In his quaint exposition of Magna Carta Burghley evidently gave not a flicker of thought to the appeal, but clearly the nobility of trial by indictment lay in its important consequence: that in matters of life and limb there existed between the Crown and the subject a shield borne by his neighbours. Attempts to remove this shield were hated and short-lived. It had been tried in 1496, when Parliament enabled felonies to be presented by information; but the statute barely outlived Empson and Dudley. Then in 1650 Parliament established a High Court of Justice which could proceed on the mere word of the Attorney-General; this was one of several good reasons for thinking it contrary to the spirit of English justice.[18]

---

15 If an appeal was discontinued, the Crown could arraign the appellee on the declaration (without indictment): Staunford, *Plees*, ff. 147v-48; Hale, *Pleas*, II, pp.149*-50*; *Reade* v *Rochforth* (1556), Dy. 120, 131.
16 Coke, *Institutes*, III, p.136.
17 Quoted by Nicholas Fuller in *Omer's Case* (1608), HLS, MS 118, f. 187 (translated).
18 11 Hen. VII, c.3 (repealed by 1 Hen. VIII, c.6); An Act for establishing an High Court of Justice, 26 Mar. 1650: *Acts and Ordinances of the Interregnum*, ed C.H. Firth and R.S. Rait (1911), II, pp.364-7.

264 The Legal Profession and the Common Law

The 'presentment'[19] by twelve could be made in a number of ways. Important in homicide cases — and the only form of communal presentment to have survived in England today — was the finding by an inquest before the coroner upon the view of a dead body that the death had been occasioned by a named person. This operated as an indictment on which the accused could be arraigned for homicide. To conform with constitutional principle it had to be the finding of at least twelve men.[20] Another mode of presentment by twelve was that by the jury in a leet or sheriff's tourn.[21] The most usual body of indictors, however, was the grand jury. At least one grand jury was summoned to appear at every assizes and sessions for the purpose of finding indictments. Each jury was composed of twelve or more substantial freeholders, sworn to present all crimes committed in their county such as were listed in their charge. A majority decision of twelve or more sufficed, and so it became usual to summon an odd number greater than twelve; in later times normally twenty-three.[22] The grand jurors could, as invited, present of their own knowledge, but since they were not omniscient the bulk of their findings were based on draft indictments (called 'bills') prepared by the clerks on behalf of the prosecutors. In considering bills they heard only Crown evidence, since their task was not to convict but to decide whether the Crown had a case to go forward. If they thought there was a case, they found the bill 'true' and endorsed it *'billa vera'*. Some thought this required such a belief in the truth of the accusation that the burden of proof was the same as for a trial jury.[23] Others took it to indicate only that the case was 'meet' or 'fit' to put the accused on trial, which called for a 'strong and pregnant presumption'.[24] Hale required only a prima facie case, made out on a balance of probabilities, though by Blackstone's time a 'thorough persuasion' was needed.[25] Grand juries were at times strongly

19 All indictments were presentments, but usage reserved the latter term for those made from the jurors' own knowledge (i.e. without bills): Lambard, *Eirenarcha* (1581), p.383; Blackstone, *Commentaries*, IV, p.301. The latter were made in the form of a note which the clerk drew into an indictment: *A Guide to Juries* (1703 edn), p.39; J. Gonson, *Charge to the Grand Jury of Westminster* (1729), p.25. But not all presentments were indictments: e.g. presentments of suicide by a coroner's jury: Hale, *Pleas*, II, pp.152-3.
20 *Cobat's Case* (1368), cited in Hale, *Pleas*, II, pp.60-1.
21 See below nn.89-90.
22 [J. Somers], *The Security of English-men's Lives* (1766 edn), p.11, says 23 or 25; *Form and Method*, p.12, says 17, 19 or 21.
23 Somers, *Security*, pp.83-107; [J. Hawles], *The English-man's Right* (1680), pp.47-8; *Guide to Juries*, pp.40-81, 105-108.
24 Babington, *Advice to Grand Jurors*, pp.119, 124-5.
25 Hale, *Pleas*, II, p.157; *R. v Earl of Shaftesbury* (1681), *State Trials*, VIII, at col. 770, *per* Pemberton C.J. ('probable cause'); J. Hawkins, *Charge to the Grand Jury of Middlesex* (1770), pp.24-8; Blackstone, *Commentaries*, IV, p.303; Eden, *Principles*, p.322n.

independent, at others meekly subservient or even superfluous, but it is difficult to assess their work because bills not found true were not supposed to be preserved. When the grand jury was not satisfied, the bill was endorsed with the non-committal word *ignoramus* (or, after 1732, 'not found'). The bill did not then become an indictment, but could be laid before another grand jury later; there was no official reason for preserving or recording it. Even a finding of *billa vera* was not a verdict, and so another indictment could always be found for the same offence; only when a trial tury had given a verdict on one indictment were proceedings on other indictments for the same offence precluded. Sometimes a man was indicted both by the grand jury and by a coroner's jury, and in that case he could be tried upon either or (as was usual at the Old Bailey) upon both together.[26]

The decline of the grand jury began at the beginning of our period, with the introduction of regular pre-trial examination. Eventually the preliminary proceedings before the justices were to supplant it entirely, though until they became indispensable it was necessary to retain both systems. But long before the completion of the process (in 1933 in England), the idea gained ground that the grand jurors' work was 'but matter of course, a ceremony; matter of form',[27] a view strongly resisted by pamphleteers but difficult to dispel in practice. By the end of our period only about one bill in seven was found not true; eighty years later, however, the proportion had dropped to one in twenty-seven.[28] By the latter date it might well have been said that the sifting of prosecutions had passed effectively to the justices; but the statistics show that in 1800 the grand jury still exercised a substantial, if decreasing, parallel responsibility.

Information
Misdemeanours could be, and often were, prosecuted by indictment in the same way as felonies; but the safeguards which the constitution guaranteed the subject in matters of life and death were relaxed in lesser cases to the extent that an alternative was allowed. The alternative was the mere 'information' of an individual, dispensing with the collectivity of a presentment of record and with the oath. Whereas an indictment began (until 1915) 'the jurors for our lord the king on their oath present that ...', an information was recorded with the opening words 'be it remembered that X gives the court here to understand and to be informed that ...'. The principle that felonies could not be prosecuted upon bare information[29] remained inviolate save for the experiments of 1496 and 1650 mentioned above. In non-capital cases, however, prosecution by information was well-established before 1550. The genus included a number of species, some

26 Hale, *Pleas*, II, p.61; *R. v Culliford* (1704), 1 Salk. 382.
27 *Guide to Juries*, p.41.
28 Radzinowicz, *History*, I, p.92; F.W. Maitland, *Justice and Police* (1885), p.139.
29 Hale founded it on a case of 1291: *Pleas*, II, pp.156-149*.

of which were essentially civil and can be distinguished by the kind of process which followed. Criminal informations could be laid either by a common person or by a law officer such as the Attorney-General. The common person could inform either for the Crown, or 'as well for himself as for our lord the king' (the *qui tam* formula). The *qui tam* prosecution was a creature of statute, designed to encourage law enforcement by giving informers a share of the penalty, and the race of 'common informers' to which the procedure gave rise played an interesting if not very worthy part in the history of economic regulation.[30] The information by a law officer was called an *ex officio* information, and was in daily use in Star Chamber and the conciliar courts. Because it bypassed the grand jury, it was a useful way of commencing unpopular prosecutions and attracted some obloquy.

A private individual could file an information in King's Bench or Star Chamber on behalf of the king, a form of proceeding which had the double attraction that it avoided the grand jury and that the prosecutor did not pay the costs. As a result of alleged misuse in the second half of the seventeenth century, the criminal information came under such odium that in 1691 its legality was seriously challenged in King's Bench. The court, however, thought the matter so clear that it upheld the information without bothering to hear argument in favour.[31] The objection was seen to be, not to informations as such, but to their abuse. That problem was attacked in 1692 by Parliament, which forbade the filing of informations in King's Bench without leave of the court, and also made the prosecutor liable to costs. Thereafter informations were effectively confined to those 'gross and serious misdemeanours which deserve the most public animadversion', such as riot or sedition.[32] The indictment remained the most proper way of initiating any prosecution at common law.[33]

II THE MODES OF TRIAL

Of the two principal types of criminal trial which developed in Europe when human judgment began to replace irrational proofs such as the ordeal, the most widespread was the 'inquisition'.[34] In its usual form, as nurtured by the Laws Civil and Canon, the inquisitorial procedure centred upon an official inquisitor or judge who directed all the proceedings, often in secret,

30 See M.W. Beresford, 'The Common Informer, Penal Statutes, and Economic Regulation', *Economic History Review*, 2nd ser., X (1957), pp.221-37; G.R. Elton, 'Informing for Profit' in *Star Chamber Stories* (1958), pp.78-113; T.G. Barnes, *Somerset 1625-1640* (Cambridge, Mass 1961), pp.54-6.
31 *R.* v *Berchet* (1690), 5 Mod. 459, 1 Show. K.B. 106.
32 4 & 5 Wm & Mary, c.18; Blackstone, *Commentaries*, IV, p.309.
33 For summary procedure see below p.270.
34 A. Esmein, *History of Continental Criminal Procedure*, transl. J. Simpson (1914); Holdsworth, *History*, III, pp.620-23; V, pp.170-78; Langbein, *Prosecuting Crime*, pp.129-251.

gathered the evidence and gave the judgment. Emphasis was placed on written evidence, and especially on confessions extracted under torture. The second type of trial, more or less peculiar to England, was 'trial by jury'. Under the common-law system, the judge merely presided over a public inquest by twelve ordinary folk sworn to find the truth, before whom the accuser and the accused pleaded to issue and produced their evidence and arguments much as they would in a civil suit. The common-law trial was by personal confrontation, that is, the production of oral evidence in the presence of the accused. Torture, though it was occasionally resorted to behind the scenes, was contrary to English law. Well might constitutional writers from Fortescue to Blackstone praise trial by jury as the palladium of English liberties.[35] Well might Englishmen read into chapter 29 of Magna Carta a fundamental right to jury trial, and inherit an invincible hatred of Romano-Canonical justice. But it is not for historians to indulge in panegyrics or exaggerations. The jury was not available in all criminal cases in England, nor altogether spotless when it was available. Jurymen were at least as liable to prejudice as judges, and more susceptible to intimidation and bribery. If juries freed Sir Nicholas Throckmorton and the Seven Bishops, they also convicted Sir Thomas More and Sir Walter Raleigh. Stephen thought they could be as unjust and tyrannical as Star Chamber.[36] Henry VIII tacitly mocked the Civil Law and torture when he brought maritime crime within the common law, but evidently it was easier to convict pirates by jury.[37] Nevertheless, the blessings of Magna Carta provided a ready argument when other modes of trial were attacked. The least attractive feature of ecclesiastical inquisition-procedure was the oath *ex officio*, whereby a man might be compelled to accuse (and virtually convict) himself; it was one of the principal reasons for Coke's hostility towards these courts and the High Commission in particular.[38] Coke approved of Star Chamber, but that also proceeded by examination and interrogation in the same vein. The absence of juries in Star Chamber, though not the main grievance, provided a convenient constitutional objection when the court was swept away and its business significantly remitted to 'due punishment and correction by the common law of the land and in the ordinary course of justice'.[39] The pretended High Court of Justice, which was as much an affront to the common law as Star Chamber, brought upon itself the constant objection that the judges decided the facts

35 J. Fortescue, *De Laudibus Legum Anglie*, ed S.B. Chrimes (Cambridge 1949), pp.69-73; Lambard, *Eirènarcha*, pp.436-7; Blackstone, *Commentaries*, IV, p.350.
36 Stephen, *History*, I, p.426.
37 28 Hen. VIII, c.15; Blackstone, *Commentaries*, IV, p.269.
38 See J.H. Wigmore, 'The Privilege against Self-Crimination: its History', *Harvard Law Review*, XV (1902), pp.610-23; R.G. Usher, *The Rise and Fall of the High Commission* (1913).
39 16 Chas I, c.10. See also *Lilburne's Case* (1637), *State Trials*, III, col.1315.

as well as the law but could not be challenged as if they were jurors.

For all practical purposes, the jury was the only form of criminal trial *at common law* in the period 1550-1800, at least if we regard Star Chamber as outside the common law. Summary 'trial' according to martial law was unconstitutional in time of peace, and (at any rate after the Petition of Right of 1628) even rebels taken in open insurrection were tried for treason at common law.[40] Vestigial survivals of earlier modes of trial, such as infangthief,[41] survived in theory but were not practically significant. Battle, according to Staunford, was 'not so disused that it could not be brought back into use today if the defendant so wished', but it was only waged (as a gesture of bravado) in one or two cases, and no battle was fought in a criminal case in our period. A gauntlet thrown into a startled Court of King's Bench in 1818 provided the occasion for its belated abolition.[42] Yet despite the prevalence of the jury over its precursors, and the resentment of interference with the right to a jury, the legislature had recognized since the fifteenth century that it was too solemn and slow, and perhaps too favourable to defendants, to be allowed without exception in all cases. So, throughout our period, grew a list of novel crimes which, by statute, were triable 'summarily': that is, by magistrates alone. Here, perhaps, England came nearest the inquistion; but there is no need to suppose conscious imitation of other systems,[43] and the idea was never extended to felonies.

Trial by jury
Nearly all lawyers in our period traced the right to trial by jury to chapter 29 of Magna Carta. But the key phrase 'judgment of his peers' was given a restricted exposition. Peers, for this purpose, were of two classes only: temporal lords of Parliament, and commoners. A peer of the realm indicted for treason or felony could only be tried by other peers of the realm, and the form of trial differed somewhat from that of a commoner in that the triers did not take an oath (and so were not 'jurors'), and unanimity was unnecessary so long as there was a majority of at least twelve.[44] The privilege did not extend to misdemeanours. Whereas a lord of Parliament

40 Smith, *De Republica*, p.44; Coke, *Institutes*, III, p.52; Hale, *Pleas*, I, p.499; L. Boynton, 'Martial Law and the Petition of Right', *English Historical Review*, LXXIX (1964), pp.255-84.
41 Hale, *Pleas*, II, p.71. The last instance of such a trial for theft was at Halifax in 1650: Stephen, *History*, I, pp.265-70.
42 Staunford, *Plees*, f.177 (translated); Smith, *De Republica*, pp.49, 93; *Lord Rea* v *Ramsey* (1631), *State Trials*, III, col. 483; *Ashford* v *Thornton* (1818), 1 B. & Ald. 405; 59 Geo. III, c.46; G. Neilson, *Trial by Combat* (Glasgow 1890), pp.322-34.
43 Langbein, *Prosecuting Crime*, pp.63-4.
44 See L.O. Pike, *Constitutional History of the House of Lords* (1894), pp.209-28. See also 7 Wm III, c.3, ss 10-11.

indicted for felony had to pray trial 'by God and my peers', every other subject sought trial 'by God and the country', which meant those men of the county where the indictment was found who were qualified to serve on the jury. The only qualification was that they should be freeholders to the value of 40*s*. or (in a city or town) owners of 40*s*. worth of goods.[45] There was no age limit, but women were by custom excluded. The jurors did not have to be 'peers' of the accused in any particular sense; an esquire could be tried by merchants.[46]

The advantages which jury trial were supposed to confer on the accused were principally two. First, since the jurors in giving a general verdict were judges of law as well as fact, they could override strained or unpopular interpretations of the law or of the evidence by government-minded judges.[47] Second, they could mitigate the rigours of the penal system by 'pious perjury' — the merciful use of 'partial verdicts' or false acquittals contrary to the evidence. The precise extent of these advantages is difficult to quantify, but it seems that from the sixteenth to the eighteenth centuries the acquittal-rate (whatever the reasons for acquittal) was between one-quarter and one-half of those indicted. Since the essence of these advantages was that a man's fate rested in the hands not of royal officials but of his neighbours, the theory counted for little if in practice those neighbours were not free to follow their own minds. How free, then, were juries in deciding upon their verdicts?

Once jurors became judges of fact, who adjudicated upon the evidence given in open court rather than on their own private knowledge, it was possible to criticize their verdicts as being against the evidence. The common law enabled a false verdict in a civil suit to be upset by an action of attaint against the jury, and there are statements in the law books that the Crown (but not a convict)[48] could bring attaint in respect of a perverse verdict on indictment. No one seems very sure that such an action was ever brought, but if 'attaint' is used loosely to denote any proceeding against jurors then it was common enough in the century after 1550. Trial judges dissatisfied with acquittals would either fine the jurors instantly, or bind them over to appear in Star Chamber, which took an active interest in misconduct by jurymen. Sir Thomas Smith writes as if such proceedings were rarely pursued to a conclusion, and says that when they were they were

---

45 2 Hen. V, c.3; 19 Hen. VII, c.13; 23 Hen. VIII, c.13. The old rule that some jurors should be 'of the hundred' was obsolete by Hale's time.
46 *R.* v *Thomas* (1554), Dy. 99. An alien, however, could by statute claim trial by a jury *de medietate linguae* (that is, one-half foreigners): see *R.* v *Sherleys* (1557), Dy. 144.
47 Hawles, *English-man's Right*, pp.10-18; *Guide to Juries, passim*. Horne Tooke's acquittal in 1794 was commemorated by medals inscribed: 'Not guilty say the jury, equal judges of law and fact'.
48 P. 10 Hen. IV, Fitzherbert, *Abridgement*, tit. 'Attaint', pl.60, 64; 12 Rep. 23. The reason was that two juries (24 in all) had already passed on him.

accounted very tyrannical; while in 1554 all the judges of England held that trial judges had no power to fine jurors for false verdicts.[49] But the records suggest that both kinds of proceeding were common enough under Elizabeth I and the early Stuarts. The Star-Chamber jurisdiction passed in 1641 to King's Bench, which followed its 'tyrannical' example until it was finally and conclusively decided in 1670 that it was contrary to law to punish jurors for their verdicts.[50] The trial judge could, alternatively, seek to prevent rather than cure by refusing to accept a verdict which had been agreed upon.[51] Some Jacobean judges would even examine the jurors individually to see whether one would give way.[52] This practice ceased at about the same time as the fining. As late as 1680 it was asserted that

> such a slavish fear attends many jurors, that let the court but direct to find guilty, or not guilty ... right or wrong accordingly they will bring in their verdict ... as the court sums up, they find; as if juries were appointed for no other purpose but to echo back what the bench would have done.

From about that time, however, trial judges generally respected the newer principle that the purpose of their address to the jury was not to direct but to 'recapitulate and sum the heads of the evidence', and to state the law in a manner 'hypothetical, not coercive'.[53]

Summary conviction
At common law the judges of superior courts could convict summarily (that is, without indictment or jury) only in respect of offences committed in open court, where knowledge of the offence was conveyed through their own senses. The idea was taken up in statutes which gave justices of the peace the power to punish offences committed in their view out of court; and then (but well before 1550) to punish offences which, though not done in their presence, they discovered by 'examination'.[54] In these latter statutes there was no attempt to disguise the departure from common law; 'examination' was contrasted with 'inquest' and 'presentment' and there was no need for a grand or trial jury. The tendency to confer summary powers on justices accelerated in the seventeenth and eighteenth centuries, and led Blackstone to issue the warning that 'it has of late been so far extended as, if a check be

49 Smith, *De Republica*, pp.87-8; BL, Harl. MS 5141(a) (hereafter cited as Dalison, Reports), f.27.
50 *R.* v *Bushell* (1670), Vaugh. 146. Cf. *R.* v *Leach* (1664), T. Ray. 98; *R.* v *Hood* (1666), Kel. 50; *R.* v *Windham* (1667), 2 Keb. 180.
51 R. Crompton, *Loffice et auctoritie de Justices de Peace* (1617 edn), p.114, pl.6 (c.1572); *R.* v *Mansell* (1584), 1 And. 103, 104; *R.* v *Chichester* (1671), Aleyn 12.
52 BL, Add. MS 25228, f.41, pl.850 (1620).
53 Hawles, *English-man's Right*, pp.36, 9-10. See also *Guide to Juries*, pp.20-22.
54 15 Ric. II, c.2; 13 Hen. IV, c.7; J.C. Fox, *History of Contempt of Court* (Oxford 1927), pp. 70-83; Langbein, *Prosecuting Crime*, pp.64-75.

not timely given, to threaten the disuse of our admirable and truly English trial by jury, except only in capital cases'.[55] Blackstone's fears were premature, for they are still voiced today; but they represented a hostile reaction to summary process from the superior courts, which had already erected a wholesome supervisory jurisdiction.

The foundation of the review of summary convictions was the ability to remove records from inferior courts into King's Bench and there to quash the convictions if patent defects were found. The power was there in Elizabeth I's time,[56] but was not commonly used until the later seventeenth century. Its foremost protagonist was Holt C.J., who considered that 'all acts which subject men to new and other trials than those by which they ought to be tried by the common law, being contrary to the rights and liberties of Englishmen as they were settled by Magna Carta, ought to be taken strictly'.[57] King's Bench could not re-examine the merits of the conviction, but could only examine the record to ensure that the proceedings were warranted by law; if the record was good on its face, it was incontrovertible. The main lines of attack were to show that the justices had not pursued the statutory power exactly, or that the accused had not been given an opportunity to attend and defend himself. The latter requirement was a noble piece of judicial law-making attributed to Hale, but not settled till 1703; it did not necessitate the presence of the accused, but only that he should receive a due summons.[58] The principle of 'natural justice' so established has become the foundation of what is now Administrative Law. Some thought the work of King's Bench undermined too far the authority of the justices, and Parliament tried experiments in excluding it.[59] The compromise solution was to provide for an appeal to quarter sessions, often by way of rehearing; this gave the accused a better chance of making his point, and saved the justices' face by keeping the matter within the county; the device was first tried in 1670,[60] and became very common in the next century. Each statute, however, had its own variations, and summary jurisdiction was not homogenized until 1848.[61]

III CRIMINAL JURISDICTION

All criminal jurisdiction in England was in constitutional theory derived

---

55 Blackstone, *Commentaries*, IV, p.281.
56 *Gardner's Case* (1592 or 1601), 5 Rep. 72, Cro. Eliz. 822.
57 *R. v Chandler* (1702), 1 Ld. Raym. 581.
58 *R. v Dyer* (1703), 1 Salk. 181, 6 Mod. 41. For all the law on the subject see W. Boscawen, *Convictions on Penal Statutes* (1792); W. Paley, *Law and Practice of Summary Convictions* (1814).
59 For a judicial retaliation see *R. v Moreley* (1760), 2 Burr. 1040.
60 Game Act 1670, 22 & 23 Chas II, c.25.
61 11 & 12 Vict., c.43; Stephen, *History*, I, pp.122-6.

from the king, as the fountain of justice and the principal conservator of the peace. Nevertheless, the king could not properly exercise such jurisdiction in person, because he could not be a judge when he was also a party. It had therefore to be delegated. This was done either by grant or by prescription (immemorial usage). As far as the regular courts were concerned, the grant had to be by letters patent conferring either a permanent judicial office in a court of known jurisdiction or a commission to exercise the jurisdiction set out in the patent. The Crown was held to be limited by law (or rather by long usage) in granting commissions, and could not grant a commission which would change the law: for instance, by giving judges power to proceed against notorious offenders without indictment, or to determine minor trespasses.[62] Commissions, restricted in time and space, account for nearly all criminal jurisdiction in the period 1550-1800. The only exceptions worth noticing in a general account are (i) the Court of King's Bench; (ii) those justices of the peace who derived their authority from borough charters or Acts of Parliament; (iii) ecclesiastical courts; and (iv) franchise jurisdictions, such as courts leet. The simple picture was distorted by legislation. Parliament could not only confer or remove jurisdiction in the case of an existing office or institution, but could alter the jurisdiction of those who held or would in the future hold a particular type of commission; it was very sparing, however, in the creation of new criminal tribunals.

Parliament
Parliament had criminal jurisdiction in respect of peers and proceedings by impeachment. Peers were tried either in full Parliament, or by triers presided over by the High Steward; the peer was indicted in the normal way by a grand jury, and the indictment removed by *certiorari* before the High Steward, who received a commission of oyer and terminer to try the one case. Impeachment was not confined to peers, though it was arguable that Magna Carta precluded the trial by peers of a commoner for a capital offence.[63] Between its revival in 1621 and the last instance in 1805 there were over fifty impeachments, two-thirds of them against peers.[64] The House of Commons acted in effect as grand jury, and its presentment (called 'articles') was tried by the House of Lords.

King's Bench
The Court of King's Bench was the only one of the three superior

62 12 Edw. III, *Liber Assisarum*, pl.5; Coke, *Institutes*, IV, pp.163-4; Hawkins, *Pleas*, II, ch. 1, ss 7-8; Stephen, *History*, I, pp.109-10.
63 Blackstone, *Commentaries*, IV, p.259. Cf. *R. v Blair* (1689), *State Trials*, XII, col. 207, which broke the rule.
64 See C.G.C. Tite, *Impeachment and Parliamentary Judicature in Early Stuart England* (1974); P.J. Marshall, *The Impeachment of Warren Hastings* (Oxford 1965).

common-law courts in Westminster Hall to possess a criminal jurisdiction, and that it possessed without stint. It was regarded as an eyre in the county where it sat (usually Middlesex), and as such had unlimited jurisdiction to try indictments. It was the only court which could try appeals of felony. It could remove into its purview the record of any inferior criminal court, and quash the conviction or proceed with the trial if it had not taken place. When Star Chamber was abolished in 1641, King's Bench inherited so much of its jurisdiction as was considered worth preserving.[65]

As a court of first instance, it could try indictments found before itself by a grand jury of Middlesex, or informations filed in the Crown Office, or indictments removed by *certiorari* from inferior courts. It was rare throughout our period for indictments to be removed before trial; the *certiorari* was not available as of right, and was generally refused in respect of trials before the superior judges at the Old Bailey or assizes. After removal, the court would either try the case 'at bar' by a jury of the county where it was found, or send the case back to the county to be tried at *nisi prius*: a situation in which the commissioners of *nisi prius* had not only criminal jurisdiction but the power to give judgment. In cases arising in Middlesex, the trial could take place in term-time at the King's Bench bar before the full court and a Middlesex jury; it was possible for all the judges to address the jury.[66] This seems to have occurred only in cases of some importance, such as criminal informations for offences against public order or morality. The run-of-the-mill Middlesex cases were heard at the Middlesex sessions or the Old Bailey, or (in vacations) by a single King's Bench judge sitting at *nisi prius*.

As a court of review, King's Bench was primarily concerned in the early part of the period with formal defects in indictments and with allowances of pardons. By 1700 the emphasis had shifted to summary convictions and settlement cases. The reason for the decline of the more serious business is that better methods were being developed for reviewing convictions on indictment on their merits, and therefore it became less necessary to poke around for technical flaws.

Assizes
Until their abolition in 1971[67] assizes were for most ordinary purposes the principal criminal courts in the country. Despite their longevity and

65 R. v *Edgerley* (1641), March N.C. 131; R. v *Johnson* (1686), Comb. 36, *per* Herbert C.J.; R. v *Abraham* (1689), Comb. 141, *per* Holt C.J.; Hawkins, *Pleas*, II, ch. 3, s.4.
66 E.g. R. v *Taverner* (1616), 3 Bulst. 171; R. v *Gibbons* (1651), *State Trials*, V, col. 366.
67 Courts Act 1971, c.23, s.1. From about 1916 until 1971 a composite short-form commission had been used. The 1971 Act restrains only commissions of assize, not gaol delivery or oyer and terminer; but the three types had long been inseparable.

regularity, assizes were not permanent institutions in the same sense as King's Bench. The assize judges, though most of them were judges of the superior courts, derived all their authority from the commissions which they received ad hoc for each circuit. The country was divided into six circuits,[68] and (save in the extreme north) there were two assizes each year; the first in the Lent and the second in the Long Vacation. Two commissioners, who had to hold the degree of serjeant, were assigned to each circuit. The commission of assize itself, ironically, conferred no criminal jurisdiction because it only empowered the judges to take the 'petty' assizes; these were all obsolete by 1550 save for novel disseisin, which was in decline. But it had become the practice in medieval times, and was enjoined by statute,[69] that the assize commissioners should deliver the gaols on their way. The assize judges therefore received, in addition to their assize commission, the two principal criminal commissions of oyer and terminer and gaol delivery.

The commission of general oyer and terminer[70] was issued to the two assize judges together with the principal justices in the county concerned and commanded them to inquire into, hear and determine all offences committed in the county. The commission of general gaol delivery issued only to the assize judges, with the clerk of assize as associate, and commanded them to deliver the gaols in the county. The jurisdiction conferred by each commission was unlimited in subject matter, but there were procedural distinctions. The commissioners of oyer and terminer could try only indictments found before themselves, because the words 'inquire, hear and determine' were held to be conjunctive. This restriction did not apply to the commissioners of gaol delivery, but they could try only persons already committed to the gaol (including those released on bail).[71] The latter had the additional power to 'deliver by proclamation' all the prisoners against whom no indictments had been found by the end of their session.

68 The Home, Midland, Norfolk, Oxford, Northern and Western. See Cockburn, *Assizes*, pp.23-48, and Map I. There were also two Welsh circuits (North and South).
69 Statute of Northampton, 2 Edw. III, c.2; 4 Edw. III, c.2.
70 There were also special commissions (limited by person, place or subject-matter): e.g. those for the Lord High Steward (trial of peers), state trials of commoners, the Court of the Verge (offences within 12 miles of the royal household), Justice Seats of the Forests, University Courts and Admiralty Sessions.
71 Bro. N.C. 37 (1555); *Anon.* (1584), 1 And. 111; *R.* v *Pursell* (1590), Cro. Eliz. 179; Hale, *Pleas,* II, pp.34-5. It was once argued that the jurisdiction extended only to those in gaol at the time of the commission: 1 And. 111. The distinction between the commissions is discussed in Dalison, Reports, f.27v (where Staunford J. opposes the orthodox view) and f.29v; 'Justice Jones his opinion touching the commissions by which the Justices sit at Newgate' (*c.*1635): CUL, MS Ll.3.11, ff.208-11. The forms of the commissions will be found in Coke, *Institutes*, IV, pp.162-3, 168; Holdsworth, *History*, I, pp.669-70.

Criminal Courts and Procedure, 1550-1800

The combined effect of these commissions was to give the assize judges unlimited criminal jurisdiction within the counties comprised in their circuit and for the duration of that circuit.

In cases of felony, the jurisdiction of assizes overlapped with that of quarter sessions. In practice, however, it was settled custom near the beginning of our period for capital felonies to be reserved to the assize judges. The custom was by no means always observed in the seventeenth century, and it had no legal foundation, but the assertions of Lambard, Dalton and Bacon[72] as to the general rule are borne out by the bulk of records.[73] It may have evolved because the justices had acquired so much minor work by statute that they could not cope and, therefore, almost by default, left serious cases to the assizes. Alternatively, the custom may have been imosed from above, either to secure a more professional or awesome tribunal for capital cases or to emphasize that the justices' role in serious criminal cases was that of prosecutor rather than judge. There are indications of the latter two views in the Marian Bail and committal statutes, which require certification to the justices of gaol delivery (not to the sessions), and in the 'case of difficulty' proviso inserted in commissions of the peace after 1590.[74] The practical consequence was that, for most of the period 1550-1800, the Crown side of assizes was chiefly occupied with murder, robbery, burglary and grand larceny, together with other serious offences such as rape, coining and witchcraft. Of these, it seems that the various forms of theft accounted for about three-quarters of the calendar.[75] Less serious offences, such as petty larceny, were divided between assizes and quarter sessions, presumably as efficiency and convenience demanded.

The assizes were, of course, far more than superior criminal courts. Of their civil jurisdiction, their supervision of the justices and of local government, and of their place in religious and political history, it would be impertinent here to say more than that an excellent full-length study was published in 1972.[76]

Sessions of the peace

Justices of the peace for counties derived their judicial authority from the commissions of the peace, which were issued to most of the knights and

---

72 Lambard, *Eirenarcha* (1588 edn), p.549; Dalton, *Countrey Justice* (1630 edn), p.49; F. Bacon, *Use of the Law* (1639 edn), p.12. Langbein, *Prosecuting Crime*, p.105, traced the passage to the 1588 edition of Lambard.
73 Barnes, *Somerset*, pp.50-4; Cockburn, *Assizes*, pp.90-9.
74 1 & 2 P. & M., c.13; 2 & 3 P. & M., c.10; Hale, *Pleas*, II, p.46; Blackstone, *Commentaries*, IV, p.268; Barnes, *Somerset*, p.53; Cockburn, *Assizes*, pp.90, 91; Langbein, *Prosecuting Crime*, pp.104-18.
75 Cockburn, *Assizes*, pp.97-8, and Table I.
76 J.S. Cockburn, *A History of English Assizes 1558-1714* (Cambridge 1972).

principal gentry and lawyers within each county. The medieval form of the commission, after slight revision in 1590, remained in use until 1878. The first *assignavimus* clause appointed the persons named to keep the peace in the county; this conferred no trial jurisdiction, but empowered each individual justice to make inquiries, issue warrants, take informations, record examinations under the Marian statutes and take recognizances to keep the peace. The second *assignavimus* appointed the same persons and any two of them, whereof (*quorum*) one was to be a justice named in the *quorum* sub-clause, to make inquiry concerning all felonies, trespasses and a host of other offences, committed within the county, and to receive indictments and hear and determine the same. This was effectively a commission of oyer and terminer, but the list of offences was archaic and misleading; for instance, murder was not mentioned, and it had been questioned whether it was included in 'felonies'.[77] At the end of this clause was a proviso, that if a case of difficulty should arise they were not to proceed to judgment except in the presence of a judge of either bench or of assize. The third clause, the charge, commanded the justices diligently to apply themselves to the premises; the fourth recited the calling of jurors by the sheriff; and the fifth the appointment of a *custos rotulorum*.

By virtue of the second *assignavimus* the justices held their general sessions of the peace. They were called 'quarter' sessions because they were directed by statute to be held at the four seasons of Michaelmas (week after 29 September), Epiphany, Easter and the translation of St Thomas (week after 7 July).[78] They were supposed to last for three days at least,[79] and to follow the procedure of the common law. At least one of the justices had to be one of those named in the *quorum* sub-clause. In 1550 the justices 'of the quorum' were invariably the legally qualified justices, but soon afterwards the quorum was 'debased' by the insertion of more and more lay justices until in the end only one was omitted for form's sake.[80] This development was associated with the loss of more serious cases to the assizes and the difficulty of assembling justices at sessions. The jurisdiction to try indictable offences was almost coextensive with that of assizes, excluding treason, perjury, forgery and a few other offences. The sessions also made orders touching public works, the poor, wage and price regulation and

---

77 A. Fitzherbert, *The newe Boke of Justices of the peas* (1538), f.21; Crompton, *Justice*, p.19; *R.* v *Buckler* (1551), Dy. 69. Fitzherbert's view was expressly denied by Hales and Portman JJ. in 1553: Dalison, Reports, f.10v.
78 2 Hen. V, c.4.
79 12 Ric. II, c.10. These statutory provisions were often ignored: Lambard, *Eirenarcha*, pp.482-91.
80 Blackstone, *Commentaries*, I, p.340; J.H. Gleason, *The Justices of the Peace in England 1558-1640* (Oxford 1969), pp.48-51, 104-8, 137-8; Langbein, *Prosecuting Crime*, pp.112-18.

other matters of local government.[81] If all who were supposed to had attended, there would have been an impressive gathering of three or four hundred people at quarter sessions, including everyone who mattered in the county.

The Webbs showed how different the practice might be from the theory in the seventeenth and eighteenth centuries.[82] There was constant difficulty in some parts in gathering together the quorum of two justices, and quarter sessions sometimes failed to be held for this reason. The constables and other officers were often negligent, and constables' presentments eventually ceased altogether. In many places there was no proper courtroom, and the sessions would proceed in a tavern or adjourn from house to house. We have already seen that serious crime was given up to the assizes; what remained for trial did not occupy more than a few hours, and the local-governmernt work which occupied most of the time could be transacted in private. In some counties there was no chairman of quarter sessions, the justices being free to proceed as they thought fit. If a lawyer was present, he would doubtless rule on points of law, but there was no sanction for this. At Hereford assizes in 1663 Hyde C.J. told the lay justices to abide by the legal rulings of lawyer justices 'and not (as it is commonly practised) put to the vote of many ignorant justices on the bench according to their fancy and opinion'.[83] So long as the record was properly made up there was no appeal; one need not, therefore, suppose that what transpired was always as formal and regular as legal theory required.

In some places quarter sessions were held independently of the county commissions of the peace. The archbishop of York and the bishops of Durham and Ely held sessions within their liberties by statutory authority.[84] Many cities and boroughs held sessions by virtue of their charters, which constituted the mayor and some of the aldermen or jurats as permanent justices, and usually provided for the appointment of a legally-qualified and salaried justice called a 'recorder'. Some boroughs had no jurisdiction in felony, others had; some were concurrent with, some exclusive of, the county sessions. These permanent sessions were affected

81 For the quarter sessions' functions in general see E.G. Dowdall, *A Hundred Years of Quarter Sessions* (Cambridge 1932); Barnes, *Somerset*, ch. 3, esp. pp.68-81; E. Moir, *Local Government in Gloucestershire 1775-1800* (Bristol 1969), pp.85-107; F.G. Emmison, *Elizabethan Life: Disorder* (Chelmsford 1970); A.H. Smith, *County and Court: Government and Politics in Norfolk 1558-1603* (Oxford 1974), esp. pp.47-138.
82 S. and B. Webb, *English Local Government: Parish and County* (1906), pp.421-79.
83 'Henry Townshend's "Notes on the Office of a Justice of Peace" 1661-63', ed R.D. Hunt, *Worcs. Hist. Soc. Misc.*, II (1967), pp.113-14.
84 27 Hen. VIII, c.24.

neither by the issuing of a new county commission of the peace nor by the demise of the Crown.

In some counties the justices held 'special' sessions between the quarter sessions to prevent delays; Lambard thought they should be held more often,[85] but no doubt they were rare outside the metropolis. What came in the nineteenth century to be called 'petty sessions' were originally called 'private' sessions, because they did not transact public business such as trials on indictment. They were held by virtue of the first *assignavimus*, whereas special sessions were held (like quarter sessions) under the second. They could be used for summary proceedings, but were chiefly for administrative business, such as licensing and poor relief.

Anomalies in London and Middlesex

Long before the establishment of the Central Criminal Court in 1834, the metropolis afforded the most important exception to the general scheme of criminal jurisdiction. There were no assizes for London or Middlesex. The Middlesex sessions, held for most of the period at Hicks' Hall in Clerkenwell,[86] competed in term time with King's Bench. Because of the presence of the latter, Middlesex was relieved from holding sessions quarterly; but, ironically, King's Bench tried so few criminal cases that the county was obliged to hold eight rather than four sessions a year. The liberty of the City of Westminster held distinct sessions, out of term in Westminster Hall. Sessions of the peace for the City of London were held at Newgate or the Guildhall. The 'Old Bailey' was the popular name for the Justice Hall adjoining Newgate prison, where commissions to deliver that gaol were executed. Newgate was the principal gaol for both Middlesex and London, and so the commissions of gaol delivery gave jurisdiction in both counties and were usually accompanied by separate oyer and terminer commissions for both counties. Until 1785 the Middlesex oyer and terminer could not be executed during term time, because of the presence of King's Bench in the county. The Old Bailey commissions issued to the Lord Mayor and some of the aldermen, the Recorder of London, the Common Serjeant, all the common-law judges and various dignitaries and lay justices. They issued as often as eleven times a year in the earlier part of our period, but towards the end there were eight regular sessions each year. At the Old Bailey were also held Admiralty sessions by virtue of special commissions of oyer and terminer to the Lord High Admiral's surrogate and other judges, to try crimes committed outside counties and within the admiralty jurisdiction.

85 Lambard, *Eirenarcha*, pp.500-503. See also Hawkins, *Pleas*, II, ch. 8, s.47.
86 Hicks' Hall was built in 1612, the new Clerkenwell Sessions Court in 1779. For much information about the sessions in the 18th century see B.H. Davis, *A Proof of Eminence: The Life of Sir John Hawkins* (Bloomington 1973), pp.175-299.

Tourns and leets

The sheriff's tourn and the court leet (which was a species of tourn in private hands) had lost most of their former importance by 1550, their work having been assumed by the justices' sessions.[87] They were never abolished, however, and in some places continued actively. Their common-law jurisdiction was to inquire into and present all felonies, and misdemeanours of a public nature such as affrays and blood-sheds.[88] Since Magna Carta, however, they had been forbidden to proceed further with felonies and their presentments had to be passed to a superior court. In the case of the tourn, the sheriff was supposed to hand in his indictments at quarter sessions; in the case of the leet, the presentment was supposed to be engrossed in a tripartite indenture and delivered to the assize judges.[89] Alternatively, the presentment could be sent to the grand jury for them to find as an indictment.[90] This power to present felonies was probably almost obsolete in our period. But the misdemeanour jurisdiction continued. The presentment of the jury was held to be 'as a gospel' because it could not be traversed; it operated as a summary conviction without trial or even 'examination'.[91] It was an archaic embarrassment, and in 1776 it was held that the conviction could be removed into King's Bench and traversed there, for otherwise the leet would have 'a power superior to that of any other jurisdiction in the kingdom'.[92] The only punishments which could be imposed were fines and amercements, not imprisonment. The most remarkable feature of leets to this day is that, although they are royal courts of record, they can be bought and sold privately with the manors to which they are appendant.

Ecclesiastical courts

Although they did not belong to the common-law scheme of jurisdiction just described, and proceeded in a different tradition without indictments or juries, the courts of the Church exercised a good deal of criminal jurisdiction during our period. They had the severe limitation that they could try only offences not cognizable at common law, but this left a substantial residue. The only capital offence within their purview was heresy, punishable until 1677 with death by fire; a few heretics were burned

---

87 Hale, *Pleas*, II, pp.69-71; Hawkins, *Pleas*, II, chs 10-11; Blackstone, *Commentaries*, IV, p.273; S. and B. Webb, *Manor and Borough*, I (1908), pp.21-30; Holdsworth, *History*, I, pp.134-8; Barnes, *Somerset*, pp.48-9.
88 M. 22 Edw. IV, 22, pl.2; M.1 Ric. III, 1, pl.1; T. 6 Hen. VII, 4, pl.4; P.11 Hen. VII, 22, pl.11.
89 1 Edw. III, c.17 (leet); 1 Edw. IV, c.2 (tourn).
90 P.27 Hen. VIII, 2, pl. 6.
91 H. 21 Edw. III, Fitzherbert, *Abridgement*, tit. 'Barre', pl.271; P.8 Edw. IV, 5, pl.17; M. 2 Ric. III, 11, pl.25; T. 20 Hen. VII, Keil. 66, pl.8; Dy. 13; Hale, *Pleas*, II, p.155; Hawkins, *Pleas*, II, ch. 10, s.76. See also J. Ritson, *The Jurisdiction of the Court Leet* (1809).
92 *R. v Roupell* (1776), 1 Cowp. 458.

in our period, but the jurisdiction was not quantitatively significant.[93] More important in practice was the punishment of moral offences in the archidiaconal courts.[94] The sins most commonly dealt with were fornication and other offences against sexual morality; but the list included 'spiritual' defamation, drunkenness, bad language and other manifestations of discordant or dissolute living. The Church courts also, of course, devoted much time to ecclesiastical discipline; to church attendance, recusancy, liturgy, ornament and such like. The usual punishment was penance, the full form of which was performed in church in a white sheet, but which might be varied to suit the crime; a common form was the reading of a public confession. The object was to shame rather than pain the offender, and to edify the congregation. Sometimes, however, the penance was commuted to a money payment, which was tantamount to a fine. The ultimate sanction was excommunication, and so the courts lacked teeth to deal with the irreligious; throughout our period there was a tendency for business other than ecclesiastical discipline to be transferred to the sessions.

IV THE TRIAL FOR FELONY[95]

Most of the persons indicted at the assizes or sessions would already have

93 12 Rep. 93; Holdsworth, *History*, I, p.618. Abolished by 29 Chas II, c.9.
94 Holdsworth, *History*, I, pp.616-21; R.A. Marchant, *The Church Under the Law 1560-1640* (Cambridge 1969); P. Hair, *Before the Bawdy Court 1300-1800* (1972); F.G. Emmison, *Elizabethan Life: Morals and the Church Courts* (Chelmsford 1973). See also Usher, *High Commission*.
95 The following section draws heavily on a series of formularies showing how clerks were to order proceedings at criminal sessions. The oldest is: (i) *Hic sequuntur regule atque ordines nonnulle observande tam in sessionibus pacis quam in sessionibus gaole deliberacionis* (c.1550): Bodleian Lib., MS *e Museo* 57, ff.87v-89. The remainder distinguish sessions of the peace from sessions of gaol delivery. For gaol delivery or assizes: (ii) 'The manner and form of proceedings at the Assizes and General Gaol Delivery holden by his Majesty's Justices according to the Law and Custom of England' (temp. Jas I): BL, Lansd. MS 569, ff.5-20; Bodleian Lib., Rawl. MS C.271, f.3; (iii) 'Here follows the Order of the Gaol Delivery' (c.1610): BL, Harl. MS 1603, ff.75-78; (iv) T.W., *Clerk of Assize*; (v) *Form and Method*; (vi) *Crown Circuit Companion*. For quarter sessions: (vii) 'Instructions for Proceedings at the Sessions of the Peace' (temp. Jas I): BL, Lansd. MS 569, ff.1-5; (viii) Richard Bragge, *Regule per Clericum ad Generalem Sessionem Pacis Observande* (temp. Chas II): in *Quarter Sessions Order Book 1642-49*, ed B.C. Redwood, *Sussex Rec. Soc.*, LIV (1954), pp.210-14; (ix) 'Directions to hold a Sessions for a Port' (c.1690): in M. Reed, 'The Keeping of Sessions of the Peace in Hastings', *Sussex Archaeological Collections*, C (1962), pp.55-59; (x) *Crown Circuit Companion*, pp.29-86. Other forms for use at sessions, not consulted by the writer: Bodleian Lib., Rawl. MS B. 257, f.77 (Kent, temp. Jas I or Chas I); Rawl. MS D. 1136 (temp. Chas II); 'The form and manner how to hold a General Sessions' in J.W., *Officium Clerici Pacis* (1686 edn), pp.2-11.

been in custody, having been committed to gaol to await trial. Anyone could arrest on suspicion of felony, though it was always prudent to seek the aid of a constable or procure a justice's warrant. At the beginning of the period there was some doubt as to the propriety of issuing a warrant to arrest for felony before indictment, because if a justice had no personal knowledge he had no ground to justify an arrest; but by Hale's time at the latest the practice had become commonplace.[96] It was requisite that within three days after any arrest the prisoner be examined before a justice; any detention beyond that period was an actionable false imprisonment.[97] At the examination the accused was accompanied by the person who arrested him and his accusers. If it appeared that a felony had been committed, the justice had no authority to release the accused but was to write down 'the examination of the said prisoner, and information of them that bring him, of the fact and circumstances thereof' for certification to the next gaol delivery. He was then to bind over the complainants to give evidence, and either commit the suspect to gaol by *mittimus* or release him on bail.[98] A single justice was forbidden to grant bail in cases of felony, lest he be tempted by corruption; but two justices, one being of the quorum, could bail for any offence except treason, murder or arson, so long as the guilt was not virtually certain (as where the accused had confessed or been taken red-handed).[99] Suspects who had not been found were indicted upon information given, and process issued against them which could result in outlawry.

From the bail certificates, depositions and gaol calendar, the clerks could prepare a calendar of the prisoners to be tried and a note of those who were bound to prosecute and give evidence. From this material the clerks would busy themselves before the assizes or sessions in drawing bills of indictment. The first business of the court, once the commissions had been publicly read and those due to attend summoned, was to swear and charge the grand jury. The grand jurors' oath was:

You shall diligently inquire and true presentment make of all such

---

96 H. 14 Hen. VIII, 16, pl.3; Coke, *Institutes*, IV, pp. 177-8; Hale, *Pleas*, II, pp.79-80, 107; Hawkins, *Pleas*, II, ch. 13, ss 11, 18-20; Blackstone, *Commentaries*, IV, p.290.
97 *Scavage* v *Tateham* (1601), Cro. Eliz. 829; *Morgan* v *Lloyd* (1649), HLS, MS 106, pp.528-32; Hale, *Pleas*, II, pp.120-21; Hawkins, *Pleas*, II, ch. 16, ss 3, 12.
98 1 & 2 P. & M., c.13; 2 & 3 P. & M., c.10; Smith, *De Republica*, p.72; Dalton, *Countrey Justice*, pp.295-304. For the power to release see Langbein, *Prosecuting Crime*, pp.7-8; Hawkins, *Pleas*, II, ch. 16, s.22.
99 Statute of Westminster I, c.15; 3 Hen. VII, c.3; Staunford, *Plees*, ff.71-77v; Crompton, *Justice*, pp.152-3; Dalton, *Countrey Justice*, pp.304-26; Hale, *Pleas*, II, pp.136-40; Hawkins, *Pleas*, II, ch. 15, ss 54-64. Blackstone said that bail in capital cases was exceptional: *Commentaries*, IV, p.296. It was argued in 1552 that a sheriff or constable acting alone could bail suspects at common law: Dalison, Reports, f.6.

matters and things as shall be given you in charge. The king's majesty's counsel, your fellows', and your own, you shall well and truly observe and keep secret. You shall present no man for envy, hatred, or malice; neither shall you leave any man unpresented for love, fear, favour, or affection, profit, lucre, gain, or any hope thereof; but in all things you shall present the truth, the whole truth, and nothing but the truth. So help you God.

After the charge, the prosecutors and witnesses were called and sworn and sent into the grand-jury room with the bills of indictment. The secrecy enjoined by the oath was generally observed, primarily to protect accusers in the event of an *ignoramus*; but the hearing was occasionally conducted in public at the request of the prosecutor[100] and prosecuting counsel were often admitted at the discretion of the grand jury.[101] The grand jury probably spent as much time on a case as the trial jury, at least in the first half of the period, and they continued their work while trials were taking place in open court, returning at intervals to feed the court with fresh indictments.

Arraignment and plea

As soon as convenient after the indictments were found, the persons indicted were 'arraigned' before the court. The arraignment corresponded to the pleading stage in civil suits, the reading of the indictment being in effect the declaration of the Crown. The prisoner, whom we shall call John Style, was called to the bar and addressed by the clerk: 'John Style, hold up thy hand'. This was not a mere ceremony, but an acknowledgment by the prisoner that he was the person indicted.[102] The clerk then read the indictment, paraphrasing it into English and into the second person: 'Thou art here indicted by the name of John Style, late of London, yeoman, for that thou ...'. It was necessary that the indictment itself be in Latin,[103] but the prisoner was not entitled to have it read in Latin,[104] nor to have a copy of the original, unless he could assign some error in law upon hearing

---

100 Hale, *Pleas*, II, p.159; *R. v Earl of Shaftesbury* (1681), *State Trials*, VIII, col. 771. The latter case was attacked in Somers, *Security*, pp.31-50. It was the last instance: E. Christian at Blackstone, *Commentaries*, IV, p.302n.
101 [J. Hawles], *Remarks upon the Tryals of Fitzharris [and others]* (1689), pp.20-21; *State Trials*, V, col. 972n; ibid., VIII, col. 773n.
102 *R. v Lilburne* (1653), *State Trials*, V, at col. 416; *R. v Harrison* (1660), ibid., at col. 996; Hale, *Pleas*, II, p.219; Blackstone, *Commentaries*, IV, p.323; Eden, *Principles*, pp.186-7.
103 36 Edw. III, c.15 (as interpreted); *R. v Humfrey* (1607), Exeter Coll. Oxford, MS 93, f.110; *Anon.* (1618), HLS, MS 2072, f.91; Hale, *Pleas*, II, p.169. English was introduced by 4 Geo. II, c.26.
104 *R. v Vane* (1661), *State Trials*, VI, col. 132.

it.[105] This seemingly harsh rule was to prevent trifling exceptions to grammar or form. After reading the indictment, the clerk asked: 'How sayest thou, John Style, art thou guilty of this felony as it is laid in the indictment whereof thou standest indicted or not guilty?' If the prisoner denied the charge he pleaded 'not guilty', to which the clerk replied: 'Culprit, how wilt thou be tried?' The word 'culprit' was not a prejudicial insult, but a corruption of the law-French *'culpable: prist'*, apparently meaning that the Crown was ready to prove the prisoner guilty. This etymology has understandably caused misgivings, because in law no such reply was called for, nor was it entered of record; but no other explanation makes sense.[106]

To the clerk's question the law permitted but one answer: 'By God and the country'. The form was essential, and it was not sufficient to say 'according to the laws of the land' or 'by God and honest men' or 'by twelve men according to the constitutions of the law'.[107] If the prisoner refused to use the required words, this was as much a standing mute as if he had failed to plead.[108] Any prisoner disposed to prevaricate was given due warning of the awful fate of those who stood mute of malice. In cases of high treason, petty larceny and misdemeanour, and in appeals of felony, it was tantamount to a conviction and judgment followed accordingly. In cases of petty treason and felony, the prisoner was adjudged to receive the *peine forte et dure*, whereby he was half-starved and pressed to death. This was perhaps the most barbaric feature of common-law procedure, and resulted from a grisly misunderstanding of a statute of 1275. Babington remarked that the full sentence as described in the year-books was 'so severe, that (I think) never English man as yet (though many were pressed to death) had the heart to execute it according to the letter'; gaolers instead tried to coerce wilful mutes into pleading by tying their thumbs with whipcord.[109] Prisoners chose this penalty in order to protect their

105 Hale, *Pleas*, II, p.236; *R. v Rosewell* (1684), *State Trials*, X, at cols 266-8; *R. v Charnock* (1696), ibid., XII, at cols 1381-83; M. Foster, *Crown Law* (Oxford 1762), p.228. But he could have it repeated, and by indulgence might copy it from dictation: *R. v Gibbons* (1651), *State Trials*, V, at col. 268; *R. v Ratcliffe* (1746), Fost. 40.
106 Hale, *Pleas*, II, pp.219, 258; *Form and Method*, p.23; Blackstone, *Commentaries*, IV, p.339; Stephen, *History*, I, p.297n. Doubters: D. Barrington, *Observations on the Ancient Statutes* (1775 edn), p.419n; Christian's note to Blackstone (1800 edn), at p.340.
107 *R.v. Abington* (1586), *State Trials*, I, col. 1143; *R. v. Harrison* (1660), ibid., V, col. 999; *R. v Axtel* (1660), ibid., col. 1008. Axtel's objection was that God was not 'locally present'. Other prisoners would only put themselves on God: e.g. *R. v Peters* (1660), ibid., col. 1007; *R. v James* (1661), ibid., VI, col. 75. See also below, p. 333; 9 Rep. 32.
108 P. 4 Edw. IV, 11, pl.18; T. 14 Edw. IV, 7, pl.10; Hale, *Pleas*, II, p.258.
109 Babington, *Advice to Grand Jurors*, p.192; *R. v Thorely* (1672), Kel. 27; Barrington, *Observations*, pp. 82-8.

dependents from the forfeiture which attended conviction. Pressing continued at least until 1741, but by a statute of 1772 standing mute of malice was made equivalent to conviction in all cases. Inexplicably, there are two cases of standing mute of malice between 1772 and 1800; the prisoners threw away their chance of acquittal for no obvious reason.[110]

Instead of pleading not guilty, the prisoner could plead a 'dilatory' or 'declinatory' plea, such as a plea to the jurisdiction, a plea in abatement for want of addition or some other defect in the indictment, or a plea of sanctuary (virtually obsolete by 1550) or clergy.[111] These were 'dilatory' pleas because, if unsuccessful, the prisoner still had to answer the indictment. In capital cases, however, this was also true of pleas in bar; sentence of death could be given only after a conviction on the general issue. The pleas in bar were three: autrefoits acquit, autrefoits attaint (or convict) and a pardon. Other forms of pleading were forbidden, because a felony could not be confessed and avoided. A third possibility was to demur to the indictment for insufficiency. In civil cases a demurrer amounted to a confession of the facts, and so an unsuccessful demurrer lost the case; Staunford, Hale and Hawkins thought this was also true of a demurrer to an indictment, though Blackstone thought otherwise.[112] Demurrers were rare, because the same advantages were available (without the risks) upon motion in arrest of judgment.

The prisoner who had no defence to make could confess the indictment by pleading 'guilty', which the clerk recorded by writing '*cogn[ovit]*' (he confessed) upon it. The court was supposed to ensure that a prisoner did not plead guilty from fear or ignorance, and in cases of doubt to persuade him to plead not guilty.[113] Nevertheless, there is some evidence of 'plea-bargaining'. Lambard condemned the practice of accepting a half-confession, by which a prisoner, protesting his innocence, put himself on the king's mercy in return for a reduced penalty; but the practice continued well into the seventeenth century.[114]

The trial: impanelling the jury
When John Style had pleaded not guilty and put himself on the country, the clerk replied 'God send thee a good deliverance', and wrote on the indictment *'po. se'* (*ponit se super patriam*). The prisoner was then entitled to have any irons or shackles removed, for at common law he was to be free

110 Barrington, *Observations*, p.86 (instance at Cambridge, 1741); 12 Geo. III, c.20; 1 Lea. 83; E. Christian at Blackstone, *Commentaries*, IV, p.328n.
111 As to clergy see below p. 292-3.
112 Staunford, *Plees*, f.150v; Hale, *Pleas*, II, p.257; Hawkins, *Pleas*, II, ch.31, s.5; Blackstone, *Commentaries*, IV, p.334.
113 Staunford, *Plees*, f.142; Hale, *Pleas*, II, p.225; Blackstone, *Commentaries*, IV, p.329.
114 Lambard, *Eirenarcha*, pp.522-3; Hawkins, *Pleas*, II, ch.31, s.3. Cf. the plea *non vult contendere*: *R. v Templeman* (1702), 7 Mod. 40.

from any duress during his trial.[115] He was also, in appropriate cases, allowed to sit and to have pen and paper; but in the vast majority of cases trials were too rapid to permit of this indulgence. The clerk then arraigned another prisoner on the next indictment, and so on until there were sufficient for the first jury to try. There was no rule that each prisoner should have a distinct jury, and the usual practice until the late seventeenth century was to arraign about half a dozen at a time. Of course, the trials were conducted separately, unless several men were arraigned jointly on the same indictment; but the jurors had to carry each case in their minds until all the trials were over, when they would if necessary retire to consider them all together. When enough prisoners had been arraigned, the jury was impanelled.

The names of those on the sheriff's panel were called, and as they appeared their names were marked with a dot by the clerk. When they had gathered, the clerk informed the prisoners of their right to challenge the jurors as their names were called, and then read out the names again. As each juror stepped forward, the crier reported '*Vous avez* Richard Roe' (or whatever his name was), and Richard Roe was sworn:

> You shall well and truly try and true deliverance make between our sovereign lord the king and the prisoners at the bar whom you shall have in charge, and a true verdict give according to your evidence. So help you God.

The clerk marked his name '*Jur[atus]*' (sworn). When twelve were so marked, the clerk commanded the crier (in law-French): '*Countez*'. The crier then counted them, as the clerk read over for the third time the names marked *Jur'*: '[A.B.] one, [C.D.] two, [E.F.] three ... twelve. Good men and true, stand together and hear your charge'.[116] The crier then made proclamation for evidence against John Style, Style was asked to raise his hand for identification, and he was given into their charge: 'Look upon the prisoner you that be sworn, and hearken to his cause. You shall understand that he is here indicted ... (reciting the indictment in English, in the third person, the plea of not guilty, and the charge to inquire whether he was guilty or not) ... Hear your evidence'. The trial could then commence.

A prisoner in capital cases was entitled at common law to thirty-six 'peremptory' challenges: that is, without cause shown. By statute this had been reduced before 1550 to twenty, though in 1555 prisoners accused of

---

115 Staunford, *Plees*, f.78; Coke, *Institutes*, II, p.315; III, p.34; Hale, *Pleas*, II, p.219; Kel. 9, 10; *State Trials*, V, at cols 979-81(f); *R. v Waite* (1743), 1 Lea. 28, 36; Eden, *Principles*, pp.187-8.
116 Smith, *De Republica*, p.79; R. Bernard, *The Legall Proceeding in Man-Shire against Sinne* (1630), p.233. In many accounts '*countez*' is corrupted to 'count these'; as to which see also Blackstone, *Commentaries*, IV, p.340n.

treason were restored to their three dozen.[117] If prisoners exercised their full rights of challenge, it could be time-consuming and might delay the trial, because thirty-two potential jurors were needed to ensure that twelve would be left.[118] If all the prisoners 'severed' their challenges, by taking them in turns, it would become virtually impossible to try them; for, if there were six, a panel of 132 would be needed to exhaust the challenges. This could be a means of achieving separate juries.[119] In practice, however, challenges were rare. Either prisoners did not know the jurors or anything against them, or did not act quickly enough, or were simply too over-awed to understand what the clerk had told them. The Crown could not challenge potential jurors peremptorily, but could require them to 'stand by', which meant that their names were passed over; only when the panel was exhausted were the names called again, and then the Crown would have to show cause or acquiesce. In practice this could give the Crown a greater control over the composition of the jury than the prisoner had; but, like the challenge, it does not seem to have been widely exercised.

The trial: presentation of the case
Throughout the period 1550-1800 prisoners indicted for felony were in law denied the assistance of counsel in presenting their case unless a point of law arose upon the evidence. The rule did not apply to appeals of felony, nor to misdemeanours, and this made it appear all the more anomalous. St Germain had explained that the judge bore the responsibility for seeing that the proceedings were sufficient in law, to which Staunford added the more realistic (and prophetically true) reason that trials would take too long if men of law were allowed; no-one could better speak about the facts than the prisoner himself. This was a typically medieval view of a trial, as an inquest, an administrative process to collect verdicts; lawyers were concerned wth law, not with disputes about facts. The rule might have disappeared sooner if the possibility of lengthening trials had not been administratively unthinkable. As the King's Bench said in 1602, when refusing counsel to a scrivener indicted for forgery: 'It would be a dangerous precedent, for every prisoner would demand it if it were now allowed'. Two more reasons were put forward in the early seventeenth century. Coke, borrowing from Roman or Scots Law, said that in capital cases the evidence against the prisoner should be so manifest that it could not be contradicted. And

117 22 Hen. VIII, c.14; 32 Hen. VIII, c.3; 33 Hen. VIII, c. 23; 1 & 2 P. & M., c.10. At common law the prisoner was treated as mute of malice after challenging 36; but after these statutes, challenges over 20 were disregarded and the jury sworn: Hale, *Pleas,* II, pp.269-70.
118 *R.* v *Harman* (1619), HLS, MS 106, f.38; *R.* v *Vane* (1661), *State Trials,* VI, col. 132.
119 T. 9 Edw. IV, 27, pl.40; *R.* v *Salisbury* (1554), Plowd. 100; *R.* v *Dennis and May* (1557), Dalison, Reports, f.42v; *Trial of the Regicides* (1660), Kel. 9, resoln 8; *Form and Method,* p.29; Foster, *Crown Law,* pp.106-7.

Pulton thought that if the party conducted his own defence, 'peradventure his conscience will prick him to utter the truth, or his countenance or gesture will show some tokens thereof, or by his simple speeches somewhat may be drawn from him to bolt out the verity of the cause', which would not happen if counsel did the speaking.[120]

Both Coke and Pulton confused the forensic presentation of the case with what we would regard as evidence. The prisoner was not competent to give evidence on oath, but his speech would serve the same purpose and it was desirable that he should deliver it in person; the prisoner's own account of himself would certainly weigh heavily with the jury. Perhaps the rule led to rough or even good justice in ordinary cases involving intelligent defendants; most prisoners asking for counsel probably hoped for some legal trick to be worked on their behalf rather than for eloquent advocacy. In most cases the Crown did not have counsel either. Perhaps points in the prisoner's favour were fairly taken by the judges or clerks or learned spectators.[121] Contemporaries might well have argued, as we now argue in relation to pre-trial interrogation, that the innocent man has nothing to lose, everything to gain, from telling his story himself. But the denial of counsel seems to have been unfair in Tudor and Stuart state trials, when the Crown was represented by the best advocates of the day.

The relaxation of the rule denying counsel accompanied the establishment of rules of evidence and trial procedure, and the cessation of the practice of questioning the prisoner during the trial. By a statute of 1695 prisoners indicted of treason were given a right to counsel for matters of fact as well as of law,[122] and thereafter the exclusion in felony cases was scarcely supportable. Foster somehow found the rule tolerable, but during the eighteenth century it became normal for counsel to be permitted to conduct the case or to prompt the accused.[123] Perhaps the greatest advantage to the defence, as Pulton had foreseen, was that it shut the mouth of the prisoner; no longer did the jury expect to hear satisfactory explanations from the defendant's own lips, and his counsel could run

120 *St Germain's Doctor and Student*, ed T.F.T. Plucknett & J.L. Barton, Selden Soc. XCI (1974), pp.284-6; Staunford, *Plees*, f.151v; *R*. v *Boothe* (1602), BL, Add. MS 25203, ff.569v-70 (translated); Coke, *Institutes*, III, p.137; *R*. v *Thomas* (1613), 2 Bulst. 147, *per* Coke C.J.; F. Pulton, *De Pace Regni* (1609), pp.184-5. Smith (*De Republica*, p.51) wrote as if it were somehow disloyal to argue against the Crown.
121 See, e.g., 'Newgate Reports', below, pp. 329, 331, 332, 334; *R*. v *Mason* (1756), Fost. 132.
122 7 & 8 Wm III, c.3. Extended to impeachment by 20 Geo. III, c.30. As to questioning the prisoner, see Wigmore, 'The Privilege against Self-Crimination', at pp.629, 633-4.
123 Foster, *Crown Law*, p.231; Blackstone, *Commentaries*, IV, pp.354-6; Eden, *Principles*, pp.156-61; Stephen, *History*, I, p.424. There are numerous instances in Leach's reports. It did not become a right until 1836: 6 & 7 Wm IV, c.114.

defences which the accused in person would never have got away with.

The Crown witnesses were called in by the crier, who reported as each one came in : *'Vous avez* Robert Downe' (or whatever his name was), and gave him the oath: 'The evidence you shall give to this jury between our sovereign lord the king and the prisoner at the bar shall be the truth, the whole truth, and nothing but the truth. So help you God'. The witness was then asked what he could say for the king, and was helped along by questions from the judge, the king's counsel (if any were present) and (occasionally) the jurors. In the earlier part of the period there might be a running altercation with the accused as he contradicted statements made against him,[124] but in the seventeenth century it became settled practice to leave the cross-examination until the witness had finished. It was settled at the same time that witnesses should not be asked leading questions during the examination-in-chief, but that greater latitude would be allowed in cross-examination.[125]

When all the Crown witnesses had finished,[126] the accused could call witnesses. There had once been a school of thought that defence witnesses were no more permissible than counsel, because the prosecution case ought to be unanswerable; but we are told that Queen Mary I personally instructed Morgan C.J. that this was an error and that 'whosoever could be brought in favour of the subject should be heard'. Her majesty's view of the matter was not clearly law until the end of the sixteenth century.[127] Even when such witnesses came to be allowed as of course, they were not (until 1695 in treason, 1702 in felony) sworn. Instead they were exhorted to stand in fear of God and tell the truth. Their evidence seems to have been given the same weight as if it had been sworn,[128] though if it turned out more favourable to the Crown an oath was hurriedly administered.[129] The distinction

124 Smith, *De Republica*, p.80; *R.* v *Abington* (1586), *State Trials*, I, col. 1143; *R.* v *Udall* (1590), ibid., col. 1278; Holdsworth, *History*, IX, pp.226-8.
125 *R.* v *Rosewell* (1684), *State Trials*, X, at col. 190, *per* Jeffreys C.J.; *R.* v *Hardy* (1794), ibid., XXIV, at cols 659-60, 754-6.
126 For the course see *R.* v *Raleigh* (1603), *State Trials*, II, at col. 4, *per* Popham C.J.; *R.* v *Axtell* (1660), ibid., V, at col. 1149, *per* Bridgman C.B.; *R.* v *Wakeman* (1679), ibid., VII, at col. 609, *per* North C.J. Cf. W. Sheppard, *Epitome of the Laws of this Nation* (1656), p.1051, who says that the prisoner spoke first and then the Crown witnesses were called.
127 *R.* v *Throckmorton* (1554), *State Trials*, I, at cols 887-8 (but he was not allowed to call witnesses); *R.* v *Udall* (1590), ibid., at cols 1281, 1304; Holdsworth, *History*, V, pp.192-4. The exclusionary rule was of Civil Law origin: Stephen, *History*, I, pp.350-4.
128 Coke, *Institutes*, III, p. 79; Crompton, *Justice*, p.110, pl.12; Dalton, *Countrey Justice*, pp.300-301; *R.* v *Moseley* (1647), *The Harleian Miscellany*, ed W. Oldys and T. Park, III, pp.499-502; *R.* v *Harvey* (1660), *State Trials*, V, col. 1197; *R.* v *Hurdman* (1661), *Worcs. Hist. Soc. Misc.*, II, p.95; Hale, *Pleas*, II, p.283; G. Duncomb, *Trials per Pais* (1766 edn), II, ch. 16; 7 & 8 Wm III, c.3, s.1; 1 Anne, st.2, c.9, s.3.
129 *R.* v *Tindal* (1633), Cro. Car. 291.

between Crown and defence witnesses was such that a Crown witness might be punished if he gave evidence to acquit the prisoner.[130]

Throughout our period most criminal trials were conducted with great rapidity during very long sittings.[131] It was, indeed, so rare for a case to last more than a few hours that it was not fully settled until the end of the eighteenth century that a criminal court had the power to adjourn a case overnight.[132]

Evidence

In the sixteenth century few recognizable rules of evidence were applied in criminal cases. Staunford, indeed, offers but one laconic remark on the whole subject: 'Anyone may be admitted to give evidence for the king'.[133] If this indicates anything, it is that there was rather a law of witnesses than of evidence. 'The law', said Bacon, 'leaveth both supply of testimony and the discerning and credit of testimony, wholly to the juries' consciences and understandings'.[134] All the evidence was given orally in open court. But, there being no exclusionary rules, hearsay was regularly admitted:[135] the written depositions could be read in evidence even though the deponent was available to give oral testimony,[136] and it was common for the constable and examining justice to give an account of their inquiries and findings. It is doubtful whether the presumption of innocence had been formulated; one writer of James I's time thought a man could be convicted without any Crown witnesses, the indictment being sufficient

130 Dalton, *Countrey Justice*, p.301, citing a case before Popham C.J. at Cambridge.
131 Cockburn, *Assizes*, pp.110-11. After-dinner sittings were sometimes disgraced by drunkenness, somnolence and noise; at the Old Bailey they continued into the middle of the 19th century.
132 E. Christian at Blackstone, *Commentaries*, IV, p.360n; *R. v Tooke* (1795), *State Trials*, XXV, at cols 128-32 (12-hour sitting). In 1798 an Irish state trial lasted for 24 hours without a break: ibid., XXVII, col. 364.
133 Staunford, *Plees*, f.163 (translated).
134 Holdsworth, *History*, I, p.333.
135 *R. v Thomas* (1554), Dy. 99; *R. v Udall* (1590), *State Trials*, I, at col. 1282 ('There was much said, to prove that the testimony of a man absent was sufficient, if it were proved to be his upon the oaths of others').
136 *R. v Throckmorton* (1554), *State Trials*, I, at col. 875; *Anon.* (1556), Dalison, Reports, f.37 (Serjeants' Inn); *R. v Duke of Norfolk* (1571), *State Trials*, I, at col. 992; *R. v Udall* (1590), ibid., at cols 1279-81, 1283, 1302-3; *R. v Raleigh* (1603), ibid., II, at cols 15-16; *R. v Harman* (1619), HLS, MS 106, f.38. A reaction against the practice may be discerned in 5 & 6 Edw. VI, c.11; 1 & 2 P. & M., c.10, s.11 (discussed in Dalison, Reports, f.37); Smith, *De Republica*, pp.79-80. It is difficult to know which school of thought prevailed in ordinary cases. In state trials the judges openly admitted the fear that a deponent might retract his accusation if called: see, e.g., *State Trials*, II, at col. 16, *per* Popham C.J.

evidence against him.[137] Nevertheless, without good eye-witness accounts of ordinary criminal trials in the early period it is difficult to say how the system normally operated.

The absence of defence counsel from important criminal trials, and the prevalence of the general issue, hindered the growth of rules of evidence in criminal cases. It seems that the strict common-law rules of evidence first manifested themselves in civil cases, and were extended to criminal trials by analogy in the later seventeenth century. By Hale's time depositions were used only if the deponent were dead or too ill to be produced;[138] and the courts began to entertain frequent objections to other kinds of hearsay evidence. The 'hearsay rule' belongs at the very earliest to the period 1675-1690, and even at the beginning of the eighteenth century Serjeant Hawkins thought hearsay could be used to lead into or augment direct evidence.[139]

By introducing exclusionary rules, the courts were able to use the nascent law of evidence, as in medieval litigation special pleading had been used, to prevent the misleading of jurors. Between the time of Staunford and that of Lord Mansfield the courts reversed their attitude to the role of the jury. Staunford excluded no evidence; its weight was for the jury. But Lord Mansfield believed it was not for courts of law 'to consider how far the minds of men may be capable of resisting temptation, but to take the most anxious care that they shall not be exposed to any temptation at all'.[140]

A recurring problem was raised by the use of accomplices' evidence. The law had long recognized the utility of giving immunity to accomplices who revealed crimes committed by their principals. The medieval technique, called 'approvement', was for the accomplice to confess on arraignment and offer to appeal his confederates; if the court agreed, he received a pardon. It was never abolished, but it went out of use before 1550 because it

---

137 BL, Add. MS 25228, f.12v, pl.225. See also *R.* v *Raleigh* (1603), *State Trials*, II, at col. 18, *per* Warburton J. ('so many horse-stealers may escape, if they may not be condemned without witnesses'). Cf., to the contrary, Smith, *De Republica*, p.76; *Guide to Juries*, pp.22-3, 81.

138 *R.* v *Lord Morley* (1666), Kel. 55, resolns 4-6; *R.* v *Bromwich* (1666), 1 Lev. 180, 2 Keb. 19; *R.* v *Thatcher* (1676), T. Jo. 53; Hale, *Pleas*, I, p.305; II, pp.52, 284; Duncomb, *Trials per Pais*, II, ch. 16. By the 1690s it was thought that depositions were evidence only by virtue of the Marian legislation: see *R.* v *Paine* (1695), 5 Mod. 163, Comb. 281; *R.* v *Kirk* (1699), 12 Mod. 304. For the civil rule, see *Fortescue* v *Coake* (1616), Godb. 193.

139 J.H. Wigmore, 'History of the Hearsay Rule', *Harvard Law Rev.* XVII (1904), at p.445; Hawkins, *Pleas*, II, ch. 46, s.14. Some earlier hints of the rule: *R.* v *Love* (1651), *State Trials*, V, at cols 77-81; *R.* v *Moders* (1663), ibid., VI, at col. 276 ('hearsays must condemn no man'); *R.* v *Langhorn* (1679), ibid., VII, at col. 441, *per* Atkins J. ('that is no evidence against the prisoner, because it is by hear-say') and Scroggs C.J. ('the jury ought to take notice, that what another man said is no evidence against the prisoner'); *R.* v *Lord Russell* (1683), ibid., IX, at col. 613.

140 *Anon.* (1775), cited by Cowper at 1 Lea. 130.

was extremely dangerous; the court could, in its discretion, sentence the approver on his confession. In its place there developed in the seventeenth century the practice of 'turning king's evidence', whereby an accomplice was promised a pardon in return for evidence against the principal offenders. Hale C.J. had been of the opinion that such a bargain disabled the accomplice from giving evidence,[141] but his highmindedness did not prevail. The accomplice did not acquire a right to a pardon by turning king's evidence, but there was an 'implied confidence' which gave him 'an equitable title to a recommendation for the king's mercy'.[142] By the middle of the eighteenth century the courts had decided that such evidence ought not normally to be admitted without corroboration;[143] had the notion existed a century earlier it would, in Stephen's view, have prevented all the unjust convictions in the state trials of 1678-80.[144]

Verdict and allocutus
When the prisoners in its charge had been tried, the jury was asked to consider its verdicts. In difficult cases the judges summed up the evidence, but in the main the judges simply put the jurors in mind of their duty and left the matter entirely to them. Thus, in a state trial as late as 1661, the Lord Chief Justice was content to say: 'You have heard the evidence, you are to find the matter of fact as it is laid before you, whereof you are the proper judges, and I pray God direct you'.[145] If the jurors wished to retire, they were given into the custody of a jury bailiff, who was sworn to keep them without fire or refreshment and free from outside influence. While the jury was out, more prisoners could be arraigned and tried.

On their return, the jurors were directed to look upon the prisoner and say whether he was guilty or not. The foreman announced the verdict. If it was 'guilty', the clerk asked them to say what property the convict had, so that it could be seized; the usual reply was 'none to our knowledge', because the inquiry would in fact be carried out by the sheriff. The clerk then wrote on the indictment: *cul[pabilis] ca [talla] nul [la]* ('guilty, no chattels'). If the verdict was 'not guilty', the clerk asked whether the accused had fled, to which a similar answer was customary. The annotation in this case was: *non cul[pabilis] nec re[traxit], q[uietus]* ('not guilty, did not flee, acquitted'). When the verdicts had all been delivered, the clerk read them out for confirmation: 'Well then, you say that John Style is guilty of the felony in

---

141 *R. v Tong* (1662), Kel. 18; Hale, *Pleas*, I, p.304.
142 *R. v Rudd* (1775), 1 Lea. 115, 119, Cowp. 331; Blackstone, *Commentaries*, IV, p.331.
143 T. Leach at Hawkins, *Pleas* (1787 edn), ch. 46, s.18; Barrington, *Observations*, p.181. Cf. Hale, *Pleas*, I, p.305 ('considerable circumstances').
144 Stephen, *History*, I, pp.400-401.
145 *R. v James* (1661), *State Trials*, VI, at col. 84. Langbein, *Prosecuting Crime*, p.50, cites a still shorter address used where a jury had even asked for advice.

manner and form as he stands indicted, and so say you all?' If none dissented, the prisoner stood convicted. In the case of an acquittal, the prisoner was made to kneel and the judge pronounced him to be discharged on paying his fees.[146] Despite acquittal, he might be bound to good behaviour or even sent to the house of correction if it appeared from the evidence that he had misbehaved. In the case of a conviction, the prisoner was led away by the gaoler. Judgment was not supposed to be given at once, but at the end of the assizes or sessions. The reason was neither to allow the judge time to reflect nor the prisoner to squirm, but to allow time to secure a pardon or prepare a motion in arrest of judgment. By the late eighteenth century, however, the practice had begun of giving judgment immediately upon conviction.[147]

Before judgment was given in cases of treason or felony, there was an indispensable[148] preliminary known as the *allocutus*. The prisoners were brought to the bar, usually in irons, and asked:

> You do remember that before this time you have been severally indicted for several felonies, upon your indictments you have been arraigned and have severally pleaded not guilty and for your trials have severally put yourselves upon God and the country, which country hath found you guilty. Now, what can you say for yourselves why according to law you should not have judgment to suffer death? What sayest thou, John Style?

The convict might take the opportunity of making a necessarily futile speech in mitigation,[149] but the legal purpose of the *allocutus* was to allow the convict to allege anything which would prevent the court from giving judgment: (i) a motion in arrest of judgment, (ii) a prayer of clergy, (iii) a prayer to allow a pardon which had been granted, or (iv) a prayer for respite by a pregnant woman.

Benefit of clergy had been extended by the medieval common law to literate laymen in all cases of murder and felony, but before 1550 statute had limited its availability to the lesser felonies and to first convictions. The statutes limiting clergy were the main reason for the scientific development of the distinctions between murder and manslaughter, robbery and larceny,

146 Fees on acquittal seem to have ranged from about 8s. to £1: W. Stubbs and G. Talmash, *The Crown Circuit Companion* (6th edn 1790), pp. 43, 718, 743; F.D. MacKinnon, *On Circuit* (1940), pp.90-91.
147 M. Madan, *Thoughts on Executive Justice* (1785), pp.82-4.
148 *R. v Geary* (1688), 2 Salk. 630, 1 Show. K.B. 131. The *allocutus* was quietly abandoned in 1967 on the assumption that it did not survive the abolition of the distinction between felony and misdemeanour.
149 By the 18th century a speech in mitigation was allowed in non-capital cases after a plea of guilty: *Crown Circuit Companion*, p.45. Ironically, there was no *allocutus* in such a case.

burglary and housebreaking, and the like; for upon such distinctions a life often depended. The requisite literacy was tested by asking the convict to read a prescribed passage from a psalter, perhaps the first verse of the *Miserere*;[150] this was the 'neck-verse', which the criminal classes presumably learned by rote. The judges could, however, achieve some control over the application of the death penalty to semi-literate convicts, either by helping them or (on the contrary) by selecting passages at random and preventing prompting.[151] Since clergy was available even after judgment, it was possible for a favoured felon to be given a hurried education in gaol so that he could return and recite his verse.[152] If one justification for clergy was that it saved 'useful' persons from the gallows, it might nevertheless be argued that a want of learning made criminal behaviour more rather than less excusable, and in 1706 Parliament extended clergy to the invincibly illiterate by abolishing the reading test.[153] Laymen could claim clergy only once, and to prevent second attempts a statute of 1490 had provided for felonious 'clerks' other than real priests to be burned in the brawn of the left thumb with a 'T' (thief) or an 'M' (manslayer). The burned thumb was not, however, a legal record; it warned the court officers to counterplead the prayer of clergy by producing the record of the previous conviction. So tedious was this procedure that some convicts doubtless had their clergy a second time.[154] Priests were exempt from branding, and in time their exemption (like clergy itself) was extended to the laity. Peers were the first to achieve immunity from the iron, by a statute of 1546, and in the following century it became customary to pardon the branding of persons 'of quality', the court granting respite for the purpose.[155] By the eighteenth century the branding was done so perfunctorily in most cases that it became 'a nice piece of absurd pageantry', and when in 1779 the judges were given power to award fines or whipping instead it went out of use altogether.[156]

150 Psalm LI, v.1. It is alluded to as the neck-verse in *The Sermons of Master Samuel Hieron* (1620), pp.222-3; Eden, *Principles*, p.192. But in *R. v Thomas* (1613), 2 Bulst. 147, verse 14 was used: *Libera me a sanguinibus, Domine*. Smith (*De Republica*, p.83) says: 'the judge commonly giveth him a psalter, and turneth to what place he will'.
151 *Anon.* (1666), Kel. 51; Cockburn, *Assizes*, pp.125, 129; 'Newgate Reports', below, p. 333.
152 E.g. *Anon.* (1561), Dy. 205, pl.6.
153 Hob. 288; 6 Anne, c.9; Blackstone, *Commentaries*, IV, p.370.
154 4 Hen. VII, c.13; *R. v Scott* (1785), 1 Lea. 401; E. Christian at Blackstone, *Commentaries*, IV, p.371n; Cockburn, *Assizes*, pp.128-9.
155 1 Edw. VI, c.12, s.14; *R. v Harman* (1620), HLS, MS 106, ff.38, 55; Babington, *Advice to Grand Jurors*, p.93.
156 Foster, *Crown Law*, p.372. Eden, *Principles*, pp.59-60, gives the impression that it could still be a real stigma. Between 1717 and 1779 it was possible to order transportation instead of branding: 4 Geo. I, c.11. The statute 19 Geo. III, c.74, s.3, did not abolish branding but made its continued use unnecessary.

Judgment

If the prisoner made no successful motion in arrest of judgment, the crier called for silence, the presiding judge[157] assumed his square cap and judgment was pronounced. It was often preceded by a homily intended for the edification of the convict and the public, but the judgment itself (now called the 'sentence') was in serious cases outside the discretion of the court.

In cases of treason and felony, the judgment was prescribed by law and could not be altered by the judge. In treason, the only judgment permitted for men until the last century was:

> You are to be drawn upon a hurdle to the place of execution, and there you are to be hanged by the neck, and being alive cut down, and your privy members to be cut off, and your bowels to be taken out of your belly and there burned, you being alive; and your head to be cut off, and your body to be divided into four quarters, and that your head and quarters be disposed of where his majesty shall think fit.

By this horrific standard only, the judgment for women in high and petty treason was more favourable: 'to be burned with fire until you are dead'. This remained law until 1790.[158] The judgment for male petty-traitors was simply to be drawn and hanged. For capital felony (excluding, that is, petty larceny) the judgment was 'to be hanged by your neck until you are dead'. Beyond these fixed details, the judge could not prescribe the manner of execution. When Felton in 1628 confessed the murder of the duke of Buckingham, he asked that his hand might be struck off as a further punishment, but the judges 'answered that it could not be, for in all murders the judgment was the same'. On the same occasion, Sir Francis Ashley, King's Serjeant, remarked in the Common Pleas that he wondered Felton was not sentenced to be hanged in chains; to which Yelverton J. answered that none but the usual sentence could be given.[159] Over a century later, the family of a murdered man asked the court to order a hanging in chains after execution, but the court ruled that it had no power to do so; the executive, however, could and did (throughout the period) order hanging in chains, the body of the deceased convict being at the king's disposal.[160]

Judgments were supposed to be carried out literally, but in fact mercy was often exercised. Traitors might be hanged until dead before the

---

157 In King's Bench, however, it was (throughout the period) the secondary justice's duty to pronounce judgment.
158 30 Geo. III, c.48. Convictions of women for *high* treason were rare; perhaps Alice Lisle and Elizabeth Gaunt (1685) were the last.
159 *Historical Collections of Private Passages of State 1618-29*, ed J. Rushworth (1659), pp.652-3; Anon. reports, CUL, MS Ee.5.17, f.254.
160 Smith, *De Republica*, p.84; *R.* v *Hale* (1741), 1 Lea. 21; *R.* v *Doyle* (1769), 1 Lea. 67; Blackstone, *Commentaries*, IV, p.201; Eden, *Principles*, pp.79-80.

mutilation began; while the terrible punishment for women who killed their husbands or counterfeited coin was usually averted by strangulation at the stake. Technically these *coups de grace* were murder, but they could hardly be punished.[161] Perhaps the most remarkable example of the insistence upon the forms of judgment occured in 1695, when an attainder for treason was reversed (somewhat too late to benefit the accused himself) on the sole ground that the record omitted after the words: *quod interiora extra ventrem trahuntur* ('that his bowels be drawn out of his belly') the necessary words: *et in conspectu eius et ipso vivente comburentur* ('and burned before his sight, he being alive'). It was said that if those words could be omitted, the court might as easily introduce Roman, Jewish or even Turkish judgments.[162]

Very few offences were punished with death at common law, though the commonest offences (homicide and theft) were among them. Parliament added a good many more, and was justly criticized for this by eighteenth-century writers. The criticisms were not usually founded on a humanitarian dislike for the death penalty so much as the observed fact that when over-used it led to excessive leniency in prosecutors, juries, judges and secretaries of state, so that the law was not enforced and criminals escaped scot-free.[163] It has been estimated that the number of convicted felons actually condemned to death, throughout our period, was between 10 and 20 per cent; while the proportion of those condemned who were actually executed probably averaged about one-half, until it dropped to one-third in the later eighteenth century.[164] Clergy and pardons allowed many to escape. Juries showed clemency by finding partial verdicts, such as clergiable larceny instead of burglary, or petty larceny instead of grand larceny. The net effect was that, even in the supposedly savage eighteenth century, only murder and particularly heinous or repeated felonies were punished with death.

The judge had greater discretion to vary punishments for misdemeanours, which were not usually fixed by law. Throughout the period the general practice was to punish petty larceny by whipping, and other misdemeanours by fine. Long terms of imprisonment were rare, since the idea of prison as a reformatory was not taken seriously until the end of the period, while the idea of prison as a punishment would have seemed an absurd expense. Life imprisonment was probably unheard of, the form being 'during the king's pleasure'.[165] The pillory was used for

161 Hale, *Pleas*, I, p.501; II, p.411; Foster, *Crown Law*, p.268; Radzinowicz, *History*, I, pp.209-13. The last instance of burning at the stake in England occurred in 1789.
162 *R. v Walcot* (1695), 4 Mod. 395. See also Smith, *De Republica*, p.84.
163 Blackstone, *Commentaries*, IV, p.4; Eden, *Principles*, pp.317-21; Madan, *Thoughts, passim*.
164 Radzinowicz, *History*, I, pp.140-51; Cockburn, *Assizes*, p.131.
165 *R. v Harrison* (1638), Cro. Car. 504, *per* Keeling Cl. Cor.

'exorbitant' misdemeanours, such as sexual offences, seditious utterances and forms of witchcraft. These undefined punishments were in practice administered lightly. The imposition of heavy discretionary punishments, such as the loss of ears or the payment of immense fines, was the primary cause of the downfall of Star Chamber; in the year of its abolition Heath J. promised that King's Bench would not make the same error.[166] In the 1680s, however, King's Bench did fall into Star-Chamber ways. The sentence passed on Titus Oates caused some consternation, and Holt and Pollexfen C.JJ. had the courage to rule it contrary to law; but the House of Lords did not share their view.[167] The provision in the Bill of Rights (1689) against the infliction of excessive fines and cruel and unusual punishments, was clearly directed against these discretionary punishments for misdemeanour; it did not affect judgments fixed by law, however cruel they were.[168]

Reprieve and pardon
If a female convict was quick with child, the judge was bound to respite judgment of death until after delivery; her condition was tried by a jury of matrons, and we learn from Hale that such juries were usually favourable whenever possible.[169] The judge was also bound to respite judgment if the convict appeared to be insane, both because it was no deterrent to punish those of unsound mind and because the convict might, if sane, have moved something in arrest of judgment.[170] In such cases judgment was not given at all for the time being. Besides these cases, judges had a wide discretion to order that a judgment which had been given should not for the time being be executed; this was called a 'reprieve'. This result could be achieved by bribing or persuading the sheriff or under-sheriff to stay execution,[171] but the only circumstance in which a formal reprieve was permissible was where the judge recommended or otherwise expected that the convict should receive a pardon. The judge himself was not competent to pardon; a pardon had to be sealed with the Great Seal on the authority of the secretary of state or the Privy Council. Where a pardon was given

---

166 *R.* v *Edgerley* (1641), March N.C. 131.
167 *R.* v *Oates* (1688), *State Trials*, X, col. 1325. See also *R.* v *Duke of Devonshire* (1687), ibid., XI, col. 1353 (judges censured for fine of £30,000).
168 Blackstone, *Commentaries*, IV, p.372; Stephen, *History*, I, p.490; A.F. Granucci, '"Nor Cruel and Unusual Punishments Inflicted": The Original Meaning', *California Law Review*, LVII (1969), pp.839-65.
169 Staunford, *Plees*, f.198v; Dalison, *Reports*, f.30 (1555); Hale, *Pleas*, II, p.413; *Form and Method*, pp.40-42; 'Newgate Reports', below, pp. 332-333.
170 Coke, *Institutes*, III, p.6; Blackstone, *Commentaries*, IV, p.24.
171 *Les Reportes del Cases in Camera Stellata 1593 to 1609*, ed W.P. Baildon (1894), p.113; *R.* v *Compton* (1625), BL, Lansd. MS 1098, f.126 (under-sheriff spared execution for £100 bribe, contrary to express direction of assize judge); Cockburn, *Assizes*, p.130.

because of doubts as to the propriety of the conviction, or on the recommendation of the jury, or because of influence, it was usually 'free' or unconditional. But the majority of pardons were granted on commuting the sentence to a period of exile in the colonies. This practice at first had no legal foundation, and required the convict's consent. It had been considered in Elizabeth's time, was in regular use by 1615,[172] and became common in the course of the seventeenth century. By the eighteenth century it was such common form that trial judges automatically prepared and returned to the secretary of state calendars of those convicted before them, marking those recommended for transportation, or for free pardons; the fortunate were then included in a 'general pardon' for the circuit or session. Over a hundred convicts were spared every year by means of pardons, the majority on condition of transportation for fourteen years. But transportation did not provide the ideal balance between justice and mercy. It was costly to the home community, which received no corresponding benefit; overseas aid was not yet regarded as a social duty. The deterrent effect was small. Although death was supposed to follow if the condition of the pardon were broken by escaping or returning, the authorities were notoriously lenient and usually granted a fresh pardon with a new term of exile.[173] In any case, seven years in America began to lose the terror it had held in James I's time and might even have been a welcome prospect for the down-at-heel. [174] Other, more useful, types of punishment were tried: under Elizabeth I, work on the galleys, and, under James I, foreign military service. In one remarkable case in George II's time a convict agreed to submit to a medical experiment involving the loss of a leg in return for a pardon, though to the credit of the surgeons none would perform it.[175] Finally (in 1779) Parliament introduced, as a regular alternative to transportation, work on the 'hulks' or in a penitential house — the origin of 'hard labour'. Blackstone was enthusiastic about this reform and hoped that thereby 'such

172 Mentioned in 39 Eliz. I, c.4. Craies attributed the idea to Sir Thomas Dale (1611): *Law Quarterly Review*, VI, p.398. In 1614 and 1615 transportations to Penguin Island were ordered at the Old Bailey: P. della Valle, *Travels into East-India* (1665 edn), pp.333-6, who relates that the 1615 contingent heard such frightening tales of the fate of their precursors that they begged to be hanged. In *R.* v *Strickland* (1617), HLS, MS 114, f.141, a convict reprieved to be sent to Virginia took fright and escaped. See further A.E. Smith, 'The Transportation of Convicts to the American Colonies in the 17th Century', *American Hist. Review*, XXXIX (1934), pp.232-49.
173 Eden, *Principles*, pp.34-7; *R.* v *P. Madan* (1780), 1 Lea. 223; Madan, *Thoughts*, pp.76-7, 94. The two Madans seem not to have been related: F. Madan, *The Madan Family* (1933), p.220.
174 Barrington, *Observations*, pp.445-6; Eden, *Principles*, pp.32-3. As alternatives, Barrington suggested the Falkland Islands, while Eden suggested the sale of convicts to redeem slaves.
175 Eden, *Principles*, pp.80-82; Madan, *Thoughts*, pp.111-15; Cockburn, *Assizes*, p.129.

a reformation may be effected in the lower classes of mankind ... as may in time supersede the necessity of capital punishment, except for very atrocious crimes'.[176] Thereafter, Parliament increasingly took upon itself to regulate the incidence of transportation and hard labour so that (as in the case of clergy) punishment ceased to represent capricious and tortuous devices for evading the fixed death penalty and came instead to represent something approaching penal policy.

V THE CORRECTION OF ERRORS

It remains to consider the means by which judgments in criminal cases could be questioned in law. The present idea of an appeal did not exist at common law, and the Court of Criminal Appeal had to await the twentieth century. There were only two ways of challenging the validity of a criminal judgment; the formal way was to show some error on the record, the better way was by special verdict or reserved case.

Error on the face of the record

The reversal of judgments for error 'on the face of the record' belonged to King's Bench, whose decisions were in turn reversible by Parliament. Proceedings in error involved making up a complete record of the case in question. Normally, the indictment with its annotations served as the only record, since the minute book which the clerk kept was in law nothing but a private memorandum. The full record was engrossed on parchment. It was written (until 1732) in Latin, and contained a minute and precise recital of the judges' commission, the names of the grand jurors and their finding the indictment, the arraignment, the process against the petty jury, the plea, the verdict, the *allocutus* and the judgment. This record was drawn up and sent into King's Bench by the clerk of the lower court on receipt either of a writ of *certiorari* or a writ of error from King's Bench. Whereas the indictment could be quashed before trial upon *certiorari* alone, a judgment following a trial at common law could be reversed only by writ of error.[177] Hale says that the practice was to sue only a writ of error, though by 1704 there had been a reversion to the older practice of removing the record by *certiorari* and then suing a writ of error *quod coram vobis residet*.[178] The writ of error was not available to quash a conviction where the convict took his clergy, because that was not a judgment,[179] nor to quash summary

---

176 Blackstone, *Commentaries*, IV, p.371; 19 Geo. III, c.74.
177 *Winchcomb* v *Goddard* (1601), Cro. Eliz. 837, *per* Popham C.J.; *R.* v *Rice* (1616), Cro. Jac. 404; *Anon.* (1661), 1 Keb. 195, pl.186; *R.* v *Porter* (1703), 1 Salk. 149, 2 Ld Raym. 937.
178 Hale, *Pleas*, II, p.210; *R.* v *Foxby* (1704), 6 Mod. 178.
179 *R.* v *Long* (1596), Cro. Eliz. 489. Technically, a 'conviction' was a verdict of guilty, whereas the 'judgment' was the sentence of the court following a verdict or upon a point of law.

convictions;[180] in these cases, therefore, the *certiorari* alone was used.

In 'the good old days when barbarous law was tempered by luck'[181] judgments might be reversed for the most trifling slips of form or want of certainty. Thus, in 1595, a murderer escaped because the indictment read that he shot the deceased '*ad sinistram partem cruris sui Anglice* the left thigh', whereas the Latin meant 'the left part of his thigh' without stating which.[182] Instances could be multiplied, and they lead one to suspect that few judgments were immune from reversal. This was the reason why prisoners were not allowed to see their indictments, and it was no doubt the reason for introducing the rule that a writ of error lay only of grace and required the *fiat* of the Attorney-General.[183] It is clear that in some cases errors were allowed only when there was some other reason for quashing the conviction, such as a doubt as to the safety of the verdict.[184] Since these other reasons are rarely mentioned in the reports, the law books are difficult to interpret. The impression given is that, notwithstanding all the checks and safeguards, numerous judgments were reversed for insubstantial reasons from what Barrington termed 'a false compassion'. Hale complained that

> It is grown to be a blemish and inconvenience in the law, and the administration thereof [that] more offenders escape by the over-easy ear given to exceptions to indictments, than by their own innocence ... to the shame of the government, and to the encouragement of villainy, and to the dishonour of God.

As late as 1771, Eden complained that in numberless instances of this kind 'the substance of justice hath been lost in the pursuit of the shadow of mercy'.[185]

The main defect of error, however, was not the punctiliousness of the forms but their emptiness. The merits of the case were irrelevant, because all that mattered was what was (or was not) entered of record. And since no evidence was entered, there could be no argument that the facts proved did not in law support the charge in the indictment. This limitation prevented

---

180 *R.* v [*Saunders*] (1669), 1 Vent. 33; *R.* v *Phorbes* (1681), T. Raym. 433; *R.* v *Lomas* (1694), Comb. 297; *R.* v *Leighton* (1708), Fort. 173. For the practice in detail see W. Hands, *The Solicitor's Practice on the Crown Side of the King's Bench* (1803), pp.27-44.
181 Maitland, *Justice and Police*, p.163.
182 *R.* v *Wye* (1595), HLS, MS 110, f.103v.
183 *R.* v *Gargrave* (1615), 1 Rolle Rep. 175; *R.* v *Allen* (1662), 1 Sid. 69; Hale MS cited in 1 Vern. 175; *R.* v *Wilkes* (1770), 4 Burr. at p.2550, *per* Ld Mansfield C.J.; Blackstone, *Commentaries*, IV, p.390.
184 'Newgate Reports', below, pp. 325-326, n. 3.
185 Barrington, *Observations*, p.248; Hale, *Pleas*, II, p.193; Eden, *Principles*, p.181.

nearly all substantive questions of law from being raised on a writ of error. Criminal appeals might have had a different history if the bill of exceptions had been allowed in criminal cases; but that hope was extinguished in the case of Sir Harry Vane in 1661.[186]

New trials

In certain situations a trial could be discontinued or set aside and a new jury summoned by a writ of *venire de novo* for a new trial. The only clear case was where the first trial was a nullity, because of misbehaviour or some formal defect. In certain cases, however, a jury might have to be discharged before verdict: for instance, if the defendant was taken ill, or one of the jurors absconded.[187] The practice was then extended to cases where the jurors could not agree,[188] or where the prosecution evidence did not come up to proof.[189] This extension infringed the rule against double jeopardy and was controversial; eventually it became acceptable in the first situation, but not in the second. There was never any attempt to extend the principle, in cases of felony, to the case where a valid but unsafe verdict had been given. In that case, it was too late to discharge the jury and there was no power to order a retrial. Logic demanded the same rule whether the unsafe verdict was for the prisoner or for the Crown. In one situation only did King's Bench relax this rule and grant a new trial: this was where a misdemeanour was tried at bar, or at *nisi prius* from King's Bench, and a conviction appeared unsafe. The first cases, in the middle of the seventeenth century, were all informations for perjury.[190]

Reserved cases

The best method of reviewing points of law arising on the evidence, and by far the most important from the point of view of criminal jurisprudence, was the 'reserved case'. This was not available as of right, but a technique adopted where the trial judge himself had doubts or where an *amicus curiae* had questioned the conviction. The prisoner was simply reprieved until the next assizes, so that the advice of the other judges could be sought in the meantime. If the judges thought the conviction wrong, a pardon was recommended. Discussions of this kind in Serjeants' Inn are reported even before 1550, and they continued until after 1800. By the eighteenth century

---

186 *R. v Vane* (1661), *State Trials*, VI, at col. 193, 1 Sid. 85, Kel. 15, resoln 5; *The Rioters' Case* (1681), 1 Vern. 175.
187 Foster, *Crown Law*, p.76; Hale, *Pleas*, II, pp.295-6.
188 Coke, *Institutes*, I, f.227v; III, p.110; Hale, *Pleas*, II, pp.295-7; *Anon.* (1698), Carth. 465; *R. v Kinloch* (1746), Fost. 16, 22-39.
189 Hale, *Pleas*, II, pp.294-5; *R. v Gardiner* (1665), Kel. 47; *R. v Jones and Bever* (1665), Kel. 52; Hawles, *English-man's Right*, p.93.
190 *Noys v Downing* (1663), 1 Keb. 484; *Primate v Jackson* (1664), 1 Lev. 10n, 1 Keb. 568, 638; *R. v Latham* (1673), 3 Keb. 143; *R. v Smith* (1681), T. Jo. 163, 2 Show. K.B. 165. New trials were never granted after acquittal.

it had become customary for the trial judge to prepare a written 'case' (a note of the evidence and of the question) for circulation to his brethren.

If legal doubts arose before conviction, it was usual to direct a 'special' verdict, whereby the jurors found the facts in detail and submitted the question of guilt to the court; this obviated the need for a pardon if the defence succeeded. The trial judge would then, if he thought fit, lay the special verdict before the 'twelve judges'.[191] Another method was for the jury to convict generally, subject to the opinion of the twelve judges; in that case a pardon was needed if the conviction was held to be wrong, but the procedure was apparently cheaper.[192] In the event of disagreement among the judges, it was known for a pardon to be recommended even if the majority of judges were against the prisoner.[193] The twelve judges did not always give reasons in public, and sometimes failed to reach any decision at all. Their meetings were purely informal, and were private. They kept no record, save for annotated books of 'cases'. Not until 1848 was the institution formalized, when Parliament erected the Court for Crown Cases Reserved.[194]

Needless to say, none of these courses could be taken upon acquittal, because a verdict of not guilty was final and could not be questioned by the Crown.

NOTE

The foregoing article was commissioned as an introductory survey of legal procedure for use by students of social history. It has since been supplemented by a number of excellent detailed studies, including: J.H. Langbein, 'The Criminal Trial before the Lawyers' (1978) 45 Univ. Chicago Law Rev. 263-316; 'Shaping the 18th Century Criminal Law: a view from the Ryder sources' (1983) 50 Univ. Chicago Law Rev. 1-136; J.G. Bellamy, *The Tudor Law of Treason* (1979); D.R. Ernst, 'The Moribund Appeal of Death' (1984) 28 A.J.L.H. 164-188; J.S. Cockburn, *Calendar of Assize Records... Introduction* (1985); J.M. Beattie, *Crime and the Courts in England* (forthcoming).

191 This expression was used for meetings of the justices of the King's Bench and Common Pleas and barons of the Exchequer, though the total number of them was not always twelve. In the 16th century the body seems rather to have included all the assize commissioners, and therefore some serjeants-at-law attended.
192 See *R.* v *Hodgson* (c.1700), 1 Lea. 6.
193 E.g. *R.* v *Dunn* (1765), 1 Lea. 57, 61; *R.* v *Shaw* (1785), ibid., 360.
194 See 'Newgate Reports', below, pp. 326-327.

10 The Court of King's Bench, c. 1450-60

This is the only known picture of an English criminal trial before the time of George III. The prisoner, removed from the fettered group in the foreground, is holding up his hand upon arraignment. At the left, a crier is swearing the jury. Sitting beneath the judges, the clerk of the crown records the proceedings on his controlment roll. *Inner Temple MS. Add. 188*

17
THE REFINEMENT OF ENGLISH CRIMINAL JURISPRUDENCE, 1500–1848

The inauguration of conferences, volumes of essays, and a journal, will provide sufficient evidence to convince historiographers that the history of crime had by 1979 become established as a distinct branch of historical science. One might even assert that the history of " crime "— whatever that means—has become a growth industry. The same could not be said of the history of criminal law. The "law" is more or less irrelevant to the enquiries of social historians, except in so far as the legal system happens to have produced the records on which they are dependent for factual information. Legal theory is an embarrassing concept for the historian who regards the law as a means by which county members and magistrates imposed their views of order on the populace. Even non-Marxist historians are rightly concerned to explore the gap between legal theory and practical reality in the administration of criminal justice, and to a certain extent this can be achieved without seeking to understand the abstractions of the lawyer in their own terms. When historians do turn their attention to the formulation or development of the criminal law, it is usually to Parliament and the incessant tinkering with statutory offences and penalties at the behest of pressure groups that they give their attention. All this makes good history, which the legal historian is most unwise to ignore. But the object of the present paper is to advance the less fashionable proposition that the substantive criminal law—what we have termed criminal jurisprudence, to distinguish it from the criminal legal system—has an independent interest of its own as a branch, not of social, but of intellectual history. Since the proposition has been denied even by the most eminent legal historians, it is not made without fear of contradiction. And there are few pioneering studies to draw upon.

So the question to be set will be a modest one. We shall not be concerned with specific principles of law, save by way of illustration, but with the means by which criminal jurisprudence could be refined: that is, the ways in which questions of criminal law could be asked, discussed and resolved. For the sake of simplicity, and to point the contrast with political history, little notice will be taken of legislative change. It is doubtful in any case whether legislation can be said to have contributed much to the scientific development of criminal law before very modern times. It was usually piecemeal, ill-drawn and concerned with adjusting penal sanctions rather than with improving doctrine. The meaning and operation of legislation was largely left to the courts, but questions of statutory interpretation give less scope to courts than do questions of case law, and we shall see the process of development more clearly by concentrating on the common law.

The present definition of murder, for instance, is a judge-made creation. If it is different from the medieval definition, which it obviously is, this is not because of legislative intervention—though the penalties have been frequently adjusted by Parliament, and the common-law penalty is no longer available in England. The changes have been not so much in the essence of the offence, which like most crimes has a timeless quality, as in the degree of sophistication of the definition. Without being too historically precise, we can well imagine a remote past when the law of homicide remained a divine secret. A man accused of killing another would be subjected to a physical ordeal, and God would decide upon his guilt. Since God did not make separate findings of fact, and since there was no way of reviewing his decision on appeal, there was no law of homicide other than the procedure governing the accusation, the test and the fate of those whom God condescended miraculously to declare guilty. Even the procedure could properly be regarded as governed by custom rather than law. There were no records, no reports, no appeals, no questions asked, and above all there were no lawyers. At this stage of history we already have what the social historian would recognize as a criminal legal system; but we have no criminal law.

Professor Milsom has taught us that legal development consists in the increasingly detailed consideration of facts.[1] A system of jurisprudence is designed to provide rational solutions to the legal problems raised by given sets of facts. Lawyers (like historians) are trained to analyze facts and to sift the relevant from the irrelevant before applying legal principles, though the task is complex because the available legal principles themselves determine what is relevant. In a simple legal system factual analysis does not proceed very far. Murder and cattle rustling are wrong and punishable, but clever lawyers' points about diminished responsibility or zoology can only be raised in prayer before the ordeal. All you have is a list of crimes; that is, a list of the kinds of accusation which in appropriate circumstances will justify trying a man with water or hot iron. The introduction of the jury does not in itself make any immediate difference: the verdict of the country is as inscrutable as the judgment of God. Jurors are, however, human. They can ask questions and be questioned. They can do injustice and be seen to do so. Trial by

---

[1] "Law and Fact in Legal Development," *University of Toronto Journal*, XVII (1967), 1.

The Refinement of English Criminal Jurisprudence

jury begins to demystify the process of adjudication and opens the way for consideration of the variable facts of actual cases.

We can summarize the story between Plantagenet and Tudor times by saying that the development of trial by jury as a hearing of evidence in open court inevitably produced a tension between judge and jury.[2] The judge heard the evidence as well as the jury and could form his own views of the case. If he thought the case clear, he might tell the jury what to do, or attempt to punish them if they got it wrong. The jury had the last word in the case, since the judge had no power to alter the verdict. But until 1670 at least jurors were liable to punishment if the verdict was considered perverse. Attempts to control the decision on the facts ultimately failed, but out of the tension were born two kinds of law: the law of evidence and the substantive criminal law. Both were aspects of decision-making which the judges managed to keep from the laymen. By the law of evidence the judges prevented unsafe or irrelevant testimony reaching the ears of the jurors. And by enlarging the scope of the substantive law the judges were able to tell the jurors what conclusion followed if they found certain facts to be true. The law of evidence in criminal cases must for the present be bypassed, though in 1600 it was little more than a nebulous body of somewhat variable practice. The creation and refinement of criminal law, on the other hand, was by then well under way.

The Indictment

The obvious starting point is the indictment. In a good indictment it was necessary to state the particulars of a known crime, and therefore the indictment represents the first stage (both procedurally and historically) in formulating the constituent elements of a criminal offence. A prisoner could take exception to his indictment on arraignment, or he could have it removed into the King's Bench by writ of *certiorari* in order to be quashed for insufficiency. King's Bench decisions to quash are enrolled on the *rex* rolls of that court (at the end of the KB 27 bundles), and the record of such a decision often specifies the error.

The procedure was available for challenging attempts to formulate new offences, though examples of such use are not plentiful.[3] Most precedents of new offences in fact passed without challenge and did not represent formal judicial decisions; for example, the famous case of Sir Charles Sedley, which established the offence of indecency and was to influence the development of obscene libel, involved a plea of guilty.[4] A

---

[2] For a detailed exposition of this theme, see T. A. Green, "The Jury and the English Law of Homicide 1200–1600," *Michigan Law Review*, LXXIV (1976), 414.

[3] E.g. *R.* v. *Ames* (1518), KB 27/1028, Rex m. 6B^d (vicar discharged from indictment for feloniously and illicitly burying a corpse); *R.* v. *Cornwall* (1591), Moore KB 302 (grand juror discharged from indictment as a common publisher of the queen's secrets).

[4] *R.* v. *Sidley* (1663), 1 Sid. 168.

more frequent use of *certiorari* was in exploring the boundaries of known offences. Some questions raised by this technique in early Tudor times were whether coinage offences extended to foreign coins,[5] whether fixtures and animals could be stolen feloniously,[6] and in whom the property of a chalice and mass vestments belonging to a parish church should be laid.[7] An analysis of all such cases in the *rex* rolls over an extended period would be profitable and not excessively difficult. Yet they are not such a deep mine of legal information as one could wish. By far the greatest number of attempts to quash indictments depended on what we should regard as formal quibbles. A few examples will illustrate the punctiliousness which the King's Bench could exhibit in these cases.

It was necessary for the caption to show sufficiently that the indictment was taken before justices or coroners having jurisdiction to take it. In 1538 a prisoner accused of treason—for saying "I set not a pudding by the king's broad seal, and all his charters be not worth a rush"—was discharged because the indictment was taken before justices of the peace who had no apparent jurisdiction to take indictments of treason.[8] And in 1589 a murderer escaped because his indictment was taken before the Herefordshire justices " apud Hereford," and it did not appear of record whether this Hereford was in Herefordshire and thus within their commission.[9] The prisoner had to be given a sufficient addition. Professor Cockburn has shown that additions were often fictitious,[10] but the only concern of the King's Bench upon *certiorari* was their legal sufficiency. Thus, an eleven-year-old scholar was discharged from an indictment for murder in 1539 on the grounds that "scholar" was no addition.[11] Details of time and place, which were likewise prone to factual inaccuracy, had to be consistent with the law. In 1536 a murderer escaped because of a slip in stating the dates. He was said to have struck the deceased on 14 April in the 26th year of King Henry VIII (1535), and the death was said to have followed on the 23rd day of the same month in the same year. Since the regnal year changed on 21 April,

---

[5] *R. v. Davy* (1536), KB 27/1100, Rex m. 7 (clipping groats); *R. v. Creyghton* (1536), KB 27/1101, Rex m. 13, Spelman, *Enditement*, pl. 22 (counterfeiting); *Anon.* (1539), Spelman, *Corone*, pl. 45 (importing forged ducats). References to Spelman are to J. H. Baker (ed.), *The Reports of Sir John Spelman*, I and II (Selden Soc., XCIII–XCIV, 1976–77).

[6] *R. v. Gardiner* (1533), discussed below; *R. v. Delarever* (1536), Spelman, *Corone*, pl. 23(2) (taking tame hart).

[7] *R. v. Watlyngton* (1499), KB 27/953, Rex m. 10^d (" goods of Warfield church " held insufficient).

[8] *R. v. Mapurley* (1538), KB 27/1109, Rex. m. 2; and two other cases in G. R. Elton, *Policy and Police* (1972), pp. 299–300.

[9] *R. v. Lenthal* (1589), Cro. Eliz. 137.

[10] J. S. Cockburn, "Trial by the Book? Fact and theory in the criminal process 1558–1625" in J. H. Baker (ed.), *Legal Records and the Historian* (1978), pp. 60–79.

[11] *R. v. Wynyard* (1539) KB 27/1109, Rex m. 13^d. See also, *Spelman reports*, II, p. *301.*

The Refinement of English Criminal Jurisprudence 307

this was construed to mean a year before the blow (1534), so that the accused could not have killed him.[12]

The Latin had to make sense throughout the indictment. Vocabulary, for example, was sometimes a problem. In about 1625 the infamous astronomer John Lambe was freed from one of his indictments for witchcraft because it said "*quod exercuit quasdam malas, execrabiles et diabolices artes anglice* witchcraft", and the Latin words were too vague to bear that sense.[13] Grammar was even more important. If two or more individuals were indicted and the verb of accusation was in the singular, all could claim to be discharged because it did not appear which of them was being accused.[14] Ambiguities could not be resolved by common sense. In 1535 another fortunate murderer escaped because the indictment said he had knocked a man's brains out at Didlington, and that the man had died at Ixburgh, "so that the accused then and there murdered him." The words "then and there" referred grammatically to Ickburgh, and not to Didlington where the fatal blow was struck.[15]

Perhaps the most extreme example of false Latin occurs in a case reported by Spelman in 1532. The prisoner was indicted of murder by a coroner's inquest upon the view of the body of Thomas Pheyse. The indictment began "*quod quidam Thomas Pheyse in pace domini regis existens . . .*" instead of "*quod quidem Thomas Pheyse in pace domini regis existens . . .*," so that the deceased was "a certain Thomas Pheyse being in the peace of the lord king." Since this Thomas Pheyse might have been a different person from the Thomas Pheyse upon whose death the coroner was sitting, it did not sufficiently appear of record that the coroner had jurisdiction to take the indictment for the death of Thomas Pheyse and so the prisoner was released. The murderer—and for all we know he was guilty—was saved by a single letter.[16]

Examples of a similar nature could be multiplied from any period in the sixteenth and seventeenth centuries, and later. Hale complained that in his time "more offenders escape by the over easy ear given to exceptions in indictments than by their own innocence . . . to the shame of the government, and to the encouragement of villainy, and to the dishonour of God."[17] The "over easy ear to exceptions" weakens the evidence of the rolls for the purposes of legal history. Although the difference between form and substance is often plain, it is by no means always so, and of course records might suffer from both formal and substantive errors at once. We know from a comparison of reports and

---

[12] *R. v. Halle* (1536), KB 27/1101, Rex m. 2^d.
[13] *R. v. Lambe* (undated), Noy 85. Lambe was murdered in 1628.
[14] *R. v. Sturgys* (1539), Spelman, *Enditement*, pl. 27.
[15] *R. v. Deynes* (1535), *ibid.*, pl. 20.
[16] *R. v. Rogers* (1532), Spelman, *Corone*, pl. 23(1).
[17] M. Hale, *Historia Placitorum Coronae* (1736), II, p. 193.

records that the court might consider errors other than those assigned,[18] and thus the record of a decision to quash is never conclusive of what appears on its face as the reason. Moreover, exceptions were recorded only when they were allowed; if they were rejected, the prosecution took its normal course.[19] A record which reveals only decisions in favour of the defendant presents a very one-sided picture.

There is an even worse historical problem posed by records of decisions to quash. We know that many slips of the very kind which we find to have been fatal in some cases were in others overlooked or even amended.[20] There was an element of discretion, and this casts some uncertainty over all the decisions. Was the eleven-year-old scholar actually released for humanitarian reasons? We know that "scholar" was held good enough three years earlier when applied to a violent Oxford don.[21] Was the gentleman who set not a pudding by the great seal discharged because the judges felt the indictment was stretching treason too far but felt it impolitic to say so explicitly? Did the courtier who was discharged on a technical ground benefit from the letter we know was written to Cromwell on his behalf?[22] Could the April 1535 killer have persuaded any court to place such an unlikely construction on his indictment if he had not managed informally to disclose something more weighty in mitigation? We do know, but only because a reporter tells us, that a judge in 1490 searched out a slip in an indictment for burglary because he had taken pity on the accused where only a few pence worth of wool had been stolen.[23]

One hundred years later, we find the King's Bench countenancing the discharge of a clerk convict for "exceptions" to the indictment, because he has been indicted "by practice" and "found guilty upon small evidence."[24] Obviously the exceptions were not related to the real ground for quashing the conviction. In a case of 1617, where a prisoner who had been convicted of some religious opinion against preaching had made an appropriate submission, the court ordered counsel to find an error so that the prisoner could be discharged.[25] And as late as 1640, when a conviction was quashed for "manifest error," the party was allowed to submit affidavits showing that the under-sheriff had packed the jury:[26] a matter irrelevant to the alleged error. These instances give

---

[18] *Spelman Reports*, II, p. *301*.
[19] *Ibid.*, at pp. *301–302*.
[20] As to amendment, see *R.* v. *Delbridge* (1618), 2 Rolle Rep. 59.
[21] *R.* v. *Weston* (1536), Spelman, *Enditement*, pl. 24.
[22] *R.* v. *Delarever* (1534), Spelman, *Corone*, pl. 23; *Enditement*, pl. 17; *Spelman Reports*, II, pp. 283–284.
[23] *R.* v. *Barbour* (1490), Brit. Lib., MS Harley 1624, f. 3, quoted in *Spelman Reports*, II, p. *301*, n. 9.
[24] *R.* v. *Longe* (1596), Cro. Eliz. 489.
[25] *R.* v. *Atwood* (1617), Harvard Law School MS 114, f. 34, quoted below, p. 326, n. 3; differently reported in Cro. Jac. 421.
[26] *R.* v. *Stevens* (1640), Cro. Car. 566.

the impression of a procedure being distorted to enable convictions to be quashed or prosecutions stifled for extra-legal reasons, which in the days before appeals was not an unworthy use of legal pedantry. Yet we cannot be confident that decisions to quash always conceal some clandestine point of non-legal substance. Hale gives no hint that the procedure might be a subterfuge for achieving justice. In many cases the ethic of the sporting contest was enough to carry the day: if the Crown did not follow the rules it could be declared " out." It is the uncertainty which blurs the evidence for the legal historian.

Even where it is possible to establish a substantive ground for quashing an indictment, it is unlikely to have been such as added greatly to the development of jurisprudence. The reason is not because the indictment contained too much form but because it contained too little of the kinds of fact upon which legal distinctions rest. Take the indictment for murder. It contained no more by way of fact than an accusation that the defendant killed another, with details of date, place, the character and value of the weapon, the location and dimensions of the wound and the interval between the blow and the death. This was dressed up with a certain amount of legal verbiage. The deceased begins the story by " being in the peace of god and the lord king," while the defendant comes along " not having the fear of god before his eyes, but being moved and seduced by the instigation of the devil." The fatal blow is struck with force and arms against the king's peace, there must be an allegation of malice aforethought, and the essential word *murdravit* must appear in the conclusion. Of these trimmings, only the last two bore any real meaning. It was established well before 1600 that the law of murder protected outlaws, infidels and confessed felons;[27] so " being in peace " meant no more than that the deceased was not an alien enemy on the battle field. In 1660 a hopeful regicide argued that he did have the fear of God before his eyes when he tried Charles I; but the argument did nothing to improve his position.[28] The sacral phrase *vi et armis* had been dispensable since a statute of 1545,[29] and the concept of force had before that been sufficiently elastic to include the starvation of a dependent. Thus the only factual allegation in the indictment which distinguished murder from any other killing was the standard phrase *ex malicia precogitata*; but no particulars were ever given of malice aforethought and so the meaning of the phrase could not arise on a motion to quash an indictment.

Any other facts necessary to constitute murder were covered by the word *murdravit*. But for the same reason, the word itself being good on

---

[27] See *Spelman Reports*, II, pp. *305–307*.
[28] *R. v. Carew* (1660), in *State Trials*, V. 1052.
[29] 37 Hen. VIII, c. 8. There was, nevertheless, a view that the phrase was still essential: Hawkins Pl. Cor. lib. II, c. 25, s. 91.

the face of the record, there could be no discussion of those facts upon the indictment itself. Since everyone knew that killing was a constituent element of murder, there was little scope for developing the law of murder through discussing indictments. This is equally true of the other felonies. An indictment for theft had to allege a forcible taking and asportation of another person's goods; but the mental element and other constituents were totally obscured behind the vital but unilluminating word *felonice*. In burglary the legal element was represented by *felonice* or *burglariter*, while in rape it was sufficient to say *felonice rapuit* without even alleging any particular form of physical violation. These curt phrases were used to the exclusion of all else. In the words of Serjeant Hawkins, "no periphrasis or circumlocution whatsoever will supply those words of art which the law hath appropriated for the description of the offence."[30] The position did not change substantially between 1500 and 1848. Indictments do not, therefore, hold the key to the detailed development of criminal jurisprudence.

The Facts Revealed by the Evidence

The refinement of criminal jurisprudence could only occur through discussion of the full facts of individual cases. In civil cases this kind of refinement was brought about by special pleading, whereby the parties could place more of the facts on record than were mentioned in the plaintiff's declaration. But special pleading was not allowed in criminal cases, and to this day the only available issue in most cases is the general issue resulting from the plea of not guilty. The prevalence of the general issue does not, and did not, preclude consideration of the facts; it merely kept them off the record. The jury would want to know whether embezzlement by a servant was felonious theft, whether stealing from a church could be burglary, whether a crime of passion was murder. Such questions depended on the construction of terms of art such as *felonice*, *burglariter* and *malicia praecogitata*. The jurors might, of course, take it upon themselves to furnish the answers, preferring their view of justice to law. Or they might ask the judges. Very likely the judges would volunteer the information in any event. The judges would also be concerned with technical discrepancies between the indictment and the evidence. Was an indictment for killing with a gun supported by evidence of killing with a bullet from a gun? Was an indictment for stealing a cow supported by evidence of stealing a heifer?[31]

Difficulties of this kind arising upon the evidence were legal difficulties, and their solution brought about a separation of function between judge and jury. The judge would direct the jury as to the law,

---

[30] Hawkins Pl. Cor. lib. II, c. 25, s. 55.
[31] Both questions were answered in the negative: Brit. Lib., MS Add. 25228, f. 15; *R. v. Cook* (1774), 1 Leach 105 (statutory offence of cow stealing).

The Refinement of English Criminal Jurisprudence 311

and the jury would decide the facts. Since, however, the evidence and the judge's directions upon it were off the record, the jury always had the last word. The autonomy of the jury became a matter of constitutional principle in the criminal libel cases of the eighteenth century. Erskine, addressing the King's Bench in the Dean of St. Asaph's Case,[32] offered this explanation:

> We all know, that by the immemorial usage of this country no man in a criminal case could ever be compelled to plead a special plea; for although our ancestors settled an accurate boundary between law and fact . . . yet a man accused of a crime had always a right to throw himself by a general plea upon the justice of his peers. . . . The reason of this distinction [from civil cases] is obvious. The rights of property depend upon various intricate rules, which require much learning to adjust, and much precision to give them stability; but crimes consist wholly in intention, and of that which passes in the breast of an Englishman as the motives of his actions, none but an English jury shall judge. It is therefore impossible, in most criminal cases, to separate law from fact.

A decade later, after Horne Tooke's acquittal, medallions were struck with the legend "Not guilty say his jury, Equal judges of law and fact." The constitutional principle that a jury may acquit perversely has not been shaken. But it is not a corollary that judges must not lay down the law. Lord Mansfield achieved much of his reputation in commercial cases by shifting the balance between judge and jury so that the judges made more law. He thought criminal justice should be subjected to a similar process of legal refinement, and in reply to Erskine he argued:

> To be free is to live under a government by law. Miserable is the condition of individuals, dangerous is the condition of the state, if there is no certain law. . . . What is contended for? That the law shall be in every particular case what any twelve men, who shall happen to be the jury, shall be inclined to think.

The difficulty had arisen in cases of seditious libel because, unlike most other forms of indictment, the indictment for libel set out the text complained of in full. On Lord Mansfield's view, it was for the jury to say whether that text had been published, but for the court to decide whether the words amounted to a libel. In most other cases, the facts relevant to a disputed point of law did not appear on the face of the record, and there could be no proceedings in error if the court gave a wrong direction on the evidence. In nearly all cases, therefore, the legal function of the trial judge was confined to informing the jury as to the law. Whether the jury acted on the judge's information was important for the prisoner but of no legal significance. If law was made at all, it was

---

[32] *R. v. Shipley* (1784), in *State Trials*, XXI, 847. The passages quoted are in col. 923 (Erskine) and col. 1040 (Mansfield).

not made by judicial decision but by a judicial declaration to juries before they retired to consider their verdicts.

To what extent could it be said that criminal jurisprudence developed through charges to juries? The answer must depend on the extent to which such charges had any influence beyond the immediate business in hand. The certainty of which Lord Mansfield spoke was not in itself achieved by giving the decision to the judge rather than the jury. The judge was not subject to reversal on appeal, and if judicial views were subject to idiosyncratic variations the discrepancies might not even come to light save by casual conversation. Nevertheless, by the middle of the sixteenth century, and doubtless long before then, it was axiomatic that criminal justice should ideally be uniform. Sir William Staundford, addressing the reader of *Plees del Coron*, stressed the importance of the *leges coronae* and the need for the studious to have a ready command of them when they were sent to hear and determine capital causes. Lambard, Crompton and Dalton in their turn emphasized the importance of legal knowledge for magistrates. But if this law was only to be found in informal directions to juries it was somewhat loose and hardly amenable to scientific development.

At the beginning of the sixteenth century the law revealed in this ephemeral manner was described as "experience."[33] By its very nature, it has now been almost wholly lost: experience was not committed to writing. In Henry VIII's reign we find a few written reports of legal questions arising at trials but they are few and far between. Caryll reports a ruling by Fyneux C. J. on accessories in 1511, and a few years later Port took down a definition of treason by the same judge.[34] Brooke, in his abridgement, reports a ruling of Fitzherbert J. at Stafford assizes on petty larceny.[35] Spelman's are perhaps the first reports since the *Liber Assisarum* to include questions of criminal law arising at assizes. From the same period we begin to have detailed reports of state trials which include the judges' rulings on treason and related procedural points; but these are often garbled, and even such a well-documented trial as that of Sir Thomas More is open to conflicting interpretations.[36]

There is similarly scattered material for later Tudor and Stuart times. Thus, in a manuscript written by a Derbyshire barrister in 1562 we find a particularly detailed instruction by Dyer C. J. at Derby assizes on the subject of accessories, with a reference to a case "in experience" in Henry VIII's time on the same subject.[37] The best examples of

---

[33] See *Spelman Reports*, II, pp. *124*, n. 4, and *300*, n. 11.
[34] *R. v. Nubolt* (1511), Keil. 161, pl. 2; MS recently sold at Sotheby's.
[35] Brooke, *Corone*, pl. 85.
[36] See J. M. Derrett, "The Trial of Sir Thomas More," *English Historical Review*, LXXIX (1964), 449; and R. S. Sylvester and G. P. Marc'hadour (ed.), *Essential Articles for the Study of Thomas More* (London, 1977), pp. 49–78.
[37] Anthony Gell's MS reports, f. 170^v. The earlier case was that of Lord Dacre, noted in contemporary chronicles and cited at length in William Dalison's MS reports.

sixteenth-century gaol delivery reporting are Plowden's reports of some proceedings in Shropshire in 1553, and of the celebrated case of Saunders and Archer in 1574.[38] Plowden's meticulous care and editorial polish reveal a more refined consideration of legal problems than are indicated by other contemporary sources. *Saunders and Archer*, a celebrated case only because Plowden made it so, is still an authority on transferred malice in murder. As a printed source it stands almost alone, and yet it can hardly have been untypical. If Plowden had reported more of the like, the history of criminal law might have been different. But the hundreds of cases which might have received the Plowden treatment were relegated to experience and thereby lost to posterity. The most visible result of this body of experience is to be seen in the treatises of Crompton, Dalton and Hale, who drew heavily on charges or rulings made at gaol deliveries.[39] It was their selection, rather than the rulings at large, which influenced the future.

The development of the uniform kind of criminal jurisprudence envisaged by Staundford and Mansfield required a further element to be introduced into criminal procedure, some mechanism by which doubts and queries could be discussed centrally and resolved consistently. The criminal legal system had grown up very differently from the civil system for this purpose. An assize judge at *nisi prius* was merely conducting the trial stage of an action begun at Westminster, and the verdict had to be transmitted back in the *postea* before judgment could be given. It was therefore possible for motions to be made to the court *in banc* between trial and judgment, so that questions of law could be discussed by the full court with ready access to libraries and the collective wisdom of the legal profession. Criminal cases, on the other hand, began and ended in the country. They could be removed into the King's Bench by *certiorari*, but we have seen the limitations of that procedure for raising points of law. The mechanisms for achieving centralized discussion were not, therefore, formal legal procedures. They were not, as in civil cases, produced in response to the manoeuvring of inventive counsel. They resulted from the need which the judges themselves felt for uniformity in the administration of criminal justice.

The Inns of Court

This centralization of discussion probably began in the inns of court. The learning exercises in the inns seem always to have been slightly in advance of the courts in opening up new areas for legal refinement. It is possible that the procedures which altered the balance between fact and law were only developed once the inns had prepared the way by creating an intellectual framework in which more detailed legal decisions could

[38] Plo. Comm. 97, 473.
[39] Below, p. 328.

be reached. The predominant subject of the readings and moots was land law. But it is now clear that criminal law occupied an important place in the curriculum. Over thirty readings on criminal subjects have survived for the period 1485 to 1545,[40] and these are but a fraction of the total number which must have been given.

The texts of readings show a degree of sophistication with which a modern law lecturer would feel more than content. They show that many questions which were once thought to have been ignored until later centuries were commonly discussed before 1530 in the halls of the inns. It is true that some of the discussions have an archaic or academic flavour. Francis Mountford, for instance, was putting to his Inner Temple audience in Henry VIII's reign the ancient Roman problem of the ball thrown over a house which strikes the hand of a barber while he is shaving a customer, so that the latter's throat is accidentally cut.[41] But the readers, themselves often magistrates, also dealt with less unlikely problems and evidently drew on practical experience of legal difficulties. Since many of the audience would themselves require legal knowledge for use at the sessions, and could not buy it in books, we may be sure that the frequent discussion of crown law was a result of general demand.

When these learning exercises were at their zenith, the inns of court were in a very real sense sources of legal development. The common learning of the inns *was* the common law. The medieval judges, who had all been readers in their time, always deferred to that learning when it was clear and generally declined to resolve the ancient doubts of the law schools. In Tudor times, however, we begin to see a new emphasis on the role of the judge. Maybe the law was still " reason " rather than the will of the justices, but it was to the justices that men looked for reasoned statements of the law for the authoritative resolution of doubts. The common law was still notionally an immutable science learned through the exercises of the inns, but the judges were beginning to take on the positive responsibility of nurturing and expounding that law. The medieval notion of law as the common learning of the profession gave way to the modern notion of law as the command or declaration of a sovereign authority. The criminal law, like the civil law, had to come under the control of the twelve judges. The change is reflected in the textbooks.

The technique of the earliest books, such as Fitzherbert, is indistinguishable from that of the later readers, such as Marrow, Mountford and Brooke. Staundford's treatment is no different in substance, but it has ostensibly become a digest of judicial authorities.

---

[40] See " Appendix One: Readings on Criminal Law c. 1450–1550," in *Spelman Reports*, II, pp. *347–350.*
[41] D. 9.2.11; Bracton f. 136ᵛ, Mountford's reading, Brit. Lib., MS Hargrave 87, f. 177; *Spelman Reports*, II. p. *33*, n. 11.

The Refinement of English Criminal Jurisprudence 315

The most influential textbooks, such as those of Staundford, Coke, Hale and Foster, were in any case the work of judges and partook of their authors' authority. There is no time here to expatiate upon the subject, but it is worth remarking that the best textbooks on criminal law were all in their time masterpieces, and have had a more lasting influence than contemporary books on other subjects. The classical writers obviously made a substantial impression on criminal jurisprudence. But the shift from the communal learning of the inns to the individual reflections of a judge's study is not consistent with the notion of centralization and uniformity.

Reserved Cases

The judicial mechanism for achieving centralized discussion of criminal law was the reserved case. The assize judge who felt doubts about a conviction would respite execution and report the difficulty to his brethren in one of the Serjeants' Inns the next term. The technique is closely associated with the inns of court discussions, but whereas those had a classroom flavour, the Serjeants' Inn cases were real cases of life and death. There is no clear evidence that the reserved case was used before the sixteenth century, though it is possible that the King's Council had exercised some kind of supervision over the administration of criminal justice.[42] The year book for 1487 reports a discussion arising from some questions posed to the judges by the Recorder of London; but the fact that several reporters noted the incident, and that the rulings were still under discussion five years later, suggests that this may have been a novelty.[43]

A possible reason for the absence of earlier reports, and the dearth of later reports, is that the reporters were not usually judges and therefore had no knowledge of these exclusive assemblies. Certainly our first collection of Serjeants' Inn rulings was the work of a judge, Sir John Spelman. The emphasis at the meetings he attended in the 1530s was on legal doctrine: for example, the definition of burglary and riot, whether repentance between the deed and the death was a defence to suicide, and the effect of provocation in a crime of passion.[44] The best sixteenth-century collection was that compiled by William Dalison, a King's Bench judge from 1556 until his early death in 1559; the many criminal

---

[42] For early examples, see 26 Lib. Ass. 23; 27 Lib. Ass. 38. See also *Spelman Reports*, I, pp. 48, 60, and II, p. *278*. The role of the Star Chamber in developing the substantive law of misdemeanour was extremely important, and depended (like that of the Chancery in civil cases) on full investigation of facts without the constraints of formality. Space forbids elaboration of this theme here, but see T. G. Barnes, "Star Chamber and the Sophistication of the Criminal Law," *Criminal Law Review* (1977), 316.
[43] See *Spelman Reports*, II, pp. *166–167*.
[44] *Ibid*, p. *302*.

cases in his unpublished reports were all points discussed in Serjeants' Inn.[45] There were no comparable collections, so far as we know, for another two centuries; but many reserved cases will be found scattered through the published and unpublished reports of the seventeenth and eighteenth centuries.

By 1600 the procedure had to some extent been regularized by the increasing use of special verdicts. Before Elizabethan times, special verdicts in Crown cases seem to have been limited to verdicts of self-defence or misadventure in homicide, in which cases they were necessary to secure the forfeiture to the Crown notwithstanding the discharge of the prisoner. Except in those situations, they had not been a vehicle for legal refinement. The kind of special verdict which set down the facts as they appeared at the trial, and left it to the court to decide whether those facts supported the indictment, seems to have developed in the time of Elizabeth I at the same time as the parallel development in civil cases.[46] The special verdict was directed by the court in difficult cases, and was probably not volunteered by the jury. Most questions were therefore settled without using it.[47] Where a special verdict was taken, therefore, the circumstances invariably dictated a reference to the twelve judges. Whether it was common thereupon to remove the record into the King's Bench by *certiorari* has not been established. The reports suggest that it was, and if this is so then the *rex* rolls from Elizabeth I's time should prove to be full of jurisprudential information; they are a completely untapped source of legal history.

Special verdicts continued in use until the last century, especially in homicide cases, but they slowly gave way to cases stated. The reason is possibly that special verdicts, being part of the record, were treated with a strictness which could at times prove seriously limiting. The judge could not alter or depart from the verdict as found, for in law he knew nothing which had not been expressly found by the jurors. Hale said that in homicide cases it was so difficult to draw a special verdict that it was very rare for a question between murder and manslaughter to be decided in favour of murder.[48] The difficulty may be illustrated by two early eighteenth-century cases.

In 1701 a smuggler was indicted for murder, and the facts as found

---

[45] Brit. Lib., MS Harley 5141. This has never been published, but the present writer has prepared an edited transcript. There are a few Serjeants' Inn cases in the reports of another Queen's Bench judge, John Clench; several texts have survived.

[46] See *Spelman Reports*, II, pp. *157–158*. The reintroduction of special verdicts in all cases was sanctioned by *Burgh* v. *Warnford* (1553), Dalison MS reports, f. 12; and *Dowman's Case* (1583), 9 Co. Rep. 1.

[47] *R.* v. *Joyner* (1664) Kelyng 30, where the court said it was dishonourable to suffer a special verdict in a plain case and directed an acquittal; M. Foster, *Crown Law* (London, 1762), p. 256.

[48] *Historia Placitorum Coronae*, II, p. 305. A later exception is *R.* v. *Oneby* (1727), 2 Ld Raym. 1485, 2 Strange 766; but there the verdict took nearly a year to draw up (2 Strange 770).

specially were that his gang had been ambushed by customs men and that one of his men had fired a fusee and killed a fellow accomplice. The court discharged the prisoner because it was not found that the fusee was fired against the customs men or anyone else, and so it might have been an accident:

> this is matter of evidence for a jury to find the fact, and not for judges to intend it . . . [for] although the jury find matter of evidence enough for them to find the fact . . . such matter, though pregnant evidence, yet it cannot be enough to impower the judge to intend the fact, or condemn him as guilty of it.[49]

And in the case of the Warden of the Fleet in 1730, where it was found that the defendant's servant had kept a prisoner without fire, chamber-pot or close-stool for six weeks so that he died, and that the defendant knew the condition of the room and saw the prisoner there two weeks before his death but turned away, the court felt it unsafe to convict the defendant of aiding and abetting in the absence of a direct finding of knowledge:

> We are to determine upon facts, and not on evidence of facts. . . . It would be the most dangerous thing in the world if we should once give into the doctrine of inferring facts from evidence, which is the proper business of a jury and not of the court.[50]

Doubtless for this reason, it became more common in the eighteenth century for the twelve judges to be asked to consider points stated informally by the trial judge after a general conviction, without recourse to a formal special verdict. This was by no means an innovation, because Coke mentions that in 1611 a case was " delivered in writing to all the judges of England to have their opinions,"[51] and it was a natural development from the oral statement of cases by assize judges in the Serjeants' Inns in the sixteenth century. To what extent the practice had survived alongside the special verdict we do not know, and in the absence of records of stated cases we could not easily find out. But the establishment of a regular practice in the eighteenth century was related to the introduction of the judge's notebook. No notebooks are known before the 1690s, and it is doubtful whether trial judges kept notes before then. The innovation probably began on the civil side, where the judge's note formed the basis of a motion for a new trial. But its value in civil cases must soon have suggested an extension to the Crown side; the judge's note in Crown cases would also be useful in preparing recommendations for pardons.

The history of the procedure has still to be established. It appears

---

[49] *R. v. Plummer* (1701), 12 Mod. Rep. 627, *per* Holt C. J. Cf. Kelyng 109, 111 (" We are not to judge the law upon evidence of a fact, but upon the fact as it is found ").
[50] *R. v. Huggins* (1730), 2 Strange 883, 886, *per* Lord Raymond C. J.
[51] *R. v. Gore* (1611), 9 Co. rep. 81.

318   *The Legal Profession and the Common Law*

that the trial judge himself drew the statement of the facts and the legal problem which confronted him, and his clerk then copied it out for circulation to the twelve judges. The case was then listed for hearing at Serjeants' Inn, or in the Exchequer Chamber, and counsel were heard. The judges usually announced their decision peremptorily, with a collegiate inscrutability more akin to Continental than English traditions, leaving reporters to supply explanations from the previous arguments. Some judges kept private collections of these cases, and a series of reserved cases from 1765 was printed by Thomas Leach. But the only official record, if so it may be called, is a series of six notebooks still in the custody of the Lord Chief Justice. The series begins in 1757,[52] and is a collection of neat transcripts of cases stated to the twelve judges with the resulting orders added. It appears to be official from the appearance in the second volume of an order signed in autograph by all the judges. East apparently made use of the manuscripts in compiling his *Pleas of the Crown* (1803), and we know for sure that they belonged to Lord Tenterden, who became Chief Justice of the King's Bench in 1818.[53] It was Lord Tenterden who brought the series to an end in 1828, because it had by then become the practice to place the original cases directly in the reporters' hands and so the decisions were all published. Finally, in 1848, the informal meetings were put on a formal footing as the Court for Crown Cases Reserved, and the cases and orders were thereafter preserved in official custody.[54]

Criminal Law and the Historian

After this outline of the techniques used for refining criminal jurisprudence, and the sources in which the results may be found, it is time to reflect on the use of this material to the legal historian. Since very few of the unpublished sources have yet been thoroughly studied, this is a largely speculative exercise. But we can attempt some preliminary comments. Although the legal system developed the means for delving further into the facts of individual cases in order to make refinements of doctrine, it does not follow that those means were commonly or consistently so used. Against the natural desire for more law and legal certainty, there was the opposing principle or policy that some matters are best left to the common sense of twelve good men and true. There is no logical way of striking the balance between these conflicting policies. The autonomy of the jury is not easily reconciled with the sovereignty of law. Nowadays, by giving a convicted person a right of appeal on points

---

[52] The writer is grateful to the Librarian of the Supreme Court and the Lord Chief Justice's clerk for allowing him to examine these books in 1974. Volume I was missing in 1974. The periods covered by the other volumes are: II (1785–1801), III (1801–14), IV (1814–18), V (1818–23), and VI (1823–28).
[53] See below, p. 327.
[54] Public Record Office, London, KB 30 and 31.

The Refinement of English Criminal Jurisprudence 319

of law, and allowing the law to be discussed upon the whole transcript of the trial evidence, we have practically abandoned the attempt to draw any line. As a result we have a criminal law of exceeding complexity to deal with situations little more complex in their essentials than those of the eighteenth or sixteenth centuries.

Whether justice is now more easily attained is not the present question. What we should note is that in the period under review these questions of policy were not seen exactly as we see them. Convicts did not have a right of appeal, except for errors on the face of the record. Juries probably did not volunteer special verdicts, and a special verdict was not directed if the law was clear. The court was the only judge of clarity, and judges were well aware that clarity was often defeated by quibbling over factual distinctions. The criminal law was therefore subjected to refinement only where the court thought it necessary or desirable to run the risk of endangering its clarity. The historian should not, therefore, assume a steady progress from vague rules of thumb to complicated and refined jurisprudence. Some problems which trouble twentieth-century lawyers were never argued at all, either because they had not yet occurred to anyone or because they were regarded as factual rather than legal problems.[55] In other areas the process could be put into reverse, by leaving all to the jury and turning a blind eye to potential legal conundrums. And to the extent that refinement was promoted by the judges, their achievements were largely at the mercy of law reporters, whose work in the field of criminal law was consistently mediocre or worse. Sir Michael Foster had reason to complain even of respectable reporters such as Coke and Strange. Referring to *R. v. Reason and Tranter* (1722)[56] he said:

> The circumstances omitted in the report are too material, and enter too far into the merits of the case to have been dropped by a gentleman of Sir John Strange's abilities and known candour, if he had not been over-studious of brevity. Imperfect reports of facts and circumstances, especially in cases where every circumstance weigheth something in the scale of justice, are the bane of all science that dependeth upon the precedents and examples of former times.[57]

The intervention of Parliament, on the other hand, tended always to be jurisprudentially retrograde. The draughtsmen of the hundreds of penal statutes passed in the eighteenth century seemed incapable of general-

---

[55] There was, for instance, no significant development in the principles governing insanity and criminal reponsibility until the nineteenth century, when advances in psychiatry provided the lawyers with new problems to argue over: see N. Walker, *Crime and Insanity in England. Volume I: the Historical Perspective* (London, 1968).
[56] 1 Strange 499.
[57] *Crown Law*, pp. 293–294. He also contrasts Coke's report of *R. v. Royly* in 12 Co. Rep. 87 with the better report in Cro. Jac. 296.

ization, and many a criminal no doubt had reason to be grateful for the arbitrary precision of statutory definitions. Sir Michael Foster, perhaps the greatest criminal lawyer of the century, contrasted acts made " upon the spur of the times " with the common law, which was " the result of the wisdom and experience of many ages." The books had become encumbered with special acts and a variety of questions touching their true extent because Parliament had produced too many " penal statutes made upon special and pressing occasions, and savouring rankly of the times."[58] The truth of his lament will be obvious to any reader of the statutes at large.

It may be helpful to illustrate some of these general remarks by taking a specific point of law and following its progress through the centuries. It is difficult to suggest a point of law which could qualify as "typical," and we are compelled to find one which is not clouded by undue complexity. Let us take the simple question of whether stealing fixtures or parts of buildings can amount to felony. The point does not seem to have been discussed in the year books or early readings. The medieval authorities established only that growing crops and trees could not be the subject of larceny, and that the non-larcenable character of land attached also to title-deeds and their boxes.[59] It might seem obvious, especially to anyone acquainted with Roman law, that buildings and fixtures should be treated in the same way; and perhaps the proposition was too obvious for discussion in the medieval period. Yet the character of the wrong was arguably different. Why should a man who stole human artefacts, such as lead from a church roof, be treated as leniently as a man who stole apples from an orchard or reaped beyond his own furrow? The man-made edifice was built from chattels, whereas natural produce and minerals had no existence apart from the land before severance. Let it be said at once that such arguments are wholly absent from the law books. But we know that the point did arise, and it must have been arguable for some such reasons. The courts had to decide between substantial justice and clear but obstructive technical doctrine.

The first relevant case to have been discovered illustrates the use of *certiorari* to quash an indictment. Both the record and the report have recently been printed.[60] Edward Gardiner was indicted in 1531 for feloniously stealing stones from the town walls of Oxford, the goods and

---

[58] *Crown Law*, pp. 299–300.
[59] 12 Lib. Ass. 32, also reported as T. 12 Edw. III, Fitzherbert, *Corone*, pl. 119 (trees); Y.B. 49 Hen. VI, 14, pl. 9, also reported as *R.* v. *Wody* (1470) 47 Selden Soc. 124 (title-deeds); readings summarized in *Spelman Reports*, II, p. *317*. Minerals were presumably treated in the same way. But according to the custom prevailing in the lead mines in the Denbigh lordship, a third offence of abstracting ore was treated as felony and the offender was to be pinned to a windlass with a knife through his hand and left to his fate.
[60] *R.* v. *Gardiner* (1533), Spelman, *Enditement*, pl. 11; *Spelman Reports*, I, p. 99, and II, p. 295.

chattels of the mayor and commonalty. The indictment was removed into the King's Bench and the record shows merely that it was quashed in 1533 for insufficiency. Spelman's report states the reason very simply as being that the stones appeared from the indictment to have been annexed to the walls and were therefore part of the freehold, which could not be stolen. The only case cited was that of taking trees, probably a reference to the year book of 1338. A formal decision such as this ought perhaps to have settled the matter. But the profession did not have ready access to the rolls, and Spelman's reports were not printed till 1977. In any case, the formal obstacle to conviction was probably removed in later years by the simple expedient of omitting from the indictment any indication that the property stolen was fixed to the freehold. Thus, the recently published calendar of Sussex indictments shows that a man was sentenced to death at East Grinstead in 1582 for stealing two sheets of lead, the property of the parishioners of Sandhurst;[61] almost certainly the lead came from the church roof, but the indictment (by omitting to say so) was good on its face. The only effect of *certiorari* had been to drive more facts off the record.

The next stage in legal development would be for questions to be raised on the evidence. We cannot know whether the fixture point was taken in the Sandhurst case. It might have been. It might even have been raised at trials before 1533. But it might just as well have been thought that sacrilege was deserving of death, and the jury ought to be left to reach a sensible verdict on the merits, without introducing legal problems which would never have occurred to their minds spontaneously. Certainly if the assize judges did not take the point, it could not be raised later, and few would be the wiser. Our present concern is not whether the prisoner could always have advantage of the rigour of the law, which clearly he could not. The question is whether the law would ever receive discussion off the record, and there is enough evidence to show that it did. The first reported case arose at the Old Bailey in 1553:

> A man was indicted at Newgate before the justices for stealing lead from a church, and the justices were in doubt whether this was felony or not. After consultation between them it was agreed by them all that it was not felony, their reason being that it was something that could not be separated from the freehold but was a thing annexed and fixed to the freehold, and therefore no felony in law. Therefore he was discharged from his arraignment for felony: but he found surety to answer for the trespass. And it was said by [Sir Robert] Broke, Recorder of London, and serjeant-at-law, to him at the bar, that his desert was as much as if it had been felony.[62]

---

[61] *R.* v. *Wynne* (1582), in Cockburn, *Sussex Indictments*, p. 171, no. 864. The Judges were Southcote and Gawdy JJ.
[62] Brit. Lib., MS Hargrave 388, f. 240 (translated from the French).

322   *The Legal Profession and the Common Law*

Here it is significant that, although the detailed arguments are not preserved, the judges unanimously overcame their feelings as to the justice of the case in order to give effect to the law as they perceived it.

Eight years later the same point arose for discussion in the Inner Temple, and was noted by Anthony Gell of that inn:

> Note that on Candlemas day [1561] Estoft put this case to Carill and Calow: a man took slabs of lead from Pontefract Castle, the castle being covered with it, and unfolded the lead outside the castle and stole it. And Carill asked whether there was any mean time between the unfolding of the lead and the taking of it; and Estoft said not. And Carill said that if a man cuts my tree and at the same time steals it, because it is annexed to the freehold [the act that is] all done at one time is not felony; but if he cut the tree at one time and let it lie and took it at another time it is felony. And Estoft said that before the justices of assize at York it *had* been taken for felony.[63]

This dictum suggests that some justices of assize had few scruples about doing rough justice, but again we see that the discussion is circumscribed by the medieval authorities. The point about the interval of time between severance and asportation had been expressly made in the 1338 case and repeated in the readings. The main interest of the report is that it shows an assize ruling being debated and criticized by the benchers of an inn of court. But Gell's note was in a private notebook and has not left his Derbyshire home to this day. The orthodox learning propounded by Carill was upheld by other judges in Elizabeth I's time and was eventually approved in print by Crompton:

> To take lead from the church which it covers is not felony, for it is part of the freehold. And so it was adjudged at Derby before Sir James Dyer at the assizes there around 20 Eliz. Reg. [and] adjudged accordingly in 30 Eliz. at Stafford assizes before Windham.[64]

What finally settled the point was not so much that it was ruled by individual judges, but that some of the rulings were approved and published by the textbook writers. The distinction taken by Carill likewise became received learning when a late edition of Dalton's *Countrey Justice* reported a ruling in 9 Charles I upon an indictment for stealing lead from Westminster Abbey. The conclusions of these writers, based on gaol delivery experience, were repeated by Hale and Blackstone with little or no amplification, and the common law may be said to have reached the limit of its development. The clarity of the law is borne out by the practice. In the Middlesex records there is an indictment of 1610 for stealing 237 pounds of lead belonging to Sir Owen Oglethorp. Although the bill does not say the lead was on the

---

[63] Anthony Gell's MS reports, f. 136 (translated from the French).
[64] R. Crompton (ed.), *Loffice et auctoritie de justices de peace* (London, 1617 ed.), f. 17, pl. 33 (translated from the French).

roof, the words "feloniously stole" were struck out and the prisoner was convicted of trespass and sentenced to the pillory:[65] a clear indication of the rule of law being applied even where formal propriety did not require it. In Old Bailey practice thereafter, tearing off and stealing lead was treated as a misdemeanour punishable by fine.[66]

The last part of the story follows from the decision of Parliament in George II's time to close what had come to be regarded as a technical loophole in the law of theft. It was all very well to exclude a 6d. capon from the ambit of grand larcency, but 3 cwt of lead was another matter. By a statute of 1731 it was made felony—and subject to seven years' transportation—to "steal, rip, cut, or break, with intent to steal, any lead, iron bar, iron gate, iron pallisade, or iron rail whatsoever, being fixed to any dwelling-house, outhouse, coach-house, stable... or to any other building whatsoever."[67] The measure might seem an obvious concession to common sense. But the decline in quality of the legal principle is deplorable. The new felony does not extend to fixtures other than those made of lead or iron, though it will be extended (again somewhat arbitrarily) to copper in 1781.[68] It does not extend to iron fixtures other than those specifically mentioned, and therefore does not include iron window casements.[69] It is not even clear whether "any other building" includes a church. By the modern principle of construction known as the *ejusdem generis* rule, it ought not to do so. In the 1780s, however, the twelve judges will rule that it does. So far as we can tell, this was the first occasion that the twelve judges were convened to discuss the stealing of fixtures, and all we have to show for it is an unreasoned ruling on the meaning of three words in a statute.[70]

In the history of this specimen point of law, the critical period for the common law seems to have been the sixteenth century, when it was still open to discussion and relatively free from known authority. By the second quarter of the seventeenth century the law was clear and no further refinement was ever thought necessary. The next step was innovative reform, at first in a piecemeal way in the eighteenth century, and then (in 1968 in England) by abolishing the distinction between realty and personalty for the purposes of the law of theft. If we had time

---

[65] *R.* v. *Yonge* (1610) in *Middlesex County Records*, II, p. 60.
[66] E.g. *R.* v. *Gwin* (1672), *ibid.*, IV, p. 37 (fined £3. 6s. 8d. for taking 90 lb. of lead belonging to the Earl of Shaftesbury); *R.* v. *Allyson*, (1679), *ibid.* 142 (fined 34s. 6d. for taking 300 lb. of lead belonging to Dr. Barebones).
[67] 4 Geo. II, c. 32.
[68] 21 Geo. III, c. 68.
[69] *R.* v. *Hedges* (1779), 1 Leach 201; *R.* v. *Senior* (1788), *ibid.* 496. In the second case the window fixture was stolen from Elm Court, the property of the benchers of the Middle Temple.
[70] *R.* v. *Parker and Easy* (1782), 2 East Pl. Cor. 592; *R.* v. *Hickman and Dyer* (1785), *ibid.* 593, 1 Leach 318; *R.* v. *Isley* (1785), 1 Leach 320n. The only point of jurisprudential interest in these cases concerned the laying of property; since it was part of the realty it could not be laid as the goods and chattels of the parishioners or churchwardens.

to follow other points of law through the centuries we should not be surprised to find wholly different patterns.

At present the legal history of crime has not been carried to the stage where definite assertions can be made at any level of generality. Perhaps it has suffered in this area, as in others, from the deterrent effect of a superabundance of unpublished and admittedly rather hieroglyphic material. Who knows what could be unearthed from the *rex* rolls and manuscript reports and notebooks? He who undertakes the search should be encouraged to stand above the minutiae, to ignore the statistics, to suppress his morbid or prurient curiosity and to attempt to answer some of the wider jurisprudential questions about the relationship between trying facts and developing the law. The line beyond which legal certainty seems more a hindrance to justice than a help is ever shifting. This moving line legal historians should be trying to trace, though as yet no one knows what shape it will describe. Although historians in general will never be seduced from the more colourful aspects of the history of criminology, it is much to be hoped that the upsurge of interest in criminal history will inspire one eccentric scholar to take up the pencil and make a start on the history of English criminal jurisprudence.

NOTE

An important monograph on the role of the trial jury in the development of criminal law has recently appeared: T.A. Green, *Verdict according to Conscience. Perspectives on the English Criminal Trial Jury 1200-1800* (1985).

18

CRIMINAL JUSTICE AT NEWGATE 1616-1627
Some Manuscript Reports in the Harvard Law School

The criminal law has hardly received generous attention from the English legal historian, and parts of the subject, especially in the post-medieval period, still lurk in the gaslight of Stephen's era. There are signs of increasing interest among local and social historians, and more records of criminal sessions are consequently finding their way to the presses. A certain amount of law is to be learned from these records—even though that is not the main object of their publication—but there is a danger that the proliferation of record material will obscure the need to understand the thinking behind the law and practice of the criminal courts. The record, though invaluable for statistical purposes, tells little or nothing about the interpretation of the terms used in the indictment, the nature of the evidence given, the rules of evidence (if any), the considerations which weighed with the jury, the influence of the judge, or the extent to which strict law might be softened by discretion. Such questions are notoriously difficult to answer, but until the answers are found there can be no history of English criminal law. The law reports in print have not afforded as much help in understanding the criminal law as they have in understanding the civil law. Reporters usually attended only in Westminster Hall, where the criminal fare was limited. Apart from the trials at bar, which probably drove most reporters into the Common Pleas or back to the Inns of Court, the criminal cases normally encountered would be appeals of felony and indictments removed into the King's Bench by *certiorari*. Appeals became less common in the sixteenth and seventeenth centuries, and were untypical in that pleading and counsel were allowed. Motions to quash occasionally involved points of substance, as where a novel offence was laid (*1*), or where a jury had already found the particular facts specially (*2*). But, since most indictments followed settled formulae, the majority of motions went to defects of form—such as the inadequacy of the addition or the

---

(*1*) E.g. *R.* v. *Holmes* (1634) Cro. Car. 376, W. Jones 351.
(*2*) E.g. *R.* v. *Mackalley* (1611) 9 Rep. 65, Cro. Jac. 279; *R.* v. *Royley* (1612) Cro. Jac. 296, Godbolt 182, 12 Rep. 87, Harvard Law School [hereafter H.L.S.] MS 109, f. 14, H.L.S. MS 2077, f. 109, H.L.S. MS 2080, ff. 79v-80; *R.* v. *Ashfield* (1623) 2 Rolle Rep. 362; *R.* v. *Holloway* (1628) Palmer 545, Cro. Car. 151, W. Jones 198, H.L.S. MS 106, f. 191v; *R.* v. *Cooke* (1638) Cro. Car. 537, W. Jones 429, H.L.S. MS 1167, pp. 166-167, 210. The special verdict was probably usually directed by the court, so that the question could be debated by the judges. See, e.g., *R.* v. *Carnabye* (1641) H.L.S. MS 113, p. 96: ". . . quia ils resolve pur aver le opinion del autres judges al Serieants Inne ils direct le matter destre trove specially".

specification of time or place, or false Latin—rather than points of law. We may well be deceived if we take such cases at their face value, for there is evidence that the court was more willing to find errors if there were some ulterior reason for so doing, such as a feeling that the conviction was unsafe on the merits (*3*). Such an approach may have been morally justifiable when there were no better ways of upsetting unsafe verdicts, but it contributed nothing to jurisprudence because like cases were presumably not always treated alike.

Where, then, was the criminal law made and developed before the establishment of the Court of Criminal Appeal?

The first "sources", if so they may be called, were the readings in court. Miss Putnam's edition of Thomas Marow's reading *De Pace* (1503) (*4*) has shown how sophisticated the criminal law was in the days before *Staundford,* but it is still not generally realised that in the late fifteenth and early sixteenth centuries there was widespread discussion of the criminal law at readings in all the Inns of Court. The loss of texts has been severe, but the writer has so far found thirty different lectures on various aspects of the criminal law delivered before 1540, none of them ever printed or even noticed in print by modern scholars. One reason for this concentration on Crown law may have been the failure of conventional processes of law-making and learning, which were based on the science of pleading, to illuminate the subject: special pleading was not generally permitted in proceedings on indictment. The men of court were closely involved in the administration of criminal justice, as local justices and commissioners if not as counsel, and the surviving readings show that they took that side of their work very seriously. The importance and content of the early readings is too large a subject to be enlarged upon here (*5*), but the influence of the Inns of Court upon the law must never be underemphasised. The Inns enjoyed an important advantage over the university law schools of today in that from the lecturers of one generation were invariably drawn the judges of the next.

The second source of criminal law was the informal discussion of cases reserved by assize judges for consultation with the other assize judges in Serjeants' Inn: a practice which evolved into the Court for Crown Cases Reserved. Cases from the sixteenth century may be found

---

(3) See *R.* v. *Longe* (1596) Cro. Eliz. 489, H.L.S. MS 105, f. 49v; *R.* v. *Atwood* (1617) H.L.S. MS 114, f. 134 ("pur ceo que le party ad fait son submission . . . le court rule que le councell de le party serchera pur auter error al intent que le party puit estre discharge"); *R.* v. *Stevens* (1640) Cro. Car. 566. If the court had taken the same view in all cases, there would have been few convictions. In *R.* v. *Delbridge* (1618) 2 Rolle Rep. 59, where a word had been omitted in joining issue, the Clerk of Assize was ordered to amend the record, "car auterment infinite indictments per negligence del clerk serra void".

(4) In *Early Treatises concerning Justices of the Peace* (1924), being vol. 7 of Oxford Studies in Social and Legal History.

(5) The writer will be attempting a preliminary account in the preface to his forthcoming edition of the *Reports of Sir John Spelman.*

scattered in the printed reports (6), though the first printed collection of reserved cases was that of Thomas Leach, which began as late as 1765 (7). There survive in manuscript, however, some important notes of Serjeants' Inn cases, the earliest of which are those of Sir John Spelman [d. 1545], Sir William Dalison [d. 1558], and Sir John Clench [d. 1607] (8). These were all written by judges who attended the discussions and noted them alongside reports of civil cases. Some of them will be published in the near future, and it seems appropriate to postpone further discussion until this has been accomplished. The reports of reserved cases underwent a decline in the eighteenth century. The question reserved by the trial judge was submitted to the central assembly (by now confined to the judges of the three common law courts) as a written "case", and usually nothing but the outcome was thought to be worth preserving. Doubtless there were normally arguments, a few of which were reported, but the profession seems to have preferred the simplicity of case and (unreasoned) answer. Until the institution of the Court for Crown Cases Reserved by statute in 1848, when official records of these decisions belatedly commenced (9), the judges kept their own books of reserved cases. The six notebooks, beginning in 1757, which are now in the custody of the Lord Chief Justice of England, may have been regarded as an official version (10). That series was brought to an end by Lord Tenterden "after the regular practice was established of placing the original cases in the reporters' hands" (11). Whatever status these volumes may have had, it is known that other judges kept similar books, some of which have survived (12).

(6) For the 16th century, see, e.g., Moo. 8, pl. 9; Dyer 179, 183, 203, 205, 214; Popham 42, 52, 96, 107; 1 And. 114; Savile 47, 59, 67; 4 Rep. 41. Dyer makes it clear that it was a meeting of assize judges (including, therefore, law officers and serjeants): see 183, 203, 214. The preparation of written cases may have been established by 1611 (see *R. v. Gore*, 9 Rep. 81), but the cases were not preserved in official custody and are now lost.

(7) *Cases in Crown Law* (1st. ed., 1789), later extended to 1815. The earlier cases in the first volume (from 1730) are Old Bailey Sessions.

(8) Spelman: Brit. Lib., MS Hargrave 388. [The writer is engaged on an edition of Spelman's Reports.] Dalison: Brit. Lib., MS Harley 5141. Clench: Yale University Library, Law MS G.R. 29.5.

(9) 11 & 12 Vict., c. 78. The cases and orders are now in the Public Record Office, classes K.B. 30 and 31.

(10) They belonged to Lords Tenterden [C.J.K.B. 1818, d. 1832] and Denman [C.J.K.B. 1832, d. 1854], but their earlier history is obscure. East used the Lord Chief Justice's manuscripts in preparing his *Pleas of the Crown* (1803): see p. xiii of the introduction. In the later 19th century they fell into private hands, and in 1901 Joyce J. purchased them and gave them to the holders of the office of Lord Chief Justice of England in perpetuity. In Vol. II, pp. 86-87, is a rule made in Hilary Term 1792, signed in autograph by all the judges. (The writer is grateful to the Librarian of the Supreme Court for bringing these books to his attention.)

(11) Note signed by Lord Denman, 27 December 1845, in Vol. VI, f. 1.

(12) Lord Denman, *ibid.*, refers to a hiatus "which will doubtless be easily supplied by Tindal C.J. and Parke B." At Harvard there is a similar odd volume, labelled "MS. Crown Cases Reserved Vol. VI" which belonged to East: H.L.S. MS 4043. This seems in turn to have been compiled from the MSS of Lawrence J. and Heath J. East, *loc. cit.* in note 10, says that each judge received a copy of the written case.

328   *The Legal Profession and the Common Law*

The third source of criminal law was the discussion of points arising at the trial itself. Although it might be objected that rulings of single judges were not authoritative, earlier writers on the criminal law—such as Crompton *(13)*, Dalton *(14)*, and Hale *(15)*—made use of such material, and Sir Matthew Hale obviously regarded Newgate practice as authoritative *(16)*. Published reports of such cases were late in appearing, the first being *Kelyng* (1708) *(17)*, which contains Old Bailey cases of Charles II's reign. By that time it was common for practitioners and judges to keep notes of evidence and of law in reporters' pocket-books, and some of the more authoritative notes (such as Kelyng's) were copied and circulated in fair manuscript copies. Foster cited from five such collections in his *Crown Law (18)*; some of these survive, and there are others, though no modern writer has used them. The object of the present study is to venture into a slightly earlier period to see what, if anything, may be found in the manuscript reports. Reports of ordinary criminal cases written from the legal point of view—excluding, that is, state trials and trials reported because of the factual interest of the evidence—are certainly not common. An opportunity of working through the manuscript law reports in the Treasure Room of the Harvard Law School has, however, revealed a few which must, by virtue of their unusual character, be of interest.

The first, and longest, group of cases is found in a volume of reports *(19)* in the handwriting of Arthur Turnour, a young barrister of the Middle Temple (later a serjeant-at-law), whose library is preserved

---

(13) An analysis of the cases cited in Crompton's *Justice of the Peace* (1617 ed.) shows the following distribution of first-instance cases: Stafford (15), Derby (5), Newgate (4), Warwick (3), Chester (3), Nottingham (2), and one each at Greenwich, Norwich, Taunton, Exeter, Rochester, and York. The dated cases are all within the period 1576-1602.

(14) Most of the first-instance cases in his *Countrey Justice* (1630 ed.) are from Cambridge Assizes, which Dalton attended as a justice: see pp. 29, 30, 305 (1615), 255 (1616), 260, 266 (1617), 93 (1618), 268, 269, 297 (1619), 46, 268 (1620), 30, 31, 262 (1621), 28, 89 (1622), 268, 269 (1624), 93, 262, 263 (1627), 32, 97 (1628), 27, 75, 98, 288, 303 (1629), 35, 130 (1630). There are also two Suffolk cases: pp. 300, 334.

(15) See *History of the Pleas of the Crown* (1778 ed.), i, 36, 369, and 513 (Aylesbury); i. 25 (Thetford) and 467 (Norwich); i. 431 (St. Alban's); i. 636 (Northampton); ii. 39 (Suffolk); ii. 311 (Oxford); ii. 358 (Cambridge). Newgate cases (1661-1673): *ibid.*, i. 373, 119, 303, 214, 477, ii. 303, 312, i. 464, 134, 483, 524, 304, 537, 555, ii. 304. [Listed in chronological order.]

(16) See, e.g., *ibid.*, i, 544: "For authorities, 1. It hath been the constant practice at Newgate . . . and this Mr. Lee, the secondary there for above thirty years, hath attested openly in court there oftentimes before myself, and divers others."

(17) J. Kelyng, *A Report of Divers Cases in Pleas of the Crown* (1708). The reports purport to be taken from the autograph manuscript in the possession of the Chief Justice's grandson. At the end were added three "modern" cases (1696-1707).

(18) See the Preface, p. iv, and pp. 231, 217, 242, 280, 292, 353, and 373. The five authors were Chapple J. (d. 1745), Denton J. (d. 1740), Dodd C.B. (d. 1716), Price J. (d. 1733), and Tracy J. (d. 1735). Some of Dodd's reports survive in MS Hargrave 70-71, and H.L.S. MS 1169.

(19) H.L.S. MS 112, pp. 295-299.

intact at Harvard. Turnour is not necessarily to be accounted the author, though it is more than likely that he was. The reporter attended a session at Newgate in the summer of 1616 (*20*), and noted the points of law which arose there, presumably for his own instruction. It is a remarkable fact that although the records of the Middlesex cases in the 1616 sessions have been calendared in print (*21*), none of the eighteen cases in the report is positively identifiable there. Neither of the two named defendants is to be found in the calendar, though their absence is explicable either by reason of the hiatus of several days in the extant records or by reason of their indictments having been found in London rather than Middlesex. The impossibility of identifying the remainder (although most of their cases probably are in the calendar) demonstrates clearly the truth of the above proposition that the records themselves do not tell us the details which interested contemporary lawyers. The other feature of general interest is that, although there are no arguments by counsel (except in the two indictments for misdemeanour), the judges nevertheless concerned themselves all the time with legal and procedural refinements, evidently before a critical audience. The initiative did not rest solely with the judges: in some cases we find the jury raising the legal question or sticking on a point of law (*22*), while in others the discussion is promoted by the clerks. The rulings seem to be in accord with the law and contemporary notions of justice, though the trial judges were less inclined to favour mere technicalities than the King's Bench seems to have been. The disinclination to assist the proven criminal to escape his deserts was tempered throughout by humanity, a quality especially evident in the 1625 case arising from an industrial strike, when the judges effected a wage settlement to the satisfaction of all concerned. The latter case shows that the court preferred discretion to fixed penalties, and the discretionary control over the exercise of benefit of clergy—which appears in a telling account of the reading-test as applied by Thomas Coventry—gave a limited control even in cases of felony. The availability of clergy underlies much of the legal discussion about the lines between burglary and simple larceny, and between murder, petit treason, and manslaughter. We are also provided with an explicit example of a jury valuing stolen goods at 10d. to reduce the offence to petit larceny. It is known from the records that only one-fifth of the prisoners indicted were sentenced to death (*23*), and the proportion actually executed was no doubt smaller.

The reports, though brief, are so plainly self-explanatory that it seems better to print them in full, with notes where appropriate, than to

(*20*) The cases at the very end seem to have been added between 1616 and the Long Vacation of 1618.
(*21*) W. Le Hardy (ed.), *Middlesex Sessions Records* [hereafter M.S.R.], Vols. III (1937) and IV (1941), cover the period 1615-1618. The records for 15-16 May and 25-26 June 1616 are lost.
(*22*) Cf. *Anon.* (1617) 2 Rolle Rep. 2; *R.* v. *Page* (1633) Cro. Car. 332.
(*23*) W. Le Hardy, M.S.R., III, p. ix.

work them into a commentary. To the 1616 reports have been added three notes of slightly later date, two of which are taken from other manuscripts in the Turnour collection (*24*), and the third from a volume primarily devoted to Star Chamber cases 1624-1640 written by a member of Gray's Inn (*25*). Abbreviations have been extended, and punctuation introduced to accord with modern usage, but the original orthography has been preserved. The passages in law-French, being readily understood, have not been translated. All the footnotes are additions by the editor.

THE REPORTS

[1] (*1*)
Matters aveignants al Sessions al Newgate

Nota que est clere per nostre livers come appeirt in *Stamford* (*2*) que si home soit atteint de felony per judgment que il ne poit estre arraigne arere apres pur auter felony pur ceo que il ad judgment del vie et member devant sinon que soyt en cas de treason. Mes est usuall al Newgate apres que home est convicte de felony per verdit pur luy arraigner arere pur auter felony. Issint nota que un convict sera auterfoits arraigne pur auter felony, mes nemi home attaint, que touts foyts est apres judgment. Issint semble que home utlage pur felony poit estre arraigne, car doit aver judgment de vye et member et le judgment sur le utlary n'est forsque pur le contempt. *Vide Perkins* fo. 6, 1 H.7. 8, et *Stanford* (*3*). *Tamen vide Fitzherbert N.B.* 144 f. (*4*), que ne sont forsque 3 brefes d'eschete et *quare utlagatus fuit* est un de eux: *ideo quere* si quant [*sic*] est utlage si ceo ne soyt un attainder, car ascuns ont dit que donques poit tryer les accessoryes. Et *quere* si home ne forfeit ses ters per le utlarye tantum, car semble per le brefe d'eschete que cy, sans ascun judgment de *sus. per coll. Ideo quere,* car *Perkins* fo. 6 dit que la doit estre judgment done de mort, nient obstant le utlary, ou auterment n'est ascun attainder. Auxi *quere,* si le principale soit convict per verdit et nul judgment done, si le accessory poit estre arraigne sur le utlary tantum devant attainder per judgment de vie. *Ideo quere.*

(*24*) H.L.S. MS 106, ff. 294v-295; H.L.S. MS 109, f. 106v.
(*25*) H.L.S. MS 1128, ff. 1v-2. The volume belonged to James Wright [1643-1713] and William Bromley [1664-1732], and remained in the possession of the Bromley-Davenport family at Baginton Hall until 1903. It was sold at the Bromley-Davenport Sale at Sotheby's on 8 May 1903, lot 414, and purchased by the Harvard Law School soon afterwards.

(*1*) H.L.S. MS 112, p. 295.
(*2*) *Plees del Corone* (1574 ed.), ff. 107v-108.
(*3*) *A Profitable Booke of Master Iohn Perkins* (1621 ed.), f. 6r; [?] H. 1 Hen. 7, 13, pl. 27; W. Staundford, *op. cit.* in last note. See also *Stone's Case* (1562) Dyer 214, pl. 48-49.
(*4*) *New Natura Brevium,* f. 144 F.

[2] (5)
Matters de Corone al Sessions de Newgate
En le vacacion apres cest terme Trin. 14 Jacobi.

Un feme que fuit un servant fuit arraigne pur embleer de divers choses de sa mistres et sur le evidence fuit prove que el avoit un trunke ove un lock in la meason de sa mistres in que el garder ses proper choses come apparell etc. et que el emblea les choses contein en l'endictment esteant en le meason et mitta eux en le truncke and then lockt the truncke lou sur un serch ils fueront trove. Le Jury en cest cas depart de le barr et reviendront et demand le advise del court, entant que ne fuit prove que le truncke fuit remove hors del meason al ascun temps. Mes Coventry (*6*) que fuit le Judge *hac vice* in le absence del Montague Recorder de London (*7*) direct le jury pur ley que ceo fuit felony, coment que les biens ne fueront remove hors del meason et lieu lou ils fueront feloniousment prise. Car ils fueront prise *animo fellonico,* que appeirt per le mitter eux en le truncke at apres denying de eux (*8*). Per que le jury trove luy culpable et accordant el avoyt judgment et fuit execute. Et Jones (*9*) le comon sergeant, esteant deputy a le Recorder al darrein sessions adevant, done autiel direction al Jury en un case l'ou un feme vient en un draper's shoppe et demand le pryce de certein clothe et made shew to buy, but while the draper was busy in serving or bargayning with some other Customer the woman conveyes a peice of stuffe under her coates; but she was not cunning enough to carry it handsomly away, for she was espied and taken with it, and for that she was arraigned and the jury was satisfied to finde her guilty, but found the stuffe but of the value of 10d. and so made it but petit larceny.

Three men were endicted of burglary, and for stealing divers goods out of the house. The evidence proved that one only brake the house and tooke the goodes, and after shared them with the rest that stood without. The jury founde hym only guilty of the Burglary that entered; the rest they found guilty of felony (*10*), so that they were capable of clergy. But Coventry was of opinion, and so directed the Jury, that forasmuch as they were all present they were all guilty of burglary. And so the jury found them (*11*).

(*5*) H.L.S. MS 112, p. 296.
(*6*) Thomas Coventry [1578-1640], who succeeded Montague as Recorder for a short time later in the year.
(*7*) Sir Henry Mountague [later Earl of Manchester, d. 1642], King's Serjeant, Recorder of London 1603-1616. He became Chief Justice of the King's Bench on Coke's removal in November 1616.
(*8*) Cf. 27 Ass., pl. 39. This accords also with the manuscript readings of Richard Littleton (1493), William Wadham (1520), and Francis Mountford (1519 or 1527).
(*9*) Thomas Jones, Common Serjeant of London [d. 1625].
(*10*) I.e. simple larceny, which was clergiable.
(*11*) The implication is that they changed their verdict upon the judge's direction, which was possible so long as the verdict was not entered of record. The direction accords with the law: M. 11 Hen. 4, 13, pl. 30, *per* Huls J.; Cromp. Just. 32; Fitz. Abr., *Corone*, pl. 187.

Two were arraigned for burglary, and another was endicted and arraigned as accessory after. And uppon the Evidence yt did not appeare that the accessory had any knowledge that the principalls had broken a house and stolne the goods which he receaved, but that he barely receaved the felons and the goods. The Jury found the principalls guilty of burglary, and the Accessory of felony only, etc. Peters (*12*) directed the Jury for law that they ought not to distinguish whether the party were accessory to the burglary or to the felony only, but Justice Stone (*13*) was in doubte. Et le jury were very much unsatisfied, yet they went and afterwards retorned and found the accessory guilty of accessory to the burglary. *Quere* if there be not a difference betweene an accessory before and an accessory after in Burglary? Also *quere,* if a man do receive and comfort one who hath murdered J.S. uppon malice forethought, without notice that yt was done uppon malice, but only that he had killed him, whether the Jury can find him accessory to Manslaughter only? It seems they cannot. *Vide* Dyer, bone cases lou le servant fuit absent et l'estranger present; et semble que si un ad receave biens al value de j^d. come accessory, nient sachant que plus fuit emblea, et en verity plus fuit emblea, est un accessory al felony et nemi al petit larceny.

A man was bound in a Recognizance to the king to give evidence against another that was to have bene arraigned and receved his Tryall at this Sessions. The endictment, being preferred the last Sessions before, was removed by *cerciorari* [p. 297] into the King's Bench, and therefore the party that was bound did forbeare his apparance. But Mr. Coventry was of opinion that he had forfeited his Recognizance, for that he was bound to give Evidence for the king, which might be in other matters as well as in that particular endictment which ys removed.

The sherifs of London have all the forfeitures and fines within the City of London by charter, and not the king. Now the case was: a man was endicted uppon a penall law which gives a penalty of 10s. and was convict, but judgment was respited untill the next Sessions, which were not to be till after Michaelmas, at which tyme there would be a change of the sherifs. And therefore yt was moved on the part of the present sherifs whether, when the judgment shalbe given in the tyme when new sherifs shalbe in office, this fine shalbe to them that are now sherifs or to those that shalbe then sherifs. And, by the better opinion, the new sherifs shall have yt.

A woman, being endicted and arraigned and convicted by verdict, was demanded what she could say why judgment should not be given against her. Who answered that she was with childe, and so praied the benefit of her belly. Whereuppon the sherif forthwith impannel'd and retorned a Jury of women, who were severally sworne and charged severally to inquire whether she were with childe or not, and whether she were

---

(*12*) Not in Le Hardy's list of magistrates.
(*13*) Either John or Thomas Stone.

quick. And they departed into a private room together with the prisoner, and afterward retorned and gave their verdict that she was not with childe. Whereupon she had her judgment of death, and was accordingly executed (*14*).

A man, being arraigned, confessed the endictment and afterward, being asked what he would say why judgment of death should not be given against him, answered that he was not guilty and that his former confession was out of Ignorance and unadvised. But Mr. Coventry cyted the example of David with the Amalekite, *Samuel* 2, cap. 1, that his blood must be uppon his owne head. And the same exhortacion he used to one that was willfull and refused to plead directly, but would be tryed by God and the Bench (*15*).

One that was convict of Manslaughter praied his Clergy, and had it (*16*). But because it was in case of blood, Coventrye tooke the booke and chose a sentence or verse himself and gave it to the Ordinary, who shewed yt to the Prisoner and gave the booke to him to reade (*17*). And Coventry gave command to remove hym from the common place where usually they stood, and to set him apart from other the standers by, to the ende no man might prompt him, and comanded him to reade alowde—which the prisoner did, distinctly and well. And then Coventrye assigned hym another place, which he also read very well. *Quere* whether this course be usuall, forasmuch as the Prisoner did reade the first place assigned him well, whether he ought to be putt to reade againe in another place? But clearly if it had bene entered, *Quod legit ut Clericus,* he ought not then to have had another assigned him.

Two men were fallen out uppon malice forethought uppon a particular and speciall matter betweene them. They were reconciled and contynued in love and friendshipp together 2 or 3 years. And afterward, uppon a soddain conference about the old busines, they fell at variance againe and the one killed the other. Whether this were murder or Manslaughter was the question. But cleerely if the quarrell had bene about some new matter it had bene but manslaughter. But it was ruled in the King's

---

(*14*) This may be *R.* v. *Alice Foster* (5-6 September 1616): M.S.R., III, 303. There were two similar cases the following year: M.S.R., IV, 116, 237. The repreive was only available if the prisoner was found quick with child, though Hale said he had "rarely found but the compassion of their sex [i.e. the jurors] is gentle to them in their verdict, if there be any colour to support a sparing verdict": *History of the Pleas of the Crown,* c. 58. See also Fitz. Abr., *Corone,* pl. 168. For a successful plea of pregnancy in 1616 see M.S.R., III, 247. See also note 23, below.

(*15*) A refusal of trial was always treated as a refusal to plead, though strictly it was not quite the same thing: see P. 4 Edw. 4, 11, pl. 18; T. 14 Edw. 4, 7, pl. 10.

(*16*) This may be *R.* v. *Godfrey* (15-16 May 1616, and later), M.S.R., III, 250.

(*17*) It was for the court, and not the ordinary, to assign the verse: T. 9 Edw. 4, 28, pl. 41; M. 2 Ric. 3, 22, pl. 53. It is interesting to see that the court might stil exercise its discretion, and that the neck-verse was not invariably selected. It looks as though the court would have been more generous if the case had not been one "of blood". A prisoner who did not read the first time might, after a hurried education, be given a second chance: *Anon.* (1561) Dyer 205, pl. 6.

Bench that where there was an ancient quarrell betweene two concerning a matter and afterward they two meete sodenly and contend about another new occasion without mencion of the former, and thereuppon heate groweth and the one killeth the other, this is murder, because the old quarrell contynued without reconciliation (*18*).

This vacacion one Harwood, by the permission of one Mr. Kareck an utter-barrister of the Middle Temple (*19*), lodged in a chamber in the Vine Court and there he built a fornace and coyned money. And, being apprehended by Mr. Calthorpe (*20*) and other gentlemen of the Temple in the very act of coyning, he was com- [p. 298] mitted to prison, and at this Sessions endicted and arraigned before Mountague Recorder of London and was found guilty, and had his judgment to be drawne and hanged. And accordingly he was executed. And Mr. Kareck was also endicted and arraigned with him for the same offence, but he was acquitted, so for this time escaped—but was hanged afterward for another offence, which was (as I remember) a Burglary (*21*).

Three men were arraigned jointly for one and the same offence. The one stood mute, viz. the first. And, by Long Clerke of the Peace of Middlesex, which was not denyed by any other, there can be no proceeding against the other two uppon this endictment.

Note also by Mr. Long, Clerk of the Peace for Middlesex, if a woman stand mute at her tryall or will not plede directly, she shall have judgment of peine fort et dure as well as a man (*22*). Which thing he affirmed that he had seene in experience often at Newgate. And also he said, and no man contradicted, that if a woman be to have judgment of peine fort et dure, she shall not have the benefit of her belly. The reason is, because of her willfull contempt of her tryall. *Vide Stamford* (*23*), que le feme n'avera le benefit de sa belly forsque un foits.

A gave *B* uppon a sodein falling out in the king's highway a blow uppon his head and felled hym to the ground. And as he lay a cart-Wheeie went over his body without the carter's knowledge, and brake 4 ribbes, whereuppon *B* presently died. Now, whether the stroake was the occasion of the death or only the occasion of the fall (and the cart the occasion of

---

(*18*) The King's Bench case may be *R.* v. *Taverner* (1616) 1 Rolle Rep. 360. Cf. Hale, H.P.C., c. 36, who puts these cases, explaining Dalton, *Countrey Justice* (1630 ed.), pp. 239-240.
(*19*) Admitted 16 February 1606/07, called to the Bar 8 July 1614, expelled 7 February 1616/17 (presumably for his criminal activities): *Middle Temple Admission Register*, I, 88; C. H. Hopwood (ed.), *Calendar of Middle Temple Records* (1903), p. 45.
(*20*) Probably Henry Calthorpe of the Middle Temple, later Recorder of London (*infra*).
(*21*) He was convicted as an accessory to burglary in December 1617, but respited then: M.S.R., IV, 302.
(*22*) Accord. *Jane Wiseman's Case* (1598) 2 Inst. 177.
(*23*) *Plees del Corone* (1574 ed.), f. 193v. This only meant that execution would not be further postponed if she became pregnant while in custody: Staundford makes this clear by saying that the gaoler should be fined for keeping her "cy remissement que el ad ewe le company d'homme". If she were pardoned, and later convicted of another felony, she could have the benefit again.

the death) it was very doubtfull uppon the evidence. But the Jury were directed for law that if the cart alone were the cause of the death, and not the blowe, that yet forasmuch as the death ensued by reason of the blow that it was manslaughter in *A* that gave that unlawfull blowe which was the occasion of the death. But it was farther said to the Jury that if they found neither the stroake nor the cart to be the occasion of the death, yet they must then finde by what meanes the death came. And afterward the Jury brought in their verdict that the bruse of the cart only was the cause of the death of *B*, and so no manslaughter in *A*. *Quere* icy whether here be any deodand in the case, forasmuch as yt is manslaughter in *A* (*24*).

A man lived in adultery with the wife of J.S. and they both conspired his death, to the end that, J.S. being taken away, they both might marry together. Now the houses of the adulterer and of J.S. joyned, so that there was but a slight partition-wall betweene a chamber in the house of the adulterer and the chamber of J.S., wherein he lodged. And the devise agreed uppon betweene the adulterer and the wife of J.S. [was] that a little hole should be made in that particion-wall, no more then would serve to putt into yt the nose of a dagge, at which hole he might shoote and kill J.S. as he should be going into bedd. Which was accordingly putt in practise, and J.S. was wounded therwith very greivously but not killed. For this fact the adulterer and the wife of J.S. both committed to the Gaole at Heartford, and at Lent assises last this matter came to be examined and tryed before Mr. Justice Houghton, who, notwithstanding that J.S. the husband was yet alive, caused an endictment to be drawne against the adulterer and also against the woman for burglary. And they were both found guilty and executed. Which, being reported to King Jeames, was commended by him for an excellent peice of justice. *Quere* si la feme fuit present et endicte come un principall, ou absent et endicte come accessory? *Quere* si la feme poit estre endicte come principall ou accessory al burglary fait en le meason son baron? Car *vide Stamford* 27 (*25*), feme covert ne poit embleer les biens son baron, et coment el prist les biens le baron et eux done al auter, le donee ne poit estre felon de eux (*26*). *Et vide* 13 Ass. 6, Broke *Corone* 77 (*27*), si home prist la feme d'un auter *cum* [p. 299] *bonis viri* ove le assent de le feme, ceo n'est felony; mes si le prisell soit encounter la volunt de la feme ceo est felony en celui que eux prist. Et en le principall case, si la feme ne poit estre principall en burglary al meason de son baron, semble que el ne poit estre accessory (*28*). *Tamen quere*, car *vide* Dyer

---

(24) This may be *R.* v. *Bull* (1617), M.S.R., IV, 142.
(25) *Plees del Corone* (1574 ed.), f. 27r; H. 21 Hen. 6, Fitz. Abr., *Corone,* pl. 455.
(26) Accord. Spelman, *Corone,* pl. 54 (not yet printed). *Aliter* if the stranger were present at the taking; he was then a felon, but the wife not.
(27) *La Graunde Abridgement* (1573), f. 182v, glossing 13 Ass., pl. 6.
(28) In the case of a servant letting in a burglar, Dalton says the servant is only guilty of larceny: *Countrey Justice* (1630 ed.), c. 99. But Hale says the servant must also be a principal burglar: H.P.C., c. 48.

fo. [ ] (*29*), que feme en cas de murder poit estre accessory al murder de son baron, et uncore el ne poit estre principall, mes ceo est petit treason en luy, *causa patet* (*30*).

Nota que a cest darrain assises al Winchester cest cas happen: que un servant que viva en le meason ove son master ala en le nuicte en le bedchamber de son master ove entent et resolucion pur luy tuer. Et il wound luy en un greivous maner, mes ne donera luy ascun mortall plage, esteant prevent per le resistance d'auters servantes en le family. Et pur cest offence un endictment fuit frame vers luy de burglary, et il avoyt judgment de mort, coment que le master recover. *Quere* le ley in ceux cases (*31*).

A man was borne deafe, and so by consequent dumme, and this man had committed a burglary and was committed to Newgate, and at the Sessions there it was resolved by the Recorder and the whole bench that in this particular case the law was deficient. For this man can not be arraigned and tryed by signes for his life (*32*). *Vide* Fitzherbert, tit. *Ley* (*33*), *homo mutus et surdus* (*34*) gage son ley per signes. *Vide Perkins* (*35*), son grant est bone et luy lyera. *Vide Stanford* 150 (*36*), si home estoit mute un enquest

---

(*29*) R. v. *Saunders* (1574) Dyer 254, 332: but it was there said that the woman was accessory to murder and not guilty of petit treason.

(*30*) There is a different version of this case written in the margin of British Library, MS Lansdowne 1098(2), f. 170*v*: "Nota en un case al Hertford Assizes devant Justice Haughton cest case happen. 2 neighbors lived so neere together that nothing parted there lodgings butt a thinn clay wall. The on neighbor fell into such a league with the others wife as between them they conspired the death of her husband. To effect which this wife acquainted her avowterer in what part of the chamber her husband was used to stand when he undrest himself to go to bedd, against which place the avowterer by agreement between the wife and him did boare a small whole throughe the wall att which he did watch against the time that the husband of the adulteress shold come to undress himself for his bedd, and when the good man cam and had undressed himself and stood in his shirt att his usuall place by the wall where the whole was boared the adulterer that had watched for him did through the hole discharge a pistoll against him, intending to kill him. Butt the adulterer nott being able to take a perfect ayme, and the goodman being in his shirt, the bullett tooke the foults of his shirt which carryed itt only through sum part of his body without doing of him mortall hurt. Butt the goodman escaping this danger, and understanding the conspiracy between his owne wife and her adulterous neighbour caused them both to be bound over to the Assizes, where Justice Houghton hearing the evidence caused the man to be indited of Burglary (the fact having bin committed in the night) and they were both found guilty and suffred. Which case and the judgment upon itt King James commended as the most rationall of any that he had heard in the common law. Per Jermin in son charge al Lancaster Assise, Lent 1647."

(*31*) This seems to be *R.* v. *Haydon and Edmunds* (T. 1618) Hutton 20. Same point, Kelyng 67.

(*32*) Hale said the point was undetermined: H.P.C., ii, c. 43. Cf. 26 Edw. 3, Broke Abr., *Corone*, pl. 217.

(*33*) Fitz. Abr., *Ley*, pl. 64; S.C., Y.B. 18 & 19 Edw. 3 (Rolls Ser.), p. 291. He took the oath by kissing the book, and Stonore C.J. warned him: "Ones forsworne, ever forlorne."

(*34*) Neither the report nor the *Abridgement* speak of a deaf person.

(*35*) *Profitable Booke* (1621 ed.), f. 5*v*, pl. 22.

(*36*) *Plees del Corone* (1574 ed.), f. 150 C, D. *Aliter* in treason: *Anon.* (1561) Dyer 205.

de office doit estre retorne pur enquirer si il estoit mute per fraud ou per l'act de Dieu. Per que semble que sil fuit per l'act de Dieu que il sera discharge. *Quere*. Mes en le principall cas le party fuit mise al meason de correction la al remayner.

[3] *(37)*

Al Sessions de Newgate cest vacacion [Summer 1618] apres le terme certein speciall verdits fueront done, un de queux fuit que un home esteant al Tower pur clipping de deniers *(38)* (que est fait treason per statute) fait un escape, et puis est reprise, per que il est endicte pur le clipping et auxy pur l'enfreinder del prison, per severall endictments. Et il est acquite del clipping et trove culpable del enfreinder del prison. Et, tout cest matter esteant trove alarge, le question fuit si cest enfreinder del prison fuit treason, il esteant acquite del principall? Et resolve que nemi, car l'acquitall del principall (esteant devant le conviccion sur l'escape) monstre sur le matter que il ne fuit unques eins pur treason. Mes s'il usset estre indicte pur lescape devant l'acquitall del treason, donques il usset estre treason solonques 7 & 8 H. 8, Crooke 187 *(39)*. Et l'acquitall apres del principall ne voet aver free luy, come est a veyer per 4 & 5 Ph. & Mar. Bendlos report.

Le second fuit: la esteant un strugling perenter deux homes, le burse d'un d'eux eschuast hors de son pocket al terr et l'auter ceo prist et alast son voy. Et le question fuit, si ceo fuit robery? Et resolve per Mountague Chief Justice et Sir Anthony Benne Recorder *(40)*, et le residue del court, que nemi, entant que le burse ne fuit prise de son person. Et uncore fuit agree que si un obviast auter home sur le voy et luy command a delyver son burse, sur que il prist son burse hors de son pocket et jecte ceo sur le ter, et l'auter prist ceo, ceo est robery, entant que le severance del burse de son person fuit pur pavour et terror fait a le owner *(41)*.

[4] *(42)*

This xxiiijth of Januarie 1624 [i.e. 1625 new style] being at the Sessions of the Peace held in the Old-Baylie before Sir John Gore Maior of London and others, there were three and thirtie embroyderers endicted for this, that contrarie to the lawes they had conspired together amongst themselves that they would not worke at theire trade under ij^s. *per diem*, viz. from 6 in the morning till 7 a clock at night, and for every hower after iiij^d. To this

---

(37) H.L.S. MS 109, f. 196v.
(38) This may be *R.* v. *Henry Reynoldes* (1618), M.S.R., IV, 368. Cf. M.S.R., IV, 347, where two suspects were discharged of assisting Reynoldes' escape from Newgate, "who was committed for clippeing of silver and did escape through a vault".
(39) *R.* v. *Cowley* (1516) Keilwey 186, pl. 3.
(40) Recorder of London 1616-1618 [d. 1618].
(41) See the old authorities collected and discussed in *Smith* v. *Desmond* [1965] A.C. 960.
(42) H.L.S. MS 1128, ff. 1v-2.

they pleaded ⟨not⟩ *(43)* guiltie. Theire counsell in extenuacion moved, that although *ignorantia juris non excusat,* yet in this case a man more learned then they might doubt whether the statute of 5 Eliz., cap. 4, had not repealed that of 2 E. 6, cap. 15. Sir Heneage Finch *(44)* Recorder said the court pittied the povertie of the menn, accepted and liked their confession of theire offence, and had consideration of the necessitie of theire labours att that tyme (for now were in hand divers robes belonging to noblemen that were going into France), and were willing that as theire masters so they, being jorniemen, should have benefitt; and therfore caused the endictment bee as for an offence at common lawe according to the booke 27 Ass. *(45)* amongst the articles there, and not upon the statute, for then the punishment there prescribed *(46)* must bee inflicted necessarily sans ascun mittigacion. Mes quant al supposicion de repeale, sans question cest statute 2 E. 6 nest repeal per [fo. 2] 5 Eliz. quant al conspiracies. Et per lorder del court ils fueront daver xx^d. manger et boyer pur chescun jour et nemy ouster, et iiij^d. pur chescun heuer de overplus et nemy ouster. Ove que touts parties fueront parbyen satisfie. Et les indictees [fueront lies] pur lour bone behaviour tanque al prochein Sessions sur lour recognizances.

[5] *(47)*

Nota at Newgate Sessions this matter fell out: Sir John Ashfield and John Bray being comming up to London at Marybone Parke Corner were sett uppon by one Robert Wright and others with purpose to have robbed them. And Bray had a blowe given hym on the side of his face wherby afterward he lost his eye; but, having a pistoll about hym charged with 2 bulletes, shott yt of and killed Wright the theef. And uppon view taken uppon the body all this speciall matter was found by the Coroner's enquest, which was certified at the Sessions at Newgate, and uppon this enquest Bray appeared. And the question was, what should be done? And uppon consideracion had of the statute of 24 H. 8, cap. 5 (which sayth that if any person or persons at any tyme hereafter be endicted or appealed of or for the death of any evill disposed person or persons attempting to murder, robbe, or burglarily to breake mansion houses as is aforesaid, that the person or persons so indicted or appealed thereof and of the same by verdit so found and tryed shall not forfeit and lose any lands, tenements,

---

(43) From what follows it seems they pleaded guilty.
(44) Recorder of London since 1620, serjeant at law [d. 1631].
(45) 27 Ass., pl. 44.
(46) £10 or 20 days imprisonment. The penalty was imposed on workmen who conspired not to work except at a certain rate. The statute of 5 Eliz. repealed all statutes concerning "the hiring, keeping, departing, working, wages, or order of servants, workmen, artificers, apprentices, and labourers."
(47) H.L.S. MS 106, ff. 294v-295. This is dated Trinity term 3 Car. 1 [probably Long Vacation 1627].

goods, or chattells for the death of any such evill disposed person in such manner slayne, but shalbe thereof and for the same fully acquitted and discharged in like maner as the same person or persons should be if he or they were lawfully acquitted of the death of the said evill disposed person or persons), it was agreed by the court that he should be arraigned uppon this endictment and that uppon his confession of it he shalbe discharged. But if the speciall matter had not bene comprised within the endictment, then he must have pleaded non culpable, and if the jury found the speciall matter, then the court ought to discharge hym. And the Recorder of London Finch was at first of opinion that, the speciall matter being conteined in the endictment, the court ought to discharge hym without any arraignment. But the other was conceyved to be the better way, and so uppon his confession he was discharged.

Reuben Hunt was endicted at the Sessions at Newgate for that he, the last day of December 2 Car., at the parish of St. Clement Danes in the com. of Middlesex, did of new erect and make a slaughterhouse and in that slaughterhouse divers oxen, cowes, sheepe and hogges and other beasts the said day and yeare and divers tymes untill the 26th. day of July caused to be killed, by reason whereof the excrementes of the said beastes so killed into the high strete and channells therof did descend and runne, wherby the ayre was corrupted and infected, to the common nusans of all his Majestie's subjects passing that way. John Stone *(48)*, being of councell for one defendant, tooke thys exception: that the offence laid in the endictment is the making and erecting of a new slaughterhouse, but this slaughterhouse is ancient, and therfore not the same entended by the endictment. 2. It appears uppon the evidence that this slaughterhouse was in leas at a certein rent and in the hands of a tenant when yt was erected, and then the offence was [not?] the act of hym that is endicted when it was first done. 3. The erection of the slaughterhouse and the contynuance of yt cannot be said to be nusans, but the running downe of the filth, and that is laid to be but as a conclusion *ex praemissis* and ys not laid in the endictment as a fact: and so, uppon the matter, no nusans is at all laid in the case at barr. Calthrop *(49)* al contrary: although yt was a slaughter-house before, yet it was not a common slaughterhouse, but only for private use for one or 2 butchers at most. But at the tyme layd in the informacion [*si.*] yt was becomme a common slaughterhouse for all, which uppon the matter is a new erecting and making of a slaughterhouse, and so the informacion [*sic*] good enough. *Vide* 14 & 15 Eliz. Dyer 319, 320 *(50)*; the new turning of the cocke made a new dyvercion of the water, although the cocke and pipe were made before in the tyme of another man. 2. Although the slaughterhouse were in the hands of a lessee when the first offence was

---

(48) Reader of the Inner Temple (Lent 1613); became a serjeant at law a few months before his death in 1640.
(49) Note 20, *supra.*
(50) *Moore* v. *Browne* (1572) Dyer 320, pl. 17.

done, yet the continuance of yt is a distinct offence and therfore he may well be found guilty for the tyme that the slaughterhouse was in the hands of the party endicted. And accordingly the court ought to sett a fine. 3. Although that the bare erection of the slaughterhouse be not in yt selfe a nusance, yet whereas by reason therof ys occasioned a defluxion and discent of filth, wherby the ayre becomes corrupted, yt is a nusance. *Vide* 4 Ass. *(51)* erection d'un lymekill. Et le defendant esteant trove culpable from the Annunciation till the 26th of July judgment was given against the party endicted and 100 markes fine sett uppon hym.*

NOTE

The Hertfordshire case reported on p. 335, *supra,* and on p. 336, note 30, is not to be found in the surviving Home Circuit files: J. S. Cockburn, *Calendar of Assize Records. Home Circuit Indictments ... Introduction* (1985), p. 13. For the rarity of such reports see *ibid.*, p. 14.

(51) 4 Ass., pl. 3.
* The above passages are reproduced by kind permission of the Harvard Law School Library.

19

THE LAW MERCHANT AND THE COMMON LAW BEFORE 1700[*]

IN 1845 a master of English commercial law wrote that there was "no part of the history of English law more obscure than that connected with the maxim that the law merchant is part of the law of the land."[1] Since then there have been detailed studies of the medieval law merchant and of the later development of English mercantile law,[2] but the precise status of the law merchant in England and the nature of the process by which it supposedly became fused with the common law remain as obscure as they were in 1845. The obscurity begins with the very concept of the "law merchant," which has been differently understood by different writers and continues to be used in widely divergent senses. Some have regarded it as a distinct and independent system of legal doctrine, akin in status to Civil or Canon law,[3] and perhaps derived from Roman law.[4] Others have supposed it to be a particular aspect of

---

[*] A preliminary version of this paper was delivered at the European University Institute, Florence, on 3 April 1979.
[1] C. Blackburn, *The Contract of Sale* (1845), p. 207; 2nd ed. (1885), p. 317.
[2] *E.g.* T. E. Scrutton, *Elements of Mercantile Law* (1891), pp. 4–16 (reprinted as "A General Survey of the History of the Law Merchant" in 3 Sel.Ess.Anglo-Amer.Leg.Hist. 7–15); A. T. Carter, "The Early History of the Law Merchant in England" (1901) 17 L.Q.R. 232–251; W. S. Holdsworth, *History of English Law*, Vol. I [1903], 1956 ed., pp. 526–544; W. Mitchell, *An Essay on the Early History of the Law Merchant* (Cambridge 1904); T. A. Street, *Foundations of Legal Liability* (Northport 1908), Vol. II, pp. 363–392; C. Gross and H. Hall, *Select Cases concerning the Law Merchant* (1908–32), 23, 46 and 49 Selden Soc.; W. A. Bewes, *The Romance of the Law Merchant* (1923); J. M. Holden, *The History of Negotiable Instruments in English Law* (1955); T. F. T. Plucknett, *Concise History of the Common Law*, 5th ed. (1956), pp. 657–670. The best account of the early development of mercantile instruments is still M. M. Postan, *Medieval Trade and Finance* (1973), Chap. II (first published in 1930); for others see Holden, *op. cit.*, p. 2.
[3] See F. M. Burdick, "What is the Law Merchant?" (1902) 2 *Columbia Law Review* 470–485 (reprinted as "Contributions of the Law Merchant to the Common Law" in 3 Sel.Ess.Anglo-Amer.Leg.Hist. 34–50).
[4] See T. E. Scrutton, *The Influence of Roman Law on the Law of England* (Cambridge 1885), pp. 177–186 (reprinted in 1 Sel.Ess.Anglo-Amer.Leg.Hist. 237–246). Carter, *op. cit.*, p. 240, says: "Possibly the law merchant was the channel through which the Roman law chiefly affected our law." And Sir Carleton Allen said the law merchant was "profoundly affected" by Roman law: *Law in the Making*, 7th ed. (Oxford 1964), p. 274. Mitchell, *op. cit.*, pp. 160–161, is guilty of equivocation on this: "Roman law was, in the main, the basis of the Law Merchant . . . But great as was the influence of Roman law, the customs and usages of the merchant himself remained the decisive factor . . . Roman law was the raw material of the Law Merchant, but that material the medieval merchant fashioned and framed as seemed good to him." (This assumes a rather surprising degree of legal erudition on the part of the medieval merchant.)

natural law, or the universal *ius gentium*, and as such akin to international law.⁵ Another school regards it as a form of immemorial custom, which by familiarity was eventually noticed by the common-law judges in the same way as the customs of gavelkind and borough English were judicially noticed, before 1926, without formal proof.⁶ Yet a fourth view, which was doubtless influenced by the seventeenth-century writer Malynes, is that the law merchant is the same thing as mercantile practice, the changeable usages of merchants.⁷ On any of these views, the law merchant could not originally have been "law" as far as the courts of common law were concerned. Whether or not it was law elsewhere, the law merchant at Westminster must have been—like foreign law or trade usage—a matter of fact to be ascertained by evidence or judicial notice. The difficult part of the story, given such assumptions as these, is that which seeks to explain how the fact somehow turned into law. It has been told in much the same way by all the modern writers, and what may be termed the orthodox version is set out most recently and cogently by Mr. Holden.⁸ In its essential features, Mr. Holden's account as far as 1700 follows Sir William Holdsworth and Judge Street, who wrote at the turn of the present century, and most of their basic assumptions may in turn be traced to the writings of Judge Cranch at the beginning of the nineteenth century. The orthodox story may be shortly summarised as follows.

Until the sixteenth century the law merchant in England was confined in operation to its own special courts, the borough and piepowder courts and the Court of Admiralty. In the sixteenth century the newly established action of *assumpsit* enabled the central royal courts to take over much of this business, the first recorded example of an action expressly founded on a bill of exchange being in an undated precedent of the 1590s in Rastell's *Entrees*, and the first reported example being in 1602. Soon after this happened, in the early seventeenth century, the pleadings in

---

⁵ This was a popular view in the seventeenth century: see Sir John Davies († 1626), quoted on p. 362 below; and the writings of Dr. Zouch, cited by Scrutton, 1 Sel.Ess.Anglo-Amer.Leg.Hist. 238–239. See also 1 Bl.Comm. 273. The doctrine has been revived by H. J. Berman and C. Kaufman, "The Law of International Commercial Transactions (*Lex Mercatoria*)" (1978) 19 *Harvard International Law Journal* 221, 224–229. ⁶ 1 Bl.Comm. 75.

⁷ G. Malynes, *Lex Mercatoria* (1622), which is not a law book but a compendium of current practice compiled by a merchant. For a judicial statement of the fourth view, see *Goodwin* v. *Robarts* (1875) L.R. 10 Ex. 337, 346, *per* Cockburn C.J., which is adopted in *Halsbury's Laws of England*, Vol. XII, 4th ed. (1975), p. 38, § 460. Postan, *op. cit.*, p. 61, says "everything which entered into the everyday practice of merchandise and was indispensable for the efficient conduct of trade was, *eo ipso*, part and parcel of merchant custom and thereby sanctioned by Law Merchant." See also Mitchell, quoted in note 4, above; and L. S. Sutherland, "The Law Merchant in England in the 17th and 18th Centuries" (1934) 17 T.R.H.S. (4th Ser.) 149–176.   ⁸ Holden, *op. cit.*, Chaps. II–III, esp. pp. 27–36.

Law Merchant and the Common Law before 1700 343

assumpsit were "simplified," following the recognition of a "novel principle" that mercantile custom could originate a legal duty upon which the plaintiff could declare in an action on the case. This, however, was attended by two technical difficulties arising from the common-law requisites of a valid custom. First, a custom had to be of immemorial antiquity; but this never gave difficulty in practice and, according to Mr. Holden, was eventually held to be unnecessary. Second, the custom had to be of local application; but in 1666, by "one of the boldest fictions known in our legal history," the courts declared that the custom was part of the law of the land and therefore applied to all persons, while in 1693 it was settled that such a custom did not need to be laid in any particular locality. The final stage was for the courts to take judicial notice of mercantile custom and to treat it as part of the law. This feat is usually attributed to Lord Mansfield:

> It was very largely as a result of Lord Mansfield's special jury system that it was found possible to "weld commercial usage into the main body of English law without the sacrifice of elasticity" [Fifoot]. His practice was to incorporate customs into his judgments, and so to establish them as binding rules for the future.[9]

Now, it is obvious from the law reports during his period of office, and from the flood of textbooks on commercial law which followed his retirement, that Lord Mansfield exerted a powerful influence on the commercial law of England and that he wished as far as possible to assimilate it to the laws of Europe. His technique involved not only special juries but the use of judicial notebooks to facilitate motions for new trials and thus to transfer many questions from the realms of fact to those of law. It is beyond the scope of the present paper to reassess this transformation, which may be illuminated by a study of Lord Mansfield's own notebooks [10] and similar unpublished sources. The present object is to reconsider the earlier and more fundamental part of the received story, which relates to the feat of incorporation rather than the subsequent detailed refinement.

It might seem absurdly heretical to question the almost universally accepted history [11] were not certain features of it very puzzling

---

[9] *Ibid.*, p. 114. See also, to the same effect, Scrutton, 3 Sel.Ess.Anglo-Amer.Leg. Hist. 13; Holdsworth, *op. cit.*, p. 572.
[10] E. Heward, "Lord Mansfield's Notebooks" (1976) 92 L.Q.R. 438–455.
[11] A. K. R. Kiralfy, *The Action on the Case* (1951), p. 169, says of the incorporation of the law merchant: "This is a substantive field of research which has been covered by Sir William Holdsworth and others and requires no further study before 1700." Against this somewhat dire warning, we may claim the support of two earlier American writers who dared to question conventional wisdom on the law merchant for reasons similar to those advanced here, but who did not

on their face. Why did it emerge as a " peculiar and novel principle " in the seventeenth century that a " custom prevailing between merchants could originate a legal duty "? [12] Is it implicit in that proposition that mercantile customs were somehow different in character from other customs, which the law had recognised since medieval times? And, if so, what kind of duty was it? It was not a " duty " in the technical sense, for which the action of debt would lie [13]; and therefore there is no analogy with the action of debt on a custom or with the seventeenth-century extension of *indebitatus assumpsit* to customary dues. Moreover, if the courts decided by a bold fiction that mercantile custom was part of the law, why did they not immediately take notice of it as law? The English courts have never admitted expert evidence as to the rules of the common law. Nor can a pure decision of law be regarded as a " fiction," which is a false pretence of fact.[14] On the other hand, there is an inherent inconsistency in supposing that mercantile custom was law and at the same time that it did not have to be immemorial. If the law merchant was not immemorial, but merely changeable usage, then it would have been difficult to square with the notion of an immutable common law. It has been suggested in modern times that " a commercial or other usage may be so often proved in courts of law that the courts will take judicial notice of it " [15]; but such a view leaves the courts in a logical trap when a usage once noticed is thought to have changed,[16] and it is probably more sound to confine the principle to immemorial local customs, such as those of gavelkind in Kent and market overt in shops in London. Shifting usages can hardly be treated as common law. They can explain contracts, but cannot create obligations. They derive such legal force as they have from incorporation, expressly or impliedly, in contracts and not from incorporation in the permanent

---

pursue the matter in historical detail: Dr. Hoffman, cited in J. Reddie, *An Historical View of the Law of Maritime Commerce* (Edinburgh 1841), pp. 427–428; J. S. Ewart, *An Exposition of the Principles of Estoppel by Representation* (Chicago 1900), p. 373. See also Sutherland, note 7 above.

[12] Holden, *op. cit.*, p. 31.

[13] *Anon.* (1668) Hard. 485, discussed on p. 360, below.

[14] Holden seems to admit this (*op. cit.*, p. 33, n. 5) when he adds the gloss, " surely this is what it amounts to? The courts declared the law merchant to be part of the ' law of the land ', *i.e.*, the common law. That it was not so, but was a separate body of doctrine with rules of its own is obvious . . ." (It is not obvious to the present writer.)

[15] *Halsbury's Laws of England*, Vol. XII, 4th ed. (1975), p. 49, § 479.

[16] See *Teheran-Europe Co. Ltd.* v. *S. T. Belton (Tractors) Ltd.* [1968] 2 Q.B. 545, 553, 558, where the Court of Appeal decided to disregard a usage which had been judicially noticed by Blackburn J., apparently on his own initiative. The " law merchant," on the other hand, cannot be extended or overridden by usage: *Edie* v. *East India Co.* (1760) 2 Burr. 1216; *Crouch* v. *Credit Foncier of England* (1873) L.R. 8 Q.B. 374, 386–387.

Law Merchant and the Common Law before 1700   345

law of the land.[17] Were it otherwise, merchants and others would be free to devise new forms of transaction which defy existing law, and entitled to have force breathed into them without the sanction of legislation. As Holt C.J. warned, in a famous passage which has been widely criticised and on this point largely misunderstood, it is not competent to private subjects thus to dictate changes in law to the courts.[18] It may be that Holt C.J.'s caution was not shared by Lord Mansfield. Professor Christian complained that the expression *lex mercatoria* had " very unfortunately led merchants to suppose that all their crude and new-fangled fashions and devices immediately become the law of the land: a notion which, perhaps, has been too much encouraged by the courts." [19] Yet Lord Mansfield's law was binding on his successors; and so, to the extent that it embodied mere current usage, it froze the practice of Georgian merchants as the permanent law of England. However, we are here concerned with the position down to the time of Holt C.J. And the central questions to be answered are these: had the " law merchant" any real existence as a source of law, and if so was it regarded by the common-law courts as law, custom or usage?

LAW MERCHANT AND THE MEDIEVAL COMMON LAW

It is possible to collect enough references to the *ley marchaunt* or *lex mercatoria* to indicate that medieval English lawyers regarded it as something different from the common law.[20] The most famous passage is in the Year Books, where Dr. Robert Stillington is reported as saying that *ley marchaunt* was the same thing as *lex naturae*, "which is a universal law throughout the world." [21] Nevertheless, it is far from clear that this law merchant was conceived of as a distinct body of substantive law. There were no doctors *in lege mercatoria*, and even the *ius gentium* was not taught

---

[17] *Halsbury's Laws of England*, Vol. XII, 4th ed. (1975), p. 4, § 405. *Cf.* the confusing assertion in H. E. Salt, " The Local Ambit of a Custom," *Cambridge Legal Essays*, ed. by Winfield and McNair (Cambridge 1926), p. 279, at p. 280, n. 3 (" a confused analogy to immemorial particular custom probably underlay the contention that the modern custom of merchants, as opposed to the ancient law merchant, could not be judicially noticed and adopted into the Common Law as a source of new rights. Of course, neither of these was required to be immemorial in the technical sense.")
[18] *Clarke* v. *Martin* (1702) 2 Ld.Raym. 757, 758 (" it amounted to the setting up of a new sort of specialty, unknown to the common law, and invented in Lombard-street, which attempted in these matters of bills of exchange to give laws to Westminster Hall "). For an anthology of strong attacks on this judgment (concerning promissory notes), see Holden, *op. cit.*, pp. 80–81.
[19] Note to 1 Bl.Comm. 75, ed. by E. Christian (1800). He concluded, " Merchants ought to take their law from the courts, and not the courts from the merchants."
[20] See F. W. Maitland, *Select Pleas in Manorial Courts* (1889) 2 Selden Soc. 132–134; Holdsworth, *op. cit.*, p. 543.
[21] *The Carrier's Case* (1473) Y.B.Pas. 13 Edw. IV, 9, pl. 5; 64 Selden Soc. 30, 32.

in the Schools. Most of the medieval literature consists in codes of mercantile procedure observed in particular cities and towns; and at this level, far from there having been a universal law throughout the world, the local variations seem as numerous as the coincidences. At the level of substantive principle, on the other hand, it is doubtful whether any distinctions were made at all between the law merchant and the common law. When medieval lawyers distinguished systems of "law" they usually had procedure in mind. Substantive justice was immutable, invariable and, of course, unattainable on earth; in the mortal world the quality of justice depended on the available mechanisms. The one surviving medieval English treatise on the *lex mercatoria* makes this point very clearly. There are, it says, only three differences between the law merchant and the common law: (i) the speed of process, (ii) the liability of pledges to answer, and (iii) the denial of wager of law as a means of establishing a negative.[22] It was the third rule which most often occasioned discussion in the common-law courts, because it enabled plaintiffs to prove informal contracts by tally or suit.[23] The difference was vital in practice, but it was a difference as to evidence and proof; there is no suggestion that the law merchant had its own substantive law of contract. Even more damaging to the traditional view is the discovery from twentieth-century record searching that the procedure of the law merchant was not at first regarded as being totally divorced from the procedure of the King's central courts.[24] In the thirteenth and early fourteenth centuries it was possible for the King to empower his own justices to proceed according to the law merchant, either by special writ or by commission[25]; and there was

---

[22] *Lex Mercatoria* [c. 1280?] printed in *The Little Red Book of Bristol*, ed. by F. B. Bickley (Bristol 1900), Vol. I, pp. 57, 58. The date is that suggested by H. G. Richardson, 37 *English Historical Review* 243 (*cf.* 17 *English Historical Review* 356).

[23] Y.B. 20 & 21 Edw. I (Rolls Series), 68; 21 & 22 Edw. I (Rolls Series), 74, 458; *Gren* v. *Berewyk* (1311) Hil. 4 Edw. II (26 Selden Soc.), 127; *Bandon's Case* (1313) 27 Selden Soc. 48, 46 Selden Soc. xxv, lxxxi–lxxxv; *Anon.* (1313) Mich. 7 Edw. II (39 Selden Soc.), 14; *Aubrey* v. *Flory* (1321) Eyre of London, 86 Selden Soc. 235, 243; *Fleta*, lib. ii, Chap. LXI (72 Selden Soc. 203); J. Fortescue, *De Laudibus Legum Anglie*, ed. by S. Chrimes (Cambridge 1949), pp. 74–77.

[24] See G. O. Sayles, 76 Selden Soc. xcvi.

[25] E.g. *Dunstable* v. *Le Bal* (1278) 46 Selden Soc. 28 (justices at Winchester commanded to administer swift justice *secundum legem mercatoriam*); *Honesti* v. *Gerardin* (1291) *ibid.* 53 (Exchequer writ ordering an account *secundum consuetudinem scaccarii et secundum legem mercatoriam*); *Bosyis* v. *Merewell* (1292) 57 Selden Soc. 70, 58 Selden Soc. cix, 76 Selden Soc. xcvi (error in King's Bench from justices at Winchester, ordered to do justice *secundum legem mercatoriam*); *Bandon's Case* (1313) 27 Selden Soc. 48, 46 Selden Soc. xxv, lxxxi, sub nom. *Comberton's Case*, *ibid.* lxxxiv (*iusticies* to recover a debt "*sicut J. secundum legem mercatoriam rationabiliter monstrare poterit quod ei reddere debeat*"; removed into the Bench and from thence in eyre); *Case of the Flemish Merchants* (1313) 3 Rym.Foed. (1727 ed.), 402, 403 (writ to Count of Flanders reciting appointment of justices according to treaty to hear and determine a dispute

Law Merchant and the Common Law before 1700 347

perhaps a body of opinion favouring the automatic application of mercantile customs as to proof where the parties had made their contract according to the law merchant.[26] In later medieval times, perhaps because of jury difficulties, perhaps because of the increasing insistence on "due process," such cases were channelled into the King's council and the writs *secundum legem mercatoriam* disappeared from the books: all, that is, except the writ of account between mercantile partners, which was known to Fitzherbert and Coke.[27]

It is against this procedural background that Dr. Stillington's remark is to be understood. The medieval law merchant was not so much a corpus of mercantile practice or commercial law as an expeditious procedure especially adapted for the needs of men who could not tarry for the common law.[28] It was essentially negative. Like the justice of the Chancery, it offered an exemption from,

---

by the law of the realm "*et similiter legem mercatoriam*"); *Dederit* v. *Abbot of Ramsey* (1315) Plac.Abbrev. 321, 46 Selden Soc. 86 (action in King's Bench for breach of a royal command relating to a suit *secundum legem mercatoriam*); *Aubrey* v. *Flory* (1321) 86 Selden Soc. 235, 243 (royal commission to justices in eyre to administer swift justice according to the law of the realm "*vel secundum legem mercatoriam*"); *Anon.* (1323) 6 Selden Soc. xxiv (writ commanding mayor's court of Bristol to investigate a prize case *secundum legem mercatoriam*; record removed into the King's Bench. In five of these cases use was made of a jury of merchants, and in the Flemish case inquiry was to be made by merchants and others. As late as 1384 the King's Bench ordered trial, in a case sent from Chancery, by a jury of merchants and others *de medietate lingue*: 6 Selden Soc. xlviii. See also *Fulham* v. *Flemyng* (1287) 55 Selden Soc. 169, 172 (action on the case in the King's Bench for seizing a ship; proof admitted *secundum legem mercatoriam*). For commissions to try maritime cases *secundum legem mercatoriam*, see 6 Selden Soc. xvi, n. 1, citing Hale.

[26] *Anon.* (1293) Y.B. 21 & 22 Edw. I (Rolls Series), 74, 458, *semble*; *Anon.* (1313) Mich. 7 Edw. II (39 Selden Soc.), 14. Sir John Davies, *The Question concerning Impositions* (1656), p. 13, cites a case to the same effect in the eyre of Derby 2 Edw. II [*sic*]; this has not been traced in the MS. reports of the eyre of Derby in 4 Edw. II. *Cf. Lowys* v. *Lowys* (1303) 46 Selden Soc. 68 (pleas at Clonmel; action of debt; plea of infancy; plaintiff replies that he is a burgess and by *consuetudo mercatoria* he can bind himself at the age of 14; rejoinder that "*contractus istud non est aliquid quod spectet ad forum mercatorium*").

[27] See the count and writ in 46 Selden Soc. lxxx; *Pylat* v. *FitzSibill* (1308) *ibid.* 78 (in Common Pleas); Fitz.N.B. 117D (*iusticies*); *Registrum Omnium Brevium*, 3rd ed. (1687), f. 135r (*iusticies*); Co.Litt. 172; S. F. C. Milsom, 80 Selden Soc. clxxxi. The existence of the writ seems to be questioned in Mich. 19 Edw. II (1678 ed.), 626, *per* Herle C.J. But the 1794 edition of Fitzherbert refers to a King's Bench precedent as late as 1616.

[28] See the statutes 11 Edw. I, *De mercatoribus* (Stat. Regn. i, 53); Ordinance of the Staples 1353, 27 Edw. III, st. 2, c. 2 (Stat. Regn. i, 334: "*soit hastive et redde proces fait devers lui, de jour en jour et de heure en heure, solonc la leie de lestaple et nemie a la comen lei*"). William Noy, reading on the Statute of Acton Burnell in 1622, said, "The wise men of the law considered that the law of merchants ought to be different from the common law, for many of their contracts consist *in aequo et bono* without solemnity, and thereon many old judgments have been given by *inspecta rei veritate* . . . and this law was made according to the rule of the merchants, according to a form wholly different from the old law of the land": Lincoln's Inn, MS. Misc. 29 (c) (translated from law French). This provides a contrast with the contrary statements of Davies and Coke, p. 362, below.

or a short circuit through, the delays of due process as embodied in the forms of action and jury system of the two benches. The context of the remark was a case in the Star Chamber in 1473 arising from an alleged felony by a foreign merchant. It had been objected that felony was a matter for the common law, to which the chancellor replied that an alien merchant was not to be delayed by the common law, "but ought to sue here; and it shall be determined according to the law of nature in the Chancery, and he ought to sue there from hour to hour and from day to day for the speeding of merchants." [29] Yet it can hardly be supposed that Dr. Stillington thought the law merchant had its own distinct principles of theft; there is no hint in the whole discussion of any such conflict or distinction, and the case later became a classic authority on the common law of larceny. The objection, and its answer, related solely to procedure: that is, whether the merchant should have been arraigned upon an indictment duly found by a grand jury. The Chancery and Star Chamber in 1473 were no more courts of natural law or mercantile law, in any specific sense, than they were courts of equity in the later sense. But they were indifferent to all laws with respect to procedure, and could therefore bypass due process. The application of the substantive law was not separated from the fact-finding process, because the chancellor combined the roles of judge and jury; but no one would have suggested that the King's chancellor in making his decrees was administering any law other than that of the kingdom of England.[30]

A second major misapprehension which underlies the traditional view is that merchants normally shunned the ordinary course of the common law and resorted to their "own" courts. That the merchants dominated the urban and fair jurisdictions is very likely, but it does not follow that they disdained to use the central courts. The rolls of the Common Pleas for the fourteenth and fifteenth centuries, especially those of the London filazers, are full of commercial cases involving city tradesmen and merchants; and the proportion of foreign names there bears witness to the international character of some of the business. The material has not been studied in detail by economic or legal historians, and so we can speak only of first impressions. Most of the actions are to recover debts, and in the case of the filazers' entries the opacity of the curt standard

---

[29] *The Carrier's Case*, note 21 above (translated from law French). The implication seems to be that the Star Chamber and the Chancery followed the same informal procedure. Perhaps it should read "[as] in the Chancery." For the conciliar jurisdiction over maritime felonies, see 6 Selden Soc. xlv.

[30] Fortescue, *op. cit.*, pp. 74–77, mentions exceptions to common-law jury procedure in the Admiralty and in courts "*ubi per legem mercatoriam proceditur*" as being nevertheless allowed as *leges Angliae*.

forms precludes us from seeing the nature of the underlying transactions; but it appears from the actions which proceeded as far as a declaration that the usual sources of the duty to pay were sealed obligations, sales and loans. The next most numerous class of actions, at any rate in the fourteenth century, is account. Our testing ground, however, must be the mercantile instrument, since it is the form of dealing which most clearly separates distinctively mercantile contracts from the rest. Why do we not find common-law actions on such instruments before the sixteenth century?

The traditional answer is that the mercantile bill was simply not recognised by the earlier common law. Professor Postan wrote that

> The courts of Common Law ignored the letter of payment, as they did other writings which were not formal bonds or covenants under seal . . . Apart from the fact that mercantile cases came comparatively rarely before the Common Law courts, the letters of payment, in so far as they were used for exchange purposes, were, in common with other contracts concluded abroad or stipulating a payment outside the Kingdom, supposed to be outside the jurisdiction of Common Law.[31]

The first reason, as we have suggested, is mistaken in fact. The second is doubtful, because the common law permitted actions of the kind mentioned, at least since the middle of the fourteenth century, by allowing the venue to be laid fictitiously in England.[32] The real reason is suggested by Professor Postan in a different passage. The mercantile instrument, by whatever name it went, was not understood or intended to create an obligation, but was simply a convenient method of discharging a pre-existing obligation.[33] It became the practice to adopt forms of words which served the second function of evidencing the terms of a contract; but the documents remained essentially evidential, not dispositive. Their extra-legal character[34] may well have been particularly convenient to merchants. It would have been easy enough for merchants to use seals, but they did not regularly do so. By avoiding the forms which could be sued upon as a matter of specialty in the common-law courts, they gave themselves more flexibility. The fact that the instruments could not in themselves be enforced was a secondary consideration in a community which depended on good credit and honour. There

---

[31] *Op. cit.*, p. 61.
[32] *E.g.* Hil. 48 Edw. III, 2, pl. 6 (Harfleur in Kent); Pas. 20 Hen. VI, 28, pl. 21 (contract made in Paris, but defendant dared not demur); Mich. 15 Edw. IV, 14, pl. 18 (Calais in Kent); *Temp.* Hen. VIII, Bro. Abr., *Faits*, pl. 95.
[33] Postan, *op. cit.*, pp. 55–56.
[34] *Ibid.* 49 (" They were extra-legal instruments, devised solely for the purposes of mercantile convenience, and they served all those purposes which mercantile convenience demanded, including that of assignment ").

is an analogy with the use or trust of land. By making arrangements outside the law, the beneficial owner of land was able to achieve many things which could not be achieved within the framework of the common law.

Whatever the merchants' reasons for using unsealed instruments, the common law was clear. Writings other than deeds under seal were matters of parol evidence, and therefore were not proffered formally in court or recorded in pleadings. This puts a very different meaning on the assertion that actions were not brought at common law on mercantile instruments. Obviously actions could not be founded on instruments which were not contracts in themselves; but there was no reason why actions should not be brought on the contracts evidenced by such instruments. If a man sold goods and took a bill of exchange in payment, his remedy if the bill was dishonoured was an action of debt against the purchaser. The action would be brought on the contract in common form, and would not mention the bill of exchange. If the defendant waged his law, the existence of the bill would never come to light. If he put himself on the country, the bill could presumably be shown in evidence to the jury, but still no mention of it would appear on the record. The common law would therefore extend to many, though not all, transactions involving mercantile instruments. It is not unlikely that it could even overcome the privity problem raised by the tripartite character of some letters of payment, because the third parties were usually factors and could properly be treated as agents. Actions of debt, of course, suffered from severe procedural limitations, which may have encouraged men to use other jurisdictions. But the supposed substantive gap in the common law is illusory, and it is probable that juries were accustomed to being shown mercantile documents long before such instruments made any formal appearance on the face of the record.

That this is not mere conjecture may be demonstrated in two ways. First, it was possible for the existence of an informal instrument such as a bill of exchange to be revealed obliquely in the course of pleading. This occurred in an action of account in 1417. The defendant put forward a tentative plea that he had received the money from a third party to take to a Lombard in London to be exchanged, and to receive letters of exchange in favour of the plaintiff, and that he had done this and sent the letters to the plaintiff. The argument turned on whether these circumstances could be pleaded, as being contrary to the plaintiff's assertion of a receipt of money *pur accompt rendre*, or whether they were merely evidence for the auditors to consider when taking the account. The defendant was allowed the plea, because receiving money for a specific purpose negatived the obligation to account[35]; and so issue was joined on the exchange.[36] Nothing turned on the existence of the bill of exchange, and the Year Book is vague as to the details, but it looks very much as though the bill had not been accepted and the payee was seeking redress by unravelling the underlying transaction. The other demonstration that the common law was not hostile to the mercantile instrument *per se* is that such an instrument could be counted on if it happened to bear a seal, even though it was not in the usual form of a bond. The common law did not object to the mercantile formula, but drew a rigid distinction between deeds and parol writings—a distinction which could not be laid aside for merchants. Thus, in 1468 we find an action of debt in the Common Pleas on an English bill to pay a person or his attorney or " the bryngar of this letter."[37] In 1536 a merchant paid £20 to another merchant to invest in prunes at Rouen and was given a sealed receipt; the death of the payee ended the venture, and the investor was allowed to bring debt on the " bill " even though it contained no formal words of obligation.[38] The only reason why the bill was mentioned in the declaration is that it was sealed and therefore amounted to a specialty.[39] Again, when a shipowner in 1541 owed money by way of exchange and sealed a bill for its payment, an action of debt was successfully brought on the bill. The bill was in a mercantile form, in which the shipowner

> acknowledged himself to owe RW the aforesaid sum of £17, which sum of £17 was for money received by exchange; and the same MM has obliged himself by the same bill well and truly to pay RW or the bearer of the same bill, at the first arrival of the same ship from the port of Danzig at any port in England [or by 6 August 1541]; to which payment MM has bound himself, his executors and assigns, in all his goods, and the aforesaid ship with her freight wheresoever she might be found, on this side of the sea or beyond; in witness of the greater truth [whereof] the aforesaid MM has caused the said bill to be made [on 8 May 1541], sealed and subscribed in the presence of SM gentleman, HC and RP merchants.[40]

Of course, it does not appear that the " bryngar of this letter " in the 1468 case, or the *lator eiusdem billae* in the 1541 case, could

---

[35] J. H. Baker, *An Introduction to English Legal History*, 2nd ed. (1979), p. 303.
[36] Y.B. 5 Hen. V, 4, pl. 10.
[37] *Spence* v. *Bryan* (1468) CP 40/829, m. 44 (issue taken upon an alleged release). The dearth of early precedents exists only because no one has made a search of the fifteenth-century plea rolls. See also Mich. 21 Edw. IV, 28 pl. 2 (debt on a Flemish bill dated according to the custom of merchants).
[38] *Core* v. *May* (1536) Dyer 20, Spelman's *Reports* (93 Selden Soc.), 132.
[39] An unsealed bill could only be disclosed indirectly: *e.g. Baynard* v. *Maltby* (1531) Spelman's *Reports*, 93 Selden Soc. 10, 94 Selden Soc. 264 (bill of account recited in a demurrer to the evidence).
[40] *Walker* v. *Myddylton* (1542) KB 27/1122, m. 105d (translated); a verdict for the plaintiff was taken by default.

have sued in the central courts, as we know they could in the Mayor's Court of London,[41] or that such actions of debt would have lain if the bills had been unsealed. But these were difficulties of a procedural character, resulting from the serious limitations of the action of debt on a contract,[42] and it is no surprise to find that in Chancery as early as the 1460s an action could be brought on a bill of exchange [43] in circumstances where the privity necessary for an action of debt was probably lacking.[44]

Decline of the mercantile courts

Towards the end of the medieval period the local mercantile courts suffered a decline. The reasons for and the extent of that decline have yet to be firmly established, but it is possible to guess. Many of the courts came under the control of legally trained recorders or stewards [45] who, wittingly or otherwise, may have substituted some of the formality of the common law for the flexible procedures which characterised the medieval law merchant. By early Tudor times actions of *assumpsit*, following exactly the formulae of Westminster Hall, are to be found even in courts of piepowder [46]; and the records of piepowder and guildhall courts could be removed into the King's Bench by writ of error, to be subjected to judicial review by common-law standards.[47] Although the King's Bench

---

[41] See *Burton* v. *Davy* (1437) 49 Selden Soc. 117.

[42] For these limitations, see W. M. McGovern, " Contract in Medieval England " (1968) 54 *Iowa Law Review* 19; (1969) 13 *American Journal of Legal History* 173.

[43] *E.g. Grene* v. *Warde*, C1/28/210, printed in W. T. Barbour, *History of Contract in Early English Equity* (Oxford 1924), pp. 212–213. W. J. Jones, *The Elizabethan Court of Chancery* (Oxford 1969), p. 381, says the sixteenth-century Chancery often handled bills of exchange. There is a case in the first decree roll: *Michael* v. *Dyas* (1545) C78/1/43 (judgment for the plaintiff where bill of exchange dishonoured).

[44] The law of debt is obscure, for the procedural reason that it rarely fell open to discussion. In *Grene* v. *Warde* the facts were that A delivered £100 at Bruges to B, who was the factor of C; B directed a bill to C witnessing the payment " after the course of marchaundise," and the action was brought against C for non-acceptance. If we analyse the situation as being that B owes A £100 and C owes B £100, and that C agrees with B to pay A £100, this was no contract because it did not discharge B's debt and so there was no *quid pro quo* : Pas. 1 Hen. VI, 43, pl. 30; McGovern, 13 A.J.L.H. 186. But if we analyse it differently by regarding B as C's agent for the purpose of lending, then there may have been no difficulty in regarding C as bound by the agent's contract made on his behalf: Mich. 8 Edw. IV, 11, pl. 9, *per* Pygot sjt (" *si* . . . *jeo face un home mon factor et mon atturney pur achater marchandise etc. en cest case s'il achate marchandise d'un home jeo serra charge per tiel contract* ").

[45] By 1466 it was held that the steward was the judge, and therefore error lay: Mich. 6 Edw. IV, 3, pl. 9, *per* Choke J.; Hil. 7 Edw. IV, 23, pl. 27, *per* Littleton J. Recorders are rarely heard of before the fifteenth century; by 1500 most cities and boroughs had inns of court men as recorders.

[46] *E.g.* KB 27/1037, m. 76 (error on a recovery in *assumpsit* in the Hereford piepowder court, 1520); *Myddelton* v. *Foxley* (1523) CP 40/1038, m. 452 (debt on a recovery in *assumpsit* in a piepowder court). See also 94 Selden Soc. *52*, n. 2.

[47] See 94 Selden Soc. *51–53*. Yet the King's Bench formally decided that the rule requiring covenants to be proved by deed, and the rule requiring fourteen days

acknowledged the propriety of some procedural flexibility in local courts, it would doubtless not have countenanced any appearance of arbitrariness. The early readers on the statute of *Quo Warranto*, indeed, maintained that a fair would be forfeited to the King if the piepowder jurisdiction was abused in that way:

> If a man has a fair and abuses the court of piepowder, all the fair and the court shall be forfeited. And the court may be abused [in various ways]. If he will not suffer the party to make defence, but condemns him upon the declaration, this is abuse and forfeiture. And likewise if he will not suffer the plaintiff to reply to the bar, but bars him without answer. And likewise if he takes a trial by proofs or by eleven men, where it should be by twelve. And likewise if the party wishes to wage his law, where he ought to do it by law, and he will not suffer him to have such trial, this is a forfeiture.[48]

The mention of special pleading, jury trial and wager of law suggests that a considerable change of practice had occurred in these courts since the thirteenth and fourteenth centuries. And there may have been other abuses than those mentioned in the quotation. The statute of 1477 concerning fair courts suggested that the courts had become so unpopular that stewards had felt the need to enlarge their jurisdiction by means of fictions, that feigned actions and embracery of jurors were rife, and that as a result merchants avoided going to those fairs where they might expect exorbitant or unfair legal action.[49] For reasons such as these the old law merchant—in the procedural sense—proved insufficiently attractive to prevent merchants having recourse to the central royal courts. Another factor in the decline of the local courts, though whether

---

between returns of writs, were not universal and did not bind local courts: 93 Selden Soc. 120, 94 Selden Soc. *258*. While this paper was in proof, the writer found a case of 1491 in Caryll's reports (Linc. Inn, MS. Maynard 86) where the plaintiff assigned an error in fact " *que touche solement le course del ley merchant.*" Hussey C.J. said, " *cest un especiall ley allowable icy, quel ne pursue le comen ley . . . dont nous ne poimus aver conusans, per que moy semble que nous covyent descryer a ceux queux sont justices, de nous certifier lour ley; et donques poimus sacher le quel cest que il assigne pur errour soit errour ou nemy.*" Kebell sjt, however, replied that the parties should join issue on any disputed point of the law merchant. The report does not resolve the doubt, but it is evident that the problem was unfamiliar. The *ley*, it will be noticed, is procedural.

[48] From Edmund Dudley's reading on *Quo Warranto* in Gray's Inn (c. 1490), Cambridge Univ. Lib. MS. Hh. 3. 10, at f. 16v (translated from law French). The same passage occurs in the later readings of William Marshall (Lincoln's Inn 1516) and John Spelman (Gray's Inn 1519).

[49] Stat. 17 Edw. IV, c. 2, which attempted to impose definite limits. See also the note on this statute in Spelman's *Reports* (93 Selden Soc.), 139, *s.v. Feiers*. Evidently a wider jurisdiction continued in some parts. In 1520 a plaintiff in error attempted to upset a judgment in a piepowder court, in *assumpsit* for a servant's wages, on the grounds that " *causa actionis sive sectae non est pro aliquibus rebus seu mercandisis in mercato emptis seu venditis*": KB 27/1037, m. 76 (no judgment).

it was a cause or an effect is less clear, is the rise of the action of *assumpsit* for money.

LAW MERCHANT AND THE ACTION OF ASSUMPSIT

The action of *assumpsit*, as is well known, was extended between 1450 and 1550 to provide the common law with an escape from the procedural shackles of debt and covenant and to enable it to provide the sort of justice which the Chancery and mercantile courts had been offering. Almost as soon as *assumpsit* became available to assert money claims, in the first half of the reign of Henry VIII, we find an action in the King's Bench rolls founded on an exchange of money. Indeed, Lawrence Tanfield's researches in 1598 led him to believe this had been the first situation where *assumpsit* had been brought for money.[50] It is very likely that in this case of 1520, as in the earliest case in Rastell[51] and other precedents from this period,[52] there had been a bill of exchange but that no formal mention was made of it, on the old ground that it was a matter of evidence rather than of obligation. But the old ground was confined to the logic of the older actions, and by the 1540s pleaders were coming to regard unsealed bills as material facts which could be mentioned in *assumpsit* declarations in order to explain the context in which an undertaking had been made or was to be inferred.

Assumpsit and mercantile instruments

In *Dolphyn* v. *Barne* (1540)[53] we can see what a substantial difference this made to the outward appearance of mercantile suits in the King's Bench records. *A* had signed a paper[54] promising to pay a

---

[50] *Blanke* v. *Spinula* (1520) KB 27/1036, m. 75; argument in *Slade's Case* (1598) in [1971] C.L.J. 58; below, p. 400.
[51] W. Rastell, *Colleccion of Entrees* (1566), f. 10r. The suggestion that this declaration imports an unmentioned bill of exchange was made by Judge Cranch in 1804: 3 Sel.Ess.Anglo-Amer.Leg.Hist. 77.
[52] E.g. *Lavandre* v. *Dele* (1519) CP 40/1024, m. 534 (*D*, having notice of a forthcoming sale of madder, *amicabiliter* told *L* that if she would deliver him the money he would buy it for her; and she delivered the money, and he promised to deliver the madder but failed to do so; *D* pleads that the contract was made with an Antwerp merchant and the money was delivered to him—which suggests that *D* may have been acting as a factor); *Mowenslowe* v. *Crowche* (1531) KB 27/1080, m. 38 (*C* bought cloth from *B* for £540 Flemish, and *M* bound himself for payment, on *C's* undertaking to indemnify him; *M* was called on to pay, and sued *C*; *C* pleads that the sale was for *M's* own use, so that *M* was not bound on his behalf; but, on a verdict for *M*, *M* recovers £400 against *C*); *Soly* v. *Perott, merchant of the Calais staple* (1547) KB 27/1143, m. 102 (*S* delivered 174½ *couronnes d'or* to *P* and *P* undertook to repay them or their value; a jury *de medietate lingue* finds for *S*, who recovers £43 12s. 6d. plus costs).
[53] KB 27/1116, m. 35d.
[54] The bill ("*cedula papiri*") read: "Be it knowen to all men that I John Barne of London oweth to Markes Colynes of Andwarp the somme of xliiij *li*. xiij *s*. iiij *d*. g., the whiche somme of xliiij *li*. xiij *s*. iiij *d*. g. I promyse to pay to the

Law Merchant and the Common Law before 1700   355

sum of Flemish money to *B* at the Cold Mart, and *C* had subscribed the paper *secundum usum mercatorum*, " I promise to see this bill contented and paid." It was alleged that *A* had the same day promised *C*, in return for 12d. paid (perhaps a fictitious allegation), that if *C* had to pay *B* on *A*'s failure to pay at the Cold Mart, *A* would pay *C*. *A* did default at the Cold Mart, and *C* paid *B* to save *A*'s credit. The action by *C* against *A* came on at the Guildhall, London, on 19 November 1540, but *A* failed to appear and so *C* recovered damages of £38 10s. 4d. (the value of the £44 13s. 4d. in Flemish money plus £4 sterling) and £4 costs. This was in effect an action on a promise to save a surety harmless, a situation where debt did not lie but *assumpsit* did [55]; the cause of action was not new, but the appearance of the mercantile details seems an almost shocking departure from precedent. *Towll* v. *Hawkyns* (1549),[56] another Cold Mart case, likewise has an appearance of extreme novelty. *A* was indebted to *B* in Flemish money and *B* was indebted to *C* in English money; in consideration that *A* should be discharged against *B*, *A* promised *C* to pay *B*'s debt to *C* in Cold Mart payments at London, and *B* delivered to *C* to the use of *A* a bill acknowledging *A*'s debt to *B*, thereby discharging *A* of the debt. *A* did not pay *C*, and so *C* sued *A*. No outcome is recorded, but the defendant by pleading *non assumpsit* took no objection at that stage to the declaration. Since *B* was not said to have been a factor or agent of either party, this was another case where debt would not have lain.

During the same decade as these two outlandish actions, the King's Bench by allowing similar use of the *assumpsit* formula took overt cognisance of a wide range of commercial transactions, including insurance and partnership agreements.[57] No doubt the court was not averse to capturing some of the business of the admiralty and borough courts and diverting mercantile business from the Council and Chancery. Yet there is no evidence of any idea that the King's Bench was incorporating some distinct body of law merchant. Apart from the mention of Dolphyn's subscription *secundum usum mercatorum*, there is no hint that the mercantile character of the transaction in itself made any difference to the result. There was no commission in these cases to proceed according to the law mer-

seide Markes or to the brynger of this bill in Colde Marte next, for the whiche payment well and truely to be payde I the seide John bynde me and my assignes. In wittenesse wherof I have wrytyn this bill and setto my hande the first day of Septembre anno domini 1538." (In 94 Selden Soc. *61, 286*, the present writer alluded to this document as a bill of exchange; but it seems closer to a promissory note, a term which was not then in use.) The subscription read: " I Henry Dolphyn promes to se this bill contented and payde at the day and tyme aforeseide by me Henry Dolphyn."

[55] See 94 Selden Soc. *282*.
[56] KB 27/1152, m. 143.
[57] 94 Selden Soc. *286*.

chant. The law merchant was not even mentioned in the declarations. The King's Bench had merely removed the procedural barriers which had in the past prevented the two benches from enforcing such transactions in a direct way. This amounted, no doubt, to a substantial change in the common law. But it was part and parcel of the general development of *assumpsit* to enable the enforcement of all parol undertakings. And, since there were no set formulae in *assumpsit*, it was possible to adapt its forms to charge the various parties to bills of exchange. The payee could sue the drawer on an undertaking by the drawer that the drawee would pay,[58] or that if the drawee did not accept the bill the drawer would pay.[59] The payee could sue the acceptor on the basis that his acceptance amounted to an undertaking to pay.[60] And the drawer could sue the drawee on an undertaking to accept and pay bills drawn on him.[61] Apart from occasional use of the phrase *secundum usum mercatorum*, which falls far short of an averment of a custom, in none of the sixteenth-century cases so far discovered was there any attempt to lay the custom of merchants in the declaration. It is true that no one has yet made a thorough search of the King's Bench rolls between 1550 and 1600. But enough has come to light, both from random searches and from a study of books of entries, to show that the bill of exchange was received into the common law without express reliance on " law merchant."

Assumpsit and the custom of merchants

This conclusion makes the seventeenth-century part of the story far more difficult to explain. The contrast between the pioneering declarations and the typical seventeenth-century declaration on a bill of exchange is considerable. And it is almost the reverse of the truth to summarise the change as one of simplification. The newer practice of setting out in full the custom of merchants in fact made declarations longer and more complicated. Had there been a process of simplification, the change would have been easier to understand. But plaintiffs are not wont to introduce complexities, with the concomitant risk of being tripped up *in banc*, unless they feel com-

---

[58] *E.g. Maynard* v. *Dyce* (1542) KB 27/1125, m. 110, abstracted below; *Tusten* v. *Clotworthy* (1600) KB 27/1361, m. 508. The writer is grateful to Mr. David Ibbetson for bringing the cases of 1600 to his attention.
[59] *E.g. Knappe* v. *Comyn* (1600) KB 27/1361, m. 360 (judgment for the plaintiff).
[60] *E.g. W. S.* v. *R. H.* (1571) Herne's *Pleader*, p. 136, citing Trin. 13 Eliz. I, m. 2021; *Lucalli* v. *Foster* (c. 1577) Brit. Lib., MS. Harley 664, f. 83; *C. W.* v. *J. B.* (1595) Rastell's *Entrees* (1596 ed.), f. 338. All these are from books of entries, in which only the declaration is copied.
[61] *E.g. Thumansen* v. *Van Prussen* (1600) KB 27/1361, m. 413 (judgment for the plaintiff); *Martin* v. *Boure* (1603) Cro.Jac. 6, citing Pas. 44 Eliz. I, m. 493 (judgment for the plaintiff affirmed in Exchequer Chamber).

pelled to do so. What, then, was the unavoidable necessity for introducing the custom of merchants as a complicating factor in declarations? The traditional story associated the changes in pleading with difficulties over consideration and privity. But this explanation will not readily fit the facts as we now see them. The earliest actions on bills of exchange do, admittedly, antedate the doctrine of consideration by that name; but when the allegation of consideration became essential, it was in these cases made in the most general terms ("*in consideratione premissorum*").[62] The changes in the declaration were not formally, and therefore probably not conceptually, linked with the insertion of this phrase. As for the doctrine of privity in the context of *assumpsit*, it was not known in anything like its modern form in the sixteenth century, and was still of very uncertain scope in the second half of the seventeenth century.[63] So chronology forbids an explanation by way of a supposed struggle to reconcile exchange transactions with a doctrine of privity of contract as such.

The problem was more likely to have been that of the implied or fictitious *assumpsit*. It was all very well to imply an *assumpsit* into every contract executory for which debt would lie,[64] but bills of exchange were not contracts executory for which debt would lie. And whilst the drawer and acceptor of a bill could reasonably be said on the facts to make an implicit but real undertaking to the payee, it was harder to find in the facts anything like a genuine promise to repay the purchaser on protest of the bill—this being effectively a quasi-contractual claim, which could only be accommodated within *assumpsit* by fiction. It seems the custom of merchants was first pushed on to the record through arguments of this kind. The first two cases known to the writer both concerned the liability of the drawer in the event of non-acceptance. In *Maynard* v. *Dyce* (1542)[65] the plaintiff (*P*) declared simply that he had delivered £100 to the defendant (*D*), for which *D* undertook that *F* would pay *P* £140 Flemish, and assigned as the breach that *F* had not paid. *D* confessed these facts, but pleaded that *X* and *Y* had delivered goods to *P* in satisfaction, with the consent of all the parties, and that *P* had received them in full satisfaction. *P* was

---

[62] E.g. *Lucalli* v. *Foster* (c. 1577), above; *Knappe* v. *Hedley* (1600) KB 27/1359, m. 621, abstracted below; *Thumansen* v. *Van Prussen* (1600), above; *Tusten* v. *Clotworthy* (1600), above; *Shepparde* v. *Becher* (1600) KB 27/1361, m. 507d, abstracted below. Thereafter it is common form, and we have seen no reported objection to it.
[63] See A. W. B. Simpson, *History of the Common Law of Contract: the Rise of Assumpsit* (Oxford 1975), pp. 475–485.
[64] This was, of course, fully debated in *Slade's Case* (1597–1602): see [1971] C.L.J. 226–227.
[65] KB 27/1125, m. 110. At the trial the plaintiff was non-suited.

driven by this plea to disclose the whole of his case by way of replication. On delivering the £100 to *D*, he had received a bill of exchange from *D* drawn on *F* for payment of the £140 Flemish at Antwerp; and afterwards, at Antwerp, *P* bought the goods from *X* and *Y* and sold them the bill of exchange in payment. The drawee, *F*, had absconded without paying. The replication concluded with a traverse to the allegation that the goods were received in satisfaction of the undertaking; but in order to make complete sense of his case *P* felt obliged to preface the replication with a statement of the immemorial custom of merchants that if merchant *A* pays money to merchant *B* and takes a bill from *B* for repayment abroad, *A* may sell the bill to merchant *C* and *B* remains chargeable. It is not clear whether *P* was suing on behalf of *X* and *Y*, or whether he had already paid *X* and *Y* to save *D*'s honour and was seeking reimbursement. In either case, his claim against *D*, though expressed as an *assumpsit*, could only be explained in fact by the custom that the drawer after sale of the bill remained chargeable and bound ("*post venditionem talis billae fuerit onerabilis et obligatus existit*") to the original payee. In *Shepparde* v. *Becher* (1600) [66] the plaintiff (*P*) declared that he had delivered £100 to the defendant (*D*) in Cheapside, to be repaid at usance in Flemish money in Middelburg; that *D* had drawn a bill of exchange on *W* in Middelburg to pay *C* or the bearer to the use of *P*; and that "in consideration of the premises" *D* undertook that if *W* did not accept the bill and pay the Flemish money *D* would repay the £100. *W* in the event refused to accept, and so *P* protested the bills. *D* pleaded *non assumpsit*, and we must suppose some difficulty at the Guildhall trial before Popham C.J., both as to the signification of "usance" and as to the reality of *D*'s undertaking to repay upon protest. The jury therefore found a special verdict setting out two immemorial customs of merchants: first, that "usance" means at the end of one month after the making of the bill [67]; and, second, that if a factor or drawee does not accept a bill or pay the contents, the drawer is under a duty to repay the sum advanced ("*solui debuisset praedictam primam summam*"). The court took advisement on this verdict for two terms, but no judgment is entered.

In the first case known to the writer in which the plaintiff began by reciting the custom of merchants in his declaration or bill, the custom was introduced in an explanatory rather than an obligatory

---

[66] KB 27/1361, m. 507d (*c.a.v.* to Hil. 1601).

[67] It is odd that this was not found as a special custom in relation to trade between London and Middelburg, because the meaning of "usance" varied with the distance between places: see p. 365, below. Malynes confirms the fact that usance between London and Middelburg was one month.

way. The custom was recited as being that masters have always accepted bills drawn on them by their factors, and that if they have not done so the bills have been protested back to the factors so that the factors should pay. The plaintiff then said that the defendant's factors received £969 from his own factor and directed bills to the defendant to pay the sum within six weeks from the arrival of *The Star of Dansk* in Newcastle; that " in consideration of the premises " and in consideration that the plaintiff would not protest the bills, the defendant accepted, subscribed *secundum usum et consuetudinem mercatorum*, and undertook to pay; that only £407 10s. had been paid, and that nevertheless the plaintiff had not protested the bills. The plaintiff recovered £620 damages by default, and the judgment was affirmed by the Exchequer Chamber on 29 June 1601.[68] It is possible that the difficulty here was one of consideration, in that a consideration not to protest a bill was meaningless without an explanation of the effect of a protest. But there is no telling from the record what errors were argued in the Exchequer Chamber, and the true explanation for the attempt to reverse the judgment may be the enormous amount of money involved rather than a legal difficulty. The precedent was probably not followed, because an " in consideration of the premises " clause was sufficient in itself.

In later cases the plaintiff's allegation of custom was aimed at explaining the *assumpsit* rather than the consideration. Thus, in the first reported case,[69] an action by the payee against the acceptor, the custom was inserted to emphasise that the act of accepting and subscribing a bill *secundum usum mercatorum* had the force of a promise. And a few years later, in an action against the drawer, the custom was put in to explain the liability of the drawer upon protest [70]—the problem which had occasioned the special verdict in *Shepparde* v. *Becher*. The customs thereafter set out by plaintiffs are all to the effect that the defendant was bound or liable (*obligatus*) or chargeable (*onerabilis*) to pay the plaintiff, and in consideration of this liability or charge he promised to pay. We must now try to establish the thinking behind this formula.

ONERABILIS ASSUMPSIT

The development suggests an analogy with *indebitatus assumpsit*, which by the 1670s was held to lie for customary debts.[71] But the

---

[68] *Knappe* v. *Hedley, Selbye and Bartram* (1600) KB 27/1359, m. 621.
[69] *Oaste* v. *Taylor* (1612) Cro.Jac. 306, 1 Rolle Abr. 6.
[70] *Mounsey* v. *Traves* (c. 1621) Vidian's *Entries*, p. 66. In *Aswel* v. *Osborn* (c. 1628) ibid. 67, the custom is set out to charge the acceptor upon protest.
[71] Baker, *Introduction to English Legal History*, p. 307.

action of *onerabilis assumpsit* (if we may so term it) was considered a different species, because the charge or obligation was not of a debt-creating kind.[72] The point was considered by the Exchequer in 1668, when debt was brought on the custom of merchants that an acceptor was chargeable. Hale C.B. conceded that debt would lie for a customary duty, but ordered further investigation into the question whether the custom of merchants was to treat the acceptor as *owing* the money or merely as having promised to pay. After search of the precedents, it was held that acceptance made the acceptor *onerabilis* and was therefore equivalent to a promise or undertaking, but that it did not create a " duty " for which debt would lie. Judgment was accordingly arrested.[73] Consistently with this conclusion, it was held shortly afterwards that *indebitatus assumpsit* would not lie on the obligation attributed to the custom of merchants, because it was not an indebtedness.[74] The plaintiff had either to bring *assumpsit* on the contract, and proffer the bill of exchange as evidence of a promise,[75] or bring *onerabilis assumpsit* and set out the custom. The latter form never became exclusive of the former, and although we shall hereafter be chiefly concerned with the *onerabilis* form, it should be noticed that the survival of the first alternative precludes any argument that the setting out of the custom of merchants in *assumpsit* can by itself be equated with the reception of a " law merchant."

In seeking the concept behind the *onerabilis* formula, we must first establish the nature of the custom on which it rested. When autonomous systems of law, such as the Canon law, were mentioned in pleading, the greatest generality was allowed. Thus, *lex ecclesiastica* is not an uncommon phrase in the plea rolls. We have already noticed some early references to *lex mercatoria* on this plane of generality, but we have suggested that this *lex*—which Fortescue

---

[72] The strange case of *Vanheath* v. *Turner* (1621), Winch 24, may indicate the contrary, but it is so obscurely reported that it is not even clear what form of action was used. Although the plaintiff's counsel said it was an action on the case, the plea of *nil debet per legem* suggests it was debt.

[73] *Anon.* (1668) Hard. 485: perhaps identifiable as *Milton's Case*, cited 2 Keb. 695, 1 Mod. 286. Twisden J. doubted the correctness of the decision: 1 Vent. 153. Debt would have lain if the bill had been sealed: see the earlier cases cited above, and *Peirson* v. *Ponuteis* (1608) 1 Bro. & Goulds. 102, Yelv. 135.

[74] *Brown* v. *London* (1669) 1 Lev. 298, 1 Vent. 152, 1 Mod. 285, 2 Keb. 695, 713, 758, 822; approved by Holt C.J. in *Stewart* v. *Hodges* (1693) 1 Salk. 125, Comb. 204, Holt 115; and *Smith* v. *Aiery* (1705) 6 Mod. 128, 129. Where, however, *A* paid money to *B* and *B* gave *A* a bill of exchange or promissory note for repayment, it was possible to bring *indebitatus assumpsit* for money lent and give the bill in evidence (in which case the custom was irrelevant): 2 Keb. 758, *per* Hale C.J.; *Bromwich* v. *Lloyd* (1698) Lutw. 1582. The same principle could have applied where money was laid out or had and received.

[75] The records do not enable us to tell exactly when this practice began, or how frequently it was followed. But the use of bills as evidence of an undertaking was approved in *Eaglechilde's Case* (1630) Hetley 167, Litt.Rep. 363, and we have speculated above that it may have been practised much earlier.

significantly reckoned among the *leges Angliae*—was conceived of as a system of procedure rather than as a body of doctrine. When we come to the specific principles adduced by plaintiffs in *assumpsit*, it is never as *lex* but always as *usus* or *consuetudo* that the customs of merchants are described. It was not law to be judicially noticed, like ecclesiastical law,[76] but custom to be averred and proved as fact. It was therefore necessary, in alleging a custom of merchants, to observe the common-law requirements for establishing customs which could be admitted as exceptions to the common law. The principal requirements were: (i) immemorial antiquity, a requirement shared with the common law, and (ii) a limitation of application, to distinguish it from the common law of the whole realm.

Antiquity

The requirement of antiquity gave little trouble in practice, but not for the reason commonly given. Customs of merchants were always alleged, from *Maynard* v. *Dyce* (1542) onwards, to have been in use from time immemorial: *a tempore cuius contrarii memoria hominum non existit*. The truth of this assertion could only have been formally challenged by traversing the existence of the custom as alleged; yet, in all the dozens of cases it has been possible to find, no such traverse was ever taken. Doubtless the existence or the details of an alleged custom could be questioned at the trial on the general issue *non assumpsit*, but proof of user since 1189 can never have been an actual evidential requirement. Yet whatever proof was admitted in practice, as a matter of law any verdict for the plaintiff necessarily included a finding that the alleged custom was immemorial. The *usus mercatorum* was not, therefore, trade usage in the modern sense. It was, in contemplation of law, unchanging and unchangeable custom.

Ambit

It was the need for some restriction on the ambit of the custom which posed the greater intellectual problem. If the law of merchants was truly universal, then it was not merely coextensive with but actually wider in scope than the geographical jurisdiction of the common law. Some seventeenth-century writers concluded from this that it must be part of the common law. At the beginning of the seventeenth century, Serjeant Davies wrote

---

[76] For the principle that Canon law was noticed in the royal courts, see " Ascertainment of Foreign Law: Certification to and by English Courts prior to 1861 " (1979) 28 I.C.L.Q. 141, 143. The same was probably true of the *lex mercatoria* in the old sense. Our seventeenth-century customs are different in character.

> *Mercatura vel societas mercatorum est magna republica* (saith Ulpian) and therefore that common-wealth of merchants hath alwayes had a peculiar and proper law to rule and govern it; this law is called the law merchant, whereof the laws of all Nations do take speciall knowledge . . . [T]he general law of Nations . . . and the law merchant . . . have been ever admitted, had [and] received by the kings and people of England in cases concerning merchants and merchandize, and so are become the law of the land in those cases.[77]

Sir Edward Coke wrote that the *lex mercatoria* " is part of laws of this realm, for the advancement and continuance of commerce and trade, which is *pro bono publico*." [78] And according to Sir Matthew Hale, " the Common Law includes . . . *Lex Mercatoria*, as it is applied under its proper Rules to the Business of Trade and Commerce "; this law merchant, like the forest law and the royal prerogative, were but branches and parts of the common law.[79] Yet none of these writers is referring to any distinct corpus of law which had been incorporated from without. The " law merchant " had become a figure of speech for what we now call mercantile law: that branch of ordinary English law which happens to govern merchants' affairs. There were several statutes dealing specifically with merchants and their privileges; and these, together with some of the ancient references to the *lex mercatoria* which have been explained above, were for Davies, Coke and Hale the principal evidences for the law merchant being part of English law. The casual references to the *ius gentium* are not borne out by such sources, since an English statute can hardly be in itself a part of the law of nations. Cowell, on the strength of the same legislation, came to the converse conclusion that the law merchant was " a privilege or speciall lawe differing from the common lawe of England." [80]

Could it be that the custom of merchants, unlike all other customs allowed by the common law, was limited to a class of persons rather than to a particular locality? This seems to be assumed in the earlier pleadings, in which the custom is alleged to apply to merchants throughout the realm. In *Maynard* v. *Dyce* (1542) the cus-

---

[77] *The Question concerning Impositions* (1656), pp. 10, 27 (written *temp.* Jac. I). There is a similar passage in his argument in *R.* v. *Cusacke* (1619) 2 Rolle Rep. 113. *Cf.* Sir Bartholomew Shower's argument in *Carter* v. *Downich* (1689) Show. 127: " It is not like a particular custom, which is confined within a certain precinct in this realm, but it is of universal extent, and concerns the whole realm; nay, reaches further, for it is *jus gentium* and concerns all countries where traffick is used." [78] Co.Litt. 182.
[79] M. Hale, *History of the Common Law of England*, ed. by C. M. Gray (Chicago 1971), p. 18. Hale, however, included local custom in the same category.
[80] *The Interpreter* (Cambridge 1607), sig. Rr3. The passage was copied verbatim in the law dictionaries of Manley, Jacob and Tomlins. *Cf.* Noy, note 28 above. Likewise Hussey C.J. in 1491, note 47 above.

tom was "*consuetudo usitata et approbata inter mercatores infra hoc regnum Angliae.*" In *Knappe* v. *Hedley* (1600) it was "*usus et consuetudo mercatorum in huiusmodi casu infra hoc regnum Angliae usitata.*" In the special verdict in *Shepparde* v. *Becher* (1600) the "*consuetudo, usus et ordo mercatorum*" was not given any local bounds at all. Now, to use the language of custom for principles which operated throughout the realm was not entirely unprecedented. There were actions founded on "customs of the realm" imposing liability for negligence on innkeepers, and householders who lit fires, and common carriers, and the phrase was used in other actions. It had, nevertheless, been pointed out more than once in the Year Books that "custom of the realm" was an illusory concept inasmuch as any immemorial usage throughout the realm was common law.[81] This difficulty soon befell the custom of England relating to merchants. If it was truly a custom of England, then it was common law which would be noticed by the judges and needed no mention in pleading.[82] If such a custom was alleged in pleading, it was to be treated as surplusage.[83] It was therefore technically better to omit it altogether, but then the plaintiff had nothing on the record and had to be sure the judges and the jury would take notice of the principle on which he relied. The desire to formulate the custom on the record may explain the survival of the custom of the realm in *assumpsit* declarations. It was a particularly useful device in framing extensions of the law, as when it was alleged successfully in two cases of 1689 that the liability of the drawer extended to any persons (including non-merchants) who drew bills *secundum usum mercatorum* in favour of other persons [84]; or when in 1693 it was established as the custom of England that the indorser is liable to a subsequent indorsee.[85]

Judicial notice of mercantile customs

The device of alleging a custom of the realm, or the omission (as in the earliest cases) of all mention of custom, was only safe in the case of well-established principles of liability. Hale C.B. warned

---

[81] Mich. 30 Edw. III, 25, *per* Finchden sjt; *Beaulieu* v. *Finglam* (1401) Pas. 2 Hen. IV, 18, pl. 6, *per curiam*; Co.Litt. 110. St. German, *Doctor and Student*, lib. i, Chap. VII (91 Selden Soc. 45–57) equates custom of the realm and common law.

[82] *Richard's Case* (1542) Dyer 54, Bro.Abr., *Custom*, pl. 59 (alleged custom of England for merchants to assign import licences by word of mouth); *Vanheath* v. *Turner* (1621) Winch 24, *per* Hobart C.J., *semble*; *Woodward* v. *Rowe* (1666) 2 Keb. 105, 132; *Carter* v. *Downich* (1689) 3 Mod. 226, Carth. 83, Show. 127 (action of covenant).

[83] *Anon.* (1668) Hard. 485, *per* Hale C.B. See also (in relation to another custom) *Rich* v. *Kneeland* (1613) Hob. 17; *Matthews* v. *Hopkin* (1665) 1 Sid. 244.

[84] *Sarsfield* v. *Witherley* (1689) Show. 125, Holt 112 (liable to payee); *Cramlington* v. *Evans* (1689) 1 Show. 4, 2 Show. 509, 2 Vent. 307, Holt 108 (liable to indorsee).   [85] *Williams* v. *Williams* (1693) **Carth. 269, 3 Salk. 68.**

in 1668 that "although we must take notice in general of the law of merchants, yet all their customs we cannot know but by information." [86] By information, he meant either "to inquire [informally] what the course has been amongst merchants" or "to direct an issue for trial of the custom amongst merchants." As he wrote elsewhere:

> either the custom or law comes in question by special pleading, and then the court use to ascertain themselves by speech with merchants . . . or else it comes in question upon the general issue, and then . . . merchants are usually jurors at the request of either party, and merchants are produced on either side to ascertain the court and jury touching the custom of merchants.[87]

These are the techniques for which Lord Mansfield C.J. is usually given the credit. We have no way of knowing how far Hale's theory was practised in the seventeenth century, but his approach seems to have been shared by Holt C.J. By the end of the century the orthodox view was that a "special" or less well-known custom of merchants had to be pleaded and proved as a local custom.[88] In 1692 Holt C.J. declared, "we take notice of the laws of merchants that are general, not of those that are particular." [89] And in 1697 the King's Bench reaffirmed the principle that a "special" custom of merchants had to be pleaded; the court would not take judicial notice of it, because if they mistook it they would set a precedent which might harm the custom.[90]

Local customs of merchants

Although, as we have just seen, the customs of merchants could in some cases be treated as common law, the majority of plaintiffs

---

[86] *Anon.* (1668) Hard. 485. See also *Hodges* v. *Steward* (1695) 3 Salk. 68, 69 ("though the court takes notice of the law merchant as part of the law of England, yet they cannot take notice of the customs of particular places"). *Cf. Peirson* v. *Ponuteis* (1608) 1 Bro. & Goulds. 102, Yelv. 135 ("the judges ought to take notice of those things that are used amongst merchants for the maintenance of traffick").

[87] *Treatise on the Admiralty Jurisdiction*, quoted with permission from the edited transcript by Mr. D. E. C. Yale, to whom the writer is extremely grateful. By "special pleading" Hale presumably meant questions raised on the pleadings (including the declaration) by demurrers, writs of error and motions *in banc*; issue was seldom, if ever, joined on the existence of a custom, though if it had been it is difficult to see why the matter should not have been dealt with by evidence and special juries. Two of Hale's rulings at the Guildhall on questions of mercantile law are noted by C. Molloy, *De Jure Maritimo* (1682 ed.), pp. 280, 281.

[88] This is plainly hinted at in *Carter* v. *Downich* (1689) Show. 127, Carth. 83, 3 Mod. 226.

[89] *Lethulier's Case* (1692) 2 Salk. 443.

[90] *Belasyse* v. *Hester* (1697) 1 Ld.Raym. 1281, 2 Lutw. 1589, 1593, *per* Powell J. ("issint que le resolucion de le court en cest case ne ledera le custome des merchants"). See also *Chandler* v. *Meade* (1705) 2 Ld.Raym. 1211, 1212.

who chose to plead a custom pleaded it as a local custom and not as a custom of the realm. The framing of general principles of liability as customs of London had begun by James I's time at the latest.[91] By the Restoration period a further refinement had been introduced. It became usual to declare on the custom of one city (usually London) operating between the merchants resident in that and in some other named city.[92] Thus, in *Death* v. *Serwonters* (1685),[93] the plaintiff alleged

> that the city of London is, and was from time whereof the memory of man is not to the contrary, an ancient city; and in the same city, that is to say in the parish of St. Mary-le-Bow in Cheap Ward, amongst merchants trading between the city of Venice in parts beyond the seas and the aforesaid city of London, a custom has been used and approved between the same merchants throughout the aforesaid time that " usance " mentioned in any bill of exchange directed by any merchants residing in Venice aforesaid to any merchants residing in London aforesaid is (and during all the aforesaid time was) a period of three months from the day of the date of such bill of exchange.

Such a bi-local custom was obviously necessary in respect of usance, which varied according to the distance between cities, but it came to be generally used for other mercantile customs. Thus, the declaration in *Death* v. *Serwonters* continued by reciting " the old and laudable custom used and approved in the aforesaid city [of London] in the parish and ward aforesaid between the merchants residing at Venice aforesaid and the merchants residing at London aforesaid " that the acceptor of a bill of exchange is chargeable to indorsees. These local customs were not legally different in character from other local customs, and so there was no objection to alleging them in such a way as to bind non-merchants.[94] In *Fairley* v. *Roch* (c. 1686)[95] the plaintiff went too far and alleged a custom of London " for merchants and others " relating to bills of exchange,

---

[91] *Oaste* v. *Taylor* (1612) Cro.Jac. 306, 1 Rolle Abr. 6; *Mounsey* v. *Traves* (c. 1621) Vidian's *Entries*, p. 66 (custom " *inter mercatores apud civitatem Lond.*"); *Aswel* v. *Osborn* (c. 1628) *ibid*. 67 (similar).

[92] E.g. *Bate* v. *Luce* (undated) Vidian's *Entries*, p. 70 (London and Venice); *Ashurst* v. *Thomas* (c. 1660) *ibid*. 33 (London and Dublin); *Clarke* v. *Robinson* (c. 1662) *ibid*. 34 (London and Amsterdam); *Aboas* v. *Raworth* (c. 1666) *ibid*. 30 (London and Amsterdam); *Colvile* v. *Cutler* (c. 1666) *ibid*. 31 (London and Gothenburg [Göteborg]); *Walkyn* v. *Butts* (1683) Clift's *Entries*, p. 897 (London and Dunkirk); *Death* v. *Serwonters* (1685), set out below (London and Venice). The custom of London was always laid in a parish and ward, but this was merely for venue purposes, since a jury could not be summoned from the city of London in general: *Bromwich* v. *Loyd* (1698) Lutw. 1582, 1585.

[93] Lutw. 885, 886 (translated from Latin).

[94] The point is raised by the pleadings in *Claxton* v. *Swift* (c. 1685) Lutw. 878, 3 Mod. 86, 2 Show. 441, but not argued.

[95] Lutw. 892.

and judgment was reversed in the Exchequer Chamber " because the custom was too general; for it is made to extend to all manner of persons throughout the world." A year later, however, a custom of London was upheld " for merchants and other residents trading in London " [96]; and shortly after that it was held that any person who drew or accepted a bill of exchange became a trader for the purpose of such a custom, even if he was a gentleman.[97] It follows that such local customs did not constitute a body of law peculiar to merchants. They followed the ordinary medieval principles of English law relating to local customs.

The reason for the prevalence of this method of framing an action of *onerabilis assumpsit* is not immediately apparent. To some extent precedents of pleading are self-perpetuating, but it is safer for the historian to assume that they reflect definite policies. One reason, clearly, was to enable mercantile law to be applied to non-merchants; but this only explains a few of the cases. A more widespread reason may have been that plaintiffs regarded it as unsafe to rely on judicial notice and preferred to have the custom left to a jury, perhaps a special jury of merchants formed by consent of the parties. They could have achieved the same object by bringing a general [98] action of *assumpsit* without mentioning any custom; but we have seen how in cases of novelty this might create uncertainty, and it was probably thought safer to spell out the principle contended for in such a way that the jury had to pronounce for or against the written formulation. It is, of course, possible—even likely—that many plaintiffs did bring general actions of *assumpsit*, or *indebitatus assumpsit*, using the bill of exchange only as evidence at the trial. The form of the record blinds us to the existence of such cases in the seventeenth century as effectively as it did in the medieval period in relation to debt and account.

Conclusion

The evidence summarised in this paper confirms the orthodox conclusion that there was no " incorporation of the law merchant " into the common law before the eighteenth century, but it does so for reasons wholly different from and largely at odds with those

---

[96] *Ewers* v. *Benchkin* (c. 1688) Lutw. 231.
[97] *Sarsfield* v. *Witherley* (1689) Show. 125, Holt 112. These cases have been misread as indicating a change of heart since *Oaste* v. *Taylor* (1612), where it was objected that the defendant was not averred to have been a merchant at the time of acceptance. But in the 1612 case the custom as laid was only for merchants, whereas in the later cases it was " for merchants and others."
[98] This might even mention a bill of exchange in setting the context for the *assumpsit*, without relying on a custom: *e.g. Vandeput* v. *Messam* (undated) Vidian's *Entries*, p. 69.

commonly stated in the legal history books. The common law had always provided remedies in commercial cases, and it adapted as fast as its formulary system would permit to the requirements of commerce. The scope of the common-law remedies, however, is only perceptible to historians after the introduction of *assumpsit*, which permitted far more of the facts to be placed on record. Even then, the variety of courses of action prevents any quantitative assessment, because plaintiffs retained the option of using more general declarations which hid relevant facts. The plaintiff in *assumpsit* could omit all mention of custom, and at the trial ask the judge and jury to notice a mercantile custom as warranting the implication of an undertaking in the circumstances. Or he could declare on a specific " custom of the realm " used by merchants, which probably had the same effect, since the allegation of such a custom, though helping to focus attention on a form of words, was surplusage. Or he could rely on an immemorial local custom, which had to be proved as fact. None of these alternatives treats the law merchant as a body of law akin to foreign law.[99] This may be why, so far as we can tell from the reports, no reliance was placed in this period on learned treatises of the law merchant or of mercantile practice or of the laws of nature, and why no calls were made on the Civil lawyers for their evidence or assistance.[1] Mercantile customs were either local facts or they were the common law of England. In so far as the judges took notice of such customs as common law, they were not taking over for their own use a pre-existing body of jurisprudence. The *lex mercatoria* in its principal medieval sense of speedy procedure was never adopted by the common law: at any rate, not until the establishment of the Commercial Court in the 1890s, and that was more a case of unconscious repetition than of borrowing. The substantive mercantile law, on the other hand, had no existence as a coherent system of principles before the common law itself developed the means of giving it expression. And that development had not proceeded very far by 1700, because the detail was still treated as a matter of fact within the province of jurors rather than judges. To the extent that there was a law merchant before Lord Mansfield, it was not an importation from the *ius gentium*, though without doubt internationally current moral views and economic practices informed this branch of the law as they informed others. Neither was it in

---

[99] As to the treatment of foreign law, see "Ascertainment of Foreign Law: Certification to and by English Courts prior to 1861" (1979) 28 I.C.L.Q. 141–151.

[1] In fact it was a familiar complaint in the 17th century that the common law in commercial matters was too remote from the actual customs of merchants: see, e.g. Sir Josiah Child, *A Discourse about Trade* (1690), p. 113.

any recognisable sense the law of the specialist mercantile courts of fairs, boroughs and admirals, though we may reasonably suppose that a dozen merchants in a piepowder or guildhall court would have administered the same kind of justice as a dozen merchants on a jury at *nisi prius*. Whatever the seventeenth-century writers may have said in vague rhetorical terms about the *lex mercatoria* in England, there was nothing arcane about it. It was in reality nothing other than a refinement of the common law which had always governed mercantile affairs. And the process of refinement was not one of borrowing ready-made law from other jurisdictions, in the way that the developed Canon law was adopted into the common law after the Reformation. It was a crystallisation of principles which had previously been left to the general knowledge and common sense of city juries. The procedures which precipitated those principles as positive law were developed, not by medieval mercantile tribunals or international conference, but by the common-law courts of the Renaissance period. And the common-law courts did not operate those procedures by "incorporating" a law merchant, in any of the usually accepted senses of that term. They used them to create it.

20

ORIGINS OF THE "DOCTRINE" OF CONSIDERATION, 1535-1585

No other doctrine in English law can compete with "consideration" for the greatest diversity and complexity of historical explanations.[1] Most of these explanations can be seen as attempts to answer two groups of questions. Was "consideration" an unbroken development of a single idea from medieval times; or was there a break with medieval thought, and perhaps a combination of different ideas? Second, was it a wholly indigenous development; and, if so, was it an incidental consequence of the exigencies of the forms of action or a direct result of juristic speculation about contractual liability? Alternatively, was it something reflected or borrowed from the canon law or the civil law? And, if so, was the influence brought to bear on the common law directly through Renaissance humanism, or indirectly by way of the canonist chancellors or ecclesiastical judges? It has been customary to seek some single answer to all these questions; but that approach in itself begs another question, for there is no reason to suppose that sixteenth-century lawyers were unanimous as to the nature, let alone the intellectual sources, of the doctrine of consideration. Indeed, the one safe assumption to begin with is that if the matter had been plain then, it would be more readily clarifiable now.

Anyone who attempts to augment, even by a few pages, all that has already been written on this vexed subject must at the outset acknowledge his own foolhardiness; for, in the apt language of our old books, *serra rette son foly demesne*. Nevertheless, there is one large evidential stone

---

1. The principal theories are to be found in the following works: Frederick Pollock, *Principles of Contract: A Treatise on the General Principles concerning the Validity of Agreements in the Law of England* (London, 1876), pp. 149–52; C. C. Langdell, *A Summary of the Law of Contracts*, 2d ed. (Boston, 1880), pp. 58–62; O. W. Holmes, *The Common Law* (1881; reprint ed. by Mark DeWolfe Howe, London and Melbourne, 1968), pp. 200–213, 222–25; J. I. Clark Hare, *The Law of Contracts* (Boston, 1887), pp. 132–36, 141; John W. Salmond, "The History of Contract," *Law Quarterly Review* 3 (1887): 171–78; John W. Salmond, *Essays in Jurisprudence and Legal History* (London, 1891), pp. 187–94, 207–24; James Barr Ames, *Lectures on Legal History and Miscellaneous Legal Essays* (Cambridge, Mass., and London, 1913), pp. 129–30, 142–48; W. T. Barbour, *History of Contract in Early English Equity* (Oxford, 1914), pp. 59–65, 160–68; C. H. S. Fifoot, *History and Sources of the Common Law* (London, 1949), pp. 395–415; A. K. Kiralfy, *The Action on the Case* (London, 1951), pp. 170–85; S. F. C. Milsom, *Historical Foundations of the Common Law* (London, 1969), pp. 309–15; W. M. McGovern, "Contract in Medieval England: The Necessity for Quid pro Quo and a Sum Certain," *American Journal of Legal History* 13 (1969): 173–201, esp. 190–97; J. L. Barton, "The Early History of Consideration," *Law Quarterly Review* 85 (1969): 372–91; A. W. B. Simpson, *A History of the Common Law of Contract* (Oxford, 1975), pp. 316–488; and S. J. Stoljar, *A History of Contract at Common Law* (Canberra, 1975), pp. 38–39.

still unturned. We have never known quite when or how "consideration" appeared in the *assumpsit* declaration, nor what legal discussion (if any) accompanied the process of its becoming a material allegation. It would be idle to expect the discovery of this missing information to end all doubt and speculation concerning the origins of the idea of consideration, if only for the very good reason that the idea seems to have been present in English law long before it acquired the name. But whether we are endeavoring to trace the idea backward or forward from its first appearance in modern guise, our most convenient focus must be the point at which the innominate idea lurking in older jurisprudence became a nominate "doctrine" capable of shaping arguments and controlling decisions. Of course, the focus will not be very sharp. The common law was not in the habit of changing overnight, and its exponents were adept at concealing any overt evidence that it had changed at all. With reasonable confidence, however, we can reduce our concentration to the half century from 1535 to 1585. By the 1580s the reports are full of discussions about consideration; usually the matter arose on a motion in arrest of judgment, but it could also be raised by a demurrer,[2] or writ of error,[3] or special verdict,[4] or argument upon the evidence.[5] Objecting to the declaration "for want of sufficient consideration" had become the lawyer's first resort in attacking any *assumpsit* action that seemed to raise some arguable point, and the procedure was already raising a wide range of questions both substantive and technical. Consideration had achieved the status of a doctrine, and could be defined as a profit to the defendant or a labor or charge to the plaintiff.[6] A mere fifty years earlier there was no trace of "consideration" in *assumpsit* declarations or in the few reported discussions relating to such actions. This fifty years, then, is the period on which attention must be fixed; and it is no accident that it is precisely the period that most previous speculation as to the history of consideration has studiously or unwittingly avoided.

2. Lucy v. Walwyn (1561), for which see below, at n. 43 and accompanying text, p. 381 (demurrer to bar); Richards v. Bartlet (1584), 1 Leo. 19, 74 *English Reports* (hereafter cited as *Eng. Rep.*) 17 (demurrer to bar); Fooly v. Preston (1586), 1 Leo. 297, 74 *Eng. Rep.* 270 (demurrer to declaration; judgment later affirmed on a writ of error: see next note).

3. Isack v. Barbour (1563), Public Record Office, King's Bench (hereafter cited as KB) 27/1207, m. 55 (quoted in n. 61, below); Page's Case (1585), Cambridge University Library (hereafter cited as C.U.L.) MS Ii. 5. 38, fols. 4v–5; Preston v. Tooley (1587), Cro. Eliz. 74, 78 *Eng. Rep.* 334; Howell v. Trevanion (1588), 1 Leo. 93, 74 *Eng. Rep.* 87, Cro. Eliz. 91, 78 *Eng. Rep.* 349.

4. Gramson v. Bower (1584), C.U.L. MS Ii. 5. 38, fols. 126–27; Fuller's Case (1586), Harvard Law School (hereafter cited as H.L.S.) MS 16, fol. 229.

5. Snowe v. Jourdan (1572), H.L.S. MS 1192, fol. 22v; Anon. (1577), Lincoln's Inn (hereafter cited as L.I.) MS Misc. 361, fol. 81; Anon. (1588), H.L.S. MS 16, fol. 423.

6. Webb's Case (1577), 4 Leo. 110, 74 *Eng. Rep.* 763; Richards v. Bartlet (1584), 1 Leo. 19, 74 *Eng. Rep.* 17. See also Coke's formulations in Stone v. Withypoll (1588), 1 Leo. 114, 74 *Eng. Rep.* 106 ("no consideration can be good, if not, that it touch either the charge of the plaintiff, or the benefit of the defendant"), Owen 94, 74 *Eng. Rep.* 924 ("consideration is the ground of every action on the case, and it ought to be either a charge to the plaintiff or a benefit to the defendant").

Origin of the "Consideration" Clause

The first appearance of the *in consideratione* clause in the *assumpsit* declaration may be dated with reasonable precision to 1539.[7] No contemporary, we may be sure, regarded it as a significant event; actions on the case were still in the fluid, experimental stage, and it would be another thirty years or more before the new phrase ousted its predecessors. The most we can hope to discover from the circumstances of its introduction is some sense of what "consideration" originally meant and of the extent to which it represented new thinking about contractual liability. In order to draw the contrast, we must first step back a little before our chosen period.

In the fifteenth century, *assumpsit* actions rarely proceeded beyond the *optulit se* stage, and therefore the precedents in the rolls are mostly of uncontested writs. Hundreds of these precedents recur in the most elementary form: "whereas, in return for [*pro*] a sum agreed or paid beforehand by Y, X had undertaken to build a house for Y, X failed to build the house." The *pro* clause here bears more than a superficial resemblance to the later consideration clause, and a discussion in 1425 suggests that it did indeed reflect a notion of reciprocity: it was because the carpenter had been paid, or could bring debt for the agreed sum, that he himself should be liable in return.[8] By the end of the century, however, the usual formula had become more sophisticated, with the *pro* clause demoted to a recital: "whereas, for a sum agreed or paid, A had agreed to build a house for B, and A had undertaken to build the house within a certain time, A had failed to build within the time as undertaken." The undertaking had been gently separated from the principal bargain, to become in effect a promise to carry out the bargain on time or (in negligence cases) in a careful manner. This verbal divorce was no doubt designed to avert technical objections to overlapping remedies, yet in so doing it introduced a new problem. The undertaking now seemed imperfectly explained; it was no longer expressed to have been made in return for the sum of money, and it was linked to the bargain only by the implication inherent in the word "and." Now, it may seem an absurd subtlety to hold that "and" did not adequately fuse the bargain and the undertaking into one single transaction, but the dilemma arose inevitably from the object of the expanded formula: either the action was founded on the bargain or covenant itself, in which case it would probably fail on formal or

---

7. The following account of the records is based on a study of the King's Bench rolls (KB 27) down to 1550, the results of which are related in more detail in *The Reports of Sir John Spelman*, ed. J. H. Baker, 2 vols., Selden Society, vols. 93 (London, 1977) and 94 (1978), 2:286–97. Forays into the Public Record Office, Common Pleas (hereafter cited as CP) 40, suggest strongly that the King's Bench led the way. It is possible that a full search will shake the details given here, and that in searching about five miles of King's Bench parchment between 1535 and 1550 the writer may have missed something significant.

8. Year Book (hereafter cited as Y. B.) Hil. 3 Hen. 6, f. 36, pl. 33 (1425), *per* Rolf, Sjt. There is no reported reply to this aspect of Rolf's argument.

evidential grounds, or it was founded on the collateral undertaking, in which case it had to be shown why that undertaking should be independently actionable. By the time of Henry VIII at the latest, pleaders seem to have been aware of this problem and increasingly they took care to avoid all mention of a precedent bargain or contract—by reciting a delivery rather than a sale of goods, or a discussion (*colloquium*) instead of a bargain—or else to give the undertaking an explanation of its own. The formulas they devised for the latter purpose are so varied as to defy classification, and include some phrases in which consideration is clearly foreshadowed;[9] but the commonest device was to say that the undertaking had been given in return for (*pro*) a small sum of money, usually twelvepence. This last device was probably in many cases a fiction and is therefore hardly a true precursor of consideration;[10] but the need for such a fiction shows the reality of the pleader's dilemma, and his uneasiness about leaving the undertaking unexplained on the face of the record.

The need for a connecting link between the recited bargain and the undertaking to perform it was the subject of an unreported King's Bench decision in *Marler v. Wilmer* (1539).[11] The plaintiff complained in the mayor's court at Coventry that he had sold goods to the defendant's testator for a sum to be paid on request, and that after the testator's death the defendant executor *super se assumpsit et fideliter promisit* to pay the sum but had not done so. The local court gave judgment for the plaintiff, upon demurrer, and the defendant brought a writ of error in the King's Bench. One of the points assigned for error was "that it does not appear in the declaration for what cause [*quam ob causam*] he made the aforesaid undertaking, either for money paid beforehand, or receipt of part of the aforesaid goods, and so *ex nudo pacto non oritur actio*." He also objected that the action should have been debt, not "deceit on the case," and that the plaintiff should have produced a deed. Unfortunately, the King's Bench proceedings end with the *scire facias* to summon the defendant in error; but it is significant that already by 1539 it could be argued that no action would lie on an undertaking without "*causa*" because it is *nudum pactum*. The declaration had to explain the under-

---

9. E.g., Browne v. Cornely (1533), KB 27/1086, m. 28 (*ob gratitudinem credenciam et benevolenciam* toward his sureties, he undertook to save them harmless; judgment for the plaintiff).
10. In at least four cases the payment was denied by protestation: Tayllor v. Kyme (1533), KB 27/1088, m. 24; Wyvell v. Frenche (1534), KB 27/1092, m. 72; Pynnok v. Fyndern (1539), KB 27/1112, m. 32; Annesley v. Kytley (1539), KB 27/1113, m. 62. In 1567 it was said to be a common-form fiction and untraversable (Lord Grey's Case, as printed in Simpson, *History of Contract*, p. 633, *per* Dyer, C.J.).
11. KB 27/1111, m. 64. This case was discovered and brought to the writer's notice by Mr. David Ibbetson of Corpus Christi College, Cambridge. Mr. Ibbetson has also persuaded the writer that he read too much into the earlier error case of Quasshe v. Skete (1538), KB 27/1109, m. 74: as to which see *Reports of Sir John Spelman*, 2:289. The objection in that case, that the plaintiff below had not set out the *causa actionis*, evidently related not to the declaration but to the curt entry of the plaint as being simply "in an action on the case."

taking, and it was not enough merely to recite a precedent bargain. The consideration required for an executor's promise would continue to give difficulty throughout the century, but the relatively simple objection in 1539 would have applied with equal force to the common declaration in *assumpsit* for the price of goods. Some linking phrase was needed between the recital and the *assumpsit* clause to explain the undertaking, and it can hardly be a mere coincidence that within a year or two of *Marler* v. *Wilmer* several new formulas had been invented for the purpose. The most common of the new devices can best be described as a *quid pro quo* clause. It was used mainly in actions to recover the price of goods, which had become the principal function of *assumpsit* by 1540. The plaintiff alleged a sale of goods for a certain sum, or a delivery of goods worth a certain sum, "for which goods [*pro quibusquidem bonis*]" the defendant undertook to pay. Thus the goods were treated as the *quid* "*pro quo*" the undertaking was given. The buyer could use the same formula, alleging that the promise to deliver was made *pro* the money paid.[12] For over twenty years the *quid pro quo* clause dominated *assumpsit* declarations, and bid fair to jostle consideration out of use.

The consideration clause that appeared in 1539 performed exactly the same linking function as the *quid pro quo* clause. At first it was simply an alternative, chosen whenever it seemed more apt or elegant than *pro*. The first recorded case illustrates this very well. The plaintiff complained that, whereas the defendant's wife had before marriage been indebted to the plaintiff for board, lodging, and a loan, the defendant in full knowledge afterwards, in consideration of his impending marriage and for twelvepence paid to him, undertook to pay off the debt, but had not done so.[13] The plaintiff's counsel had seen fit to make use of the fictional shilling in addition to the true cause, and so the *in consideratione* clause was used to avoid the repetition of *pro*, a word much more appropriate to introduce a payment than a marriage.[14] In the next instance on the King's Bench rolls, the undertaking to pay was in consideration of wrongs done and *pro* twelvepence paid; again *in consideratione* is a companion to *pro*, and it is more apt to describe a motive founded on something past.[15] In a third early case, the two phrases occur together as past and present moving causes, where a woman had asked a man to ride on a

---

12. E.g., Grey v. Botte (1544), KB 27/1133, m. 105 (judgment for the plaintiff).
13. Harvy v. Stone (1539), KB 27/1112, m. 65.
14. Marriage had often been treated as a "consideration" to raise a use, and it was more accurate to describe it so than as *quid pro quo* because there were doubtless other reasons for the marriage than the payment of the debt. See below, at n. 46 and accompanying text.
15. Phyllyp v. Heeth (1540), KB 27/1116, m. 23d. For the association of consideration with causes past or "precedent," see Dyer 49, 73 *Eng. Rep.* 108–9; and Christopher St. German, *Doctor and Student*, ed. T. F. T. Plucknett and J. L. Barton, Selden Society, vol. 91 (London, 1975), p. 229. St. German distinguishes between an "accord" (for past wrongs) and a contract. The first mention of consideration in an *assumpsit* action occurs not in a declaration, but in a plea of accord: Hewton v. Forster (1536), KB 27/1099, m. 76.

journey with her, and for (*pro*) his company and in consideration that he had lent her money, she promised to give him a ring.[16]

In the decade after 1540 there are at least thirty-two instances of consideration clauses in the King's Bench rolls, but there is little uniformity in their form or function. In one back-to-front case the *assumpsit* was the consideration for the plaintiff's promise to perform.[17] In nearly all the cases, however, the consideration was used to explain a promise to pay money. It might be a past act (often the delivery of goods), or a present bargain, or a future act. Sometimes it was combined with the word *pro*, as in the phrase *pro et in consideratione*[18] or the general, meaningless *pro diversis considerationibus*.[19] As a mere alternative to *pro* it could mean "in return for," and this sense of reciprocity is underlined in such phrases as *in consideratione et recompensatione*.[20] But it had more subtle connotations of its own: there was the sense of *causa*, itself ambiguously hovering between the two shades of meaning "because of" and (more subjectively) "having taken into consideration" or "being moved by." The latter sense is clearly manifest in the general form *pro diversis aliis causis et considerationibus ipsum E. adtunc et ibidem moventibus*.[21] It is therefore impossible to assert that the nascent phrase represented precisely the notion of *quid pro quo* or *causa*. There is a very strong case, on the other hand, for saying that it actually combined both notions, and that its triumph over the various *pro* clauses was eventually secured by its convenient ambivalence.

Attempts to Delimit Consideration

On turning to the reports, we meet with an apparent lack of concern with general principles of liability. Not only are there no discussions of the nature of "consideration" before 1560, but when the discussions do begin the profession seems already to be engulfed in a torrent of complex learning gushing out in every direction from no apparent source. Ironically, the commonest types of *assumpsit*—actions for the price of goods or services—received the least attention. Although consideration had begun in such actions, it was by now thought unnecessary for them and if alleged could not be traversed; under such liberal conditions even a conditional gift of money could be enforced.[22] We have seen that consid-

16. Turfote v. Pytcher (1543), KB 27/1130, m. 104.
17. Owtrede v. Whyte (1546), KB 27/1138, m. 24d (judgment for the plaintiff).
18. E.g., Rent v. Danyell (1549), KB 27/1150, m. 104.
19. Usually added to a money payment: e.g., Cawenfeld v. Elder (1546), KB 27/1137, m. 113d (*pro 4d. et pro aliis subsequentibus consideracionibus*); Pynnok v. Clopton (1547), KB 27/1141, m. 79 (*pro 5s. et pro aliis consideracionibus inter ipsos concordatis*); Holmes v. Harryson (1549), KB 27/1149, m. 32 (*pro 2s. et pro diversis aliis causis et consideracionibus*); Norman v. Moore (1549), KB 27/1149, m. 117 (similar).
20. Pyrry v. Appowell (1545), KB 27/1134, m. 67d.
21. Newman v. Gybbe (1549), KB 27/1152, m. 135; Kiralfy, *Action on the Case*, p. 176.
22. Not traversable: Lord Grey's Case (1567), printed in Simpson, *History of Contract*,

eration in these common cases served to link circumstances that had always given rise to liability with the undertaking that enabled *assumpsit* to be brought instead; whatever problems that caused with respect to overlapping remedies, they were not problems relating to the nature of consideration. The doubts were not as to the existence of liability, but as to the form of the remedy and the mode of proof; in the seventeenth-century common counts consideration was to become virtually meaningless, certainly unimportant. It was outside the context of sale that consideration came to be of fundamental importance, because there was no preexisting substantive law of contractual liability and so consideration not only explained the undertaking, but thereby determined whether an action would lie for its breach. This was the context in which discussion began as to what constituted a "good" consideration. Would a merely subjective motive (such as affection), or a "continuing" motive (such as kinship), give binding force to an undertaking; or must the plaintiff have done or promised something in return? If the plaintiff had done something in return, must it have been done in return for the promise; or would it be sufficient if it had been done at the defendant's request, or simply for the defendant's benefit? If the plaintiff had not done, but *promised*, something in return, was it necessary that he should subsequently have performed his promise; or would it be enough that the promise would have been performed if the defendant had not broken his promise?

Adequacy and Contemporaneity

The courts do not seem ever to have been troubled about economic disparity between consideration and promise; it was a common maxim that for a penny consideration a man could bind himself for a hundred pounds.[23] In the earlier cases past consideration is not unusual,[24] and there are also several examples of the vague general clause *pro aliis*

---

p. 633; Anon. (1572), British Library Lansdowne MS 1067, fol. 28, *per* Lovelace, Sjt.; Anon. (1577), L.I. MS Misc. 361, fol. 81, *per* Wray, J. (no need to prove any consideration beyond the debt); Smith v. Hitchcocke (1587), H.L.S. MS 16, fol. 445. Not necessary: Anon. (1581), Godb. 13, 78 *Eng. Rep.* 8; Anon. (1582), L.I. MS Misc. 488, p. 100, *per* Wray and Gawdy, JJ.; also reported, C.U.L. MS Ii. 5. 38, fol. 60; Whorwood v. Gybbons (1587), Gould. 48, 75 *Eng. Rep.* 986, sub nom. Gill v. Harewood, 1 Leo. 61, 74 *Eng. Rep.* 57. Conditional gift: Bedford v. Eyre (1559), KB 27/1192, m. 178 (upon a marriage treaty, the father undertook that *if* the plaintiff married his daughter he would pay twenty pounds; judgment for the plaintiff).

23. J. Rastell, *Exposiciones terminorum* [ca. 1525], sig. B4v ("*ex nudo pacto non oritur accio* but yf any thyng were gevyn for the xx s. though it were not but to the valew of a peny, then it was a good contract"); Howell v. Trevanion (1588), H.L.S. MS 16, fols. 423v–24, *per* Drew; Knight v. Rushworth (1596), Duck's reports, British Library Hargrave MS (hereafter cited as B.L. Harg. MS) 51, fol. 134, *per* Anderson, C.J.

24. E.g., Phyllyp v. Heeth (1540), KB 27/1116, m. 23d (injuries done); Busshewell v. Rye (1546), KB 27/1138, m. 67d (money previously received); Tyll v. Brockhouse (1548), KB 27/1147, m. 103d (goods previously taken).

considerationibus tacked on to a small prepayment.[25] By the 1580s, however, it was common learning that consideration had to be something of value; and it was a standard objection to the consideration that it was "insufficient" or "past." That position may well have been reached in a haphazard way, as defense lawyers persuaded courts to reject particularly dubious kinds of moving cause; but its attainment is significant as marking the emergence of a "doctrine" of consideration. The choice of direction open to the courts was provided by the ambiguity of the word "consideration." In the *causa* sense it might more easily encompass motives, and things past or continuing, whereas in the *quid pro quo* sense it called for some reciprocal act done or promised. Common lawyers were not wont to distinguish these senses, and in the law of uses it was already the practice to speak of "insufficient cause" to denote the absence of *quid pro quo*.

The first area of difficulty seems to have been the consideration of friendship or kinship. That "natural love and affection" should have been rejected as consideration was by no means a foregone conclusion. At the beginning, the word "consideration" was closely associated with the context of marriage;[26] and in 1549 a surety launched an action on an undertaking given "in consideration of friendship and good will."[27] The reaction is first encountered in a case of 1565 concerning uses, which Plowden argued and made into a leading case by reporting verbatim the arguments of counsel. The attack by Serjeants Fletewoode and Wray was based very much on the *quid pro quo* school of thought. Affection or kinship were of no monetary value, and they were continuing states of affairs that would continue even if no promise had been made; as recompense, therefore, they were quite illusory:

> For if a man makes a grant to John Style in consideration of his long acquaintance, or of great familiarity between them, or that they were schoolboys together in their youth, or upon such like considerations, that he will stand seised of his land to the use of him: this will not change the use, for such are not taken as considerations worthy in law to make a use, for they are not of value or recompense. For if I promise you, in consideration that you are of my great familiarity or acquaintance, or are my brother, to pay you £20 at such a day, you shall not have an action on the case or action of debt for it, for it is but a naked and barren pact and *ex*

---

25. See above, at n. 21 and accompanying text. In 1584 it was held that such general consideration could not raise a use, because it did not appear whether it was sufficient (which Coke interpreted as requiring *quid pro quo*) (Mildmay v. Standysh [1584], 1 Rep. 175, 76 *Eng. Rep.* 379; C.U.L. MS Ff. 5. 4, fol. 111).

26. See Yorke's reports, B.L. Harg. MS 388, fol. 180 (1530); Pollard's reports, ibid., fol. 76v (1532); Dyer 17, §100, 73 *Eng. Rep.* 37 (1536); Harvy v. Stone (1539), KB 27/1112, m. 65; Dyer 49, §11, 73 *Eng. Rep.* 109 (1541); and Holt v. Oxenden (1542), KB 27/1125, m. 38 (judgment for the plaintiff in *assumpsit*).

27. Rent v. Danyell (1549), KB 27/1150, m. 104 (imparlance).

nudo pacto non oritur actio, for the cause is not sufficient. And nothing is done or given from the one side, for you were my brother before and will be so afterwards, and you were of my acquaintance before and will be so afterwards.[28]

There was also an evidential reason: "the common law requires fresh cause, whereof the country may have intelligence or knowledge for the trial if need be." Plowden maintained that natural causes were sufficient consideration, and in an ingenious argument based on the law of nature and philosophy demonstrated that the continuance of male heirs was good consideration because men are more reasonable than women and have more discretion in managing affairs. His eloquence won the day, but he had not met the objections squarely and the doubts had been sown. Two years later, Dyer, C.J., seems to have been wavering; according to one report, he ruled that a father's indebtedness was no consideration for a son's promise to pay off the debt, whereas another has him declaring that "whatever goes in ease and benefit of my friend is my ease and benefit also."[29] By 1588, at any rate, the courts had ruled out "love and affection" as consideration for an *assumpsit*, apparently for the reasons advanced on the losing side in 1565.[30]

The later cases on adequacy were mostly about such trivia as forbearances to sue "for a little while,"[31] showing the party a document,[32] permitting a party to do what he was already entitled to do,[33] or releasing a nonexistent right.[34] These transparently artificial considerations were introduced for ulterior reasons: to convert debt into *assumpsit*, to extend liability to personal representatives, or to enable *assumpsit* to be brought to enforce quasi-contractual or noncontractual obligations. The parent principle, however, had more significant offspring in the doctrine that past consideration was insufficient. The objection to past consideration was close, both in spirit and in chronology, to the objection to love and affection. There had been dissent in Mary's reign as to whether a past consideration could support a use, and the context seems to have been the continuing relationship.[35] The doubt spread to *assumpsit* by 1568,

28. Sharington v. Strotton (1564–66), Plowd. 298, at 302, 75 *Eng. Rep.* 454, at 460 (translated).
29. Watton's Case (1567), C.U.L. MS Ii. 3. 14, fol. 145; Lord Grey's Case (1567), H.L.S. MS 2071, fol. 18v. (Cf. Simpson, *History of Contract*, p. 633.) These may be reports of the same case.
30. Harford v. Gardiner (1588), 2 Leo. 30, 74 *Eng. Rep.* 332. For a full discussion of the cases, see Simpson, *History of Contract*, pp. 434–37.
31. Lutwich v. Hussey (1583), Cro. Eliz. 19, 78 *Eng. Rep.* 286.
32. Sturlyn v. Albany (1587), Cro. Eliz. 67, 78 *Eng. Rep.* 327.
33. Lile v. Frencham (1587), H.L.S. MS 16, fol. 418v (permitting finder of goods to retain them until asked for them). This seems to be an attempt to use *assumpsit* instead of trover.
34. Anon. (1584), L.I. MS Misc. 487, fol. 192v (held good, because *est quiett a son mynde*). Cf. Stone v. Wythypoll (1589), Cro. Eliz. 126, 78 *Eng. Rep.* 383; and Tooley v. Windham (1590), Cro. Eliz. 206, 78 *Eng. Rep.* 463.
35. Sir Robert Brooke, *La Graunde Abridgement* (London, 1573), Feoffments al Uses, pl. 54; Simpson, *History of Contract*, pp. 453–54.

and again the context was friendship; a consideration of gratitude for a past favor was rejected, on a motion in arrest of judgment, on the ground that it had been spent when the promise was made.[36] The teaching of Fletewoode and Wray had again prevailed: something past will remain done and cannot be undone, and so it is not a fresh cause moving the promise. The decision would have threatened the growing practice of laying the consideration in the pluperfect tense and the *assumpsit* in the perfect tense, were it not for the common allegation of a "special instance and request." The precedent request linked the past event, in a reciprocal sense, with the undertaking, and thereby avoided the objection.[37] In practice, therefore, the objection to past consideration usually arose only when the pleader had for some reason omitted to lay a request.[38] In many cases the request was no doubt either fictional or (in modern language) "implied in fact"; but in theory a present consideration had to be proved. In a case of 1584, where a friend had undertaken to pay the arrears of account incurred by a beer-clerk if his master would release him, it appeared in evidence and was found specially that the release had occurred before the undertaking was made. Fuller argued that, as the issue was *non assumpsit*, the jurors ought not to enquire into the consideration. The court of Queen's Bench, however, ordered judgment to be entered for the defendant; if the consideration was not proved in evidence, said Wray, C.J., the whole action failed.[39]

Mutual Promises
It has been generally assumed that the question whether a promise could be consideration for a promise was the last important question to be asked, and that its answer in the affirmative finally transformed consideration into a doctrine based on a consensual view of contract. The hurdle, as historians have seen it, was a logical one: a promise was only of value if binding, and to say that it was binding because it was given in consideration of another promise would trap one in a vicious circle from which the only escape would be to suppose that the reciprocal promises somehow breathed life into each other at the same instant, so that they could support each other. Unfortunately for this view, no contemporary discussion has been found in which the problem is treated in those terms. One recent writer has concluded from this that the problem never entered anyone's head, and that "all talk about the recognition of 'wholly execu-

36. Hunt v. Bate (1568), Dyer 272, 73 *Eng. Rep.* 605–9. See also Hurleston v. Lord Dacre (1568), entry in British Library Harley MS 7648, fol. 114, citing Hil. 10 Eliz. 1, m. 850 (D. undertook to pay fourteen pounds *tam in consideracione laboris et industrie* of H. about his affairs *quam in recompensacione onerum et custagiorum* laid out by H. in the same; demurrer to declaration; court takes advisement until Easter term).
37. For a full discussion, see S. J. Stoljar, "The Consideration of Request," *Melbourne University Law Review* 5 (1966): 314–28.
38. E.g., Cooke's Case (1581), L.I. MS Misc. 488, p. 91; Crewe v. Curson (1582), C.U.L. MS Ii. 5. 38, fol. 56v. For the later cases see Simpson, *History of Contract*, pp. 455–58.
39. Gramson v. Bower (1584), C.U.L. MS Ii. 5. 38, fols. 126–27.

tory,' 'bilateral,' or 'consensual' contracts in [the sixteenth] century is wholly misconceived."[40] The only contemporary problem, on this view, was whether the plaintiff had to aver the performance of his own promise; and the answer lay in the "sharp distinction" between a promise and a future act. If A promised B ten pounds if B would build a house, then B had to show that he had built the house before he could sue for the ten pounds; but if A promised B ten pounds in consideration that B then and there promised to build a house, then B's promise was a sufficient consideration to bind A. This was not so much a consideration problem as that of determining whether promises were dependent or independent: a problem eventually to be solved by a mass of abstruse learning centered upon Serjeant Williams's notes to *Pordage* v. *Cole* and then lost (in England) in the confused law about conditions, warranties, and discharge by breach.[41]

Neither approach seems entirely satisfactory. It is true that mutual promises are found at an early date,[42] and that the discussions are not in terms that anyone affected toward the traditional story would wish. But it is equally true that the reported cases do reveal a consideration problem; indeed, the three most extensive early discussions of consideration arose from mutual promises.

The first reported discussion is also the very first case so far discovered in which an objection was taken to the consideration by that name. Such are the vagaries of sixteenth-century law reporting that the report is only to be found in a manuscript notebook, in private possession and hitherto unnoticed, containing reports by Anthony Gell of the Inner Temple. It concerned a mutual friend (Simon Walwyn) who had been asked by one friend (Thomas Lucy) to obtain an assignment of a lease for him from the other friend (John Swyfte). Walwyn in the event bought the lease for himself, and was sued in *assumpsit*. The declaration recited a lease of the manors of Hampton Bishop and Hatton by Queen Mary in 1554 to John Swyfte for sixteen years, and continued:

> and the aforesaid Thomas Lucy, coveting and desiring to acquire and purchase the aforesaid interest and entire estate of the aforesaid John Swyfte for some reasonable sum, to the same Thomas's own use, and having great faith in the same Simon and being fully

---

40. Simpson, *History of Contract*, pp. 461, 467. Much of the material that follows was not available in print when Simpson wrote.

41. There is a valuable account in Stoljar, *History of Contract*, pp. 147–63, which is "an abridged and much revised" version of a longer article in the *Sydney Law Review*, 2:217–52.

42. Perhaps the earliest is Fyneux v. Clyfford (1517), KB 27/1026, m. 76, in which the ingenious and elaborate bill was drawn for (perhaps by) Fineux, C.J. It was an action against a vendor of land who had sold to another; but Fineux, C.J., had not, like William Shipton in Doige's Case, been tricked into paying anything. Fineux had to lay mutual undertakings on each side, a tender of payment by himself, and then a direct assertion that the defendants schemed (*machinaverunt*) to deprive him of the bargain and sold to another. The case has not been traced beyond imparlance. Its uniqueness bears testimony to the peculiar problem raised by a wholly executory contract.

confident in him on account of the long fellowship and acquaintance which existed between the said Simon and John Swyfte, warmly requested and desired the same Simon [at such a time and place] to do whatever he could to obtain and purchase the aforesaid interest [etc.] from the said John for a reasonable sum of money for the said Thomas Lucy, to the use of him the said Thomas Lucy and his assigns.

And the said Thomas then and there promised [*pollicitus fuit*] the same Simon for his labour to be bestowed in that behalf, and for purchasing and procuring the said interest [etc.], to give and deliver to the said Simon immediately upon the purchase of the said estate and interest as aforesaid all the charges, expenses and sums of money paid and spent by him the said Simon in that behalf, and also a gelding to the value of 100s. or 100s. in cash. . . .

Whereupon the same Simon, afterwards on the same [day], in consideration that the same Thomas Lucy would pay the said Simon all his charges, expenses and sums of money paid and spent by him the said Simon in that behalf, and also in consideration of the aforesaid gelding to be delivered to him as aforesaid (or of the aforesaid sum of 100s. to be paid to the same Simon as aforesaid) . . . took upon himself and faithfully promised the said Thomas Lucy that he the same Simon would do as much as he could, with as much speed as possible, to obtain, purchase and procure the said estate and interest [etc.] for the said Thomas Lucy, to the use of him the said Thomas Lucy and his assigns.

The long declaration went on to allege a breach of the undertaking, in that Simon had not obtained the lease for Thomas but had acquired it himself. The defendant pleaded that for three weeks following the undertaking he had done all he could to obtain the lease from John Swyfte, who had utterly refused to sell it to Thomas but had (at the end of the three weeks) granted it to Simon himself, so that Simon could no longer procure it from John for Thomas. To this plea the plaintiff demurred, and the matter was argued in the King's Bench. The original ground of the demurrer was that the defendant, having undertaken to do his best, should have gone on trying for the rest of his life; his confession that he had abandoned his efforts was therefore a confession of breach. This point was not hotly pursued, because it was arguable that the words "with as much speed as possible" would make a mere demand and refusal sufficient; so the argument shifted to the declaration, and to the consideration.

Thomas Nicholls argued that the consideration was nugatory, because the defendant "was to have nothing before the obtaining and so no *quid pro quo*, but *nudum pactum*." Onslow countered with the argument that the gelding was partly "for his labor to be bestowed," and labor had been bestowed in the three weeks of negotiation; but this argument was opposed by Plowden, in a speech that our reporter has irritatingly omitted. The record shows that, after five continuances, the court gave judgment on the demurrer for the plaintiff; and upon the writ of inquiry the inquest returned damages of one hundred pounds and twenty shillings' costs, whereupon the court took advisement again for two terms. The meaning of this last adjournment is obscure, but because judgment had already been given "that the aforesaid Thomas do recover his damages" the court must have decided that the consideration was good as alleged.[43] This is not a clear case; the plaintiff's promise (or "pollicitation") is mentioned in the recital, not directly in the consideration clause, and so it could be argued that the consideration was not the promise but a future act that never fell to be performed, and that the problem was therefore one of dependency. According to Gell's report, the unsuccessful argument was apparently that something conditional on the defendant's performance was not *quid pro quo*. If A promises B that he will do x if B does y, and B in consideration of A's promise to do x undertakes to do y, but fails to do it, the consideration for B's promise logically fails because it is subject to a condition that is not fulfilled. This is a more subtle point than the historians' conundrum about a promise for a promise; but without a text of Plowden's argument we cannot be certain that the more general problem of mutual promises was not also raised. What we do know is that while *Lucy* v. *Walwyn* was depending, and during the readership of Richard Onslow (Lucy's counsel), the general point was argued in the Inner Temple. Again Anthony Gell is the source, and it is worth reproducing his report in full:

> Note that Kelway said that if I give another 20s. or a penny in consideration that he to whom the gift is made should make an assurance to me of his manor of Dale for the sum of £20 to be paid later, and if he who takes the penny does not make assurance, the other may have an action on the case and recover damages to the value of the land; because it was a contract and there was *quid pro quo*.
>
> And Thomas Gawdy said that, even if no money had been paid, but one promised the other to enfeoff him of his manor of Dale before such a day, and the other promised to pay him £20 for it, if the feoffor did not make the feoffment the other could have an action on the case notwithstanding that no money was paid. But Kelway denied this, and said that it is but *nudum pactum* upon which *non oritur actio*, without *quid pro quo*. And see *Lucy's Case*, above, well argued in a similar action on the case.[44]

---

43. Lucy v. Walwyn (1561–63), KB 27/1198, m. 183 (extracts translated in the text); Anthony Gell's manuscript reports (hereafter cited as Gell MS), fols. 154v–63v (quoted below, at text accompanying n. 60). The report ends, "Plowden argue al contrary et le grand reason que il fist fuit ceo que ouste le respondre sur *quid pro quo*." The writer is most grateful to Mrs. A. E. Gell for permission to copy the manuscript in her possession.

44. Gell MS, fol. 198 (translated). It is reported under Michaelmas term 1562, and there

Again we must lament the absence of detailed reasons, but it is clear that no less a lawyer than Robert Kelway (Keilwey) regarded mutual promises as *nudum pactum*, because the counter-promise was not *quid pro quo*, and that Anthony Gell thought this to have been the main point in *Lucy* v. *Walwyn*.

A similar division of opinion occurred in the next reported discussion, which arose from Lord Effingham's victory in an archery contest. The agreement was a ten-pound wager on the result, between the loser and a noncompetitor. As yet there was no objection of public policy to wagering contracts, and so the defendant's argument turned on the consideration. The only consideration for the defendant's promise to pay ten pounds was the plaintiff's counter-promise to pay ten pounds if the defendant won the competition. It is proper for us to note that again the counter-promise was conditioned upon an event that never happened; but that point is not expressly taken in the printed report. Mounson, J., thought a counter-promise was a good consideration because it was "reciprocal." Manwood, J., however, took the more conservative view that it was not; between the competitors, he said, there was good consideration in preparing equipment, attending the match, and "the labour in shooting and the travell in going up and down between the marks"; but between the "bettors by" there was no such consideration.[45]

The third of our discussions was occasioned by a somewhat mercenary love affair. A suitor for the hand of the defendant's sister had entered into negotiations with the defendant, and the crucial bargaining point was whether the girl was worth fifteen hundred pounds (that is, in property). She was not, and the plaintiff did not marry her; instead he brought *assumpsit* against the brother for breach of an undertaking that she was worth the sum mentioned. The consideration for the defendant's undertaking was the plaintiff's counter-promise that, if the girl was worth fifteen hundred pounds, he would pay the defendant two hundred pounds. The transaction smacks of wagering, but that point was not taken. Yelverton moved in arrest of judgment that there was no consideration because, at the time when the promise was broken (the same instant as it was made), the plaintiff had sustained no prejudice. Gawdy, J.—the same Thomas Gawdy who had advocated the recognition of mutual promises in 1562—thought there was consideration, because of the suitor's financial interest in the girl's wealth: "It seems his intent was to marry as much for the riches as for love." But Wray, C.J., and Ayloffe, J.,

---

is no express reference to the Inner Temple, but Gell often noted discussions in the inn. Keilwey (d. 1580) read in 1547, Gawdy (d. 1588) read in 1553 and 1560, and Gell (d. 1583) was reader-elect in 1563–64.

45. West v. Stowell (1577), 2 Leo. 154, 74 *Eng. Rep.* 437. The record in CP 40/1346, m. 719 (Trin., 1577), ends with an imparlance; the declaration corresponds closely to the report, the consideration being laid as a conditional past promise ("in consideracione quod [the plaintiff] assumpsisset super se et fideliter ... promisisset quod si ... [the defendant] assumpsit et ... promisit quod si. ... ").

decided there was no consideration, because the defendant had no reciprocal remedy for the two hundred pounds; if the counter-promise was not binding, it was no consideration for the defendant's promise.[46]

In so far as there is a discernible theme in these discussions, it is not the need for the plaintiff to aver performance of his counter-promise[47] but an uneasiness about the want of reciprocity or *quid pro quo*. How could a promise be consideration for another promise, when it was itself conditioned on the performance of the other promise? Could even an unconditional promise be regarded as *quid pro quo*? However readily these questions may have been answered at the end of the century, the opinions of such distinguished lawyers as Plowden, Keilwey, and Wray, in the third quarter of the century, are enough to show that the difficulties then were serious. When general statements about the effectiveness of mutual promises began to appear in the books, the explanation of their efficacy was that there were reciprocal remedies.[48] The constant repetition of that proposition in the reports indicates in itself that it was not altogether digestible. On the other hand, there was never any difficulty over "future acts" as consideration; it only became necessary to explore the distinction between promise-consideration and act-consideration, in the context of the need to aver performance by the plaintiff, once the difficulties about promise-consideration had been overcome. The value of the early discussions is not only the unsureness they reveal, but the testimony they bear to the widespread belief that good consideration was synonymous with *quid pro quo*.

Was Consideration Old Law or New?

By 1600 there were so many decisions touching the doctrine of consideration that recourse to earlier ideas was seldom necessary. To that extent the doctrine of consideration was plainly novel, so novel in fact that none of the cases after 1568 was in print until the seventeenth century. In the earliest discussions, however, lawyers saw no incongruity in citing Year Book cases for propositions about consideration: in the

---

46. Butterye v. Goodman (1583), C.U.L. MS Ii. 5. 38, fols. 85v–87. Gawdy, J., dissented from Wray, C.J., and Ayloffe, J., on a similar point in Smith v. Smith (1584), 3 Leo. 88, 74 *Eng. Rep.* 559.

47. Simpson, *History of Contract*, pp. 461 ff., in arguing that this was the question, relies on cases beginning in 1596. In the cases of 1561, 1577, and 1583 any such averment was out of the question because the plaintiff's promise never became due for performance.

48. E.g., Anon. (1579), L.I. MS Misc. 488, p. 61 ("si jeo promise al J. S. leas de mon parsonadge pur 10 li. annual rent et J. S. agrea a ceo, que en cest case si jeo ne performe ceo accordant il avera accion sur le case sur cest assumpcion, et le consideracion fuit assetts sufficient car la ad equall remedie envers lauter si le contract ne soit performe"); Anon. (1584), C.U.L. MS Ii. 5. 38, fol. 120v; Anon. (1584), ibid., fol. 159v; Fuller's Case (1586), H.L.S. MS 16, fol. 229 (either performance of act or "cross-assumption" required); Lile v. Frencham (1587), ibid., fol. 418v; Strangborough v. Warner (1589), 4 Leo. 3, 74 *Eng. Rep.* 686.

middle of the sixteenth century, Brooke and Plowden explained the nonfeasance cases of 1409 and 1425 as showing that *assumpsit* would not lie without consideration;[49] Wyndham, J., in 1581 adapted a definition of consideration from a remark of Serjeant Jenney in 1476;[50] and, in 1588, Coke professed to have based his "charge or benefit" definition on the marriage-money case of 1477.[51] Should we conclude that consideration was but an amalgam of old ideas in a new guise, or were lawyers trying to disguise, or at least authenticate, completely new ideas?

Of one thing we may be sure: the law of consideration was English. Of course, we know that St. German had some slight acquaintance with the canonist learning about *causa,* and that Plowden was able to quote a brief civilian definition of *nudum pactum*.[52] But these superficial flirtations with Romanism had no noticeable effect on the history of consideration, except perhaps on Plowden's notion of "deliberation" or intention to be bound; but that notion bore little fruit until Lord Mansfield tried unsuccessfully to revive it two centuries later, and it is now treated by English lawyers as a requirement distinct from consideration. The sixteenth-century cases contain no discussion of error or of vested pacts. Both before and after the introduction of "consideration," English lawyers admittedly made free use of the phrase *nudum pactum*;[53] but they were borrowing language, not legal doctrine. It can also be admitted that the notion of consideration to raise a use, a generation older than consideration in *assumpsit,* played an influential role;[54] indeed, it was probably not until late in Elizabeth I's reign that it occurred to anyone that there might be two "doctrines." This, however, is far from acknowledging canonist influence; the law of uses was the creation of the common-law courts, not (as so many have assumed) of canonist chancellors.[55] The most we can say of Roman influence is that St. German and Plowden

---

49. Brooke, *Abridgement,* Action sur le Case, pll. 7, 40; Plowd. 309, 75 *Eng. Rep.* 470.

50. Lord Gerard's Case (1581), L.I. MS Misc. 361, fol. 21v: "al primes il monstre que fuit un consideracion, le quel il define solonque le definition de Genney in 16 E. 4. en tiel manner: un consideracion nest que un reasonable cause pur de mover ou pur de passer chose etc." This is a reference to Y. B. Mich. 16 Edw. 4, f. 9, pl. 5 (1476), where Jenney, Sjt., explained that an accord must be pleaded with satisfaction, "car per nostre ley parols sans reason ne liera nulluy, car si jeo die a vous que jeo dona ou paya a vous xx li. a certain jour *nihil operatur* per ceux parols."

51. Stone v. Withepoole (1588), Owen 94, 74 *Eng. Rep.* 924. The case referred to is Y. B. Mich. 17 Edw. 4, f. 5, pl. 4 (1477).

52. *Doctor and Student,* pp. 228-29; Plowd. 309, 75 *Eng. Rep.* 470-71.

53. E.g., Y. B. Mich. 9 Hen. 5, f. 14, pl. 23 (1421), *per* Cokaine, J.; Y. B. Pasch. 11 Hen. 6, f. 43, pl. 30 (1433); Y. B. Trin. 17 Edw. 4, f. 4, pl. 4 (1477), *per* Townshend, Sjt.; Yorke's reports, B.L. Harg. MS 388, fol. 215 (before 1537); Gray's Inn reading, probably that of James Hales in 1537, B.L. Harg. MS 253, fol. 12; Gell MS, fol. 198 (quoted in the text accompanying n. 44); Sharington v. Strotton (1565), Plowd. 298 at 302, 305, 306, 308v; 75 *Eng. Rep.* 454, at 460, 464, 465, 470; West v. Stowell (1577), 2 Leo. 154, 74 *Eng. Rep.* 437; Cook v. Pyne (*temp.* Eliz. 1), L.I. MS Misc. 487, fol. 275v.

54. See Simpson, *History of Contract,* pp. 327-74.

55. Ibid., pp. 327-28, 372-74.

were curious to see whether foreign solutions were capable of adaptation to fill the jurisprudential void; but they did not delve very deep, and if their knowledge of other laws was so limited, it is inconceivable that the profession as a whole paid the least attention to canon or civil law.

Causa

Both in the plea rolls and in the reports, consideration was not infrequently associated with or defined in terms of "cause."[56] Some have jumped to the conclusion that this betokens some reliance on Roman conceptions of *causa*; but it seems rather that, as with *nudum pactum*, all that was borrowed was the vocabulary. And, like other borrowed words such as *injuria*, it was virtually devoid of precise technical meaning: indeed, it was probably borrowed as a nontechnical word. There is an ambiguity in the word "cause"—and also in "consideration" when used in that sense—quite distinct from the other ambiguity in "consideration" to which attention was drawn above. For, in addition to the sense of *causa promissionis*, the reason why the promise was made, it could also denote the "cause of action," the reason why the law made the promise actionable. No doubt in some minds the two coalesced, so that what made the promise actionable was the sufficiency of the reason why it was made; but no assertion in such clear terms appears in the books. If we compare three early sixteenth-century statements about the liability of carpenters for nonfeasance, we find the requirement of advance payment consistently treated as *causa* in the sense of *causa actionis* rather than *causa promissionis*:

> If I covenant with a carpenter to build a house, and pay him £20 to build the house by a certain day, and he does not build the house by the day, now I shall have a good action upon my case because of [*per cause de*] the payment of my money; and yet it sounds only in covenant, and without payment of money in this case there is no remedy. . . . And so it seems to me in the case at bar the payment of the money is the *cause of the action* on the case.[57]
>
> If I promise you to build you a house by a day, which I do not do, this is but *nudum pactum* upon which [you] shall not have an action. . . . [But] if I give certain money to someone to build me a house by a day, and he does not build it by the day, there this is a

---

56. For the association in the words of pleadings, see above, at nn. 11, 19, 21. For definitions, see, e.g., Calthorpe's Case (1574), Dyer 336b, §34, 73 *Eng. Rep.* 759 ("un consideration est un cause ou occasion meritorious . . ."); Lord Gerard's Case (1581), L.I. MS Misc. 361, fol. 22, *per* Dyer, C.J. ("un consideracion est *causa meritoria* pur que il granteroit, et poet estre appell per bien *causa reciproca*, s. un mutuall cause"); and Sydenham v. Worlington (1585), Godb. 31, 78 *Eng. Rep.* 20, *per* Peryam, J. ("it is sufficient if there be any moving cause or consideration precedent, for which cause or consideration precedent the promise was made").

57. Orwell v. Mortoft (1505), Keil. 78, pl. 25, 72 *Eng. Rep.* 239, *per* Frowyk, C.J. (translated).

> consideration why I should have an action on my case for the nonfeasance.[58]
>
> If a man comes to me and says, "Give me £10 and I will build you a barn of so much in length," now if he does not build I shall have an action on my case. It is the contrary where no money was given, for then it is but *nudum pactum*. And this is nonfeasance; but, because I have no remedy for my money, this is the *cause why* I shall have this action.[59]

When we come to *Lucy* v. *Walwyn* in 1561, we find "consideration" still being used in this sense, and may even allow ourselves a little surprise on finding talk of consideration for an action in tort:

> Always in an action on the case there must be a consideration in fact or in law. Thus, if a man menaces my villeins of my manor of Dale so that they run away from it, I shall have an action on the case because it is wrong, and against law and reason, which makes a consideration in law. And so it is for slandering me: it is a consideration in law. But if there is no consideration in fact or in law, no action on the case lies. And this is why the book is agreed in 11 Hen. 4, where one erected a school which was to the nuisance of another, and yet no action against him who erected it.... And so in our case there is no consideration in fact or in law, for he who undertook to obtain the lease was to have nothing before the obtaining; so that there is no *quid pro quo*, but only *nudum pactum*, upon which an *assumpsit* cannot be.[60]

If "consideration" were here used in its later sense, we might argue that "consideration in fact" was *quid pro quo* and that "consideration in law" was our modern duty of care. But it is obviously not used as a term of art in this passage; it means "the reason why I can sue." If the passage reflects current thought in 1561, there was evidently still no doctrine of consideration; the word was the name of the problem, not of its answer.

Again it is the plea rolls that provide the best evidence of a refinement of meaning. In 1563 an administratrix, who had been sued in London on a promise to pay the debt of the deceased, had the judgment against her reversed in the King's Bench for error because "no consideration is alleged by reason of which [she] promised and undertook to pay."[61] Considera-

---

58. Anon. (between 1526 and 1537), Yorke's reports, B.L. Harg. MS 388, fol. 215 (translated). This is the first use of the word "consideration" in a reported contract case; but it is obviously not used in the later sense.

59. Gray's Inn reading, probably that of James Hales in 1537, B.L. Harg. MS 253, fol. 12 (translated).

60. Lucy v. Walwyn (1561), Gell MS, at fol. 161, *per* Nicholls (translated). The case referred to is The Case of Gloucester School, Y. B. Hil. 11 Hen. 4, f. 47, pl. 21 (1410).

61. Isack v. Barbour (1563), KB 27/1207, m. 55: "nulla allegatur consideracio ob quam predicta Elizabetha promisit et super se assumpsit." The writer is indebted to Dr. R. H. Helmholz for bringing this case to his attention.

tion here is not only *causa promissionis*, but it seems to have acquired a technical sense, at least for the pleader. The *causa promissionis* sense had always underlain the consideration clause of the declaration, which was introduced with the object of showing cause for the undertaking. It was in this sense that past and insufficient considerations were at first recited without demur; they were sound reasons for promising. It also explains such seemingly unreciprocal considerations as natural love and affection, being found in arrears upon an account,[62] having goods in the capacity of an administrator,[63] or having goods by finding.[64] These were all held good in their time, until they were struck down by the countervailing notion of reciprocity. But the only ultimate legacy of this looser view of consideration was the *indebitatus* formula; it was to be by far the most important species of *assumpsit*, yet it was a species in which consideration in the established sense played no real part and which in the seventeenth and eighteenth centuries spread itself well beyond the bounds of "contract." Once consideration was not merely a cause, but a "reciprocal" or "mutual" cause, then the older sense of *causa* was defunct. Consideration had come to mean the price of the promise, not the motive behind it.

Quid pro Quo

The *causa reciproca* mentioned by Dyer, C.J., was better known to common lawyers as *quid pro quo*. Much controversy has raged over the suggestion, promoted by Langdell and Holmes, that consideration was somehow "derived" from *quid pro quo*. The arguments put forward by those pioneers of the law of contract now seem incredibly odd. Yet the reaction against the *quid pro quo* school has at worst been equally misconceived. In its bluntest form, the traditional learning was that *quid pro quo* was a precise and technical doctrine in the law of debt; this doctrine was then either transferred to or absorbed into the law of *assumpsit* because of the close analogy between *indebitatus assumpsit* and debt; or, according to the opposing school, it was not precisely followed in *indebitatus assumpsit* because that action was tortious in origin and there was no need to prove an indebtedness in any technical sense. This traditional learning—which has been on the wane in recent years—rests on two false assumptions. In the first place, *quid pro quo* was not a

---

62. Snowe v. Jurden (1572), KB 27/1242, m. 481; KB 27/1244, m. 228; H.L.S. MS 1192, fol. 22v; C.U.L. MS Hh. 2. 9, fol. 59. In the first action the consideration was an accounting together and being found in arrears; in the second it was altered to a being found in arrears (reciting the account in the *cum* clause) *and* twelvepence paid (probably a fiction).

63. Hudson's Case (1558), cited in Howell v. Trevanion (1588), H.L.S. MS 16, fol. 423v; Becher v. Mountjoye (1573), in E. Coke, *Booke of Entries* (London, 1614), fols. 2–3 (citing Mich. 15 & 16 Eliz. 1, m. 1959).

64. Lile v. Frencham (1587), H.L.S. MS 16, fol. 418v; C.U.L. MS Ii. 5. 38, fol. 259 (executor; case of finder put in argument); Ireland v. Higgins (1589), Cro. Eliz. 125, 78 *Eng. Rep.* 383, Owen 93, 74 *Eng. Rep.* 924, 3 Leo. 219, 74 *Eng. Rep.* 644, Het. 50, 124 *Eng. Rep.* 334 (finder of animal).

precise doctrine carefully worked out in medieval times in the context of debt. The prevalence of the general issue prevented any discussion of the basis of liability in debt, except in those rare cases where there was a tentative demurrer to a novel kind of declaration: and when that happened, as in the marriage-money cases of the fifteenth century, everyone who spoke seems to have had a different conception of *quid pro quo*. The second error lay in supposing that the notion belonged exclusively to the action of debt, and could therefore have influenced only *indebitatus assumpsit*. This was doubly wrong. First, the consideration in *indebitatus assumpsit* never was the *quid pro quo* of the debt-creating contract, but was either the indebtedness itself or something collateral (such as the fictional shilling, or a forbearance). Second, and more important, *quid pro quo* was a constituent element of a "bargain," only one side of which was remedied by debt. It had therefore been as relevant in *assumpsit* for not performing a bargain as in debt, and it continued to play a more prominent role in "special" *assumpsit* than it ever did in *indebitatus assumpsit*.

Thus, in *Doige's Case* (1442), Newton, C.J., and Fortescue, C.J., both gave as the reason for allowing *assumpsit* against a defaulting vendor of land that it achieved reciprocity of remedies: "it would be wonderful law if a bargain could be made by which one party was bound by an action of debt but was without remedy against the other."[65] One of the clerks of the King's Bench actually described the payment for the promise as *quid pro quo*.[66] In some of the early Tudor discussions of *assumpsit* to perform acts, the prepayment that was regarded as the cause of action is described as *quid pro quo*.[67] The first reported nonfeasance case where there was no prepayment, *Sukley v. Wyte* (1543), occasioned a discussion in terms of reciprocity; the word "consideration" does not appear, but Shelley, J., in reserving judgment, remarked that nothing was given in return for the undertaking "except a thing which by law he could do anyway."[68] For Keilwey, in 1562, it was only *quid pro quo* that could save a promise from being *nudum pactum*.[69] Likewise, Beaumont, also of the Inner Temple, said in a case about uses a few years later: "In every bargain there must be *quid pro quo* or else it is *nudum pactum* and no perfect bargain. If I bargain with a carpenter that he will build me a house, and he agrees to do it, but it is not agreed what he will have for his labor, this

65. [Shipton v. Dogge] (1442), Y. B. Trin. 20 Hen. 6, f. 34, pl. 4 (1442) (translated).
66. Simpson, *History of Contract*, p. 626, citing H.L.S. MS 156. William Broune or Brome was filazer for Yorkshire and Lincolnshire from 1434 to 1458 and chief clerk from 1458 to 1461.
67. Yorke's reports, B.L. Harg. MS. 388, fol. 215; Sir Anthony Fitzherbert, *La Nouvelle Natura Brevium* (London, 1534), fol. 145 G.
68. Library of Congress, Gell MS, Pasch. 34 Hen. 8, fol. 12v (translated); Simpson, *History of Contract*, pp. 631–32. These reports were written by the same Anthony Gell who is mentioned above.
69. See above, at n. 44 and accompanying text. See also Nicholls's argument, above, at text accompanying n. 60.

is a void bargain unless the money be paid immediately, or a day of payment appointed, or earnest given."[70] And Coke, who showed little interest in *assumpsit*, was sure that the consideration required to raise a use was nothing more nor less than *quid pro quo*.[71]

"Labor or Charge"

Although the notion of a bargain, or *quid pro quo*, seems to have been responsible for ousting vaguer notions of *causa* from English law, it does not explain the whole story; for, by the 1580s, it was repeatedly being stated that a promise could be supported by considerations which did not amount to *quid pro quo*.[72] The tradition of legal history was that these further considerations, usually summarized in the misleading phrase "detriment to the promisee," were a legacy of the delictual origins of *assumpsit* for nonfeasance. The cases which established that *assumpsit* lay for nonfeasance had all stressed the need for the plaintiff to show that he had been deceived out of his money, or had suffered consequential loss in reliance on the promise.[73] Ironically, the very prepayment that had been treated as *quid pro quo* was in the same cases treated as "tortious" damage: the confusion of ideas was present from the start. There is no doubt that the delictual approach held considerable sway in the reigns of Henry VII and Henry VIII. Frowyk, C.J., repeatedly stressed the deceit or "misdemeanour" as the cause of action,[74] and an illuminating moot of 1516 shows a general supposition in Gray's Inn that *assumpsit* lay only for a tort (*injuria*) that caused damage.[75] For Spelman, J., in 1532, a breach of promise was actionable in *assumpsit* because it was a "tort."[76] And declarations in *assumpsit* from this time onward nearly always alleged some form of consequential damage. In assessing this evidence, we should not deceive ourselves into confusing form and substance: the main reason for the delictual approach was to find a justification for using actions on the case instead of "general" writs of debt or covenant,

70. Bracebridge's Case (1583?), B.L. Harg. MS 9, fol. 136, *per* Beaumont "le puisne" (translated). The speaker is probably Henry Beaumont (d. 1585), who became a bencher in 1584; his elder brother Francis (d. 1598) became a bencher in 1578.
71. Mildmaye's Case (1584), 1 Rep. 175a, 76 *Eng. Rep.* 379; Wiseman v. Barnard (1585), 2 Rep. 15, 76 *Eng. Rep.* 418.
72. Webb's Case (1577), 4 Leo. 110, 74 *Eng. Rep.* 763; Baxter v. Read (1584), Treby's notes to Dyer 272 (73 *Eng. Rep.* 606) in marg.; Sydenham v. Worlington (1585), Godb. 31, 78 *Eng. Rep.* 20; Foster v. Scarlet (1587), Cro. Eliz. 70, 78 *Eng. Rep.* 330; Preston v. Tooley (1587), Cro. Eliz. 74, 78 *Eng. Rep.* 334.
73. E.g., Shipton v. Dogge (see above, at n. 65); Orwell v. Mortoft (see next note); Pykeryng v. Thurgoode (see below, at n. 76). In the last case, consequential loss alone is relied on, and deceit is no longer discussed.
74. Y. B. Mich. 20 Hen. 7, f. 8, pl. 18 (1504); Keil. 69, 77, 72 *Eng. Rep.* 229, 239. The case is Orwell v. Mortoft (1505), CP 40/972, m. 123.
75. Moot at Peter Dillon's reading, L.I. MS Misc. 486(2), fol. 7v; printed in *Reports of Sir John Spelman*, 2:272. The question was whether an action on the case lay against a carpenter for nonfeasance. Harlakenden and Hales thought not; Tingleden said that consequential physical damage was necessary; Dillon and Martin said that it was sufficient if there was *injuria*. None of the speakers took the point about prepayment and *quid pro quo*.
76. Pykeryng v. Thurgoode (1532), printed in *Reports of Sir John Spelman*, 1:5, *per* Spelman, J.

and we need not suppose that the notion of deceit denoted much more than a disappointed expectation. There does, nevertheless, seem to have been a substantive principle as well: the principle that a promisor should be liable for breaking his promise if the promisee has relied on the promise in such a way as to incur loss. The defaulting carpenter could be seen, on this view, as being liable because of the "wrong" he had done the client both by taking his money and by keeping him without a home.[77]

Having granted all this, we must face the near impossibility of linking either the delictual history or the substantive principle with the "doctrine" of consideration in the way suggested by Hare and Ames. The elements of deceit and consequential loss were never incorporated in the consideration clause, but were destined to wither away as fictions. And in the cases that established "detriment to the promisee" as good consideration, the consideration in question had nothing in common with the earlier deceit cases: it was a reciprocal future act, or a promise to act, by the plaintiff. Even the line between "detriment" consideration and *quid pro quo* was unhistorical, probably the result of a Tudor restriction of the latter, which later generations would receive as medieval.[78] Salmond was correct, therefore, in supposing a "breach of continuity" between the rationale of the nonfeasance cases and the doctrine of consideration. On the other hand, there was no breach of continuity in the development of *quid pro quo*; and so the conclusion drawn from Salmond's theory, that consideration must have been imported into English law *ab extra*, was as unnecessary as it is improbable.

Conclusion

We began with a warning against an undue desire for historical neatness. When the legal historian sees confusion or inconsistency, unless it is of his own making, he is probably looking at law being made. If a legal historian of the twenty-fourth century purported to reveal the perfect clarity of, say, the English doctrine of fundamental breach in the 1960s and 1970s, he would be a bad historian; we of the 1960s and 1970s know how many plausible ways there are of looking at the same problem, but we cannot know (as our successor will) which view will ultimately prevail, and so the state of uncertainty is itself the historical truth. It rather looks as though "consideration" was in the same plight in

---

77. Ibid.; Anon. (before 1537), Yorke's reports, B.L. Harg. MS 388, fol. 215.
78. For the uncertainty of the judges in 1458, see Y. B. Mich. 37 Hen. 6, f. 8, pl. 18 (1458). Prisot, C.J., apparently thought *quid pro quo* unnecessary to maintain debt; Danvers, J., thought a future act was *quid pro quo*; and Moyle, J., thought a future act done for a third party was "tantamount" to *quid pro quo*. The medieval uncertainty is fully discussed by McGovern, "Contract in Medieval England," pp. 173–201. The later definitions of *quid pro quo* may, ironically, have been more influenced by Roman law than consideration was: not by way of canon law or St. German, but through the revival of interest in Glanvill and Bracton.

the period we have examined. Most lawyers could identify the questions without difficulty, but the search for a clear answer was complicated and delayed in practice by divergent views about the forms of action, by the infinite variety of special declarations, and by the tireless ingenuity of opposing counsel. The survival of older ways of settling disputes had rendered a detailed law of contractual liability unnecessary, or at least unattainable, before the establishment of *assumpsit* for nonfeasance. The comfortable certainty of that old world ended when the special declarations in case, with their myriad permutations of facts, began to throw up endless questions of law that had never been posed before. These new questions required new, more precise formulations of shadowy medieval notions, and the nascent learning suddenly converged in the 1560s upon a simple phrase which was calculated merely to avoid or deflect a number of disparate problems raised by the development of *assumpsit* declarations. Contemporary sources suggest that the only novelty lay in the refinement of earlier ideas; for the spiritual sources of the law of consideration were the two simple, timeless, and ubiquitous moral principles that bargains should bind both parties and that men should be held to promises on which others have actively relied. The technical "doctrine of consideration" in which these principles came to be enshrined in the time of Elizabeth I was occasioned by nothing more arcane than the fertile ambiguity resulting from a little shift of wording by the pleader. It is true enough that the life of the law has not been scholastic logic: it has been the conversion of loose words into jargon.

NOTE

The significance of *Marler* v. *Wilmer* (p. 380, above) is explored in detail in D. Ibbetson, "Assumpsit and Debt in the early Sixteenth Century: the origins of the indebitatus count" (1982) 41 *Cambridge Law Journal* 142-161.

11 Sir Thomas Walmsley

Walmsley was the principal opponent of the King's Bench attitude towards actions on the case.

Portrait in the writer's possession

21

NEW LIGHT ON SLADE'S CASE

Slade's Case is of such significance in the history of the common law that it has, quite properly, been the subject of more scrutiny and discussion in recent years than any other case of the same age.[1] The foundation of all this discussion has been Coke's report,[2] which is the only full report in print. The accuracy and completeness of Coke's version have hardly been challenged, and the discussions have assumed that it contains almost all there is to know about the case. This assumption must be discarded if we are to understand the contemporary significance of the case.

The problem of resurrecting sixteenth and seventeenth century reports from obscurity is by no means confined to *Slade's Case*. An enormous mass of unpublished material stands in urgent need of detailed analysis and study, and when this has been done a good deal of legal history as now written will require modification. The fact that certain volumes of reports were printed, and others were not, should be an immaterial consideration to the historian; law publishers exercised no editorial functions and printed good and bad books indiscriminately. Sometimes, therefore, the best report of a leading case is only to be found in manuscript; and very often important supplementary reports remain unpublished. It is natural that practising lawyers should rely chiefly on the printed reports, as being the most accessible, and that anything which Coke reported should come to acquire the greatest authority.[3] But it is clear that legal historians, who wish not merely to retrace the law as it actually developed but to understand how and why particular decisions were made, and what effect those decisions were believed to have at the time, must begin to tackle the shelves of manuscript reports which occupy so many of our major libraries.[4]

---

[1] See A. W. B. Simpson, "The Place of Slade's Case in the History of Contract" (1958) 74 L.Q.R. 381; H. K. Lücke, "Slade's Case and the Origin of the Common Counts" (1966) 81 L.Q.R. 422, 539; 82 L.Q.R. 81; S. F. C. Milsom, *Historical Foundations of the Common Law* (1969), pp. 292–308.

[2] 4 Rep. 91; 76 E.R. 1072.

[3] *Cf.* G. D. G. Hall, "An Assize Book of the 17th Century" (1963) 7 *American Journal of Legal History* 228, 229, to the same effect.

[4] The first problem will be that of classification and listing. A valuable start has been made by Dr. L. W. Abbott, of the University of Guelph, in his *Lawyers and Law Reporting in the Sixteenth Century* (London Ph.D. Thesis: 1969), which is being prepared for the press.

The present inquiry may begin with Coke's report itself. Generations of lawyers have been aware of Bacon's criticism of the *Reports*—that they "hold too much *de proprio*"[5]—without, in most cases, being able to check its truth. Coke's reports are so often the fullest in print, and rarely is there any internal demarcation between report and comment. It is demonstrable, however, that the printed report of *Slade's Case* does reproduce what Coke wrote at the time; there is no question of an earlier factual report being elaborated for the press. Coke's draft, in his own hand, is preserved in the British Museum. The hitherto unnoticed manuscript,[6] which contains a chronological series of reports from Michaelmas Term 1591 to Trinity Term 1606,[7] with Coke's own interlineations and additions, provides the answers to several of Plucknett's queries about the genesis of the *Reports*.[8] For one thing, the reports are chronological and probably contemporary.[9] And, although not all the cases were subsequently printed,[10] those which were do not differ materially from the printed versions. The only additions of substance seem to be the transcripts from the record prefixed to the cases in the printed *Reports*. Apart from minor corrections, and one or two trifling additions, the vulgate text of *Slade's Case* is Coke's contemporary account of the decision.[11]

The only other printed reports of *Slade's Case* are the brief notes by Moore and Yelverton, which have been more of a hindrance to understanding than a help,[12] and hardly bear comparison with Coke. Searches in the British Museum, the Inns of Court, the Cambridge University Library and the Bodleian Library Oxford, have revealed about a dozen independent unpublished reports of the arguments in

[5] "A Memorial Touching the Amendment of Laws" (c. 1614) J. Spedding, *Letters and Life of Bacon* (1869), Vol. V, p. 86. *Cf.* Lord Ellesmere on the same theme: *ibid.*, Vol. VI, p. 87.
[6] MS.Harl. 6686 (700 ff.). It is in the same hand as MS.Harl. 6687, which contains Coke's annotations of *Littleton*. The volume is described vaguely in the *Catalogus Librorum Bibliothecae Harleianae* (1808), Vol. III, p. 384, and this probably accounts for its unfortunate obscurity. It comes from Coke's library: see *A Catalogue of the Library of Sir Edward Coke* (ed. W. O. Hassall, 1950), p. 22, no. 293.
[7] The period in which Coke was Attorney-General. The volume is inscribed *Liber Primus*, but on f. 1 there is a reference to a case in Easter Term 33 Eliz. "*devant*."
[8] "The Genesis of Coke's Reports" (1942) 27 *Cornell Law Quarterly* 190.
[9] Plucknett must therefore be wrong in saying (*op. cit.*, p. 200) that "the set of reports as a whole does not come from a chronologically arranged register like Plowden's and does not reproduce a single series of cases noted down as they occurred."
[10] *e.g.* the report of *Finch* v. *Throgmorton* (1598) at ff. 226v–229: see J. H. Baker, "The Common Lawyers and the Chancery", *supra*, pp. 208–209.
[11] The report is MS.Harl. 6686, ff. 526–530v. The interval before publication was less than two years.
[12] Moo. 667; Yel. 21. Dr. Lücke chides Coke for "serious omissions" on the strength of these notes (*op. cit.*, 81 L.Q.R. at p. 557; 82 L.Q.R. at p. 85). His criticisms are not supported by the MS. reports.

Slade's Case, which do provide an instructive comparison with Coke. With one doubtful exception,[13] they are all, unfortunately, anonymous; but they are none the worse for their obscurity. One manuscript, in particular, is of outstanding quality and contains meticulous reports of cases from Michaelmas Term 1598 to Hilary Term 1604 which surpass everything in print.[14] None of these reports contains a list of "resolutions," as in Coke's version, but between them they present a consistent account of the several arguments of counsel over a period of five years. They lead the reader to the irresistible conclusion that Coke's report is in fact a polished redaction of his own speeches for the plaintiff. There is no account in the printed report of the learned and persuasive arguments advanced by Bacon for the defendant. Since Coke won the argument, his attitude is not blatantly dishonest; but it is unfortunate that he created the impression that his own, successful, arguments had the force of judicial resolutions, and that the arguments on the other side were largely glossed over.[15]

This first article contains a translation of Bacon's argument, together with Laurence Tanfield's argument for the plaintiff. The text is taken from the best manuscripts, and additional material from the other reports, together with references to the printed authorities cited, is subjoined in the notes. The law French has been translated more or less literally, but punctuation has been introduced to accord as nearly as possible with modern usage. The second article, to be published in the next issue, will contain a discussion of the new material, in the light of contemporary legal opinion as revealed by other manuscript reports.

List of Manuscript Reports of Slade's Case

1. Michaelmas Term 1597.   John Dodderidge, for the defendant.
   In the Exchequer Chamber.   Edward Coke, for the plaintiff.
     A: Inner Temple, MS.Petyt 516/5, ff. 120–121v.
     B: British Museum, MS.Hargrave 5, ff. 67–68.

---

[13] MS.Hargrave 5 is identified by Edward Umfreville (at f. 1) as the work of Chief Baron Walter (1563–1630). Walter was called to the bar in 1590 and might well have reported *Slade's Case*; but there is no internal evidence to confirm his authorship. The volume is a bound collection of scattered papers in different hands.

[14] Brit.Mus.MS.Add. 25203 (695 ff.). The volume formerly belonged to St. John C.J. Partial copies exist in other collections: Brit.Mus.MS.Stowe 398 (part of Mich. 1598), Lincoln's Inn MS.Misc. 492 (1600–1604), MS.Hargrave 13 (Mich. 1600–Trin. 1601). It deserves close study and contains, *inter alia*, a lengthy report of the *Case of Monopolies*: MS.Add. 25203, ff. 543–548, 558–559v, 576v–588, 678v.

[15] Professor Dawson has reached a similar conclusion from the internal evidence of Coke's report itself: *The Oracles of the Law* (1968), pp. 69–71. But his interpretation of the word "executory," upon which his conclusion is partly based, is unacceptable. See also T. F. T. Plucknett, *Concise History of the Common Law* (1956), pp. 280–281.

C: British Museum, MS.Harl. 1697, ff. 131v–132.
D: British Museum, MS.Lansd. 1071, ff. 332v.
E: British Museum, MS.Add. 35950, ff. 175v–176v.
E$_1$: Cambridge University Library, MS.Ll.iii. 9, ff. 504v–506.
F: Cambridge University Library, MS.Dd.viii. 48, f. 1.
G: British Museum, M.S.Harl. 6809, ff. 45–46v (*Dodderidge* only).[16]

2. Michaelmas Term 1598.   *Laurence Tanfield*, for the plaintiff.
At Serjeants' Inn.   *Francis Bacon*, for the defendant.
H: British Museum, M.S.Add. 25203, ff. 12–12v (*Tanfield* only).[17]
H$_1$: British Museum, MS.Stowe 398, ff. 10v–11.
I: Cambridge University Library, MS.Dd.viii. 48, f. 33.[18]

3. 17 October 1601.   *Edward Coke*, for the plaintiff.
In the Exchequer Chamber.
J: British Museum, MS.Add. 25203, ff. 391v–394.
J$_1$: Lincoln's Inn, MS.Misc. 492, f. 314v.
K: Bodleian Library Oxford, MS.Rawl.C. 720, ff. 66–67.[19]
L: British Museum, MS.Add. 25215, ff, 2–2v.

4. 13 May 1602.   *Francis Bacon*, for the defendant.
At Serjeants' Inn.   *Edward Coke*, for the plaintiff.
M: British Museum, MS.Add. 25203, ff. 496–499.[20]
M$_1$: Lincoln's Inn, MS.Misc. 492, ff. 319–323v.

5. 9 November 1602.   *Edward Coke*, for the plaintiff.
In the King's Bench.   SIR JOHN POPHAM, C.J.
N: British Museum, MS.Add. 25203, f. 607.[21]
N$_1$: Lincoln's Inn, MS.Misc. 492, f. 323v.

At Serjeants' Inn, Michaelmas Term 1598 [22]

Before all the justices of England assembled at Serjeants' Inn, *Tanfielde* recited how John Slade had brought an action on the case against Humfrey Morley, and counted that the defendant, in consideration that the plaintiff sold him certain corn, assumed to pay £16 to the plaintiff, etc. The defendant pleaded *non assumpsit*, and the jury

---
[16] This is by far the best report of Dodderidge's argument, and preserves the pristine eloquence of the original speech. Unlike all the other reports listed here, it is in English.
[17] Printed below, in translation, at pp. 396-401.
[18] Printed below, in translation, at pp. 401-402.
[19] This is the only MS. which has previously been noticed in print: see Simpson, *op. cit.*, 74 L.Q.R. at pp. 390n., 393–394. The argument was not, as Mr. Simpson states, *in banc*.
[20] Printed below, in translation, at pp. 402-408.
[21] Printed below, in translation, at pp. 408-409.
[22] H, collated with H$_1$.

found that the defendant bought the said corn of the plaintiff for £16 to be paid at the feast of St. John next following the sale, and that *nulla alia fuit assumptio*, etc., etc. Upon which he prayed judgment for the plaintiff.

Firstly, I must answer the objections which before now have been made against my part. And first, it has been said that there is no express promise in this case, and therefore the action lies not.[23] And as to this I will show what thing an assumption is. And, as I have learned, an assumption is nothing but a mutual agreement between the parties for a thing to be performed by the defendant in consideration of some benefit which must depart from, or of some labour or prejudice which must be sustained by, the plaintiff. For if some benefit leave the plaintiff, be it to the defendant or to a stranger, this suffices; for it shall be intended at the request of the defendant. As, if a man assume, upon consideration that I give £20 to J.S., to do a thing, it is a good *assumpsit*. Likewise, in consideration that I will go to E. for the defendant, he assumes to do something, it is a good *assumpsit*, for it is a labour to me. And, in the same manner, if, in consideration that I forbear my debt, he assume, etc., for it is a prejudice. And in our case the assumption comes within this definition, wherefor I hold it to be good.

[Although there was no express promise *quoad verba*, yet the matter was thus, and it shall be pleaded as an *assumpsit*.][24] And although countrymen do not always use apt words, yet the construction of the law will make them effectual. And therefore in 5 Hen. 7[25] a man, being indebted to another, licenses the debtee to take his gold chain and to retain it until he pays the money. Although no apt words are there used,[26] the law says that this is a pledge. And it is likewise there held that if a man license me to enter into his land and

---

[23] This was Dodderidge's third reason in 1597. "First, as hath beene said, accons are grounded uppon wronges and iniuries; but yncluded, ymplied or imaginitive wrongs are no cause of accon. They must be actuall, reall and expresse . . . Secondlie, there is nothinge founde but the contract—but the bare stipulacion, as Bracton borowinge the worde out of the Civill lawe calleth it— that is, I agree you shall have my wares and you agree that I shall have your money, this is nothinge but the verye contract yt self out of which resulteth properlye the accion of debt, which is the only legittimate son of that marriage. . . ." (G). He also argued that the declaration was grounded on a deceit by the plaintiff relying on a promise, "which must be an actual promise whearunto yow gave creadict." (G). The same argument is thus reported in A: "There must be an express promise to maintain an action on the case on an *indebitatus assumpsit*, and not solely a promise implied by the contract. For whereas action of debt is created by the contract, *et inde oritur debitum*, so the original and basis of the action on the case is the promise. For this is *ipsum stipulacio*, without which the action cannot be maintained. . . . Also the promise must be actual, so that the other may give confidence and trust to it, for thus is the count. . . ."
[24] From I.   [25] *Lord Dudley* v. *Lord Powles* (1489) M. 5 Hen. 7, 1, *pl.* 1.
[26] H₁ (*Coment la apt parolls.* . . .) This seems preferable to H (*Coment les auters parolls*).

to occupy it for one month, this is a lease and not a licence, and so it must be pleaded. And here in our case the countrymen do not know how to use the apt words. For it is not used amongst them to say that " in consideration that you will do such a thing, I assume to pay you such or such sum," but still the law will make their words to be effectual.[27] And therefore in 21 Hen. 7 [28] Frowicke [C.J.] puts the case that if a man having a rent-charge would command the tenant to pay it to another, and he pay it, yet in avowry this payment is no bar; but the party is put to his action on the case, which must be an action on the case on a promise. And yet there are no words expressly proving the promise, but the construction of the law makes it a sufficient assumption.

Another matter has been objected, that a man shall not have two actions upon one wrong where both reduce the same thing in judgment, but in the action of debt and in the action on the case the same thing is reduced in judgment, wherefor the action on the case lies not.[29] But this objection is not true, for in the action of debt the debt itself is to be recovered, but in the action on the case only damages. And it may be that the jury would give less damages than the sum to which the debt amounts, and if they do so no attaint lies for too little damages. Wherefor the actions reduce several things in judgment.

Another matter has been objected,[30] that where a man has a pro-

---

[27] *Cf.* Coke in 1597: " When the plaintiff said ' You shall have my corn ' and the other said ' You shall have so much money for your corn,' these are express promises. And these words *assumpsit, promisit* and *agreeavit* are all synonymous and of one signification. Would you have every plain man use the proper words ' I assume ' and ' I take upon myself '? It is not necessary. If he says ' I promise ' or ' I agree ' it is as much as and all one. And if you will deny that there was any promise here, there is no contract either, for in every contract there is a reciprocal agreement: *actus contra actum.*" (A). " Here is an express promise, for this is my case and I shall have an action upon it. Here it is said ' You shall have my money.' This is a promise, for put it in writing and covenant lies upon it. Promise and agreement are all one, for every agreement executory is a promise." (B). For Bacon's argument to the contrary, see below, p. 61.

[28] *Abbot of Ramsey* v. *Prior of Anglesey* (1506) H. 21 Hen. 7, 12, *pl.* 13.

[29] This summarises the second limb of Dodderidge's first argument: " In the accion of the case he shall recover all the damages, which shall be no more then the valewe of the debt and damages for the deteyner. There is no more wrought by the one then by the other. In vaine then is it to have libertie of choyse whear there is no choosinge for the better. Therefore wheare the home made and free born will serve the turne, lett the straunger and late made denizen be excluded." (G). The cases cited were P. 41 Edw. 3, 10, *pl.* 5; P. 42 Edw. 3, 9, *pl.* 7; M. 37 Hen. 6, 8, *pl.* 18; M. 2 Ric. 3, 14, *pl.* 39; *Broker's Case* (1490) M. 6 Hen. 7, 7, *pl.* 14; *Core* v. *Woddye* (1537) Dyer 20.

[30] According to Coke (in 1601) this was the main point, on which all the doubt in the case depended: J. K. Coke's subsequent argument was more elaborate than Tanfield's: see 4 Rep. 94–95. In addition to the cases set out there, Coke cited *Stratton* v. *Swanlond* (1375) H. 48 Edw. 3, 6, *pl.* 11 (see A. K. R. Kiralfy, *Source Book of English Law* (1957), p. 185); T. 12 Ric. 2 (Ames Foundation), 7, *pl.* 5; *Hunt* v. *Bate* (1568) Dyer 272.

per action framed in the Register he must not resort to an action on the case.[31] But as to this the law is contrary. For sometimes a man shall have action on the case where he could have assize of novel disseisin being action real, as appears in 4 Edw. 4.[32] Likewise in 21 Hen. 7 in the *Lord Graye's Case*,[33] if one make a trench by which the water running to the mill of another is put out of its course, the party grieved may have action on the case or assize of nuisance. And in 20 Hen. 7 [34] the case was that a man bought twenty quarters of barley to be delivered at a place and day, and the vendor did not perform the contract, and an action on the case was maintainable. And although in the Book at large some opinion seems to impugn this, yet by the record the rule is thus, and so it is cited by Fitzjames [C.J.] in the case between *Core* and *Woddy*.[35] [And . . . where the Book is that three justices were against the action and one for, he cited the reports of Mr. Carrill, that afterwards judgment was given for the action with the opinion of Frowicke.] [36] And in the Book of 20 Hen. 7 Frowicke [C.J.] puts the case, if I deliver money to one to deliver over to my attorney, and he deliver it to my adversary, action on the case lies.[37] In 33 Hen. 8 [38] it is held, if a man bring a writ of debt and be barred by wager of law, and then bring an action on the case for the same money, the defendant may plead how he had already barred the plaintiff by wager of law. So that it is not doubted but that action on the case lies. But where the plaintiff has once made election of his action, and is barred in it, he may not afterwards have the other action. In 2 and 3 Phil. & Mar. between *Pecke* and *Redman*,[39] the case was that two bargained together that the one would deliver to the other twenty quarters of barley every year during their lives, and that the plaintiff would pay four shillings for each quarter. And there

---

[31] *Cf.* note 69, *infra*. This had been Dodderidge's first reason. He relied on *Orwell* v. *Mortoft* (1505) M. 20 Hen. 7, 8, *pl.* 18 (*infra*); P. 14 Hen. 8, 31, *pl.* 8; *Lord Mounteagle* v. *Countess of Worcester* (1555) Dyer 121.

[32] P. 4 Edw. 4, 2, *pl.* 2, *per* Moyle *et alios* JJ.

[33] M. 21 Hen. 7, 30, *pl.* 5.

[34] *Orwell* v. *Mortoft* (1505) M. 20 Hen. 7, 8, *pl.* 18.

[35] Dyer 20, 22: "adjudged maintainable."

[36] From I. As to John Carrill and his reports, see A. W. B. Simpson, "Keilwey's Reports" (1957) 73 L.Q.R. 89. The printed report of the 1505 case in Keil. 69, 77, supports the Year Book account; but it was not printed until 1602, and the printed case would not be cited as from Carrill. The variant Year Books in Brit.Mus.MS.Harg. 105, ff. 233, 236, and Brit.Mus.MS.Add. 35938, f. 195v, both confirm that Frowicke C.J.'s opinion was opposed to that of Kingsmill, Fisher and Vavisour JJ. Professor Kiralfy examined the record (C.P.40/972, m. 123), but could find no judgment entered: *Source Book of English Law* (1957), p. 150.

[37] This was the first reported case in point. Dodderidge had "insisted much on 20 Hen. 7, 8, where it is argued by four justices against Frowicke that where I sell you twenty quarters of barley to be delivered such a day, that if I do not deliver them, action of debt lies and not action on the case." (E).

[38] R. Brooke, *La Graunde Abridgement* (1586), f. 7v, *Accion sur le case*, *pl.* 105.

[39] (1555) Dyer 113.

it is doubted, in an action on the case brought for the non-performance of this bargain, whether the plaintiff should recover damages for the entire bargain or only in recompence of that which was past. But it was not questioned but that the action well lay.

[And he cited about thirty judgments between 21 Hen. 7 and this time that action of case brought for debt will lie.][40] And moreover there are divers precedents in this case of my part, and I vouch divers in the King's Bench [41] in T. 12 Hen. 8, *rot.* 78,[42] H. 22 Hen. 8, *rot.* 66,[43] T. 22 Hen. 8, *rot.* 64,[44] 32 Hen. 8 and 30 Hen. 8 and divers others. All of which were ruled upon this reason, inasmuch that the law gives to the party his double remedy. And when men were found too dangerous in making of their oath, this action on the case was put in ure. And moreover, inasmuch that the course of the Court has been such for so long a time, it seems hard if all their precedents should be reversed; for it has always been used that one court must yield to the customs of another.[45] And therefore in the Common Bench or Queen's Bench no *capias* lies on a recognisance, but

---

[40] From I.

[41] Coke made a great deal of the precedents (4 Rep. 93) and asserted that there were 6,000 in his favour: E. Professor Kiralfy could not trace any precedents of the kind supposed to have been found for Coke by Secondary Kemp: see *The Action on the Case* (1951), pp. 165-166. Those here cited by Tanfield are not of the same kind either, but they are cases where *assumpsit* was brought instead of debt.

[42] *Thomas Blanke* v. *Cassanus Spinula* (1520) K.B. 27/1036, m. 75 (London, Rooper). The plaintiff declared that he had delivered £100 English money to the defendant in exchange for £150 Flemish money, and that the defendant *adtunc et ibidem super se assumpsisset ac prefato Thome fideliter promisisset quod idem Cassanus solueret et deliberaret aut solui et deliberari faceret* to the plaintiff, or to his factor at Antwerp, the £150 Flemish money; and that the defendant had failed to perform his promise *machinans defraudare* the plaintiff of the Flemish money. Damages of £104 were recovered.

[43] *John Turnor* v. *Nicholas Nelethropp* (1531) K.B. 27/1078, m. 66 (London, Rooper). The plaintiff sued for the price of poultry and his salary and costs in providing poultry for the defendant. The plaintiff did not declare expressly of a sale, but that the defendant *pro quadam pecunie summa inter predictis* J.T. *et* N.N. *prius concordata tunc et ibidem super se assumps' quod idem* N.N. *fideliter satisfaceret predicto* J.T. *pro omnimodo* pultryware *per ipsum eidem* J.T. *extunc imposterum deliberandum secundum verum valorem eorundem,* and that he would pay his salary and costs. He showed divers sums owing and not paid, whereby he lost credit and the profits he might have had in trading if the assumption had been performed. The defendant pleaded *non assumpsit.*

[44] *John Whitehed* v. *John Elderton* (1530) K.B. 27/1076, m. 64 (London, Rooper). This is an early *indebitatus assumpsit* action, to recover the price of a brewer's vat. No sale is expressly alleged, but the plaintiff declared that *ubi dictus* J.E. *pro uno vase ligneo vocato* a coole fate *per predictum* J.E. *de prefato* J.W. *prius habito et recepto indebitatus fuit prefati* J.W. *in quatuor marcis sterling, predictus* J.E. *postea . . . pro quadam pecunie summa inter dictum* J.W. *et prefatum* J.E. *prius concordata tunc et ibidem super se assumps' ad solvendum prefato* J.W. *dictas quatuor marcas cum inde requisitus fuisset.* He then showed the non-payment of the four marks and the consequent loss of profits and of days of payment with his own creditors.

[45] See further 4 Rep. 93. Other cases cited by Coke in 1601 (J) were *Paston* v. *Genney* (1471) T. 11 Edw. 4, 3, *pl.* 4, *per* Genney sjt.; *The Chief Baron's Question* (1484) M. 2 Ric. 3, 7, *pl.* 13; *Digby* v. *Mountford* (1575) Dyer 342.

in the Chancery it is usual; and therefore it was held in *Paston's Case*[46] in the Exchequer that if a *capias* be awarded out of a recognisance in Chancery and the sheriff take the reconusor and suffer him to escape, he shall be charged with the escape, for the court must admit the law as it has been used in the Chancery. [Also he spoke of the late introduction of *de eiectione firme* to recover a term, and yet it is allowed for good law and remedy.][47] Wherefor I intend in our case that the party has two remedies, and therefore he may make election which he will use. As, in 31 Edw. 1, title *Voucher* 289,[48] if a man make a lease for life rendering rent and oblige himself and his heirs to warrant, and then grant the reversion, the lessee has two warranties and the one does not confound the other; but he has his election to vouch the grantee of the reversion or his lessor.

Wherefor for these causes I pray judgment for the plaintiff.

Bacon, econtra.

[*Bacon* argued to the contrary, and he imitated *Dodderidge* in his argument.

First, he said that action on the case for *assumpsit* lies where the contract and agreement is executory; not where one thing is transferred for another *in presente,* as in a simple contract for a horse, ox, etc.

And the Chancery will compel one to perform a promise, not to perform a contract.

And he answered all the ancient authorities of Hen. 7 that they were brought for conversion, not because the plaintiff *fidem adhibens promissioni,* etc., as in the principal case.

And he argued that the defendant would be deprived of the benefit of wager of law. And said that *Deus veritas est.* In secret things, the trial of them is *per Deum et victoriam,* as in battle, or *Deum et partem,* as in wager of law. And that anciently there was a third trial by *lotgager.* But, as St. Paul says,[49] *finis omnis controversie est iuramentum*: either of the judge, or of the party, or of the jury. It behoves him to have twelve hands with him, 33 Hen. 6,[50] or he cannot wage his law.

Also the conveyance shall not be traversed in wager of law,

---

[46] *Clement Paston's Case* (1579) cited Yelv. 42.
[47] From I. Likewise Coke in 1597: " In *eiectione firme* a man could not recover possession until 14 Hen. 7, but now it is allowed without any question inasmuch that there are many precedents in the point." (B). This is an allusion to Fitz.N.B. 220H. As to the date, *cf.* T. F. T. Plucknett, *Concise History of the Common Law* (1956 ed.), pp. 373, 574.
[48] *L.* v. *M.* (1302) A. Fitzherbert, *La Graunde Abridgement* (1565), f. 206a, *Voucher, pl.* 289.
[49] *Epistle to the Hebrews,* vi, 16.
[50] H. 33 Hen. 6, 8, *pl.* 23, *per* Nedham sjt. Dodderidge had also cited M. 9 Hen. 3, Fitz.Abr.,*Ley, pl.* 78. (G).

because the defendant shall not be deprived of his wager of law:[51] 8 Hen. 6,[52] 22 Edw. 4.[53] And 49 Edw. 3,[54] 9 Eliz. Dyer,[55] simple contract debts are not forfeited to the Queen, because a subject shall not wage his law against her. See the Statute 5 Hen. 4 [c. 8] for such like material.

It was a question when the action on the case commenced, and LORD ANDERSON [C.J., C.P.] said that it commenced by the last chapter of the Statute of Westminster II.[56] [57]

At Serjeants' Inn, 13 May 1602 [58]

Before all the justices of England assembled at Serjeants' Inn on Ascension Day, being the thirteenth day of May, *Bacon* recited the case between *Slade* and *Morely* . . . and it seemed to him that the action on the case does not lie. And in the argument of this he proved his intent by three reasons. Firstly, that there lacks substance and matter here upon which to ground an action on the case. Secondly, that the action lacks form; and therefore where there is a writ in the Register framed and formed for this case, this action on the case lies not. Thirdly, the subject is by this ousted from the benefit of law if action on the case should be maintained, wherefor in respect of this mischief he ought to sue action of debt.

As to the first reason, a contract is not a ground for an action on the case. For action on the case must be grounded on deceit or breach of promise, but in debt on a contract there is no deceit or breach of promise supposed. For a bargain is in any manner a thing executed and not executory as an *assumpsit* is. For a bargain changes the property of each part, and therefore in action of debt it is alleged that the defendant detains the money or thing demanded as if it were his before; to wit, that the plaintiff had the property of it by the contract. Wherefor Bracton says that *contractus est permutatio rerum*. And therefore when the plaintiff demands only that which was his before, it cannot be said that he is deceived by the defendant; but that the defendant detains that of which the property was in the plaintiff. And

---

[51] This is better explained by Dodderidge: "If a man doe bringe an accon of debt uppon a contract, the defendant shall not travers the contract for that he maye wage his lawe. But in those accons of debt, detynew, or accoumpt in which he cannot wage his lawe, he shall not answer to the poynte of the wrytt (for that he is ousted of his benefitt by *ley gadger*) but shall travers the conveyance, which otherwise is not traversable. For the lawe taketh from hym no benefitt but geveth hym as good." (G). He cited M. 12 Edw. 4, 11, *pl.* 2; M. 13 Edw. 4, 4, *pl.* 9; M. 21 Edw. 4, 55, *pl.* 27.
[52] M. 8 Hen. 6, 5, *pl.* 13.
[53] See P. 22 Edw. 4, 2, *pl.* 8; *ibid.*, 7, *pl.* 20.
[54] H. 49 Edw. 3, 5, *pl.* 8, *per* Hanymer and Holt sjts.
[55] *Anon.* (1569) Dyer 262, *pl.* 31 (Star Chamber).
[56] Presumably a mistake for 13 Edw. 1, c. 24, *in consimili casu*.
[57] From I.
[58] M collated with M$_1$.

in 3 Hen. 6, 36,[59] and 11 Hen. 4, 33,[60] an *assumpsit* is called a parol covenant. And therefore when a man covenants by writing to pay a sum of money, he to whom the covenant is made shall have action of debt and not action of covenant, since the deed is a mere obligation. Likewise of the other part, when this covenant is made by parol it sounds only in the nature of the contract and not in the nature of a promise, and therefore the plaintiff shall be put to his action of debt and shall be ousted from the action on the case. And we put that a man, in consideration of certain corn delivered to him by the plaintiff, will acknowledge himself to be indebted in £20; these are the usual words of an obligation, and it is clear that had they been put into writing no action could be maintained upon them save an action of debt. And, for the same reason, when such a promise or acknowledgment is made by parol without any writing yet it is solely in the nature of debt and therefore no other action except writ of debt lies for it. And 45 Edw. 4 [61] it is said that upon a promise broken a man shall have suit in Court Christian *pro lesione fidei*; but it is clear that if a man make a contract with another, though the money be not paid at the day, no suit *pro lesione fidei* lies for this in Court Christian. And in 21 Hen. 7, 41,[62] it is held that if a man promise to enfeoff me of certain land and do not do it accordingly, I shall have action on the case or *subpena* in Chancery at my election. And by the one I shall recover damages, and by the other the Chancellor will compel the party by imprisonment to execute the feoffment. But if a man contract with another to give him a certain sum of money for a certain quantity of corn, if the money be not paid still no *subpena* lies to compel the defendant to pay the money; but he must sue for it by writ of debt.[63]

And so it appears that there is a great diversity between the nature of the action of debt and action on the case. For the action on the case implies wrong, bad conscience and deceit, wherefor in 20 Hen. 7, 9,[64] Frowicke [C.J.] calls it "misdemeanour."[65] And the action on

---

[59] *W.B.* v. *Watkins* (1425) H. 3 Hen. 6, 36, *pl.* 33.
[60] *The Carpenter's Case* (1409) M. 11 Hen. 4, 33, *pl.* 60; (f. 186 in the 1575 edition).
[61] Evidently a mistake. M₁ says 45 Edw. 3, but this was probably an extempore correction by the transcriber. The most likely case is M. 20 Edw. 4, 10, *pl.* 9, where in prohibition to Court Christian the defendant pleaded that he was not suing for debt on a contract, but for the breach of faith in not paying as promised. Brian C.J. held the plea bad, since the faith was pledged upon a temporal matter.
[62] M. 21 Hen. 7, 41, *pl.* 66, *per* Fineux C.J. His words were "*ieo aver accion sur mon case et ne besoigne suer sub pena, etc.*"
[63] Coke replied: "It is clear enough that *subpena* does not lie in the one case or the other, nor in any case where there is some remedy by the common law." (M).   [64] *Orwell* v. *Mortoft*, notes 34–36, *supra*.

[65] For footnote please see p. 404.

the case is an action of trespass, for which cause the law does not suffer that the defendant shall wage his law in this action. Wherefor, when the nature and ground of these actions is so different, it is not reason that upon a contract for which properly an action of debt lies, action on the case should be maintained.

But he said that sometimes when a contract is mixed with collateral matter an action on the case shall be maintained upon it. As, if a man contract to pay me £10 in angels or crowns or in some other special coin, I may have action on the case inasmuch that here it is not a nude contract but it is mixed with another collateral circumstance. Likewise if I sell a horse to another, he shall have action of debt for the horse; but if it be added over to the contract that the horse shall be broken and taught ready for the field, there he shall have action on the case. Likewise if to the contract be added a special place of delivery or payment, to wit that the defendant must deliver the thing or pay the money at such a place, action on the case lies; for in writ of debt the plaintiff shall recover the money, but neither the place nor the other collateral circumstances before-mentioned shall be respected in the action of debt. Also it seemed to him that if the contract be distracted and divided unto several days, action on the case shall lie well. And these diversities, as he said, will reconcile all the cases objected of the contrary part. Such as the case in 21 Hen. 6, 55,[66] for there was a contract for two pipes of wine, and this was to be delivered at a certain place. And in *Norwood's Case*, Com. 180,[67] there was a place appointed for the delivery of the corn, and also the contract was distracted in several days. And in *Pecke* and *Redman's Case*, 2 and 3 Phil. and Mar., Dyer 113, the barley was to be delivered to the plaintiff annually, so that there was again a distraction of the contract. And the same reasons can be attributed to 5 Mar., Brooke *Accion sur le case* 108, for there the marriage money was to be paid in four years. But it seems that if a man contract to pay money at one day, though a time certain be limited, this is not so forcible to change the nature of the action as the limiting of the place or the distracting of the contract unto several days.[68] And the reason why the

---

[65] Likewise Dodderidge: "20 Hen. 7, 9, it is said by Frowicke that in a case where debt lies yet action on the case may lie for the misdemeanour or deceit. But here is no deceit, but solely a detainer." (B). Coke replied to Bacon's argument: "It is clear that when a man contracts with another to pay money or to do anything, and does not perform it, this is a deceit." (M). Dodderidge apparently conceded that the non-delivery of goods was a "secondary fraud" (D), but the reporter commented that this was no different from the non-payment of money.

[66] *Tailboys* v. *Sherman* (1443) T. 21 Hen. 6, 55, *pl.* 12.

[67] *Norwood* v. *Read* (1558) Plowd. 180.

[68] Coke answered thus: "Without question it is not the place or the distraction of days which makes the deceit, but the non-performance of the contract. And if action on the case will lie where the money is to be paid at twenty several days,

law in these cases allows action on the case is because it will not put him to two actions, to wit to the action of debt to recover the money and then to the action on the case because it was not paid at the due place. Wherefor he concluded this first reason, that the matter is insufficient to bring action on the case.

And as to the second, it seemed to him that the action is not maintainable because it wants form. For the law favours order and abhors confusion. And therefore the Register must not be confounded, but men must sue by the writs in the Register and not frame actions of their own head.[69] And therefore when the Register appoints debt a proper action to give remedy to the plaintiff for his grievance, he must not pursue an action on the case. He agreed that often a man may sue at his election several actions for one same thing, for as is commonly said *bonum est simplex et malum est multiplex*. And therefore the same act in several respects may give cause for several actions. But he said that where there is any other remedy no action on the case lies. For this is only a supplemental action and therefore it does not lie in cases where there is a proper action unless the matter digress in some way from the nature of the proper action. As, 11 Hen. 4,[70] and 33 Hen. 6,[71] if a man stop my way I shall have assize of nuisance, but if he straighten the way and do not stop it entirely, inasmuch that this digresses somewhat from the nature of the assize of nuisance, an action on the case lies. In the case of the way stopped, if this be done by a stranger and not by the tenant of the soil no assize lies and therefore I shall have action on the case.

Also he agreed that sometimes an action on the case lies in such cases where there is also a formal writ in the Register. But this is

for the same reason it will lie if it be to be paid at six days, and for a like reason if it be payable at four or two days. And what diversity can be put as to the maintenance of this action, whether the money be payable at two days or one? For this conceit being pursued will be reduced to *non quantum*." (M).

[69] *Cf.* Dodderidge: "Wheare there is a readie framed wrytt of forme in the Register, sufficiently able to deduce to judgment the wronge and the damage and throughlie to punish the one and to satisfie the other, there shall the partie plaintiff never have recourse to the wrytt without forme to satisfie the same damage and punishe the same wronge. But heare is a readie framed wrytt in the Register, the accon of debt: the naturall remedye, the wrytt of forme. Theirfore here is no place for the accon uppon the case, the wrytt without form, the usurped remedie." (G). "Yf the accon uppon the case have thus incroached uppon the accon of dett, why shoulde it not incroache hearafter uppon other accons of forme and so make a confusion of the Regester, which is said in the Comentaries [Plo. 77, 228] to be for such matters of wryttes the foundacion and groundes of the lawe?" (G). Dodderidge expatiated on the history of wrlts, said the Register was compiled for Edward I ("the English Justinian"), and that the action on the case was a new-found action (B, D, G). But Coke replied that there were many actions in the Register of later date, including *assumpsit*.
[70] *Popham* v. *Prior of Bremour* (1410) T. 11 Hen. 4, 82, *pl*. 28; (ff. 235-236 in the 1575 edition).
[71] *Right's Case* (1455) T. 33 Hen. 6, 26, *pl*. 10.

where the writ in the Register is of higher nature and more penal to the defendant than action on the case. For the law will not compel any man to pursue his wrong in extremity; but, if he will, he may well refuse the remedy which is more penal to the defendant and pursue a milder action. And therefore when a man has cause to pursue appeal of mayhem he may have action on the case. And so where he has cause to sue a writ of *rescous* he may well have action on the case. And likewise where he may have assize of nuisance or trespass *quare vi et armis* he may waive it and take action on the case. For in these cases the other actions are greater and higher than action on the case. But action on the case is greater and higher and more penal to the defendant than action of debt. For in action of debt the defendant wages his law, but not in action on the case, which proves that it is the higher action. Also action on the case supposes a tort and deceit in the defendant. And therefore, although the plaintiff may forego his right in taking his remedy by inferior action, yet he may not at his pleasure use an action superior to that which is proper to his case.[72] Wherefor, etc.

And as to the last reason, he objected that the action on the case does not lie, for then the defendant shall be ousted from his law, which is a defence of which the law is very tender. And therefore he observed three reasons for which principally the law allows that the defendant may discharge himself of a debt by doing his law. The first is for expedition, for several matters are briefly determined by wager of law which would depend longer if they were tried by inquest. The second reason is because the defendant shall not be surprised in his proof. For contracts are often made in secret and it would be most inconvenient that on every private bargain between men they were compelled to call unto them a notary or witnesses to prove the bargain. And therefore the law has allowed that the defendant in such a case may discharge himself by his oath. The third reason is because such private contracts are difficult to be tried by juries. And of this the law has great regard, for the trials in our law by inquests are stricter than the trial of any other law. For an inquest of necessity gives a verdict, and cannot give a *non liquet*, whether or not the parties will give evidence. Secondly, a majority [*pluralitye*] of voices does not hold in the verdict, but it behoves all of them to accord in their verdict or otherwise it is not good. Thirdly, the jurors are in duress until they have given their verdict. All which matters being considered, it is a great reason to provide as far as may be that the issues to be tried by juries shall be upon plain and clear matter. And there-

---

[72] Coke replied: "It seems that the writ of debt is of a higher nature than action on the case, for by it the duty itself is to be recovered, and by the other nothing except damages for the breach of promise." (M).

fore the law allows that a man may discharge himself of these secret contracts by wager of law rather than put him upon the trial of an inquest. For though the contract be made in the presence of witnesses, yet the proof of it is very dangerous and uncertain, when the wresting or mistaking of a word may alter the whole substance of the contract. And therefore it is very reasonable to put this on the oath of the party himself. And this is according to the law of God, for *finis omnis controversie est iuramentum*.[73] And where it is said that this trial by wager of law is an occasion of great perjury when the party for his own profit is tempted to say contrary to the truth,[74] surely the mischief is not so great of this part as of the other. For where by wager of law the defendant himself may be perjured, the trial of such secret matters by inquest gives occasion to twelve jurors and also to several witnesses to be forsworn. And for these causes the law gives great favour to the trial by wager of law. And therefore the Queen's prerogative shall not oust a man of his law, as appears by 49 Edw. 3, 5,[75] 16 Edw. 4, 4;[76] and 9 Eliz., Dyer 262:[77] if I be indebted to another upon a simple contract and the debtee is *felo de se* or outlawed, yet the debt shall not be forfeited because the debtor must not be ousted of his law.

POPHAM [C.J., K.B.] That is not law.
WALMSLEY [J., C.P.] But still the books are thus.
POPHAM [C.J., K.B.] But the books are against law.

To which several other justices assented.[78]

And it is no wonder how this trial has obtained such respect in law, being so indifferent as it is. For the law has provided that it shall be made by the oath of a true and credible person, for he who has been attainted of a false oath by writ of attaint shall not be received to do his law: as 33 Hen. 6, 32[79] is. Also it must be made *duodena manu*, for the oath of the party himself is not sufficient, but he must be sworn with eleven others who will swear that they think the oath of the party himself true.[80] Wherefor it seems, in respect of the mis-

---

[73] Note 49, *supra*.
[74] So argued Coke: "At this day wager of law is too common, and the consciences of men exceeding bad and hasty to commit perjury for profit. And by allowing this action you will lead their souls away from such devilish perils." (L). *Cf.* 4 Rep. 95.
[75] H. 49 Edw. 3, 5, *pl.* 8, *per* Hanymer and Holt sjts.
[76] *B.* v. *T.* (1476) P. 16 Edw. 4, 4, *pl.* 9, *semble*, *per* Brian C.J., reporter's note.
[77] *Anon.* (1569) Dyer 262, *pl.* 31 (Star Chamber).
[78] See the further authorities collected at 4 Rep. 95, where Coke asserts that Anderson C.J., C.P., was of the same opinion as Popham C.J. The three cases cited by Bacon are there dismissed as "sudden opinions."
[79] M. 33 Hen. 6, 32, *pl.* 6, *per* Littleton sjt.
[80] Dodderidge attached special significance to the number twelve: "Wager of law is one of the trials appointed by the law, and it is a twelve-handed trial ... which trial has resemblance to the trial by jury and the trial by demurrer. For

chief which would ensue to the defendant in this case to be ousted of his wager of law, the action on the case does not lie.[81]

As to the precedents, he confessed that several had been shown him of which the most ancient are in 8 Hen. 6 [82] and after. But all the precedents until 22 Hen. 8 are upon an *assumpsit liberare* and not upon *assumpsit soluere*. But after 22 Hen. 8 there have been several precedents [83] that action on the case has been maintained upon an *assumpsit soluere*. But these have been adjudged solely in the King's Bench. And also several of them may be answered with the diversities shown before, or because a place of payment was appointed or because the contract was distracted unto several separate days of payment. Whereby he concluded that the action on the case does not lie.

In the King's Bench, 9 November 1602 [84]

Memorandum, that the ninth day of November this Term, *Cooke* the Queen's Attorney-General moved the case between *Slade* and *Morley* . . . and inasmuch that the case had depended a long time and had been argued and debated in this Court and also so often before all the justices of England and the barons of the Exchequer, who had conferred about it amongst themselves, he prayed their resolution and judgment in the case.

And POPHAM the Chief Justice answered that they had conferred and advised of the case and that they had resolved it, and that they were agreed:

Firstly, that every contract executory implies in itself a promise or *assumpsit*.

Secondly, that although upon such a contract an action of debt lies to recover the duty, yet the plaintiff may well have an action on the case upon the *assumpsit*.

And that they had resolved this not only upon the precedents of this Court, but also upon reason, and upon the precedents of all the courts that the Queen has. For as well in the Common Bench as the Exchequer there are several precedents which concur with this resolution.

---

whereas the law is tried by twelve reverend judges and matters in fact by twelve jurors, so the trial by wager of law is *duodecima manu*, by the party himself and eleven others." (A). The magical quality of twelve as a topic of jurisprudence is exhausted by Coke in Co.Litt. 155.

[81] Coke had already made the point that this argument was *petitio principii*: "for if the action on the case lies by law, then this does not deprive the defendant of any benefit." (B).

[82] Professor Kiralfy cites two entries of this date in actions of *assumpsit* to deliver seisin: *The Action on the Case* (1951), p. 182.

[83] Notes 43 and 44, *supra*.

[84] N. *Cf.* Moo. 667, Yelv. 21.

But whether upon such *assumpsit* an action on the case will lie against the executors of him that made it, he said that they were not resolved.

And all this that was delivered by the Chief Justice was affirmed by the other justices to be thus agreed. Wherefor POPHAM [C.J.] *ex assensu sociorum* commanded judgment to be entered for the plaintiff.

PART II

THE number of extant reports of *Slade's Case*, by different hands, indicates the significance which the case possessed for contemporary lawyers. Its subsequent significance was assured by its inclusion in Coke's *Reports*, an honour which entitled it to all the attention which posterity is obliged to bestow on leading cases; but, for three centuries, the more that was written about it the more difficult it became to remember or to imagine what it had meant when it was decided. The case has been partially redeemed from its oblivion by recent studies, but it is becoming plain that it is still not understood, and perhaps will not be fully understood for some years to come. It is hoped that the publication of some of the leading arguments in the case, in the last issue of this *Journal*,[1] will help to bring understanding within closer reach. Those arguments, however, presuppose a familiarity with the problems the case was intended to solve. Although part of the background may be learned from the published reports and Year Books, the story which they reveal is neither complete nor clear. The older cases are too sparse, too badly reported and cover too many years for any safe general conclusions to be drawn from them. They are relevant to the investigation in so far as they formed part of the Elizabethan lawyers' common education, providing a starting point for further discussion, and a recourse for those who sought authority for everything in their old books. But the burning questions in the minds of those who awaited the final pronouncement in *Slade's Case* were not Year Book questions, or ancient moot points, but new questions which had only come to the fore in the preceding ten or fifteen years. No doubt the best lawyers of that time understood those questions more clearly than a legal historian ever will; but now that so much manuscript material has found its way into accessible libraries it is at least possible for us to read more widely than they could, and to review their authorities with detachment. This commentary is based on a study of the manuscript reports for the last decade of the sixteenth century, together with the printed reports and a few of the relevant plea rolls.

[1] *Supra*, pp. 396-409.

Law and the interstices of procedure

The details of the early history of the action of *assumpsit* to recover money have still to be culled from the plea rolls, but it is now established that each of the distinct types of declaration was in use by the second quarter of the sixteenth century. The declarations may be classified as: (1) those which specified a *contract* [2] as the consideration for the promise to pay, and (2) those which stated the consideration to be an indebtedness.[3] The latter (*indebitatus*) forms of declaration sometimes set out the contract which gave rise to the indebtedness, and sometimes they did not. The promise was the primary cause of action, and since the indebtedness was regarded as matter of "inducement" it was not essential to go into detail.[4] Professor Lücke has explained the practical and doctrinal difficulties which were occasioned by allowing plaintiffs to declare too generally in *indebitatus assumpsit*[5]; and how, according to Moore's brief report,[6] the general declaration was outlawed in *Slade's Case*. But this interpretation of the case is not corroborated by any of the better reports, and the point was not argued at all. It is safe to conclude that the pleading problem was not in issue in *Slade's Case*; it was settled, in fact, six years afterwards by a further decision of the Exchequer Chamber.[7]

The main difference between the two types of count seems to have been one of tense. Indebtedness was a continuing state, and was therefore a present consideration to support a promise subsequent to the contract; but a contract laid in the pluperfect tense could not in itself be a present consideration for a promise laid in the perfect tense, unless it had been moved by a "special instance and request."[8] It is doubtful whether this reflected any difference of substance, since the contract necessarily created a state of indebtedness, even if it were not expressly alleged in the pleadings, and that state continued until the debt was discharged. Of course, good

---

[2] This word will be used here in the sense in which it was used in and before the sixteenth century: *i.e.*, a transaction *re* creating a debt.

[3] See *Whitehed* v. *Elderton* (1530), *supra*, p. 400, note 44.

[4] *Hughes* v. *Robotham* (1593) Poph. 30, at p. 31, *per* Gawdy J. In forbearance *assumpsit* the general declaration was considered good even in the Common Pleas: *Smyth* v. *Bocher* (M.1595) B.M. MS.Harg. 7, pt. i, f. 119v, *per* Anderson C.J.

[5] 81 L.Q.R. at pp. 551 *et seq.*, 82 L.Q.R. at pp. 85 *et seq.*

[6] Moo. 667. See also 10 Rep. 68b.

[7] *Woodford* v. *Deacon* (P.1608) Cro.Jac. 206 (said to have been a unanimous decision). See also *Gardiner* v. *Bellingham* (1614) Hob. 5, 1 Ro.Rep. 24.

[8] See Lücke in 81 L.Q.R. at pp. 437–445. *Cf. Sheffield* v. *Rise* (M.1594) Moo. 367, where it was said that the words *adtunc et ibidem* made the contract "*entendible al temps del assumpsit*," notwithstanding the difference in tenses. See the question argued by the judges in *Pillesworth* v. *Feake* (P. 1602) as reported in B.M. MS.Add. 25203, f. 479. *Anon.* (1572) Dal. 84, affords further proof that a change of tense was not equivalent to the use of the word "*postea*."

lawyers were astute to take advantage of grammatical or verbal slips in declarations if it would serve their clients to do so, and to that extent the forms were of practical importance. Professor Lücke concluded from this that problems of procedure and pleading were of " overriding importance " and that the substantive principles were " merely the by-products of procedural rulings." [9] This, it is submitted, gives a misleading impression of Elizabethan jurisprudence. The emphasis given to forms of pleading arose from the fact that the issues to be tried were those raised by the words of the pleadings, and not otherwise; but, unless a pleader slipped up and used inappropriate words, the issue would normally be one of substance. The debate leading to *Slade's Case* certainly does not reveal any obsession with formalism in pleading; it was about substantive remedies, not the accidents of procedure.

THE CONTROVERSY BETWEEN THE COURTS

The debate was primarily about the propriety of using *assumpsit* to recover debts. That it became, towards the end of the sixteenth century, a debate not merely between individual lawyers but between the two principal common law courts, is too well known to need repeating. Yet the reason for this division of judicial opinion across Westminster Hall is not immediately apparent. It is unlikely that the debate was principally motivated by the jealous preservation of jurisdictional boundaries for the sake of revenue from fees.[10] It is true that the action of debt was part of the Common Pleas monopoly, in which it may have felt some proprietary interest,[11] but by Elizabethan times it was established that the King's Bench could entertain bills of debt against defendants in the custody of the Marshal; and, since King's Bench fees were lower than those in the Common Pleas, the jurisdictional victory had already been won. It may seem a miracle that the Common Pleas survived at all, but it was kept going by the vested interests of the attorneys who had been admitted to the court and brought their business to it. Had the members of that court not enjoyed a sublime confidence in the stability of their business, any consideration of fees would have been more likely to motivate profitable innovation in the Common Pleas than in the King's Bench.

---

[9] 81 L.Q.R. at p. 422.
[10] *Cf.* S. F. C. Milsom, *Historical Foundations of the Common Law* (1969), p. 297: " debt was still the staple of the common pleas, and more than intellectual symmetry was visibly at stake over this development in the king's bench."
[11] *Ibid.*, p. 302: the Common Pleas " sought . . . to defend what it no doubt still regarded as its own property."

The debate seems rather to have been symptomatic of a more intellectual conflict, a final confrontation between the old learning and the new. It may perhaps be regarded as the last stand of Tudor legal conservatives against the legal renaissance of the sixteenth century, and the reformation of the old Year Book learning which this entailed. The Common Pleas, complacent about its paramount position in the judicial system, and proud of the medieval heritage preserved (not without personal profit) by its attorneys and serjeants, represented the conservative standpoint. The King's Bench, newly enriched by the extension of its business through the use of the *latitat*, and now vying with its sister court to become a second court of common pleas, was inevitably cast in a progressive role. Although the King's Bench was in theory the superior court, being nominally held *coram rege seipso*, yet it still lacked the status of the tribunal which Coke venerated as the " lock and key of the common law." [12]

The spirit of the Common Pleas was manifested in the counting, the law French, the coifs and hoods—symbols of continuity from ancient times. It was embodied most of all in one person, Thomas Walmsley, one of the justices of the court from 1589 to 1611. Again and again he is found in the law reports stoutly resisting all kinds of innovation. It is tempting to see some connection between his devotion to the old common law and his suspected sympathies for the old religion.[13] Yet it would be just as wrong to brand the Common Pleas judges as unthinking reactionaries, insensible to the public good, as it would be to see all Elizabethan Papists in the same light. Their judicial speeches are often marked by a sincere anxiety to explain the particular benefits to be derived from the old law, and the particular dangers inherent in the innovations contended for. Thus, to return to the present instance, the whole point of *Slade's Case* would be missed if the action of debt were dismissed as an inconvenient archaism, bound to give way in due course to a newer remedy. There is some evidence that, in the sixteenth century, pleading in the action of debt was *less* strict than in *assumpsit* [14]: and it will be argued later, also contrary to the received view, that there was much to be said for

---

[12] 4 Inst. 99.

[13] Although he conformed, he came from a Catholic family and was believed to harbour recusant sympathies: see M. Brigg, " The Walmsleys of Dunkenhalgh " (1969) *Transactions of the Lancashire and Cheshire Antiquarian Society*, pp. 73–82. The present writer is indebted to Miss Brigg for supplementary information on this point.

[14] *Anon.* (1582) B.M. MS.Lansd. 1084, f. 59 The plaintiff declared on a promise to pay £40 for wine, the jury found a promise to pay £20, and this was held to be a verdict for the defendant: " *pur ceo que il doit prover un assumpsit absolutement et precisement en cest accon come il ad count, et nient semblable al dett sur contract l'ou le plaintiff recovera dett solonque ceo que est trove pur lui.*" *Cf.* Simpson in 74 L.Q.R. at p. 381.

wager of law.[15] Reform is always easier to vindicate than conservation, it has the advantage of seeming (in retrospect) inevitable and it also tends to favour plaintiffs. To the extent that the King's Bench attitude favoured plaintiffs, the inference that *its* motives were partly mercenary may be justifiable. At least the Common Pleas judges must be credited, in their attempts to safeguard what they saw as the interests of the public in general (including defendants), with a genuine and rational belief in the merits of the law they strove to conserve.

The Common Pleas' view

The essence of the Common Pleas' objection to the indiscriminate use of actions on the case was that they were (by definition) special remedies, to be brought into operation only in cases where the general writs in the Register were inappropriate.[16] In the words of Walmsley J.:

> Action on the case is so called from *cadendo*, because something happens in it which does not happen in other cases. For where you have an ordinary action of debt, you may not have action on the case unless upon special cause. As, in this case, if the money were payable at Michaelmas and for non-payment of it the other will forfeit his bond of £20, or such similar *casual* or special thing, action on the case lies. Otherwise not.[17]

The etymological reason was supported by the historical. According to the views of the day, the action on the case derived from the Statute of Westminster II, c. 24, *In consimili casu*.[18] And by the tenor of that statute, the Chancery clerks were to draw special writs only where there was no existing writ to meet the case. Since the statute was passed to prevent a failure of justice for want of a remedy, it could have no application in cases where a remedy existed at common law.[19]

---

[15] *Infra*, pp. 424-426. These are the "two difficulties" to which Blackstone ascribed the eclipse of debt by case: Bla.Comm. iii, 154.

[16] This was no new suggestion: see *Orwell* v. *Mortoft* (1505) 20 Hen. 7, 8, *pl.* 18, per Kingsmill J.: P. 14 Hen. 8, 31, *pl.* 8, per Brooke J.; *Pickering* v. *Thoroughgood* (1532) B.M. MS.Harg. 388, f. 67v, 74 L.Q.R. at p. 383. *Cf. Jordan's Case* (1535) M. 27 Hen. 8, 24, *pl.* 3, *per curiam*.

[17] *Paramour* v. *Payne* (M.1595) B.M. MS.Harl. 4552, f. 92 (translated). The example was probably taken from the Year Books: *cf.* M. 20 Hen. 7, 8, *pl.* 18, per Frowicke C.J.

[18] Plucknett attributed the doctrine to Lambard: 31 *Columbia Law Review* at p. 781. The relevant passage is in W. Lambard, *Archeion* (1635), p. 61; it is not in the pirated edition of D. Frere, entitled *Archion* (1635). Lambard may have taken it from a case of 1553 in *Dalison's Reports*, B.M. MS.Harl. 5141, f. 13 (Lambard's copy), where the statute was alluded to as enabling the clerks to devise an action not in the Register. Lambard's views would have been known to the profession in the 1590s.

[19] *Wade* v. *Braunch* (1596) 2 And. 53. Lücke's argument (81 L.Q.R. at p. 428) that the reasoning in this case was fallacious, is not entirely acceptable—Elizabethan lawyers would not have regarded the statute as spent when the first writ on the case was sealed, because each action on the case was different and had to be warranted by the statute.

The Register was of great antiquity and authority, and not to be "confounded" by new remedies for which no legal authority could be found.[20] It was not permissible for litigants to "fly from the Register, and invent actions and writs of their own heads, which is insufferable."[21] The historical premiss was probably accepted without question; it was never challenged in the reported cases.

Another weighty argument, leading to the same conclusion, derived from the nascent "doctrine" of consideration, the principle that a parol undertaking was only of legal force if some recompense were given in exchange for it. But a promise to pay a debt was a promise to perform a duty which the law imposed on the promisor independently of the promise, and was therefore *nudum pactum*.[22] This was so whether the promise was contemporaneous with the contract, or subsequent to it. Where the promise was subsequent, the consideration was open to the obvious objection that it was "executed" or past.[23] In the case of a contemporaneous promise, however, it could be suggested that the benefit which constituted the *quid pro quo* for the contract was at the same time consideration for the promise.[24] This led on to the two main questions to be discussed in *Slade's Case*. The first was whether such a promise could be inferred from the mere entry into a contract, since it was rare for contracting parties to use express words of promise. The second was whether a contract and a contemporaneous promise to perform it could give rise simultaneously to two distinct forms of action to achieve the same end. The Common Pleas answered both in the negative.

[20] *Williams* v. *Williams* (P.1596) B.M. MS.Harg. 7, pt. i, f. 188, MS.Harg. 51, f. 78, *per* Anderson C.J. The first MS. is a volume of Common Pleas reports (T.1594–T.1599) attributed by Edward Umfreville to Humfrey Were: see 9 C.B. at p. 193. Were was a Reader of the Inner Temple (Lent 1613), not a serjeant, as Umfreville states. There are several inferior copies in the British Museum and Lincoln's Inn. The second MS. is a less significant volume of reports by Nicholas Duck, Reader of Lincoln's Inn (Lent 1617).
[21] *Ibid.*, Were's version, *per* Walmsley J.
[22] *Ibid.*, *per* Anderson C.J.; *Turgys* v. *Becher* (T.1596) as reported in B.M. MS.Lansd. 1084, f. 120v, MS.Harl. 1631, f. 55, MS.Harl. 1697, f. 107v, U.L.C. MS.Gg. iii. 25 f. 80 ("*c'est nudum pactum eo que il que fist le promise n'ad benifitt per ceo*"), MS.Ii. v. 13, f. 59 ("*quant il promise de payer ceo sur le contract, n'est pluis que ceo que le ley voet sans son promise, et un n'est de aver remedy per accon sur le case, mes ou le ley n'ad provide a luy ascun auter remedy*").
[23] *Turgys* v. *Becher* (T.1596) as reported in B.M. MS.Lansd. 1084, f. 120v, per Anderson C.J.: "*le det esteant due devant, il fuit chose execut sur que assumpsit ne veut estre mainteyn.*" *Cf.* Were's report (MS.Harg. 7, pt. i, f. 204): "*Mes s'il fuit un promise fait apres le bargayne ou contract donques* Walmesley *et auters semble que le ley voet estre auterment. . . .*" See also S.C., B.M. MS.Harl. 1624, f. 298v; *Michell* v. *Dunsden* (P.1595) B.M. MS.Lansd. 1076, f. 153v, MS.Harg. 7, pt. i, f. 84, MS.Add. 25211, f. 97v, U.L.C. MS.Ee. iii. 2, f. 60.
[24] See Lücke in 81 L.Q.R. at pp. 543–545, as to pleading delivery of goods as consideration for a promise to pay for them. This, apparently, did not necessarily indicate that a contract had been made. See also *Taylor* v. *Lodington* (M.1593) B.M. MS.Harl. 1588, f. 183v.

A third argument was that the action on the case deprived defendants in debt of their birthright to wage their law, in subversion of the old common law.[25] This was really ancillary to the first two arguments, because, as Coke pointed out, if the action on the case was warranted by the law, its consequences could not be regarded as subverting the law.[26] Clearly, however, the replacement of debt by the action on the case was principally motivated, from the plaintiff's point of view, by the desire to avoid wager of law.

Each of these arguments will be returned to later.[27] None of them, it may be seen, necessitated the conclusion that " no single state of affairs should give rise to two separate causes of action." [28] The objection was not to two different causes of action arising on the same facts, but to the same *cause* of action giving rise to two different *forms of action*. The former was not uncommon, but the latter would " confound " the Register. This being so, the Common Pleas were content to allow actions on the case in situations where debt would lie, provided there was something collateral or additional to the mere contract or indebtedness, which would provide consideration for an undertaking to pay, and which would therefore amount to a distinct cause of action. Suitable additional factors were: an agreement to pay in a certain place or by several instalments [29] or in specified coin,[30] a forbearance to sue for a fixed time,[31] or a payment or set-off of a smaller sum of money.[32] Since the action of debt lay only to recover the liquidated sum owed, it gave no remedy in respect of these additional factors, and so an action on the case was legitimate. The action on the case, being tortious in nature, was also appropriate to

---

[25] *Williams* v. *Williams* (P. 1596) B.M. MS.Harg. 7, pt. i, f. 188, *per* Owen J.; *Turgys* v. *Becher* (T.1596) B.M. MS.Lansd. 1084, f. 120v, MS.Harg. 7, pt. i, f. 204, U.L.C. MS.Ii.v. 13, f. 59; *Paine* v. *Perramour* (M.1596) Inner Temple MS.Barr. 7, f. 10; *Michelbourne* v. *Burrell* (P.1597) U.L.C. MS.Gg.vi. 29, f. 135.
[26] *Supra*, p. 408, note 81.
[27] *Infra*, pp. 421-426.
[28] Simpson, in 74 L.Q.R. at p. 382. The present writer respectfully agrees with Milsom, *op. cit.*, p. 296: " the mere availability of debt was not in itself a bar to *assumpsit*, so long as there was some basis for the *assumpsit* action apart from the debt itself."
[29] *Pecke* v. *Redman* (P.1555) Dyer 113, *semble*; *Anon.* (T.1557) Bro.N.C. 6, Action sur le case pl. 108; *Tanfeild's Case* (*ante* 1574) cited Linc.Inn. MS.Mayn. 77, f. 325; *Hunt* v. *Sone* (M.1587) Cro.Eliz. 118; *Anon.* (P.1594) U.L.C. MS.Ll.iii 9, f. 400v; *Anon.* (1599) B.M. MS.Lansd. 1074, f. 287; *Taylor* v. *Foster* (H.1601) Cro.Eliz. 776, 807. Since debt did not lie until all the instalments had been incurred, hardship could result if an action on the case were not allowed. See also *Rudder* v. *Price* (1791) 1 Hy.Bl. 547, where the old cases are reviewed and criticised.
[30] See Bacon's argument, *supra*, pp. 404-405.
[31] *Whorwood* v. *Gybbons* (P.1587) Goulds. 48: *Sturges* v. *Beecher*, next note; *infra*, notes 36 and 37.
[32] *Sturges* v. *Beecher* (T.1596) U.L.C. MS.Gg. iii. 25, f. 80: "*le esteant in dett n'est consideration sur que de grounder assumpsit sans doner de longer jour, ou abatinge de part del debt.*" For examples from the records, see A. K. Kiralfy, *The Action on the Case* (1951), pp. 184-185.

recover special loss flowing from the non-payment: for instance, if the debt were in wares or grain and after the failure to deliver the market values rose [33] or the plaintiff's family went hungry [34] or the plaintiff suffered in his business.[35]

Pleaders introduced various combinations of such factors into all declarations in *assumpsit* for money, and sometimes, one may safely guess, they were fictitious. But the Common Pleas frowned on subterfuge, and required any such matter to be genuine. A forbearance to sue for a very short time, such as a quarter of an hour, or an hour, would not be good consideration for a promise to pay the debt.[36] Neither, it would seem, would a forbearance to sue for a day; because "the plaintiff must forbear so long, willy nilly, for he cannot have any remedy or recovery in so short a time." [37] The Common Pleas therefore required the period of forbearance to be specified. In a case of 1596 a nominal payment of threepence was dismissed as being only "a bait to draw him into the bargain." [38] It was common form to allege a loss of profits from prospective bargains in general, as a result of the non-payment,[39] but as this was rarely the subject of objection or judicial discussion it was probably mere form in most cases and so little weight attached to it. Since every creditor could justify such a general allegation, it added nothing to the complaint of debt. Another standard formula was the allegation that the defendant refused to pay deceitfully in order to defraud the plaintiff of his money. This, if true, added a trespassory element to the nonfeasance; yet in most cases it must have been mere form, and so it would avail the plaintiff nothing in the Common Pleas. A failure to perform an obligation was not *ipso facto* fraudulent. Walmsley J., indeed, said it was "plain dealing" for a man to pay nothing when he had no money with which to pay.[40]

---

[33] *Norman* v. *Some* (M.1594) B.M. MS.Harg. 7, pt. i, f. 37 and U.L.C. MS.Ee. iii. 2, f. 34: "*Nota per curiam que accion de dett ne serra convert en accion sur le case si le plaintiff n'ad susteyne damage pluis que ordinarye, come pur wares ou frument vend et nemi deliver et les marketts ryse etc. Car en tiels speciall cases de extraordinarye damages susteyne dette poit estre convert en assumpsit.*"

[34] *Frisland's Case* (H.1596) B.M. MS.Harg. 51, f. 66v and MS.Harl. 1631, f. 210, per Walmsley J.: "*il doit aver monstre ascun extraordinary endamagement sicome pur non deliverance del wheate ses children fueront famished.*"

[35] For examples from the King's Bench rolls, see A. K. R. Kiralfy, *op. cit.*, p. 169.

[36] *Lutwich* v. *Hussey* (P.1583) Cro.Eliz. 19; *Sackford* v. *Phillips* (P.1594) Cro.Eliz. 455, Owen 109; *Purslowe* v. *Tisdale* (P.1600) Inner Temple MS.Barr. 6, f. 56v, Cro.Eliz. 758.

[37] *Milles* v. *Raynton* (M.1600) B.M. MS.Add. 25203, f. 244v, per Walmsley J. See also Inner Temple MS.Barr. 6, f. 86v, MS.Barr. 7, f. 16v. His brethren were divided as to a forbearance for a week out of term time.

[38] *Frisland's Case, supra*, note 34.

[39] See, *e.g.*, Milsom, *op. cit.*, at p. 299.

[40] *Anon.* (P.1596) B.M. MS.Harg. 51, f. 82. Accord. *Duppa* v. *Jones* (T.1602) B.M. MS.Lansd. 1074, f. 413, per Anderson C.J. and Walmsley J.: *infra*, p. 427. *Cf.* the argument *supra*, p. 404, note 65.

The King's Bench view

The judges of the King's Bench had persuaded themselves that actions on the case could properly be used to recover debts and avoid wager of law, and they therefore treated any formula which brought the non-payment of a debt into the realms of trespass as valid. They were not so fastidious as their brethren across the Hall about nominal or unspecified forbearances [41] or formal allegations of deceit. They did not insist on juries finding an express promise to pay the debt before giving judgment for the plaintiff, because, as they said, the debt itself " imported " an undertaking to pay [42]: it was an " assumption in law " if not in words.[43]

The theoretical distinction between the action of debt and that of *assumpsit* was sufficiently preserved, in their view, by the unchallenged fact that juries could only award unliquidated damages in a trespass action. The award might be less than,[44] and in practice often exceeded,[45] the debt. The reality of the King's Bench practice was betrayed by a careless clerk who entered an *indebitatus assumpsit* action in the same roll which contains *Slade's Case*. He described the action as a plea of debt, and the judgment entered was that the plaintiff should recover his debt and also damages for its detention.[46] Such a confusion of theory and practice would have been heresy in the Common Pleas.

The principal authority advanced for the King's Bench view was the continuous practice of the court itself. When pressed to expound their doctrine rationally, the judges seem to have been less than confident. In *Colson* v. *Cotton* [47] the court discussed the effect of an *assumpsit* to pay £10 in consideration of the sale and delivery of barley worth £10. Fenner J. admitted that there might have been a " question " if the sale had been *pro* £10, so that debt would have

---

[41] *May* v. *Alvares* (P.1595) Cro.Eliz. 387; *Palmer* v. *Randz* (P.1599) Hetley 62, B.M. MS.Add. 25203, f. 63, MS.Add. 35951, f. 86.
[42] *Estrigge* v. *Owles* (T.1588) 3 Leo. 200, at p. 201; *Barkley* v. *Foster* (P.1597) Inner Temple MS.Petyt 516/5, f. 102. *Cf. Norwood* v. *Read* (1558) 1 Plo. 180.
[43] *Edwards* v. *Burre* (1573) Dalison 108, *per* Wray C.J.; *Escrigg* v. *Owles* (1589) as reported in B.M. MS.Lansd. 1104, f. 119.
[44] *Coleman's Case* (M.1595) U.L.C. MS.Gg. v. 3, f. 46: " *En accion sur le case damages solement sont demand, et ceux doient estre asses per le jurors, et nient obstant que appiert que le plaintiff duist aver x li. si l'assumpsit fuit performe, uncore le jurors poient done meindre some s'ils voile, et est bon.*" In *Barkley* v. *Foster* (H.1597) B.M. MS.Harl. 4552, f. 111, Popham C.J. said that "*le plaintiff icy in l'accion sur le case ne recovera in damages forsque tant come il est prejudice per le non payment al jour lymit.*" The reporter added: " *Mes quere coment il ceo intend.*"
[45] Sometimes only 6d. or 1s. above the debt was awarded: *e.g.*, K.B. 27/1336, mm. 79, 126. In *Slade's Case* the sum awarded was equal to the sum owed.
[46] *Shackleton* v. *Grene* (H.1596) K.B. 27/1336, m. 68: " *Ideo consideratum est quod J. S. recuperet versus H. G. debitum suum predictum necnon viginti solidos pro dampnis suis. . . .*"
[47] (M.1596) B.M. MS.Harl. 1697, f. 121v, U.L.C. MS.Gg. iii 25, f. 124v.

lain, but as £10 was only stated as the value of the barley and not the contract price the plaintiff had judgment. This looks like a technical quibble, seized upon by a court very much on the defensive. The judges even felt unsure of themselves on the question of the contemporaneous implied *assumpsit*, and put it down to *communis error* rather than defend it on its merits: " Every debt is an *assumpsit* in itself. And so are infinite precedents upon search here found in this court in the time of Henry VIII, although this is now contradicted by the Common Bench. And if this be error, the ' community ' of it makes it law." [48] In another report of this same speech of Popham C.J., he is credited with the following specimen of logic-chopping:

> Although it be error, yet the long use and multitude of precedents must draw it into a law, for *communis error facit ius*. . . . And where [the judges of the Common Pleas] say that there must be a special *assumpsit*, otherwise no action on the case lies, he answered that the acceptance of the money delivered or lent to him *is* express *assumpsit*. They agree that in such a case account or debt lies. If debt lies, then there is a consideration *de necessario*; and, if consideration, then a promise, for each of them follows the one the other.[49]

If this was the best summary of the King's Bench attack on what was perhaps the weakest part of the Common Pleas' case, then a King's Bench victory was very far from inevitable.

THE COURTS JOIN BATTLE 1585–97

The difference between the courts—by no means confined to the sphere of debt [50]—had resulted, by the middle of Queen Elizabeth I's reign, in an unsatisfactory deadlock. When the judges discussed these matters at dinner, or found each other directing juries in different ways on circuit, they must have craved some final solution. But there was no way in which the two opposing sides could be brought into direct conflict until the establishment of the new Exchequer Chamber, to review judgments of the King's Bench, in 1585.[51]

---

[48] *Barkley* v. *Foster* (P.1597) U.L.C. MS.Gg. vi 29, f. 69 (translated). Even this argument is false, because the implied promise doctrine nowhere appears on the record, and so there were no " precedents " of the kind referred to.

[49] *Barkley* v. *Foster* (P.1597) B.M. MS.Harl. 4552, f. 110 (translated). See the other reports in B.M. MS.Lansd. 1071, f. 230, MS.Lansd. 1104, f. 166v, MS.Harl. 4558, f. 25, and Inner Temple MS.Petyt 516/5, f. 102.

[50] *Cf.* (1) (Detinue and case). *Eason* v. *Newman* (M.1596) Cro.Eliz. 495, Moo. 460, Goulds. 152; *Hyne* v. *Tanner* (M.1597) Inner Temple MS.Petyt 516/5, f. 138v; *Anon.* (M.1599) B.M. MS.Lansd. 1074, f. 325; *Holcroft* v. *Beard* (M.1600) B.M. MS.Add. 25203, f. 251v. (2) (Nuisance and case). *Alston* v. *Pamphyn* (P.1596) Cro.Eliz. 466; *Beswick* v. *Cunden* (M.1596) Cro.Eliz. 520, Moo. 450; *Crattendon's Case* (M.1599) B.M. MS.Lansd. 1074, f. 332v; *Cantrell* v. *Church* (T.1601) Cro.Eliz. 845, Noy 37. (3) (Account and case). *Holiday* v. *Hicks* (1598–1600) Cro.Eliz. 638, 661, 746. There are numerous additional reports of the leading cases in manuscript.

[51] By the 27 Eliz. 1, c. 8, as amended by the 31 Eliz. 1, c. 1.

The new tribunal took ten years to find its teeth, a long delay which cannot comfortably be attributed to mere lethargy. Professor Lücke detected an apparent change of mind by Wray C.J.K.B., but decided that " to assume that the change occurred between 1588 and 1591 would be fanciful in the extreme; at any rate, it would have removed the major cause for the conflict between the King's Bench and the Common Pleas." [52] Manuscript evidence now suggests, however, that the postponement of hostilities on the debt issue was the result of just such a change of mind by Wray C.J. A few years afterwards, Owen J.C.P. claimed to have spoken to Wray C.J. (as the " chief supporter " of the King's Bench " error ") and persuaded him that it was unjust to oust defendants of their law by actions on the case. According to Owen J., " Wray, upon this, said that he would never maintain this action again, and truly he never adjudged this afterwards." [53] Whether or not this claim can be verified, it seems more than mere coincidence that battle was not joined in the Exchequer Chamber until shortly after Wray's death in 1592. In Easter Term 1592 it was reported in the Common Pleas that the King's Bench were prepared to allow case on a mere loan of money,[54] and by 1593 some of the writs of error to reverse *assumpsit* for debt against executors were pending.[55] Wray's successor, Sir John Popham, had no qualms about the " error," and two of the first Exchequer Chamber cases were brought to reverse Popham C.J.'s judgments. The proximity of the leading cases to each other in time has been disguised by the length of the protracted deliberations which followed; but in fact they all began within nine months of each other, in 1595 and 1596.

The first reported Exchequer Chamber case arising out of the dispute was *Turgys* v. *Becher*. The pleadings were in the *indebitatus* form, setting out the contract of sale.[56] Writs of error were received by the King's Bench on 27 October 1595 and again on 25 January 1596, and the case was argued before all the justices of the Common

---

[52] 81 L.Q.R. at p. 556.
[53] *Beecher* v. *Sturges* (T.1596) B.M. MS.Harg. 7, pt. i, f. 204 (translated). Owen was not then a judge, but he had taken the coif in 1589, and was a fellow member with Wray of Serjeants' Inn Fleet Street.
[54] *Anon.* (P.1592) B.M. MS.Lansd. 1067, f. 170: "*Accion sur le case port sur apprompt, et per curiam ne gist, car partie avera accion de dett. Mes per Glanvill aliter tenetur in Banco Regis.*"
[55] *May* v. *Cardwydin* (M.1593) B.M. MS.Lansd. 1071, f. 260: "*Nota que est dit que mults breve d'error sont pendantes en le chequer chamber sur tiels judgments dones en bank le roi.*" For the dispute over executors, see below, pp. 428-429.
[56] Trin. 37 Eliz. 1, K.B. 27/1334, m. 606: " *quod cum* W. B. . . . *indebitatus fuit* [to the intestate T.] *in* [£30] *adtunc remanentis eidem* T. *insolutis per* W. B. *pro c. quarteriis tritici predicto* W. B. *per ipsum* T. *tunc prius venditis, predictus* W. B. *adtunc . . . in consideracione inde super se assumpsit* [to pay]." And another similar sale of wheat for £25. The plaintiff had judgment for £60 and costs.

Pleas and barons of the Exchequer in Trinity Term 1596. Since there were no circumstances additional to the contract on which to found a special action on the case, all the judges (after some hesitation by Clerke B.) agreed that the King's Bench judgment should be reversed. Anderson C.J. even refused to hear argument to the contrary.[57] Within months of the writ of error in this case, further writs were brought to reverse two judgments in *assumpsit* in cases which had been tried before Popham C.J. in London. In both cases the consideration pleaded was the contract itself. The first was similar to *Slade's Case*,[58] but no report of any discussion has been found. The second was *Paramour* v. *Payne*,[59] in which the declaration was similar to the last, except that it showed a bargain and sale without a delivery. The argument, in Michaelmas Term, went over the same ground as before, and a similar conclusion was reached.[60]

Before these two cases reached the Exchequer Chamber, John Slade had (in Michaelmas Term 1595) preferred his bill against Humfrey Morley, who pleaded *non assumpsit* in Hilary Term 1596. The *assumpsit* on which issue had been taken was a promise to pay £16 in consideration of a bargain and sale of certain crops for that sum. The issue was tried during Lent at Exeter Castle, the commissioners of *nisi prius* being Fenner J.K.B. and Walmsley J.C.P.[61] It is not difficult to imagine the kind of disagreement which occurred at Exeter, the outcome of which was the special verdict finding the contract proved but no other promise or *assumpsit*. This verdict was contrived to put on the record for consideration by the judges the question whether a debt imported an *assumpsit* in itself. Probably a test case was envisaged.[62] Then Popham C.J. strategically forestalled

---

[57] B.M. MS.Harg. 7, pt. i, f. 204: "Anderson *noluit audire argumentum del contrary part, car il dit la ne poit estre ascun reason omnino fait a mainteiner ceo.*" The only printed report (Moo. 694) is quite inadequate. Other reports are: B.M. MS.Harl. 1624, f. 298v, MS.Harl. 1631, f. 55, MS.Harl. 1697, f. 107v, MS.Harl. 4998, f. 177v, MS.Lansd. 1084, f. 120v, Inner Temple MS.Barr. 7, f. 8, Linc. Inn MS.Misc. 490, f. 706v, U.L.C. MS.Dd. x. 51, f. 78, MS.Ee. vi. 17, f. 112v, MS.Gg. ii. 5, ff. 431v, 469, MS.Ii. v. 13, ff. 59, 102.

[58] *Myles* v. *Smythe*, Mich. 37 & 38 Eliz. 1, K.B. 27/1335, m. 742. This was an action on a promise to pay £7 for a pack of wool bargained, sold and delivered to the defendant at his request. The plaintiff recovered £7 10s. damages. There is a note on the record that the writ of error was received on 23 January 1596.

[59] Mich. 37 & 38 Eliz. 1, K.B. 27/1335, m. 664. This was an action on a promise to pay separate sums of money for divers goods sold and bargained to the defendant at his request. The jury found part of the claim false, but the plaintiff had judgment for the remainder. The writ of error was received on 16 February 1596.

[60] The only printed report (Moo. 703) is unhelpful. Other reports are: B.M. MS.Harl. 1631, f. 71v, MS.Harl. 4552, f. 92, Inner Temple MS.Barr. 7, f. 10, U.L.C. MS.Dd. x. 51, f. 52, MS.Gg. ii. 5, f. 444v.

[61] Hil. 38 Eliz. 1, K.B. 27/1336, m. 305. The record is accurately printed in 4 Rep. 91.

[62] *Cf.* the special verdict in *Eason* v. *Newman* (M.1596) Moo. 460.

the statutory court of Exchequer Chamber by referring the matter, before judgment, to all the judges of England in the old informal "Exchequer Chamber." By thus staying judgment, no writ of error could be brought until the matter had been decided by the English judiciary as a whole.

The first reported argument in the Exchequer Chamber was not until 9 October 1597, when John Dodderidge moved the case for the defendant, saying it had been adjourned thither because of its difficulty. Dodderidge was a Devon man,[63] and had perhaps been engaged in the case from the beginning. His opponent was the Attorney-General, Coke, whose services may well have been procured by Popham C.J.; Coke's arguments closely followed Popham C.J.'s *communis error* argument, and stressed the importance of upholding the practice of each court even when it differed from that of other courts. The next debate took place at Serjeants' Inn a year later, when Laurence Tanfield[64] took the place of Coke, and Francis Bacon[65] took over from Dodderidge as counsel for the defendant. There is no trace of the case in the reports for the three years ensuing, presumably because the private consultations between the judges[66] were not leading towards a consensus of opinion. The legal world was kept in suspense; in one case the court would not allow discussion of the point because *Slade's Case* was still pending.[67] On 17 October 1601 the case was moved again by Coke, and Bacon's reply on 13 May 1602 has been printed above.[68]

No report of the judicial conferences has come to light, and no decision is known to have been given in the Exchequer Chamber. The content of the debate must therefore be deduced from the arguments of counsel.

THE ARGUMENTS IN SLADE'S CASE

The arguments as reported ranged beyond the technical question raised by the special verdict, and encompassed the vexed general question of the propriety of using actions on the case instead of the action of debt. The latter question divided itself into two: the first touching the sanctity of the Register, the second touching the advantages of wager of law.

---

[63] His father was a Barnstaple merchant; he (the lawyer) was buried (not far from Bracton) in Exeter Cathedral, where his effigy may still be seen. He was later a judge of the King's Bench; but in 1597 he was still an utter barrister, aged 42.
[64] Reader of the Inner Temple; later Chief Baron. His argument is printed *supra*, pp. 396-401.
[65] Bencher of Gray's Inn and the Queen's counsel extraordinary; later Lord Chancellor.
[66] Referred to in 4 Rep. 93a.
[67] *Burley* v. *Wisse* (1601) Bodl.Lib. MS.Rawl. A. 415, f. 15.
[68] *Supra*, pp. 402-408.

1. "*Every contract executory imports in itself an* assumpsit"

These famous words of Popham C.J. in delivering the judgment of the King's Bench in 1602 [69] have been the subject of much misunderstanding. Until fairly recent times it was basic teaching in the law schools that they marked the final recognition of the action on the case to enforce mutual promises [70]; a complete misinterpretation of the word "executory," which has now been exploded.[71] There has also been speculation as to whether the difficulty of "importing" an *assumpsit* was a difficulty over contemporaneous implied promises or subsequent fictional promises [72]; a doubt which arose partly from our not knowing that contemporaries saw this as a question separate from the more important question of remedies. The traditional view was that the promise had been fictional: "a monstrous fiction, and one extremely characteristic of the pedantic, subtle, sophistical spirit of the age." [73] But the arguments reveal that this was not so at all, and that the question was much less sophisticated than has been supposed. Did a contract contain in itself an undertaking to perform the duty which it generated, even though the contracting parties did not use the express words "I promise" or "I undertake"? In so far as that question has anything to do with "implied" [74] promises, it has to do with the *Moorcock* type of implication and not with any figments of juristic imagination.[75]

---

[69] *Ibid.*, p. 66; 4 Rep. 94a, Moo. 667. Popham did not invent the phrase: *cf.* note 42, *supra*.

[70] In Cambridge by Professors Winfield and Hollond: lecture notes in the Squire Law Library. In Oxford by Professor Holdsworth: *History of English Law*, Vol. 3 (3rd ed., 1923), pp. 445, 451. In London by Professors Jenks, Potter and Kiralfy: E. Jenks, *Short History of English Law* (6th ed., 1949), p. 305; H. Potter, *Historical Introduction to English Law* (4th ed., 1958), p. 465; A. K. R. Kiralfy, *The English Legal System* (4th ed., 1967), p. 69. See also J. P. Dawson, *Oracles of the Law* (1968), p. 71 (who incorrectly blames Plucknett).

[71] By Professors Plucknett and Milsom. See also Simpson in 74 L.Q.R. at p. 391.

[72] See J. Ames, *Lectures on Legal History* (1913), pp. 150–152 (still an important passage); Plucknett, *op. cit.*, pp. 644–646; S. F. C. Milsom, "Not Doing is No Trespass" [1954] C.L.J. 105, at pp. 111–112; Lücke, *op. cit.*, 81 L.Q.R. at pp. 553–554; S. F. C. Milsom, *Historical Foundations of the Common Law* (1969), pp. 303–304. Much of the difficulty stems from *Anon.* (1572) Dal. 84, where it it said that a *subsequent* promise must be pleaded; but it is not said that a subsequent promise would be implied by the court. It cannot be taken as representing the later King's Bench view. Plucknett incorrectly read the word "subsequent" into *Edwards* v. *Burre* (1573) Dal. 104, and *Slade's Case* itself. With respect to Lücke's persuasive argument (82 L.Q.R. at p. 82), *adtunc et ibidem* cannot mean the same as *postea*, notwithstanding the change of tense: see *Sheffield* v. *Rise*, note 8, *supra*; and *Anon.* (1572) Dal. 84. We can avoid some of the difficulties if we ask, not whether the promise had to be *subsequent* to the contract, but whether it had to be *separate* from it.

[73] W. F. Finlason, note to J. Reeves, *History of English Law* (1869 ed.), Vol. 3, p. 751. Reeves did not make this mistake himself, but most subsequent writers have assumed that the imported promise was a King's Bench fiction.

[74] Coke actually altered the word "implied" to "imported," which conveys the meaning more precisely. See his draft in B.M. MS.Harl. 6686.

[75] Accord. J. Reeves, *History of English Law* (1869 ed.), Vol. 3, p. 752; Ames, *op. cit.*, p. 152; P. H. Winfield, *The Law of Quasi-Contract* (1952), pp. 6–7;

Dodderidge bravely submitted that an action of trespass would not lie on an imaginary promise,[76] but Coke's denial that the imported promise was "imaginary"[77] was virtually unanswerable. Ordinary laymen do not use terms of art when making their bargains. If what they say and do amounts to an undertaking, then the law will so account it, and it may be so pleaded. Bacon does not seem to have troubled himself with finding an answer to such a sensible proposition.

Although this point had been in issue between the courts in preceding years, it did not go to the root of the differences, and its determination in favour of the King's Bench did not settle the main issue.

2. *Action on the case instead of debt*

The principal bone of contention between the courts, as revealed by the events of the previous decade, was whether a plaintiff might resort to an action on the case when he had a " proper action framed in the Register."[78] It seems to have been accepted without demur that the action on the case originated with the Statute of Westminster II,[79] and Dodderidge, as an eminent legal antiquary, seized upon the opportunity to expatiate on his subject: on the history of the Register, on the achievements of Edward I (the " English Justinian "), even on the *formulae iuris* of ancient Rome.[80] Coke wisely kept away from these topics, with which Dodderidge undoubtedly had a greater familiarity. Yet, given the historical premiss, the conclusions of the Common Pleas judges seem unimpeachable. Coke's instances in which actions on the case had been allowed notwithstanding the availability of an older writ were nearly all effectively distinguished by Bacon, on the grounds that there had in each case been alleged some collateral matter or actual deceit. This aspect of the argument is overlooked in Coke's printed report of the case—probably a tacit admission that he knew it to be against him. For all his learning, his case was " indefensible."[81] To cover himself, he urged on the judges

J. F. Wilson, *Principles of the Law of Contract* (1957), pp. 9–10; Simpson, 74 L.Q.R. at pp. 394–395. There remains the difficulty whether the implied *assumpsit* is the same *assumpsit* as that expressed in the declaration. Lücke argued that it was not, but the argument leads to insuperable difficulties: 81 L.Q.R. at pp. 554–555. On the view advanced here, there is no objection to holding the contrary; the jurors did not find the *assumpsit* not proved, only that there was no promise apart from the contract.

[76] *Supra.* p. 397, note 23.
[77] *Supra*, p. 398, note 27; 74 L.Q.R. at p. 394. Coke dismissed the point as deserving no discussion, and gave it little prominence in his report.
[78] *Ibid.*, pp. 398-399; 4 Rep. 92b.
[79] This was stated by Anderson C.J. at Serjeants' Inn, and apparently not contradicted: *supra*, p. 402.
[80] B.M. MS.Harl. 6809, f. 46. Dodderidge was a leading light in the Elizabethan Society of Antiquaries.
[81] Plucknett, *op. cit.*, p. 647. Simpson says it was " a mere perversion of authority " (74 L.Q.R. at p. 393). Lord Loughborough C.J. attacked Coke's arguments on

the principle that courts would follow a multitude of precedents even if they disagreed with them. That Coke, as well as Popham, should have been driven to rely on *communis error* is proof of his diffidence in the strength of their legal reasoning.

3. *Wager of law and perjury*

It has been commonly, and no doubt correctly, assumed that the main reason for extending *assumpsit* into the area served by the action of debt was the desire to evade wager of law—which was not so much a mode of trial as a bar which operated even if the oath were demonstrably false.[82] Coke, naturally, relied on the prevalence of perjury, and invited the judges to save the souls of defendants from damnation.

To modern eyes, the farce which compurgation had seemingly become through the offices of the "knights of the post"[83] should have been a self-evident objection to its continuance. But these characters are not referred to in the argument, and their assistance was probably considered desirable "for the ease of the subject."[84] The use of professional wagermen was approved and sanctioned by the courts, and the porter or court-keeper was allowed fees for finding them,[85] though it is likely that the courts had a discretion to withhold their sanction in appropriate cases. In 1602 a defendant tendered his law for the exceptionally large sum of £500:

> and because the sum was so great the court refused to take his law then and willed him to bring some of his neighbours, because the plaintiff was there to prove the debt. And att two other daies hee came againe with his neighbours, and the plaintiff came allso and was non suited.[86]

similar grounds as long ago as 1791: *Rudder* v. *Price*, 1 Hy.Bl. 547, at pp. 550–551.

[82] *Anon.* (P.1587) B.M. MS.Lansd. 1076, f. 122v, Goulds. 51. Reeves represented the dispute leading to *Slade's Case* as being entirely about wager of law: *History of English Law* (1869 ed.), Vol. 3, p. 750.

[83] See *A True Collection of the King's offices and Fees* (temp. Jac. I), B.M. MS.Harl. 829, f. 116v: "there is an officer in the Common Place will gett yow them to fill up the number which be called knights of the post." The name derives from the post, or pillory, a professional hazard encountered by such men. See also E. S., *The Discoverie of the Knights of the Poste* (1597) S.T.C. 21489; *New English Dictionary*, s.v. "post-knight"; E. Partridge, *A Dictionary of Slang* (1963), p. 460. [For an early reference, see C1/369/92.]

[84] T. Powell, *The Attorneys Academy* (1623), p. 132: "But there is an officer heere for the ease of the subject, who will furnish . . . twelve such compurgators as occasion shall require." Such assistance was needed when the defendant wished to do his law *instanter* to prevent a non-suit; he would fail if he did not produce 12 hands at once: *Anon.* (T.1595) B.M. MS.Lansd. 1076, r. 184v.

[85] See the reports on court fees in G. T., *Attourney of the Court of Common Pleas* (1648), pp. 85, 86, 103, 146 and 173. (The fees were claimed as having been received since 1569 at least.) If the defendant paid the fee for 12, and the officer only produced eight, his law failed: *Anon.* (temp. Eliz. 1) U.L.C. MS.Gg. v. 4, f. 87v.

[86] *Barnham and Cartwright* v. *Barrett* (T.1602) B.M. MS.Lansd. 1074, f. 410. In Easter Term 1609 it was reported that "*ore le court ad fait ordre, que ou le*

This last case is a reminder that, in this period, most actions on simple contracts were brought for comparatively small sums. Slade's action was brought for £16. The use of conditioned bonds was still widespread, and merchants preferred the efficacious securities of statutes and recognisances. In most cases, therefore, wager of law operated only in relation to small debts—debts which had probably been contracted by word of mouth, and possibly paid off in private.[87] In this kind of case there were genuine difficulties of proof. The parties themselves could not give evidence at all, and if there were no other witnesses the jurors would have to hazard their consciences on a guess. The worst hardship arose when there was evidence of a debt, but no evidence of its discharge; if the defendant could not wage his law, he might have to pay twice. Wray's conversion by Owen had proceeded from this argument. It was customary in London to pay a merchant in advance for wares to be supplied over a long period, and it was not usual to take an acquittance. If, after supplying the wares for several years, the merchant sued for the price, the customer would have no evidence of the prepayment to put to the jury.[88] It was also hard, argued Owen J., to impose on chapmen the burden of proving every individual payment made by them to London merchants for wares they were known to have received.[89]

Coke's answer to this argument was that people ought to take acquittances at their peril, or at least pay their debts in the presence of witnesses. But this was not realistic advice, and in any case the knights of the post could have rendered assistance here *qua* witnesses, just as they had helped out defendants *qua* oath-helpers. At this very period, Lord Keeper Egerton was refusing to enforce unwritten agreements in the Chancery, " considering the plenty of witnesses nowadays, which were *testes diabolica*." [90] Presumably a fraudulent debtor would more readily buy another man's conscience than endanger his own soul, and would therefore prefer to remain mute and hire witnesses than to swear falsely with the support of wagermen.

The latter point, it is submitted, is crucial. The potential perjury under discussion was not that of the knights of the post, but of dishonest debtors. The theory of wager of law, wrote Coke, was that

summe est petit et ne amount at 40 li. ou pluis il avera desouth 6, mes lou il amount al 40 li. il avera 6 al meins, et ceux doient estre de ses neighboures queux melieux conusont le person de luy que jure": Petit's Reports, collection by T. Tourneur, MS. *penes* Sir John Neale, p. 301; Leeds Public Lib. MS.SRF/942.06. c.685, f. 1081.

[87] *Cf.* S. E. Thorne, "Tudor Social Transformation and Legal Change" (1951) 26 N.Y.U.L.R. 10, at pp. 19-21.   [88] *Loc. cit., supra*, note 53.
[89] S.C., B.M. MS.Harl. 1624, f. 298v: "*Et* Owen *dit que le inconvenience fuit grand pur le chapmen que buy wares dell Londoners car ills sera arct de prover le payment de chescun particuler some que ills ont paid.*"
[90] *Anon.* (1603) Cary 27.

"the law presumeth that no man will forswear himself for any worldly thing "[91]; and his argument in *Slade's Case* was that this presumption had been rebutted by experience. It is unnecessary to decide whether Coke's strictures on the moral values of his contemporaries were well founded; for, assuming that perjury was a widespread practical problem, it does not follow that it worked more injustice through wager of law than it did through jury trials in which the parties were not competent witnesses. This is the reason why medieval statutes defended the use of wager of law in appropriate cases, as a safeguard against perjured jurors.[92] Moreover, the fact that some debtors were rogues was no reason for denying justice to the honest man who was not in debt but had difficulty in establishing the fact. The court was not interested in the mumbled recitations of the oath-helpers; they were an indispensable ceremony, but no more. But the court did take steps to reach the conscience of the defendant himself, who was reminded of the sanctity of an oath before he was sworn.[93] The reports are full of cases in which defendants upon examination revealed the truth of their case and sought guidance whether it was " safe " for them to wage their law.[94]

There is no clear evidence that wager of law did not work well, or that the merits of the debate about the burden of proof lay all on Coke's side. It must not, therefore, be assumed that the corruptions of legal doctrine in *Slade's Case* were justifiable on the grounds that wager of law was an evil to be destroyed by any means available.

THE MYSTERY OF SLADE'S CASE

Mr. Simpson has justly described the decision of the Court of King's Bench in *Slade's Case* as an " astonishing act of judicial legislation."[95] It is impossible, even with the best accounts of the speeches before us, to understand how the decision was ever consented to; and

---

[91] Co.Litt. 295a.
[92] See Plucknett, *op. cit.*, p. 160; W. M. McGovern, " Contract in Medieval England: Wager of Law and the Effect of Death " (1968) 54 *Iowa Law Review* 19, at p. 38, notes 125–129.
[93] 4 Rep. 95a; B.M. MS.Harl. 6686, f. 530 ("*les judges sans bone admonition et due examination del partie ne admitt luy a [ley gager]*"). In 1647 it was said that " the judges will admonish him to be well advised, and tell him the danger of taking a false oath ": W. Style, *Practical Register* (1657), p. 349. See also McGovern, *op. cit.*, at pp. 27–28.
[94] *Anon.* (1587) Goulds. 57, B.M. MS.Lansd. 1076, f. 123v; *Millington* v. *Burges* (1587) Goulds. 65; *Anon.* (1588) 3 Leo. 212; *Anon.* (1588) 4 Leo. 81; *Sanderson* v. *Ekins* (1588 or 1590) 3 Leo. 258, Goulds. 80; *Arnold Rutton's Case* (P.1592) B.M. MS.Lansd. 1076, f. 148v; *Anon.* (M.1594) *ibid.*, f. 178v; *Blocke's Case* (H.1597) B.M. MS.Harg. 7, pt. ii, f. 65; *Flower* v. *Flower* (M.1597) B.M. MS.Lansd. 1076, f. 166, MS.Harl. 1631, f. 271; *Oliver Hagger's Case* (1598) U.L.C. MS.Ll. iii. 10, f. 60v. In *Flower's Case* the defendant " *monstre al court le veritie del case, craving lour advise s'il poet jure safement.*"
[95] 74 L.Q.R. at p. 392.

this difficulty at once prompts the question whether it really did reflect a judicial agreement.

The retreat of the Common Pleas

Coke related the decision as being that of all the judges of England,[96] and the same impression is conveyed by Popham C.J. in his curt announcement of 9 November 1602.[97] Nevertheless, searches have failed to reveal any intimation by the judges of the Common Pleas that they had reversed their former opinions, or even that they had reluctantly decided not to press their views. What is more, the statutory Exchequer Chamber continued to reverse King's Bench judgments in *assumpsit* for debt while the informal assembly was considering *Slade's Case*,[98] and in 1601 Walmsley J. was still attacking the action on the case as " only a wrench to defraud the common law." [99] More remarkable than this, in Trinity Term 1602, by which time any supposed agreement between the courts ought to have been concluded, both Anderson C.J. and Walmsley J. repeated their doctrine in unambiguous terms:

> Cleerly the action will not lye, for the debt is hereby not changed and these new devises of accions of the case cannot be mainteined. For there ought to be no accions of the case but grounded upon some fraud, for so are the words of the writt, " *machinans* [*defraudare*] etc." What fraud is here committed? [1]

If Moore is to be trusted at all, the weight of opinion in the Exchequer Chamber at the first argument, in Michaelmas Term 1597, was with the Common Pleas.[2] The changes in the composition of the court during the next five years cannot be made to explain any change of heart. Anderson C.J. and Walmsley J. both survived the dispute. Their brethren Owen and Beaumont JJ. died in 1598, and were succeeded by Glanvill and Kingsmill JJ. Glanvill J.'s views on the subject have not come to light, but Kingsmill J. was true to the old cause.[3]

Assuming that the Common Pleas judges remained unmoved by Coke's advocacy, did they have a substantial majority against them?

---

[96] 4 Rep. 93.
[97] Baker, *supra*, p. 66; Moo. 667.
[98] *Maylard* v. *Kester* (M.1599) Moo. 711; *Powell* v. *Preston* (H.1601) Inner Temple MS.Barr. 6, f. 126; *Simcocke* v. *Payne* (P.1601) B.M. MS.Add. 25203, f. 320, MS.Lansd. 1067, f. 184v, Inner Temple MS.Barr. 6, f. 166, Cro.Eliz. 786. The point was taken in the Exchequer Chamber by Altham as late as Easter Term 1602: *Pillesworth* v. *Feake*, as reported in B.M. MS.Add. 25203, f. 479v.
[99] *Simcocke* v. *Payne* (P.1601) B.M. MS.Add. 25203, f. 320.
[1] *Duppa* v. *Jones* (T.1602) B.M. MS.Lansd. 1074, f. 413, Linc. Inn. MS. Mayn. 87, f. 309. Was this an attempt to divert attention from the imported promise point, which they had lost?
[2] Moo. 433.
[3] *Simcocke* v. *Payne, supra*, note 98.

All would have depended on the barons of the Exchequer. Clerke B. seems to have sympathised with the King's Bench,[4] and Ewens B. (who died while the case was pending) likewise.[5] But Peryam C.B., a former Common Pleas judge, and Savile B. were traditionalists.[6] The Chief Baron had even sided with Walmsley J. in his dissent from the Exchequer Chamber decision which allowed case to be brought instead of the assize of nuisance.[7]

The judges of England seem, therefore, to have been more or less evenly divided on the question, and this probably accounts for the fact that they never (apparently) convened to deliver their opinions *seriatim*. Had they done so, it is certain that it would have attracted publicity and that accounts of it would survive. The decision appears, on the face of it, to have been a decision of the King's Bench alone. Yet it did put an end to the controversy. Morley did not purchase a writ of error, and with his debt to the lawyers added to his debt to Slade it is not surprising. And the Common Pleas judges, if they were not privy to the decision announced by Popham C.J., certainly made no further struggle to reverse King's Bench judgments in the Exchequer Chamber. Why they should have given way—if only by their silence—remains an unsolved mystery.

The liability of executors

An important chapter in the history of *assumpsit* for money is that which relates to the liability of executors to pay the contract debts of the deceased. The King's Bench thought that a debtor by simple contract should have no more right to defeat his creditors by dying than had a debtor by specialty; and so they allowed *assumpsit* to be brought against the executors of such debtors.[8] The Common Pleas

---

[4] *Turgys* v. *Becher, supra*, note 56; *Paramour* v. *Payne* (M.1596) U.L.C. MS.Gg. vi. 29, f. 133v; *Stubbings* v. *Rotheram* (M.1595) Cro.Eliz. 454. In the first case, he hesitated but did not actually dissent.
[5] *Paramour* v. *Payne* (M.1596) U.L.C. MS.Gg. vi. 29, f. 133v.
[6] *Anon.* (probably *Milles* v. *Raynton*) (M.1600) as reported in B.M. MS.Lansd. 1074, f. 363v, Linc. Inn MS.Mayn. 87, f. 253v; *Simcocke* v. *Payne, supra*, note 98.
[7] *Churche* v. *Cantrell* (M.1601) B.M. MS.Add. 25203, f. 395. The reporter said of their dissent " *non multum contradixerunt*." The decision was not regarded as final: see *Gamford* v. *Nightingale* (1605) Noy 112; three cases in Rolle Abr., Vol. 1, p. 104.
[8] *Cleymond* v. *Vincent*, M. 12 Hen. 8, 11, *pl.* 3; *Norwood* v. *Read* (M.1557) Plo. 180; *Cottington* v. *Hulett* (M.1588) Cro.Eliz. 59; *May* v. *Cardwydin* (M.1593) B.M. MS.Lansd. 1071, f. 260; *Hughes* v. *Robotham* (T.1593) Poph. 30, at p. 32, *per* Popham C.J.; *Harper* v. *Belfield* (H.1594) B.M. MS.Lansd. 1071, f. 269; *Anon.* (M.1595) U.L.C. MS.Gg. v. 3, f. 45v; *Gaywood* v. *Gent* (H.1596) B.M. MS.Harl. 1697, f. 96v, MS.Add. 35950, f. 93v, (*sub nom. Gawod* v. *Bankes*) MS.Harl. 1624, f. 291, (*sub nom. Gawoode* v. *Binkes*) U.L.C. MS.Gg. v. 3, f. 99v, (*sub nom. Camond* v. *Jent*) U.L.C. MS.Ee. vi. 17, f. 61v, U.L.C. MS.Gg. iii. 25, f. 55v, Rolle Abr., Vol. 1, p. 14, (*sub nom. Gowode* v. *Binkes*) Owen 56; *Thorneton* v. *Kempe* (T.1596) U.L.C. MS.Gg. iii. 25, f. 79v; *Perke* v. *Loveden* (H.1601) B.M. MS.Add. 25203, f. 285, MS.Lansd. 1067, f. 195; *Hogg*

New Light on Slade's Case 429

at one time showed signs of following the same course, since it involved no conflict with the action of debt and was therefore within the province of actions on the case. Dyer C.J. said that his predecessor Montague C.J. had brought the practice with him when he was translated from the King's Bench, and in 1580 Dyer C.J. admitted that it had been adjudged before himself and his companions that *assumpsit* lay against executors on a simple contract.[9] But later on, at least by the time of Anderson C.J., the Common Pleas had reverted to their original view that such an action could not be allowed, in the absence of special damage or consideration which would bind the executors.[10] The statutory Exchequer Chamber had, therefore, consistently reversed King's Bench judgments against executors.[11] In 1595 Popham C.J. had offered to make an Exchequer Chamber case of the matter " and so try the law "[12]; he probably had in mind an assembly of all the judges, but there is no record of the assembly having taken place. A judgment against executors was still considered reversible in 1601.[13]

Since the creditor could not sue the executors in debt, this question was a very important one, and it occupies many pages in the reports. It may well have been thought that it ought to have been resolved in *Slade's Case*. Indeed, according to Yelverton[14] it was. But the report of the case in the British Museum manuscript Add. 25203, which is in other respects far superior to the printed reports, makes it clear that Popham C.J. expressly left the question open.[15] Obviously, however, the defeat of the Common Pleas' doctrine in *Slade's Case* removed the objections based on the want of any collateral consideration. The maxim *actio personalis moritur cum persona* provided ammunition for some parting shots, and of course Walmsley J.

---

v. *Jackson* (M.1601) B.M. MS.Add. 25203, f. 396; *Wright* v. *Green* (P.1602) Linc. Inn MS.Mayn. 82, f. 36v.

[9] *Anon.* (M.1571) B.M. MS.Add. 25211, f. 10v; *Anon.* (P.1580) B.M. MS.Lansd. 1084, f. 54v. Fitzherbert J. had attacked the King's Bench practice in 1535: T. 27 Hen. 8, 23, *pl.* 21. See also 37 Hen. 8, Bro.Ab. *Action sur le case, pl.* 4.

[10] Gawdy J. referred in 1588 to a recent judgment to this effect: Owen 95. *Cf. Edwards* v. *Burre* (1573) Dal. 104: *sed quaere* whether the reporter's note is contemporaneous. The later view was affirmed in *Anon.* (T.1594) U.L.C. MS.Ii. v. 25, f. 7.

[11] The first reported case is *Griggs* v. *Helhouse* (M.1595), cited Cro.Eliz. 454, Moo. 691; reported (under various titles) in B.M. MS.Lansd. 1084, f. 114, MS.Harl. 1631, f. 144v, U.L.C. MS.Ee. vi. 17, f. 57, Inner Temple MS.Petyt 516/5, f. 26, MS.Barr. 7, f. 6. See also *Stubbings* v. *Rotheram* (M.1595) Cro.Eliz. 454, Moo. 691; *Jordan's Case* (H.1596) Owen 57; *Serle* v. *Rosse* (H.1596) Cro.Eliz. 459; *Mathew's Case* (1595) Moo. 702. All these cases are more fully reported in MSS.

[12] *Payne* v. *Hyde* (M.1596) B.M. MS.Harl. 1697, f. 118, U.L.C. MS.Gg. iii. 25, f. 112, Goulds. 154.

[13] *Perke* v. *Loveden* (H.1601) B.M. MS.Add. 25203, f. 285: " Gawdy *dit a* Fenner, *si nous done judgment pur le plaintiff . . . voet estre reverse en l'eschequer chamber.*"

[14] Yelv. 20.

[15] *Supra*, p. 409.

never changed his mind.[16] But in 1611 the matter was settled with minimal opposition from the Common Pleas.[17] Tanfield C.B. observed, significantly, that " there was no reason that there should be a difference betwixt the Courts; it would be a scandall to the Common law, that they differed in opinion." [18]

What Slade's Case did not decide

The foregoing evidence raises suspicions that many of the principles of law which have traditionally been ascribed to the decision in *Slade's Case* cannot properly be so ascribed. First, we must lay aside Coke's "resolutions," in so far as they appear from their relationship with independent manuscript reports to be the heads of his own argument. In so doing, we must beware of assuming that any resolutions were ever handed down from an assembly of *all* the judges. Then we find that the problem of general declarations, a problem which Professor Lücke considers to have been central to *Slade's Case,* was not even discussed, and does not seem to have been resolved until 1608.[19] Neither was there any discussion of the vexed question whether the *indebitatus assumpsit* declaration, setting out a subsequent promise, was not bad on the face of it, because the performance of an existing duty is no consideration.[20] Since this kind of declaration was to become common form in the seventeenth-century " common counts," the solution of this outstanding difficulty needs to be accounted for. Some explanation is still required for the failure of the *Slade's Case* type of declaration to survive, and for its replacement with a form which, to say the least, was of doubtful legal validity.[21] Another very familiar story tells how *Slade's Case* directly enabled actions of *assumpsit* to be brought to enforce quasi-contractual obligations, by the expedient of implying a subsequent promise to pay

---

[16] See *Kercher's Case* (1611) Godb. 176. He may have absented himself from the discussion in *Pinchon's Case*; his name is not included in Coke's list of the judges present.

[17] *Meane* v. *Peacher* (P.1611) Ro.Ab. i. 14; *Pinchon's Case* (M.1611) 9 Rep. 86; *Kercher's Case,* last note. There was little debate in *Pinchon's Case,* but Coke " *voet les students pur observer que ceo est adjudge per touts les justices et barons de touts les courts* ": Linc. Inn MS.Mayn. 62, f. 148. One is tempted to add " (by way of contrast to *Slade's Case*)."

[18] *Kercher's Case* (1611) Godb. 176.

[19] *Supra,* p. 410, note 7. By this time Coke had become Chief Justice of the Common Pleas.

[20] Some books treat this problem as having been solved in *Slade's Case*: e.g. Chitty on Contracts (23rd ed., 1968), s. 115, note 51, s. 117; Anson's *Law of Contract* (23rd ed., 1969), p. 89.

[21] The difficulty was aired in *Hodge* v. *Vavisour* (M.1612) 3 Bulst. 222, 1 Rolle Rep. 413, and the common form of count was approved. But Rolle was dissatisfied with the decision, since there was no consideration for the new promise. The problem was still worrying the House of Lords in 1922: *Spencer* v. *Hemmerde* [1922] 2 A.C. 507, at p. 524, *per* Lord Sumner.

what was due.[22] Some such connection may have been in the minds of the judges responsible for the innovation, but this is far from clear.[23] It *is* clear, however, that nothing could be further from the principle in *Slade's Case*. The notion that an executory contract, in the old technical sense, imported an *assumpsit* in itself, does not lead logically to the implication of fictional subsequent promises in cases where there is no contract at all.[24]

It is debatable whether the decision even settled the controversy between the courts over the replacement of debt by *assumpsit*. That something happened to silence the Common Pleas is clear, but surely it was not Coke's strained ingenuity. Can it really be that " all but a few sentimental antiquarians turned from [debt] with joy to a new action wherein trial by jury flourished " ?[25] The abandonment of wager of law only exacerbated the problems which led to the Statute of Frauds and Perjuries in 1677. Was it really a victory for " more modern, more rational, more pragmatic principles " over " fifteenth-century legal positivism " ?[26] Reason and pragmatism were hardly on Coke's side. The most we can imagine is that the Common Pleas judges reluctantly gave way in order to end the " scandal " of uncertainty. Maybe they admitted that on the pleadings alone, with their allegations of deceit and special loss, they had been hard pressed to find good reasons for reversing King's Bench judgments.[27] Intact though their own reasoning remained, there was no satisfactory way of imposing it on unwilling King's Bench judges, even with the aid of a court of error. The special verdict in *Slade's Case*, ironically, concentrated attention on a side issue and thereby failed to precipitate an authoritative solution of the central question. Suppose the Exeter jury had found a different verdict: that there was a contract, and a promise, but no deceit or damage other than the outstanding debt. Coke would not so easily have wriggled out of that. The result might have been quite different. On the " imported " *assumpsit* issue, however, Bacon was almost bound to lose.

Our difficulties are deepened by the fact that, in the absence of an Exchequer Chamber decision, the profession in 1602 probably had

---

[22] T. E. Street, *Foundations of Legal Liability* (1906), Vol. 3, p. 187; Holdsworth, *op. cit.*, Vol. 3, pp. 446–447; Plucknett, *op. cit.*, p. 648; J. F. Wilson, *Principles of the Law of Contract* (1957), pp. 8–9; S. J. Stoljar, *Law of Quasi-Contract* (1964), pp. 10–11; R. Goff and G. Jones, *Law of Restitution* (1966), pp. 6–8; Anson's *Law of Contract* (23rd ed., 1969), pp. 616, 621. *Cf.* R. M. Jackson, *The History of Quasi-Contract in English Law* (1936), pp. 39 *et seq.*

[23] See *City of London* v. *Goree* (1676) 3 Keb. 677; *Howard* v. *Wood* (1679) 1 Freem. 473, at p. 479, *per* Pemberton J.; *Shuttleworth* v. *Garrett* (1689) Comb. 151, *per* Holt C.J. The references to *Slade's Case* are obscure.

[24] *Accord.* Fifoot, *op. cit.*, pp. 361–362; W. J. V. Windeyer, *Lectures on Legal History* (2nd ed., 1949), p. 121.

[25] H. G. Hanbury, *English Courts of Law* (1944), p. 93.

[26] Lücke, *op. cit.*, 82 L.Q.R. at pp. 94–95.

[27] *Cf.* Simpson, *op. cit.*, 74 L.Q.R. at p. 389.

no clear idea of the outcome of the debate. Since the principal arguments on both sides had been addressed to the wider issues, no doubt those were the issues which contemporaries expected *Slade's Case* to solve. The publication of Coke's version in 1604 must have given many lawyers their only knowledge of the long-awaited "resolutions"; for Popham's announcement did nothing to further jurisprudence. Misled by the published reports, by the corrupting influence of hearsay, and by the unchecked association of similar ideas, seventeenth-century lawyers cannot be blamed if they read into the "decision" many things which were not there. If that be true, the development of the law of contract—and quasi-contract—in the seventeenth century stemmed not from any solemn, considered, declaration of legal principle in *Slade's Case*, but from the doctrinal confusion caused by the failure of the judges to reach a reasoned settlement. In that confusion the old debate was forgotten; only an isolated purist would try to resume it.[28]

Conclusion

Perhaps the effect of this "new light" on *Slade's Case* has been merely to throw into deeper contrast the shadows which surround it. Some day the chance discovery of a dormant text may lighten that darkness and dispel all the mystery. But it could be that the shadows are an important part of the picture, and that they worry us only because we have tried to make the past tidier than it was, tried to be wiser than the generation we have sought to understand. If that seems an unsatisfactory ending, at least it is hoped that Coke's report of the case will no longer be accepted at face value; and that in due course someone will have the patience to resurrect the legal history of the sixteenth and seventeenth centuries from the dusty manuscripts in which for the present so much of it lies in sleep.

NOTE

For still more new light, and a possible solution to the "mystery", see now D. Ibbetson, "Sixteenth Century Contract Law: *Slade's Case* in perspective" (1984) 4 *Oxford Journal of Legal Studies* 295-317.

---

[28] *Edgecomb* v. *Dee* (1670) Vaugh. 89, at p. 101; *Anon*. (1673) 1 Mod. 163, *per* Vaughan C.J. He said *Slade's Case* was an "illegal resolution . . . grounded upon reasons not fit for a declamation, much less for a decision of law." Lord Mansfield appears to criticise the decision, in *Moses* v. *Macferlan* (1760) 5 Burr. 1005, at p. 1008.

IV

THE TUDOR LEGAL TRANSFORMATION

22

THE DARK AGE OF
ENGLISH LEGAL HISTORY, 1500-1700

IF anniversaries are anything to go by, 1972 is an appropriate year in which to hold this conference of legal historians. On 20 November we remember the accession to the Throne, seven hundred years ago, of our "English Justinian"—perhaps we should say our Welsh Justinian—whose legislative achievements are central to the historical study of English law. Three centuries later, in 1572, an equally important era commenced with the admission to the Inner Temple of Edward Coke and the call to the Bar of his future rival Thomas Egerton. Another journey of three centuries transports us to 1872 and the appearance at the head of the Moral Sciences Tripos list at Cambridge of a name too well-known to us to need mention; he was about to follow Coke's path to the Inns of Court, later to return to Cambridge and lay the foundations of our science.

These three anniversaries, besides reminding us of three particularly memorable men, suggest also a few thoughts about the study of legal history. Few would contend that English legal history should follow the Roman example by ending with its Justinian, and yet it is not a grave distortion to assert that much of what happened after his death, or at least after the death of his son Edward II, has been seriously neglected by historians of the law. One reason may be that we are still, in some ways, too near the Tudors and Stuarts to appreciate fully their distance. We use, almost without question, the anachronistic word "medieval" as denoting pre-Renaissance times; when, from the modern point of view, the Renaissance period has a much better claim to be regarded as a middle age.

We are told that the Renaissance gave man an awareness of his past, and if ever the history of English legal history comes to be written the story will begin in the first Elizabethan age—the age of William Lambard, John Dodderidge, Francis Tate and Roger Owen.[1] But those first legal antiquaries were preoccupied with dark and distant problems about the origins of the common law and its Englishness: problems which they had even less hope of solving than we have. Coke's devotion to things medieval, far from being crabbed pedantry, reflected this Renaissance spirit of enquiry. But he would have had difficulty in understanding why we have come together for this conference; his beloved "antiquities"[2] were a guide not to the past but to the present. The sense of continuity which they conveyed was of rhetorical and emotional and political, rather than historical, value.

---

[1] See R. J. Shoeck, "The Elizabethan Society of Antiquaries and the Lawyers" (1954) 199 *Notes and Queries* 417.

[2] Co.Litt. 244v. His unpublished notebooks are crammed with historical matter. For Coke's contribution to the "Norman yoke" controversy, see his *Reading on Fines* (1592) and the prefaces to Parts 3, 6, and 8 of the *Reports*.

The position was much the same when Hale wrote his *History of the Common Law*. Hale was doubtless a better historian than Coke, but history for him ended in a remote past. Hale's hero was Edward I. Of the later period he had little or nothing to say by way of history. The changes that had taken place in four centuries were not so much in the law, wrote Hale, as in the conditions of society;[3] and the Year Books and Tudor reports were still sources, not of history, but of living law.

Lawyers have always been bemused by the apparent continuity of their heritage into a way of thinking which inhibits historical understanding. "Pure" historians, on the other hand, have often fled in despair from the mysteries of the law which permeates their history. The first man to overcome both difficulties to the satisfaction of both disciplines remains an inspiration to us all. But Maitland left the impression that he did not care too much for the law of the sixteenth century.[4] Perhaps his youthful distaste for the antique features of the law he had read in chambers made the more recent legal history offensive to his palate: "Who shall interest us in contingent remainders, or the Statute of Uses, while Chinese metaphysics remain unexplored?"[5] Or it may be simply that he was compelled to begin at the beginning, and was not spared to proceed further than he did. He abandoned the idea (which Pollock favoured) of carrying the *History of English Law* beyond 1272, because the source material for the later period was not yet in proper shape. The Year Books, he wrote, needed a complete and tolerable new edition, and the plea rolls were "of so unwieldy a bulk that we can hardly hope that much will ever be known about them".[6] If it was too late for Maitland's contemporaries to be early English,[7] it was yet too early for them to be Perpendicular.

Historians since Maitland have gone far towards explaining the development of Tudor and Stuart legal institutions, but the study of legal thought and jurisprudence during the same period is still in its infancy. Most of our knowledge has been derived from printed sources, many of them miserably unable to bear the responsibility. Holdsworth, who wrote more (quantitatively) than any other writer on the subject, did not fully appreciate the value of manuscripts. He did not use the plea rolls as sources of legal history. Of the unpublished sixteenth-century reports he had little to say, save his comment on a list compiled as long ago as 1834, that "doubtless a systematic search would reveal other manuscripts".[8] He seems to have been unaware of the wealth of new material these manuscripts contained, perhaps thinking that most of the texts were substantially available in print. We should not be too hard on Holdsworth for failing to see what no one

---

[3] Preface to H. Rolle, *Abridgment des Plusieurs Cases* (1668) sig. a2.
[4] Cf. *Letters of F. W. Maitland* (ed. C. H. S. Fifoot, Cambridge, 1965) 1 SSSS no. 233.
[5] CP i.190.
[6] PM Introduction and ii.673.
[7] *Township and Borough* (Cambridge, 1898) 21, alluding to *Patience* by W. S. Gilbert.
[8] HEL v.369.

The Dark Age of English Legal History, 1500-1700   437

of his generation could see; there was more than enough material in print for a pioneer to work on. But so long as the sources were ignored it was inevitable that legends and misinterpretations should flourish.

The sixteenth century is surely one of the most interesting and vital periods in the history of the common law. If the twelfth and thirteenth centuries saw the birth of the common law, the sixteenth century witnessed its renaissance—or at least its reformation. To what extent the common law was influenced by *the* Renaissance is a question which, for the moment, must be laid aside.[9]

But that there were great changes is manifest.[10] The land law was changed almost beyond recognition by the resuscitation for fiscal purposes of the defunct feudal system, the perfection of the common recovery and the consequent challenge to conveyancers, the effects of the agrarian revolution, and the transformation of the use. Mercantile law assumed a new importance in an expanding world. The criminal law became more efficient with the abolition of abjuration, the severe restriction of sanctuary, the harnessing of benefit of clergy to secular policy, and the improvement of pre-trial procedure. The forms of action were virtually replaced by formless actions on the case, which would later divide into a new scheme of forms of action. Old courts acquired new functions and more business. New courts rose up, and a new profession. We cannot fully understand the later common law unless we first understand this Tudor legal revolution, but we still know little about its underlying causes. The deceptive proximity of the sixteenth century (compared with the so-called middle ages), and the professional tendency to confuse law and history, easily generated assumptions that what became law must have been "right": that it was the inevitable consequence of the relentless march of progress. It is always difficult to resist the temptation merely to set out how the story unfolded itself, as if it were all preordained. The losing arguments are soon forgotten, because in law they have been shown to be false. But the rightness of a legal argument is a matter of law, not of fact; and, although the law may have been settled for four centuries, the questions of historical fact remain open. In answering these questions, we find the legal sources more rather than less helpful. In an age less tied up in precedent, Tudor lawyers (like their predecessors) were as anxious to know how a case had been presented, and why it had proceeded in a particular way, as they were to know the outcome of the argument.

[9] Meanwhile, see F. W. Maitland, *English Law and the Renaissance* (Cambridge, 1901; reprinted in AALH i.168–203 and, with few of the many notes, in *Selected Historical Essays* (ed. Helen M. Cam, Cambridge, 1958) 135–51); Holdsworth, HEL iv.252–93; H. D. Hazeltine "The Renaissance and the Laws of Europe" in *Cambridge Legal Essays* (ed. P. H. Winfield and A. D. McNair, Cambridge, 1926) 165–9; T. F. T. Plucknett, "The Legal Profession in the History of English Law" (1932) 48 LQR 328; H. E. Bell, *Maitland* (London, 1965) 130–37; S. E. Thorne, "English Law and the Renaissance" in *La Storia del Diritto nel quadro delle scienze storiche* (Florence, 1966) 437–45; E. W. Ives, "The Common Lawyers in pre-Reformation England" (1968) 18 TRHS/V 145; G. R. Elton, "Reform by Statute: Thomas Starkey's *Dialogue* and Thomas Cromwell's Policy" (1968) 54 PBA 165, esp. at 176–80 (reprint, *Studies in Tudor and Stuart Politics and Government* (Cambridge, 1974) ii.236, 246–50).

[10] See S. E. Thorne, "Tudor Social Transformation and Legal Change" (1951) 26 *New York University Law Review* 10.

Two instances involving Coke may serve to illustrate the dangers of orthodoxy. It has generally been assumed that Coke was "wrong" in his quarrel with Ellesmere's Chancery, because Ellesmere and equity were held to prevail. The victory of the Chancery was necessary, wrote Maitland, if we were to have a Court of Equity at all.[11] But in fact the dispute did not turn on the relationship between law and equity in the abstract. It concerned the finality of a judgment at law where the unsuccessful party failed to seek equitable relief before judgment was given against him. On this narrower question, all the law and much of the equity were on Coke's side. He lost for political and personal reasons.[12] It may be questioned whether his defeat was constitutional, and whether (even in the seventeenth century) the King, acting on the advice of his counsel (not of his judges), could override a decision of the Exchequer Chamber. The matter was fully re-argued in 1670 in *R. v. Standish*. On this occasion, Twisden J. explained:

> Ellesmere had great power, and did much prevail in his time. And the reference in 14 Jac. was made to such persons as he that desired it would have, and they were all great practisers in the Chancery (at least except Sir John Walter [who] had not the spirit of infallibility). Beside, those persons were no court. The reason Ellesmere gave, that they would not undo the judgment but only examine the corrupt conscience of the party, is an eluding of the statute.

Kelyng C. J. took the same view, but hoped they could avoid the "stirr and heat there was in Lord Coke's time". In the event Hale C. J. persuaded his brethren that the statute of praemunire was intended to restrain ecclesiastical appeals only. Hale was, of course, correct in his interpretation of fourteenth-century history and of law. But Twisden's factual explanation of the events of 1616 is very persuasive, and is far easier to reconcile to the evidence than the Bacon-Ellesmere versions of the story.[13]

The other example is provided by *Slade's Case*, in which Coke's argument prevailed and was therefore treated by later lawyers as if it had been unanswerable. *Slade's Case* became, in the textbooks of law and history, the ultimate source of numerous principles of contract and quasi-contract. The professional tradition derived almost entirely from Coke's own report of the case, which, despite its brusque treatment of Bacon's arguments on the losing side, was the only full report to be printed. But in this case the law was against Coke; and justice was probably against him also, in that wager of law occasioned less perjury than jury trials in which the parties were not competent witnesses.[14] The "victory" in this case may simply have been the result of Morley's disinclination to bring error and so give the Common Pleas judges a stronger voice. The foremost judicial opponent of

---

[11] *Constitutional History of England* (Cambridge, 1908) 270.
[12] See "The Common Lawyers and the Chancery: 1616", above, p. 205.
[13] The best report (the source of the quotations above) is in Treby's MS. Reports, Middle Temple Library, 458–61, 602–3. See also 1 Mod. 59, 94; 2 Keb. 661, 787; 1 Lev. 241; 1 Sid. 463.
[14] See "New Light on Slade's Case" [1971] CLJ 213.

the new approach, Walmsley J., complained afterwards that

> Slade and Morlye was not resolved upon argument or reasons delivered [i.e. by the judges] but, the justices being assembled, it was asked of each of what opinion he was, and thus it was ruled by the majority opinion.[15]

This was an irregular way of proceeding, a manoeuvre by Popham C. J. which his successors were to rue. Vaughan C. J. attacked the "decision" as "an illegal resolution . . . grounded upon reasons not fit for a declamation, much less for a decision of law."[16] And Hale C. J. thought it was "hardly brought in (for it was by a capitulation and agreement among the judges)," and that it had "done more hurt than ever it did or will do good."[17] In 1671 he proclaimed actions on the case to be "one of the great grievances of the nation: for, two men cannot talk together but one fellow or other, who stands in a corner, swears a promise. . . ."[18] "It were well," he concluded, "if a law were made that no promise should bind, unless there were some signal ceremony, or that wager of law did ly upon a promise. For, the common law was a wise law, that men should wage their law in debt on a contract."[19] These observations escaped the press, but they were almost certainly among the principal motive forces behind the Statute of Frauds and Perjuries 1677, which for certain classes of debt required written evidence.

In both these instances the conventional view became unacceptable after a little delving into unfamiliar, unpublished legal sources. One cannot work for long on these sources without being almost helplessly conscious of the vast store of unworked material which has survived. It is impossible to spend an afternoon with a pile of manuscript law reports without finding something new, some detail perhaps which will not fit into the textbook stories, or which suggests a new and unforeseen story of its own. Before saying any more about this material, a little space may be devoted to the difficulties of research even in the printed books of the period.

THE PRINTED LAW BOOKS

THE first defect in our knowledge of the printed law books—and it is hardly a trifling defect—is that we know very little about the law printers and their work. The monopoly of printing common law books, first granted to Richard Tottell in 1556,[20] was the subject of almost continuous Chancery litigation with the London stationers for well over a century. The public records contain, in consequence, several bundles of papers from which the business practices of these printers may in part be reconstructed and

---
[15] BM Hargrave MS. 29, f.94.
[16] Vaughan 89, 101; cf. 1 Mod. 163 (1673).
[17] *Anon.* (1672) Treby's MS. Reports 747.
[18] *Buckridge* v. *Shirley, ibid.* 651.
[19] *Anon.* (1672) *ibid.* 747; cf. *Anon.* (1672) *ibid.* 775.
[20] Pat. 2 & 3 Ph. & Mar., pt 1, m.28, renewed in 1559 for life. The earlier patent of 1553 (Pat. 7 Ed. 6, pt 3, m.29) conferred copyright privileges but not a monopoly.

valuable information unearthed concerning the mechanics of law publishing and the solus agreements by which the printers were financed after 1669.[21] Of the craftsmanship of these men we know far less than advances in bibliographical and typographical science have qualified us to discover, though Mr Howard J. Graham has made a useful start on the work of the earlier law printers. *Beale* has been a most useful work of reference, but it contains numerous errors and quite a few omissions, and the way is wide open for a new edition by professional bibliographers. For the period after 1600 we do not even have a *Beale*.

The second defect is that little work has been done to discover the extent and manner of the use of printed law books before, say, 1700. If, as will be suggested later, many printed law books are of slight value as evidence of the facts recorded in them, their principal value to the legal historian is that they show what lawyers read and may therefore reveal the source of certain ideas. But this kind of information is not fully within reach until research tells us about lawyers' libraries, their contents, and the use made of them. Very few lawyers' libraries of early date have been reconstructed, and some of those which have are exceptional in size or character.[22] After 1680 there are numerous printed catalogues of law libraries, drawn up by auctioneers;[23] before that date search must be made in wills and inventories and manuscript catalogues. The labour would probably be worth while. The sale catalogues are often marked with prices, and the fluctuation in price tells a great deal about the use made of law books. (Thus, the sale in 1797 of a *Statham* for four shillings and a set of *Term Reports* for seven guineas, in the same sale,[24] tells its own story about the decline in the study of Year Books and old abridgments.) Then there is the evidence of the books themselves, which contain much real evidence about their owners. Dr Knafla has pioneered the study of manuscript marginalia in printed law books in an examination of some of Egerton's books preserved in the Henry E. Huntington Library;[25] his results suggest there may be more to be learned from similar studies.

Textual Problems

(i) *Works prepared for the press by their authors*

It might be thought that works edited by their authors would present few, if any, textual difficulties, since what we read is presumably what the

---

[21] I hope to publish a summary of this story in the near future, in an account of the printing of the Year Books.

[22] E.g. the immense library at Holkham: W. O. Hassall (ed.), *A Catalogue of the Library of Sir Edward Coke* (New Haven, 1950). See also E. W. Ives "A Lawyer's Library in 1500" (1969) 85 LQR 104 (Serjeant Keble, 1500). For an inventory of William Rastell's library, seized in 1562, see (1844) 31 *Law Magazine* 57–8 (24 law books and 17 others). There is an inventory of 1572 (William Dalison, jun.) in Kent Archives Office MS. U.552.E.1/2, mm.8–9. See further R. J. Shoeck, "The Libraries of Common Lawyers in Renaissance England" (1962) 6 *Manuscripta* 155.

[23] The best collection is in the British Museum.

[24] Sir Henry Gould sale, lots 917, 1152.

[25] L. A. Knafla, "The Law Studies of an Elizabethan Student" (1969) 32 *Huntington Library Quarterly* 221. Other collections which merit study are those of Sir Edward Coke (deposited by the Earl of Leicester in the Inner Temple) and Sir John Popham (at Littlecote House).

The Dark Age of English Legal History, 1500-1700

author wished us to read. But, while the text may be taken as a faithful representation of the author's personal opinions, and whether or not it was later accepted as an authoritative source of *law*, it is not necessarily to be relied on for any statements of *fact* it contains. The evidence may be hearsay. At least an effort should be made to ascertain the date, purpose, and method of composition, the sources drawn upon by the author, and the extent to which he was in a position to know the truth. It may be possible to find answers to such questions if the author left his notes or his manuscript sources behind. Coke's notebooks, for instance, enable some conclusions to be drawn concerning the sources of his *Reports* and the way in which they were compiled.[26] The solution is more difficult where the author did not leave such obvious clues, but hidden clues are often waiting to be uncovered. Thus, Mr Graham has shown how important facts relating to the composition of Fitzherbert's *Graunde Abridgement* could be deduced from a study of the almost contemporary *Tabula* and the *Liber Assisarum*.[27] Even if one accepts statements about authorship on trust from title-pages, the number of major law books prepared for the press by their authors before 1700 is small. We must exclude *Littleton's Tenures, Brooke's Abridgement*, and Coke's last three *Institutes*; all except possibly one Year Book;[28] and most of the later reports. Plowden's *Commentaries* are the only reports known to have been published in print by their author in the sixteenth century. And, apart from Coke, only three other reporters seem to have edited their own reports for publication before 1660: John Clayton, author of the almost forgotten small volume of cases decided at York (1651), Edward Bulstrode (1657-9), and William Style (1658).

(ii) *Works published posthumously*

When examining a work printed after its author's death there is obviously a need for more care in establishing the correctness of the text. In many cases the exemplar used will have been one which the author would not have wished to be published, and the printer will not normally have improved it. It will be remembered that the appearance in print (in 1585) of Dyer's notes, in their imperfect state, was an event which so alarmed Coke that it persuaded him to prepare his own reports for the press while he was alive.[29] Moreover, many of the collections ascribed to eminent men were either not their work at all or were crude notes collected in their youth or for transient purposes, and found among their papers after their death. *Rolle's Abridgment* was castigated by contemporaries as "nothing but a collection of year-books and little things noted when he made his common

---

[26] See "Coke's Notebooks and the Sources of his Reports", above, p. 177.
[27] "The Book that 'made' the Common Law: the first Printing of Fitzherbert's *La Graunde Abridgement*, 1514–1516" (1958) 51 *Law Library Journal* 100.
[28] Pynson's undated edition of 14 H.8 (STC 9945, Beale R.418) is the only nearly contemporary printed Year Book. Pynson died in 1530, and Pollard and Redgrave assign a date as early as c. 1525, a mere three years after the reports were taken. The only copy known is Rastell's, in Lincoln's Inn.
[29] This is the inference to be drawn from 8 Rep. preface xxxii–xxxiii, 10 Rep. preface xxxiv.

place book".[30] Vaughan C. J. said

> he wished it had never bin printed, for there are so many contradicting judgments in it that it makes the law ridiculous, and 'twas pitty there was not more paines taken with it before it was printed, to expung[e] those judgments which were not law, or to reconcile 'em to such as were law.[31]

Similar criticisms were made of many of the volumes of reports which appeared during the printing rush of the Interregnum, when the law printers' monopoly was in de facto abeyance. As early as 1653, in the preface to *Gouldsborough's Reports,* W. S[tyle?] alluded to the "trick, played by the subtle Gamesters of this serpentine age" of fathering spurious offspring upon dead men, and assured the reader that the present reports were under the author's hand and were such as "were he living he would not blush to own". Bulstrode and Grimstone spared no words in castigating the "flying reports" which had "surreptitiously crept forth",[32] and Style said the press had brought forth many births, but there was not a father alive to own many of them.[33] Francis North, later Chief Justice of the Common Pleas, said of this period:

> there was no copy so absurd but somebody would print it. Imperfect transcripts came out under great names that were a reproach to them; and some were so unskilfully printed that they could hardly be made use of.[34]

Some of these volumes were merely collections from other sources, or common-place books. Thus, *Noy's Reports* were identified by Twisden J. as a copy of an abridgment of the original reports of Noy made by Serjeant Evan Size (or Seys) when he was a student.[35] The practice of collecting cases explains why some cases verbally identical will be found in two or even three different books. One case, for example, appears three times in exactly the same words in Leonard's collections alone.[36] Typically the reports are greatly abridged, or are mere notes and scraps, and represent the lowest standard of this kind of material.

Rarely do we have the author's autograph copy for comparison. Dyer's own manuscript is said to have belonged to Coke,[37] but it is now lost. Croke's autograph notebooks of reports have survived in the Earl of Verulam's library, formerly at Gorhambury.[38] The judge's "small and close" hand justified their description by his son-in-law and editor Sir

---

[30] Treby's MS. Reports 514, per Twisden J. (1670).
[31] *Anon.* (1673) Roger North's MS. Reports, BM Add. MS. 32527, f.29.
[32] E. Bulstrode, *Reports* (1657), epistle dedicatory to Part I; H. Grimstone, Part I of *Croke's Reports* (1657), preface.
[33] *Narrationes Modernae or Modern Reports* (1658), epistle dedicatory.
[34] Speech in the case concerning the privilege of the law printers (1669): BM Add. MS. 32519, f.211v.
[35] Treby's MS. Reports 433; same point, 2 Keb. 652, 1 Vent. 81.
[36] *Anon.* (1566) 3 Leo. 13, 4 Leo. 167, 224. It should be observed that even the publisher did not pretend that any of these reports were *by* Leonard.
[37] See above, p. 187 n.57.
[38] Hertfordshire Record Office, Verulam MSS. XXII.A.6, C–E, and XII.A.14.

Harbottle Grimstone as *"folia sybillina,* as difficult as excellent."[39] There are other manuscripts which are said to collate exactly with parts of Croke, which invites the question whether Croke or his representatives lent out the notebooks to be copied, or whether Croke's collection is itself second-hand.

Since the printers often worked from inferior copies it is often possible to construct a better text from manuscripts. In the case of the more dubious texts, it is common to find different parts in different collections and apparently by different hands, thereby raising textual problems of frightening complexity. It seems to have been rare for the law printers of later times to engage professional help in editing the manuscripts, although during the Interregnum the necessity of having texts translated from law French into English at least compelled someone familiar with the law to consider what, if anything, the text meant. Perhaps we should be grateful that the texts were not corrupted still further by editors. But there were exceptions which warn us to be on our guard. A striking early example is afforded by Redman's masterpiece, his edition of the *Quadragesimus* or Year Book of 40 Edward III. This not only shows signs of textual comparison, but contains numerous and sometimes copious comments on the cases, in addition to mere cross-references.[40] That these interpolations belong to the sixteenth rather than the fourteenth century was overlooked even by Coke, who quoted one of them as an example of the mode of citing cases in the time of Edward III.[41] Redman's enterprising experiment is unique among the Year Books; perhaps it failed because readers preferred to make their own comments. Nevertheless, it shows how the printed word may deceive.

MANUSCRIPT SOURCES

SAVE for a few works of outstanding merit and timeless fame, the only claim which the printed law books can make to our particular attention arises from the incidental distinction of their having been printed. Publication obviously increased their importance as sources of law in later ages. But it is not a very relevant factor in assessing their evidential value, and might be held against the bulk of them, were we to heed the unanimous opinion of those seventeenth-century lawyers who knew good from bad. The printed books cannot, in any case, lay claim to our exclusive attention. Compared with the mass of unpublished material which has been preserved

---

[39] Part I of *Croke's Reports* (1657), preface sig. a3.
[40] See the *Telos* in Redman's edition, STC 9587. Bolland noticed this, but thought only references had been added: *Manual of Year Book Studies* (Cambridge, 1925) 69. Turner wrongly attributed the additions to Tottell: *Year Book 4 Edward II* (1911/1914) 26 SS xvi. See also T. Ellis Lewis, 46 LQR 343–4, who was misled by the 1679 edition.
[41] 10 Rep. preface xxi, referring to STC 9587, f.[xvi], misprinted as "xiii". Holdsworth attached some weight to the passage: HEL v.373.

in our older libraries, or sold to our wealthier neighbours, the printed matter is but a meagre and not very representative selection from the treasures which remain. These treasures cannot, like Tutankhamen's tomb, be laid open in a momentary flash of discovery; but, with so many of the doors still sealed, one can soon experience some of the excitement of the explorer at the prospect of what may be found in an unopened book. And, as Maitland said of the public records, the territory to be explored is "free to all, like the air and the sunlight".[42]

There are many more possibilities than it is feasible to indicate in a short space; only the three major classes of manuscript will therefore be discussed.

1. *Plea rolls*

We know something of the importance of the later common law records through the labours of Professors Kiralfy and Milsom.[43] They are the key to the development of the forms of action and to their replacement by the infinitely variable actions on the case, and to the forms of pleading. But our whetted appetite soon becomes nagging starvation when we contemplate the million or so membranes occupied by the records of the two principal common law courts between 1500 and 1650. How can anyone enter the Public Record Office with hope in his heart when to search the rolls of the Common Law courts for one year involves scanning up to 10,000 long skins of parchment, closely written on both sides? It would be profitable to know how Coke acquired his mastery of the forbidding rolls of Elizabeth and 1–14 James I, in spite of his admission that the judicial records (unlike the reports) were *thesauri absconditi*.[44] The one man who might have helped us, as he probably helped Coke, has long since passed away and taken his secrets with him. Richard Brownlow (d. 1638), prothonotary of the Common Pleas for forty-six years, knew more about these records than perhaps anyone ever will again; but the wise old man who looks down on us from his memorial in Belton Church is as silent as the Sphinx.

The collections of entries made by the prothonotaries and others provide some short-cuts, but they were not written for the ease of historians and they pose more questions than they resolve. A new collection, based on an original study of the plea rolls with the problems of legal history in mind, is an indispensable preliminary to a complete history of sixteenth-century law. It would demand the greater part of a man's academic career, assuming that is is within one man's competence at all. The earlier King's Bench rolls might be the easiest to start with, perhaps those of Henry VII and

---

[42] CP i.496.
[43] E.g. A. K. R. Kiralfy, *The Action on the Case* (London, 1951); Milsom, *Foundations* 271–352.
[44] 10 Rep. 75. See also *Reports of Judgments delivered by Sir Orlando Bridgman* (ed. S. Bannister, London, 1823) 349: "In the time of Sir Edward Coke, and before him, there was not the freedom of access to records which there has been since." The judges probably had access to the records without fee.

The Dark Age of English Legal History, 1500-1700

Henry VIII.[45] Until the latter part of Henry VIII's reign the bundles of rolls rarely contain more than a hundred membranes and so they are relatively simple to peruse. This was the period of greatest innovation, and the King's Bench is thought to have led the way. The results of such a study, however, would be inconclusive until they could be compared with the results of a parallel review of the cumbersome *De Banco* rolls.[46]

2. Readings and Moots

Professor Thorne's study of the fifteenth-century readings[47] has taught us all what valuable sources of information they are. There is reason to think that the later readings are no less valuable, although they have been almost totally overlooked by modern scholars.[48] Coke, it is true, decried the later readings as "liker rather to riddles than lectures, which when they are opened they vanish away like smoake".[49] No doubt his strictures are applicable to some of the weaker perfomances, but they could not fairly be used to describe his own readings, or those of comparable merit. Of the thousand or more readings given between 1500 and 1700,[50] if only one quarter merited our notice there would be enough material for countless books and theses. Of course, not all have survived, and we may be fortunate if we can salvage more than one-fifth of the total. Yet, in the nature of things, many of those which have survived are those which someone thought to be worth preserving.

The readings of Henry VII's and Henry VIII's time provide us, *inter alia*, with vital information relating to the history of criminal law and procedure; they desperately need publication. The later readings were normally delivered on the "modern" statutes: that is, the statutes passed after the time of Edward I. Many were given on the legislation of Henry VIII. The most obviously interesting are the lectures on uses, among which may be noticed those of Edmund Knightley (1523) and Thomas Audley (1526) on the statute of Henry VII, and of John Brograve (1576), Richard Shuttleworth (1583), Francis Bacon (1588), Edward Coke (1592), Thomas Richardson (1613), Edward Estcourt (1618), Robert Tanfield (1623), and Arthur Tourneur (1633). Of similar interest are the lectures on wills, which include those of James Dyer (1552), Ambrose Gilbert (1556), Robert Nowell (1561), John Popham (1568), Robert Gardiner (1575), Henry Blanchard (1581), John Shurley (1588), Hugh Hare (1591), Augustine Nicholls (1602),

---

[45] Since the delivery of the lecture, the writer has been through the King's Bench rolls KB 27/980 to 1120 (1506–41). The results of this investigation will appear in the introduction to *The Reports of Sir John Spelman*. [Printed in 94 SS, in 1978.]

[46] Dr Sue S. Walker's valuable *Checklist of Research in British Legal Manuscripts* (1974), the outcome of a conference on plea roll studies in Chicago on 13–14 April 1973, does not reveal much interest in the legal content of the later common-law plea rolls.

[47] *Readings and Moots at the Inns of Court* i (1952/1954) 71 SS. See also his edition of Robert Constable's reading on *Prerogativa Regis* (New Haven and London, 1949) with notes from other readings.

[48] Cf. W. R. Prest, *The Inns of Court under Elizabeth I and the earlier Stuarts* (London, 1972) 119–30.

[49] Co. Litt. 280. Thorne, *Readings*, 71 SS xvii, seems to accept Coke's criticism.

[50] Two were delivered each year in four inns. (This excludes readings in Chancery, fewer of which were reported.) Towards 1700 many readers defaulted.

and Henry Sherfield (1623). Another popular statute was the 32 Hen.VIII, c.28, of leases, which was chosen by William Symmonds (1549), John Kitchin (1562), Edward Fenner (1576), Thomas Egerton (1582), Thomas Wentworth (1611), Richard Reynell (1614), John Hutchins (1634), and William le Hunt (1667). That is a very random selection of lectures on but three statutes; but it indicates the wealth of almost unknown[51] legal literature which awaits investigation.

The reports of moots are valuable not as legal decisions but as an indication of the educational background of a Tudor lawyer. Many of the points argued are not to be found answered in Littleton or the Year Books, because the academic coverage was necessarily more comprehensive than that provided by the accidents of litigation and more modern than that provided by the old books. Yet all this learning, some of which may have been almost axiomatic to anyone who had been through the course, is hidden away in unpublished (and virtually unread) notebooks. None of these moots have been printed since 1602.[52] The material is less plentiful than the readings, and it dies out rather earlier. Most of the material for Henry VIII's reign is of Gray's Inn provenance.[53]

3. Reports of cases

More important even than the two preceding classes of manuscript are the unprinted reports. Much of their importance is simply a matter of quantity. For every printed volume of cases there are perhaps half a dozen or a dozen unpublished volumes which provide reports of cases—sometimes of whole terms—not in print, and of otherwise unknown speeches and observations in cases which were printed from inferior texts.

(i) *1500–1590*

The greater part of the sixteenth century is poorly served by printed reports. Only seven years of Henry VIII were printed as "Year Books", to which "Keilwey" added another ten; without counting missing terms in these seventeen years, this leaves more than half the years of Henry VIII's reign without reports in Year Book form. A few more cases are to be found in Dyer, which begins in earnest in 28 Hen.VIII. To these must be added a group of about fifty notes in abridged form which are usually associated with the name of Serjeant Bendlowes, a few of which have also strayed into *Anderson* and *Moore*.

There is, strangely enough, only one known manuscript corresponding

---

[51] For a modern study of a later reading see Gareth H. Jones, *History of the Law of Charity 1532–1827* (Cambridge, 1969) 22–101, 229–50 (Francis Moore on charitable uses).

[52] Professor Thorne is said to be editing a volume of moots for the Selden Society. The 1602 collection is Keil. 102v–137, which was probably printed unwittingly because Serjeant Croke did not appreciate its nature.

[53] See Bodl. Lib. Rawl. MS. C.705; BM Add. MS. 35939; Harvard Law School MS. 125(1); BM Harl. MS. 5103 (by William Coke), Harg. MS. 253 (perhaps by William Yelverton). For Middle Temple moots in this reign see Bodl. Lib. Rawl. MS. C.707; Harvard Law School MS. 125(2). For the Inner Temple: BM Harl. MS. 1691. Nothing is known to survive from Lincoln's Inn.

The Dark Age of English Legal History, 1500-1700   447

to any of the printed Year Books of Henry VIII, and it is probably misleading to apply the term "Year Books" to any of the other sixteenth-century manuscripts.[54] Neither is there any trace of the original Keilwey manuscript from which John Croke published the reports of 1-3, 5-10, 21 Henry VIII in 1602.[55] Mr Simpson has identified the collection from which these reports were taken as that known in the sixteenth century as "Carrell's Reports".[56] Carrell's collection certainly contained much that is not in the 1602 volume;[57] and it continued until at least 27 Hen.VIII,[58] by which time Serjeant Carrell was dead. Some of the later reports seem to be by the serjeant's son, John Carrell, Attorney of the Duchy of Lancaster;[59] but it is possible that the serjeant wrote the earlier part.[60] Fortunately there are some surviving copies of extracts from Carrell's collection;[61] these ought to be published without delay to supplement the printed reports. A few of the Henry VII cases were printed in the Year Books of that reign.

These reports are, however, by no means the only reports of Henry VIII's reign. At least four other series were used in compiling a volume which formerly belonged to Sir Christopher Yelverton and is now MS.Hargrave 388 in the British Museum. The principal source has been identified both from internal and external[62] evidence as the reports of Sir John Spelman, justice of the King's Bench. Spelman's autograph book was handed down in the family at least until the time of Sir Clement Spelman (d.1679),[63] and it was known to Bishop Burnet; but its subsequent fate is unknown. Study of the Yelverton copy shows that the original text must have been arranged alphabetically and not chronologically, though the copyist made things difficult for later generations by rearranging part of the material (presumably so much as Spelman had dated) in chronological order to give the series a more conventional appearance. It is not impossible to reconstruct

---

[54] Cf. J. Nicholson, *Register of Manuscripts of Year Books extant* (London, Historical Manuscripts Commission for Selden Society, 1956) 26-8. The one Year Book MS. is not listed by Nicholson; it is the Gell MS. in the Library of Congress.

[55] *Relationes quorundam Casuum selectorum ex Libris Robert Keilwey*, STC 14901. The earliest, and best, manuscript text is in the Huntington Library, MS. EL.6108-6138. Cf. note 61, below.

[56] "Keilwey's Reports" (1957) 73 LQR 89. Keilwey himself in 1558 reported to counsel a case *"in son liuer de Reports de Serieant Carell"*: Dyer 174v.

[57] See e.g. Arthur Tourneur's Reports, BM Harg. MS.30, f.71: "Cest ieo ad de veiell reportes. Mr Carrell ad reporte en son lyuer de Reportes que il fuit cite in anno 22 H.8 que un Wise fuit indite de felony . . ."

[58] In BM Lansd. MS. 1084, f.3, is a case abridged as "27 H.8 lib. Carell". See also a case of 26 Hen. VIII cited from "un liuer report per Carrill" in Inner Temple Petyt MS. 511/13, f.58.

[59] See BM Harl. MS. 1691, f.98: "Hec habui ex libro Magistri Johannis Caryll Attornati ducatis Lancastriae viri valde pii ac docti ac interioris templi socii."

[60] See Dyer 174v (note 56 above) and Lansd. MS. 1084, f.3, "per Frowike et Grauntham de libro de reportes de seriant Carell". (Presumably a collection of Inner Temple moot cases similar to that printed in Keil. 102v-137.) Both Carrells were of the Inner Temple.

[61] Cambridge UL MS. Gg.iii.26, ff.97-108 ("cases in temps H. septimi ex libro Roberti Kiloway", including some which are in print); BM Harl. MS. 1691, ff.67-90 (4-11 H.7), ff.98-107 (H.8), ff.111-112 (moot cases "de libro alio Magistri Carell"); Harl. MS. 1624, ff.1-33 (4-6 H.7), 33v-55r (1-11 H.8).

[62] See note 64 below. The author refers to himself by name on f.57v, where he records his appointment as a judge. There is much material relating to Spelman's part of Norfolk, and to Gray's Inn. The Spelman portion of Harg. MS. 388 seems to end at f.154. The brief selection in Cambridge UL MS. Gg.ii.5, f.29 (which is in alphabetical order) is headed "Certaine cases in temps H.8 Reporte per Spilman". Other citations of Spelman by Coke and others correspond with passages in Harg. MS. 388.

[63] See the note cited in W. Dugdale, *Origines Juridiciales* (1680 ed.) 137, which shows that the MS. belonged to Clement Spelman in 1663. Spelman B. cited the MS. in 1676: 73 SS 414, Kelyng 56.

a substantial part of the original work from this mangled and inaccurate version. The importance of the collection has been demonstrated by Mr Simpson,[64] and it merits publication.[65]

The scribe of MS.Harg.388 also inserted in his collection a few cases (14–26 Henry VIII) from a source identified as "Pollarde", reports possibly by the John Pollard who became a serjeant in 1547. They cannot be the work of Sir Lewis Pollard, the judge, who died in 1526. They are poorer in quality than Spelman's but were arranged in similar fashion.

A third collection used by the same scribe contains Somerset and Gray's Inn material, and may be identified as the work of Serjeant Roger Yorke. Three other copies of these reports are known.[66] They seem to be neither chronologically nor alphabetically arranged, but the cases are grouped under random subject headings.

There is yet a fourth collection copied into the Yelverton manuscript, of which other copies are known; as yet it is not possible to identify the author.[67]

Perhaps of the same type was the volume sold in Umfreville's sale of 1758 as "Judge Elliot's common place, temp.Hen.VIII."[68]

One example of the new method found its way into print: the new cases added by Robert Brooke in his *Graunde Abridgment*. The intention, apparently, was that new case law should be recorded in such a way as to augment the abridgments rather than the Year Books, and these alphabetical collections indicate a brief triumph of the abridgment over the chronological register as the most convenient way of storing law. The new method did not survive, however, and before the end of the century lawyers had gone to the trouble of rearranging *Spelman* and *Pollarde*, just as some lawyers distilled cases from the printed abridgments to produce Year Books in miniature.

The next batch of reports carries us from the end of Henry VIII's reign through the much shorter reigns of Edward VI and Philip and Mary, into the reign of Elizabeth. This period is well served by *Plowden* and *Dyer*, but the former was limited to exceptionally full reports of a few select leading cases argued upon demurrer or special verdict, and does not present a typical picture of litigation during this period. The unpublished store does not compare well in quantity with these two great works, since it is characterised by the note form. These reports, which usually begin "*Nota que . . .*", make no pretence of recording legal arguments; they

---

[64] "The Reports of John Spelman" (1956) 72 LQR 334–8. The spelling of the judge's name varies.
[65] The writer has begun to prepare an edition for the Selden Society. [Printed in 93 SS.]
[66] BM Harg. MS. 388, ff.155–216; Harg. MS. 3, ff.1–21; Lansd. MS. 1072, ff 4–35 (lacks first 14 cases); Gonville and Caius College, Cambridge, MS. 601 (titled "De abrig' Rogeri Yorke seruientis ad legem"). The identification is confirmed by two notes in the first person.
[67] It is headed "En temps H.8", and the last case begins "Nota per Baron Hales . . .": Harg. MS. 388, ff.217–239v; Lansd. MS. 1072, ff.35–48. It is followed in both MSS. by cases "En temps Phillip et Mary", which also occur in Harg. MS. 3, ff.24–32. In all three MSS. this collection is found next to Yorke's, though it cannot be his since he died in 1536.
[68] *A Catalogue of a Genuine Collection of Law Manuscripts* 42, lot 89.

The Dark Age of English Legal History, 1500-1700 449

simply note resolutions or dicta in summary form. Two series, however, deserve special mention and ought to be considered for publication. One contains, apparently, the residue of Dyer's collections which were not printed; it will be recalled that Dyer did not himself select the cases for the press, and therefore it is arguable that everything he left deserves attention. (Some limited use of them was made by Mr Vaillant in his edition of *Dyer*.) Certainly the contents of the surviving copies make rewarding reading, part of them providing a unique record of the work of a mid-sixteenth-century circuit judge.[69]

The other important collections for the middle of the century are those attributed to William Dalison, justice of the Queen's Bench for three years from 1556 to 1559. One of these collections seems to have survived in only one copy, which was made by William Lambard in 1569.[70] It contains good reports of cases from 6 Edw.VI to the end of Philip and Mary, including some most useful Serjeants' Inn discussions on criminal law. Lambard occasionally cited these reports in his own printed works, and his identification is entitled to some weight since he was related by marriage to the Dalisons.[71] The second series circulated far more widely, and its attribution to Dalison is less certain. The many variant copies are distinguishable by the fact that they all begin in Michaelmas Term 38 Hen.VIII (1546), the last term of that King. Some versions are associated with Dalison's name, others with the name of Richard Harpur, Justice of the Queen's Bench 1567–1576/77; and several continue beyond the lifetime of both. Dr Abbott has tentatively suggested that Harpur was the author, and that the association with Dalison is false.[72] Although it may be rash to challenge this thesis before it has been fully developed in print, the opposite conclusion seems at least tenable. The confusion is all a result of the practice of "collecting" cases as a preliminary to beginning a new series of reports. Many of the early Elizabethan reports began with a selection of abridged cases from the collection which starts in 38 Hen.VIII; these abridged or selected cases must be further from the original reports than the fuller versions. Three copies of fuller versions have been inspected. They are far from being identical; but one of them is bound as *Dalison's Reports*,[73] and another is stated to have been copied in 1583 from the reports of Justice Dalison.[74] Of the multitude of abridged and paraphrased versions,

---

[69] Inner Temple Petyt MS. 511/13, ff.34–48 ("certaine cases which are probablie thought to be of the Lord Diers collection in his circuite" from Mary to 23 Eliz. I); *ibid*. ff.49–70 ("Here followe certaine cases of the Lord Diers collection which for some private reasons hee thought not fitt to make them vulgarr"); BM Harg. MS. 26, ff.166v–174. See also above, p. 187.

[70] Harl. MS. 5141, ff.1–45. At f.14v (after Edw. VI) is the colophon "Gulielmus Lamberdus transcripsit 1569" and at f.45 the final colophon "Huiusque ex libro Willelmi Dallison conscript' Willelmus Lambert Examinavit 1569."

[71] He married Sylvestria, widow of the judge's son.

[72] In "Lawyers and Law Reporting in the Sixteenth Century", London Ph.D. thesis, 1969. This was published by the Athlone Press in 1973, as *Law Reporting in England 1485–1585*. On pp.123–6 is a useful list of Harpur MSS.

[73] Bodl. Lib. Rawl. MS. C.112.

[74] BM Add. MS. 24845. The date 5 December 1583 appears at the end of 1 Mary. Both the Edw. VI and the Marian sections end "finis secundum Dalison Justice del Banck le Roy."

some are attributed to Dalison;[75] some to Harpur;[76] and some to others.[77] There are even abridged versions of Harpur.[78] Since Dalison died in 1559, and Harpur not until 1577, it is more likely that the latter abridged the former than vice versa. There is, of course, the difficulty that the Lambard text overlaps in date with this series and has a different content, and so it may be wrong to associate Dalison with the second series at all. Whatever the answer may be, these series are well worth publication even if they are not up to the standard of Dyer and Plowden.

By the time of Elizabeth I many, if not most, of the judges were keeping reports of some kind. No doubt most of them were intended for private reference only, and it is only fair to give the authors due allowance for this; but it is also wholly proper that we should delve into them and concern ourselves with what judges put into their private notes. Most of the notes are lost; we know of the former existence of reports by Wray C. J., Peryam C. B., Wyndham J., Manwood C. B., and others. Of the survivors, some were printed in the following century (for instance, *Anderson*), and some were never printed (for instance, *Harpur* and *Clench*). It is impossible in a short compass to begin to describe all the other series written by serjeants, readers, barristers, and young students.

(ii) *1590–1640*

In the fascinating half-century between 1590 and the Civil War, when litigation reached a peak and the finishing touches were made to the new jurisprudence, law reporting became a routine occupation for keen young lawyers and part of the way of life of some of their elders. There are too many series to describe or evaluate here, but it might be helpful to attempt to identify the main characteristics of the different kinds of report which may be encountered.

(a) *Notes and brief reports*

A majority, or at least a substantial minority, of the reporters in this period continued the tradition of taking what are better described as notes of cases than reports. This was probably all that the average student desired to have or was prepared to produce. The notes were sometimes derived from a wide variety of sources, but only rarely does the writer oblige us by specifying them. It would be incorrect to assume that such notes were necessarily scribbled down by someone sitting in court. Undoubtedly there were facili-

---

[75] E.g. the printed "Dalison" and BM Add. MS. 35941, ff.261v–268v ("Ascuns cases hors del reports del Dalison Justice del bank le Roy").
[76] See BM Harg. MSS. 6, 8, 10 (note by Umfreville), 374 (note by Hargrave); Lansd. MSS. 1060, 1072, 1121; Lincoln's Inn Misc. MS. 791. The true limits of Harpur's reports are probably 2–19 Eliz.I.
[77] In the Verulam collection (Hertfordshire Record Office) is a small selection by William Lewis. A different series of abridged cases is BM Add. 35940.
[78] E.g. Verulam MS. XII.A.6A, f.74, "Cases ex libro Harp[er]" abridged by George Croke.

ties for writing,[79] but most of the crowd of lawyers at the bar were unable to sit down, let alone write continuously, and would have had to carry away a general impression of what had happened for entry into their notebooks later in the day. We ought not even to assume that the writer was an eye-witness. Often he was noting what a friend had told him, or what was going round the inns, or was simply copying or abridging what somebody else had written down (sometimes years before the copy was made). For all their imperfections, these notes are still useful provided they are not used in isolation. They show what ordinary lawyers felt to be the kernel of a case—what they regarded as worth using again—and they may occasionally supply the best evidence of something quite significant which the loss of better texts has otherwise obscured. It would be pointless to try to draw a line between a note and a report, though most of the printed "reports" of this period (including *Croke*) could best be classified as notes. Obviously notebooks kept by judges or senior practitioners, such as Coke, Croke, Hyde, and Fleming, command particular notice; and these better writers often expand into the style of a reporter when the need arises. Coke's extensive notebooks provide perfect examples of the whole range of reports from brief notes, some attributable to hearsay, to fully minuted discussions.

(b) *Minute record of arguments*

At least two extant series of King's Bench reports preserve a uniformly detailed and minute account of what must have been virtually all the business of moment transacted at the bar of the King's Bench during the period covered. Neither of them were published, perhaps because they were too bulky, and they are both anonymous.

The first extends from Michaelmas Term 1598 to Hilary Term 1604. In the most complete copy, which belonged to St. John C. J. in the seventeenth century,[80] these five years occupy 1,390 neat and closely written pages. This seems to be a professional copy by a law stationer, and other partial copies are known to exist.[81] It gives by far the fullest and most obviously reliable accounts of the cases during this period, including *Slade's Case* and the *Case of Monopolies*, and the reports are preferable to Coke's as factual records of what was spoken in court.[82]

The second series extends from Easter Term 1629 to Easter Term 1638. Two full copies have been seen. In the Cambridge University Library copy

---

[79] Below, 452. A drawing in the Print Room of the British Museum shows the Court of King's Bench in about 1600, and there is a wooden gallery on poles at the side of the court, in which (presumably) students could sit to make notes. The curious frontispiece to G. Billinghurst, *Arcana Clericalia or the Misteries of Clerkshipp* (1674), shows six reporters wearing cloaks and *standing* on either side of the bench, with their long reporters' notebooks in their left hands and pens in their right hands.

[80] BM Add. MS. 25203.

[81] BM Stowe MS. 398 (part of Mich. 1598 only); Harg. MS. 13 (Mich. 1600–Trin.1601); Lincoln's Inn Misc. MS. 492 (1600–1604); Exeter College, Oxford, MS. 144 (Pasch. 1598–Pasch. 1599); Harvard Law School MS. 2076 (Mich. 1600–Mich. 1602); Yale Law School MS. G.R.29/12 (Trin. 1598–Pasch. 1599).

[82] See "New Light on Slade's Case", above, p. 393ff.

452 *The Legal Profession and the Common Law*

the series fills two large volumes containing between them 2,392 pages.[83] They are written in a large scrivener's hand, and have a full index. The other full copy, in the Hardwicke collection, is closely written and covers 968 pages.[84] Other partial copies are known.[85] The quality is similar to the earlier series, though sometimes the note form is resorted to. Occasionally the writer acknowledged that reports were based on hearsay; his chief informants being "Mr Heath" (probably Edward Heath, of the Inner Temple), "Mr Ellis" (probably William Ellis of Gray's Inn), and "T.H." or "Thomas Hard[re]s" (of Gray's Inn). These relate to courts which the writer did not attend, and the fact that he notes the source suggests that they are exceptional. The Exchequer reports related by Hardres show that this reporter had attended in that court (if only briefly) well before his printed series begins.[86]

The style of these two series is reminiscent of the Year Books, in so far as the arguments are treated as being instructive in themselves and worth recording in verbatim form even where they were not followed immediately by judgment. The wealth of detail shows that the reporter must have taken full notes in court; no one could have committed so much material, complete with references, to memory. The author of the second collection indicates as much when he says of a case heard in 1635, that he would make a summary report (although the case was well argued) because *"ieo ne la poy escrier pur le malvesity de mon penne"*.[87] This circumstance poses two or three questions.

Firstly, one would like to know whether either of these reporters had recourse to the novel art of stenography. The art had been popularised by John Willis, whose manual had apparently passed through ten editions between 1602 and 1632.[88] Similar techniques had been available even at the date of the earlier series, for in 1588 Dr Timothy Bright had published his rare treatise on *Characterie* to enable his readers to "write orations of publike actions of speech . . . verbatim." This had been followed in 1590 by Peter Bales' textbook, in which he wrote that "Brachygraphy, or the art of writing as fast as a man speaketh tractably . . . is in effect very easy."[89] It is not yet possible to demonstrate that any of these systems were used by lawyers before the Restoration period, but the possibility cannot be dismissed. Whether or not this was so, the text which remains cannot be verbatim because it is in law French, and the actual words have probably been redrawn in the traditional phraseology of the reports. By

---

[83] MS. Gg.ii.19, 20.
[84] BM Add. MS. 35958.
[85] BM Add. MS. 35968, 35969 (Serjeant Waller's copy, lacks first five years and last term); Harl. MS. 4811 (Robert Paynell's copy, lacks first five years).
[86] The printed series begins in 1655. In the MS. are some Exchequer cases of Michaelmas Term 1637 related by "T.H." Hardres was called to the bar of Gray's Inn in 1636.
[87] *Allen* v. *Nash*, BM Add. MS. 35958, f.317v. The case is even more briefly reported in W. Jones 393.
[88] *Art of Stenographie*, STC 25744-7 (some of the editions not recorded).
[89] T. Bright, *Characterie, an arte of shorte, swifte and secrete writing by Character* (London, 1588) STC 3742 (reprinted in 1888); P. Bales, *The writing schoolemaster* (London, 1590) STC 1312.

1700 over twenty authors had written manuals of short-writing and the technique was widely practised;[90] Sir George Treby wrote stenographical memoranda in his reports, and other legal notes in such form are known.[91]

The second question is whether the writers enjoyed any special privilege of sitting within the bar of the King's Bench, so that they could write at the table. There were no seats outside the bar, though it may have been possible to write in the gallery. If the writers did have special privileges, they were either clerks or officers of the court, or persons recognised and encouraged by the court as reporters. This brings us to the more important question whether any of the reports in this period were in any sense official.

(c) *The official reporters*

The two series just mentioned might be thought to provide in themselves a good prima facie case for supposing the existence of official reporters in the King's Bench. Whether or not the reporter had publication in mind, the reports certainly were widely circulated within a short time of their publication. Is there any evidence to corroborate such a supposition?

It is well-known that Bacon persuaded James I in 1617 to appoint two official law reporters at a stipend of £100.[92] The writs of appointment provided, most significantly, that the reporters should be allocated convenient seats in court. Turner discovered that the two first appointees, Edward Writington and Thomas Hetley of Gray's Inn, actually began work sitting in Chancery at the feet of Lord Keeper Bacon, and were still in receipt of their salaries in 1619.[93] Moreover, in one of the accounts of the general call of serjeants which was held in October 1623, Mr Serjeant-elect Hetley is described as *"un des reporters del ley"*,[94] which suggests that he had continued in that capacity until 1623 at least. The fruits of his labour, however, are lost. There is, of course, a series of reports from 3–7 Charles I which was printed in 1657 with Serjeant Hetley's name on the title-page and the statement that he was appointed by the King and the Judges for one of the Reporters of the Law. But there are no known reports from 1617 to 1623 bearing Hetley's name. Even the printed series is probably not by Hetley, but by Humphrey Mackworth;[95] the statements on the

---

[90] See I. Pitman, *History of Shorthand* (4th ed., London, 1918) 9–40. The methods were variously known as characatery, brachygraphy, tachygraphy, semigraphy, stenography, cryptography, thoography, and short-writing.

[91] MS. in Middle Temple, *passim*. Sir Dudley Ryder's notebooks (1717–55) are in shorthand; they have been deposited in Lincoln's Inn (Misc. MSS. 861–78) by Lord Harrowby. The writer's copy of Savile's *Reports* (1688) has some shorthand notes in the index. A small volume at present in the possession of Winifred A. Myers Ltd contains some reports of James I's time in shorthand; but it seems to have been written later, and was probably transcribed in this way from a longhand exemplar.

[92] The writ of privy seal was enrolled as a patent: C.66/2147, no.2 (printed in 26 SS xxii–xxiii and as *Ordinatio qua constituuntur lez Reporters de lege* in Rymer's *Foedera* xvii.27 (Reprint vii, pt iii, 19). See also J. W. Wallace, *The Reporters* (4th ed., Boston, Mass., 1882) 270–71.

[93] See 26 SS xix–xxiii.

[94] Cambridge UL MS. Gg.v.6, f.216v.

[95] Thus in three copies, some of the terms are headed "Ex relacione Humphridi Mackworth": BM Add. MS. 35957, ff.126–239; Add. MS. 35962, ff.2–470; Harg. MS. 362, ff.97v–217 (ends Hil. 1629). Many other copies are known: e.g. BM Lansd. MS. 1085; Cambridge UL MS. Mm.vi.67, f.182, continuing in MS.Dd.iii.46; MS. Ii.v.35; MS. Mm.vi.12 (ends Pasch. 1628); Inner Temple Barrington MSS. 8, 12; Harvard Law School MSS. 1125, 1178, 1195.

title-page were bookseller's puffs. Some of the same reports are also to be found in *"Littleton"*, which seem to be no more the work of the future Lord Keeper than of the official reporter.[96] No reports known to be by Writington have survived either.[97]

It is perfectly clear that neither Hetley nor Writington was responsible for the series from 1629 to 1638 with which this discussion began. Hetley died in 1637, and the anonymous author revealed himself as a member of the Inner Temple when he recorded the elevation of *"Mr Gardiner de nostre meason"* to the Recordership of London.[98] The only further obvious clues to authorship which this reporter left are that his father died in or immediately before Michaelmas Term 1635,[99] and that he regarded Viscount Savage (d.1635) as his "treshonorable amie".[100] Whether he was in any way Hetley's successor can only be proved if some unknown record comes to light; but there are no known texts bearing the judicial fiat contemplated by the Baconian scheme.

(d) *Verbatim drafts of speeches*

The fourth type of "report" does not belong to the same class as those just described and is perhaps not properly so described. A few examples may be found of copies of single speeches, written (and often signed) by the counsel who delivered them, in English, either to assist themselves in court or to preserve their wit and learning for future reference. The phenomenon seems to have been confined to the later years of Elizabeth I and the reign of James I. Coke's report of *Shelley's Case*, in its original state before the publication of the first part of the *Reports* in 1600, was in this form. It was primarily a polished account of Coke's own speech, with a signed dedication to Lord Buckhurst, and was copied and distributed widely in the profession.[101] Other examples of the same species are Dodderidge's argument in *Slade's Case* (1598),[102] Bacon's argument in

---

[96] Umfreville was probably correct when he observed (in a note in Harg. MS. 362, f.3v) that "many of these cases from P.3 C.1 are printed most incorrectly in the Book falsely called Hetley's Reports and Winch and Littleton. The Book called Winch's Reports is no more than a Bad abbreviated impression of the Reports of Allestree tempore Jacobi as Hetley and parts of Littleton are of him and Mackworth in C.B. tempore Caroli, but neither of the three are genuine." See also Umfreville's note in Lansd. MS. 1091. Sylvester Douglas wrote of "Hetley": "Whether it was he or the Lord Keeper Littleton, who was really the author of those reports (many of them being exact duplicates of those ascribed to Littleton), they are so far from bearing any marks of peculiar skill, information, or authenticity": *Reports of Cases in the King's Bench* (2nd ed., London, 1786) preface xi. Cambridge UL MS. Ii.v.22 is attributed to Littleton; for reports attributed to Winch, see BM Add. MS. 25197, Lansd. MS. 1091, Cambridge UL MS. Ii.v.34, Yale Law School MS. G.R.29/22.

[97] Turner attempts to father on him some of Widdrington's Reports, but he is not convincing: 26 SS xix–xx. For Widdrington's work, see BM Harg. MSS.38, 39, Lansd. MSS. 1083, 1092.

[98] BM Add. MS. 35958, f.314; Harl. MS. 4811, f.125.

[99] "Nota jeo fuit absent grand part de cest terme [M.11 Car.1] per encheson del mort mon beau pere": Add. MS. 35958, f.297; Add. MS. 35968, f.568; Harl. MS. 4811, f.119.

[100] "Nota en ceo terme [M.11 Car.1] mon treshonourable amie le seigniour [Viscount] Savage chancellor al Roigne mor[ust]": Add. MS. 35958, f.314; Harl. MS. 4811, f.125 (slightly corrupt). Thomas, Viscount Savage of Rock-Savage, Cheshire, buried at Macclesfield in the same county. The word *amie* may denote patronage, but it is rather vague.

[101] See above, p. 189.

[102] BM Harl. MS. 6809, ff.45–46v, parts of which are printed above, pp. 396-409 (text "G").

12 Manuscript law reports

The passage illustrated records the death of Viscount Savage and various legal appointments in Michaelmas term 1635.

Cambridge University Library, MS Gg. 2. 20, fo. 765ᵛ (upper part)

13 Reporters in the Court of King's Bench, c. 1675

This engraving shows groups of reporters standing at the side of the bench, writing in oblong notebooks of the kind which still survive. At the table the chief clerk and secondary, wearing round bonnets, write their remembrances.

Bodleian Library, Oxford

The Dark Age of English Legal History, 1500-1700 455

Lord Zouch's Case (1603),[103] Fuller's argument in the *Case of Monopolies* (1602),[104] Yelverton's argument in *Zangis* v. *Whiskeard*,[105] and Davenport's argument in *Shuttleworth* v. *Bolton*.[106]

These oddities show us precisely how lawyers phrased their arguments in the vernacular. The actual performances may not have been equal to the eloquence of these written drafts; indeed, some maintained that nothing in Coke's report of his argument in *Shelley's Case* had been spoken in open court.[107] Perhaps they indicated what the speaker had wanted to say, rather than what he did say, in the manner of those ancient historians who reported not what great men said but what they ought to have said, or might have said if they had been better prepared. Nevertheless, we derive from these texts a clearer notion of what a legal argument sounded like than we can guess from the convenient stereotyped and inanimate law-French phrases of the conventional reporter.

(iii) *1640-1700*

The last division of the period under review has been better served by modern scholarship in so far as a collection of reports from this period has been published this century. Mr D. E. C. Yale's edition of Lord Nottingham's *Case Book*[108] is the only volume of reports between the Year Books and 1700 to have been edited and published in the present century. For the last edition of a collection of seventeenth-century common law reports, we have to go back as far as 1823, when Saxe Bannister published a selection of the judgments of Sir Orlando Bridgman. Needless to say, the manuscript material has not yet been exhausted.

The decade of the Civil War is poorly served by reports, probably because the work of the courts dwindled and the Inns of Court all but closed down. March's *New Reports* end in Trinity Term 1642, and *Style* and *Aleyn* both begin again in 1646. It is doubtful whether much of the gap can be filled from unprinted sources. Rolle reported cases from the 1640s and inserted them in his *Abridgment*. Another good source is Hargrave MS. 42, described by Umfreville (a former owner) as "very judiciously and carefully taken"; it extends from 1639 to 1652, with a gap between Trinity Term 1642 and Hilary Term 1646. The reporter noted the trial and execution of Charles I without comment, but betrayed royalist (or at least conservative) sentiments by continuing to date his reports by the regnal years of Charles II. The author may be identified with reasonable

---

[103] Printed by Henry Owen in (1901) 14 *Y Cymmrodor* 33-41, from BM Harl. MS. 141.
[104] Noy 172-85. Cf. Inner Temple Petyt MS. 516/5, ff.347-362v. Another copy in Phillipps MS. 11125(1), now in Leeds Public Library (MS. SRF.942.06.c.685).
[105] BM Harg. MS. 29, ff.116-25.
[106] Cambridge UL MS. Ee.iii.45, ff.74v-83.
[107] 1 And. 71.
[108] (1954/1957) 73 SS and (1961-2/1961) 79 SS.

confidence as Thomas Twisden of the Inner Temple, later a judge.[109]

During the Interregnum there are several good series of reports to supplement *Style*, *Aleyn* and *Hardres*. Thomas Cory, Chief Prothonotary of the Common Pleas, filled a substantial volume with reports written in a peculiar crabbed hand which only a prothonotary could have developed, and which requires immense patience to decipher.[110] Francis North also took reports during this period,[111] according to a system of censorship which Roger North disclosed in the original draft of his *Life of Lord Keeper Guildford*, but which he evidently thought it politic to omit from the printed version:

> I have heard him say, that if the most stupid judge, such as Archer, said anything that closed with his reason, he noted it, and if the most accute judge said what he in his own reason did not approve, he took no notice of it. And if a serjeant or other councel said that was notable and new to him, he set it down.[112]

The quality of reporting in the Restoration period was not generally good, but nevertheless the best reports are still unpublished. Two series deserve special mention, as they were written in some detail by future chief justices and are full of interesting memoranda about events in the legal world. One is the work of George Treby between 1667 and 1672, which fills two folio volumes of 782 pages, now in the Middle Temple Library. Treby is mainly remembered for his learned annotations to *Dyer*—including the famous "brickbat" case—which betoken a close study of manuscript reports and readings, and which contain the only printed specimens of several forgotten collections. His own reports, which have been referred to once or twice above, add greatly to his credit. The other noteworthy series is the work of Edward Ward, and is in two parts. The first part consists of two volumes of reports from 1660 to 1678, and the second of five notebooks of cases from 1673 to 1697. They are all in Lincoln's Inn Library.[113] In the same collection is a third set of notebooks (1674–1714), some of which contain Ward's judicial notes as Chief Baron of the Exchequer.[114] These are amongst the earliest examples of a class of record which seems never to have been used by legal historians: the

---

[109] Cf. BM Add. MS. 10169, called *Twisden's Reports*, which is an alphabetical abridgment of Year Books and later cases, some of them identifiable in Harg. MS. 42. At Harg. MS. 42, f.104v, the reporter says "*I* moved in arest de judgment ..."; the same case is reported in Sty. 175, where Twisden is the counsel who moves in arrest of judgment. The existence of reports by Twisden is alluded to in DNB.
    The history of Twisden's extensive law library is still obscure. Some of his manuscripts were dispersed in 1924, when the Harvard Law School purchased five of them: MSS. 1165–6, 1171 (Hutton), 1195 ("Hetley"), 1207 (Lane, Rolle). The last volume was removed from Bradbourne, Kent, the Twisden seat, on the death of Sir John Twisden, the last baronet, by T. L. Hodges (d. 1857).

[110] BM Harg. MS. 23. There is a copy by Prothonotary Moyle, if anything even less legible, in Lincoln's Inn Misc. MS 586.

[111] Lincoln's Inn Hill MS. 82 (1658); later reports lost, some copied by Roger North in BM Add. MS. 32521 ("An extract out of his Lordship's court books of divers cases which came afore him as Judge"). See also Add. MS. 32523, f.33.

[112] BM Add. MS. 32508, f.59. John Archer (d. 1682) became a judge in 1659 and was reconstituted by Charles II in 1663.

[113] Misc. MSS. 499–500, 555–9.

[114] Misc. MSS. 510–40 (1674–1714). One of the cases is printed in J. Rayner, *Cases concerning Tithes* (1783), i, "Authorities", p. xxxiv; ii.361.

The Dark Age of English Legal History, 1500-1700   457

judge's notebook. Several have been preserved from the period 1700–1875. Although they might be regarded as having a semi-official character, since they supplement the record with notes of evidence and arguments, they were never regarded as public records and they remained in private ownership. Amongst the examples noticed (though outside our period) may be mentioned those of Dudley Ryder,[115] Nathaniel Gundry,[116] Thomas Burnet,[117] Lord Hardwicke,[118] Thomas Denison,[119] Martin Wright,[120] Lord Denman,[121] Sir Cresswell Cresswell,[122] J. F. Pollock,[123] T. N. Talfourd,[124] Samuel Martin,[125] and J. S. Keating.[126]

There would be little point in merely listing all the unprinted reports from the period 1660–1700, and this brief selection may be brought to an end with a note on Lord Raymond. The reports published under his name mark the transition from the generally poor seventeenth-century reports to the modern methods of reporting which were perfected in the eighteenth century. The reports were not printed until 1743, and the title was "Reports of Cases taken *and collected* by Lord Raymond." It is not generally realised that even such an authoritative series as this is of dubious authorship. The first volume is full of reports communicated by others: *ex relatione* Place, Nott, Mather, Daly, Salkeld, Jacob, Shelley, Northey, Lutwyche, Cheshyre, Thornhill, Peere Williams, Bury and Pengelly.[127] Many of these were reporters in their own right, and the cases in Lord Raymond really come from these other series. Worse still, surviving manuscripts suggest that quite a number of the better reports, including *Ashby* v. *White* itself, were written not by Lord Raymond (whose contributions are marked "R.R.") but by Serjeant (later Chief Baron) Pengelly.[128]

THE STUDY OF LEGAL MANUSCRIPTS

IT is easier to extol the wonders of our manuscript heritage than it is to begin to indicate how one can go about rescuing it from oblivion. The task certainly requires more trained scholars than are at present engaged upon it. Yet the potential recruit is easily discouraged. He has virtually no biblio-

---

[115] (1717–56), Lincoln's Inn Misc. MSS. 861–80, deposited by Lord Harrowby. The notebooks relate mostly to the period before Ryder became Chief Justice in 1754.
[116] (1722–42), Lincoln's Inn Misc. MSS. 31–45.
[117] (1730–51), Lincoln's Inn Hill MSS. 37–48. Burnet became a judge in 1741.
[118] (1733–56), BM Add. MSS. 36028–69. Sir Philip Yorke became Chief Justice of the Common Pleas in 1733 and Lord Chancellor in 1737.
[119] (c.1736–1758), Harvard Law School, uncatalogued. Some of them are more like reports.
[120] (1740–54), Inner Temple Petyt MS. 509.
[121] (1832–49), Lincoln's Inn Misc. MSS. 609–703.
[122] (1842–57), deposited in the Inner Temple.
[123] (1848–58), divided between the Middle Temple, the Squire Law Library (Cambridge), and BM Add. MS. 43839, 43840.
[124] (1849–53), Reading Public Library.
[125] (1850), BM Add. MS. 43646.
[126] (1859–75), Squire Law Library, Cambridge.
[127] See Wallace, *Reporters* 402.
[128] See BM Add. MS. 35987 and Harg. MS. 66.

graphies, glossaries, or palaeographical guides to help him find and read his material. He must learn the language and palaeography himself by slow and painful perseverance. The challenge of deciphering texts written in an unfamiliar tongue, abbreviated almost beyond recognition, and disguised in hands not illustrated in any of the textbooks on Tudor or Stuart handwriting—and often not intended to be read by anyone but the writer—is more likely to deter than to stimulate those to whom it is presented.

The first requirement, if further work in this field is to be undertaken on anything like an encouraging scale, is a book or booklet devoted to the problems of reading later legal texts. Students of the public records are well catered for; Latin abbreviations and the set hands of the courts and official departments are comparatively easy to conquer with the printed aids. What is now urgently needed is a glossary of later law-French, with some guidance as to the ways in which it was contracted in writing, and a collection of facsimiles of specimen private law-hands of the later period.

The second requirement is a union catalogue of legal manuscripts, or at least further work towards adequately listing and cataloguing all collections of such material. The old catalogues of the collections in the British Museum, the university and college libraries, and Lincoln's Inn library, will not suffice for this purpose. In the Harleian Catalogue, for instance, a Year Book may be missed under a description such as "Adversaria Juridica", or Sir Edward Coke's autograph notebook passed over as "precedents and cases in law." Some collections are not catalogued in print at all: for instance the immensely important Ellesmere collection in the Henry E. Huntington Library, San Marino.[129] This conference brought to the writer's attention an interesting small collection of legal manuscripts in the Wynnstay MSS. at the National Library of Wales. The publication (since this paper was delivered) of a detailed catalogue of the manuscripts in the Inner Temple Library, compiled by the late Dr Conway Davies, is most encouraging. It is much to be wished that other institutions will be spurred to follow this example.

A third difficulty arises from the scattering of the material. Originally most of it was in London, but then it was not generally accessible because it belonged to numerous private owners. The great collectors of the seventeenth to the nineteenth centuries deserve our eternal gratitude for accumulating many of these smaller collections at a time when their contents were little valued. The libraries of Maynard, Hale, Glynne, Bishop Moore, Hardwicke, and Hargrave, are still the nucleus of all the legal manuscripts in public collections in England. Unfortunately, other large collections have themselves been dispersed. Francis Tate (d.1616),

---

[129] There is a microfilm copy of the old Bridgewater shelf-list in the University Library, Cambridge. Since the delivery of the paper, I was able to visit the Harvard Law School and Yale University. The collection at Harvard is far more extensive than De Ricci's *Census* indicates; whilst Yale has an important collection of Hale MSS., purchased from the Hale family in recent times, and including over twenty volumes of reports (nowhere described in print).

The Dark Age of English Legal History, 1500-1700   459

one of the earliest collectors, owned a library which rivalled that of his friend Robert Cotton (now in the British Museum). It was mainly composed, as far as we can tell, of medieval legal manuscripts—including the unique copy of the *Mirror of Justices* and the famous *Liber Luffield*. This library was dispersed in the seventeenth century, and only about a dozen legal items can now be traced in Cambridge, Oxford, and London. Edward Umfreville (d.1758) not only built up an enormous collection of post-medieval legal manuscripts in the eighteenth century, but actually read them and made notes and indices throughout his collection. But he made insufficient financial provision for his issue, and therefore his manuscripts were dispersed at auction (in 1758 and 1792). Fortunately, about half of them have found their way into the British Museum *via* Lord Lansdowne and Francis Hargrave; the other half are almost all lost. The vast and important collection of Lord Somers was divided between Sir Joseph Jekyll and the Yorkes; the former portion was dispersed in 1739, and the latter destroyed by a fire in Lincoln's Inn on 27 June 1752.[130] Only a few odd volumes can now be traced. The largest collection of all was that formed in the last century by Sir Thomas Phillipps, whose library of over 40,000 manuscripts included at least 600 of interest to legal historians. Most of these were sold at auction sales between 1893 and the present, and over half have disappeared once more.[131] One consequence of the Phillipps sales, and other large-scale auction sales at the end of the last and in the present century, is that a considerable share of the material has crossed the Atlantic at the behest of librarians with more foresight or (latterly) more funds than their English counterparts.[132] It is also safe to assume that material still lurks in old country houses: the best known, if under-explored, example being Serjeant Thynne's collection at Longleat.

The wide dispersal of the material makes study extremely difficult. The nature of legal research necessitates the use of a multitude of texts, since it is nearly always desirable to read as far as possible all the literature and case law on a given subject in a given period. At present such work cannot, for most practical purposes, be done with any degree of thoroughness; and the Englishman is at a particular disadvantage because of the expense of getting to and staying in the United States and the lack of any research funds. One answer to these problems would be to film as much of the material as possible, and make it available to scholars and librarians in microfiche. A project is already under discussion to publish manuscript Year Books, readings, and reports in microfiche, and to produce a cumulative listing as the work proceeds. If this project is successful, many of

---

[130] See C. E. Wright (ed.) *Fontes Harleiani* (1972) 308–9. The catalogue in Harl. MS. 7191 indicates the richness of Somers' collection. Several volumes survive, presumably from the Jekyll portion.

[131] The writer is indebted to Dr A. N. L. Munby, Librarian of King's College, Cambridge, for permitting him to study his annotated set of Phillipps catalogues. Some of the Year Books are now in the British Museum. The largest collection of Phillipps' legal manuscripts is in the Harvard Law School.

[132] Before the last War, legal manuscripts on paper tended to sell for shillings rather than pounds. No attempt was made to buy them for the principal English libraries.

the above difficulties will disappear, and also editors might be relieved of the need to print original texts alongside their translations—thus freeing more badly needed space for the publication of edited material.

One final suggestion concerns the manuscripts which have been lost. These probably represent the greater part, at least in quantitative terms, of all that once existed. Mention has already been made of the loss of Lord Somers' collection. Other libraries are known to have been destroyed in their entirety. For instance, Sir John Vaughan lost all his books and manuscripts in the Great Fire of 1666, which swept through the northeastern corner of the Inner Temple.[133] Sir William Jones lost three volumes of his reports while crossing to Ireland.[134] Probably far more volumes were simply thrown away by ignorant descendants, who did not realise that (generally speaking) the less legible a manuscript, the more likely it is to be of historical importance. It is not impossible to reconstruct some of these libraries, and it is by no means a futile exercise to try to calculate what has gone missing; and there is always the slight hope that research of this kind may now and then lead to the discovery of something which has survived.

The study of this Dark Age of English legal history has only just begun, and the prospect, though challenging, is not entirely hopeful. There are far more questions than answers, and many more questions than we have yet learned to ask. There are few volunteers coming forward who can add some feeling for the common law to their expertise in history. The sources remain in an appalling state of intellectual, if not physical, neglect. But some day a history of the law of Renaissance England will be written from the material which is now coming to our notice. It may well read very differently from our present textbooks, and it may contain a few surprises. For anyone who will contribute to this work, there is a lifetime of rewarding study ahead.

---

[133] See Lincoln's Inn Misc. MS. 499, f.435, *per* Vaughan C.J. at his installation: "[Vaughan] disable luy mesme pur cy grand liew per reason del discontinuance de son study occasion'd partment per les guerres en les darrain temps et le seizing de son study et sequestring de son estate, et partment per le grand losse que il sustayne en le darrain few en Londres en quel son study et ses liures et papers que il ad retrieve a sequestracion fueront ure." Cf. the obituary by Serjeant Waller in BM Add. MS. 36076 f.301v: "[Vaughan] fuit en tresgrand rationall parts et bien studdye en le veiell ley et yeare bookes mes nemy mult verse in les novell reports ayant este sequester in the times pur son loyaltie al roy et plunder de mults . . . et ayant mults de son livres et manuscripts burnt in le inner Temple per fire que happen la."

[134] BM Add. MS. 35958, f.233, *per* Jones J.: "iav null authority in point car en mon passage en Ireland ieo perde 3 report-books MS."

23

ENGLISH LAW AND THE RENAISSANCE*

IN HIS famous Rede lecture of 1901, Maitland posed the question why the medieval law of England survived the period when (as he said) old creeds were crumbling everywhere and Roman law was pushing German law out of Germany.[1] Much controversy has reigned since Maitland's time not only about his conclusions and his evidence, but also about the precise gist of his question—since it is not wholly clear what assumptions he was making about the nature of the so-called "Reception" of Roman law in Europe or about the extent to which the medieval common law really did survive in England. It is not the purpose of this paper to provide yet another interpretation of Maitland, but rather to re-examine from a different viewpoint the subject which he opened.

As was appropriate to the occasion, Maitland attacked his subject with a broad brush and vivid colours, without tracing the minutiae of legal change. He himself emphasised that he was merely raising questions to be considered when further work had been done on the unpublished sources; and he did not have a later opportunity to elaborate or revise his initial sketch. The lecture nevertheless made a deep impression on legal history, and (without doubt unintentionally) drew attention away from the internal changes in the common law, changes the nature and chronology of which were not fully perceptible in 1901. Recent research suggests that the medieval common law, though surviving in an organic sense, actually underwent a substantial reformation in the Renaissance period. And, where Maitland (with proper chronological caution) chose to speak of "the age of the Renaissance," we can now define the period more precisely. It seems that many of the more remarkable developments began in the half century between the 1490s and the 1540s,[2] even if they did not all bear full fruit until the Elizabethan period. That is not inconsistent with Maitland's view of things. He had argued on an earlier occasion that the transformation of the English legal system

---

* The James Ford Special Lecture delivered before the University of Oxford on 4 May 1984. Earlier versions were presented at the universities of Edinburgh, Chicago and California (at Berkeley).
[1] F. W. Maitland, *English Law and the Renaissance* (Cambridge, 1901).
[2] See the introduction to *The Reports of Sir John Spelman*, Vol. II (1978), in Selden Society Vol. XCIV.

under the Tudors helped to explain its survival in a rapidly changing world. But it does invite further reflection.

So far no single explanation has been produced for the early-Tudor transformation of the common law. Probably no simple thesis could satisfy every question. At one time it was fashionable to suppose that all legal change could be explained by social or economic factors, or by political events. Certainly the legal historian ignores such things at his peril. But the search for explanations external to the reasoning of the law itself is so fraught with difficulties that it is legitimate to question whether it is always necessary or correct. History is not in its nature tidy, and it should not be forgotten that law has an intellectual as well as a social history.

Let us first consider (briefly) legislation, the species of change most readily susceptible of "external" explanation. The most important—at least, the most often discussed—of the statutes in our period were the Statute of Uses and the Statute of Wills. We can now give them a fairly satisfying political explanation, as compromises between the identifiable interests of the crown and the more important landowners. Yet it is clear that in order to understand fully the legal issues and the form which the solution took it is necessary to understand the currents of legal thought in the preceding fifty years, since the significant but less frequently discussed statute of Richard III.[3] The fictional livery of seisin was indeed an impressive display of legislative magic—and disturbing magic it proved to be when it ran loose—but the thinking behind it was far from revolutionary, because the tendency of the law since 1484 and even earlier had been to assimilate the legal position of the beneficiary to that of the freeholder.[4] Many of the cases in which that tendency can be traced had little or nothing to do, explicitly or implicitly, with crown revenue. No more did the statute of Richard III. The apparently clear political event, and the surrounding economic circumstances, explain the timing of the legislation: but the thinking behind the legislation was part of a much broader movement, rooted in the rise of feoffments to uses in the previous century and the manifold legal problems which this occasioned.

While on the subject of purely political explanations for legislative change, a similar observation may be made concerning the changes associated with the Reformation. Actually the legislation of the 1530s had little direct effect on everyday law, and such jurisdictional adjustments as took place had been on the way since the previous century.[5] The larger legal context, however, shows that even the

---

[3] 1 Ric. III, c.1.
[4] 94 Selden Soc. *192–203*.
[5] Ibid., pp. *64–70*.

break with Rome was not as revolutionary as some have represented it to be. Had not Huse C.J. in 1485 asserted that the king of England was answerable directly to God, and was superior to the pope within his realm?[6] This is not to suggest that the break with Rome, or fiscal feudalism, can be explained purely in terms of legal reasoning, which would be an absurd proposition: but it would be as absurd to treat them as purely political in origin. One could hardly account for the Reformation solely in terms of Henry VIII's succession problem, without reference to developments in theology—which, of course, were not confined to England. Likewise, the legisation of Henry VIII cannot be fully understood without reference to the course of common-law reasoning in the preceding period, much of which is innocent of Tudor politics.

The reforms in the land law may, alternatively, be approached in terms of social change. Uses had become popular in order to achieve greater freedom of disposition, and this seems to have been just as important as evading feudal dues. Disputes about the legal status of the beneficiary are paralleled by disputes about the status of the tenant for years and the copyholder,[7] occupiers who likewise (but for different reasons) were seen as beneficial owners but lacked freehold status. All came under the wing of the common law in the Tudor period, and the explanation may well be that the social position and expectations of such tenants had changed. The perfection of the common recovery in the 1480s[8] was no doubt also a result of social pressure on lawyers to loosen and reframe entails to suit changing family circumstances. However, if we turn from the law of property to contract and tort, we find equally large changes which are much less amenable to explanation in terms of external forces. The establishment of assumpsit as a remedy for non-performance of parol agreements, and for not paying money, opened up a new commercial jurisdiction in the King's Bench and represented the beginning of our modern law of contract.[9] But how are we to account for it? At present we do not really know whether the change extended new remedies to any class of persons, or whether it was simply a matter of redistributing jurisdiction. There was undoubtedly a general increase in litigation, and in the amounts of money claimed, during the sixteenth century; but, while such changes are presumably capable of socio-economic explanation, they do not of themselves explain changes in the law or in the character of the remedies provided. Some

---

[6] Y.B. Hil. 1 Hen. VII, fo. 10, pl. 10.
[7] 94 Selden Soc. *180–187*.
[8] *Ibid.*, pp. *204–206*.
[9] *Ibid.*, pp. *255–298*. The development was perhaps not confined to the King's Bench. In the Common Pleas London cases were always numerous, but the proportion of such cases seems to rise during the 16th century.

urban courts are known to have declined in our period, but it is becoming apparent that other local courts flourished and indeed expanded their business in step with the central courts. Some contract business may have passed to Westminster from the church courts: certainly the decline of *laesio fidei* can be plotted dramatically against the rise of assumpsit. There might be some perverse pleasure to be derived from linking the origins of the modern law of contract to Queen Katharine's inability to produce a son; but that possibility has been laid to rest by research which shows that the graph is illusory. The litigants, and their suits, were not of the same type.[10] Then there is the problem that some at least of the assumpsit business represented no more than a rearrangement of the remedies provided in the central courts themselves, chiefly so as to ensure compulsory jury trial and remove the risk of wager of law. As a result of these jurisdictional and procedural complications, we still lack a comprehensive picture of what was going on, and consequently a comprehensive social or economic explanation for the changes is out of the question. Nevertheless, even if such an explanation could be found, it is inherently unlikely that it would also explain the principal development in the law of tort. The action for defamatory words develops term by term alongside assumpsit,[11] and yet it can hardly have developed in response to commercial pressure or changed economic conditions. The church courts again leap to mind, but there is a similar problem in correlating the kinds of case generally found in spiritual and lay courts. Those who would interpret the common law solely by reference to economic or social theories face a severe challenge here, especially if the chronological coincidence of all the changes is to be accommodated.

A third approach, which would have the advantage of solving the chronological problem, might be to attribute all the changes to outstanding legal personalities—to individuals who took an interest (or, if we are inclined to cynicism, had an interest) in reform. Certainly many of the changes mentioned above occurred under the chief justiceship (1495–1525) of Sir John Fyneux, whose son-in-law John Rooper had a personal interest in the success of the King's Bench.[12] Judicial co-operation was of course essential in effecting the reforms in the law; and the internecine conflicts between the courts over actions on the case shows how common-law reform, and

---

[10] R. H. Helmholz, "Assumpsit and *Laesio Fidei*" (1975) 91 L.Q.R. 406. For related problems, see S. E. Thorne, "Tudor Social Transformation and Legal Change" (1951) 26 N.Y.U. Law Rev. 10. [*Essays in English Legal History*, 197.]

[11] 94 Selden Soc. *236–244*. A major study of this transition, by Professor R. H. Helmholz, is shortly to be published by the Selden Society.

[12] 94 Selden Soc. *53–57*; M. Blatcher, *The Court of King's Bench 1450–1550* (1978), pp. 7–9, 146, 149–150. *Cf.* the note of caution in E. W. Ives, *The Common Lawyers of pre-Reformation England* (Cambridge, 1983), pp. 209–216.

resistance to it, can be associated with identifiable groups of judges. Nevertheless, no one has yet dared to attribute the transformation of the common law to the vision (or avarice) of a few individual lawyers. The officials who benefited from changes in the legal system are seen rather as having reacted productively to forces outside their control.

In so far as the changes were merely jurisdictional or procedural illusions—changes of form rather than substance—the main cause was probably not social, economic or political, but intellectual. The growing influence of the inns of court and chancery—to which belonged not only learned counsel and lesser practitioners but also a good proportion of their clients—led everyone concerned to want litigation conducted by rational procedures, and according to known rules, in courts run by professionals. And in so far as the changes were substantive developments of legal principle, the form and perhaps the timing of the innovations may have been controlled by the same law schools, where abstract doctrine was discussed both before and after actual cases arose. Law schools are not indifferent to real life; but they do give law an intellectual life of its own, and their logic is sometimes stronger than pressures from the changing world outside. The logic of the common law, in particular, has rarely admitted openly to the possibility of change. Alterations in the common law therefore have to be accommodated on an intellectual level, and that is why existing doctrine inevitably controls the shape and speed of any reform. Here, by a different route, we join Maitland. It was the inns of court which answered his question—whatever it was—about English law and the Renaissance.

But the existence of the inns of court does not in itself solve the central problem of chronology. They had been teaching and discussing law since the fourteenth century, and would continue to do so until 1642. Yet fiscal feudalism, the changes in security of tenure, the new law of contract, the torts of defamation and conversion, and much more, all emerge in the same narrow period. Is it a mere coincidence that it was also the age of many other changes—the age of Reformation, of Renaissance (in England), and of revolution in natural science and the arts? If at this time there were "in the air" thoughts and feelings which transcended national boundaries, we cannot be so sure of answering our legal problem by looking merely at English circumstances and English thought. Now, Maitland told us that in the first place; but he may have overstated the danger of a Reception of Roman law in England, and he may have overstated the impact of the Reception in Europe. If the curtain inscribed "Reception" is drawn aside, it may be possible to see that the changes taking place on the Continent had more in common with those in England than has ever been thought arguable. Some

Continental legal historians have already begun to question whether what has been called the Reception can properly be viewed simply as the displacement of old local custom by the law of Justinian. There was no more a Roman Yoke in France or Germany than there had been a Reception of Norman law in England in 1066. What changed most was not the law as a body of principles, but the learned treatment of legal disputes by the doctors of law who advised and adjudicated in real cases. Courts which had been governed by laymen were replaced by courts composed of professional lawyers, who naturally used the materials available to them in their texts and glosses when arguing and deciding cases. Now, was that process any different in kind from the process whereby common lawyers took questions from the laymen on the jury (or the burgesses in the portman-moot) and argued about them in the king's courts? Their learning was not that of Rome and Bologna, but of Holborn and the Temple; yet the process of increasing sophistication is present in both systems at the same period.

The difficulties in pursuing this question are appalling because of the gulf which has existed between the work of English legal historians and that of their continental counterparts.[13] So different are their training and traditions that comparison seems virtually impossible. Civilians and canonists are taught to revere texts before judicial decisions, and their legal history is largely a study of texts, their authors and commentators, and the relationship between them. Cases are of interest only as showing how texts were used in dealing with real problems. Common lawyers, by contrast, have few texts, and work largely from the reports and records of real cases arising before the royal courts. Such texts as they have are usually assumed to reflect the jurisprudence of the courts, or else to be speculative works of doubtful scientific value. The magnitude of these differences between historians can hardly be exaggerated. But the extent to which those differences represent the historical reality of the fourteenth, fifteenth and sixteenth centuries has also been exaggerated, on both sides of the channel.

"Doctrine" in England

The lack of any institutional writer on English law between Bracton and Coke creates the initial impression of a profound gulf between English and Continental lawyers. But the existence of even one book

---

[13] An attempt is now being made to bridge this gap. Under the leadership of Professor H. Coing, and with the assistance of the Gerda Henkel Stiftung, eight working parties were established in 1982 to investigate common questions in Anglo-American and Continental legal history and to produce a series of exploratory volumes. It is hoped that publication of the series will begin in 1986.

such as the *New Tenures* by Sir Thomas Littleton (d. 1481)[14] should put us on our guard. Although Littleton chose to write in plain language in order to instruct his son, the book shows that fifteenth-century judges were capable of viewing legal rules in the abstract, of giving them an intellectual existence separate from the exigencies of the forms of action and the rules of pleading.[15] Littleton for that reason reads very differently from the year books, in which questions of principle usually arise in a very roundabout way. Yet Littleton was not an eccentric genius, ahead of his time or remote from his profession. Littleton the author is the same Littleton whose arguments appear, in garbled law French, in the year books. His book was deservedly admired, but as an essay in the exposition of abstract law it was hardly unique; it was just the most famous and successful example of an enormous and much neglected genre of doctrine found in the reports of readings and moots in the inns of court. Of hundreds of surviving texts from the 1420s to the 1670s, only a handful have been printed. We see in them, nevertheless, the same kind of analytical treatment as in the more polished phrases of Littleton, the same assumption that the common law can be expounded rationally, and a degree of legal sophistication which the year books do not prepare us for. Both the *New Tenures* and the readings reflect the same kind of learning as is glimpsed more dimly in the year books, but they are not necessarily derived from it. Littleton the author never cites a case, and the readers do so sparingly. They rely on "reason" rather than authority, on the inherent rightness of the reasoning rather than the impressiveness of the footnotes. They show lawyers thinking about the law as a coherent whole, rather than as a series of accidental and unconnected byproducts of litigation. It would be anachronistic, therefore, to treat the medieval common law as if it were purely case-law. The year books and readings, and Littleton, show us that English law was the common learning of a learned profession. The learning of that profession was centred on its law schools as much as on Westminster Hall, and we know that the academic discipline of the early-Tudor inns was as rigorous as that of any university. Their *quaestiones* and *lecturae* have almost exact parallels in the academical teaching of doctors of law, and fulfilled a similar role in shaping the *communis opinio* which our common lawyers termed "common erudition."[16] Not without reason were the inns of court and chancery called the third university of England; and we should not assume (because of

---

[14] For the date of composition of the book, and a brief bibliography, see the entry in *Biographical Dictionary of the Common Law*, ed. A. W. B. Simpson (1984), pp. 315–317.
[15] *Cf.* A. W. B. Simpson, "The Rise and Fall of the Legal Treatise" (1981) 48 Univ. Chicago Law Rev. 632, at pp. 634–635, 643–644, to the same effect.
[16] For this phrase, see 94 Selden Soc. *161*.

later history) that the medieval professors there had less influence in England than the professors of Italy and France had in their countries. It is true that the cases put in the inns sometimes had an air of academic unreality:

> How could a man become a villein every other day of his life?
> In what circumstances could a man sue his own executors?
> Could a woman justice of the peace commit her own husband?

Such hypothetical cases belonged more to the classroom than the world of practice, though any law teacher knows that his most imaginative examination questions have a habit of coming true. In our period, however, there was no separation between academical and vocational training. The Littletons and Fitzherberts who graced the bench had, after all, been lecturers in the Temple and Gray's Inn themselves. Lecturing was an indispensable qualification for the coif, and thus for the judicial bench. The notebooks of students destined for the coif—men such as John Port (d. 1540),[17] John Spelman (d. 1545)[18] and Roger Yorke (d. 1535)[19]—show clearly enough that in the time of Henry VII and Henry VIII what was said as law in the inns was as noteworthy as what was said in court.[20] Indeed, in one well-known instance—the establishment of assumpsit as a remedy for nonfeasance—the prime authority was not a case, but the dictum of a judge in Gray's Inn hall.[21]

Continental "Jurisprudence"

If, next, we look across and beyond the English Channel, we find that by 1500, Italian and French lawyers were beginning to take a considerable interest in decided cases.[22] This is not altogether surprising in countries where courts were coming under the domination of doctors of law. So long as courts were composed of laymen, and had to take advice from outside, the doctor's *consilia* obviously attracted more interest than the judicial sentence: just as in medieval

---

[17] The autograph notebook of Sir John Port came to light in 1979 and is now in the H. E. Huntington Library, San Marino, California. It contains voluminous student notes from the 1490s, but later additions include cases in the King's Bench when Port was a judge there. An edition of its principal contents is in an advanced stage of preparation.

[18] See the introduction to *The Reports of Sir John Spelman*, vol. I (1977), in Selden Society Vol. XCIII.

[19] Yorke's notebook is known from four manuscript copies, but has not yet been edited. It contains reports down to the 1530s, but is mainly devoted to Gray's Inn material. See 93 Selden Soc. xxvii; 94 Selden Soc. *137, 172.*

[20] 94 Selden Soc. *124.*

[21] *Ibid.*, pp. 269–270. The remark was made by Fyneux C.J. in 1499 "in greis Inne": Fitz. Abr., *Action sur le case,* pl. 45 (in the 1514 ed. only). The reference to the inn was omitted from later editions, and from Y.B. Mich. 21 Hen. VII, fo. 41, pl. 66, in which the passage was interpolated.

[22] See J. P. Dawson, *Oracles of the Law,* (Ann Arbor, 1968), pp. 144–145 (Italy), 218–232 (Germany), 290–339 (France); *Handbuch der Quellen und Literatur der neuren Europäischen Privatrechtsgeschichte,* ed. H. Coing, Vol. II, part 2 (Munich, 1976), pp. 1113–1445. The latter contains full bibliographies of printed reports.

England the arguments and opinions of the serjeants and judges *in banc* were more interesting to lawyers than the verdict of the jurors which settled the dispute in hand. When, however, courts were composed of doctors, their collegiate decision had at once both judicial and doctrinal force—more force than the considered opinion of a single doctor.[23] The fusion of judicial and doctoral authority produced a new and potent compound.

The first Continental reports were those produced by auditors of the papal Rota in the 1330s.[24] And of these the earliest to be printed (covering a few months in 1336-37) were the work of an English doctor of law, Thomas Fastolf,[25] who was almost certainly the brother of Serjeant Nicholas Fastolf. It is doubtlesss a mere coincidence that one of the earliest reporters at Avignon[26] was closely related to a serjeant whose name appears in the year books of Edward II; but nevertheless, like those English reports, the *decisiones rotae* contain the arguments and opinions of named lawyers in actual cases. They proved to be very influential. The first instance of direct imitation occurs with the *Distinctiones capellae* collected by Jean Corsier in the 1390s as official of the archbishopric of Toulouse.[27] And the first temporal imitation was the work of Guy Pape, a councillor of the *parlement* of Dauphiné from 1444 to 1487. Pape collected decisions throughout his judicial career, and the result was printed in Grenoble in 1490. He says he followed the form of the decisions of the Rota, and that his purpose had been to record doubtful cases which had been resolved by advisement, together with practice cases, for future reference by judges and practitioners.[28] Pape's work at Grenoble was continued by François Marc from 1502 to 1508, and in Marc's reports more of the facts of the cases are

---

[23] G. Ermini, "Giurisprudenza della Rota Romana come fattore costitivo delle jus commune" in *Studi in Onore di Francesco Scaduto* (Florence, 1936), Vol. I, pp. 283-298, who cites Gomes (1557) to the effect that opinions of the Rota were held *communis* "non solum propter eius authoritatem, sed etiam propter numerum doctorum in ea militantium."

[24] For a full survey see A. Fliniaux, "Les anciennes collections de Decisiones Rotae" (1925) 4 R.H.D. (4th ser.) 61-93, 382-410; G. Dolezalek and K. W. Nörr, "Die Rechtsprechungssammlungen der mittelalterlichen Rota" in Coing, *op. cit.* in n. 22, Vol. I, pp. 849-856.

[25] The *decisiones* of "Falstoli" were first printed in *Decisiones sive conclusiones antique dominorum de Rota* (Rome, 1475), ff. 263-274v. Two manuscripts have been discovered. The compiler has been identified as Thomas Fastolf (d. 1361), an auditor of the Rota in the 1330s and 1340s, who became bishop of St. David's in 1352. In a paper delivered to the 7th International Congress of Medieval Canon Law, at Cambridge, on 23 July 1984, the writer argued that Fastolf belonged to the circle of East Anglian lawyers associated with William Bateman (d. 1355), founder of Trinity Hall.

[26] The only known contender for primacy of place is William Bateman himself. See G. Dolezalek, "Quaestiones motae in Rota: Richterliche Beratungsnotizen aus dem vierzehnten Jahrhundert" in *Proceedings of the Fifth International Congress of Medieval Canon Law*, ed. S. Kuttner and K. Pennington (Vatican, 1980), pp. 99-114.

[27] *Decisiones capelle sedis archiepiscopalis Tholose* (Lyon 1508), printed with additions by Dr. Étienne D'Aufrère. The author is identifiable from the preface.

[28] Guido Papa, *Decisiones Grationopolitane* (1490). Pape mentions actual cases in only 20 per cent. of the "decisions": Dawson, *Oracles of the Law*, p. 299.

given.[29] Meanwhile, reporting had reached Italy; and it is the reports from the kingdom of Naples which provide the most striking comparison with English law reports. The Sacro Regio Consiglio was erected in Naples in the 1440s by King Alfonso I of Aragon, and is thought to have been modelled in part on the papal Rota. There was a flourishing law faculty at Naples, and the Consiglio was from the start dominated by doctors of law. The first printed collection of its decisions was compiled by Matteo d'Afflitto (1448–1528), a councillor in the 1490s.[30] D'Afflitto gives the facts of each case in detail before arraying the conflicting authorities and arguments, often distinguishing the views of individual councillors. The *dubia* which the royal council were asked to settle were differences between the old doctors in the texts and glosses; but the new doctors relied also on decisions of the Rota and of the council itself. Previous decisions were not binding but were usually followed. There was a mixture of reasons for this. First, there was the personal authority of the doctors themselves—and that is why their names, sometimes with an appraisal of their qualities, are given in the reports.[31] Then there was the feeling that matters which had been several times adjudged in one way ought to be treated as settled, for the sake of consistency.[32] And to these factual reasons for respecting decisions was soon added a legal concept. When the court was a superior court of last resort, such as a royal council or parliament, it exercised sovereign power and its decisions were equivalent to imperial rescripts or papal decretals. It was therefore said by Neapolitan lawyers that the royal council exercised the king's authority—*Sacrum Consilium repraesentat perso-*

---

[29] *Nove decisiones supreme curie Parlamenti Delphina. Per magnificum quondam dominum Franciscum Marcum* (Grenoble, 1532).

[30] Matthaeus de Afflictis, *Decisiones Neapolitane* (Naples, 1508). D'Afflitto was followed in Naples by Antonio Capece (d. 1545), Gian Tommaso Minadoi (d. 1555) and Tommaso Grammatico (d. 1556), all of them lords of the Sacro Regio Consiglio. The Neapolitan reporters were greatly respected elsewhere in Europe. The writer has a collected edition of D'Afflitto, Capece and Grammatico printed in Lyon in 1566.

[31] D'Afflitto treated with respect the decisions of certain councillors, such as Antonio di Gennaro, Giovanni Antonio Palmieri and Carlo di Ruggiero, and was particularly respectful towards Antonio d'Alessandro (d. 1499), the vice-prothonotary, "doctissimus iurisconsultus . . . qui me ob suas virtutes nimia charitate dilexit, et me coram nostris superioribus extollebat, qui multum ingenium meum erudivit, et ab eo multa docui, cuius anima requiescat cum sanctis angelis et praesentiam Dei videat" (dec. 257). But he was not afraid to dissent even from his master: *e.g.*, dec. 195 ("Dicebat dominus Antonius de Alexandro viceprotonotarius . . . Ego autem et dominus Marcellus de Gaieta et quidam alii consiliarii dicebamus contrarium . . . Dicebat dominus Antonius . . . tamen ego et dominus Marcellus et dominus Carolus de Rogeriis et dominus Iacobus de Gello dicebamus . . ."), dec. 263 ("Dicebat dominus Antonius de Alexandro, et tres domini vel quatuor secuti sunt eum, . . . sed ego dicebam . . . Et ideo ego fui in voto contrario solus . . . Tamen salubrior est mea opinio").

[32] See, *e.g.*, dec. 383, §6–8 ("Domini de consilio dixerunt quod semper fuit observatum tam in Magna Curia Vicariae quam in Sacro Consilio quod . . . Et ego alias audivi a doctoribus antiquis Sacri Consilii quod ita per eos fuit observatum, et illi dicebant quod ita ab aliis doctoribus fuit observatum et iudicatum. Et ita affirmaverunt omnes domini de Consilio seniores . . . Et ego etiam vidi sic pluries fuisse iudicatum in Magna Curia Vicariae et in Sacro Consilio. Ideo minime sunt mutanda quae antiquam interpretationem habuerunt . . . et maxime quando sic iudicatum fuit per Consilium, ubi semper sunt aliqui doctores valentissimi in iure . . .").

nam regiam[33]—and consequently its decision had the force of law—*nova decisio Sacri Consilii habet vim legis, et sic facit jus.*[34] It was doubtless a similar sentiment which had stirred reporters at Avignon and Paris in the fourteenth century. Indeed, the principal Parisian reporter said as much: *curia parlamenti repraesentat regem.*[35]

After 1500, *decisiones* were published in profusion across Europe: at first in Italy and France, though reporting soon began to spread northwards to Germany and even Scotland—where the Reichskammergericht (1495) and the Court of Session (1532) provided the necessary central conciliar tribunals. In the low countries, reports were not printed until the seventeenth century; but manuscript evidence shows that case-notes were being taken as early as the 1530s in the Grand Conseil de Malines.[36] It appears, moreover, from the writings of Nicolas Everaerts (1462–1532) that decisions of such supreme courts were thought to have greater authority than *communis opinio*, and could be likened to imperial decrees.[37]

At this point we may recall Maitland's dictum that the Star Chamber could have done for England the Romanising which the Reichskammergericht did for Germany and which the Court of Session seemed to have done for Scotland.[38] But "Romanising" was only one aspect—maybe only a side-effect—of the Renaissance legal revolution. The effect of entrusting sovereign judicial power to learned tribunals was not merely to import Roman procedures and scholarship, but to give the decisions of such tribunals the force of law and thus to create a new kind of legal authority.

BACK TO ENGLAND

The development of Continental jurisprudence in newly established

---

[33] D'Afflitto, dec. 149, §6. *Cf.* Grammatico, dec. 76, §34 ("*Et ideo, omnibus pro et contra bene ruminatis per Sacrum Consilium, solitum et consuetum iudicare nedum per iuris tramites sed etiam secundum veritatem et equitatem naturalem: cum habeat supremam iurisdictionem et principem ipsum repraesentat*," citing Baldus). The reference to conciliar equity suggests an obvious English parallel.

[34] D'Afflitto, dec. 169, §9 ("... *ista est nova decisio Sacri Consilii, quae habet vim legis, et sic facit ius*," citing Baldus, Alessandro, "Abbas" and Andrea d'Isernia). *Cf.* dec. 190, §7 ("*Et in hoc versatur aequitas Sacri Consilii. Et ita sub nomine regio fuit sententiatum.* . . . *Haec sic notavi in specie, quia iste articulus erat dubius et nunc est decisus per sententiam regis cum Consilio, quae facit ius universale in regno*"); dec. 383, §8 ("*doctores valentissimi in iure, quorum sententiae . . . quia proferuntur sub nomine regiae maiestatis habent vim generalis legis in regno*," citing Baldus, Hostiensis and Butrio).

[35] *Quaestiones Iohannis Galli*, ed. M. Boulet (Paris, 1944), p. lxx. and qu. 18. (These reports by Jean le Coq, king's advocate, are the only Continental reports to have been edited together with the corresponding records.) A contemporary of le Coq (cited *ibid.*,p. lix, n.9) said that the decisions of the Burgundian council "*sont dictes coustumes approuvés qui valent lois et emportent force lois en Bourgoingne*".

[36] P. Godding, "L'origine et l'authorité des recueils de jurisprudence dans les Pays-Bas méridionaux (13ᵉ–18ᵉ siècles)" in *Rapports belges au 8ᵉ congrès international de droit comparé* (1970), pp. 1–37, at 15–16.

[37] *Ibid.*, pp. 29–30.

[38] *English Law and the Renaissance*, pp. 19–20.

papal and royal courts may, in an unexpected way, help to illuminate what was happening in England. The most obvious parallels with the Continental *decisiones,* written by royal councillors over the course of a professional lifetime, were the reports by Edmund Plowden (1518–85) and Sir Edward Coke (1552–1634), and to a lesser extent their predecessors John Caryll (d. 1523), Sir John Spelman (d. 1545) and Sir James Dyer (1512–82): the work, in each case, of a learned lawyer's lifetime, compilations of cases selected to illustrate points of law settled by the central courts. Plowden in particular stands apart from the year-book tradition[39] in the way he chose cases for their decisiveness. In contrast, the year books were not first and foremost books of judicial decisions. The judicial indecision was often more interesting to the reporter; and in any case the books served primarily as guides to the science and technique of pleading, illustrating what should be done in court as much as elucidating legal principles. The reason is not that the reports were defective, or that the reporters were inattentive to what was happening, but that contemporaries did not see what we would look for. Courts were simply not perceived as having a strong decision-making role. This does not mean that medieval decisions were less binding than Tudor or Victorian decisions. Rather that the judges were very much less inclined to reach decisions at all if the law was unclear. Perhaps because of the fear that a wrong decision *would* be binding, no decision would be reached in a case of balanced merits. We nowadays give a single judge the power—nay the duty—to decide cases entirely by himself, subject to appeal; and even in the Court of Appeal a majority of two can bind over one hundred brethren, subject always to the House of Lords (where three against two can bind the entire English judiciary). A medieval judge, on the other hand, had no more individual authority to declare the law than an individual serjeant, or a reader lecturing in the Temple. Certainly he had no authority to question what the profession in general thought the law to be; and whether he was sitting on the bench or at the dinner table would have been considered an irrelevant circumstance. Common erudition did not emanate from the judges alone: it was inherited wisdom, refined in the inns of court as well as in Westminster Hall, accepted by virtue of its inherent rightness rather than because a court had declared it to be right. A full court could give expression to common learning; but the court was not the same as the judge. It was a corporate body, with a common seal, and spoke in the records with one voice. It was its own

---

[39] From this tradition may be partly excepted the year books of 12–14 Hen. VIII, in which most of the cases were of the decisive category; but the records were not printed, and the texts (which were obviously not prepared for the press by their unknown author) are unpolished and defective. The writer has prepared an edition of these books, together with the relevant records.

court of appeal before judgment, because its judgments (if formally correct) were final. Every opportunity for exploring doubts was therefore given before judgment was entered. If the judges of one bench had doubts, they could consult the other bench across the hall. If the doubts persisted, they might adjourn for a confabulation in Serjeants' Inn or a full-scale public moot in the Exchequer Chamber. If, after all that, they still had qualms—they did nothing. Judicial inaction was not seen as a dereliction of duty, as it would be today, because it encouraged and helped parties to settle their differences when the merits were balanced. That is by no means less wise or fair than our system, under which—even if the law is doubtful at the outset—the winner takes all. But it was a necessary assumption of the medieval system that men could and should live within a framework of relatively simple law. The judge's role can conveniently be likened in the modern world to that of a football referee, though a medieval judge would have found the comparison with idle sport most *inconvenient*. There is no great body of referee-jurisprudence continually refining the laws of the game, perhaps because teams are not represented on the field by counsel, but more likely because the ethics of sport demand clear rules which layman can grasp and which cannot easily be bent. (For the same reason, no doubt, there is no equity jurisdiction in sport.) The medieval attitude to litigation was not dissimilar. The parties were the contestants, and so long as they adhered strictly to the rules—which everyone knew—they were left to play the game unimpeded. No one looked to litigation as a means of creating or refining legal rules, any more than one watches chess matches in the hope that new or more sophisticated rules of chess will emerge. The law of the land, like the laws of chess, was there to begin with.

JUDICIAL DECISION-MAKING

The biggest changes in English law during the Renaissance period were perhaps not in the details of doctrine but in the procedures which enabled the law to become more detailed. They can be attributed to a greater willingness on the part of royal courts (including Parliament) to decide points of law which had not been settled or raised before, and a corresponding tendency to employ procedures which encouraged them to do so. Some of the changes were simply shifts of jurisdiction to and between the central courts, and these can be paralleled by the growth of royal conciliar courts on the Continent. Others were the result of removing questions from juries and placing them as points of law before the court, in the expectation that the court would decide them. Here the parallel, though less obvious, is with the changes which brought doubts before courts of doctors instead of lay judges.

In point of detail the English story could not be more different from Continental legal history. But in the shift of emphasis from *doctrine* (or common learning) to *jurisprudence* (or judge-made law) the similarity is striking. On the Continent the change is marked by the increasing publication of *decisiones*, and in England—where law reporting had passed through an earlier stage—by the greater decisiveness of reports such as Plowden's and Coke's. It is also reflected in the English textbooks. Littleton relied on reason and common learning, and disdained to cite precedents.[40] Sir William Staundford (1509–58), holding the same judicial office as Littleton less than a century later,[41] wrote books so crammed with references and quotations that he seemed incapable of venturing an opinion unless it could be derived from someone else. In that sense Staundford was the first modern legal textbook writer. His works belong to our world, Littleton's to the world we have lost.

The shift is further reflected in England in the rise of judicial majority-rule. Maitland once said that one of the world's great books which had still to be written was "The History of the Majority."[42] He was thinking primarily of corporations and political institutions, and much of the material for such a book has been amassed since Maitland wrote. But the history of the judicial majority needs also to be written. Although the English Parliament and royal council, and its Continental counterparts, seem always to have followed the majority principle,[43] it was much less acceptable in the courts of common law before the sixteenth century. It had been ruled out for juries in the fourteenth century.[44] And, although we occasionally hear of judgments being entered without judicial unanimity, the

[40] The few citations in the printed text are all interpolations. Littleton did, on the other hand, regard the general opinion of the readers in the inns of court as authority (see s.481). Coke, commenting on s.481, felt obliged to remark that the position had changed since the 15th century: "new readings have not that honour, for that they are so obscure and dark" (Co.Litt. 280b).
[41] Both were justices of the Common Pleas: Littleton from 1466 to 1481, Staundford from 1554 to 1558. Staundford saw *Les plees del coron* published in 1557. His *An exposition of the kinges prerogative* was published posthumously in 1567.
[42] *Township and Borough* (Cambridge, 1898), p. 34.
[43] For Parliament, see N. Pronay and J. Taylor, *Parliamentary Texts of the late Middle Ages* (Oxford, 1980), pp. 74, 87, 107; Y.B. Mich. 15 Edw. IV, fo. 2. pl. 2, *per* Littleton J. In the 15th-century council the problem seems rather to have been that of ensuring that the majority prevailed over a powerful minority: *Rot. Parl.*, Vol. IV, p. 201, no. 17, para. [4]; p. 343, no. 27, para. 13. The first case in D'Afflitto contained a full discussion in 1496 of whether the president of the council could pass sentence according to a minority opinion if the minority seemed more learned; it was held that he should not, though there were precedents for so doing. This was the familiar conundrum of whether the *sanior pars* (or *valentior pars*) was preferable to a numerical majority: the majoritarian principle was itself taken for granted.
[44] Y.B. Mich. 41 Edw. III, fo. 31, pl. 36.

usual consequence of disagreement was adjournment.[45] There may have been a distinction between different types of case; but certainly where parties demurred on a point of law the usual outcome before the sixteenth century was an indecision.[46] By the end of that century, however, it was not at all uncommon for judgment to be given (even on demurrer) by a majority of those present, whether or not they were an absolute majority of the whole court. Thus, in a case of 1593, where the four[47] judges of the King's Bench were evenly divided, we are told that judgment was withheld until one day when Popham C.J. was absent and the two who disagreed with him seized their opportunity.[48] Moreover, in the case of proceedings in error, a bare majority in the court of error could prevail over the majority of the judges of England. This possibility seems to have attracted no comment in earlier times, because it was unthinkable; but by the early seventeenth century it had come to pass, albeit to the consternation of some contemporaries. In this apparent change in the philosophy of judicial lawmaking—the details of which have still to be traced—we may perceive a further indication of the shift from common learning, or professional consensus, towards a more positive view of authority.

This brings us, finally, back to the reports. The reason why Plowden is so different from the typical year book is not merely that he was the first reporter to revise his own proofs, though that was itself a major improvement. It is that he deliberately refrained from reporting inconclusive or extempore discussions, and published only the set-piece debates resulting from formal demurrers, special verdicts, writs of error and motions *in banc* after trial: cases where a point of law had been settled by a final judgment of record. His method, he announced, led to "most firmeness and suretie of law."[49] There was nothing new in the kind of case selected by Plowden. What was new was the assumption that it was the only kind of case worth reporting. There was, moreover, an increase in that kind of case during the early Tudor period. In the seven years from 1517 to 1523 the Common Pleas rolls record seventy-seven demurrers, of which twenty-five were successful, ten unsuccessful and fifty-two undecided.[50] Despite the high proportion of undecided cases, a

---

[45] For the importance of securing unanimity (at least in public) in a controversial case, see *Lord Dacre's Case* (1535) in 93 Selden Soc. 228–230; 94 Selden Soc. *140, 201.*
[46] What follows is discussed in more detail above, pp. 166-169.
[47] The fact that four was commonly the number of judges in each bench tells its own story about the attitude to majorities.
[48] *Bartlett* v. *Wright* (1593) Cro.Eliz. 300, pl. 12, *ad finem.*
[49] *Les Comentaries* (1571), prologue, sig. B; 94 Selden Soc. *155.*
[50] This figure is based on a study of the plea rolls, CP 40/1017–1041. No earlier figures are yet available. Professor M. S. Arnold has estimated that about one-third of 14th century demurrers were decided; but the proportion may have dropped in the 15th century.

decision-rate of 45 per cent. exceeds anything that might have been expected in the fifteenth century. Moreover, ten of the twenty-five successful demurrers attracted the notice of law reporters, whereas only eight of the fifty-two undecided cases were reported: decisions were becoming more memorable than indecisions. Also developed during the same period were motions in arrest of judgment—not always visible in the records, but productive of important legal decisions about the scope of actions on the case.[51] And in the middle of the century special verdicts were revived and extended in scope,[52] so that still more new questions could be posed for the courts. No figures are available, but the reports indicate a noticeable increase in the use of all these devices in Elizabethan times.[53]

These procedural changes suggest that litigants, as advised by their lawyers, did not merely want their disputes settled: they wanted them settled with reasons, and they wanted the judges to elaborate the law. That process resembles in its essential characteristics the reception of learned law on the Continent. In so far as that was a reception of the techniques and reasoning processes of the doctors of law, rather than of ancient Roman principles as such, we may say that England also had a reception: but it was a reception of Inns of Court Law. What brought about this seemingly universal desire for more detailed law, and for greater judicial authority in making it, may have something to do with Renaissance humanism, at any rate with the applied humanism of the legal profession: but this is too large and difficult a question to resolve at present.[54]

Whatever the causes of the supranational movement or tendency which has been tentatively identified above, they obviously will not explain the detailed course of change in each country, any more than a study of the *Corpus Juris* or its glosses will explain why German law was different from French or Italian law. Particular changes in municipal law have to be explained, as in the past, by a combination of different social, political and economic causes; by the inexorable processes of legal reasoning, the unexpected successes of forensic ingenuity, and even now and then by mistakes and accidents of fate. On the broader plane, however, Maitland's difficulty may at last have disappeared. England was sailing with the jurisprudential tide, not against it; and the tough law of the inns of court, however impervious to Roman influence, was indeed susceptible to new ways of thinking about the legal process and the jurisprudence of the courts.

---

[51] 94 Selden Soc. *157–159*.   [52] *Ibid.*, pp. *114, 158.*
[53] For examples of the use of all these devices in exploring the doctrine of consideration between the 1560s and 1580s, see above, p. 370.
[54] It may be that "humanism" itself should be traced to the new spirit of enquiry among lawyers: see D. R. Kelley, *Foundations of Modern Historical Scholarship* (New York, 1970).

INDEX OF NAMES

Abbot, Charles, Lord Tenterden, 318, 327
Abdy, Prof., 26, 184
Adderly, –, prothonotary, 255, 256
Afflitto, Matteo d', 470-1, 474 n. 43
Aldeburgh, Richard de, 173
Alessandro, Antonio d', 470 n. 31
Alfonso I, king of Aragon, 470
Amsterdam, Holland, 365 n. 92
Anderson, Edmund, 194, 402, 420, 427, 429
Antwerp, Flanders, 354 n. 54, 358
Apsley, Michael, 212-13
Archer, John, 456
Argentré (Argentrius), Bertrand d', 236
Arnisoeus, Henning, 240
Arnold, M.S., 4
Ash, Joseph, 254
Ashfield, John, 338
Ashley, Francis, 294
Atkins, Thomas, 91 n. 60
Audley, Thomas, 79, 80, 445
Avignon, papal court at, 469
Ayloffe, William, 382
Ayrault (Erodius), Pierre, 236

Babham, John, 108 n. 60
Babington, William, 15
Babington, Zachary, 283
Bacon, Francis (d. 1626), Viscount St Alban's, 235, 289, 454-5
–, argument in Slade's Case, 395, 396, 401-2, 402-8, 421
–, chancellorship, 226-7, 453
–, reading, 34, 445
–, relations with Coke and Egerton, 205 ff.
Bacon, Francis (d. 1657), 35
Bacon, Francis (fl. 1662), 36
Bacon, Nicholas, 52
Baker, David, 130 n. 25
Baker, John, 90
Balaam's ass, 105
Baldock, Robert, 37
Baldwin, John, 31
Bale, John, 235
Bannister, Saxe, 455
Barnard, Richard, 256
Barnard's Inn, 56 n. 33, 58, 61 n. 53, 62
Barons, Peter, 21 n. 53
Basset, Richard, 96 n. 84
Bateman, William, 469 n. 25
Battandier, Claude de, 236

Baudouin (Balduinus), François, 236
Beaumont, Francis, 427
Beaumont, Henry, 388, 389 n. 70
Bede, 235
Beka, Jean de, 236
Belbin, Anthony, 256
Belton, Leices, church, 444
Bendlowes, William, 181, 185, 187, 446
Benn (Ben, Benne), Anthony, 219, 337
Bérault, Josia, 236
Berkeley, William, earl of Nottingham, 92
Blackstone, William, 37, 122, 264, 267, 270-1, 284, 297-8
Blagge, Robert, 83
Blanchard, Henry, 445
Boccalini, Traiano, 240
Bolton, Richard, 82 n. 23
Bouchel (Bochellus), Laurent, 236
Boulenger (Bulenger), Jules-César, 236
Bourchier, John, Lord Fitzwaren, 92
Bowen, Catherine D., 204
Boys, John, 32
Bracton, 402
Bradshaw, John, 199
Bramston, John, 121, 210, 239
Braunscombe, –, 14
Bray, John, 338
Brecknock, recorder of, 32
Bree, Alice and William, 17
Bretton, –, 14
Brewode, John, 31
Bridgman, John, 120, 188
Bridgman, Orlando, 455
Bridgwater, Som, prior of, 93
Bright, Timothy, 452
Brighton, Sussex, pier, 154
Britanny, customs of, 236 n. 40
Brograve, John, 33, 445
Broke, Richard, 112 n. 88
Brooke, David, 72 n. 94
Broughton, Richard, 131-2
Broune, William, 27 n. 11
Browker, Hugh, 256
Brownlow, Richard, 142, 250, 252, 255, 444
Bruce, John, 179
Brugge, Thomas, 31
Bruneau (Brunellus), Jean, 237
Bryan, Thomas, 33
Bryncheley, William, 3

478 The Legal Profession and the Common Law

Brystall, Robert, 82 n. 23
Buc, George, 7
Buckhurst, Lord, *see* Sackville
Buckingham, duke of, *see* Stafford; Villiers
Budé (Budaeus), Guillaume, 236
Bulstrode, Edward, 441, 442
Burghley, Lord, *see* Cecil
Burgundy, customs of, 236 n. 48
Burman (Booreman), Thomas, 66 n. 74
Burnet, Thomas, 457
Burton, Andrew, 135
Bury St Edmund's, Suff, monastery, 104
Bury, Thomas, 457

Caesar, Julius, dictator of Rome, 237
Caesar, Julius (d. 1636), 223 n. 25
Callis, Robert, 34
Calthorpe, Henry, 334, 339
Camden, William, 235, 237, 239
Capell, Edward, 21 n. 53
Cary, Richard, 193
Cambridge, Cambs, assizes, 289 n. 130, 328 n. 14
Cambridge university, 8, 9, 177
–, colleges: Catharine Hall, 48; Clare Hall, 49; Gonville Hall, 49; King's, 48, 55; Magdalene, 213-5; Queens', 48; Sidney Sussex, 234; Trinity Hall, 49, 52
–, law faculty, 469 n. 25
–, proctors, 49
Caryll, John (d. 1523), 96, 312, 399, 447, 472
Caryll, John (d. 1566), 322
Cassanaeus, *see* Chasseneux
Cassy, John, 3, 5 n. 10
Catte, John, 62
Caxton, William, 75
Cecil, William, Lord Burghley, 263
Chaloner, John, 32
Chamberlayne, Edward, 68
Charles I, king of England, 196, 309, 455
Charles II, king of England, 51
Chasseneux (Cassanaeus), Barthélemi de, 236
Chaucer, Geoffrey, 6, 30, 100, 102, 235
Cherletoun, Robert de, 4
Cheseman, Edward, 82
Cheshire, attorneys in, 145
Chesshyre, John, 457
Cheyne, John, 108 n. 60
Chichester, see of, 58
Chichester, Ralph of, 235
Chokier, Jean a, 237
Cholmeley, Randle, 72 n. 94
Cholmeley, Roger, 59 n. 45
Chopin, René, 236

Christian, Edward, 346
Clamenges, Mathieu Nicolas de, 235
Clare, earl of, *see* Holles
Clay, Edmund de, 4 n. 5
Clayton, John, 441
Clement's Inn, 11, 18-19, 57, 68 n. 83, 73, 83 n. 25, 111
Clench, John, 316 n. 45, 327
Clerke, Robert, 428
Clerkenwell, Midd, Hicks Hall in, 278
Clifford, Henry, Lord Clifford, 57
Clifford's Inn, 4, 11, 18, 56, 57, 67, 77 n. 8, 117 n. 19
Cockburn, J.S., 306
Codin, George, 235
Coke, Edward, 196-8, 202-3, 435, 442
–, on Chancery, 205-29, 438
–, on consideration, 384, 389
–, on counsel for felony, 286-7
–, on courts, 161-3, 169
–, on judges, 119, 206-7
–, on legal profession, 7, 88, 113
–, on lex mercatoria, 362
–, on readings, 35, 37, 445
–, on year books, 443
–, Slade's Case, 393 ff., 408, 409 ff., 421 ff., 438
–, writings: Entries, 193-4; Institutes, 195-8, 234; Points dangerous et absurd, 210 n. 34; reading, 445; reports, 177-204, 393-5, 441, 454, 458, 472, 474
Coke, Robert, 197, 198
Coke, Roger, 197
Coke, Thomas, 25 n. 3
Coke, William, 22, 446 n. 33
Cold Mart, 355
Coleridge, Samuel Taylor, 123
Colles, Nicholas, 88 n. 45
Colyns, John, 87 n. 43
Coningsby, Humfrey, 86
Constable, Robert, 96
Cooke, George, 251
Cooke, John, of Gray's Inn, 35
Cooke, John, of Inner Temple, 255, 256
Coppin, George, 224
Copwode, John, 83
Coras, Jean de, 236
Corsier, Jean, 469
Cory, Thomas, 245, 246 nn. 1 & 3, 249 n. 1, 250-1, 252, 255, 456
Cotton, Robert, 234, 459
Cotton, Thomas, 241
Courtney, Francis, 211-12, 216-18
Coventry, Warw, mayor's court, 372
Coventry, Thomas, 57, 227-8, 329, 331-3

Index of Names

Cowell (Couel), John, 235, 240, 362
Cressingham (Great), Norf, 86
Cresswell, Cresswell, 457
Crofton, William, 50 n. 16, 110 n. 71
Croke, George, 213, 442-3, 450 n. 78, 451
Croke, John, 217, 447
Crompton, Richard, 312, 313, 322, 328
Crompton, Thomas, 256
Cromwell, Thomas, 308
Crosby, William, 3
Crowche, William, 86
Crowcombe, Som, 232-3
Cujas, Jacques, 236

Dacre, Thomas, Lord, 92
Dallison, William, 187, 315-6, 327, 449-50
Dalton, John, 27 n. 11
Dalton, Michael, 312, 313, 322, 328
Daly, –, 457
Danzig, 351
Dauphiné, parlement of, 236 n. 56, 469
Davenport, Humfrey, 455
Davies, John, 119, 361-2
De Afflictis, *see* Afflitto
Dean, Glouces, forest of, 234
Deerhurst, Glouces, 5 n. 10
Delves, John de, 14
Denbigh lordship, lead mines, 320 n. 59
Denison, Thomas, 457
Denman, Thomas, Lord Denman, 327 n. 10-12, 457
Denys, Thomas, 17
Derby, Derbs, assizes, 312, 322
Derby, earl of, *see* Stanley
Devereux, Robert, earl of Essex, 201
Devon, litigious county, 85 n. 39
Didlington, Norf, 307
Dillon, Peter, 33
Dodderidge, John, 51, 214 n. 58, 215, 227, 239, 241, 395 ff., 401, 402 n. 51, 404 n. 65, 405 n. 69, 407 n. 80, 421 ff., 435, 454
Drake, Francis, 202
Dublin, Ireland, 365 n. 92
Duck, Nicholas, 414 n. 20
Dudley (Dodeley), Edmund, 22 n. 58, 31-2, 33, 353
Dugdale, William
Dunham, W.H., 12
Dunkirk, France, 365 n. 92
Durham, bishop of, 277
Dyer, James, 113, 138, 312, 377, 385 n. 56, 387, 429
–, reading, 445
–, reports, 187, 193 n. 81, 441, 442, 446, 448-9, 472

448-9, 472
Dykes, Alexander, 62

East, Edward Hyde, 318, 327 nn. 10 & 12
Eden, William, Lord Auckland, 299
Edgar, Thomas, 36
Edward I, king of England, 423, 435
Effingham, Lord, *see* Howard
Egerton, Thomas, Lord Ellesmere, Viscount Brackley, 113, 119, 141-3, 185, 425, 435, 438, 440
–, 'bane of the law', 210
–, chancellorship, 209-11, 218 n. 88, 223-4
–, Coke and, 201, 205-29
–, illness, 218
–, library, 458
–, reading, 446
–, retirement, 224-5
Egypt, grasshoppers of, 142
Eldon, Lord, *see* Scott
Elizabeth I, queen of England, 51, 202-3
Ellesmere, Lord, *see* Egerton
Ellis, William, 36, 452
Ely, see of, 53, 277
Elyot, Richard, 111, 448
Elyot, Thomas, 23
Empson, Richard, 103
Erneley, John, 80, 96 n. 84
Erskine, Thomas, 311
Essex, earl of, *see* Devereux
Estcourt, Edmund, 445
Estoft, [?John], 322
Everaerts, Nicolas, 471
Ewens, Matthew, 428
Exeter, Devon, 420, 421 n. 63
Eyre, William, 86

Fabri, Jean-Rodolphe, 235
Fairechild, John, 92 n. 63
Falkland Islands, 297 n. 174
Farmer, George, 252, 253, 256
Fastolf, Nicholas and Thomas, 469
Fawkes (Faux), Guy, 202
Felton, John, 294
Fenner, Edward, 140, 417, 420, 446
Fermour, William, 83
Finch, Heneage (d. 1631), 338, 339
Finch, Heneage (d. 1682), earl of Nottingham, 55, 247, 455
Finch, John, 118, 252-3
Fitzherbert, Anthony, 22, 32, 96-7, 168, 312, 314
Fitzjames, John, 399
Fitz John, moot called, 25
Fitzwaren, *see* Bourchier

Flanders, money of, 355, 357-8
Fleming, Thomas, 210, 262
Fletewoode, William, 376, 378
Forcadel (Forcatulus), Étienne, 236
Forde, Rhys, 131
Fortescue, John, 3, 7, 45, 66, 78, 88, 93-4, 96, 98, 100, 102, 267, 388
Foster, Michael, 319-20, 328
France, 236, 469
Franchis, Vincent de, 236
Frice, John, 17
Frowyk, Thomas, 389, 398, 399, 403
Fuller, Nicholas, 455
Furnival's Inn, 16, 17, 19 n. 42, 56, 62, 64, 65, 67, 92, 94
Fyncham, –, 14
Fyneux, John, 33, 84 n. 32, 312, 379 n. 42, 464, 468 n. 21
Fyssher, William, 87 n. 42

Gaill, Andreas von, 236
Gardiner, Edward, 320-1
Gardiner, Robert, 445
Gardiner, Thomas, 454
Garnet, Henry, 202
Gascoigne, William, 3, 5
Gawdy, Francis, 251
Gawdy, Thomas (d. 1588), 381, 382, 383 n. 46
Gell, Anthony, 312, 322, 379, 381, 388 n. 68
Gentili, Alberico, 237
George I, king of Great Britain, 183
Germany, 236, 471
Germoni, Anastasio, 237
Germyn, –, attorney, 138
Gilbert, Ambrose, 445
Girard, Bernard de, sieur de Haillan, 240
Glantham, Thomas, 87 n. 42
Glanvill, John (d. 1600), 427
Glanvill, John (d. 1661), 233
Glanvill, Richard, 211-12, 216-18
Glynn, John, 253
Godbold, John, 36
Godefroy (Gothofredus), Denis, 236
Googe, Barnaby, 214-15
Gore, John, 337
Gorhambury, Herts, 442
Gorphyn, Walter, 92
Göteborg (Gothenburg), 365 n. 92
Gouldsborough, John, 250, 256
Gower, John, 30, 174-5
Graham, Howard J., 440, 441
Gray's Inn, 3, 5, 7, 50 n. 15, 63, 94
–, carols, 29

–, 'college', 50 n. 16, 56
–, constitution, 64, 69, 71
–, extraparochial, 61 n. 53
–, library, 72 n. 94
–, moots, 19, 20, 21, 22, 25, 446
–, readings, 31 ff.
–, title, 58
Greene, John, 134 n. 43
Grenoble, Dauphiné, 469
Grey, Susan, countess of Kent, 138
Grimstone, Harbottle, 442-3
Grinstead (East), Sussex, 321
Grotius, Hugo, 233 n. 17, 235, 237
Guevara, Antonio de, 240
Gulston, John, 246 n. 2, 253 nn. 1-2, 256
Gundry, Nathaniel, 457

Hadley, James, 96 n. 84
Hakewill, William, 219, 240
Hale, Matthew, 199, 436, 438, 439
–, on criminal law, 264, 271, 284, 290, 291, 296, 299, 307, 313, 316, 328
–, on mercantile law, 360, 362, 363-4
Hales, Alys and Christopher, 22
Hales, James, 32
Halifax, Yorks, 268 n. 41
Halle, Edward, 32
Halsequell, Nicholas, 135 n. 46
Hamilton (Hambleton), James, marquess Hamilton, 252
Hampton Bishop, Heref, 379
Hankeforde, William, 3
Hardres, Thomas, 36, 452
Hardwicke, Lord, see Yorke, Philip
Hare, Hugh, 445
Harewood, Yorks, 5 n. 10
Hargrave, Francis, 459
Harley, Robert, earl of Oxford, 180-1
Harman, Henry, 83
Harpur, Richard, 449-50
Harvey, Francis, 147
Harvie, John, 27 n. 11
Hatton, Christopher, 114
Haverhill, Suff, 97 n. 87
Hawkins, William, 284, 290, 310
Heath, Edward, 452
Heath, Robert, 252
Heed, William, 81 n. 19
Heigham, Clement, 110 n. 71
Heinsius, Daniel, 236
Hele, John, 111, 216
Henley, Walter, 20, 21 n. 54
Hereford, Herefs, 306
Herne, Edward, 141
Hertford, Herts, assizes, 335-6

Index of Names

Hetley, Thomas, 232, 453
Heyron, John, 87 n. 42
Hill, John, 17; see also Hulle
Hitcham, Robert, 148, 159
Hobart, James and Walter, 96 n. 79
Hobbe and John, moot called, 21, 25
Hoccleve, Thomas, 30
Holborn, Barnard's Inn (q.v.)
–, Cursitors' Inn, 52
–, Furnival's Inn (q.v.)
–, Gray's Inn (q.v.)
–, Harflew Inn, 52
–, Lincoln's Inn (q.v.)
–, St Andrew's church, 26
–, Staple Inn (q.v.)
–, Thavies Inn (q.v.)
Holden, M., 322-4
Holdsworth, William Searle, 342, 436-7
Holkham, Norf, 178, 440 n. 22
Holles, John, earl of Clare, 57
Holt, John, 262, 271, 296, 317, 345, 364
Hoo, William of, 104
Hoppyng, Charles, 17
Hornchurch, Essex, 83 n. 29
Hotman (Hotoman), François, 236
Hotman, Jean, 237
Houghton, Robert, 335, 336 n. 30
Howard, Charles, Lord Howard of Effingham, 382
Howard, John, duke of Norfolk, 92
Hudson, William, 113, 134, 142
Hulle, John, 4
Huls, Hugh, 3, 5 n. 10
Hungate, Richard, 7 n. 8
Hunston, Thomas, 22 n. 58
Hunt, Reuben, 339
Huntingdon, Henry of, 235
Hurdley, Montgoms, 131
Huse (Hussey), William, 31 n. 4, 463
Hutchins, John, 446
Hutton, Richard, 210, 211 n. 40, 221, 225, 227, 252-3
Hyde, Robert, 277
Hyll, Robert, 3

Ickburgh, Norf, 307
Ingoldesby, John, 62
Inner Temple, 3, 5-7, 106
–, benchers, 90
–, buildings, 247
–, 'college', 50 n. 16
–, fires, 248, 460
–, governors, 63
–, moots, 19, 20-1, 25
Ireby, Anthony, 204

Ireland, 197 n. 12, 201
Irish sea, 460
Isaac and Jacob, moot called, 21, 25
Italy, 235-6, 470-1
Ives, E.W., 97

Jacob and Esau, moot called, 21, 25
Jacob, Mr, reporter, 457
Jakes, Thomas, 84 n. 32
James I, king of England, 206, 215, 218-23, 225, 336 n. 30
Jekyll, Joseph, 459
Jenney, William, 384
Jenour, John, 84
Jones, Charles, 240
Jones, Edmund, 32, 37
Jones, Thomas, 331
Jones, William, 37, 460

Kareck, Richard, 334
Katherine of Aragon, queen of England, 464
Keating, Henry Singer, 457
Keble, Joseph, 36
Keilwey (Kaylway, Kelway), Robert, 25, 187, 381-3, 388, 446-7
Kelyng, John, 328, 438
Kempe, Henry, 253
Kentwell Hall, see Long Melford
Kikeby, –, 14
Kingsmill, George, 427
Kiralfy, A.K.R., 444
Kitchin, John, 446
Knightley, Edmund, 22 n. 58, 90, 445
Knyght, John, 92
Knyvett, Francis, 27
Kyrkeby, –, 14

Lambard, William, 235, 284, 413 n. 18, 435, 449
Lambe, John, 307
Lancaster, William, 97
Lane, William, 97
Langbein, J.H., 260
Langland, John, 105
Langland, Luke, 97
Lansdowne, marquess of, see Petty
Leach, Thomas, 318, 327
Leech, Solomon, 145
LeHunt, William, 446
Leicester, Robert of, 104
Leland, John, 235
Levinz, Creswell, 64 n. 66
Lewes, Sussex, prior of, 92
Lewis, William, 450 n. 77
Ley, James, 51, 115, 116

Lincoln, dean and chapter of, 58
Lincoln's Inn, 4-5, 50 n. 15, 57, 60 n. 47, 62, 67
–, arms, 48 n. 11
–, calls to bar, 8, 91
–, extraparochial, 61 n. 53
–, fire in, 459
–, immemorial in law, 68 n. 53
–, moots, 20, 25 ff.
–, pecunes, contribution to, 171, 172
–, Serle Court, 65 n. 70
–, title, 58
Lindenbrog, Friedrich, 237
Lindley, Nathaniel, 54
Littleton, Edward, Baron Lyttleton of Mounslow, 116, 231-41, 454
Littleton, Thomas, 116, 180-1, 231, 234, 467, 474
Littleton, Timothy, 231 n. 4, 232
Lockhart, Alan, 253-4, 256
Loktoun, John, 4
Lombardy, litigant from, 350
London, churches and religious houses: Greyfriars, 110 n. 71; St Clement's parish, 61 n. 53; St Dunstan in West, 53; St John's priory, 93; St Paul's, 102
–, city: common serjeant, 31; customs, 365-6; Guildhall, 102; mayor's court, 352; sheriffs, 332
–, colleges and companies, 47-8: Barber Surgeons, 50-1; College of Physicians, 50; Doctors' Commons, 52-3; see also the inns of court and chancery under their respective names
–, places in or near: Chancery Lane, Serjeants' Inn in, 53, 56, 61 n. 53; Cheapside, 358; Cheap Ward, 365; Covent Garden, 274; Fleet Street, 163, Serjeants' Inn in, 54, 61 n. 53; Newgate, 278, 321, 328-40; Newgate Street (Rainbow Tavern in), 59 n. 45; Old Bailey, 278, 297 n. 172, 321, 323, 328-40; Outer Temple, 3
–, Temple: church, 110 n. 71, 247, 248; Elm Court, 73, 323 n. 69; privileges, 61; title, 58-9; Vine Court, 334; see also Inner Temple; Middle Temple
Long, Mr, clerk of peace, 334
Longleat House, Wilts, 459
Long Melford, Suff, Kentwell Hall in, 243, 247
Loupe, Vincent de la, 240
Lucas, John, 83
Lücke, H.K., 430
Lucy, Thomas, 379-80, 381
Ludlow, Salop, 132

Lutwyche, Edward, 457
Lyndesell, Richard, 27
Lyndwood, William, 235
Lyons Inn, 17, 57, 63, 65, 67 n. 77
Lyster, Richard, 81

Macclesfield, Cheshire, 454 n. 100
Macdonnell, G.P., 204
Machiavelli, Niccolò, 240
Mackworth, Humfrey, 232 n. 10, 453
Maggi (Magius), Ottaviano, 237
Maitland, F.W., 13, 46, 74, 157, 164, 173, 228, 435 ff., 444, 461, 465, 474, 476
Malines, Grand Conseil de, 471
Malvern hills, 105
Malynes, Gerard, 342
Man, Isle of, 202
Mansfield, Lord, see Murray
Manwood, Roger, 106, 133, 194, 382, 450
Map, Walter, 153, 161
Marc, François, 469
Markham, John, 14
Marow, Thomas, 326
Marselaer, Frederik van, 237
Martin, Samuel, 457
Mary I, queen of England, 288
Marylebone Park Corner, Midd, 338
Mather, Mr, reporter, 457
Maxey, John, 92
Maycote, Richard and Robert, 82
Maynard, John, 116, 199, 238
Mead, Thomas, 194
Metcalfe, Miles, 31
Middelburg, 358
Middlesex cases, 273, 278
Middle Temple, 3, 5-7
–, arms, 48 n. 11
–, calls to bar, 91
–, customs, 8
–, treasurer, 63
Mildmay, Anthony, 216
Mildmay, Walter, 202
Milsom, S.F.C., 111, 304, 444
Montague, Edward, 429
Montague, Henry, 109, 224-5, 331, 334, 337
Moore, Francis, 217
Moore, John, 26, 183-4, 204
More, Thomas, 80, 312
Morgan, Richard, 288
Morisot, Claude-Barthélemi, 233 n. 17, 236
Morley, Humfrey, 396 ff., 420 ff.
Mounson, Robert, 382

Index of Names

Mountague, *see* Montague
Mountford, Francis, 90, 314
Moyle, Robert, 246 n. 3, 249 n. 1, 252-3, 256
Moyle, Walter, 172
Moyn, Thomas, 21 n. 53
Murray, William, earl of Mansfield, 290, 311-12, 343, 364, 367

Naples, Italy, 470-1
Nares, R., 179
Nevyll, Thomas, 21 n. 54
Newcastle, Northumb, 359
New Inn, 4 n. 8, 50 n. 15, 56, 57, 60 n. 47, 77 nn. 8 & 10
Newnam, Newnham, –, 14
Newton, Richard, 15 n. 28, 388
Nicholls, Augustine, 445
Nicholls, Thomas, 380-1
Norfolk, 85
Norfolk, duke of, *see* Howard
Normandy, customs of, 236
North, Francis, 245, 254-5, 442, 456
North, Roger, 116, 456
Northey, Edward, 457
Norwich, Norf, 234
Norwich, Richard de, 3
Nott, Fetiplace, 457
Nottingham, earl of, *see* Berkeley; Finch, Heneage
Nowell, Robert, 445
Noy, William, 89 n. 51, 107, 108 n. 62, 240, 241, 347 n. 28, 442

Oates, Titus, 296
Ocean Island, 155 n. 5
Oglethorp, Owen, 322-3
Onley, Edward, 138
Only, John, 21 n. 53
Onslow, Richard, 381
Overton, Guthlac, 93
Owen, Roger, 102, 435
Owen, Thomas, 419, 425, 427
Oxford, 231-4, 237, 238, 320-1
Oxford, Simon of, 12

Pakyngton, John, 90
Palmes, Guy, 96 n. 84
Pangbourne, Berks, 245 n. 4
Pape, Guy de la, 236, 469
Paris, parlement de, 471
Paris, Matthew, 235, 237
Pasquale (Paschalius), Carlo, 237
Pasquier, Étienne, 236-7
Paston, John, 50 n. 16

Pateshall, Simon de, 165
Pekham, Piers, 81
Pelham, Edmund, 34
Pemberton, Francis, 248, 255
Pengelly, Thomas, 457
Penguin Island, 297 n. 172
Pepys, John, 197
Perpoint, Leonard, 97
Peryam, William, 187, 428, 450
Peters, Mr, J.P. Middlesex, 332
Petty, William, marquess of Lansdowne, 459
Pheasant, Peter, 200
Pheyse, Thomas, 307
Phillipps, Thomas, 180 n. 14, 459
Phillips, Edward, 210-11
Philoxenus, 237
Pickering, Danby, 37
Plowden, Edmund, 178, 181, 185, 313, 376-7, 381, 383-4, 441, 448, 472, 474
Plucknett, T.F.T., 12, 177-8, 195, 260
Pole, William, 107
Pollard, Richard, 448
Pollexfen, Henry, 296
Pollock, Frederick, 436
Pollock, Jonathan Frederick, 457
Polstede, John, 87 n. 42
Pontefract, Yorks, 322
Popelinière, Lancelot-Voisin de la, 237
Popham, John, 139-40, 194, 209, 312, 358, 407-8, 419-21, 422, 427-9, 439, 445, 475
Port, John, 19, 22 n. 61, 468
Porter, William, 22 n. 61, 83
Portman, Walter, 172-3
Postan, M.M., 349
Prince, Richard, 129-34
Prisot, John, 172
Prynne, William, 238
Pulton, Ferdinando, 287
Puttenham, George, 107
Pynchebek, Thomas de, 4
Pynsent, John, 253, 256

Ragueau, François, 237
Rainsford, Richard, 251
Raleigh, Walter, 202
Rashdall, Hastings, 22
Rauchbar, Andreas, 236
Ravenscroft, James, 147
Raymond, Robert, Lord Raymond, 457
Raymond, Thomas, 36
Redman, Robert, 443
Reynell, Richard, 446

Ribadeneira, Pedro de, 240
Richardson, Thomas, 146, 238 n. 81, 445
Rikhill, William, 16
Robinson, Thomas, 243-55
Rolle, Henry, 121, 238, 241, 441-2
Roper (Rooper), John, 83, 464
Rouclyff, Brian, 96 n. 84
Roudon, Walter, 86, 87
Rouen, Normandy, 351
Rusburgh, Richard, 27 n. 13
Ruswell, –, 212-13
Ryder, Dudley, 453 n. 91, 457

Sackville, Thomas, Lord Buckhurst, 189, 454
St German, Christopher, 215-16, 384-5
St John, Oliver, 451
St Lancelot, 26
St Milburga, 26
St Paul, 401
St Thomas a Becket, 26
Salamanca, Diego Pérez de, 240
Salkeld, William, 457
Salter, John, 86
Sambiagio, Giovanni-Battista da, 235
San Giorgio, Giovanni Antonio da, 235
Sandhurst, Kent, 321
Saumaise (Salmasius), Claude de, 237
Savage, Thomas, Viscount Savage, 454
Savaron, Jean, 240
Savile, John, 428
Saxony, law of, 236 n. 39
Scotland, 46 n. 4, 220, 471
Scott, John, Lord Eldon, 65
Scott, Zachary, 25
Scroggs, William, 245 n. 1, 251
Sedley, Charles, 305
Segar, Simon, 5, 29, 32
Selden, John, 231, 235, 238, 239, 241
Serres, Jean de, 240
Servin, Louis, 240
Seys (Size), Evan, 442
Seyssel, Claude de, 240
Shelley, William, 388
Shelley, Mr, 457
Sherfield, Henry, 446
Shilton, Richard, 207 n. 20
Shrewsbury, Salop, 129
Shurley, John, 445
Shuttleworth, Richard, 445
Simon, Jocelyn, Lord Simon, 229
Simpson, A.W.B., 3, 426, 447, 448
Size, *see* Seys
Skene, John, 235
Skipwyth, William, 13
Skrene, William, 117 n. 19

Slade, John, 396 ff., 420 ff.
Smith, Thomas, 23, 235, 269
Somers, John, Lord Somers, 459
Sonde, Reynold, 83
Southampton, earl of, *see* Wriothesley
Southworth, Oliver, 82 n. 23, 84 n. 32
Spaldington, Yorks, 173 nn. 13 & 14
Spelman, Clement, 447
Spelman, Henry, 31, 89 n. 49, 235
Spelman, John, 20, 28, 32, 33-4, 187, 312, 315, 321, 327, 389, 447-8, 468, 472
Sprouse, 'famous solicitor', 141 n. 75
Stafford, Staffs, assizes, 312, 322
Stafford, Henry (d. 1521), duke of Buckingham, 92
Stafford, Henry (d. 1523), earl of Wiltshire, 97
Stamford, *see* Staunford
Stanley, George, Lord Strange, 92
Stanley, Thomas, earl of Derby, 92
Staple Inn, 56-7, 60 n. 47, 61 n.53, 63-4, 77 n. 8, 83, 243, 245
Star of Dansk, ship, 359
Starkey, Humfrey, 5
Staunford (Stamford, Staundford), William, 262, 268, 284, 286, 312, 314-15, 326, 474
Stephen, James Fitzjames, 267, 291
Stillington, Robert, 345, 347, 348
Stone, John, 339
Stone, Mr, J.P. Middlesex, 332
Strafford, earl of, *see* Wentworth
Strand Inn, 50 n. 15, 60 n. 117, 77 n. 8, 96 n. 84
Strange, *see* Stanley, George
Strange, John, 319
Strode, George, 198
Style, William, 441, 442
Suffolk, 85
Sulyard, Eustace and William, 58
Swayn, –, 14
Swyfte, John, 379-80
Symmonds, William, 129, 446

Talfourd, Thomas Noon, 457
Tame, Edward, 21 n. 53
Tanfield, Laurence, 354, 395, 396-401, 421, 430
Tanfield, Robert, 445
Tate, Francis, 435, 458-9
Tempest, William, 256
Temple, *see under* London
Tenterden, Lord, *see* Abbot
Thatcher, Thomas, 32
Thavies Inn, 57, 61 n. 53

Index of Names

Thirnyng, William, 4
Thomas, J.H., 177
Thorne, S.E., 25, 31, 445
Thornhill, Mr, 457
Thou, Jacques-Auguste de, 240
Thurlow (Great), Suffolk, 97 n. 87
Thursby, William, 253-4
Thurston, John, 187
Thynne, Thomas, Viscount Weymouth, 198 n. 18
Tillet (Tilius), Jean de, 237
Tindal, John, 214, 217
Tiraqueau, Andrée, 237
Tooke, Horne, 311
Tottell, Richard, 439
Toulouse, archbishopric of, 469
Tourneur, Timothy, 199, 206, 210, 211 n. 40, 218 n. 88, 221-2, 223, 224, 225
Tourneur, *see also* Turnour
Townesend, George, 453, 456
Trevanion, John, 173
Trottescliffe, Kent, 50 n. 16, 110 n. 71
Tufold, Thomas, 63 n. 62
Turner, G.J., 173
Turnour (Tourneur), Arthur, 328-9, 445
Twisden, Thomas, 438, 442, 456
Twyford (West), Midddlesex, 252 n. 3
Twyford, Henry, 183

Ulpian, 118
Umfreville, Edward, 455, 459
Underhill, Thomas, 97

Vaillant, John, 449
Valerius Maximus, 237
Vane, Harry, 300
Vaughan, John, 439, 442, 460
Vavasour, Andrew, 107, 113
Vavasour, John, 171-3
Vavasour, William, 173
Venice, Italy, 365
Villadiego, Gundisalvus de, 237
Villiers, George, duke of Buckingham, 294
Virginia, 297 n. 172
Vowell, William, 92

Wadham, John, 4
Wakeb' (or Wakel'), –, 14
Wales, marches of, 129-31, 202
Waller, Thomas, 253 n. 2, 256
Walmsley, Thomas, 194, 209, 407, 412, 413, 416, 420, 427-9, 439
Walsingham, Thomas of, 235
Walter, John, 238, 241, 395 n. 13, 438

Walwyn, Simon, 379-80
Warburton, Peter, 27
Ward, Edward, 255, 456
Warszewicki, Krysztof, 237
Watford, Herts, 5 n. 10
Wedderburn, Alexander, 107 n. 51
Wells, dean and chapter, 93
Wentworth, Thomas, earl of Strafford, 239
Wentworth, Thomas, of Lincoln's Inn, 446
Were, Humfrey, 414 n. 20
Wesenbeck, Matthew, 236
Westminster, Middlesex, abbey, 322
–, hall, galleries in, 174-5
–, liberty, 278
Weston, John, 4 n. 8
Wetherden, Suff, 86
Whitelocke, Bulstrode, 232
Whyte, John (fl. 1400), 29 n. 19
Whyte, John (fl. 1480), 87 n. 42
Williams, John, 227
Williams, Peere, 457
Williamson, John, 96 n. 84
Willis, John, 452
Willoughby, Richard de, 13
Wiltshire, earl of, *see* Stafford
Winchester, Hants, assizes, 336; college, 150
Windebank, Francis, 196, 197
Windsor, Elizabeth, 107
Winford, Thomas, 254-5, 256
Winwood, Ralph, 213 n. 53
Woderove, John, 3
Wolsey, Thomas, 80, 106, 208
Worsley, Charles, 65
Wray, Christopher, 185, 186-7, 376, 378, 382, 383, 419, 425, 450
Wright, Martin, 457
Wriothesley, Henry, earl of Southampton, 201
Writington, Edward, 453
Wye, Richard, 90, 97, 110 n. 71
Wyllenhale, Robert, 62
Wyndham, Ann, 198
Wyndham, Francis, 187, 384, 450
Wyndham, Hugh and Wadham, 198
Wynter, Thomas, 202
Wyrley, Humphrey, 254, 256

Yale, D.E.C., 455
Yelverton, Christopher, 447
Yelverton, Henry, 294, 429
Yelverton, William, 446 n. 33
York, archbishop of, 277
York, dean and chapter, 54

York, city, 31, 322
Yorke, Philip, earl of Hardwicke, 457
Yorke, Roger, 22 n. 61, 448, 468

Zasius, Ulrich, 236
Zouche, Richard, 235

INDEX OF SUBJECTS

abridgments, 440, 441, 448
academy of history, proposed, 51
accessory to felony, 331, 332, 335-6
account, action of, 349, 350-1
account between partners, 347
accountants, 92-3
accomplices, 290-1
action on the case, *see* case, actions on
actions, *see* double remedies; election; representative action
additions, 306
adjournment, 157, 160, 165, 166 n. 60, 244, 289
administrative law, 271
admiralty, 234, 278
adultery, damages for, 234
advocates, civilian, 46 n. 4, 52-3, 103, 104, 118 n. 25, 121
affray, 279
allocutus, 292
ambassadors, 237
angel, as fee, 105
annuity, for counsel, 101-04
antiquaries, 51, 435
appeal of felony, 202, 262, 273, 286
appellate jurisdiction, 277, 298, 300; *see also* Court of Appeal; Exchequer Chamber
apprentice of law, 13, 88-90, 108, 112 n. 83
–, 'of Common Bench', 3 n. 2, 173
–, 'of the court', 162
apprentices of London, treason by, 202
apprenticii nobiliores, 6
apprise, 12
approvement, 290-1
archidiaconal courts, 280
arms, grants of, 48, 83-4
arraignment, 282-4
–, without indictment, 261, 263 n. 15
arrest, 61, 281
arrest of judgment, 370
assizes, 166, 273-5
–, judicial rulings at, 312-13, 328
associations, unincorporated, 45-74
assumpsit, definition of, 397, 403
assumpsit, action of, 463-4
–, common counts, 430
–, consideration, 369-91, 397, 410, 414
–, declaration in, 371-4, 410-11, 416
–, executors' liability, 428-30
–, fees, to recover, 120, 137-41, 144-9

–, indebitatus count, 359-60, 410, 419 n. 56, 430
–, lawyers, against, 104-5
–, local courts, in, 352, 353 n. 49
–, mercantile cases, 354-66
–, reading on, 33
attainder and conviction, 330
attaint, action of, 269, 407
attorney-general, removal of, 185 n. 43
attorneys, 84-88, 100-01
–, career prospects, 245-6
–, 'hugging' of, 118
–, husbandman as, 86
–, members of inns, 17, 18, 117-18
–, number of, 85-6, 143
–, qualifications, 144
–, thrown over bar, 84, 126, 251-2
auditors, 92-3
auterfoitz acquit, convict, 262, 284

bail, 281
bar of court, picking or casting over, 84, 126, 251-2
bar of inn of chancery, 18
bar (outer bar) of inn of court, 18, 20, 91 n. 56, 111 n. 79
–, bar bond, 64 n. 66
–, call to, 9-10, 77-78, 111-12, 143
bar, practice at, qualification for, 89-90, 109-112, 127-35
bar, *see also* barrister at law
barbers, 50
barrator, common, 149
barrister at law, degree of, 10-11, 69-70, 76, 88 n. 48, 89, 91-2, 109-12, 134-5
–, esquire, 123 n. 61
–, rights of audience, 127-35
–, solicitor, as, 137, 147-8; distinguished from, 100, 112-16
–, title 'at law', 91, 101 n. 8, 109 n. 65, 112 nn. 86-7
battle, trial by, 164-5, 268
bencher, degree of, 10-11, 69-70, 90, 112
benefit of clergy, *see* clergy
bill of exceptions, 300
bill of exchange, 342, 349-52, 354-66
billa vera, 264-5
branding, 293
briefs to counsel, 116
burglary, 308, 315, 331, 332, 335, 336

488 The Legal Profession and the Common Law

burning, sentence of death by, 280, 294, 295

Canon law, books of, 235, 469; see also ecclesiastical law
carols, 29-30
case, actions on, origin, 402, 413, 423
–, scope, 398-400, 403-4, 413
–, reading on, 32
–, see also assumpsit
case law, 466, 468-76; see also precedent; reports of cases
case stated, 301, 317-18, 327
casus placitorum, 11-12
'caterpillars of the commonwealth', 141
causa, 372, 374, 384, 385-7
causidicus, degree of, 112 n. 85
Central Criminal Court, 154, 278
certiorari, 271-3, 298-9, 305, 306, 313, 316, 320-1, 325, 332
challenge, 285-6
chambers, business in, 54 n. 27, 79, 162-3
champerty, 119
chancellors, 80
Chancery, court of, contract jurisdiction, 107-8, 352, 401, 403, 425
–, –, error in, 227
–, –, jurisdiction after judgment at law, 202, 205-29, 438
–, –, litigation in, 56, 65, 85 n. 39
–, –, medieval, 347-8
–, –, officers of, 52, 80, 81-2
–, –, overloaded with business, 223
–, –, practice of, 401
–, –, prerogative, associated with, 218, 222, 225
–, –, record, not a court of, 209
–, –, reporters in, 453, 455
–, –, soliciting causes in, 139, 145, 146
charitable trust, 57-8
charter of incorporation, 47-55
Christmas in inns of court, 28-30
church, property of, 306, 323 n. 70
church, see also Canon law; ecclesiastical courts and law; heresy; parishes; pope; reformation; sacrilege; simony
circuit cases, 449 n. 69; see also assizes
Civil (Roman) law, Bracton and, 397 n. 23
–, case from, 314
–, consideration and, 369, 384-5, 390 n. 78
–, courts of, 207
–, evidence in, 286

–, James I and, 205, 220
–, knowledge of, 235
–, law merchant and, 241
–, liberal professions, idea of, 119, 121 n. 45
–, procedure of, 266-7
–, see also honorarium; nudum pactum
civil war, 35, 231-4
clergy, benefit of, 292-3, 329, 333
clergy employed in courts, 80, 81
clerk of assize, 260, 274, 281
clerk of market, 185 n. 42
clerk of the peace, 82
clerks of courts, see under Chancery; Common Pleas; King's Bench; Exchequer
coinage offences, 306, 334, 337
coinage, see also mint
collar of SS., 185 n. 40, 224
colleges, 47-9, 50, 55
colloquium, 372
comitiva, 48, 49-50
commissions, 160, 166, 272
–, assize, of, 273-5
–, law merchant, to follow, 346
–, military, 201
–, peace, of, 275-8
–, Old Bailey, for, 278
–, sewers, of, 34, 216
common learning (eruditon), 169, 314, 467-472-3, 474
Common Pleas, bar of, 78
–, conservatism of, 411-13
–, dispute with King's Bench, 411-13, 417 f 427 ff.
–, mercantile suits in, 348-9
–, officers of, 81, 84, 243-56, 444, 456
–, origin of, 158
–, suits by inns, 62-4
common recovery, 463
commonplace books, 181; see also abridgments
communis error, 418
company, meaning of, 46 n. 6, 49-50
comparative law, 231-41
conciliar jurisdictions, counsel in, 129-32
–, on continent, 468-71, 473
–, see also council
conscience, 208, 214, 227; see also equity
consideration, 357, 359, 369-91, 397, 410, 414
conspiracy to strike, 337-8
constable and marshal, court of, 202
constables, 260, 261, 277
constitutional law, see administrative law; liberty of subject; natural justice;

Index of Subjects

parliament; prerogative
consultation of lawyers, 101-2, 115-116
contempt of court, 163, 261
contract, definition of, 402
–, executory, 378-9, 401, 408, 422
–, implied promise, 422-3
–, terms, construction of, 397-8, 417, 423
–, *see also* assumpsit; consideration; debt
conversion, 401
conveyancing, 12, 88, 114, 243
coram rege, 158
coroner's inquest, 264, 307
corporate personality, 46-9, 54-5, 165
Council in Marches of Wales, 129-32
council, king's, and inns of court, 60; *see also* conciliar jurisdictions; Star Chamber
counsel, counsellors at law, 68 n. 83, 69, 76, 99-123
–, approached through solicitor, 115-16
–, duties of, 103-4
–, liberal profession, 118-19, 123
–, not liable for bad advice, 122
–, signature to pleas, 128-9
counsel in criminal cases, 286-8, 338, 339
county court, 164-5
court, authority of, 468-76
–, contempt of, 163, 261
–, course of, 159, 400
–, men of, 68 n. 83
–, nature of, 153-68
–, open, 162
–, 'sitting in', 154-5
–, *see also particular courts*
Court for Crown Cases Reserved, 301, 318, 326-7
Court of Appeal, 154, 155, 472
courtholders, 87-8
courts of criminal jurisdiction, 271-80
crib in court, 173-4
criminal information, *see* information
criminal jurisdiction, 271-80
criminal law, 31, 303-24, 325-30, 449
criminal procedure, 289-301
crown, source of judicial authority, 159-60; *see also* prerogative
Crown Court, 154
'culprit', 283
curia, 155, 156, 160-1, 164
curia regis, 157-8, 161
curia villae, 164
curiales (men of court), 162 n. 32
cursitors, 52
custody before trial, *see under* imprisonment
custom, 342, 343-4, 347, 356-66
–, of realm, 362-3, 367

damages in assumpsit, 398, 399-400, 417
dancing, medieval, 29-30
day in court, 160
death penalty, 294-5, 297, 329
debt, action of, basis of, 397 n. 23, 402-3
–, –, jurisdiction over, 411
–, –, on mercantile instrument, 351-2, 360
–, –, on retaining, 103, 105, 107, 119 n. 28, 120-1, 123
–, –, relationship with assumpsit, 393-432
deceit, as element in action on case, 402-4, 406, 416, 427
decisiones rotae, 469, 470
decisions, *see* majority; precedent; *and under* judge
defamation, 111-12, 134-5, 464
demaunde, 12
demurrer, 167, 168, 193 n. 86, 284, 370, 372, 380, 475-6
deodand, 335
depositions, 289, 290
detinue, 418 n. 50
dilatory plea, 284
direction, *see under* judge (relationship with jury)
doctor of laws, 89 n. 52
Doctors' Commons, 52-3
double remedies, rule against, 398-400, 405-6, 413-4
duke, degradation of, 185 n. 43

ecclesiastical courts, 206, 267, 279-80
ecclesiastical law, 361; *see also* Canon law
entries, 193-4
–, books of, 247, 248-9
election of remedies, 401, 405; *see also* double remedies
entails, 463
equity, 208, 210 n. 35, 219-20, 227, 438; *see also* Chancery; conscience
error, proceedings in, 165, 169, 352, 370, 372, 475
–, in criminal cases, 295, 298-300, **306-9**, 325-6
eruditus in lege, 60, 76-7, 87 n. 42, 109, 110, 111, 112 n. 83; *see also* juris peritus; legis peritus
evidence, law of, 286-91, 310-11; *see also* innocence; proof
exceptions, *see* bill of exceptions
exchange of currency, *see* bill of exchange
Exchequer, barons of, 80, 428
–, chancellor of, 202
–, green wax, 185 n. 42

–, officers of, 81, 83
–, origin of, 158
–, quominus in, 131
–, record of reasons, 193
–, reports in, 452
–, soliciting causes in, 142
Exchequer Chamber, informal meeting, 167-8, 318, 421, 427-8, 438
–, statutory tribunal, 168-9, 418-20, 429
executors, 428-30, 468
'executory' contract, 378-9, 401, 408, 422
'experience' in criminal cases, 312-13

Faculty of Advocates, 46 n. 4
fair, 353
false judgement, 165; see also error
fees, 143-4
–, contingent, 107, 121
–, counsel, of, 101, 102, 104-8
–, court officers, of, 82
–, honorarium doctrine, 118-23
–, payable in advance, 120, 122
–, solicitors, of, 137-41, 147-9
fellowship, 46, 49, 165-6
felony, 261, 275, 276, 279, 292, 294; see also appeal
fictions, 343-4
–, assumpsit, in, 357, 372, 373, 387 n. 62, 422
–, day of court, 160
–, transactions in court, 163
–, venue, as to, 349
final concord, 166 n. 57
fixtures, stealing, 320-3
forest law, 185 n. 42, 238, 241
forfeiture for alienation, 185 n. 43
formalism, 295, 299, 306-08, 325-6
French language, see law French

galleries in courts, 174-5
gaol delivery, 274-5
general issue, 283, 310, 311
gentlemen, lawyers as, 86, 88, 97, 118, 123 n. 61
gift to fluctuating body, 72 n. 96
God, peace and fear of, 309
–, trial by, 283, 333
graduation, notion of, 9, 89
grand jury, 217, 260, 263-5, 281-2
'grasshoppers of Egypt', 142
green wax, 185 n. 42
gunpowder plot, 197 n. 9, 202

habeas corpus, 211-16, 241
hanging, death by; see also death penalty

hearsay testimony, 289, 290
heresy, 279-80
High Commission, 206, 267
High Court of Justice (1650), 263, 267-8
High Court of Justice (1875), 154, 155
homicide, see manslaughter; murder
homo eruditus in lege, see eruditus in lege
honorarium, 118-23
'hostels' (inns of court), 3 n. 2, 13
House of Lords, 157, 239
hove-dance, 30
humanism, 476
husband and wife, see marriage; widows; wife

ignoramus, 265
impeachment, 272
imprisonment, before trial, 281
–, punishment, as, 295
indebitatus assumpsit, see under assumpsit
indictment, 73, 263-5, 281-3, 305-10, 325-6
infangthief, 268
information, criminal, 263, 265-6
inheritance customs, 185 n. 43
injuria, 389
innocence, presumption of, 289-90
inns of chancery, admissions, number of, 95
–, audit in, 68
–, barristers of, 18
–, chamber rent, 64
–, constitutions, 64
–, dues recovered by, 62-4, 67-8
–, extraparochiality, 61
–, inferior status of, 3, 4, 7, 117
–, learning exercises in, 11, 16-19
–, legal status of, 45-74
–, litigation by, 62-6
–, members, contract between, 67
–, –, 'learned in law', 87
–, –, numbers, 93-5
–, –, prothonotaries as, 245, 255-6
–, moots in, 16-17, 18-19
–, nuisance to, 61, 65
–, ownership of, 56-8
–, pension, 67
–, pensioner, 63, 65
–, principals, 18-19, 62-5, 67, 68
–, readings in, 11, 16, 67 n. 77, 91
–, statutes of, 18, 19 n. 43, 67
–, supervision by chancellor, 67 n. 77
–, treasurer, 63, 65
inns of court, 3-74, 93-8, 313-14, 465-8
–, admissions, number of, 95-6, 114

–, ancients of, 69
–, auctioneer expelled from, 60 n. 49
–, bar (q.v.)
–, barrister (q.v.); *see also* inner barristers, below
–, bencher (q.v.)
–, butlers of, 25-7
–, building agreements by, 71, 74
–, constitutions, 7, 10, 45-74
–, contractual capacity of, 71-3
–, control by council, 60
–, cupboard cases, 20
–, dues recovered by, 62-4, 94
–, endowments, 59
–, exhibitions to study at, 96-7
–, extraparochiality, 61
–, governors of, 63
–, grand company, 69
–, grand day, 37
–, immemorial in law, 69-70
–, influence on law, 313-14, 326, 465-8
–, inner barristers, 11, 20, 21-2, 26, 91
–, inquiry of 1854, 73-4
–, investments of, 72, 73
–, learning exercises in, 3 n. 2, 7-23, 445-6; *see also* moots; readings
–, legal status of, 45-74, 132
–, libraries of, 72
–, litigation by, 62-6
–, members, age on admission, 96
–, –, attorneys as, 86-7
–, –, contract between, 67, 68
–, –, court officers as, 82-3
–, –, expulsion of, 60, 66, 68, 97
–, –, legal status of, 60, 76-7, 110-11
–, –, numbers of, 93-6
–, –, supervision of studies of, 8
–, –, taxation of, 61
–, –, yeomen as, 97
–, moot cases, 20-1, 25-8, 468
–, moots, 14-16, 19-22, 25-7, 238
–, pension roll, 72 n. 96
–, privileges of, 59-62
–, property of, 56-9, 65
–, readers, 36, 89, 91
–, readings, 14-15, 31-7, 90, 313-14, 322, 326, 467-8
–, revels, 28-30
–, seals of, 59
–, Senate of, 45 n. 3
–, silver of, 65, 72
–, songs of, 28-9
–, taxation of, 62
–, treasurer, 63, 64
–, visitors of, 67, 70-1

inquisition, 266-7
insanity, 296, 319 n. 55
insimul computaverunt, 63-4
insurance, reading on, 36-7
international law, *see* law of nations
interregnum, 455-6, 460 n. 133

jointures, reading on, 33
'jour', 160
judges, decisions, *see* majority
–, development of law by, 314, 315-18, 468-76
–, dismissal of, 224
–, installation ceremony, 245, 251
–, notebooks of, 317-18, 343, 456-7
–, qualifications of, 79-80
–, relationship with jury, 269-70, 285, 305, 310-12, 316-17, 318-19, 329, 331
–, suing in own court, 166
–, *see also* court
judgment, effect of, 332
–, entry of, 163, 166
–, in criminal cases, 294-6
–, *see also* arrest of judgment
judicial authority, *see under* judges (development of law by)
judicial review, of inns of court, 66-7, 70-1
–, of summary convictions, 271
juris peritus, 108; *see also* eruditus in lege; legis peritus
juris professor, 104
jurisdiction, criminal, 271-80
–, notion of, 156-60
–, redistribution of, 411, 463
jury, petty, 267-70, 305, 324
–, –, autonomy of, 311-12, 318-19
–, –, charge to, 285
–, –, verdict, 167, 291-2
jury, *see also* grand jury; *and under* judges (relationship with jury)
justices of the peace, 260-1, 270-1, 275-8

king, as judge, 220, 239; *see also* prerogative
King's Bench, bill procedure, 411-12
–, criminal jurisdiction, 266, 270, 272-3, 298-300, 305-9, 313, 316
–, dispute with Common Pleas, 411-13, 417 ff., 427 ff.
–, growth of business, 464-5
–, informations in, 266, 270
–, mercantile jurisdiction, 354-5

–, officers of, 81, 83
–, Wales, jurisdiction in, 32
king's council, see council; Star Chamber
king's counsel, gown of, 36
king's evidence, 291
king's serjeant, slander of, 111
knights of the post, 424

laesio fidei, 403, 464
larceny, 275, 306, 310, 320-23, 331
Latin language, 282, 299, 307, 326; see also maxims
law, wager of, see wager of law
law and fact, see under judges (relationship with jury)
law and procedure, 346-8
law French, 17, 20, 22, 23, 35, 193, 458
law merchant, 56, 341-68
law of nations, 237, 362
law of nature (lex naturae), 342, 345, 348
law officers of crown, 79-80; and see attorney-general; solicitor-general
Law Society, 53
lawyers, see legal profession
learned in law, see eruditus in lege; legis peritus
leases, readings on, 446
leet, 264, 279
legal change, 315-18, 435-9, 462-3
legal fiction, see fiction
legal profession, 75-98
–, definition of, 75-8, 99-100
–, etiquette of, 107, 114-16, 118, 121
–, see also consultation; eruditus in lege; inns; serjeants
legis peritus, 86, 88-9
legislation, see statutes
lex naturae, see law of nature
liberty of subject, 202; and see habeas corpus
libraries of lawyers, 440, 458-9
licence and lease, 397-8
licentiatus juris, 112
lien, counsel's, 122
liveries, 101, 102, 106
livery companies, 47, 82
local government, 276-7
lords, see peer; seigniorial courts
love and affection, consideration of, 376-7

mainour, 261
maintenance, justification of, 77, 101, 106, 109-11, 112-14, 135-49
majority, judicial, 155, 167-9, 194, 472-3, 474-5
mandamus, 66, 112 n. 87
manorial courts, see seigniorial courts
manslaughter, 333, 334-5
manuscripts, importance of, 436-7, 439, 443-60
marginalia, 440
market, clerk of, 185 n. 42
marriage as consideration, 373 n. 14, 376, 382-3
marriage, see also wife
martial law, 268
matrons, jury of, 296, 332-3
maxims, communis error facit jus, 418
–, ex nudo pacto non oritur actio, 372, 376-7, 381
mayhem, 406
medical practitioners, see physicians; surgeons
memory, 161-2
'men of court', 68 n. 83
mercantile courts, 352-4
mercantile law, see law merchant
mercantile usage, 342, 344-5
mint, royal, 185 n. 42
mirth and solace, song of, 29
misdemeanour, 261, 265, 268, 279, 286, 295-6, 300
mitigation of sentence, speech in, 292, 338
money, 404; see also bill of exchange
moots, see under inns
mortmain, 36, 55 n. 29
motions in banc, see arrest of judgment; new trial
murder, 306, 307, 309-10, 313, 316-17, 333-4, 336
mute on arraignment, 283, 334, 336-7

natura brevium, 18-19, 238
natural justice, principles of, 271
natural law, see law of nature
neck-verse, 293, 333
new trial, motion for, 300, 317
nisi prius, criminal case at, 273
notaries, 88
nudum pactum, 372, 376-7, 380, 381-2, 384-6, 388, 414
nuisance, 386
–, action on case for, 399, 405, 406, 418 n. 50
–, public, 339-40
–, to inn of chancery, 61, 65
oaths, of allegiance, 135 n. 48
–, of grand jurors, 281-2
–, of trial jurors, 285

Index of Subjects

—, of witnesses, 288
—, ex officio, 267
obituaries by Coke, 185
obscene libel, 305
offices, sale of, 245-55
onerabilis assumpsit, 359-61
outlawry, 330
oyer and terminer, 274-5, 276

pardon, 291, 296-7, 300-01
parishes, gift to, 72 n. 96
—, inns not in, 61
parliament, 185 n. 42, 202, 222, 272
—, law of, 234, 238-9, 241
partnership, 347
paupers, advice to, 106
pecunes (pekons), 171-5
peer, degradation of, 185 n. 43
peers, trial by, 160, 239, 268-9
peine forte et dure, 219, 283-4, 334
penance, 280
perjury, 300
personal property, ownership of, 72-3
pettifoggers, 143
petty larceny, 329, 331
petty sessions, 278
petty treason, 294, 334
physicians, 50, 100, 103 n. 23, 117 n. 17, 123
piepowder, courts of, 352-4
placea (court), 161
plea-bargaining, 284
plea rolls, 436, 444-5; *see also* record
pleading, assumpsit, in, 379, 383
—, criminal cases, in, 282-4, 333
—, drawn by counsel, 115
—, expertise in, 246-7, 248-9
—, record of, 163; *see also* entries
pledge, 397
police function, 260-1
pope, 463; *see also* rota
praecipe writ, 156
praemunire, 209, 215-21, 223, 438
precedent, binding force of, 470
precedents vouched from records, 400, 408
pregnancy, plea of, 296, 332-3, 334
prerogative, royal, 185, 196, 202
—, whether arguable at bar, 205
—, whether determinable by judges, 206-7, 220-1
—, wager of law and, 407
prerogative rule, 206-7, 221-2
prescription, by inns of court, 68-70
presentment of offences, 264, 279
pressing, *see* peine

printing of law books, 439-43
prison-breach, 337
privity of contract, 350, 352, 357
proctors, 53, 121
—, of university, 49
prohibition, 211
proof, burden of, 264, 289-90
proof, problems of, 406-7, 425, 439
prosecution of crime, 259-61
protestation, 372 n. 10
proxies, 197 n. 12
punishments, 294-6, 297-8
purveyance, 185 n. 42

quaestiones de statutis, 3 n. 2, 14, 20
quarter sessions, 271, 275, 276-8
quasi-contract, 430-1
qui tam proceedings, 266
quid pro quo, 373, 374, 376, 380-3, 386, 387-90
quo warranto, 33, 157
quominus, 131
quorum, 276, 277

readings, *see under* inns
reception of Roman law, 461, 465-6, 468-9, 471, 476
recognizance, 332
record, 162, 164, 166 n. 57, 298-300; *see also* entries; formalism; Latin
recusants, 185
reformation, 462-3
register of writs, 398-9, 405, 414, 423-4
remedies, *see* double remedies; election; writs
renaissance, law and, 435-76
'report', exercise, 11, 18-19
reports of cases, criminal cases, 312-13, 315-16
—, manuscripts, 393-5, 409, 446-57
—, official, 453-4
—, printing of, 383, 440-2
—, prothonotaries, by, 250-1
—, spurious, 442
reporters, *see index of names*
representative action, 65
reprieve, 296
reserved crown cases, 300-01, 315-18, 326-7
retainer of lawyers, 101-08, 123
'reward', 101
rhetoric, 23
robbery, 262, 357
rolls, *see* record
Roman law, *see* Canon law; Civil law;

reception
rota, papal, 167, 469
rote learning, 19
Royal Society, 51, 55

sacrilege, 321, 322
sanior pars, 474 n. 43
scandalum magnatum, 140
'scholar', as addition, 306, 308
scriveners, 88
seals, 48, 50, 59
secretary of state, in court, 213 n. 53
seigniorial courts, 156, 157, 159, 164-5
sentencing, 294-6
serjeants at law, 3-4, 78-80, 89, 100, 101-2, 104-5, 106, 251
serjeants' inns, 53-4, 78-9
—, criminal cases discussed in, 300-01, 315-18, 326-7
settlement of chattels, 72
sewers, commissions of, 34, 216
sheriff's tourn, 264, 279
ship-money, 240
shorthand, systems of, 452-3
simony, 36
si non omnes, 166
six clerks, 52
slaughterhouse, erection of, 339-40
societas, 48, 49, 165-6
Society of Judges and Serjeants, 53
solicitor-general, appointment of, 202-3
solicitors, 76, 92-3, 100, 112-14, 125-49
—, attorneys as, 136, 138-42, 145-7
—, barristers as, 137, 147-8
—, common (or general) and private, 144-5, 148-9
special jury, 364, 366
special pleading, 310, 311
special verdict, 301, 316-17, 325, 327, 338-9, 370, 420-1, 476
Star Chamber, 141-2, 144-6, 158-9, 202, 219, 220-2, 266-70, 273, 296, 348, 471
status, *see* gentlemen; peer; *and under* barrister at law (esquire)
statutes of inns of chancery, 18, 19 n. 43, 67
statutes, parliamentary, construction of, 185, 194-5
—, criminal legislation, 303-4, 319-20, 323
steward, lord high, 160, 272
strike by embroiderers, 337-8
study of law, *see under* inns of chancery (learning); inns of court (learning)
suitors of court, 165
summary procedure and conviction, 268, 270-1, 298-9
summing up, 270, 291
surgeons, 50-1, 100, 117, 297
surgery, books of, 82
swan-mark, 185 n. 43

taxation and inns of court, 61-2
textbooks, *see* treatises
theft, *see* larceny
titledeeds, theft of, 320
tort, breach of promise as, 389
—, consideration in, 386
torture, 267
tourn, sheriff's, 264, 279
transportation, 297-8, 323
treason, 201-2, 239, 287, 294-5, 306, 308, 312; *see also* petty treason
trespass on the case, *see* case
treatises, 231-41, 313, 314-5, 467, 474
trial by jury, 267, 268-70, 305; *see also* jury
trial procedure, 260, 280-93, 310-13, 328, 330-40, 370
trusts, 56-9, 74

unanimity, 167-8
uncertainty in law, 390-1
universities, conveyancing taught in, 12
—, degrees in, 9, 89, 108 n. 62
—, history not taught in, 51
—, incorporation of, 48, 49
—, inns compared with, 7, 45
—, learning exercises, 9
—, proctors, 49
usance, 358, 365
uses, 377, 384, 389
—, readings on, 32, 33, 34, 445
usury, 36

venire de novo, 300
verdict, 167, 291-2; *see also* special verdict
vi et armis, 309
view, 155 n. 5
villein every other day, 468
visitatorial jurisdiction, 67, 70-1, 234
voucher to warranty, 164

wagering contract, 382
wager of law, 105, 107, 346, 399, 401-2, 406-8, 415, 424-6, 431
widows, 185 n. 43
wife, theft by, 331, 335
wills, law of, 445-6
witchcraft, 307

Index of Subjects

witnesses, 288-9
women, as justices of peace, 468
—, punishment of, 294, 295, 296, 332-3, 334
writs, original, 160; *see also* register of writs

year books, 13, 32, 168, 171-2, 175, 195, 443, 467, 475